Formations of the Unconscious

Jacques Lacan

Formations of the Unconscious

The Seminar of Jacques Lacan
Book V

Edited by Jacques-Alain Miller

Translated by Russell Grigg

polity

First published in French as *Le Séminaire de Jacques Lacan. Livre V. Les formations de l'inconscient (1957–1958)* © Éditions du Seuil, 1998

English translation © Polity Press 2017
This English edition © Polity Press 2017
First published in English in 2017
This paperback edition published in 2020

Polity Press
65 Bridge Street
Cambridge CB2 1UR, UK

Polity Press
101 Station Landing
Suite 300
Medford, MA 02155, USA

ISBN-13: 978-0-7456-6037-0
ISBN-13: 978-0-7456-6038-7 (pb)

A catalogue record for this book is available from the British Library.

Library of Congress Cataloging-in-Publication Data

Names: Lacan, Jacques, 1901-1981, author. | Miller, Jacques-Alain, editor.
Title: Formations of the unconscious : the seminar of Jacques Lacan, Book V / Jacques Lacan, Jacques-Alain Miller ; translated by Russell Crigg.
Other titles: Seminaire de Jacques Lacan. English
Description: Malden, MA : Polity, 2017. | First published in language as Le Seminaire. Livre V. Les formations de l'inconscient (1957-1958). | Includes bibliographical references and index.
Identifiers: LCCN 2016039422 | ISBN 9780745660370 (hardback)
Subjects: LCSH: Subconsciousness. | Psychoanalysis. | BISAC: PSYCHOLOGY / Movements / Psychoanalysis.
Classification: LCC BF315 .L33 2017 | DDC 154.2--dc23 LC record available at https://lccn.loc.gov/2016039422

Typeset in 10.5/12 Times New Roman
by Servis Filmsetting Ltd, Stockport, Cheshire
Printed in Great Britain by CPI Group (UK) Ltd, Croydon

The publisher has used its best endeavours to ensure that the URLs for external websites referred to in this book are correct and active at the time of going to press. However, the publisher has no responsibility for the websites and can make no guarantee that a site will remain live or that the content is or will remain appropriate.

Every effort has been made to trace all copyright holders, but if any have been inadvertently overlooked the publisher will be pleased to include any necessary credits in any subsequent reprint or edition.

For further information on Polity, visit our website: politybooks.com

Contents

THE DIALECTIC OF DESIRE AND DEMAND IN THE CLINICAL STUDY AND TREATMENT OF THE NEUROSES

APPENDICES

Translator's Preface

Throughout this Seminar, the French terms '*trait d'esprit*', its synonym '*mot d'esprit*' and the less common '*esprit*' have most often been translated as witticism, occasionally as wit or joke. As Lacan mentions (p. 13), *trait d'esprit* is his preferred translation for Freud's '*Witz*', though he doesn't follow this practice consistently and often uses the more common expression '*mot d'esprit*', which is how '*Witz*' in Freud's *Der Witz und seine Beziehung zum Unbewussten* (*Jokes and Their Relation to the Unconscious*) has been rendered in the two major French translations.

It is true that 'witticism' is not in widespread use in English and carries the connotation of refined and intellectual forms of humour, as James Strachey noted in his preface to *Jokes and Their Relation to the Unconscious*, published in *The Standard Edition of the Complete Works of Sigmund Freud*. However, not only is 'joke' closer to the French terms '*blague*' and '*histoire drôle*', but it is also true that, in this Seminar in which Lacan emphasizes connotations of the finesse of language, the choice of the word 'witticism' is not out of place. I have very occasionally translated '*trait d'esprit*' and '*mot d'esprit*' as joke, when it has been clear that a joke is what Lacan has in mind.

Many of the choices I have made for the translation of crucial terms of Lacan's are discussed in the translator's endnotes as they arise.

The numbers in the margins of this translation refer to the pagination of the French edition published by Éditions du Seuil in 1998.

I owe thanks to the following people: Yael Baldwin, for her valuable comments on the entire translation; Bruce Fink, whose thoughts on ways to render Lacan into good English have always been greatly appreciated; Adrian Price, who sent me detailed comments on parts of the translation; and Geoffrey Young, who generously sent me his own translation of this Seminar when he heard that I was working on the authorized version.

I do not doubt that the translation could still be improved and I invite anyone who has suggestions or corrections to write to me directly or contact me via the publisher.

Abbreviations

Écrits Jacques Lacan, *Écrits: The First Complete Edition in English*, translated by Bruce Fink in collaboration with Héloïse Fink and Russell Grigg (New York: W. W. Norton, 2006).

SE Sigmund Freud, *Standard Edition of the Complete Psychological Works of Sigmund Freud* (24 volumes), translated and edited by James Strachey in collaboration with Anna Freud, assisted by Alix Strachey and Alan Tyson (London: The Hogarth Press and the Institute of Psycho-Analysis, 1953–74). All quotations of Freud are from this edition.

Words followed by an asterisk (*) are found in English in the original.

Book V

Formations of the Unconscious

1957–1958

THE FREUDIAN
STRUCTURES OF WIT

I

THE FAMILLIONAIRE

Points from previous Seminars
Schema of *Witz*
Wit and its national traditions
Confirmation by the Other
What can only be seen by looking away

This year I have taken 'formations of the unconscious' as my topic.

Those of you, and I think this includes most of you, who were at our scientific meeting last night are already up to date and aware that the questions I raise here concern – directly, this time – the function in the unconscious of what in previous years I have been developing as the signifier.

Some of you – I express myself like this because my ambitions are modest – have, I hope, read the article entitled '*L'instance de la lettre dans l'inconscient*' ['The Instance of the Letter in the Unconscious'] that I published in the third issue of the journal *La psychanalyse*. Those who had the stamina for it will be well prepared, or better prepared than the others, to follow the discussion. Moreover, my hope, a modest one, or so it seems to me, is that you who make the effort to listen to what I have to say also make the effort to read what I write, since in the end it's for you that I write it. Those of you who have not done so would therefore do well to read it, especially as I will be referring to it constantly. I am obliged to assume you are familiar with what has already been said.

In thinking about those of you who have come unprepared in any of these ways, I am going to tell you what I will limit myself to today and what the object of this introductory lesson to our topic will be.

In the first instance, I will necessarily briefly and allusively, because I cannot go back to square one, recall several major [*ponctuant*] points from previous years that initiated and foreshadowed what I have to tell you about the function of signifiers in the unconscious.

10   Then, as a pause for those whose minds may be left a little out of breath by this brief reminder, I will explain to you what the schema I will be referring to over the course of our theoretical experience this year means.

And then I will finish with an example. It's the first example that Freud employs in his book on witticisms. I am not doing this as an illustration, but because a witticism is always particular – there is no such thing as a witticism in the abstract. I will make a start at showing, in this respect, how witticisms happen to be the best point of entry into our topic, that of formations of the unconscious. This is not only the best point of entry but also the most striking form in which Freud himself indicates the unconscious's relations with signifiers and their techniques.

These, then, are my three parts. You know, then, what to expect from what I am going to explain to you, and this should also spare you some mental effort.

1

The first year of my Seminar, devoted to Freud's writings on technique, essentially consisted in introducing you to the notion of the function of the symbolic as alone capable of explaining what can be called the determination as to meaning insofar as it relates to the fundamental reality of Freudian experience.

Since 'determination as to meaning' is on this occasion nothing but a definition of reason, let me remind you that this reason is to be found at the very origins of the possibility of analysis. It's because something has become tied to something like speech that discourse can untie the knot.

I pointed out to you in this respect the distance separating speech, insofar as it's filled by a subject's being, from the empty discourse that drones away over the actions of humans. These actions are rendered impenetrable by the imagining of motives that are irrational, inasmuch as they are only rationalized from the ego's perspective of misrecognition. As I also taught you in that first year, the ego is itself a function of the symbolic relation and is apt to be affected by it in its density and functions of synthesis – all also made from a mirage, but a captivating mirage. This is only possible because of the gap opened up in human beings by the original, biological pres-
11   ence of death in them, owing to what I have called the prematurity of birth. This is the point where the symbolic intrudes.

That was where we had come to at the juncture of my first and second Seminars.

The second Seminar highlighted the factor of repetitive insistence arising from the unconscious. I identified its consistence with the structure of the signifying chain, and this is what I tried to get you to see by giving you a model of it in the form of the so-called syntax of α, β, γ, δ.

You now have a written exposition of this in my article, 'The Purloined Letter', which gives a brief summary of this syntax. Despite the criticisms it has received, some of which were justified – there are two minor mistakes that should be corrected in a future edition – you should still manage to find it useful for a long while to come. I am even convinced that it will change with age, and that you will find it less difficult to refer to in several months' time, or even by the end of the year. I say this in answer to the laudable efforts that have been made by certain people seeking to limit its significance. It was in any case an opportunity for them to put themselves to the test, and this is precisely all I look for. Whatever dead-end they might have found in it, these gymnastics have nevertheless been useful to them. They will have the opportunity for more gymnastics in what I will have occasion to show them this year.

Of course, as the people who have made this effort stressed to me, even in writing, each of these four terms is marked by a fundamental ambiguity. But that is precisely what makes it a valuable example. With these groupings we have set off down the path of what forms current speculation on groups and sets. These researches are founded on the principle that one starts with complex structures, simple structures merely presenting themselves as special cases. I won't go back over how these little letters are created but it's clear that, following operations by means of which we can define them, we end up with something extremely simple. Each of them is effectively defined on the basis of the relations between two terms in [one of] two pairs of terms, the pair including [configurations] that go from symmetrical to dissymmetrical and from dissymmetrical to symmetrical [see *Écrits*, pp. 47–50], and then the pair that goes from same to different and from different to same. We have here, then, a group of four signifiers [α, β, γ, δ] with the property that each of them can be analysed in terms of its relations with the other three. To confirm this analysis, incidentally, I would add that according to Roman Jakobson, in his own words which I heard from him when I met him recently, four is the minimum number of signifiers necessary for the primary, elementary conditions of linguistic analysis. Now, as you will see, the latter has the closest of relationships to analysis as such. They are indistinguishable, even. If we look closely, they are essentially no different from one another.

12

In the third year of my Seminar, I spoke about psychosis insofar as it's founded on a primordial deficiency of a signifier. I showed what sort of subduction of the real arises when, induced by vital invocation, the real comes to take its place within this deficiency of a signifier, which we were speaking about last night in terms of *Verwerfung* and that, I agree, is not free of difficulties – which is why we will have to return to it this year. I nevertheless believe that the Seminar on psychosis made it possible for you to understand, if not the ultimate mainspring, at least the essential mechanism by which the Other, the big Other, the Other as the seat of speech, is reduced to the imaginary other. It involves the suppletion of the symbolic by the imaginary.

As a consequence, you grasped how it is that we are able to conceptualize the effect of total foreignness of the real produced at moments of rupture in the psychotic's delusional dialogue, which is his sole means of maintaining within himself what I will call a certain kind of intransitivity of the subject. It seems quite natural to us. 'I am thinking, therefore I am', as we say, intransitively. For sure, this is where the difficulty lies for the psychotic, precisely because of the reduction of the duality of the Other with a big O and the other with a little o, the Other as the seat of speech and guarantor of truth, and the dual other, the one whom the subject finds himself faced with as his own image. The disappearance of this double aspect is precisely what makes it so difficult for the psychotic to maintain himself in the human real, that is to say, in the symbolic real.

Over the course of that third year, dealing with the dimension of what I call dialogue, insofar as it makes it possible for a subject to sustain himself, I illustrated it with no more, no less than an example from the first scene of Racine's *Athaliah*. This is a Seminar that I would have quite liked to return to and write up, had I had the time.

Nevertheless, I think that you won't have forgotten the extraordinary first dialogue of the play, where one sees this Abner come forward, prototype of the false friend and double agent, coming to test the water right from the word go. His 'Yes, I come into his temple to adore the Eternal Lord' [Act 1, Scene 1] initially sounds like some sort of attempt at seduction. The way in which we crowned this play has no doubt made us forget all these resonances somewhat, but do admire how extraordinary it is. I stressed how, for his part, the High Priest put in a few essential signifiers – 'And God found faithful in all his threats', or, again, 'Why do you renounce the promises of heaven?' The term 'heaven', and also several other well-chosen words, are nothing but pure signifiers. I stressed their total emptiness. Jehoiada skewers, as it were, his opponent to the point of henceforth transforming him into this pathetic earthworm who, as I said, re-enters the ranks of the procession and serves as the bait for Athaliah, who ends up falling for this little game.

The signifier's relation to the signified, so palpable in this dramatic dialogue, led me to refer to Ferdinand de Saussure's famous schema in which you see the double parallel flow of signifiers and signifieds, distinct and destined to perpetually slide over one another. It was in reference to this that I fabricated the image, borrowed from the upholsterer's craft, of the quilting point. There does have to be some point, effectively, at which the fabric of one becomes attached to the fabric of the other, so that we know where we stand, at least with respect to the possible limits of the sliding. There are quilting points, then, but they leave some elasticity in the links between the two terms.

We will pick things up from here this year, once I have told you where the dialogue between Jehoiada and Abner, in parallel and symmetrically with this, ends up – namely, with the fact that the only real subject that stands up is the subject who speaks in the name of speech. You won't have forgotten the plane on which Jehoiada speaks – 'Hear how this God replies to you through my mouth.' There is no subject except in reference to this Other. This is symbolic of what exists in all valid speech.

Similarly, in the fourth year of my Seminar, I wanted to show you that the only object is a metonymic object, the object of desire being the object of the Other's desire, and desire always being desire for some Other thing, very precisely for what is lacking, a, the primordially lost object, insofar as Freud shows it to us as always having to be refound. Similarly, the only meaning is metaphorical meaning, meaning emerging only from the substitution of one signifier for another in the symbolic chain.

This is connoted in the work I was talking about before, which I invited you to read, 'The Instance of the Letter in the Unconscious'. The following symbols are those for metonymy and metaphor, respectively.

$$f(S \dots S')\, S'' \cong S\,(-)\, s$$

$$f\!\left(\frac{S'}{S}\right) S'' \cong S\,(+)\, s$$

In the first formula, S is linked to S′ in the chain's combination, both of them in relation to S″, the result of which is to put S in a certain metonymic relationship with s at the level of signification.

14

Similarly, the substitution of S′ for S in relation to S″ results in the relationship S(+)s, which here indicates – this is easier to say than in the case of metonymy – the emergence or creation of meaning.

This, then, is where we are. We are now going to start on what will be the object of our research this year.

2

I have constructed a schema for investigating this object and I am now going to tell you what, at least for today, it can be used to connote.

If we have to find a way to examine the signifying chain's relations with the signified chain, it would be by means of the crude image of the quilting point.

For it to be valid, you would still have to ask where the upholsterer is. He is obviously somewhere, but the place where we could put him in the schema would, nevertheless, be far too simplistic.

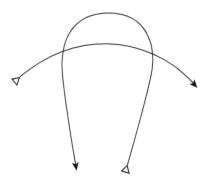

Since, between the signifying chain and the flow of the signified, there is, as it were, a reciprocal sliding, which is what is essential in their relationship, and since, despite this sliding, there is a liaison or coherence between these two currents, and we have to grasp where it appears, it may occur to us that this sliding, if sliding there be, is necessarily a relative sliding. Displacement in one produces displacement in the other. Thus, it must be through something like the intersecting of the two lines in opposite directions, in a sort of ideal present, that we will find an exemplary schema.

This, then, is what we might focus our speculations on.

All the same, whatever importance this notion of the present must possess for us, a discourse is not a punctiform event, à la Russell, if I can put it like that. A discourse not only has a substance, a texture, but it takes time, it has a dimension in time, a thickness. We absolutely cannot be satisfied with an instantaneous present, our entire experience runs counter to it, as does everything that we have said. We can present this immediately through the experience of speech. For instance, if I begin a sentence, you will not understand its meaning until I have got to the end. It's completely necessary – this is the definition of a sentence – that I say the final word for you to understand what the first was about. This provides us with the most tangible example of what can be called the *nachträglich* action of a signifier. This is precisely what I am constantly showing you in the text of analytic experience itself, on an infinitely grander scale, when we are dealing with the history of the past.

Moreover, one thing is clear – this is one way of putting it – which I stress in a precise manner in 'The Instance of the Letter in the Unconscious'. I ask you to refer to it provisionally. I expressed it in the form of a topological metaphor, if I can put it like that. It's impossible to represent the signifier, the signified and the subject on the same plane. This is neither mysterious nor opaque. It's demonstrable in a very simple way in the text with respect to the Cartesian cogito. I will refrain from returning to it now because we will come across it in a different form.

The aim of this reminder is simply to justify the two lines that we are now going to work with.

The little stopper stands for the beginning of the trajectory, and the tip of the arrow is its end. You will recognize my first line here, which the other hooks onto once it has crossed it twice.

Note that you cannot confuse what these two lines previously represented [in Saussure's diagram] – namely the signifier and the signified – with what they represent here, which is slightly different, for now we are going to place ourselves entirely at the level of the signifier. The effects on the signified are elsewhere; they are not directly represented. In this schema, we see the two states or functions that we can apprehend in a sequence of signifiers.

The first line [which goes from left to right] represents the signifying chain insofar as it remains completely permeable to the properly signifying effects of metaphor and metonymy, which implies the possible actualization of signifying effects at all levels, and down to the phonemic level in particular. The phonological element is in effect what puns, word plays and so on are based on. In short, it's the signifying material we analysts constantly have to play with. Apart from those of you who have come here for the first time, you will have some idea of this, and this is why today we will start exploring the subject of the unconscious by way of wit, *Witz*.

16

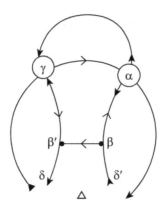

The other line [from right to left] is the line of rational discourse, into which a number of reference points or fixed things are already integrated. These things can only be properly grasped in this case at the level of the usage of signifiers, that is, at the level of what concretely, in the use of discourse, constitutes fixed points. As you know, they are a long way from corresponding univocally to a thing. No one single semanteme corresponds to one single thing. Most of the time, a semanteme corresponds to a wide variety of things. We are pausing here at the level of the semanteme, that is, at what is fixed and defined by usage.

This, then, is the line of common, everyday discourse, such as is admitted into the code of the discourse that I will call the discourse of reality we all share. This is also the level at which the fewest meanings are created, since meaning is already there and in some way already given. Most of the time this discourse only consists of a subtle mixture of received ideas. It's precisely at this level that the famous empty discourse is produced, which is what a number of my remarks on the function of speech and the field of language were based on.

As you can plainly see, this line is the individual subject's concrete discourse, the discourse of the person who speaks and makes himself understood. It's discourse that can be recorded on a disk, whereas the former [line] is everything that this includes by way of possibilities of decomposition, reinterpretation, resonance, and metaphorical and metonymic effects. They go in opposite directions, for the simple reason that they slide over one another. But one intersects the other. And they intersect at two perfectly recognizable points.

If we start with discourse, the first point at which it meets the properly signifying chain is what I have just been explaining to you from the point of view of the signifier, namely the bundle of usages. I will call this the code, at a point here marked α.

17

The code really has to be somewhere here if the discourse is to be capable of being heard. This code is very obviously located in the big Other, that is, in the Other insofar as it's the companion of language. It's absolutely necessary that this big Other exist, and, I beg you to take note of this, there is absolutely no need to call it by the idiotic and delusional name 'collective consciousness'. An Other is an Other. One is enough for a language to be a living language – so much so that this Other is able to constitute the first moment all on its own. The fact that there is one person who remains and is able to speak his own language to himself is enough for there to be he himself plus not only one Other but even two, in any case someone who understands him. One can still make word plays in a language of which one is the sole possessor.

That, then, is the initial encounter, which occurs at the level of what I am calling the code. The second intersection, which closes the circle and constitutes meaning properly so-called, and constitutes it on the basis of the code that it initially encountered, occurs at this endpoint labelled γ. As you can see, two arrows terminate there, and I will dispense with telling you today what the second one is. The result of the conjunction of discourse with the signifier as the medium that creates meaning is the message.

Meaning comes into being in the message. The truth that is there to be announced, if truth there be, is here. Most of the time no truth is announced, for the simple reason that most often discourse absolutely does not go via the signifying chain and is the pure and simple purring of repetition, idle chatter, short-circuiting between β and β'. The discourse says absolutely nothing, apart from indicating to you that I am a speaking animal. This is everyday discourse, words put together for the purpose of saying nothing, owing to which you reassure yourself that you are not simply dealing, opposite you, with what man is in his natural state, namely a ferocious beast.

The two points – the minimum nodal points for the short-circuit of discourse – are easily recognizable. There is, on the one hand, at β', the object in the sense of the metonymic object I spoke to you about last year. There is, on the other hand, at β, the *I* insofar as it indicates the place in discourse itself of the one who is speaking.

In this schema it's possible to put our finger, in a tangible way, on what binds and what distinguishes statement [*énoncé*] and utterance [*énonciation*]. This is a truth that is perfectly and immediately accessible to linguistic experience, but which in Freudian experience coincides with the distinction that exists, at least in principle, between the *I* that is nothing other than the place of him who is speaking in the discourse chain, which moreover doesn't even need

18

to be designated by an *I*, and, on the other hand, the message, which, to exist, requires the apparatus of this schema as an absolute minimum. It's totally impossible to bring out a message or a statement of any kind whatsoever, in a radiating and concentric manner, on the basis of any subject, without this entire complexity – and this is for the good reason that speech specifically presupposes the existence of a signifying chain.

Its genesis is far from simple to obtain – we spent a year getting there. It presumes the existence of a network of uses, in other words, of usage for a given language. It presumes as well an entire mechanism that makes it the case that – whatever you say in thinking about it, or in not thinking about it, whatever you formulate – once you have mounted the treadmill of idle chatter, your discourse always says more than what you are saying.

Moreover, solely by virtue of the fact that it's speech, discourse is founded on the existence somewhere of this reference point that is the plane of truth – of truth as distinct from reality, which brings into play the possible emergence of new meanings introduced into the world or reality. These are not meanings that are already there, but meanings that are brought about by speech and that speech literally brings into the world.

Here you have, radiating out from the message on the one hand and from the *I* on the other, these little fins which indicate two divergent directions. From the *I*, one goes towards the metonymic object and the second towards the Other. Symmetrically, following the return path of discourse, the message goes towards the metonymic object and towards the Other. This is all provisional, I ask you to take note, but you will see that these two lines that may look like they are self-evident, the one that goes from the *I* towards the Other, and the one that goes from the *I* towards the metonymic object, will be very useful to us.

You will also see what the other two lines, which are incredibly fascinating, correspond to, those that go from the message towards the code and from the code towards the message. Effectively, the return line exists and, if it did not exist, there would not be the slightest hope of creating meaning, as the schema shows you. The essential dimension that witticisms [*trait d'esprit*] bring us right into is at work specifically in the interplay between message and code, thus also in the return from the code to the message.

We will stay at this point for a number of seminars so that we can see everything that is extraordinarily suggestive and indicative that may occur there.

This will also give us a further opportunity to grasp how the metonymic object, this famous object that we started looking at last

19

year, this object that is never there, that is always situated elsewhere, that is always something else, is in a relationship of dependence.

Let's now turn to the *Witz*.

3

'*Witz*' has been translated into French as *trait d'esprit*. '*Mot d'esprit*' has also been used. I'll spare you the reasons why I prefer the former translation. But '*Witz*' also means *esprit*. The term is therefore immediately presented to us with an extreme ambiguity.

Traits d'esprit, witticisms, are sometimes an object of disparagement – they are light, not serious, fanciful and capricious. What about *esprit*? Here, on the other hand, one pauses and thinks twice before speaking of it in the same way.

It's fitting that all these ambiguities should be left open to '*esprit*', including even '*esprit*' in the broad sense, as in the *esprit* that obviously serves all too often as an ensign for doubtful merchandise, the *esprit* of spiritualism. But the notion of *esprit* nonetheless has a centre of gravity, which for us resides in *esprit* in the sense in which one speaks of an *homme spirituel*, a witty man, and does so even if he does not have a terribly good reputation. We centre *esprit* on the *trait d'esprit*, that is, on what in it seems the most contingent, the most outdated and the most open to criticism. It's indeed part of the genius of psychoanalysis to do things like that, and this is why we should not be astonished that the one point in Freud's work where he mentions what is elsewhere honoured with a capital letter, namely, *Esprit*, is in his work on *Witz*. There is, nonetheless, a relationship between the two poles of the term, which has always been a source of disagreement.

It would be amusing to evoke the English tradition with you. 'Wit' is even more clearly ambiguous than '*Witz*', and even more than '*esprit*' in French. Discussions have flourished on true, authentic wit – in a word, good wit – and also on bad wit, that is, the wit with which charlatans entertain their audience. How are they to be distinguished? We would have to refer to the difficulties that critics have got themselves into. After the eighteenth century with Addison, Pope, and so on, this discussion continues into the early nineteenth century with the English Romantic school, where the question of wit could not fail to be put on the agenda. Hazlitt's writings are very significant in this regard. It was Coleridge, whom we will have occasion to discuss, who went the furthest in this direction.

Equally, I could speak of the German tradition. In particular the promotion of *esprit* to the highest plane of literary Christianity

20

followed a strictly parallel evolution in Germany. The question of *Witz* is there at the heart of all Romantic speculation, which will hold our interest as much from a historical point of view as from that of the situation of analysis.

What is altogether striking is that there is nothing in France that corresponds to this interest by critics in the question of *Witz* or wit.* The only people who have taken any serious interest in the matter are poets. In the nineteenth century, not only is the question a live one for them, but it's at the heart of the work of Baudelaire and Mallarmé. Elsewhere, it has only ever been present, even in essays, from the standpoint of criticism, I mean from the standpoint of an intellectual formulation of the problem.

I leave to one side the main tradition, the Spanish one, because it's too important for us not to have to return to it frequently later on.

The decisive point is this – whatever you read on the problem of *Witz* or wit,* the fact is that you will always arrive at tangible impasses, which only time prevents me from developing today. I'll come back to this. I will omit this part of my talk, but later I will prove to you what a leap, what a sharp rupture, what a difference in quality and results, characterize Freud's work.

Freud did not carry out the enquiry I have just been alluding to on the European tradition of *Witz*. He tells us what his sources are, and they are clear – there are three very sensible, very readable books by good German professors from minor universities who had the time to reflect peacefully and who wrote these things that were not at all pedantic. They are Kruno Fischer, Theodor Vischer and Theodor Lipps, a Munich professor whose work is the best of the three, and who goes quite far, to the point of lending a hand to Freud's research. Simply put, if Herr Lipps had not been so worried about the respectability of *Witz*, if he hadn't wanted there to be false wit and true wit, he would certainly have gone a lot further. This, on the contrary, was never something that held Freud back. He had already formed the habit of compromising himself, and this is why he was able to see much more clearly. It's also because he saw the structural relations that exist between *Witz* and the unconscious.

On what plane did he see them? Uniquely on a plane that can be called formal. I mean 'formal', not in the sense of pretty forms, curves and everything with which people try to drown you in the blackest obscurantism, but in the sense in which one speaks of form in literary theory, for example. There is effectively yet another tradition that I have not spoken to you about, but this is also because I will have to come back to it often, a recent tradition, which is the Czech tradition. Your ignorance leads you to think that the reference to formalism has a vague meaning. Not at all. 'Formalism' has an extremely precise meaning – it's a school of literary criticism, which the state apparatus located in the land of the Sputnik has been persecuting for some time now. Be that as it may, Freud places himself at the level of this formalism, that is, of a structural theory of the signifier as such, and the result is not in doubt – it's even thoroughly convincing. This is a key that makes it possible to go much further.

Having asked you to read my articles from time to time, I do not really need to ask you to read Freud's book, *Der Witz und seine Beziehung zum Unbewussten*. Since I am talking about *Witz* this year, this seems to me to be the least one can do. You will see that the economy of this book is founded on the fact that Freud starts with the technique of witticisms, and constantly returns to it. What does this mean for him? It's a matter of a 'verbal technique', as they say. I say, more precisely, a 'technique of the signifier'.

Because Freud begins with the technique of the signifier, and because he constantly returns to it, he really does unpack the problem. He brings out distinct levels, and we suddenly see, with the greatest clarity, what you have to know how to distinguish if you are to avoid getting lost in perpetual confusions over the signified, in thoughts that you are unable to extract yourself from. You will see, for example, that there is the problem of witticisms and the problem of the comic, and these are not at all the same thing. Similarly, the problem of the comic and the problem of laughter, even though these sometimes go together, and even though all three get confused, are not at all the same problem.

In short, to clarify the problem of wit, Freud starts with signifying technique, and we too will start from there along with him.   22

What is curious is that this takes place at a level about which absolutely nothing indicates that it's at the level of the unconscious. But, for deep reasons which have to do with the very nature of what is at issue in *Witz*, it's precisely by looking there that we will see most clearly what is not completely there but is off to the side – namely, the unconscious. The unconscious, in fact, is only ever illuminated and only reveals itself when you look away a little. This is something that you will rediscover in *Witz* all the time, for it's in its very nature – you look away and this makes it possible for you to see what is not there.

Let's begin, then, along with Freud, with the keys to the technique of the signifier.

Freud didn't go to too much trouble to look for examples – almost all the ones he gives, and they may strike us as a bit banal and unequal in value, are taken from these three professors, and this is why I spoke of the esteem in which I hold them. But there is, nevertheless, another author in whom Freud truly is steeped – Heinrich Heine – and it's from this source that he takes his first example.

There is a marvellous quip that comes from the mouth of Hirsch-Hyacinth, a Jew from Hamburg, lottery ticket agent, hard-working and half starved, whom Heine encounters in the baths at Lucca. If you want to undertake a comprehensive reading of Freud's *Witz*, you will need to read *Reisebilder, Travel Pictures*. It's astonishing that it's not a classic. In it you will discover, in the part set in Italy, a passage in which this indescribable character features, and whose properties I hope I still have time to say something about today.

In the course of their conversation, Hirsch-Hyacinth declares to Heine that he had the honour of treating the corns of the great Rothschild, Nathan the Wise. While he is trimming his corns, he says to himself that he, Hirsch-Hyacinth, is an important man. He is effectively thinking that during this procedure Nathan the Wise was mulling over the various letters that he would be sending to kings, and that if he, Hirsch-Hyacinth, should trim his corns a little too closely, this would result in an irritation in the upper regions that would in turn cause Nathan to clip the hide of kings a little more.

And thus, one thing leads to another. Hirsch-Hyacinth goes on to talk about another Rothschild that he knew, Salomon Rothschild. One day, when he announces himself as Hirsch-Hyacinth, he receives a reply in nonchalant terms, 'I am a lottery-agent myself, for the Rothschild lottery, I do not want any colleague of mine in the kitchen.' And, Hirsch-Hyacinth exclaims, 'He treated me in quite a famillionaire manner.'

This is where Freud pauses.

What is 'famillionaire'? Is it a neologism, a slip of the tongue, a witticism? It's a witticism, for sure, but the simple fact that I am able to ask these other two questions already introduces us to a fundamental ambiguity concerning signifiers in the unconscious.

What does Freud say? That we can recognize here the mechanism of condensation, that it's materialized in the material of the signifiers and that it involves a sort of stamping together, by means of some machinery or other, of two lines of the signifying chain. Freud completes the witticism with a very nice signifying schema on which '*familiär*' is first entered, then, underneath, '*Millionär*'. Phonetically, '*är*' is on both lines, '*mili*' also; things get condensed and, in the interval between the two, '*familionär*' appears.

| famili | är |
mili	onär
faMILIon	ÄR

Let's try and see what this produces using the schema on the blackboard. I am obliged to move quickly here, but I have something to point out to you.

Discourse can obviously be schematized by saying that it starts from the *I* and goes to the Other. It's more correct to recognize that, whatever we might think, all discourse starts from the Other, α, that it's reflected by the *I* at β, since the latter must play some part in the matter, that it returns to the Other at a second moment – hence the invoking of the Other, 'I was on completely familiar terms with Salomon Rothschild' – and that it then heads off towards the message, γ.

But don't forget that the reason this schema is interesting is that there are two lines and that things circulate at one and the same time along the line of the signifying chain. Owing to the mysterious property of the phonemes that are in both words, something correlatively stirs within the signifiers – there is an unsettling of the elementary signifying chain as such. Three moments can also be distinguished on the side of the chain.

At the first moment the message takes shape.

At the second moment, the chain is reflected by the metonymic object at β', 'my millionaire'. In effect, what is involved for Hirsch-Hyacinth is the schematized, metonymic object that belongs to him. He is 'his' millionaire, but at the same time he is not, because the case is, indeed, rather that the millionaire owns him. Result – it doesn't go through and this is precisely why, at the second moment, 'millionaire' is reflected back at β', at the same time as the other term, the 'familiar' manner, arrives at α.

At the third moment, 'millionaire' and 'familiar' meet and come together in the message at γ to form 'famillionaire'.

This schema may strike you as a frivolous one to provide, even though a good one because I am the one who put it together. However, as it falls into place over the course of the year, maybe you will say to yourselves that it has been useful for something. In particular, owing to the topographical requirements it presents us with, it enables us to proceed in a measured way as far as the signifier is concerned. In the way it's constructed, however you run through it, it limits all our steps – I mean that with every step we have to take, the schema requires us to take no more than three elementary ones. This is what the little stoppers at the beginning and the arrowheads are defined for, as are the [directional] fins along the segments, which always have to be in an intermediary, second position. The others either start or end.

Thus, in three moments, the two chains – that of discourse and that of the signifier – have ended up converging on the same point,

24

which is that of the message. This makes it the case that Herr Hirsch-Hyacinth was treated in a completely 'famillionaire' manner.

This message is completely incongruous, in the sense that it's not received, it's not in the code. That is the crux of the matter. To be sure, the message is in theory designed to be distinct from the code, but here, it's on the actual plane of the signifier that it's manifestly in violation of the code.

The definition of 'witticism' I propose rests, first, on the fact that the message is produced at a particular level of signifying production, that it's differentiated and distinguished from the code, and that it assumes its value as a message by virtue of this distinction and this differentiation. The message lies in its difference from the code.

How is this difference confirmed? This is where the second plane comes in. This difference is confirmed as a witticism by the Other. This is indispensable and it's in Freud.

There are two things in Freud's book on witticisms – the emphasis on the signifying technique, and the explicit reference to the Other as a third party. This reference, which I have been drilling into you for ages, is absolutely spelt out by Freud, especially in the second part of his work, but necessarily from the outset.

For instance, Freud is constantly stressing the difference between witticisms and the comic, which is due to the fact that the comic is dual. The comic is a dual relation, and there has to be a third Other for witticisms to exist. Confirmation by the Other as third party, whether supported or not by an individual person, is essential here. The Other lobs it back, he places the message in the code as a witticism, he says in the code, 'This is a witticism'. If no one does this, there is no witticism. If no one observes it, if 'famillionaire' is a slip, there is no witticism. It's therefore necessary that the Other codify it as a witticism, that it be inscribed in the code through the Other's intervention.

The third element of my definition is that witticisms are related to something that is profoundly located at the level of meaning. I am not saying that this is *a* truth, for the subtle allusions to some kind of psychology of millionaires and parasites – even though they contribute greatly to our pleasure, we will come back to this – do not explain the production of 'famillionaire'. I am saying it's *the* truth.

I put it to you, as of today, that the essence of witticisms – if we wish to seek it, and seek it with Freud, for he will take us as far as is possible in the direction where its crux lies, since it's a question of its crux, and crux there is – resides in their relation to a radical dimension, which essentially depends on truth, namely, what I called in my article 'The Instance of the Letter', the dimension of truth's alibi.

No matter how close we get to the essence of witticisms, which never fail to produce a kind of mental double vision in us, what is always at issue, and which is what witticisms explicitly do, is this – they designate, and always off to the side, what is only ever seen by looking elsewhere.

This is where we will pick things up next time. I am clearly ending with something left up in the air, with an enigma. I think, however, that I have at least set the terms that, as I will show you in what is to come, we must necessarily rally to.

6 November 1957

II

THE *FAT-MILLIONAIRE*

Substitution, condensation and metaphor
'*Atterré*'
From jokes to slips and to the forgetting of names
Ruins and metonymic sparks
The parasite and his master

Let me pick up the discussion from where I left off last time, at the point at which Hirsch-Hyacinth, talking to the author of *Reisebilder*, whom he met at the baths of Lucca, says to him, 'As true as God shall grant me all good things, I was sitting with Salomon Rothschild, and he treated me quite like an equal, he was completely famillionaire.'

1

We will begin, then, with the word 'famillionaire', which, all in all, had its moment of fame and fortune. It's known for being Freud's starting point, and I will thereby attempt to show you how he approaches witticisms.

If his analysis is of use to us and if this point is exemplary, it's because it shows us – and, sadly, we need this badly – the indisputable importance of the signifier in what, with Freud, we can call unconscious mechanisms.

It's surprising to see that when they grapple with the delicate subject of aphasia, that is, with speech deficits, neurologists, whose discipline doesn't prepare them for this particularly well, make remarkably steady progress in what might be called their linguistic training. Psychoanalysts, on the other hand, whose entire art and technique rest on the use of speech, have never paid it the least bit of attention, despite the fact that Freud's references to philology are not simply humanistic references displaying his culture or his reading, but grow organically from his research work.

Since at least the majority of you will have had a look at Freud's work on *Witz* since we last met, you will have seen that his entire argument revolves around the technique of witticisms as a linguistic technique. While the meaning and signification that emerge in witticisms seem to him to deserve to be compared to the unconscious, this is based solely on their function of creating pleasure. I am hammering away at this, since everything that I have to say about witticisms refers to it – the essential element always and uniquely revolves around structural analogies that can only be conceptualized on the linguistic plane, and that appear between the technical or verbal aspect of witticisms and the mechanisms specific to the unconscious which he discovered, giving them such names as 'condensation' and 'displacement' – I will limit myself to those two today.

This is where we are. Hirsch-Hyacinth, one of Heinrich Heine's fictional characters, recounts what happened to him. To cleave to the segment that I picked out to begin with, a very clear utterance is produced at the outset, elevating what follows, putting it on display and exalting it. It's an invocation addressed to the universal Witness and to the subject's personal relations with this Witness, that is, with God. 'As true as God shall grant me all good things' – this is both undeniably significant with respect to its meaning and ironic because of what in reality is shown to be lacking. Then what follows – 'I was sitting next to Salomon Rothschild, totally like an equal' – makes the object emerge. This 'totally' [*tout à fait*] contains something that is quite significant. Whenever we invoke a totality, it's because we are not totally certain that it actually obtains. You find this at many levels, I would even say at all [*tous*] levels, in the use of the notion of totality.

Finally, the unexpected phenomenon, the scandal when it comes to enunciation, is produced, namely, this novel message, and we don't yet know what it is, for we can't name it yet – 'in quite a famillionaire manner, quite famillionairely'.

Is this a bungled act or a successful one? A slip or a poetic creation? We don't know. Maybe it's both at once. But it's fitting to think about the formation of the phenomenon strictly on the plane of the signifier. Effectively, as I declared last time, there is a signifying function here that is specific to witticisms, involving a signifier that is not included in the code, that is, not in any of the signifying formations that, in the signifier's signified-creating functions, have accumulated up to that point. Something new appears, which can be conceived of as tied to the very mainspring of what we can call the progress of, or the changes in, language, but which requires that before we get to it we think about its very formation in order to locate it in relation to the signifier's formative mechanism.

The essential phenomenon is the nodal point [*noeud*] at which 'famillionaire', this new and paradoxical signifier, appears. Freud begins with it and returns to it repeatedly. He asks us to dwell on it and, right till the end of his speculations on witticisms, as you will see, he doesn't fail to reflect on it as an essential phenomenon. It's the technical phenomenon that distinguishes witticisms. That is the central phenomenon. He teaches us about the level that is specifically ours, the level of relations with the unconscious, while simultaneously clarifying from a new perspective what leads him into the tendencies – this is the word used in this work – as well as what is there around it and radiating out from it, the comic, laughter and so on. If we fail to reflect on this, we will be unable to validly articulate the consequences and accompaniments of the phenom-enon as well as its sources and reference points.

Let's think, then, about 'famillionaire'. There are several ways of going about it. The aim of my schema is to make it possible for you to do this, but also to allow you to inscribe on it the different planes of elaboration involving the signifier – I have chosen the word 'elab-oration' because it's emphasized by Freud. So as not to give you too great a surprise, let's start at the level of meaning.

What happens when 'famillionaire' appears? We initially experi-ence something like an aiming towards meaning, a meaning that is ironic, even satirical. Less apparent, unfolding in the after-effects of the phenomenon, propagating itself in the world in its wake, an object also emerges, one that tends towards the comic, the absurd and nonsense. This is the character of the famillionaire, insofar as it ridicules the millionaire, and begins to take shape as a figure.

It doesn't take much to show you in what direction he begins to be incarnated. Freud himself points out to us in passing that Heinrich Heine, redoubling his witticism, calls the millionaire the *Millionarr*, which in German means something like the scatter-brained mil-lionaire. Along the same line of turning famillionaire into a noun, in French we could say, '*le fat-millionaire*', with a hyphen, the con-ceited millionaire.

This approach shows you that we are not inhuman. This is a good thing, as long as we do not go too much further in that direction. It's the kind of step that shouldn't be rushed. We mustn't understand too quickly because, by understanding too quickly, we don't under-stand a thing. Such considerations do not explain the phenomenon, or in what way the latter is connected to the general economy of signifiers.

2

On this point, I must insist that you all familiarize yourselves with the examples I gave in 'The Instance of the Letter' of what I call the essential functions of the signifier, insofar as it's by means of them that the ploughshare of the signifier ploughs the signified into the real, literally evoking it, making it emerge, working it and creating it. They concern the functions of metaphor and metonymy.

It seems that for some people it's my style, let's say, that makes it impossible to read the article.

I regret it, but there's nothing I can do about it – my style is what it is. I ask them to make an effort here. I will just add that whatever deficiencies have been introduced by my own personal doing, there is also something – perhaps they are half-aware of this – that corresponds to the very object in question in the difficulties of this style. Since the point in the article is to speak in a valid way about the creative functions that signifiers exercise over signifieds, namely, not simply to speak about speech but to speak wholly in keeping with speech, as it were, so as to evoke its very functions, perhaps there are internal necessities of style that are required – such as conciseness, allusion, and even a few barbs, which are elements needed for entering the field where they dominate not only its avenues but its entire texture. I hope that what I have to say this year will demonstrate this. We shall return to it concerning a certain style that I will not hesitate to call by its name, as ambiguous as it may seem, namely, mannerism. I will try to show you that it not only has a great tradition behind it but that it also serves an irreplaceable function.

That was only a parenthesis to bring us back to my text.

In it, then, you will see that what I call, following Roman Jakobson who invented them, the metaphorical and metonymic functions of language can be very simply expressed in the register of signifiers.

As I have already stated several times over the course of previous years, the characteristics of signifiers are those of the existence of an articulated chain, and, as I add in this article, they tend to form closed groups, that is, groups formed by a series of rings linked together to form chains, which themselves link up like rings with other chains. The general form of my schema also evokes this a little, without presenting it directly. The existence of these chains implies that the connections or links between signifiers involve two dimensions, one that can be called the combination, continuity or concatenation of the chain, and one of substitution, whose possibilities are always implicit in each element of the chain. This second dimension is left out of the linear definitions that are given of the relationship between signifiers and signifieds.

In other words, in every linguistic act, while the diachronic dimension is essential, synchrony is also implied or evoked by the permanent possibility of substitution inherent in each of the signifying terms.

Last time I wrote two formulas up on the board for you, one that gave a representation of combination and the other an image of the relationship of substitution that is always implicit in every signifying articulation. We need no extraordinary powers of intuition to see that there must be some relationship between the formula for metaphor and what Freud gives us with the schema of the formation of 'famillionaire'.

What might his schema mean? It could mean that something has fallen out in the interval, which has been eluded in the articulation of meaning, at the same time as something has occurred that has compressed or concertinaed 'familiar' and 'millionaire' into one another to produce 'famillionaire', which is what is left. There is, here, a sort of special case of the function of substitution, a special case whose traces remain in some way. Condensation is, if you will, a specific form of what can occur at the level of substitution as a function.

It would be good if you keep in mind, starting now, my lengthy commentary on a metaphor, that of Booz's sheaf, '*Sa gerbe n'était point avare ni haineuse*', 'His sheaf was neither miserly nor hateful', showing how the fact that 'his sheaf' replaces the term 'Booz' forms the metaphor here. Owing to this metaphor, a meaning emerges around the figure of Booz, the meaning of the advent of his paternity, with everything that can radiate and spring from it, by virtue of the fact that he comes to it in an unlikely, belated, unforeseen, providential and divine manner. This metaphor is there in the poem precisely to show the advent of a new meaning around Booz, this character who seemed to have been excluded, foreclosed from it.

It's in the relationship of substitution that metaphor's creative mainspring, creative force or power to engender – that's the word for it! – lies.

Metaphor has a completely general function. I would even say that it's the possibility of substitution that allows the engendering, so to speak, of the world of meaning to be conceived. It's here, and nowhere else, that we must grasp the entire history of language, namely the changes in function owing to which a language is constituted.

If some day we wished to give a model or example of the genesis and appearance of a language in the midst of the unformed reality of the world as it was before anyone spoke, we would need to assume the existence of an original, irreducible given, which would of course be the smallest possible signifying chain. I won't insist on this 'smallest possible' today, but I have already given you enough indications about this for you to know that it's by way of metaphor, by the play of the substitution of one signifier for another in a given place, that the possibility is created not only of signifying developments but also of the emergence of ever new meanings, always tending towards refining, complicating, deepening and giving its sense of depth to what in the real is nothing but pure opacity.

To illustrate this, I would like to give an example of what might be called the evolution of meaning, where we almost always find the mechanism of substitution. As is my wont, I let chance provide me with examples. And, indeed, one was provided to me by someone close to me who, while working on a translation, had to look up the meaning of the word '*atterré*' in the dictionary, and was surprised to realize that he had never understood the actual meaning of the word until then. In effect, '*atterré*' did not originally, nor in many of its uses, have the meaning of stricken with terror, but that of *mis-à-terre*, knocked to the ground or brought to the ground.

In Bossuet, '*atterrer*' literally means to knock to the ground. In other, slightly later texts we see the weight of '*terreur*', which purists would say contaminates, changes the meaning of the word '*atterré*'. The purists are indisputably wrong about this. There isn't any such contamination. Even if, all of a sudden, following this reminder about the etymological meaning of the word '*atterré*', some of you are under the illusion that '*atterrer*' obviously means nothing other than turn towards the ground, bring to the ground, or place at the level of the ground – in other words, fill with consternation – the fact remains that the word's current usage implies a backdrop of terror.

Take another word that bears a certain relationship to the original meaning of the word '*atterré*'. This is purely conventional, because there is no origin of the word '*atterré*', but let's agree [for the sake of argument] that it's the word '*abattu*', brought down, killed, demoralized or exhausted, insofar as it effectively evokes what the word '*atterré*' might evoke for us in its purportedly pure meaning.

The word '*atterré*' is, then, substituted for the word '*abattu*'. It's a metaphor.

It's a metaphor that doesn't look like one, since we start with the hypothesis that they originally meant the same thing, thrown to the ground or on the ground. This is what I ask you to notice – it's not because the meaning of '*atterré*' changes the meaning of '*abattu*' in any way that the word is fertile, generating new meaning.

33

However, saying that someone has been *atterré* is not the same thing as saying that someone has been *abattu* and, however much terror is implied, it doesn't mean terrorized either. There is an extra nuance, something new, a new meaning. A new nuance of terror is thereby introduced into the psychological and already metaphorical meaning of the word '*abattu*'.

It's self-evident that, psychologically speaking, no one is '*atterré*', or '*abattu*', in the strict sense. This is something that we cannot say so long as there are no words, and these words are a product of a metaphor – namely, what happens when a tree is felled, *abattu*, or when a wrestler is taken down [*mis à terre*], *atterré*, a second metaphor.

But what is interesting about the thing is seeing that terror, *terreur*, is introduced by earth [*terre*], which is in '*atterré*'. In other words, a metaphor is not an injection of meaning – as if that were possible, as if meanings existed in a reservoir somewhere [just waiting to be injected]. If the word '*atterré*' brings a new meaning with it, it's not insofar as it has a signification, but insofar as it's a signifier. It's because it contains a phoneme that is also found in the word '*terreur*'. It's by way of the signifier, that of equivocation or homonymy – that is, by way of the most meaningless thing there is – that the word comes to create this nuance of meaning, this nuance of terror, which it's going to introduce or inject into the already metaphorical meaning of the word '*abattu*'.

In other words, it's in the relationship of one signifier to another signifier that a certain relationship of *signifier over signified* will be engendered. The distinction between the two is essential.

$$\frac{S}{S'} \to \frac{S}{s}$$

It's on the basis of the signifier-to-signifier relationship, of the link between this signifier over here and that signifier over there – on the basis of a relationship between signifiers alone, that is, the homonymic relationship, between '*atterré*' and '*terreur*' – that the action of creating signification, namely, the nuancing by 'terror' of what already existed by way of meaning on a metaphorical basis, is going to occur.

This exemplifies for us what happens at the level of metaphor. The metaphorical pathway presides not only over the creation and evolution of a language, but also over the creation and evolution of meaning as such, I mean over meaning insofar as it's not only perceived, but insofar as the subject is included therein, that is, insofar as meaning enriches our lives.

34

I would again like to point out to you just the beginning of a pathway which connects up with what we see happening in the unconscious.

I have already indicated to you the essential role of the hook, '*terre*', which we must regard purely as a signifier, and the role of the homonymic domain in which metaphors operate, whether we see it or not. But something else is happening as well. I do not know if you will grasp it immediately. You will grasp it better once you have seen it elaborated. This is just the start of an essential pathway.

The nuance of signification that '*atterré*' brings with it, to the full extent that it's constituted and affirmed, implies – notice this – a degree of domination and a certain taming of your terror. Terror is not only named but also attenuated, and indeed it's this that enables you, moreover, to keep the ambiguity of the word '*atterré*' in your mind. You say to yourself that, after all, '*atterré*' does indeed have a relationship with the ground, *la terre*, that the terror in it is not complete, that the *abattement*, felling, in the sense in which it's unambiguous for you, is prevalent, and that terror is just a shade of meaning.

In short, terror remains partly in the shadows on this occasion, it's not observed head on and is grasped by the intermediary aspect of a depression. What has happened is completely forgotten up till the very moment I remind you of it. The model is, as such, not included in the circuit. In other words, insofar as the nuance '*atterré*' has become established in usage, insofar as it has become meaning and usage of meaning, the signifier is, let's use the word, repressed in the strict sense of the term. Once the use of the word '*atterré*' became established in its current nuance, the model was no longer within reach – unless we looked it up in a dictionary or in a scholarly study – but, as '*terre*', or '*terra*', was repressed.

I've got a bit ahead of myself here, because this is a mode of thinking that you are not very accustomed to yet, but I think that this will save us the trouble of coming back to it again. You will see the extent to which this beginning finds confirmation in our analysis of the phenomena.

3

Let's come back to our '*famillionaire*' and to the point of metaphorical conjunction or condensation at which we saw it form.

It's useful to begin by separating the thing from its context, namely, from the fact that it's Hirsch-Hyacinth, that is, the mind of Heine, that created it. We will ultimately seek its genesis much

35

further back in Heinrich Heine's antecedents and relations with the Rothschild family. We would even need to reread the entire history of the Rothschild family to be completely sure not to make any mistakes. But we are not at that point yet, we are at 'famillionaire'.

Let's isolate it for a moment. Let's zoom in for a close-up on this 'famillionaire'. After all, it might have been born elsewhere than in Heinrich Heine's imagination. Perhaps he didn't make it up when he was sitting in front of a blank sheet of paper, pen in hand. Perhaps it was one evening, during one of those strolls around Paris that I will discuss, that it popped into his head. There is even every chance that it was in a state of fatigue or twilight. 'Famillionaire' might also have been a slip; it's quite conceivable.

I have already referred to a slip that I gathered as it rolled off the tongue of one of my patients. I have others, too, but I will come back to this one because one must always return to the same things until they have been exhausted. Then one can move on to other things. This is the patient who, in the course of recounting his history and associations on my couch, mentioned the period in his life when, with his companion whom he ended up marrying through the good offices of the Mayor, he was living merely *maritablement*, maritably.

All of you will have already grasped that this can be inscribed on Freud's schema – on top we write *'maritalement'*, which means that one is not married, and underneath we write an adverb in which the situations of married and unmarried people come together perfectly: *'misérablement'*, miserably. This gives *'maritablement'*. It's not said, which is much better than being said. You can see here to what extent the message goes beyond, not the messenger – for it's truly the messenger of the gods who is speaking through the mouth of this innocent man – but the medium of speech.

The context, as Freud would say, completely rules out the possibility that my patient was making a joke, and you wouldn't know about it if on this occasion I hadn't been the Other with a big O, that is the listener, and not only the attentive listener, but the listener who hears [*entendant*], in the true sense of the term. The fact remains that, when put in its place, which is precisely in the Other, it's a particularly sensational and brilliant witticism.

Freud gave us countless examples of the close connection between witticisms and slips in *The Psychopathology of Everyday Life*. In certain circumstances a slip can so closely resemble a witticism that Freud himself is obliged to say, and we are obliged to take his word for it, that the context excludes the possibility that the patient in question was trying to make a joke.

Somewhere in the book, Freud gives the example of a woman who, in speaking of the respective situations of men and women,

36

says, 'For a woman to be of interest to men she has to be pretty' – which is not true of everyone, she implies in her sentence – 'but for a man it suffices that he have his five straight limbs'.

Expressions like this are not always entirely translatable, and I am quite often obliged to completely transpose them, that is, to re-create the slips in French. Here it would almost be necessary to use the expression 'completely stiff'. The word *'droit'*, 'straight', is not in common usage, so much so that it isn't in common usage in German either. Freud has to gloss the four and five members to explain the genesis of the thing. The ever-so-slightly suggestive overtone is undeniable. What Freud shows us, in any case, is that the slip doesn't quite go *straight to the point*, any more in German than in French. Moreover, the context rules out the possibility, according to him, that the woman could have been so crude deliberately. It's quite clearly a slip, but you see how closely it resembles a witticism.

It could therefore be a witticism, it could be a slip, and I would even say that it could even just purely and simply be something stupid, something linguistically naive. After all, for my patient, who was a particularly likeable man, *maritablement* was not even a true slip, since the word was clearly part and parcel of his own personal lexicon – he did not in the slightest think he was saying anything extraordinary. There are people who wander through life like that, who sometimes occupy quite high positions, and who utter words of this kind. A famous film producer used to come out with words like that by the bucketful, it seems, all day long. He used to say, for example, to conclude some of his imperious remarks, 'And then, that's how it is, it's signed with a "No".' It was not a slip; it was the simple result of ignorance and stupidity.

Since we have been speaking about parapraxes, which in all of this is what interests us most, let's take a bit of a look at what is going on at this level. Let's return to the parapraxis that we have gone over several times now in order to emphasize the signifier's essential function, the original parapraxis, so to speak, the one that is at the core of Freudian theory, the one that opens *The Psychopathology of Everyday Life* and had been published previously – namely, the forgetting of a proper name, in this instance, 'Signorelli'.

At first sight, a case of forgetting and what I have just been speaking to you about are not the same thing. But if what I am explaining to you carries any weight, if the mechanism or metabolism of the signifier is truly the crux and mainspring of formations of the unconscious, we should be able to find all of them in one of them. What differs outwardly must display its unity inwardly. 37

In forgetting a name, instead of seeing a word like 'famillionaire' emerge, we have the contrary – something goes missing. What does the analysis that Freud provides of the forgetting of proper names and foreign names, to boot, show us?

We read *The Psychopathology of Everyday Life* as if it were the newspaper, and we know so much about it that we don't think it's worth pausing over. These things were, however, Freud's steps, and each of his steps deserves to be examined. They are the vehicle of his teachings, rich in consequences. Let me point out to you in passing that names – proper names – are situated at the level of the message. We will have to come back to the implications of this later, for I cannot tell you everything at once, unlike 'today's psychoanalysts' who are so knowledgeable that they say everything at once, speaking of the *I* and the ego [*moi*] as if these things had no complexity at all, mixing everything up. I bring you some titbits, to which I will return, and which I will develop further for you later.

The proper name in question is a foreign name, in the sense that its elements are foreign to Freud's own language. '*Signor*' is not a German word, and Freud stresses that this is not unimportant. He doesn't tell us why, but the fact that he singles it out in the initial chapter proves that he thinks it's a particularly striking facet of the reality he is addressing. If Freud states this, it's because this introduces another dimension than that of proper names as such, which is always more or less attached to cabbalistic signs. If a name were absolutely proper and particular, it would have no homeland.

There is another fact that Freud immediately emphasizes just as much, whereas we don't usually dwell on it. What strikes him as remarkable, in effect, in the forgetting of a proper name that he mentions at the beginning of *The Psychopathology of Everyday Life* is that this forgetting is not an absolute forgetting – a hole or gap – but that other names present themselves in its place. It's here that is located, for him, what is found at the beginning of every science, namely, astonishment. One can only be truly astonished by what one has already begun, however little, to pick up on already, otherwise one doesn't dwell on it at all because one doesn't perceive anything. But Freud, forewarned by his experience with neurotics, perceives that the fact that substitutions occur is worth dwelling on.

38   Now I need to pick up the pace a bit, and spell out for you the entire economy of Freud's analysis of this forgetting of a name, which is a parapraxis, in the sense in which the name has dropped out.

Everything is centred on what we can call a metonymic approximation. Why? Because what re-emerges first are replacement names – 'Botticelli', 'Boltraffio'. There is no doubt but that Freud locates the phenomenon on the metonymic level. We can grasp this in the fact – this is why I am making a detour via the analysis of a case of forgetting – that the emergence of these names in the place of the forgotten 'Signorelli' is located at the level of a formation involving, not substitution this time, but combination. In the analysis of the case that Freud gives, there is no perceptible relationship between 'Signorelli', 'Boltraffio' and 'Botticelli', except indirect relationships linked solely to phenomena involving signifiers.

I am initially restricting myself to what Freud tells us, which stands out by its rigour. This is one of the clearest demonstrations he ever gives of the mechanisms at work in a phenomenon of formation and deformation linked to the unconscious. It leaves absolutely nothing to be desired with respect to clarity. As for me, I am forced here, for the clarity of my own account, to present this analysis to you indirectly, by saying, 'This is what Freud says.'

He tells us why 'Botticelli' appears. The last half of the name, '-elli', is the remnant of 'Signorelli', rendered incomplete by the fact that the 'Signor' has been forgotten. 'Bo' is the incomplete remnant of 'Bosnia-Herzegovina', 'Herr' having been repressed. It's this same repression that explains that 'Boltraffio' connects the 'Bo' of 'Bosnia-Herzegovina' with 'Trafoi', the name of the locality in which Freud had learned that one of his patients had committed suicide because of sexual impotence.

This latter theme had come up in the course of a conversation Freud had with someone on the train from Ragusa to Herzegovina, which immediately preceded the forgetting of the name. His interlocutor was telling him about the Turks of Bosnia-Herzegovina, these Muslims, ever so endearing, who, when their doctor has been unsuccessful at curing them, tell him, '*Herr*, Sir, we know that you have done everything you could.' The '*Herr*' here has its own weight and significant accent – it's at the limit of the sayable, it's the absolute *Herr*, which is death, this death that, as La Rochefoucauld says, like the sun, one cannot look at directly. And, in effect, Freud is no more able to than anyone else.

Death is here rendered present to Freud twice over. It's rendered present through the incident concerning his function as a doctor. It's also made blatantly present through a specific link, which has quite a personal aspect, between death and sexual potency. It's highly likely that this link, which is undeniable in the text, is not only in the object, that is, not only in what is rendered present to him by his patient's suicide.

What do we have before us? Nothing but a pure and simple combination of signifiers. They are the metonymic ruins of the object in question. The object is behind the various specific elements that are at play there in the immediate past. Who lies behind that? The

39

absolute *Herr*, death. The word moves on, fades away, withdraws, is repelled, and is, strictly speaking, *unterdrückt*.

There are two words that Freud plays with in an ambiguous manner. The first is '*unterdrückt*', which I have already translated for you as 'fallen into the lower regions' [*tombé dans les dessous*]. The second is '*verdrängt*'.

If we situate this forgetting on our schema, *Herr* has fled the level of the metonymic object, and for a very good reason, which is that it was liable to be a little too present after Freud's conversations on the train. We rediscover, as an *ersatz*, the debris or ruins of this metonymic object, namely, this 'Bo-' that comes along and combines with the other ruins of the name which is repressed at that moment, namely '-elli', which doesn't figure in the other substitute name [Boltraffio].

This is the trace or clue that we have of the metonymic level. It's what makes it possible for us to rediscover the chain of the phenomenon in discourse. It's here that, in analysis, what we call free association is located, insofar as it enables us to track what happens in the unconscious.

Since this object is metonymic, it's already fractured. Everything that occurs in the order of language is always already accomplished. If the metonymic object fractures so readily, it's because, as a metonymic object, it's never anything but a fragment of the reality it represents. That's not all. In effect, '*Signor*' is not to be found amongst the traces, the fragments of the fractured metonymic object. This is what needs to be explained now.

If '*Signor*' cannot be evoked, if this is what makes Freud unable to retrieve the name 'Signorelli', it's because he is implicated in it. He is obviously implicated indirectly by way of '*Herr*'. '*Herr*' has in fact been uttered at a particularly significant moment of the function that it could take on as the absolute *Herr,* the representative of death, which on this occasion is *unterdrück*. *Signor* is implicated only insofar as it's a simple translation of '*Herr*'. This is where we encounter anew the level of substitution.

Substitution is the articulation, the signifying means whereby metaphorical action is instituted. This doesn't mean that substitution is metaphor. If I teach you to proceed down all these pathways in an articulated manner here, it's so that you don't constantly misuse words. To say that a metaphor is produced at the level of substitution means that substitution is one possible way to articulate signifiers, that metaphors exercise their function of creating signifieds in the place where substitution can occur, but they are two different things. Similarly, metonymy and combination are two different things.

I will spell it out for you, as an aside, because such non-distinctions lead to what are called misuses of language. In what is defined in the terms of mathematical logic as a set or a subset when that set has only one member, the set in question must not be confused with this one member. This is a typical example of the misuse of language. This may be useful to those who have criticized my inventions involving α, β, γ and δ.

Coming back to what takes place at the level of '*Signor*' and '*Herr*', the substitutive link in question is a substitution that is called heteronymous. This is what happens in every translation – the translation of one term into a foreign language on the substitutive axis, in the comparison required by the existence of different linguistic systems, is called a heteronymous substitution. You are going to tell me that it isn't a metaphor. I agree, I only need establish one thing, which is that it's a substitution.

Note that I am only following what you are forced to admit in reading the text. In other words, I want to get you to extract from your knowledge the fact that you knew it. Moreover, I am not innovating here – you must accept all of this if you accept Freud's text.

Therefore, if '*Signor*' is implicated or involved, there is indeed something that binds it to what the phenomenon of metonymic decomposition is a sign of, here at the place at which it's produced. '*Signor*' is implicated as a substitute for '*Herr*'.

There is nothing more I need to establish in order to tell you that if '*Herr*' has gone off that way, in the direction of the βs, '*Signor*', as indicated by the direction of the arrows, has gone off in the direction of α – γ. Not only has it gone off in that direction, but we can allow for the moment, till I come back to it, that it rebounds like a ball back and forth between code and message. It goes around in circles in what can be called memory. Remember what I gave you a glimpse of in the past, when I said that we should conceive of the mechanism of forgetting, and, by the same token, of analytic remembering, as like the memory of a machine. What is in the memory of a machine, in effect, goes round in circles until one needs it – it's obliged to go round in circles, for memory cannot be built into a machine in any other way. Curiously enough, we find an application of this in the fact that we can think of '*Signor*' as in constant rotation between code and message, until it's refound.

By the same token, you will see there the slight nuance that we can discern between the *unterdrückt*, on the one hand, and the *verdrängt*, on the other. Whereas *unterdrückt* need happen but once and for all, under conditions to which a being, at the level of his mortal condition, cannot descend, something else is going on when '*Signor*' is maintained in the circuit without being able to re-enter

41

it for a certain period of time. It's necessary for us to admit what Freud admits, namely, the existence of a special force that maintains it there, that is, strictly speaking, a *Verdrängung*.

Now that I have shown you where I wanted to get to regarding this precise point, I will return to the relations between metaphor and substitution. Although, in effect, there is only a substitution between '*Herr*' and '*Signor*', there is also a metaphor. Whenever there is a substitution, there is a metaphorical effect or induction as well.

For someone who is German-speaking, saying '*Signor*' is not quite the same thing as saying '*Herr*'. I would go even further – it's never insignificant when our bilingual patients, or those who simply know another language, having something to say, suddenly change languages. This change of register is always, you can be sure of it, much more convenient for them, and never occurs without a reason. If the patient really is a polyglot, it has a meaning. If he knows the language he is referring to imperfectly, then naturally it has another meaning. If he is bilingual from birth, it has yet another. But in each case, it has one.

I provisionally told you that in substituting '*Signor*' for '*Herr*' there was no metaphor, but simply a heteronymic substitution. I am coming back to this to say that on this occasion, on the contrary, '*Signor*', given the whole context it's attached to, namely, the painter Signorelli, the Orvieto frescoes and the evocation of the last things, represents the most beautiful elaborations there are of this impossible-to-confront reality that is death. It's precisely through recounting a thousand fictions – I am using 'fiction' here in its most veridical sense – on the subject of final things that we metaphorize, or tame, the confrontation with death and bring it into language. It's therefore clear that '*Signor*' here, insofar as it's attached to the context of 'Signorelli', really does represent a metaphor.

42   This is what we have arrived at, and it enables us to reapply, point by point, the phenomenon of *Witz* to the forgetting of a name, since we have found that they share a topography.

'Famillionaire' is a positive production, but the point at which it's produced is the same hole as the one that the phenomenon of a slip displays. I could take another example, and perform the demonstration again. By way of homework, I could give you the task of spelling out the example of Latin verse mentioned by one of Freud's interlocutors – '*Exoriare ex nostris ossibus ultor*' – where the speaker changed the order a bit – the '*ex*' is between '*nostris*' and '*ossibus*' – and also drops the second word, which is indispensable for the scansion, '*aliquis*', which he is unable to articulate. You can only truly understand the phenomenon by referring it to this same grid or framework.

It comprises two levels – the combinatory level, with the special point at which the metonymic object as such is produced, and the substitutive level, with the special point at which the two chains meet, that of discourse and that of the signifying chain in a pure state, where the message is produced. '*Signor*' is repressed, *verdrängt*, in the message-code circuit, whereas '*Herr*' is *unterdrückt* at the level of discourse. Indeed, the preceding discourse captures '*Herr*', and what puts us on the track of the lost signifier are the metonymic ruins of the object.

This is what the analysis of Freud's example of the forgetting of a name yields. Now we can see more clearly what we are able to make of 'famillionaire', this formation that, in itself, has something ambiguous about it.

4

The creation of a witticism, as we have seen, belongs to the same order as the production of a linguistic symptom like the forgetting of a name.

If the two are superimposable and have the same signifying economy, then we should find what, at the level of witticisms, complements – I hinted at something about their double function earlier – their aim with respect to meaning, their disturbing, disruptive neologistic function. What complements it is to be found on the side of what may be called dissolution of the object.

It's no longer a question just of 'he welcomed me like an equal, completely famillionairely', but of the emergence of this fantastical and pathetic character that we can call 'the famillionaire'. He is like one of these creations that a certain fantastic poetry enables us to imagine, halfway between a '*fou-millionaire*', a 'mad-millionaire', and a millipede. This would be a kind of human type whose specimens one could imagine moving, living and growing in the interstices of things, a mycetoma or some analogous parasite. Even without going that far, the word could be assimilated into language in the same way as, for some time now, '*une respectueuse*' has meant a whore.

These sorts of creations have a value of their own, which is that of introducing us to a domain that was previously unexplored. They bring out what we might call a verbal being. But a verbal being is still a being, and it increasingly tends to become embodied. 'Famillionaire' has thus played, it seems to me, many roles, not simply in the imagination of poets, but in history as well.

There are many creations that have come closer to it than

43

'famillionaire'. Gide makes the entire story of his *Prometheus Misbound* revolve around what is not really a god but a machine, namely the banker Zeus, whom he calls the 'Miglionaire'. Should it be pronounced in French or in Italian? We can't tell, but for my part I think it has to be pronounced in Italian. I will show you the essential function, in Freud, of the *Miglionnaire* in the creation of a witticism.

If we now examine 'famillionaire', we see that the direction I am indicating is not achieved at the level of Heine's text. In no way does the latter give it freedom or independence as a substantive. If I translated it just before as 'completely famillionairely', it was so as to point out to you that Heine remains at the adverbial level. We can make a play on words here and appeal to language – there is a world of difference between the *manner* of being and the direction I was showing you, namely, a manner of *being*. You can see that there is continuity between the two. Heine remains at the level of the *manner* of being when he writes '*ganz famillionär*'.

What does Heine's 'completely famillionairely' bring us? Without us in any way ending up with a being of poetry, it's an extraordinarily rich, swarming and proliferating term, much like what we find at the level of metonymic decomposition.

Heinrich Heine's creation deserves to be put back here in its context, *The Baths of Lucca*, in which we encounter, along with Hirsch-Hyacinth, the Marquis Cristoforo di Gumpelino, a very fashionable man who lavishes all manner of courtesy and attentiveness on beautiful women, to which is added the fabulous familiarity of Hirsch-Hyacinth clinging to his heels.

44   The latter's function as a parasite, valet, manservant or doorman evokes another possible decomposition of the word for us, the '*affamillionaire*', 'famine-llionaire', stressing Gumpelino's hungering for success, the hunger that is no longer the *auri sacra fames*, but that of acceding to the highest spheres, a satisfaction which had previously been denied him. I don't want to allude to something still further in the background – namely, the sad, heartrending function of women in the life of this caricature of a marquis.

We could trace the possible signification of the word in yet another way by decomposing it thus – '*fat-millionaire*', 'conceited millionaire'. The '*fat-millionaire*' is both Hirsch-Hyacinth and Gumpelino. And it's far more than that, because behind them lie Heinrich Heine's singularly *famillionaire* relations, including those he had with the Rothschilds.

You can see, then, the two axes of metaphorical creation in this witticism. There is the axis of meaning, insofar as this word hits home, moves us, is rich in psychological significations and immediately hits the nail on the head, owing to its improvisation, and captures our attention through a talent that is at the limit of poetic creation. But there is another side, which may not be immediately perceived – by virtue of the combinations that we could extend indefinitely, the word is crawling with all the needs that proliferate around an object.

I alluded to *fames*. There is also '*fama*', namely, the need to shine and be famous that hounds the character of Hirsch-Hyacinth's master. There is also the fundamental 'infamy' of this servile familiarity, which, in the scene at the baths of Lucca, results in the fact that Hirsch-Hyacinth gives his master one of those purges only he knows how to prepare, giving Gumpelino agonizing stomach cramps at the very moment the poor fellow finally receives from his beloved lady the letter that, in other circumstances, would have enabled him to realize his fondest wishes. This hugely farcical scene exposes the underside of this infamous familiarity. It really does give the formation of the witticism its weight, its meaning, its ties, its front and back, its metaphorical aspect and its metonymic aspect. This is, however, not the essence.

We have now seen both sides, the ins and the outs of it. There is, on the one hand, the creation of meaning by 'famillionaire', which also implies a waste product, something that is repressed. It's necessarily something connected to Heinrich Heine, and it will start, just like '*Signor*' did, circulating between code and message. On the other hand, there is the metonymic thing, with all the scraps of meaning, sparks and splatters that are produced around the creation of the word 'famillionaire', and which constitute its influence, its weight, which for us establish its literary value. The fact remains that the only thing that matters, the centre of the phenomenon, is what happens at the level of signifying creation, which makes it a witticism. Everything that happens around it puts us on the scent of its function, but must not be confused with the phenomenon's centre of gravity. 45

What gives the phenomenon its tone and weight must be sought out in its very centre, sought out, that is, on the one hand at the level of the conjunction of signifiers and, on the other, at the level – as I have already pointed out – of the confirmation that the Other gives this creation. It's the Other who gives the signifying creation its value as a signifier in its own right, its value as a signifier in relation to the phenomenon of signifying creation. It's the Other's confirmation that distinguishes a witticism from the pure and simple phenomenon of a symptom, for example. A witticism resides in the shift to this second function.

But if it weren't for everything that I have just told you today, that is, if it weren't for what occurs at the level of signifying conjunction, which is the essential phenomenon, and at the level of what this conjunction develops insofar as it shares in the fundamental dimensions of the signifier, namely, metaphor and metonymy, then no confirmation of a witticism would be possible. There would be no means of distinguishing it from the comic, from a joke, or from a crude explosion of laughter.

In order to understand what is at issue in witticisms as signifying phenomena, we need to have identified all their facets, particularities, ties, and ins and outs at the level of the signifier. Witticisms are located at such an elevated level of signifying elaboration that Freud paused there to perceive a specific example of formations of the unconscious. This, too, is what holds our interest.

You must be beginning to glimpse their importance, since you have been able to observe that they make it possible for us to enter further, and in a rigorous manner, into the analysis of a properly psychopathological phenomenon, namely, parapraxes.

13 November 1957

III

THE *MIGLIONAIRE*

From Kant to Jakobson
The repressed in witticisms
The forgetting of a name, a failed metaphor
The appeal to a signifier
The young woman and the count

So, we have now started on this year's topic, having begun with witticisms.

Last time, we started analysing the first example Freud brought up, which was in the form of this word 'famillionaire' attributed by Heinrich Heine to the character of Hirsch-Hyacinth. It is a poetic creation full of meaning, and it is no accident that Freud found himself in the position of choosing this example from the context of poetic creation. As usually happens, moreover, I have found this example to be particularly apt for demonstrating what I wish to demonstrate here.

The analysis of the psychological phenomenon involved in witticisms leads us, as you will have no doubt seen, to the level of a signifying articulation which, as interesting as it is to so many of you – at least I hope it is – may nevertheless appear to be quite puzzling, as you can easily imagine. What is surprising and baffling here is also the central thread running through this return to analytic experience which I want to undertake with you and which concerns the place and, up to a point, the existence of the subject.

1

Someone who was clearly far from being uninformed, neither uninformed about this question nor uninformed about what I am trying to contribute to it, asked me, 'But then, what becomes of the subject? Where is he?'

The response was easy. Since it was a philosopher who asked this question at the French Society of Philosophy, where I was speaking, I was tempted to reply, 'I'll refer the question back to you, I leave it to the philosophers to respond on this point. There's no question of my doing all the work myself.'

To be sure, the notion of the subject needs to be revised on the basis of Freudian experience. There's no surprise there. On the other hand, given the essential contribution Freud made, would we have ever expected to see minds, and especially the minds of psychoanalysts, even more strongly attached to a notion of the subject that is embodied in some particular way of conceptualizing the ego, no less? This is just returning to what we might call grammatical confusion over the issue of the subject.

Of course, nothing in our experience authorizes us to maintain that the ego should be identified with a power of synthesis. Is there even any need to resort to Freudian experience to see this? A simple and sincere inspection of the life of each and every one of us makes it possible to glimpse the fact that this so-called power of synthesis is less than ineffective. As a matter of fact, fiction aside, there is really no more common experience than that not only are our reasons for doing things incoherent, but we don't know what those reasons are and are fundamentally alienated from them. Freud brings us the notion of a subject that operates beyond this. He shows us the mainsprings and the action of this subject within us that is so difficult to grasp. Something there that should have caught people's attention is that this subject – which introduces a hidden, secret unity into what, at the level of the most common experience, appears to be profoundly divided, profoundly bewitched and profoundly alienated in relation to our very motives – is other.

Is this other subject merely some kind of double or, as has been said, a bad ego insofar as it effectively hides lots of surprising tendencies? Or is it another ego or, as you might take me to be saying, a true ego? Is that what it is about? Is it simply a double? Another ego, purely and simply, one that we can think of as structured like the experiential ego? That is the question, and that too is why we are going to explore it this year at the level of and under the title of 'formations of the unconscious'.

To be sure, the question answers itself – the subject isn't structured in the same way as the ego of experience. What is present in the subject has its own laws. Its formations have not only a specific style but also a specific structure. Freud investigates this structure and reveals it at the level of neuroses, symptoms, dreams, bungled actions and witticisms, and he detects that there is just the one, homogeneous structure. This is his fundamental argument for treating witticisms as a manifestation of the unconscious. It is the crux of what he lays out for us on the topic of witticisms, and this is why I have chosen them as our way in.

Witticisms are structured and organized according to the same laws as those we found in dreams. Freud detects these laws in the structure of witticisms, enumerates them and spells them out. They are the laws of condensation, *Verdichtung*, displacement, *Verschiebung*, and a third element that belongs to this list, and which at the end of my article I call '*égard aux nécessités de la mise en scène*', 'considerations of representability', to translate '*Rücksicht auf Darstellung*'. But naming them isn't the point. The key to his analysis is the recognition of common structural laws. This is how we can tell that a process, as he expresses it, has been drawn into the unconscious – it is structured according to laws of this kind. This is what is involved where the unconscious is concerned.

Now, there is something that happens at the level of what I teach you. It is that now – that is, after Freud – we are in a position to grasp that this unconscious structure, by which a phenomenon is recognized as belonging to the unconscious, completely coincides with everything that through linguistic analysis we can identify as the essential ways that meaning, insofar as it is created by combining signifiers, is formed. This outcome is all the more convincing for having come as a complete surprise.

The notion of signifying elements acquired its full meaning, in the concrete evolution of linguistics, when the notion of the phoneme was isolated. It means that we can take language at the level of a doubly defined elementary register – as a diachronic chain and, within this chain, as the permanent possibility of substitution in the synchronic sense. It also means that we can detect, at the level of the functions of signifiers, an original power as the location for a certain creation of what is called meaning. Without any need for us to labour away any further at this conception, which in itself is very rich in its psychological implications, it is complemented by what Freud already prepared for us at the point where the field of linguistics meets the field specific to analysis, insofar as the psychological effects by which meaning is created are, as he showed us, nothing but formations of the unconscious.

We can grasp and situate here a fact about the place of man that had been overlooked till then. It is obvious that for man there is a heterogeneity, a diversity and a variability of objects that is truly surprising in comparison with biological objects. Every living organism's existence is correlated with a singular set of objects in the world of a particular style. But where man is concerned, this set has a super-abundant and luxuriant variety. Furthermore, human objects, the world of human objects, cannot be grasped as biological objects. Now, it turns out that in this context this fact has to be placed in a close, even indissoluble, relationship with the human being's submission to or subduction by the phenomenon of language.

To be sure, this did in fact emerge, but only up to a point and, in a way, it remained masked. Effectively, what can be grasped at the level of concrete discourse in relation to creating meaning is always in an ambiguous position, given that language is turned towards objects that already bear within themselves something of the creation they have received from language itself. This became the object of an entire tradition, even an entire philosophical rhetoric – that of critique in the broadest sense of the term – which poses the question, 'What is the value of language?' What do these connections represent in relation to the connections that they appear to lead to, even put in place for reflecting, and which are the connections with the real?

This is effectively the question raised by a philosophical tradition whose highest point can be defined as Kant's critical philosophy, which can be interpreted as the most profound questioning of every form of the real, insofar as it is subject to the a priori categories not only of the aesthetic but also of the logic. This was a pivotal moment, one at which human meditation made a new start and rediscovered what was not at all perceived in that way of raising the question at the level of logical discourse and enquiring into the correspondence between the real and a certain syntax of the circle of intention, insofar as it is completed in every sentence. We must take this up again, underneath and across this critique, on the basis of the action of speech in this creative chain where it is always liable to engender new meaning – by way of metaphor, in the most obvious manner, or by way of metonymy, in a manner that has stayed profoundly masked till quite recently. I will explain why when the time comes.

This introduction has already been difficult enough and so I will go back to my 'famillionaire' example and try to finish analysing it.

2

We got as far as the idea that in the course of an intentional discourse in which the subject presents himself as wanting to say something, something happens that goes beyond his will and that looks like an accident, a paradox, or even a scandal.

This neo-formation, a witticism, appears with features that are not at all negative, whereas they could be considered a sort of stumbling or bungled action – I have shown you things that oddly resemble this at the level of a pure and simple slip of the tongue. On the contrary, under the conditions in which this accident occurs it gets registered and valued as a signifying phenomenon that creates a meaning.

A signifying neo-formation presents a sort of collapse of signifiers, which, as Freud says, get compressed and concertinaed into one another. The result is the creation of signification, whose nuances and enigma I have shown you, between an evocation of a properly metaphorical *manner* of being – 'He treated me quite famillionairely' – and an evocation of a manner of *being*, of verbal being, that almost comes to life in the odd form the phantom of which I tried to raise for you with the character of the 'famillionaire'.

The word 'famillionaire' makes its entry into the world as the representative of a being that for us is highly likely to adopt a reality and a weight that, for us, are infinitely more substantial than those of the millionaire, which are more indistinct. I have shown you how much force it retains, lively enough to really represent a character typical of a specific historical period. I pointed out to you, finally, that it wasn't only Heine who had invented it, and I spoke to you about Gide's *Prometheus Misbound* and his 'Miglionaire'.

It would be extremely interesting to dwell for a moment on this creation of Gide's. His 'Miglionaire' is Zeus the banker. Nothing is more surprising than the creation of this character. The memory this work of Gide's leaves us with is perhaps eclipsed by the extraordinary brilliance of *Paludes*, of which it is nevertheless a sort of double. We have the same character in both cases. They have many overlapping characteristics. In any case, this Miglionaire turns out to engage in some odd conduct with his semblables, since it is there that we see the idea of the gratuitous act emerge.

Effectively, Zeus the banker is unable to have a real and authentic exchange with anyone at all, insofar as he is identified here with absolute power, with money as a 'pure signifier' that calls into question the existence of any possibly meaningful exchange. The only way he has of escaping from his solitude is by doing the following. He goes out into the street with an envelope containing a five-hundred franc note, which was worth something back then, in one hand and in the other a slap in the face, as it were. He drops the envelope and a passer-by obligingly picks it up for him. He asks the latter to write a name and an address on the envelope, in return for which he gives him a slap in the face – and since he isn't Zeus for nothing, it is a tremendous slap, one that leaves the subject dizzy

52

and wounded. He then slips away and sends the contents of the envelope to the person whose name was written down by the person he has just roughed up.

Thus, he finds himself in the position of having made no choice himself, and of having offset a gratuitous evil spell by bestowing a gift that he plays no part in. Through his actions he is trying to restore the circuit of exchange that it was not possible to introduce just any old how or from just any angle. Zeus tries to become a part of it by making some kind of forced entry, by incurring a sort of debt in which he plays no part. The rest of the novel shows how the two characters never end up putting together what they owe one another. As a result, one ends up almost blind in one eye and the other dies.

That is the whole storyline of the novel, which is profoundly instructive, moral and useful for what I am trying to show here.

Our Heinrich Heine has, then, managed to create a character out of which, with the signifier 'famillionaire', he generates two dimensions – one of metaphorical creation, plus a sort of new metonymic object, the famillionaire – whose place we can locate on our schema. As I showed you last time, even though our attention isn't drawn to this aspect of the thing, we can find in it all the debris or scraps typical of reflecting on an object used in any metaphorical creation. This is the underside of the signifiers, all those signifying fragments into which the term 'famillionaire' shatters – *'fames'*, *'fama'*, *'famulus'*, 'infamy' and, ultimately, whatever you want, whatever Hirsch-Hyacinth actually is for this caricature of a master, Cristoforo di Gumpelino. Whenever we are dealing with a formation of the unconscious, we have to systematically search for what I call the debris of the metonymic object.

For reasons that are very clear in analytic experience, this debris proves to be particularly important when the metaphorical creation has not been successful – I mean when nothing comes of it, as in the case I presented to you of the forgetting of a name. When the name 'Signorelli' is forgotten and leaves a hollow or makes a hole at the level of metaphor, the metonymic debris becomes all-important for refinding its traces. When the term *'Herr'* disappears, the metonymic context in which it has been isolated, namely the context 'Bosnia-Herzegovina', makes it possible to restore it.

Let's return to our 'famillionaire', a neo-formation produced at the level of the message. I pointed out to you that, when it comes to witticisms, we should find metonymic correspondences to these paradoxical formations no less than those corresponding to the conjuring-away or disappearance of *'Signor'* when it comes to the forgetting of a name. That is where we ended. How are we to conceptualize what happens at the level of 'famillionaire' insofar as the metaphor, which is a witty one here, works? There must be something that in some way marks the residue or scraps of the metaphorical creation.

A child could tell you straightaway. If we stop being fascinated by the 'thingification' aspect that always makes us treat the phenomenon of language as if an object were involved, we will learn to say simple and obvious things in the same way mathematicians do when they work with their little symbols, x and y, a and b, without thinking of anything, without thinking of what they signify. What is rejected? What marks the remainder and residue of metaphorical creation at the level of metaphor? It is clear that it is the word 'familiar'.

Since the word 'familiar' didn't come and 'famillionaire' came in its place, we have to conclude that the word 'familiar' has gone somewhere and has met with the same fate as that reserved for the 'Signor' of 'Signorelli', which, as I explained to you last time, went off and followed its own little circular circuit somewhere in unconscious memory.

We won't be at all astonished to learn that this is how it is. The word 'familiar' undergoes a fate that corresponds closely to the mechanism of repression in the usual sense – I mean in the sense in which we experience it, and which corresponds to a prior, let's say personal, historical experience, one that goes back a long way. Of course, it is no longer the being of Hirsch-Hyacinth that is then involved, but that of his creator, Heinrich Heine.

If in Heinrich Heine's poetical creation the word 'famillionaire' unfolded in such a felicitous manner, it doesn't really matter what the circumstances in which he discovered it were. Perhaps it didn't come to him while he was at his desk but was invented during one of those solitary walks in night-time Paris he would have taken, after the meetings he had in the 1830s with Baron James de Rothschild, who treated him like an equal and in a manner that was 'completely famillionaire'. It doesn't make any difference, it works well, it's good.

Don't imagine that I am going any further than Freud did. At around a third of the way into the book you will see that he comes back to the example of 'famillionaire' at the level of what he calls the tendencies of the mind and identifies the sources of the formation of this ingeniously invented witticism. He informs us that this creation of Heine's corresponds to something in his past and in his personal family relations. Behind Salomon de Rothschild, whom he calls into question in his fiction, there is effectively another 'famillionaire' who is from his own family this time, Salomon Heine, his uncle. The

54

latter played the most oppressive of roles in his life over the entire course of his existence. Not only did he treat him extremely poorly, not giving him the concrete assistance he could have expected from him, but he stood in the way of the realization of his great love, the love he had for his cousin – he was unable to marry her for the essentially 'famillionaire' reason that his uncle was a millionaire while he wasn't. Heine always considered as a betrayal what was merely the consequence of a family impasse profoundly marked by 'millionarity'.

The word 'familiar', which happens to have the major signifying function here in the repression that matches the witty creation by Heine, an artist of language, shows us, in an obvious way, an underlying personal signifier. What makes it underlying is tied to the word, not to anything that the standing signification may have confusedly accumulated over the poet's life with respect to dissatisfaction and to a singularly difficult position in relation to women in general. If this is a factor here, it enters by way of the signifier 'familiar' as such. In this example, there is no other way of grasping the action or impact of the unconscious than by showing that the signification is closely tied to the presence of the signifying term 'familiar'.

Remarks such as these are designed to show you that the path we are taking, that of linking the entire economy of what is registered in the unconscious to combinations of signifiers, takes us far, launching us into a regression that doesn't go on ad infinitum, but leads us all the way back to the origins of language. Effectively, we have to consider all human significations as having been created metaphorically at one time or another through the conjunction of signifiers.

55   Considerations such as these are certainly not devoid of interest – we always have a lot to learn from the history of signifiers. Identifying the term *'famille'* [family], as what is repressed at the level of the metaphor's formation is well suited to serve, in passing, as an illustration of this.

Effectively, unless you have read Freud, or have simply maintained some homogeneity between the way you think while you are in analysis and the way you read a text, you don't think of *'famille'* in the term *'famillionaire'*, any more than you think of *'terre'* [ground], in the term *'atterré'* [dismayed or distressed]. The more real you make the term *'atterré'*, the more you will drift into the sense of terror and the more *'terre'* will be avoided, whereas it is the active element in the signifying use of the term *'atterré'* as a metaphor. It's the same here. The further you go in the direction of *'famillionaire'*, the more you think about *'famillionaire'*, that is, about the millionaire having become transcendent, as it were – having become something that exists in being and no longer just as a sign, pure and simple – the more '*famille*' tends to elude you as the active term in the creation of the word '*famillionaire*'. Take an interest, then, in this term '*famille*', just as I have, at the level of the signifier and its history, by opening the Littré dictionary.

The Littré, as Charles Chassé tells us, is where Mallarmé got all his ideas from. The funny thing is that he is right. He is right in the particular context he, no less than his interlocutors, is caught up in, and this gives him the feeling that he is breaking down doors. Of course, he is breaking this door down because it isn't open. If everyone thought about what poetry is, there would be nothing surprising in the realization that Mallarmé took a keen interest in signifiers. But no one has ever broached the question of what poetry really is. People oscillate between some vague and obscure theory of similes and reference to musical terms of one kind or another, by means of which one seeks to explain Mallarmé's so-called lack of meaning. In short, one is completely unaware that there must be a way to define poetry as a function of its relationship to signifiers. As soon as one formulates poetry in a slightly more rigorous way, as Mallarmé did, it is much less surprising that it should be called into question in his more obscure sonnets.

That said, I doubt that anyone will ever make the discovery that I too got my ideas from the Littré dictionary on the grounds that I open it.

I open it, then, and I can inform you of this, which I suppose a number of you know already, but which is of interest all the same – in French, the term '*familial*' was a neologism in 1881. Close consultation of some good authors who have addressed the issue 56 has made it possible for me to date this word's appearance at 1865. We didn't have this adjective before that date. Why not?

According to Littré's definition, '*familial*' is used to refer to the family at the level, he says, of political science. The word '*familial*' is thus tied to the context in which one says, for example, '*allocations familiales*' [family welfare benefits]. The adjective came into being, then, when it was possible to treat the family as an object at the level of an interesting political reality, that is, insofar as the family no longer had the same structuring function for the subject it had had up till then, as an integral part of the very bases of one's discourse, without it even occurring to one to isolate it. It was insofar as it was drawn from this level and became subject to a particular technical use that something as simple as its adjectival correlate could appear. This is perhaps not unrelated, as you won't have failed to notice, to the very usage of the signifier '*famille*'.

Be that as it may, it seems that the value of this term which, as I have just been saying, was introduced into the circuit of the repressed was absolutely not the same in Heinrich Heine's day as in ours. In effect, the sole fact that the term '*familial*' not only wasn't in use in the same context but didn't even exist at this period is enough to change the axis of the signifying function linked to the term '*famille*'. This nuance should not be neglected in this case.

It's because we neglect things of this kind that we are capable of imagining that we understand ancient texts as their contemporaries understood them. It is, however, quite likely that a naive reading of Homer will not correspond to its true meaning in any way. It is certainly not for nothing that people dedicate themselves to an exhaustive study of Homer's vocabulary in the hope of approximately situating the dimension of meaning at work in his poems in its proper place. But the fact is that the latter retain their meaning even though a good part of what is improperly called the mental world – which is the world of meanings – of Homeric heroes in all probability escapes us completely and most probably must escape us more or less definitively. The distance between the signifier and the signified makes it possible for us to understand that plausible meanings can always be attributed to a well-formed concatenation, which is precisely what characterizes poetry, probably down to the end of time.

I think I have covered just about everything that can be said about the phenomenon of the creation of witticisms in its own register. Perhaps this will mean we can more precisely formulate what is involved in the forgetting of a name, which I spoke about last week.

57

3

What is the forgetting of a name? In this case, there is the fact that the subject poses the question to the Other, and to the Other itself qua Other – 'Who painted the Orvieto frescoes?' And nothing comes to him.

I would like you to notice in this case the amount of care I am taking to give an accurate formulation. On the grounds that analysis reveals that the reason the subject doesn't come up with the name of the painter of the Orvieto frescoes is that '*Signor*' is missing, you may think that it is '*Signor*' that has been forgotten. This isn't true. It isn't '*Signor*' he is looking for, but 'Signorelli', and it is 'Signorelli' that has been forgotten. '*Signor*' is the repressed signifying scrap of something that occurs in the place in which 'Signorelli' isn't found.

Do understand the rigorous character of what I am telling you. Recalling 'Signorelli' and recalling '*Signor*' are not the same thing. Once 'Signorelli' has become the name of a painter, one no longer thinks about '*Signor*'. '*Signor*' is detached here from 'Signorelli' by the action of decomposition characteristic of metaphor, and insofar as the name is caught up in the play of metaphor that resulted in its being forgotten.

Our analysis enables us to reconstruct the connection of '*Signor*' with '*Herr*' in a metaphorical creation that targets the meaning lying beyond '*Herr*', which it assumed in the course of Freud's conversation with the person who was accompanying him on his little journey to the Bay of Kotor. '*Herr*' became the symbol of the place at which his mastery as a physician fails, that of the absolute master, that is to say, of an ailment that he cannot cure – the patient committed suicide despite his efforts – and, in short, of the death and impotence that threaten him, Freud, personally. It was in the metaphorical creation that the shattering of 'Signorelli' occurred, and this made it possible for the '*Signor*' element to go elsewhere. One should therefore not say that it was '*Signor*' that was forgotten, when it was 'Signorelli'. '*Signor*' is what we find at the level of the metaphorical waste product, qua repressed. '*Signor*' was repressed, but it was not forgotten. It doesn't have to be forgotten, since it did not exist beforehand.

If 'Signorelli' was so susceptible to fragmentation and '*Signor*' to becoming detached, it was because for Freud 'Signorelli' was a word in a foreign language. It is striking – you will easily observe this even if you have only the slightest experience with foreign languages – that you much more easily discern the component parts of signifiers in another language than your own. When you start to learn a language you become aware of the rules for the composition of words – which you overlook in your own language. In your own language, you do not think of words by breaking them down into root and suffix, whereas you do it quite spontaneously when you learn a foreign language. It is for this reason that a foreign word is more easily fragmented and usable in its component signifiers than any given word of your own language. This merely helps the process along. It can occur with the words of your own language, but the reason Freud started with the forgetting of a foreign name is that the example was readily available and conclusive.

What, then, is there in the place of the name 'Signorelli' that you do not find? An attempt at metaphorical creation was made in that place. What appears here as the forgetting of a name is what is appreciated in the place of '*famillionaire*'. There would have been nothing there at all if Heinrich Heine had said, 'He received me as a complete equal, completely, . . . um . . . um.' This is precisely what happens at the level at which Freud is searching for the name 'Signorelli'. There is something that doesn't emerge, that isn't created. He is looking for 'Signorelli' and he looks for it unduly. Why? Because at the level at which he is looking for 'Signorelli', which he expects to be in that place because of the earlier conversation, what is called to that place is a metaphor that would mediate between the topic of the conversation as it is unfolding and what he rejects, namely death.

This is precisely what is involved when he turns his thoughts towards the frescoes at Orvieto, namely, what he himself calls the last things. What is called for is an eschatological elaboration, if one may use this term. This would be the only way in which he could broach this abhorrent and, as it were, unthinkable term in his thinking, which he has to dwell on because death exists and limits his being as a man as well as his action as a doctor and forms an absolutely irrefutable limit to all his thoughts. Now, no metaphor occurs to him on his way to expounding on these last things. Freud rejects all eschatology, except when it takes the form of his admiration for the painted frescoes at Orvieto. And nothing comes.

In the place where he looks for the painter – ultimately, it's about the painter, about naming the painter – nothing is produced, no metaphor succeeds and no equivalent to 'Signorelli' can be found. 'Signorelli' was called for at that moment in quite a different signifying form from that of a simple name. It was invited to enter into play in the manner in which, in 'atterré', the root 'terre' fulfils its function – that is to say, it shatters and is elided. The existence somewhere of the term 'Signor' is the consequence of the unsuccessful metaphor that Freud appeals to for help at that moment and whose effects must be indicated on the schema at the level of the metonymic object.

Freud had no trouble retrieving from memory the object in question, the object that was represented or painted in the last things. 'Not only could I not find the name "Signorelli", but I have never visualized the Orvieto frescoes so clearly, and I am not particularly imaginative' [SE 3: 290–1]. We know that this is true from all sorts of other characteristics, from the form of his dreams for instance. And if Freud succeeded in making all these discoveries, it is most likely because he was much more open and permeable to symbolic play than to imaginary play. He himself notes the intensification of the image at the level of memory, the more intense recalling of the object in question, namely the painting, including the very image of Signorelli himself, who is there adopting the pose in which, in paintings of that period, the donors and sometimes the painter appear. Signorelli is in the painting, and Freud visualizes him.

There is, then, no forgetting pure and simple, no global forgetting of the object. There is, on the contrary, a relationship between the intense revivification of a number of its imaginary components and the loss of certain other components, which are signifying components at the symbolic level. We find here a sign of what is happening at the level of the metonymic object.

We can, then, formulate more or less as follows what happens when a name is forgotten:

$$\frac{X}{Signor} \cdot \frac{Signor}{Herr}$$

We rediscover here the formula for metaphor insofar as it operates by means of a mechanism of substituting one signifier S for another signifier S'. What is the consequence of this substitution? A change in meaning is produced at the level of S' – the meaning of S', say s', becomes the new meaning, which we shall call s, insofar as it corresponds to big S. So as not to leave you in any doubt, for you might think that in this topology small s is the meaning of big S, I would add that the S has to have come into a relation with S' in order for the little s to be able to produce, as such, what I will call s''. It is the creation of this meaning that is the aim of the functioning of a metaphor. A metaphor is always successful when, once it has been made, the terms are simplified and cancel one another out, just as when you multiply fractions. The meaning is produced at this moment, having entered into operation in the subject.

It is inasmuch as '*atterré*' comes to signify what it signifies for us in practice, namely, more or less touched by terror, that '*terre*' – which, on the one hand, serves as an intermediary between '*atterré*' and '*abattu*', and this is the most absolute distinction, for there is no reason for '*atterré*' to replace '*abattu*', and, on the other, contributes '*terreur*' as a homonym – can be simplified on both sides. This phenomenon is similar to what occurs at the level of the forgetting of a name.

This isn't about the loss of the name 'Signorelli'. It's about the loss of an X that I am introducing here because we are going to learn how to recognize it and make use of it. This X marks the appeal to signifying creation. We will come across its place in the economy of other unconscious formations. To tell you what it is straightaway, it is what happens at the level of what we call desire in a dream. We see it here, in a straightforward manner, in the place where Freud should have found 'Signorelli'.

Freud finds nothing there, not just because 'Signorelli' has disappeared, but because at this level he would have had to create something that corresponded to what for him is in question, namely, the last things. Insofar as this X is present, a metaphorical formation tends to be produced, and we see this in the fact that the term

'*Signor*' appears at the level of two opposed signifying terms. The value S′ is there twice, and it is as such that it undergoes repression. Nothing is produced at the level of the X, which is why Freud doesn't find the name, and why '*Herr*' plays the role and occupies the place of the metonymic object, the object that cannot be named and that is only named through its connections. Death is the absolute *Herr*. But when one speaks of *Herr*, one isn't speaking about death, because one cannot speak of death and because death is very precisely both the limit of all speech and probably also the place in which it originates.

There you have what it leads to, then, when you relate the formation of witticisms point by point to this unconscious formation whose form you can now see better. It looks negative. In fact, it isn't negative. The forgetting of a name isn't simply a negation, it is a lack, but – we always tend to go too fast – the lack of a name. It isn't because the name isn't grasped that there is a lack. No, the lack is the lack of this name.

61　　Searching for the name, we encounter a lack in the place where it should be serving its function and can no longer serve it, for a new meaning is required, one that demands a new metaphorical creation. This is why 'Signorelli' was not recovered, but, on the contrary, one encounters fragments there where they have to be recovered in the analysis, where they play the function of the second term in the metaphor, namely the term that is elided in metaphor.

This might sound like gobbledygook, but it doesn't matter so long as you simply let yourselves be carried along by what appears. It may sound like gobbledygook to you, but it is rich in consequences. If you remember it when you need to remember it, you will be able to shed light on what occurs in the analysis of this or that unconscious formation and explain it in a satisfactory manner. On the other hand, by eliding it and not taking it into account, you are led to entifications that are summary and crude and, if not constantly producing mistakes, at least to sustaining mistakes in word identification that play such an important role in the construction of a certain psychology, a feeble one at that.

4

Let's return to our witticism and to what we should make of it. To conclude, I want to introduce a distinction that returns to where I started, namely, the question of the subject.

Thought is always led back to making the subject the person who is designated as such in discourse. I would observe that there is another term opposed to this one. It is the opposition between what I will call the speaking present [*le dire du présent*] and the present speaking [*le présent du dire*].

This looks like a play on words. It's nothing of the sort.

'The speaking present' refers to what says 'I' in discourse. Along with a series of other particles – 'here', 'now' and other taboo words in our psychoanalytic vocabulary – it serves to locate the presence of the speaker in discourse, to situate him in his actuality as speaker at the level of the message.

You need only the slightest experience of language to see that the present speaking – namely, what is there, now, in discourse – is a completely different thing. The present speaking can be read in all sorts of modes and registers and has no in-principle relationship with the present insofar as it is designated in the discourse as the present of the person who is enunciating the discourse, who is variable, and where the words for it have only the value of a particle. 'I' has no more value than 'here' or 'now'. The proof of this is that when you, my interlocutor, speak to me of 'here' or 'now', you are not speaking of the same 'here' or 'now' as I am. In any case, your *I* is clearly not the same as mine.

I am going to give you an illustration of the present speaking straightaway by means of the shortest witticism I know, which introduces us to another dimension than the metaphorical dimension.

The latter dimension corresponds to condensation. I spoke to you a little while ago about displacement, which is what the metonymic dimension corresponds to. The reason I haven't explored it yet is that it is much more difficult to grasp, but this witticism is particularly well suited to give you a sense of it.

The metonymic dimension, insofar as it makes a contribution to witticisms, plays upon contexts and usage. It operates by associating elements already preserved in the treasure trove of metonymies. A word may be linked in different ways in different contexts, and this will give it two completely different meanings. By using it in a certain context with the meaning it has in another, we are in the metonymic dimension.

I will give you a prime example in the form of a witticism that I will let you think about before I discuss it.

Heinrich Heine is with the poet Frédéric Soulié at a salon, and the latter says to him, talking about a person who was rolling in money, a character who occupied an important position at the time, as you can see, and who was very popular, 'You see, my friend, the cult of the Golden Calf isn't yet over.' 'Oh!' Heinrich Heine replies after looking the person over, 'For a calf he strikes me as being a bit past it.'

62

That's an example of a metonymic witticism. I will dissect it next time, but already you can see that it is a witticism insofar as the word 'calf' is being used, and uniquely being used, in two different metonymic contexts. It adds nothing to the signification of the witticism to say what it means, namely that the person is a cow. It's amusing to say this, but it is a witticism only insofar as, from one reply to the next, 'calf' is used in two different contexts.

It can be demonstrated ultra-quickly that witticisms operate at the level of the play of signifiers.

A young woman in the making, in whom we can recognize all the qualities of a true education – one that consists in her not using but knowing vulgar language – is invited to her first surprise party by a ladies' man, who, after a moment of bored silence, says to her during a dance that has, moreover, not yet ended, '*Vous avez vu, mademoiselle, que je suis comte.*' 'You have noticed, Mademoiselle, that I am a count.' '*Ahhht!*' she simply replies [thereby highlighting that a '*comte*' without a 't' is a '*con*', an idiot].

You won't have read this story in any of the small, specialist collections. Perhaps you will have heard it directly from the mouth of the young woman herself, who was quite pleased with herself, I have to say. But the nature of the story is exemplary nonetheless, for it is the incarnation par excellence of what I have been calling the speaking present. There is no 'I', the *I* isn't named. Nothing exemplifies the speaking present, as opposed to the present speaking, more than a pure and simple exclamation. Exclamations are paradigmatic of the presence of discourse insofar as the person whose discourse it is completely effaces his own present. His present is, if I may say so, retained entirely in the present of discourse.

However, at the level of creation, this subject displays great presence of mind, since something like that isn't premeditated, it just pops out like that, and that's how you recognize that someone is witty. She makes a simple modification to the code which consists in adding a small 't' to it, which draws its value from the context, if I can put it like that – namely, that the count doesn't make her content, apart from the fact that the count, if he is, as I say, so little pleasing, may notice nothing. This trait is therefore completely gratuitous, but nonetheless you see the elementary mechanism of wit here, namely that this slight transgression of the code is, all by itself, taken as a new value enabling the required meaning to be created instantaneously.

What is this meaning? It may seem to you that it is not in doubt, but, after all, this well-bred young woman doesn't tell her count that he was what he was minus a 't'. She tells him nothing of the kind. The meaning to be created remains suspended somewhere between the ego and the Other. This is an indication that something remains to be desired, at least for the moment. Moreover, the text isn't at all transposable – if the text had said that he was a Marquis, this creation would not have been possible. According to the good old formula that apparently gave our fathers such pleasure last century, you would ask, 'How are you?', and you would give the [meaningless] reply, '*Et toile à matelas!*' It was best not to reply, '*Et toile à édredon!*' You'll tell me they were days of simple pleasures.

'Ahhht!' – there you have wit in its shortest, undeniably phonematic form. This is the shortest composition that you can give a phoneme. Two distinctive traits are required, the shortest formula of a phoneme being this – either a consonant following a vowel or a vowel following a consonant. A consonant following a vowel is the classic formula, and that is what we find here. This is enough to construct an utterance having the value of a message, insofar as it makes a paradoxical reference to actual word usage, and provided that it directs the Other's thoughts to an instantaneous grasp of the meaning.

64

That's what we call being witty. It is also what primes the properly combinatory element on which all metaphors rely. If I have spoken extensively about metaphor today, again it is by mapping out the mechanism of substitution. The mechanism has the four terms I gave you in 'The Instance of the Letter'. It is uniquely, at least in its form, the essential operation of intelligence, which consists in formulating the correlate of a proportion established with an X.

An intelligence test is perhaps nothing but that. It's just that it isn't enough just to say that man differs from animals by his intelligence. Perhaps man does differ from animals by his intelligence, but perhaps in this fact the introduction of signifying formulations was primordial.

To put in its proper place the question of men's supposed intelligence as the source of their reality plus X, you would have to start by asking yourself this – intelligence with respect to what? What is there to understand? Where the real is concerned, is it so much a question of understanding? If it is purely and simply about a relationship to reality, surely our discourse must come to the point of re-establishing it in its existence as reality, that is, it must, strictly speaking, culminate in nothing. Moreover, this is what discourse does in general. If we arrive at something else, if one can even speak about a story culminating in knowledge of some kind, it is inasmuch as discourse has brought about an essential transformation.

That is what it's about, and perhaps it's quite simply about these four small terms linked together in a particular way, by what are called 'relations of proportion'. Once again we have a tendency to entify these relations. We believe that we find them in objects. But where in objects are these relations of proportion, if we haven't introduced them with the help of our little signifiers?

It remains the case that the very possibility of metaphorical play is founded on the existence of having something to substitute. The basis for this is the signifying chain as the principle of combination and locus of metonymy.

This is what I will attempt to elaborate next time.

20 November 1957

IV

THE GOLDEN CALF

Need and refusal
Formalizing metonymy
No metaphor without metonymy
Maupassant's double vision
Fénéon's decentring

We left things last time at the point where I showed you the main-spring of one form of witticism, in what I call the metaphorical function, and was about to take up a second aspect in the register of the metonymic function.

You might be surprised at this way of going about it, consisting as it does in starting off with an example and then gradually developing functional relations which as a result do not seem to possess any general relationship to the matter at hand. It stems from a necessity inherent in our subject, whose palpable element I will have an opportunity to show you. Let's say that everything that is at the level of the unconscious insofar as it is structured by language confronts us with the following phenomenon – it is neither the genre nor the class but only specific examples that enable us to grasp the most significant properties.

This is an inversion of our usual analytic perspective – analytic in the sense of the analysis of mental functions. It could be called a failure of the concept, in the abstract sense of the term. More precisely, we need to find another way of grasping it than grasping it conceptually. This is what I was alluding to when I mentioned Mannerism one day, and this feature is entirely appropriate in our field. Given the terrain over which we roam, we're obliged to proceed by misusing concepts rather than using them – and this is due to the domain in which the structurations in question move.

Since the term 'prelogical' is liable to create confusion, I recommend you cross it off your list of categories in advance, given what it's been turned into – namely, a psychological property. We're dealing here with structural properties of language, which are prior to any question that we can put to language about the legitimacy of any aim that it, language, suggests to us. As you know, this is just what philosophers have made the object of anxious enquiry, owing to which we have come to a sort of compromise that goes more or less as follows – if language shows that we can hardly say anything about anything unless it's a being of language, it is with the aim of bringing about a 'for-us' that can be called 'objectivity'. This is undoubtedly a bit too swift as a way of summarizing the entire enterprise that goes from formal logic to transcendental logic, but it is just intended to tell you at the outset that we place ourselves in a different field.

When Freud speaks about the unconscious, he doesn't say that it is structured in a certain way, but he says it nevertheless, inasmuch as the laws that he proposes, the compositional laws of the unconscious, exactly match some of the most fundamental laws of the composition of discourse. Also, all sorts of elements involved in ordinary discourse are missing from the way in which the unconscious is articulated – the link of causality, he tells us, concerning dreams, or negation, and then he returns to it immediately afterwards and shows us that it finds expression in the dream in some other way. This is the field that is already circled, defined, circumscribed, explored and even ploughed by Freud. This is what we are returning to in trying to formulate – let's go even further – in trying to formalize what a moment ago I called the primordial structuring laws of language.

If there's anything that the Freudian experience tells us, it is that we are determined by laws in the very depths of ourselves, as we rightly or wrongly say, adopting an image – let's simply say, at the level of what lies within us beyond our conceptual grasp of ourselves, beyond the idea that we have of ourselves and draw upon, that we hold onto more or less well, and that we sometimes hasten a little too prematurely to make our fate by speaking of synthesis and total personality. And let's not forget that these are all terms that are precisely subject to challenge by the Freudian experience.

Indeed, Freud teaches us – and I will have to make this a signed frontispiece – about the distance, the gap even, that exists between the structuring of desire and the structuring of needs. And while Freudian experience has come to the point of referring to a metapsychology of needs, this certainly has nothing self-evident about it, and one might even describe it as unexpected in relation to what is most obvious, for the entire experience instituted and defined by Freud shows, at every turn, to what extent the structure of desires is determined by something other than needs. Needs only come to us refracted, broken and fragmented, and they are structured precisely by all these mechanisms like condensation, displacement and so on, according to the manifestations of psychical life in which they are reflected – mechanisms which presuppose still other intermediaries and mechanisms in which we recognize a number of the laws that we will come to before the end of the Seminar this year, and which I call laws of the signifier.

These laws prevail here, and in witticisms we learn about a certain way of using them, in a kind of mental game, with the question mark that introducing the term *'esprit'* calls for. What is *'esprit'*? What is *'ingenius'* in Latin? What is *'ingenio'* in Spanish, since I referred to the concept? What is this thing that intervenes here and is different from the function of judgement? We can only work out its place once we have spelled out and clarified the method. What is this method? What is its basic aim?

We have already emphasized the ambiguity of witticisms and slips, a basic and in some way constitutive ambiguity. Depending on the circumstances, what is produced may tend towards the sort of psychological accident that slips are, by which we would remain perplexed without Freud's analysis, or rather, on the contrary, it may be taken up and ratified as having been heard by the Other at the level of a specific signifying value – such as the one that has been acquired by the neologistic, paradoxical and scandalous term, 'famillionaire'. The specific signifying function of this word is to designate not only this or that but also some sort of beyond. What is fundamental in what is signified here isn't linked solely to the impasse in the subject's relations with his millionaire protector. We're faced with a certain relationship that fails, with what introduces, into ongoing human relationships, a type of essential impasse that resides in the fact that no desire can ever be received or admitted by the Other save through all sorts of interventions that refract it and turn it into something other than what it is, an object of exchange, and, frankly, right from the outset, submit the process of making a demand to the necessity of refusal.

I will take the liberty of introducing the actual level at which this question arises of translating a demand into an utterance which has an effect by recounting an amusing if not witty story whose register extends well beyond a small, momentary laugh. It's the story that you are all no doubt familiar with about the masochist and the sadist – 'Hurt me!' says the former to the latter, who replies, 'No!'

I see it doesn't make you laugh. No matter. Some people laugh, though. In any case, the story isn't meant to make you laugh. I simply ask you to notice that something unfolds at a level that has nothing witty about it. Effectively, who are better made for one another than the masochist and the sadist? Sure – but, as you can

68

see from this little story, they get along as long as they don't speak to one another.

It isn't out of spite that the sadist answers, 'No'. His response is a feature of his sadistic character. And as soon as one has spoken he is obliged to reply at the level of speech. Therefore, inasmuch as we have moved onto the level of speech, what should result in the most profound understanding leads to what a moment ago I called the dialectic of refusal that is necessary for sustaining what, in its essence as demand, manifests itself through speech.

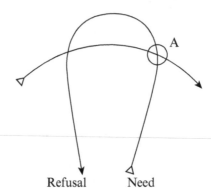

Refusal   Need

In other words, as you can observe in this schema, there is a symmetry between the two elements of the circuit – a closed loop, which is the circle of discourse, and an open loop. Something is uttered by the subject and, coming to the point at which there is a bifurcation at A, it loops back upon itself as an articulated sentence, a ring of discourse [see graph, p. 10]. On the other hand, if what is presented as a demand doesn't respect the essential symmetry I was talking about and describes a circuit that goes directly from his need to the object of his desire, then the sentence ends on a 'No'. Let's say that need, if we locate it at the point delta prime, necessarily encounters the Other's response, which for the moment we'll call a 'refusal'.

What is presented here merely as a paradox, which only our schema makes it possible to locate, no doubt deserves to be gone into in more detail. Let's now return to the chain of our propositions about the different phases of a witticism.

69   **1**

Today, then, I'll introduce the metonymic phase.

To give you an immediate idea of it, I gave you an example in the form of a story where you can see everything that differentiates it from 'famillionaire'. There is, then, a dialogue between Heinrich Heine and the poet Frédéric Soulié, almost his contemporary, which is recounted in Kuno Fischer's book, which was, I believe, reasonably well known at the time. A group gathers in a salon around an elderly gentleman basking in the reflected aura of his financial power. 'Look!' says Frédéric Soulié to someone who was barely his senior, and whom he admired, 'Look how the nineteenth century worships the Golden Calf!' To which Heinrich Heine replies, looking with a disdainful eye at the object drawn to his attention, 'Yes, but this one strikes me as a bit old for that' [*SE* 8: 47–8].

What does this witticism signify? What gives it its bite? What is its mainspring?

On the topic of witticisms, Freud, as you know, places us on this level from the outset – witticisms are to be sought where they are, namely, in their text. Nothing is more striking – this man who has been attributed with being a genius at probing what lies beyond, as it were, psychological hypotheses, always sets out on the contrary from the opposite point, namely the materiality of signifiers, treating them as a given, existing in and for themselves. We have a clear example in his analysis of witticisms. Not only does he consistently begin with a technique, but he has confidence that the elements of his technique will uncover the mainspring.

What is the first thing he does? He proceeds to carry out what he calls an attempt at reduction. If we translate the wit of 'famillionaire' into its expanded sense, decompose what it involves and then read the elements – that is, if we say, 'as familiar as one can be with a millionaire' – everything belonging to the witticism vanishes or disappears. This shows clearly that what is at issue lies in the relationship between the fundamental ambiguity specific to metaphor and the function that a signifier acquires when it is substituted for another signifier, one that is latent in the chain through positional similarity or simultaneity.

Having started by examining witticisms at the metaphorical level, Freud finds himself faced with a new variety with the story of the Golden Calf, where one can sense a difference and, as he isn't one to spare us the detours of his approach to the phenomena, he tells us to think about describing it as a 'conceptual joke' as opposed to a 'verbal joke'. But he soon realizes that this distinction is totally inadequate, and that, here, what one should rely on is what is called the form, namely the combining of signifiers. He therefore undertakes anew to submit the example in question to the technique of reduction, making it accountable for what is subjacent to this debatable form, namely subjective agreement that it is a witticism. He

70

encounters something here that doesn't yield to analysis in the same way 'famillionaire' does.

Sharing each of his approaches in his thinking with us, he pauses for a moment – following Kuno Fischer who remained at this level – at the protasis, that is, at the contribution by Heine's interlocutor, Frédéric Soulié. He detects something metaphorical in the Golden Calf and, to be sure, the expression does have a double value – on the one hand, as a symbol of intrigue and, on the other, as a symbol of the power of money. Does this mean that this gentleman receives all these tributes because he is rich? Wouldn't this obscure the mainspring of what this is about? Freud quickly becomes aware of what is fallacious in such an approach. The richness of this example deserves close scrutiny.

It is certain that in what we are initially given to set the scene for this Golden Calf the notion of the matter is implicated. Without going into how all the verbal uses of this undeniably metaphorical term came to be established, suffice it to say that, while the Golden Calf has the closest of relations with the relationship between signifiers and images that forms the aspect under which idolatry effectively comes to be established, ultimately it is only located within a perspective where being recognized by the god who announces himself as 'I am that I am' – namely, the god of the Jews – demands that one renounce not only idolatry pure and simple, that is, the worship of statues, but also, subsequently, the naming, par excellence, of every imaged hypostasis – that is, the renunciation of what presents itself as the very origin of signifiers, and this in order to seek their essential beyond the refusal of which is precisely what gives the Golden Calf its value.

Thus, it is only through what is already a shift that the Golden Calf comes to acquire a metaphorical use. The topical regression that from a religious perspective is involved in substituting the imaginary for the symbolic, which underpins the idolatry, secondarily acquires the metaphorical value of expressing what people other than I have called the fetishistic value of gold, which I do not mention without reason here, since precisely this fetishistic function – we will have to come back to this – is itself only conceivable in the signifying dimension of metonymy.

71 Here, then, we have the Golden Calf laden with all the intrications and entanglements of the symbolic function with the imaginary. Is this where the *Witz* resides? No. This isn't at all the place where it is located. The witticism, as Freud is aware, is in Heinrich Heine's riposte, and the latter at least consists precisely in subverting, if not annulling, all the references that underpin the metaphor of the Golden Calf, designating him as someone who is suddenly reduced

to the quality of being no more than a vealer worth [*un veau qui vaut*] so much the pound. Suddenly, this calf is taken for what it is, a living being that the market, itself effectively instituted through the reign of gold, reduces to being only sold as stock, a head of cattle, whereby it is possible to emphasize that he is clearly no longer under the age limit for a vealer – which, according to the definition that Littré gives, is a calf in its first year, and which a butchery purist would define as a calf that has not stopped suckling its mother, 'a calf under its mother'. I allowed myself to say that only in France is this purism respected.

There is no way of reducing the fact that this calf isn't a calf, or that this calf is a bit old to be a calf. With or without the Golden Calf in the background, it's still a witticism. Freud thus grasps a difference between the story about the *famillionaire* and this one – the first is analysable, the second is unanalysable. And yet they're both witticisms. What does this mean if not that these are undoubtedly two separate dimensions of the experience of witticisms? What is present here, as Freud himself tells us, looks like sleight of hand, a trick or faulty reasoning. Yet it's a trait common to an entire category of witticisms distinct from the category in which *famillionaire* is inscribed and in which one takes, as one might crudely put it, a word in a different sense from the sense in which it was intended.

Another story belonging to the same category as the Golden Calf refers to the confiscation by Napoleon III of all the property of the house of Orléans when he ascended to the throne. 'It's the first flight [*vol*] of the Eagle,' someone said, and everyone was delighted with its ambiguity; there was no need to spell it out. Here, there's no question of speaking of a witticism of thought, since it is a witticism of words based on the ambiguity that enables us to take a word in a different sense.

It is, moreover, potentially amusing to probe into what underlies such words and, because this word is recorded in French, Freud takes care to specify the double meaning of '*vol*' as action, as the means of locomotion of birds, and as the removal, abduction or theft of property. It's good to bear in mind what Freud elides here – I am not saying he was unaware of it – which is that one of the meanings was historically borrowed from the other and that towards the thirteenth or fourteenth century the term '*volerie*' [hunting with birds] had passed from the usage whereby a falcon or a quail flies [*vole*], to the usage that designates this violation of one of the essential laws of property, known as theft [*vol*].

72

This was no accident. I'm not saying it occurs in every language, but it had already occurred in Latin, where '*volare*' took on the same meaning from the same origin. I take this opportunity to stress something which isn't unrelated to what we are familiar with, namely what I will call the euphemistic modes of expressing what, in speech, represents the 'violation' [*viol*] of one's word or a contract. It's not for nothing that the word '*viol*' is borrowed from the register of an abduction [*rapt*] which has nothing to do with what we properly and juridically call theft [*vol*].

Let's leave it there and return to why I introduce the term 'metonymy' here.

2

Beyond these elusive ambiguities of meaning, I think we effectively need to search for another reference if we are to define this second register of witticisms, unify its mechanism with the first kind and locate their common mainspring. Freud shows us the way without quite finding the formula for it.

What point would there be in talking about Freud if we didn't try to derive the maximum benefit from what he contributed? It's up to us to move it along a little further by giving it this formalization, and our experience will tell us whether it is right and whether this is the right direction for organizing the phenomena.

It's a question that is rich with consequences, not only for everything concerning our therapeutics but also for our conception of modes of the unconscious. It is absolutely decisive whether there is a particular structure, whether this structure is the structure of signifiers and whether the latter imposes its grid on everything that has to do with human needs.

I have already presented metonymy on several occasions, most notably in the article called 'The Instance of the Letter in the Unconscious' [*Écrits*, 412–41]. There I deliberately gave an example drawn from our common experience of grammar that draws on your memories of your secondary-school studies. No one could say that you were exactly filled to the brim with the study of the figures of rhetoric – in actual fact, no great fuss has been made of them till now. Metonymy was at the time relegated to the end, under the auspices of a much-underrated Quintilian. Nonetheless, given the point we're at with respect to our conception of forms of discourse, I took 'thirty sails', spoken in the place of 'thirty ships'. There's a literary background to this choice, since, as you are aware, these thirty sails can be found in a certain monologue in *Le Cid*, a reference we'll perhaps do something with later.

In 'thirty sails' it's not simply a matter of taking the part for the whole, as you've been told with reference to the real, for it is rarely the case that ships have only one sail. We don't know what to do with these thirty sails – either there are thirty of them and there aren't thirty ships, or there are thirty ships and there are more than thirty sails. That is why I say one has to refer to the word-for-word [*mot-à-mot*] correspondence. That said, I am only presenting you with the problematic aspect of the thing, to be sure, and we need to go deeper into the nature of how it differs from metaphor – for you could say to me that it really is a metaphor. Why isn't it one? Indeed, that is the question.

For a while now I have been hearing from time to time that some of you, in the course of your everyday life, are suddenly struck by encountering something you no longer know whether to classify as metaphor or as metonymy. This is sometimes followed by some excessive disturbance in your organism, a sharp rolling from the port of metaphor to the starboard of metonymy, causing some of you to feel a bit seasick. I've also been told, in connection with Booz, that 'His sheaf was neither miserly nor hateful', which I presented to you as a metaphor, could actually be a metonymy. Still, I think that in my article I clearly showed what this sheaf is, and how much it is something other than part of his property. Insofar as it is precisely a substitute for the father, it brings out the entire dimension of biological fecundity that underlies the spirit of the poem, and it's no accident that on the horizon and further out, in the firmament, the sharp cutting edge of the celestial sickle emerges, evoking castration in the background.

Let's return to our thirty sails and try to pinpoint, once and for all, what it is that I'm calling the metonymic function.

Concerning metaphor, I think I've sufficiently stressed, though not without leaving a number of puzzles, that substitution is its structural source. Metaphor is the result of the function that is brought to a signifier S insofar as this signifier is substituted for another in a signifying chain.

As for metonymy, it is the result of the function that a signifier S adopts when it relates to another signifier along the length of the signifying chain. The function that a sail has in relation to a ship exists along the signifying chain and not in reference to the real – along the length of the chain and not in a substitution. It's thus a question, in the clearest way, of the transfer of signification along the chain.

This is why formal representations or formulas are always liable to place extra demands on you. Someone recently reminded me that at one time I said I was seeking to devise a rubber logic for you to use. It's actually something like that that is involved here. This topographical structuring invariably leaves gaps because it's made up of these ambiguities. Let me say in passing that this is unavoidable.

Then again, if we do manage to develop this topographical structuring well enough, we won't be able to avoid a remainder of extra
requirements, no matter how much a univocal formalization is an
ideal for you – if indeed a univocal formalization is an ideal for
you at all – for some ambiguities are irreducible to the level of the
structure of language that we're trying to define.

Let me also say in passing that the notion of metalanguage is
very often employed in the most inadequate of fashions, insofar
as people misrecognize the following – either a metalanguage has
formal requirements that displace the total structuring phenomenon
in which it has to be situated, or the metalanguage itself conserves
the ambiguities of language. In other words, there is no such thing
as a metalanguage, there are formalizations – either at the level of
logic, or at the level of this signifying structure whose autonomous
level I've been trying to uncover for you. There is no such thing as
a metalanguage in the sense in which it would mean, for example,
a complete mathematization of the phenomenon of language, and
this is so precisely because there's no way of formalizing any further
than what's given as the primitive structure of language. Still, not
only can this formalization be demanded, it is necessary.

It's necessary here, for instance. In effect, the notion of the substitution of one signifier for another requires that its place already
be defined. This is a positional substitution, and position requires a
signifying chain, that is, a combinatory succession. I'm not saying
it requires every one of its features. I'm saying that this combinatory succession is characterized by elements I will call, for instance,
intransitivity, alternation and repetition.

If we go into the constitution of a signifying chain at this original, minimal level, we'll end up a long way off today's topic. There
are minimal requirements. I'm not saying I claim to have completely
got to them all yet, although I have already given you enough for
me to suggest some formulas as a basis for some reflection drawn on
particular examples – which, in this domain and no doubt for essential reasons, we must draw upon for all our teachings.

We will proceed in this way once again, observing, even if this
sounds like a play on words, that these sails [*voiles*] veil [*voilent*] our
view, every bit as much as they designate that they don't enter with
their full rights as sails, at full sail, into the use we are putting them
to. These are sails that rarely slacken. What is reduced in their scope
and in their sign can be rediscovered if one evokes 'a village of thirty
souls', where the souls are placed there for the shadows of what
they represent, lighter than a term suggesting an excessive presence
of inhabitants. As in the title of a famous novel, rather than being
beings who are not there, these souls may be dead souls. Similarly,

75

'thirty fires' [for thirty households] also represents a certain degradation or minimization of meaning, for these fires are as much extinguished fires as they are fires about which we say there is no smoke without fire – and it's not for nothing that these fires reappear in a usage that says metonymically what it is that they stand in for.

You will tell me no doubt that I am relying on a reference to meaning to show the difference. I don't believe so, and I'd point out to you that what I started from is the following – metonymy is the fundamental structure within which something new and creative, which is metaphor, can be produced. Even if something of metonymic origin is placed in the position of substitution, as in the case of 'thirty sails', it's different from a metaphor. In short, there would be no metaphor if there were no metonymy.

The chain in which the position at which the metaphorical phenomenon occurs is defined is in a sort of shifting or equivocation where metonymy is concerned. 'There would be no metaphor if there were no metonymy' comes back to me as an echo, and not by chance by any means, of the comic invocation Jarry puts into the mouth of Father Ubu, 'Long live Poland, for without Poland there'd be no Poles!' This is the very essence of our subject. It's a witticism and – this is what's funny – it refers precisely to the metonymic function. You'd be on the wrong track if you thought that what's funny here relates to, for instance, the role the Poles have played in the misfortunes of Poland, which are only too well known. It's just as funny if I say, 'Long live France, Monsieur, for without France there would be no French!' Similarly, if I say, 'Long live Christianity, because without Christianity there'd be no Christians!' And even, 'Long live Christ!', and so on.

76

One cannot fail to recognize the metonymic dimension in these examples. Every relationship of derivation and every use of a suffix or an ending in inflected languages uses the contiguity of the chain for signifying purposes. The aphasic's experience is indicative here, for instance. There are precisely two types of aphasia, and when we're at the level of disturbances of contiguity – that is, of the metonymic function – the subject has the greatest difficulty with the relation between words and adjectives, between 'benefit' or 'beneficence' and 'beneficent' and also 'benefaction'. It's here in the metonymic Other that this lightning flash occurs, casting a light that's not only comical but also rather farcical.

It's important to try to grasp the signifying chain's properties, and I've tried to find some terms of reference that make it possible to grasp what I would like to describe as the effect of the signifying chain, an effect inherent in its nature as signifying chain, and which one may call its meaning.

3

Last year, it was by means of an analogical reference – it might have seemed metaphorical to you, but I stressed that it wasn't and that it was intended to be taken to the letter of the metonymic chain – that I situated the essence of all fetishistic displacements of desire, its fixation, in other words, before, after or alongside, or at any rate on the threshold of, its natural object. This was about establishing the fundamental phenomenon that we can call the radical perversion of human desires.

I would now like to indicate another dimension of the metonymic chain, which I will call the sliding of meaning. I've already pointed out how it is related to the literary procedure typically referred to by the term 'realism'.

There is no reason why one cannot have all sorts of experiences in this domain, and I subjected myself to the experience of taking a novel from the realist period and rereading it to see what features might help you grasp the original something that the metonymic use of the signifying chain introduces into the dimension of meaning. Thus, I turned, at random, to a novel by Maupassant, *Bel-Ami*.

It makes for pleasant reading. Try it some time. Having made a start, I was quite surprised to find in it what I'm attempting to designate here when I talk about sliding. We see our hero, Georges Duroy, setting out from the top of the rue Notre-Dame-de-Lorette.

77

> When the woman behind the till had given him the change for his five-franc piece, Georges Duroy left the restaurant. A good-looking man, with the poise of an ex-cavalry N.C.O., he drew himself up, twirled his moustache with a familiar military gesture, and quickly glanced around at the remaining diners with one of those looks of a handsome young man on the lookout for prey. [p.105]

That is how the novel begins. It doesn't seem like much, but it goes on from one moment to the next, from one encounter to another, and you witness, in the clearest of ways, a sort of shift. This shift carries off a fairly basic being, I would say, if we think of him at the point to which he has been reduced at the beginning of the novel, because this five-franc piece is all he has left. It gradually leads this being, then, who has been reduced to the most direct of needs, to an immediate preoccupation with love and hunger, into a series of good and bad incidents, but generally good, for he's not only a handsome fellow, but a lucky one. It places him in a circle, a system of displays of exchange, in which the metonymic subversion of primitive elements is accomplished, and which, as soon as they're satisfied, are alienated in a series of situations in which he is never able to get his bearings or find any repose. And it conveys him from success to success and to an almost total alienation from what is his own person.

The storyline of the novel, in an overview like this, doesn't actually amount to much because everything is in the detail, I mean in the way in which the novelist never goes beyond what's happening in the sequence of events and records them in the most concrete terms possible, just as he constantly places not only the hero but everything around him in a position that is invariably double so that at every moment one has double vision with respect to the object, no matter how proximate it is.

I will take as an example the meal at the restaurant, which is one of the first moments in the rise in this character's fortunes.

> Succulent Ostend oysters were brought in, looking like dainty little ears enclosed in shells and melting between the tongue and the palate like salty titbits.
>
> After the soup came a trout as pink-fleshed as a young girl; tongues began to wag. [. . .]
>
> They had reached the stage of witty suggestiveness, of words, veiled yet revealing, that are like a hand lifting up a skirt, the stage of clever allusions, skilfully hidden impropriety, shamelessly brazen hypocrisy, cryptic words that cover naked images and which fill the eye and the mind with a sudden vision of what dares not be said openly and enables smart society to enjoy a subtle, mysterious sort of lovemaking, a sort of marriage of impure minds, by simultaneously conjuring up, with words as sensual and disturbing as a sexual embrace, the secret, shameful desire for body to clasp body. The roast had now appeared, partridges . . . [pp. 105–8]

78

Note that they ate this roast, the partridges, the poultry terrine and all the rest 'without tasting it properly, without realizing what they were eating, entirely absorbed in what they were saying, immersed in thoughts of love' [pp. 108–9].

This constant diversion which means you don't know whether it's the flesh of a young girl or a trout that's on the table makes it possible for the so-called realist description to dispense with any unfathomable reference to any meaning or trans-meaning whatsoever, poetic or moral or other. This throws enough light, or so it seems to me, on what I'm pointing to when I say that any discourse aiming at grasping reality is obliged to view things from the perspective of the perpetual sliding of meaning. This is what gives it its value and also what makes it the case that literary realism doesn't exist. In an effort to get a tighter grip on reality by articulating it in discourse, all one ever manages to do is show what is disorganizing and even perverse in what the introduction of discourse adds to this reality.

If that seems a bit impressionistic, I'd like to try out something else with you. Since we're trying to remain, not at the level at which discourse corresponds to the real, but at which it simply claims to connote it, follow it or be its annalist – with two *ns* – let's see what this produces. I've taken the series *Novels in Three Lines*, which Félix Fénéon, a no doubt worthy author whom I don't have time to introduce, used to write for the newspaper *Le Matin*. There's no doubt that they were not collected haphazardly, since a special talent is apparent there. Let's try to find out what it is, taking them at random.

For having thrown a few stones at the police, three pious ladies of Hérissart have been fined by the magistrates in Doullens.

As Mr Poulbot, a primary school teacher in Île-Saint-Denis, rang the bell for the return to class, the bell fell, almost scalping him.

In Clichy, an elegant young man threw himself under a hansom cab with rubber tyres and then, unhurt, under a truck, which crushed him to pieces.

A young woman was seated on the ground in Choisy-le-Roi. The only identifying word her amnesia enabled her to say was: 'Model.'

The corpse of the sexagenarian Dorlay was swinging from a tree in Arcueil with the sign, 'Too old to work'.

In relation to the mystery of Luzarches, the examining magistrate Dupuy deposed the suspect Averlant; but she was mad.

Mangin, from Verdun, was trudging along behind the coffin. He didn't make it to the cemetery that day. Death overtook him on the way.

The valet Silot, from Neuilly, settled an entertaining woman into his absent master's house then disappeared, taking everything but her.

While pretending to search through her savings for rare coins, two swindlers took 1,800 francs of the ordinary kind from a woman in Malakoff.

At the beach at Saint-Anne [Finistère], two bathers were drowning. A bather jumped in. And Mr Étienne then had three people to save.

What makes them funny? Here we have facts, described with an impersonal rigour and the fewest words possible. I would say the entire art consists simply in this extreme reduction. What is comical, when we read 'Mangin, from Verdun, was trudging along behind a coffin. He didn't make it to the cemetery that day. Death took him by surprise on the way', absolutely fails to touch our own journey towards the cemetery, however diverse the methods employed to make the journey. The effect wouldn't appear if these things were said in a more lengthy fashion, I mean if it was all drowned in a flood of words.

It's because of what I've been calling the 'sliding of meaning' that we literally don't know where to stop, at what point, in these sentences which we encounter in their rigour, in order to locate their centre of gravity or point of equilibrium. This is just what I would call their decentring. There is no morality here. Anything that could be in any way exemplary is carefully effaced. This is the whole art of composition in these *Novels in Three Lines* – their style's art of detachment. Nevertheless, what's recounted is still a sequence of events, one whose coordinates are given to us in a completely rigorous manner. This is another quality of the style.

That is what I was getting at in trying to show you that along the horizontal dimension of the chain, discourse is really a skating rink, just as useful to study as the figures of skating, and along which meaning slides. It is a light, infinite band no doubt, which perhaps, because it is so reduced, appears to be nothing at all, but which is manifest in the order of witticisms in their ridiculous, degrading and disorganizing dimension.   80

It is along this dimension that the type of witticism like the 'flight of the eagle' is located, that is, where discourse meets the signifying chain. This is also the case with 'famillionaire', except that the latter is inscribed at the meeting point at gamma, whereas the other one simply takes place a bit further on.

Frédéric Soulié contributes something that obviously goes in the direction of locating it over on the side of the *I*, while he appeals to Heinrich Heine to be his witness as the Other. At the beginning of any witticism there's always an appeal to the Other as the locus of verification. 'As true', Hirsch-Hyacinth begins, 'as God shall grant me all good things.' The reference to God may well be ironic, but it is fundamental. Here Soulié invokes a Heinrich Heine who, I will tell you, is much more prestigious than he is himself – without giving you the history of Frédéric Soulié, though the article devoted to him in *Larousse* is a nice one. Soulié says to him, 'Don't you see, my dear master?' and so on. Here, the appeal, the invocation, tends to fall on the side of Heinrich Heine's *I*, which is the pivotal point of the matter.

We have, then, passed through the *I* and returned with 'Golden Calf' at A, the locus of usage and metonymy, for, while the Golden Calf is a metaphor it is a dead one, it has passed into language – and earlier, incidentally, we displayed its sources, origins and mode of production. It is ultimately a commonplace that Soulié sends to the locus of the message via the classic alpha–gamma pathway. We have two characters here, but you know that there might just as easily have been only one, since the Other, merely because the dimension of speech exists, exists in each of us. Moreover, when Soulié describes the financier as a Golden Calf, it's because he's conscious of a usage that to us seems no longer accepted, but I found it in *Littré* – a gentleman may be called a Golden Calf [*Veau d'or*] if he is filthy rich [*cousu d'or*] and, for that reason, the object of universal admiration. There's no ambiguity [in French], and none in the German either.

At this moment – that is, here, between gamma and alpha – there is a referral from the message back to the code, that is, along the line of the signifying chain and, in a way metonymically, the term is picked up again on a plane which is no longer the one along which it had been sent, and this makes it possible to see the collapse, reduction or devaluation of meaning brought about in metonymy quite clearly.

81   This leads me, at the end of today's lesson, to introduce the following, which may perhaps seem paradoxical – that metonymy is, strictly speaking, the locus where we must situate the dimension that is primordial in and essential to human language and that lies at the opposite end of the dimension of meaning – namely, the dimension of value.

The value dimension becomes apparent, in contrast with the meaning dimension. It is another aspect, another register. It refers to the diversity of objects already constituted by language, into which the magnetic field of each person's needs, with their contradictions, is introduced.

Some of you are, I believe, fairly familiar with *Das Kapital*. I am not talking about the entire text – who's read *Capital*! – but with the first book, which almost everyone has read. A prodigious first book, superabundant, revealing someone – and this is rare – who sustains an articulated philosophical discourse. I urge you to go to the page where, at the level of the formulation of the so-called 'theory of the particular form of the value of merchandise', Marx shows himself, in a note, to be a precursor of the mirror stage.

On this page Marx formulates the following proposition – no quantitative relations of value can be established without the prior establishment of a general equivalence. It's not simply a question of equating so many yards of cloth, it's the equivalence between cloth and clothes which has to be structured, that is, that clothes can come to represent the value of cloth. It's thus not a matter of the clothes that can be worn but of the fact that clothes can come to be the signifier of the value of cloth. In other words, the equivalence necessary from the start of the analysis, and on which what is called value is based, presupposes, on the part of both terms in play, abandoning a very important part of their meaning.

The meaning effect of the metonymic line is located along this dimension.

We shall subsequently see what the use of bringing this meaning effect into play in the two registers of metaphor and metonymy is. Together they refer to an essential dimension that enables us to refind the plane of the unconscious – the dimension of the Other, to which we necessarily appeal, insofar as the Other is the locus, receiver and pivotal point of witticisms.

That's what we'll do next time.

27 November 1957

V

A BIT-OF-SENSE AND
THE STEP-OF-SENSE

Knots of signification and pleasure
Need, demand, desire
Benefits of ingratitude
Misunderstanding and misrecognition
Subjectivity

When Freud comes to the second, synthetic part of his work on witticisms, he enquires into the source of the pleasure they produce.

It's becoming more and more essential that you read this text at least once. I stress this for anyone who might think he is excused from doing so. It's the only way you can become familiar with this work, short of me reading it to you myself, which, I imagine, wouldn't be to your liking. Although this will decidedly lower your attention level, I will read out some extracts, since this is the only way you will realize how closely and how frequently the formulas I bring you – or am trying to – follow the questions Freud raises.

Nevertheless, do be aware that Freud's approach is often circuitous. While he refers to standard themes under various psychological or other headings, the manner in which he exploits them introduces an implicit theme that is just as important as, and even more important than, the themes that serve as his explicit references and which he and his readers have in common. The way he makes use of them, in fact, and you'd really have to have never opened the text not to be aware of this, brings out a dimension that no one had ever suggested before him. This dimension is precisely that of the signifier. I am going to show its role.

1

I'll go straight to the issue that we will occupy ourselves with today – what, Freud asks, is a witticism's source of pleasure?

In language that is too widespread in our day and that certain people would employ, one could say that the source of pleasure in a witticism is to be found in its formal aspect. Fortunately, these are not the terms Freud uses. On the contrary, he goes so far as to say, with much more precision, that the true source of pleasure yielded by a witticism is that it's funny.

It nevertheless remains the case that the pleasure we get from hearing a witticism is centred elsewhere. Are we not aware of the direction in which Freud is looking for this source throughout his analysis? The ambiguity inherent in the act of making a joke prevents us from recognizing where the pleasure comes from, and it takes all the effort of his analysis to show us.

It's quite essential here to follow the way he proceeds. In a manner consistent with a system of explicit references that becomes increasingly apparent as the work progresses, the primitive source of pleasure is referred to a playful period of infantile activity, to the early playing with words that refers us directly to the acquisition of language as pure signifiers, to verbal play and to the practice that we might almost describe as the pure utterance of word forms. Is it a pure and simple question of a return to playing with signifiers as such at a period before they are mastered, whereas reason will gradually oblige the subject, through education and what is learned from reality, to bring mastery and criticism to the use of signifiers? Does the principal source of the pleasure in witticisms lie, then, in this difference? If that were how Freud's contribution could be summed up, the whole thing would appear pretty simple, but this is far from being the case.

While Freud tells us that this is the source of the pleasure, he also shows us the paths down which this pleasure passes – they're former paths, ones that are still there, existing potentially, virtually, and still sustaining something. They are what is liberated by the operation of witticisms, as is their privilege by comparison with the paths that the subject's progress towards the adult state has brought to the forefront of the regulation of thought. Going down these paths immediately takes witticisms – and this is where all of Freud's earlier analysis [in Part A] of their mainspring and mechanisms comes in – down these structuring paths that are the very paths of the unconscious.

In other words, and Freud himself expresses it this way, a witticism has two sides.

On the one hand, there are signifiers in action, with this freedom that maximizes their possibilities of fundamental ambiguity. In a word, here we find the original feature of signifiers in relation to meaning, the essential polyvalence and creative function that they have in relation to meaning, and the touch of the arbitrary that they bring to it.

The other aspect is that of the unconscious. That signifiers in action evoke, all by themselves, the entire order of the unconscious is well enough indicated, as Freud sees it, by the fact that the structures revealed in witticisms – their constitution, crystallization and functioning – are none other than the very ones he discovered in his initial apprehension of the unconscious at the level of dreams, bungled actions – or successful actions, however you want to take it – and at the level of symptoms, even, and which we've tried to formulate more precisely by using the terms 'metaphor' and 'metonymy'. These forms are the same for all language use and also for the structuring by language we encounter in the unconscious. They are the most general forms, of which condensation, displacement and the other mechanisms Freud emphasizes in the structures of the unconscious are in a way merely applications. It may not be in our mental habits to confer the structure of speech on the unconscious in this way, but it corresponds to what's effectively dynamic in the relation of the unconscious to desire.

This commonality between the unconscious and the structure of speech, insofar as it's regulated by the laws of the signifier, is precisely what we're trying to get a better understanding of and illustrate by means of our recourse to Freud's text on witticisms. This is what we're going to attempt to examine in more detail today.

Stressing what might be called the autonomy of the laws of the signifier, and saying that they're primary in relation to the mechanism for the creation of meaning, does not, of course, exempt us from asking how to conceptualize not only the appearance of meaning but also, to parody a rather awkwardly produced formula from the school of logical positivism, the 'meaning of meaning' – not that this latter expression makes any sense. What do we mean when we talk of meaning?

Moreover, in the chapter on the mechanism of pleasure, doesn't Freud repeatedly refer to this formula, so widespread in connection with witticisms, of 'sense in nonsense'? This formula, which had been put forward by many authors in the past, records the two visible sides of pleasure – a witticism immediately strikes one as nonsense, it grabs you and then compensates you with the emergence, inside this very nonsense, of some secret meaning or other that is, moreover, always so difficult to characterize.

From another perspective, it has been said that the way has been paved for meaning's emergence by the nonsense that in the moment confuses and confounds us. This is perhaps closer to the way it works, and Freud is doubtless inclined to concede that there is more to it. That is to say that the role of nonsense is to trick us for a moment, long enough for a previously unnoticed meaning to hit us as we get the joke. This meaning also fades very quickly. It's fleeting, a flash of meaning, similar in nature to the moment of confusion when we were struck by the nonsense.

Effectively, if you take a closer look, you'll notice that Freud goes so far as to reject the term 'nonsense'. This is what I'd like us to think about today, since it's quite characteristic of these approximations to avoid precisely the final term, the ultimate mainspring of the mechanism at work. Formulas like this no doubt have a seductive psychological appeal to them, but they are not strictly speaking correct.

I'm going to propose that we not take the reference to children as our point of departure. We know that children can take pleasure in these verbal games, that one can therefore refer to something of this order, give sense and weight to the psychogenesis of the mechanism of wit and bestow charm on this primitive and distant ludic activity – and rest content with that. But, if we think about this in some other way than by going along with established routine, it's perhaps not a reference that we should be all that happy with, since it's also uncertain whether the pleasure of wit, in which children only remotely take part, can be completely explained by appealing to fantasy [*fantaisie*].

In order to make the link between the use of signifiers and what we might call satisfaction or pleasure, I'm going to return to a reference that may seem elementary. Even if we do refer to children, it must nevertheless not be forgotten that in the beginning signifiers have a purpose – they are made for expressing a demand. Okay, so let's stop for a moment at the mainspring of demand.

2

What is demand? Demand is what in need gets conveyed by means of signifiers addressed to the Other. I pointed out to you last time that this reference merits an effort on our part to explore the different moments in it.

These moments are so underexplored that a distinguished representative of the psychoanalytic hierarchy devoted an entire article of a dozen or so pages – I have alluded to it somewhere in one of

87   my own articles – to marvelling at the virtues of what he calls 'the
       wording', an English word corresponding to what in French we more
       awkwardly call '*le passage au verbal*' or '*la verbalisation*'. It's obvi-
       ously more elegant in English. A patient of his had been particularly
       irritated by an intervention he had made. He had uttered something
       to the effect that she had unusual or even strong 'demands', which
       has an even more insistent emphasis in English than in French. She
       had been literally bowled over, as if by an accusation or a denuncia-
       tion. But when he repeated the same interpretation a few moments
       later using the word 'needs', '*besoins*', he found someone who quite
       docilely accepted his interpretation. And the author is amazed by it.

       The mountain the author in question makes out of this discovery
       clearly shows us how primitive the state of this art of wording still
       is inside analysis, or at least inside certain analytic circles. For, in
       actual fact, there you have it all – demand is in itself so relative to the
       Other that the Other is immediately in the position of accusing and
       rejecting the subject, whereas by invoking need he authenticates,
       assumes and ratifies it, he assumes it and is already beginning to
       recognize it, which in itself is an essential form of satisfaction. The
       mechanism of demand brings the Other to oppose it by nature – you
       could even say that, by its very nature, demand requires opposition
       for it to be sustained as demand. The introduction of language into
       communication is being constantly illustrated by the way in which
       the Other agrees to a demand.

       Let's think about this. The system of needs enters the dimension
       of language where it's remodelled, but it's also permanently pouring
       into the signifying complex, which is why demand is essentially
       something that by its very nature presents itself as capable of being
       excessive. It's not for nothing that children ask for the moon. They
       ask for the moon because it's in the nature of a need expressed via a
       signifying system to ask for the moon. And incidentally, don't ever
       hesitate to promise it to them. And incidentally, we ourselves are
       very close to having it. But at the end of the day we haven't got it yet.

       The most important thing to emphasize is the following – what
       happens with a demand for a need to be satisfied? We respond to the
       demand, we give our neighbour what he demands, but what mouse
       hole does it have to pass through? What reduction in his aspirations
       must he lower himself to in order for his demand to be approved?

88   The phenomenon of need highlights this quite well when it appears
       in a naked form. I would even say that to have access to need qua
       need, we have to refer, beyond the subject, to some kind of Other
       called Christ who identifies with the poor. This is true of those who
       practise Christian charity, but also of the rest as well. The man of
       desire, Molière's Don Juan, of course gives the beggar what he asks

him for, and it's not for nothing that he adds, 'for the love of humanity'. The response to a demand, granting a demand, is ultimately
referred to an Other beyond the person there in front of you. One
of the stories Freud treats as pivotal in his analysis of witticisms, the
one about salmon mayonnaise, gives the best illustration of this.

It's about a character who, having given a beggar the money he
needs in order to repay some debt or other, make some payment,
is outraged when he sees him putting the object of his generosity to
another use. It's a very funny story. Some time after the good deed,
he comes across him in a restaurant where he is helping himself to
salmon mayonnaise – something regarded as a sign of extravagant
expenditure. You need to give it a bit of a Viennese accent, which
the story calls for. He says, 'What? Is this what I gave you money
for? To buy yourself salmon mayonnaise?' The other then makes a
joke of it by responding, 'But I don't understand. When I don't have
any money, I can't have salmon mayonnaise, and when I do have
some money, I can't have any either! So when am I supposed to eat
salmon mayonnaise?' [*SE* 8: 49–50]

Every example of a witticism is made even more significant by its
particularity, by what is special in the story and unable to be generalized. It's by way of this particularity that we come to the very
mainspring of the domain we're examining.

This story is no less relevant than any other, for they all place us
at the very heart of the problem, namely, the relationship between
signifiers and desire. Desire is profoundly changed in its emphasis, subverted and rendered ambiguous by its passage through the
pathways of the signifier. Let's take a close look at what this means.
Satisfaction is always granted in the name of a certain register that
brings the Other into play beyond the person making the demand,
and it's precisely this that profoundly perverts the system of demand
and response to demand.

Clothe the naked, feed the hungry, visit the sick – I don't need to
remind you of the seven, eight or nine works of mercy. The terms
themselves are striking enough. Clothe the naked – if a demand was
something that was to be maintained at its most direct point, why
not dress the naked men or women in Christian Dior? This happens
from time to time, but usually it's because one has undressed them
in the first place. Similarly, feed the hungry – why not get them
drunk? This isn't done, it would harm them, they are used to being
sober and you mustn't disturb them. As for visiting the sick, there's
Sacha Guitry's quip, 'Paying a visit always pleases, if not when you
arrive, then at least when you leave.'

The topic of demand is thus at the heart of my remarks today.
Let's try, then, to schematize what happens during this pause,

89

which, in some way, through a singular, zigzag pathway, as it were, renders the communication of a demand out of phase with respect to gaining access to satisfaction.

So that we can put this little schema to use, I'll ask you to refer to something which, while it's only mythical, is nonetheless profoundly true.

Let's assume what must exist somewhere, all the same, even if only on our schema – namely, a demand that is met. That's what matters, ultimately – if Freud introduced a new dimension into our considerations on man, I wouldn't say that it's that something succeeds regardless, but that something meant to succeed gets through. The desire that should go through, leaves, somewhere, not only traces but also a circuit that insists.

Let's start, then, with something that supposedly represents a demand that gets through. Since childhood really does exist, we may think of it as a refuge for this demand that goes through. The child articulates something that for him is still only an uncertain articulation, but he takes pleasure in it – this is what Freud refers to, moreover. The young subject directs his demand somewhere. Where does it come from when it has not yet entered into play? Let's say that something starts to take shape at this point we'll call delta or capital D, for 'Demand'.

What does this describe for us? It describes the function of need. Something gets expressed, coming from the subject, and I'll make it the line of his need. It ends here, in A, where it also crosses the curved line of what we've identified as discourse, consisting of the mobilization of previously existing material. I didn't invent the line of discourse where the stock of signifiers, very limited at this moment, comes into play inasmuch as the subject correlatively articulates something.

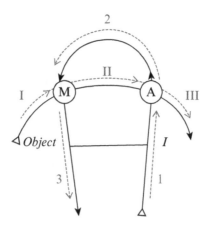

Look at these things. They unfold on two planes – that of the young subject's intention, however confused you might suppose it to be, insofar as he makes an appeal, and that of signifiers, however disorganized you might suppose their use to be, inasmuch as they are mobilized by his efforts and his appeal. The line of signifiers advances apace with the intention, until both reach the intersections A and M, whose usefulness for understanding the retroactive effect of a sentence as it comes to a close I've already pointed out to you.

Note that these two lines don't cross before the end of the second moment. In other words, whoever's saying something says both more and less than what he has to say. The reference to the tentative character of a child's first use of language comes into its own here.

There is simultaneous progression along both lines and a twofold completion at the end of the second moment. What began as need will be called demand, while the signifiers will come to a close on what, in as approximate a manner as you like, completes the demand's meaning, which constitutes the message that the Other evokes – let's say the mother, granting the existence of good mothers from time to time. Instituting the Other thus coexists with the completion of the message. They are determined at one and the same time, one as message and the other as Other.

At the third moment, we see the two curved lines extend beyond both A and M. I will indicate, at least hypothetically, the names we can give these endpoints and indicate where we can locate them on the structuring of demand that I'm trying to situate as the foundation of the initial use of signifiers for expressing desire.

As the most useful reference point for what we will try to develop later, I would ask you to consider, at least provisionally, the ideal case where demand encounters what extends it at this third moment, namely, the Other who takes it up at the level of its message.

Now, what we have to consider here with respect to demand cannot exactly be confused with the satisfaction of a need, for using signifiers transforms the way this need manifests itself. With the addition of signifiers, it undergoes a minimal transformation – a minimal metaphor, in a word – and this makes it the case that what is signified is something beyond raw need and is remodelled through the use of signifiers. Henceforth, from this beginning, what enters into the creation of the signified isn't purely and simply the translation of need, but the recapture, reassumption and remodelling of need, the creation of a desire other than a need. It's a need with signifiers. Just as socialism – as Lenin used to say – is probably something quite nice, but the perfect society has electricity as well, so, here, in the expression of need, there are signifiers as well.

On the other hand, with respect to signifiers, at the third moment there's certainly something that corresponds to the miraculous appearance – we have effectively made the assumption that it's miraculous, fully satisfying – of the satisfaction in the Other of the new message that has been created. This normally results in what Freud presents to us as the pleasure we get in the deployment of signifiers. In this ideal case of success, the Other enters into prolonging the deployment of signifiers. What prolongs the effect of signifiers is when they are resolved into their own authentic pleasure, the pleasure we get from using signifiers. You can inscribe this at the end of the [horizontal] line.

I ask you to grant as a hypothesis for a moment that the ordinary usage of 'demand' as such is underpinned by an original reference to what we may call the complete success, the initial success, the mythical success, or the primordial and archaic form of the deployment of signifiers. This hypothesis will underlie everything we are going to try to conceptualize concerning what happens in actual cases in which signifiers come into play.

Inasmuch as the fully successful passage of demand into the real creates both the message and the Other at one and the same time, it results, on the one hand, in a remodelling of the signifieds, something introduced by the use of signifiers as such, and, on the other, it directly prolongs the authentic pleasure in the deployment of signifiers. The two alternate. On the one hand, there is the deployment of signifiers that we effectively find, with Freud, at the origin of verbal play and that constitutes an original pleasure that is always ready to surface. On the other, there is what happens in opposition to this. Let's see what is involved.

The originality of this is well masked and appears not merely in the response to demand but in the verbal demand itself. This original something that transforms need renders it more complex and places it on the plane of what, starting now, I will call desire.

What is desire? Desire is characterized by an essential shift in relation to everything that is purely and simply of the order of the imaginary direction of need – need that demand introduces into another order, the symbolic order, with all the disruptions that this is liable to bring about.

The reason I ask you to refer to this initial myth is that we will have to build on it for what is to come, otherwise everything Freud formulates concerning the specific mechanism of the pleasure of witticisms will be rendered incomprehensible. The novelty that appears as an essential dimension in the signified through the introduction of signifiers is found everywhere. Freud emphasizes it at every turn in manifestations of the unconscious.

Freud occasionally tells us that something called surprise appears at the level of formations of the unconscious. We shouldn't take this as an accident of this discovery but rather as a fundamental aspect of its essence. The phenomenon of surprise has something originary about it – whether it's produced in a formation of the unconscious, insofar as it shocks the subject by its surprising character, but, equally, where you provoke this sentiment of surprise in the subject when you unveil it to him. Freud makes this point on all sorts of occasions, whether it's in *The Interpretation of Dreams*, *The Psychopathology of Everyday Life*, or, at every moment, in the text of *Jokes and their Relationship to the Unconscious*. The dimension of surprise is consubstantial with what desire is essentially, once it has passed to the level of the unconscious.

This dimension is a dimension that desire carries with it as a specific condition of the emergence of desire as desire. It's the very dimension by which desire is able to enter the unconscious. Not every desire is effectively capable of entering the unconscious. The only desires that enter the unconscious are those that, having been symbolized, can, on entering the unconscious, be preserved in their symbolic form – that is, in the form of this indestructible trace, examples of which Freud turns to again in *Witz*. They are desires that never fade, that don't possess the character of impermanence characteristic of all forms of dissatisfaction, but, on the contrary, are supported by the symbolic structure, which maintains them at a certain level of circulation of signifiers, which I have designated as having to be situated on this schema in the circuit between the message and the Other, where it occupies a function that varies according to the effects it has where it emerges. We must use these same pathways to conceptualize the rotating circuit of the unconscious insofar as it's there and always ready to reappear.

93

New meaning emerges through the action of a metaphor when, taking original circuits, it enters the everyday, banal and accepted circuit of metonymy. In a witticism, it's there for all to see that the ball flies back and forth between the message and the Other, and that this produces the effect of originality that is one of the latter's characteristic features.

Let's now go into greater detail so we can try to grasp and understand this.

3

What happens once we leave the primordial, mythic level of the initial establishment of demand in its characteristic form?

Let's consider an absolutely fundamental theme that runs through stories involving jokes. All you ever see are beggars whom one grants things to. Either they are granted what they haven't asked for, or having been given what they asked for they put it to a different use, or they behave with a special kind of insolence towards the person who has given it to them, reproducing in the relationship between requester and solicited the blessed dimension of ingratitude, in the absence of which granting any request would be truly unbearable. Note, as our friend Mannoni has very pertinently pointed out in an excellent work, how the normal mechanism of granting a request provokes new demands again and again.

What is this demand, ultimately, inasmuch as it reaches the listener, whose ear it was intended for? Let's do a bit of etymology. Although the essential dimension that we must refer to does not lie in the usage of signifiers, a bit of etymology is, however, apt to enlighten us here. '*Demande*', which is so marked by themes of insistence in the concrete use of the term, even more so in English than in other languages, but also in other languages, is originally '*demandare*', to confide in.

94

Demand is thus placed on the level of a shared register and language and succeeds in handing all of one's self and all one's needs over to an Other from whom the signifying material for every demand is itself borrowed, and it thereby assumes a different tone. This displacement is especially imposed on demand in particular because of how it effectively functions. This is where we find the origin of the materials that have been employed metaphorically, as you can see in the progress of a language.

For us, this is quite an instructive fact regarding what is involved in the famous complex of dependence I mentioned earlier. Effectively, in Mannoni's terms, when the person making the demand is able to think that the Other has truly granted one of his demands, there is effectively no longer any limit – it becomes normal to entrust all one's needs to him. Hence the benefits of ingratitude, as I just mentioned, which puts an end to what otherwise can't be stopped.

But, equally, the experienced beggar isn't in the habit of presenting his demand so nakedly. A demand has nothing confiding about it. The subject knows only too well what he is dealing with in the other's mind, and this is why he disguises his demand. He demands something that he needs in the name of something else that he sometimes also needs, but which will be more easily admitted as a pretext for the demand. If he needs to, if he doesn't have this other thing, he will just simply invent it and he will above all take into account what the Other's system is in formulating his demand. He will address himself to a charity worker in one way, to a banker in another, in another to a marriage broker, and in yet another way to any of these characters who are so amusingly portrayed in this book on *Witz*. That is, his desire will be taken up and remodelled not just in the system of signifiers, but in the system of signifiers such as it is installed or instituted in the Other.

The formulation of his demand thus begins in the Other. It's initially deflected [1] onto this, namely the *I*, which has already been in an active state in his discourse for a long time. The *I* proffers the demand, deflecting it back [2] to the Other, and it will travel via the circuit A–M and arrive [3] at the message. This is the appeal, the intention and the secondary circuit of need. It isn't necessary to emphasize its rationality too much, apart from emphasizing its control by the system of the Other. Of course, the latter already implies all sorts of factors that, purely for the case at hand, we are warranted in describing as rational. Let's say that even if it is rational to take them into account, there is nevertheless no implica-   95
tion that they actually are rational in structure.

What happens along the chain of signifiers, according to the three moments we see described here? Something remobilizes the entire apparatus and the entire material, and initially arrives [I] here, at M. Then, it doesn't head towards the Other [A] straightaway, but is deflected [II] towards something which, at the second moment, corresponded to the appeal to the Other – namely, the object. This is an object that is admissible to the Other, the object of what the Other is willing to desire, in short, the metonymic object. Once it's deflected towards this object, it converges, at the third moment [III], on the message.

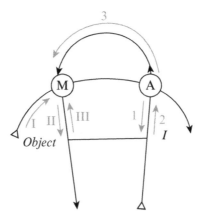

Here we don't find ourselves, then, in the happy state of satisfaction we had reached at the end of the three moments of the initial mythical representation of demand and its success which, with its surprising novelty and pleasure, is satisfying in itself. On the contrary, we find ourselves coming to a stop at a message that in itself possesses a character of ambiguity. This message is a formulation which is alienated from the very beginning insofar at it sets out from the Other, and which terminates on this side at what is, in some way, the Other's desire. The message is the meeting point of the two. On the one hand, the appeal has been evoked from the Other itself. On the other, all sorts of conventional elements are introduced into its very signifying apparatus, elements which form what I will call the communal or displacement nature of objects, insofar as the latter are profoundly reworked by the Other's world. And it's striking to see that at the third moment, as we have seen, discourse circulates between the tip and the tail of the arrow. This can culminate in what we call a lapsus, a slip of the tongue.

It's doubtful that meaning formed in this way is univocal. It's so doubtful that misunderstandings and misrecognitions are a fundamental feature of language, forming one of its essential elements. Witticisms exploit the ambiguity of this formation of messages. They are formed, in various ways, on the basis of this point.

I won't sketch out again, today, the variety of forms in which messages that are constituted in an essentially ambiguous form structurally are capable of being taken up and treated in a way that, as Freud tells us, ultimately aims at restoring the ideal pathway ending in the surprise of something novel, on the one hand, and in the pleasure of the play of signifiers, on the other. This is the point of a witticism. The point of a witticism is in effect to re-evoke for us the dimension by which desire, if it does not recapture, at least indicates everything that has been lost along the way, namely, on the one hand, what scraps it has left behind at the level of the metonymic chain and, on the other, what it has not fully actualized at the level of metaphor.

While we call 'natural metaphor' what took place earlier in the ideal transition by which desire reaches the Other, where desire is formed in the subject and is directed to the Other which takes it up, here we find ourselves at a more evolved level. Effectively, these two things known as the *I*, on the one hand, and the profoundly transformed, metonymic object, on the other, have already intervened in the subject's psychology. From that point on, we are no longer dealing with a natural metaphor, but with the ordinary use of one, whether it succeeds or fails in the ambiguity of the message, which now is to be highlighted under the conditions that remain in the natural state.

An entire aspect of desire continues to circulate in the form of scraps of signifiers in the unconscious. In the case of a joke, through a sort of forcing, a happy shadow or reflection of former satisfaction is conveyed. An astonishing success, one purely achieved by signifiers. Let's say that something happens the effect of which is, very precisely, to reproduce the initial pleasure of the satisfied demand even as it accedes to an original novelty. That is what a joke, essentially, accomplishes. How does it manage it?

This schema may help us appreciate that the completion of the initial curve of the signifying chain also extends what in intentional need passes into discourse. How so? Via a joke. But how is a joke going to come to light? Here again we find the dimensions of sense and nonsense – but we should examine them more closely.

If the indications regarding the metonymic function I gave last time were directed at anything, it was at what equalization, levelling out and equivalences are produced simply by the unfolding of the signifying chain. There is an effacement or reduction of meaning, but this isn't to say that it's nonsense. I borrowed a Marxist reference in this connection – bringing two objects of need into operation in such a way that one becomes the measure of the value of the other, effaces what is specifically related to need from the object and thereby introduces it into the order of value. From the point of view of sense, this might be called, using a neologism that is also ambiguous, the de-sense [*dé-sens*]. Today, let's simply call it 'the bit-of-sense' ['*le peu-de-sens*']. Once you have this key in hand, the meaning of the metonymic chain will not fail to appear for you.

The 'bit-of-sense' is exactly what the majority of witticisms play on. We are not dealing with nonsense, for in a witticism we aren't one of those noble souls who, immediately following the great desert by which they are inhabited, reveal to us the great mysteries of general absurdity. If the discourse of the beautiful soul hasn't succeeded in ennobling our feelings, it has recently nobelled a writer. His address on nonsense remains the shallowest [*vain*] I've ever heard. It's absolutely not the case that there is a play on nonsense every time equivocation is introduced. If you recall the story of the calf – this calf I was having fun with last time almost to the point of giving Heinrich Heine's response for him – let's say that this 'veal's value' was almost nothing at the time it was talked about. Moreover, everything you can find in plays on words, and very specifically those called conceptual plays on words, consists in playing upon how bad words are at maintaining a full sense. It's this 'bit-of-sense', as such, that is taken up, and it's here that something occurs that reduces the message to its scope, insofar as the message is both a success and a failure, but always a form necessary for any formulation of a demand. The message questions the

Other over this bit-of-sense. The dimension of the Other is essential here.

Freud dwells on the fact, as if it were something completely primordial that pertains to the very nature of jokes, that no joke exists in isolation. Even if we have forged it or invented it ourselves, even if the joke is our own invention and it's not that the joke invented us, we feel the need to put it to the Other. A joke is indissociable from the Other, who is charged with authenticating it.

What is this Other? Why this Other? What is this need for the Other? I don't know whether we will have enough time today to define it and establish its structure and limits, but, at the point we have come to, I would simply say this. What in a joke is communicated to the Other essentially plays out, in a manner that is particularly cunning, along the dimension of this bit-of-sense. We need to keep in full view here the nature of what is at issue. A *Witz* is never about provoking the pathetic invocation of some fundamental absurdity like the one I was alluding to before when I referred to the work of one of the Great Woolly Thinkers of our time. It's always a matter of suggesting the dimension of the bit-of-sense by questioning value as such and by summoning it, as it were, to realize its value dimension, reveal itself as true value. Note that this is a ruse of language, for the more value reveals itself as true value, the more it will reveal itself to be supported by what I am calling the bit-of-sense. It can only respond in the sense of the bit-of-sense, and this is where the nature of the message specific to a joke lies, that is, that by which here at the level of the message I resume, with the Other, the interrupted path of metonymy, and ask it this question – 'What does that all mean?'

A joke is only complete once it gets beyond this point – that is, only after the Other has taken the joke on board, responded to it and authenticated it as a joke. A joke requires that the Other has perceived what is there as a demand for sense – that is, as an evocation of a sense that lies beyond – in this vehicle for this question about the bit-of-sense. In all of that, something marked by the sign of the Other has effectively remained. This sign marks every formulation of desire with its profound ambiguity, above all linking desire, as such, to the necessities and ambiguities of a signifier, to homonymy – that is, to homophony. The Other replies to this on the upper circuit, which goes from A to the message, by authenticating . . . but what?

Shall we say that it authenticates whatever nonsense it contains? Here too I'm going to insist. I don't think it's necessary to maintain this term 'nonsense', which only makes sense from the perspective of reason or critique, that is, of precisely what is avoided in this circuit.

I propose the formula 'step-of-sense', *'pas-de-sens'* – just as one says *'pas de vis'*, screw thread, *'pas de quatre'*, four step, *'Pas-de-Suse'*, the Pass of Susa, or the *'Pas de Calais'*, the Strait of Dover.

This step-of-sense is, strictly speaking, what is actualized in metaphor. It's the subject's intention, his need, which introduces the 'step-of-sense' into metaphors beyond metonymic use and beyond anything commensurable, beyond any received values to be satisfied. Removing one element from its place and substituting another – I would almost say any other – for it, introduces this 'beyond need' in relation to every formulated desire, which is always at the origin of metaphor.

99

What do witticisms have to do with this? They indicate nothing more than the very dimension of the 'step' as such, strictly speaking. This is the form of the 'step', as it were. It's the 'step' voided of every kind of need. It's where what, in a witticism, can nevertheless manifest what is latent in my desire in me, and it's something that may resonate in the Other, though not necessarily. What's important in witticisms is that the dimension of the 'step-of-sense' be picked up and authenticated.

This is what displacement corresponds to. Novelty only emerges beyond the object at the same time as the step-of-sense does, and at the same time for both subjects. There's a subject and there's the Other. It's the subject who addresses the Other, who communicates the novelty to him as a joke. He travels along the segment of the metonymic dimension, he then gets the bit-of-sense received as such, the Other authenticates the step-of-sense within it, and pleasure is released for the subject.

The subject reaps pleasure inasmuch as he has succeeded in surprising the Other with his joke – and, indeed, this is the same original pleasure that the infantile, mythical, archaic, primordial subject I mentioned before obtains from his first use of signifiers.

I'll stop at this point. I hope it doesn't seem too artificial or too pedantic to you. My apologies to anyone who gets a headache from these sorts of little exercises on the high wire, not that I believe you incapable of grasping these things mentally. I don't think that what Kant calls your *Mutterwitz*, your good sense, is so degraded by the medical, psychological, analytic and whatever other studies you've pursued that you are incapable of following me down these paths with some simple allusions. Nevertheless, the laws of my teaching don't render the dismantling, one way or another, of these stages or essential moments in the progress of subjectivity in jokes off limits.

'Subjectivity' – that's the word I come to now, because up till the present day, and even still today, while working through the signifiers' pathways with you, something has been missing in the midst of it all – and not without reason, as you will see. It's not for nothing that in the midst of it all, today, we only ever find quasi-absent subjects, various kinds of support for using signifiers to put the ball back in the other's court. And yet, what is more essential to the dimension of jokes than subjectivity?

When I say 'subjectivity', I am saying that nowhere can the purpose of a joke be grasped. Even what a joke designates beyond what it expresses, even the feature of essential, internal allusion is an allusion to nothing other than the necessary requirement of the step-of-sense. And yet, in this total absence of a purpose, something ultimately underpins the joke, which is the liveliest of the lively, the most embraced of the embraced, and which makes it such a subjective thing. As Freud says somewhere, there is an essential subjective conditionality here, and the word 'sovereign' is here, emerging between the lines. 'The only joke', he says, in one of these formulas whose acerbic character can be found in almost no other literary author – I've never seen this comment made by anyone else – 'The only joke is one that I myself recognize as a joke.'

And yet I need the other. The entire chapter following the one on 'The Mechanism of Pleasure', which I have been speaking about today, namely, 'The Motives of Jokes – Jokes as a Social Process' – it has been translated into French as '*mobiles*', I have never understood why – has this other as an essential reference. There is no pleasure in a joke without this other, who is there also as a subject. Everything comes back to the relations between two subjects, the one Freud calls the first person of a joke, the one who makes it, and the one to whom, he says, it's absolutely essential that it be communicated [*SE* 8: 100].

What sort of other does this suggest? To say it here and now, at this level the other, with its characteristic features that are ungraspable anywhere else with such clarity, is strictly speaking what I am calling the Other with a capital O.

I hope to show you this next time.

4 December 1957

VI

WHOAH, NEDDY!

Exorcizing the topic of thought
Queneau tells a joke
The joke machine
The Other between the real and the symbolic
Being of like mind

I have some very important things to tell you today.

I ended last time on the subject's role in jokes, giving full weight to the word 'subject'. I am hoping that, on the grounds that we use it here, it has not become something that you wipe your feet on. When one uses the word 'subject', it generally carries lively, very personal and sometimes emotional reactions from those who cleave above all to objectivity.

Also, we had come to this sort of point of intersection located here at what I call A – that is, the Other. As the locus of the code, it is the locus that a message in the form of a joke reaches by following the path on our schema that goes from the message to the Other where the simple succession of signifiers in a chain, as the foundation of what is produced at the level of discourse, gets registered. At this level the essential something I have been calling 'the bit-of-sense' issues from the text of the sentence.

Last time I mentioned, without dwelling on it, the Other's confirmation of the bit-of-sense in a sentence, which is always more or less apparent in a joke. I limited myself to saying that what is transmitted from the Other, here [at A], in the circle that comes back to the level of the message, confirms the message and constitutes the joke, inasmuch as the Other, having received what is presented as a bit-of-sense, transforms it into what I have called, in an equivocal and ambiguous manner, the 'step-of-sense'.

What I stressed thereby is neither the absence of sense nor nonsense, but exactly the step that corresponds to a glimpse into what

102   sense reveals about its own procedure and what is always metaphorical and allusive in it. Thus it is that, once need has been through
the dialectic of demand introduced by the existence of signifiers, it is
never encountered again. Everything that is language proceeds via
a series of steps like those of Achilles who never catches up to the
tortoise – it aims at re-creating a full sense which, however, it never
achieves, which is always somewhere else.

This is the schema I came to in the final quarter of an hour of
our last session. It seems my discourse flagged a little. From what
some people told me, I wasn't finishing sentences. And yet, when I
read my text, I didn't find they lacked a tail. Because I am trying to
project myself into something difficult to communicate step by step,
there will necessarily be some stumbling. My apologies if it happens
again today.

1

We have come to the point where we need to enquire into the
Other's function and, in a word, essence, at this intersection that I
have designated quite well by calling it the 'step-of-sense'.

This step-of-sense is in some ways a partial retrieval of the ideal
plenitude, purely and simply realized, of demand, which is where
we started from as the point of departure of our dialectic. By what
transmutation, transubstantiation or subtle operation of communion, as it were, can this step-of-sense be embraced by the Other?
What is this Other?

Our enquiry bears upon this junction that is indicated well
enough by Freud's problematic when he speaks about jokes with
that capacity he has to leave the question in suspense, and which
means that, undeniably, of all the varied attempts carried out over
the course of ages to get a good grip on the mystery-question of
jokes – however many of these attempts I read, and I haven't held
back, and whichever author I turn to, even going back to the fertile
Romantic period – I truly see no one who has brought together even
the most basic, material elements of the question.

Consider this, for instance, which Freud thinks about. On the one
hand, he says, with that sovereign tone of his that cuts through the
ordinary, blushing timidity of scientific discourse, 'The only joke
103   is one that I recognize is a joke.' It's what he calls the irreducible
'subjective conditionality' of jokes. Indeed, it is the subject who is
speaking there, Freud says. On the other hand, he highlights the
fact that as soon as I am in possession of something that qualifies
as a joke, I am all in a hurry to try it out on the Other – and, what's

more, to provide him with the context. This is even a condition for me to be able to enjoy its pleasure to the full. And it would not be difficult for me to reveal the play of mirrors in the background whereby, when I tell a joke – if I really am seeking the culmination, repose and acceptance of my pleasure in the Other's consent – the possibility remains on the horizon that this Other will recount the joke in turn, transmit it to others and so on and so on.

Let's grab the dilemma by the horns. On the one hand, the only joke is one that I myself experience as one. But, on the other, nothing in my acceptance of it is in any way sufficient in this respect – the pleasure in a joke is only complete in the Other and through the Other. Let's say – on condition that we pay careful attention to what we say and don't imply any simplification by this term – that a joke has to be communicated. This assumes that at the end of the communication we leave an opening without knowing what may come and fill it.

Freud's observation, then, confronts us with an essential question, which we have come across before. What is this Other which, in some way, is the subject's correlate? We find affirmation of this correlation here in what is a real need inscribed in the phenomenon. But we are already familiar with the form of this relation between subject and Other, and have been ever since we insisted, here, on the necessary form in which our reflection proposes the term 'subjectivity' to us.

I have alluded to the sort of objection that might occur to minds trained in a certain discipline, and which, on the grounds that psychoanalysis presents itself as a science, would introduce the requirement that we only ever speak of things that are objectifiable, namely, things on which experience can agree. Simply by virtue of speaking about the subject, analytic experience supposedly becomes something subjective and non-scientific. Implied in the term 'subject' is the notion, which at a certain level is a good one, that what is there underneath the object – which makes it possible to give the object support and which, also, lies beyond the object as well as behind it – presents us with a sort of unknowable substance, something resistant to objectification, which your education and psychological training has given you the arms to fight against. This naturally leads to other forms of objection that are even more crude. I want to mention the identification of the term 'subjective' with the distorting effects of feelings about the experience of another person, and also introduce, moreover, some kind of mirage of transparency that founds the subject on the immanence of consciousness itself which people rely on a little too quickly to sum up the theme of the Cartesian cogito. In short, a series of entanglements. They are only there to get between us and what we are describing when we bring the subjectivity in our experience into play.

104

Subjectivity cannot be eliminated from our experience as analysts. The concept is confirmed in a way that completely bypasses the ways in which one could object to it. As an analyst, just as for anyone who goes down the path of a certain dialogue, one has to take subjectivity into consideration in one's calculations when dealing with the other who is capable of introducing errors of his own into his own calculations, and not try to provoke them, as such. I give you this formula, and it clearly expresses something tangible that even a passing reference to chess, or even to the game of odds and evens, suffices to confirm.

When we express it in these terms, subjectivity seems to appear in two ways – there is no point in going back over all this here, I have already emphasized it elsewhere. It certainly seems to me that subjectivity can be seen reflected in what is produced whenever there is confrontation or camouflage in either fight or display. I illustrated this in its day with some ethological examples that I don't think I need return to. Fighting between animals, even display between the sexes, present us with phenomena of reciprocal approaching and fascinating erection in which a sort of natural coaptation is apparent. One thus observes forms of conduct that are reciprocal in nature and that tend towards an embrace – therefore, at the motor level called behaviourist. The spectacle of an animal that appears to be performing a dance is very striking.

This is also what, in this case, leaves something ambiguous in the notion of intersubjectivity, which, having briefly emerged from the opposition between two subjects, as it were, is liable to disappear again in an attempt at objectification. The reciprocal fascination can very easily be thought of merely as subject to a cyclical regulation isolatable in the instinctual process, which, following an appetitive stage, enables consummation to be achieved and the sought-for end to be reached. We can reduce everything here to an innate mechanism of relays, to the point where it fades into the general obscurity of the teleology of living things.

This is all completely different once we introduce any resistances whatsoever, in the form of a signifying chain, into the problem. The signifying chain as such introduces an essential heterogeneity here. Hear 'heterogeneity' with the emphasis on 'heteros', which signifies 'inspired' in Greek, and whose true acceptation in Latin is remainder, residue. Once we bring signifiers into play, as soon as two subjects address one another and relate to one another through the intermediary of a signifying chain, there is a remainder, and the kind of subjectivity that is established is of another order, inasmuch as it refers to the locus of truth as such.

Consequently, my behaviour is no longer deceptive but provocative. The A is included in it, and this means that even a lie has to appeal to truth and that the truth itself may seem not to be in the register of truth. Recall this example, 'Why do you tell me you are going to Cracow when you really are going to Cracow?' This can mean that truth has need of lies. Later, when I lay my cards on the table, my good faith makes me reliant on the Other's evaluation insofar as he may be planning to take my strategy by surprise even as I am in the process of showing it to him. The detection of bluffing and deception is also at the mercy of the Other's bad faith.

These essential dimensions are apparent in simple experiences of everyday life. However, even though they are woven into our daily life, we will be no less inclined to avoid them as long as analytic experience and Freud's position have not shown us this hetero-dimension of signifiers at play on their own, autonomously. As long as we have not felt this and become aware of it, we will not fail to think that signifiers are there to serve the outpourings of consciousness.

Freud's entire thought is rife with the heterogeneity of the ways signifiers function – namely, with the radical character of the speaking subject's relation to the Other. Now, prior to Freud, this relation was hidden by the fact that we took for granted that the subject speaks, as it were, according to his good or bad consciousness, that he never speaks without intending a meaning, and that his intention lies behind his lying – or his sincerity, it makes no difference. Now, this intention is equally ridiculous whether the subject thinks he is lying or telling the truth, for he is deluding himself no less in his efforts to confess than in his efforts to deceive.

Until now intention has been confused with the dimension of consciousness, because it seemed that consciousness was inherent in what the subject has to say in terms of signification.

The least one could take for granted till now was that a subject always had a meaning to state, and that as a consequence consciousness was inherent in it. Objections to the idea of the Freudian unconscious have always found their last resort here. How could the existence of *Traumgedanken* [dream-thoughts] have been foreseen before Freud, dream-thoughts such as he presents to us, thoughts that our usual intuitions understand as thoughts that are not thoughts? This is why we now need to carry out a veritable exorcism of the topic of thought.

If the topic of the Cartesian cogito clearly is still so powerful, its harmfulness, as it were, derives from the fact that it is always inflected. This 'I am thinking, therefore I am' is difficult to grasp at the height of its mainspring – and anyway perhaps it is only a joke.

106

But let's leave that alone, for we are not at the point of displaying the relations philosophy has with jokes. The Cartesian cogito is not effectively experienced in each of us as an 'I am thinking, therefore I am', but as an 'I am as I think', which naturally assumes, behind it, an 'I think as I breathe'.

One only need, on this matter, engage in the slightest of reflective experiences on what supports the mental activity of those around us. Since we are scientists, let me speak of those who are dedicated to doing major scientific work. We can very readily form the impression that there are, on average, probably not all that many more thoughts in action in this cogitating body overall than there are in that of any hardworking cleaning lady beset by the most immediate necessities for her subsistence. In itself thought has absolutely nothing to do with the significance of the discourse conveyed. Moreover, the more consistent and coherent the discourse is, the more it appears to lend itself to all sorts of gaps with respect to what can be reasonably defined as a question posed by the subject to his existence as a subject.

At the end of the day, we are confronted with the following, which is that a subject thinks in us, and thinks according to laws that turn out to be the same as those that organize the signifying chain. This signifier-in-action in us is called the unconscious. It was named as such by Freud. And it is so original, so separate from anything at work in our tendencies that Freud repeats to us in a thousand different ways that it involves *another psychical scene*. This term is repeated at every turn in the *Traumdeutung*.

Freud actually borrowed this term from Fechner, and I have already had occasion to emphasize the uniqueness of the Fechnerian context, which is far from being reducible to the observation of psychophysical parallelism, or even to the strange extrapolations he went in for regarding the existence, which he affirms, of the domain of consciousness. The term 'other psychical scene' that Freud borrows from his thorough reading of Fechner is always correlated by him with the strict heterogeneity of the laws concerning the unconscious in comparison with everything that can be referred to in the domain of the preconscious, that is, in the domain of the comprehensible, of meaning.

The Other that's at issue, which Freud also calls 'reference of the psychical scene' concerning jokes, is the one that today we have to question. It is the one that Freud constantly brings us back to concerning the pathways and the very process of jokes.

There is no possibility, for us, he notes, of a joke emerging without an element of surprise. It is even more striking in German – '*Seine volle Wirkung auf den Hörer nur zu äussern, wenn er ihm neu ist, ihm als Überraschung ehtgegentritt.'* This can be translated as: 'They only produce their full effect on the hearer if they are new to him, if they come as a surprise to him' [*SE* 8: 154].

There is something that must render the subject foreign to the immediate content of the sentence, and that is sometimes presented by means of what looks like nonsense. This is the nonsense in relation to signification which makes you say momentarily, 'I don't understand, I am confused, this sentence has no real content', marking a break in the subject's assent in relation to what he accepts. That's the first stage, Freud tells us, in the natural preparation for a joke, which will subsequently constitute a sort of pleasure-generator, a 'pleasurogenic'.

What is going on at this level? What is the order of the Other that is invoked in the subject? Since there is, also, something immediate in the subject that one does by means of a joke, the technique of this movement must tell us something about what mode of the Other has to be struck here in the subject.

This is what we are going to think about today.

2

I have only referred to jokes related by Freud himself till now, or almost only. I am now going to introduce a joke that has a different provenance. It hasn't been specially chosen, either. When I decided to explore the question of *Witz* or wit* with you this year, I carried out a small investigation. It will come as no surprise at all that I began by questioning a poet. It was a poet who introduces the dimension of an especially playful wit that runs through his work, as much through his prose as through more poetic forms, and it's a wit that he brings even when he happens to be talking about mathematics, for he is also a mathematician. I am referring to Raymond Queneau.

When we were having our first exchange of remarks on the matter he told me a joke. It's not only in analytic experience itself that things that fit like a glove come one's way. Having spent an entire year talking to you about the signifying function of horses, here, once again, we have a horse making its way into our field of attention in quite a curious way.

The joke that Queneau told me is not one that you will know. He took it as an example of what we might call long jokes as opposed to short jokes. This is, to be sure, very much an initial classification. 'Brevity', Jean-Paul Richter, quoted by Freud, says somewhere, 'is the body and soul of wit', to which we can add the sentence in

Hamlet where it is said that if brevity is 'the soul of wit', 'tedious-ness' is no less 'its limbs and outward flourishes' [*SE* 8: 13]. Both things are true; both authors knew what they were talking about. You'll see whether the term 'long joke' is appropriate here, for there is a witticism in there somewhere.

Here, then, is the joke. It's a joke about exams, about university entrance exams, if you will. We have a candidate and we have an examiner.

'Tell me', says the examiner, 'about the battle of Marengo.'
The candidate pauses for a moment, with a dreamy air. 'The battle of Marengo ... ? Bodies everywhere! It's terrible ... Wounded everywhere! It's horrible ... '
'But', says the examiner, 'can't you tell me anything more precise about this battle?'
The candidate thinks for a moment, then replies, 'A horse rears and whinnies.'
The examiner, surprised, seeks to test him a little further and says, 'In that case, can you tell me about the battle of Fontenoy?'
'The battle of Fontenoy? ... Dead soldiers, wounded sol-diers! Everywhere! All of that, and more.'
The examiner, interested, says, 'But, young man, could you give me some more precise details about this battle of Fontenoy?'
'Oh!' says the candidate. 'A horse rears and whinnies.'
The examiner, strategically, asks the candidate to talk about the battle of Trafalgar. The candidate replies, 'Dead every-where! A bloodbath ... Wounded everywhere! Hundreds of them ... '
'But, my good man, can't you tell me anything more precise about this battle?'
'A horse –'
'Excuse me, I would have you note that the battle of Trafalgar was a naval battle.'
'Whoah! Whoah!' says the candidate. 'Back up, Neddy!'

To my mind, the value of this joke is that it enables us to disman-tle, I believe, what is going on in a joke.

I think that the entirety of the joke's wittiness lies in its punchline. There would be no reason for the tale itself to come to an end, were it to consist solely of this kind of playing or sparring in which two interlocutors are opposed – and, moreover, no matter how far you extend it, the effect is produced immediately.

109

Prior to the punchline, this is a joke that makes us laugh because it is comical. I don't want to go any deeper into the question of the comic, because so many enormous and particularly obscure things have been proffered on this matter, ever since Mr Bergson wrote a book on laughter about which the only thing that can be said is that it is readable.

What does the comic consist in? For the moment let's just limit ourselves to the observation that it is bound up with a dual situation. It is because the candidate is there with the examiner that this joust unfolds in which their arms are obviously so radically different and also that this something liable to produce in us what we call 'lively amusement' is created. Is it the subject's lack of knowledge that makes us laugh? I am not convinced. Obviously, the fact that he produces these first truths about what can be called a battle, which no one ever mentions, at least not when taking a history exam, ought to give us pause for a moment's thought. But we can't go into that, for it would take us into questions concerning the nature of the comic, and I do not know whether we will have the opportunity to go there, unless it is to complete our examination of Freud's book.

This book effectively ends with a chapter on the comic in which it is striking to see Freud suddenly miles below his usual perspicacity, so much so that the question is rather why he says nothing more than the worst of authors focused on the most elementary notion of the comic and why in some ways he refused to do more. This will no doubt make us more indulgent towards our psychoanalytic colleagues who also lack a sense of the comic, to the point where it seems to be ruled out for anyone exercising the profession.

Insofar as we experience a lively comical effect with this joke, the comic concerns the preliminary part about the battles. It's against this background that the punchline comes, which makes the joke witty in the strict sense of the term.

110

Please note the following. Even if some of you are not particularly receptive to what makes this joke witty, there is wit there nevertheless. It is lurking there at one point, namely the point at which it suddenly breaks free from the constraints of the format and the candidate does something that is almost unbelievable if we were to put ourselves momentarily in a position where we situated this joke in a real-life context. The subject all of a sudden seems to be leaning back and pulling on the reins. It's an image that in a flash takes on an almost phobic value. The moment is in any case of a kind, or so it seems, with what can be drawn from various childhood experiences beginning with phobias and extending to all sorts of excesses of imaginary life that we have such difficulty fathoming. It is not so rare to see reports, in recollections from a subject's life, of attraction to a big horse, or an image of this same horse descending from tapestries, or this horse entering a dormitory where the subject is there with fifty friends. The punchline therefore turns us into observers of the sudden emergence in this joke of the signifying fantasy of the horse.

Call this joke what you will, comical or poetic, but it surely deserves to be called witty, if, as Freud says, you are the final arbiter. Consequently, we may call it a funny story. It is, nevertheless, true that we are no longer surprised by the fact that its content coincides with an image borrowed from an observed and recognized form at the level of unconscious phenomena.

Moreover, the fact that this aspect of it is so clear is what gives the story its value. Am I saying that this is sufficient to make it a joke?

Here, then, are these two moments, broken down into what I will call its preparation and its punchline. Are we going to leave it there? We could leave it there at the level of what can be called the Freudian analysis of *Witz*. We would have no more difficulty, I think, highlighting these two moments or aspects of the phenomenon in another joke, but here they are especially distinct.

What makes the thing not simply poetical or funny but truly witty in character follows the retrograde or retroactive path of what in our schema I call the 'step-of-sense'. However elusive or ungraspable the punchline of this joke is, it is nevertheless heading towards something. It's perhaps forcing things a little bit, no doubt, to spell it out, but so as to indicate this direction, I am going to have to do it nevertheless – the specific feature to which the subject returns with the sort of insistence that in another context would no longer be wit but humour, namely this horse rearing and whinnying, but that may be what we truly relish in the joke.

111

Of all the history that we have integrated into our experience, formation and culture, let's say that this image here is the most essential of all. We cannot take more than three steps in a museum and look at the paintings of battles without seeing this horse up on its hind legs, whinnying. The horse entered the history of war with a certain splendour. The moment at which men sat astride this animal was a milestone. At the time, with the Achaeans' arrival on horseback, this brought real and enormous progress. These men suddenly had an extraordinary tactical superiority in comparison with horses harnessed to chariots – right up to the First World War when the horse disappeared, when it was rendered practically obsolete by other weapons. Thus, from the Achaean period to the First World War, the horse was effectively something absolutely essential to this interhuman commerce known as war.

The fact that it has consequently been the central image of certain conceptions of history that we can bring together under the rubric of battle history is a phenomenon whose significant character we are inclined to have a liking for, to the extent that this age has passed and has been progressively purified as the discipline of history has advanced. Ultimately, an entire history is summed up in that image, which strikes us as futile in the light of this funny story. The indication of meaning that it harbours implies that in the end there is no real need to worry oneself over a battle, neither Marengo, nor Fontenoy, perhaps with a little more justification concerning Trafalgar.

Of course, none of this is there in the story. There is no question of extracting any wise lessons concerning the teaching of history. It doesn't teach but shows that the step-of-sense tends in the direction of a reduction in the value, an exorcism, of this fascinating element.

In what sense does this story act? And in what sense does it satisfy us, in what sense does it give us pleasure?

Introducing signifiers into our significations leaves a margin that makes us remain in bondage to them. Something escapes us beyond the bonds that the chain of signifiers maintains for us. The simple fact that this refrain that is repeated from the start of the joke – namely, 'The dead! The wounded!' – makes us laugh is indication enough of the extent to which we are refused access to reality as soon as we penetrate it by means of signifiers.

This joke will simply serve as a point of reference here. Freud stresses that whenever it is a matter of the transmission of a joke and the satisfaction it is capable of bringing, there are always three people involved. The comic can make do with a play between two. In the case of a joke there are three. The Other, who is the second, is located in different places. He is sometimes the second person in the story, without our knowing, and without our even needing to know, whether it is the schoolboy or the examiner. He is also you, when I am recounting it to you. 112

Effectively, during the first part it is necessary for you to allow yourself to be taken for a bit of a ride. At first the joke elicits your various sympathies, either for the candidate or for the examiner, and it fascinates you or it makes you hostile – although really what is drawn upon in this joke is not so much our hostility as a certain captivation by the game the candidate is engaged in with the examiner, where the latter has a surprise in store for him. The same game is also sketched out in other kinds of tendentious jokes of a smutty or sexual kind. In fact, it's not so much a matter of getting around whatever resistance and repugnance lies within you as it is, on the contrary, of starting to activate it. Far from extinguishing something in you that you might object to, if a good joke is going to be smutty, there is already something at the start that will indicate to you that we are entering this domain. And so you prepare yourself either to consent or resist, but there is certainly something in you that emerges at the dual level. This is how, here, you let yourself get caught up in the prestige and display aspect foreshadowed by the register and the order of the joke.

Of course, what arrives unexpectedly at the end is invariably located on the plane of language. The playful side of words is developed much further here and is even so dismantled that we see, on the one hand, a pure signifier, the horse as it happens, and, on the other, the playful element in signifiers which presents itself in the form of a cliché that is much more difficult to locate, but where it is nevertheless obvious that that is all the joke contains. What surprises you is the fundamental equivocation, the passage from one meaning to another through the intermediary of the support of signifiers, as the examples I have previously given indicate. There's a hole here that makes you wait for the stage at which it hits you that what is being communicated is a joke.

As a general rule, it always hits you at a different spot from the place your attention – or agreement or opposition – has initially been attracted to and lured by, and this occurs whatever effects are at play, such as nonsense effects, comical effects or effects of smutty participation in a sexually exciting narration. Let's say that this dual game is only ever a preparation, one that enables both what is always imaginary, reflexive and collusive in the communication, and the bringing into play of a certain tendency in which the subject is the second person to be separated into two opposing poles. This is no more than the joke's support. Similarly, everything that attracts the subject's attention and everything that is alert at the level of consciousness is only the base whose role is to enable the move onto another plane, which is always present as more or less enigmatic. This is where the surprise occurs, and it's here, then, that we find ourselves at the level of the unconscious.

Given that the issue is always bound up with the mechanism of language on a plane on which the Other seeks and is sought, on which the Other is joined, on which the Other is the aim and on which the Other is reached by means of a joke – given this, how should we define this Other?

3

Let's pause for a moment at our schema and say some very simple things, some first truths.

You can use this schema as a grid or framework for locating the signifying elements as such. When we take the various modes or forms that establish the basis for our classifications of jokes, we find ourselves led to enumerate something like the following – word plays, puns in the strict sense, word plays via transposition or displacement of meaning and jokes via transposition or displacement of meaning, jokes via a small modification to a word that is sufficient to throw light on something and bring out an unexpected dimension. Whatever classificatory elements we choose, we tend, along with Freud, to reduce them to terms that are recorded in the register of signifiers. Imagine, then, a machine.

This machine is located somewhere at A or M. It receives data from both sides. It has the capability to dismantle the means of access by which both the construction of the term 'famillionaire' and the passage from the Golden Calf to the butcher's veal are achieved. Let's suppose that it is sufficiently complex for an exhaustive analysis of the signifiers' components. Will it be up to the task of authenticating a joke, as such? Of calculating and replying, 'This is a joke'? That is, of ratifying a message in relation to the code correctly, so that we remain within the limits, at least the possible limits, of what we call a joke?

I am producing this imaginary machine for purely humorous reasons, and it goes without saying that there's no question of making one. But what does that mean? Is it enough to say that we have to be in the presence of a person? That may be self-evident, and we're quite happy with that. Saying so corresponds to experience more or less, overall. But given that the unconscious exists for us, with its enigma, 'a person' is a response that needs to be broken down.

We can start by saying that we have to be in the presence of a real subject. It's effectively in meaning, in a direction for meaning, that jokes play their part. Now, as we have already indicated, this meaning is only conceivable in relation to the interaction between a signifier and a need. Therefore, the absence of the dimension of need in a machine is an objection and an obstacle to its ratifying a joke in any way at all.

Is it possible for us to say, though, that this real subject has to have needs that are homogeneous with our own? It is not necessarily assumed that we must impose this requirement from the outset of our exercise. Effectively, the need is nowhere designated in jokes. On the contrary, jokes point to the distance that exists between a need and whatever is put into play in a discourse. Whatever is articulated in a discourse takes us, by virtue of this very fact, to a series of reactions that is an infinity away from what a need is, strictly speaking.

Here, then, is an initial definition – the subject must be a real subject. God, animal or man? We have no idea!

114

What I am saying is so true that stories about the supernatural, which do not exist for no reason in human folklore, in no way exclude the possibility of making a joke with fairies or devils, namely with a subject said to have quite different relations, in its own reality, from those defined by human needs. You will tell me no doubt that these verbal beings, beings of thought, are nevertheless fabricated out of human images. I don't disagree, and indeed that's the issue. Effectively, we find ourselves between the following two elements. First, having dealings with a real subject, namely a living subject. Second, a living subject that understands language and, moreover, that possesses a stock of what is verbally exchanged – usages, uses, locutions, terms – without which there would be no question of entering into communication with him via language.

What do jokes suggest to us and in some way put us in touch with?

Bear in mind that these images are present in the human economy in a disconnected way, with an apparent freedom between them which makes possible all kinds of coalescences, exchanges, condensations and displacements, the juggling that we see at the origin of so many manifestations that make for the richness and heterogeneity of the human world in relation to biological reality. From an analytic perspective, we very often inscribe this freedom in a system of reference that leads us to consider it as being conditioned by an initial lesion concerning the interrelationship between man and his entourage, which I have attempted to designate by the prematurity of birth, and which means that it is via the image of the other that man finds unification of his movements, even the most elementary of them. Whether this starts here or somewhere else, what is certain is that these images, in their characteristic state of anarchy in the human order, in the human species, are activated, caught up in and used through the operation of signifiers. This is the way in which they enter into what's involved in a joke.

It is these images, which have become more or less everyday signifying elements, more or less ratified in what I have called the metonymic treasure trove, that are at play in jokes. It's the Other that possesses this treasure trove. It is assumed that the Other knows the multiplicity of signifying combinations, moreover completely abridged, elided and, let's say, even purified with respect to their signification. All metaphorical implications are already piled up and compressed in language. It's a matter of everything that language bears within itself, which manifests itself at moments of significant creation and is already there, latent, in a non-active state. That's what I am invoking in a joke, that's what I am seeking to awaken in the Other and in some way I am relying on the Other to support it. In a word, I only ever address the Other by assuming that what I bring into play in my joke is already contained in it.

Take one of Freud's examples. It's a quip by a witty man, famous in Viennese society, about a bad writer who floods the newspapers with his idle and interminable output on Napoleon and his descendants. As this writer has the particular physical characteristic of being a redhead, our wit skewers him with the words '*rote Fadian*', which signifies that he's redheaded and that he speaks drivel, '*rouquin filandreux*', as it has been translated into French [*SE* 8: 22ff].

What makes the joke a joke is the reference to the red thread, '*roter Faden*', a metaphor which is itself poetical and which, as you know, Goethe borrowed from a practice of the British Navy. The red thread effectively makes it possible to recognize the smallest piece of rope, even and above all stolen rope, stolen from vessels of His British Majesty at a time when sailing ships used rope a lot. This red thread definitively authenticated ownership of the material. The metaphor is certainly more famous for German-speaking subjects than it may be for us, but I suppose that quite a number of you are familiar, at least via this quotation, and perhaps even without being aware that you are, with this passage from *Elective Affinities*. This retort, very much in the style of the time, which was found very funny at a particular moment and in a particular context referred to as cultural, whether rightly or wrongly, lodges itself in the play between the red thread and the ropey character who utters banalities. This is what makes something work as a successful wisecrack or joke. That's where I'm going with this.

Freud says somewhere that something that finds satisfaction under the cover of wit is the subject's aggressive tendency – otherwise it would never show itself. One would not allow oneself to be so rude about a literary colleague. It is only possible under the cover of wit. That's just one aspect of the question, but it is obvious that there is a very great difference between purely and simply proffering an insult and expressing oneself in this register, for in expressing oneself in this register one is appealing to all sorts of things in the Other that are supposedly part of its usage, of its most everyday code.

I chose this example to give you a perspective taken from a specific moment in the history of Viennese society. In this context, reference to Goethe's red thread is immediately accessible to everybody, and up to a point it flatters the desire for recognition in all of us by offering us a shared symbol we are all familiar with.

There's also something else indicated in the tendency of this joke that calls into question not only the person ridiculed but also a very particular value in the social order. As Freud emphasizes, the essayist who approaches history from the perspective of anecdotes has a

116

habit of including basic ideas in which the author's own insufficien-
cies, the poverty of his categories and even the laziness of his writing
are only too apparent. In short, it's a confused style at the borders
of history that he is taking aim at here, one whose writings clutter
the newspapers of the day. Undoubtedly, this tendency, quite well
characterized in this joke, is not over, is not finished, but still it is
what gives this joke its value and its impact.

We are, then, in a position to say that far from its being the case
that the subject here with us has to be a real living creature, this
Other is essentially a symbolic locus.

The Other is the locus of the treasure trove of, let's say, the sentences or even the received ideas without which jokes cannot have
value or impact. But at the same time let's observe that no particular
signification is emphasized therein. On the contrary, this common
treasure trove of categories presents a characteristic that we can
describe as abstract. I am alluding here very precisely to this element
of transmission which makes it the case that there is something there
that, in a way, is supra-individual, and that is tied by an absolutely
undeniable community to everything that has been in preparation
ever since the origins of culture. What one is addressing when one
attacks a subject at the level of the equivocations of signifiers has, as
it were, a singularly immortal characteristic. This is really the other
term of the question.

The question of knowing who the Other is arises between two
poles. For us this Other has to be a real, living being, one made
of flesh, even though it is not his flesh that I'm arousing. But, on
the other hand, there is also something quasi anonymous, which is
present in what I refer to as I reach out to him and arouse his pleasure at the same time as my own.

What is the mainspring that lies there between the two poles of
the real and the symbolic? It's the function of the Other. It's this
function that is, strictly speaking, brought into play. I have of
course said enough about it to be able to say that this Other is the
Other as the locus of signifiers, but I have only extracted a direction
for meaning from this locus of signifiers, only a step-of-sense, which
is where, in the final analysis, the active mainspring lies.

We may say that a joke appears like a Spanish inn here. Or,
more exactly, it's the contrary of one, for in a Spanish inn you have
to bring your own food and they bring you wine, whereas here I
have to bring the wine of speech, since I won't find it here, even
if – an image that is more or less comical and ridiculous – I were to
consume my adversary.

The wine of speech is always present in everything I say. A joke
is usually present, ambient in everything I recount as soon as I

117

speak, for I necessarily speak in the double register of metonymy and metaphor. The bit-of-sense and the step-of-sense are always in the process of crossing over one another, just as a thousand shuttles cross back and forth, as Freud mentions in the *Traumdeutung*. But also, this wine of speech usually seeps into the sand. What is produced between the Other and me in a joke is, as it were, a very special communion between the bit-of-sense and the step-of-sense. This communion is no doubt more specifically humanizing than any other, but it is humanizing precisely because we begin at a level which, on both sides, is very inhuman.

If I invite the Other to this communion, it is because I have even greater need of his assistance because he is the vase or Grail. This Grail is empty. I mean that I address nothing in the Other that is specified, nothing that unites us in any kind of communion that might lead to any kind of agreement in desire or judgement. It is solely a form.

118

By what is this form constituted? It is constituted by what is always at issue in jokes, what in Freud are called inhibitions. It is not for nothing that when I prepare a joke I evoke something in the Other that tends to set him in a certain direction. This is still nothing more than a shell in comparison with something more profoundly linked to the stock of metonyms without which, in this order, I am absolutely unable to communicate anything to the Other.

In other words, in order for a joke to make the Other laugh, as Bergson says somewhere, and it's the only good thing that there is in *Laughter*, you have to have a lot in common, you have to belong to the same church.

What does that mean? The very term '*paroisse*', parish, is of no small help to our making progress in understanding the question. I do not know if you know what the origin of the word '*paroisse*' is. It's quite unusual, but ever since etymologists turned their attention to the matter, they have been unable to learn by what miracle a thing that at the outset was '*parodia*' – namely, people who are not from our house, I mean our house here on earth, who are from another world and who have their roots in another world, namely Christians, for the term appeared with Christianity – was, as it were, metaphorized by another term which recorded its signifying element in 'khi', which reappears in the Italian '*parrocchia*'. This other term is the Greek 'πάροχος', which means the purveyor, the intendant to whom the functionaries of the Empire knew that they had to address themselves so as to procure from him pretty well everything that a functionary of the Empire might desire, and in the blessed days of the Pax Romana that could go a very long way indeed.

We are here, then, at the level designated by the ambiguous term '*paroisse*', which clearly shows the limits of the field in which a joke will work. You can see that jokes don't have the same effect always and everywhere, since the one about the red thread has only a feeble effect upon you in comparison with the earlier joke about the candidate at an exam. Given that you are the public that you are, it was quite natural that something as much from our shared background as the baccalaureate or any other exam should be the kind of thing to serve as the container for what was being conveyed, namely a direction for meaning. Undoubtedly, inasmuch as this direction doesn't result in any meaning, it is only the distance that always remains there between every actual meaning and what I could call an ideal of full-sense.

119

I would add one more play on words. The manner in which this Other is constituted at the level of a joke is something that we are familiar with from Freud's use – he calls it 'the censor' – which bears upon 'sense' or meaning. The Other is constituted as a filter that puts order into, and places an obstacle before, what can be accepted or simply even heard. There are things that cannot be heard, or which habitually are never heard any more, and which a joke strives to make heard somewhere, as an echo. To get them to be echoed back, it uses precisely the thing that forms an obstacle to it, like some sort of reflecting concavity. I had already come to this metaphor earlier, and something inside it was resisting, something that is comprised entirely of a series of imaginary crystallizations in the subject.

We are not surprised to see things occur at this level. The little other, to call him by his name, contributes to the possibility of a joke, but it's within the subject's resistance – which for once, and this is highly instructive for us, I am rather seeking to provoke – that something that makes itself heard will resonate much further, and this means that the joke will resonate directly in the unconscious.

11 December 1957

UNE FEMME DE NON-RECEVOIR, OR: A FLAT REFUSAL

Duplicating the graph
Laughter, an imaginary phenomenon
An Other of one's own
The return to jouissance in Aristophanes
Comic love

Last time I spoke to you about the Grail. You are the Grail, which I'm solidifying by placing your contradictions on alert in all sorts of ways, with the aim of getting you to authenticate 'in spirit', so to speak, the fact that I am conveying this message to you. The essence of this Grail consists in its very defects.

Since it's always a good idea to go back over even the best understood of things, I am going to attempt to materialize on the blackboard what I was saying to you last time.

1

What I was saying to you last time was about the Other, this damned Other, who, when one communicates a *Witz*, completes and, in a way, fulfils the gap formed by the insolubility of desire. It can be said that a *Witz* restores an essentially unsatisfied demand its jouissance, under the double and moreover identical aspects of surprise and pleasure – the pleasure of surprise and the surprise in pleasure.

Last time I stressed the process of immobilizing the Other and forming what I called 'the empty Grail'. This is represented in Freud by what he calls the joke's 'façade' [*SE* 8: 55]. It diverts the Other's attention away from the path down which the joke is heading, it attaches the inhibition somewhere in order to leave another path open somewhere else for the witty words to take.

This, then, is more or less how the thing might be schematized. The path goes from speech, here condensed into a message, to the Other to whom it is addressed. An obstacle, a gap or a flaw in the message is authenticated by the Other as a witticism, but it is thereby restored to the subject himself, and forms the indispensable complement to the desire specific to witticisms.

This, then, is the schema we have been using. The Other, the message, the I and the metonymic object are here [see the graphs on pages 10 and 80]. We have already covered these points, which I assume you know. The Other is indispensable for closing the loop that is discourse insofar as it arrives at the message in a position to satisfy, at least symbolically, the fundamentally insoluble character of demand as such. This circuit is the authentication by the Other of what is, in short, an allusion to the fact that once man enters the symbolic world no demand can be attained except through an infinite succession of steps-of-sense. By virtue of the fact that his desire is caught up in the mechanism of language, man, a new Achilles in search of another tortoise, is destined to this never-to-be-satisfied, infinite approach linked to the very mechanism of desire, which we shall simply call discursiveness.

While the Other is essential to the final, symbolically satisfying step, the instantaneous moment of a joke – when it comes off – it is nevertheless worth remembering that the Other also exists. He exists in the same way that what we call the subject exists, circulating somewhere as in the game of pass the parcel. Don't imagine that there is a subject at the start of need – need is not yet a subject. Where is he, then? Perhaps I can say more about this today.

The subject is the entire system and, perhaps, something in the system. The Other is the same, he is constructed in the same way, and this is why he is able to relay my discourse.

I am going to encounter certain specific conditions that will have to be representable on my schema if it is going to be of any use. These conditions are the ones we spoke about last time. Take note of the directions on the segments. Here there are vectors that go from the I towards the object and towards the Other [$\beta \to \beta'$, $\beta \to \alpha$], and vectors that go from the message towards the Other and towards the object [$\gamma \to \alpha, \gamma \to \beta'$], for there is a strong relationship of symmetry between the message and the I, just as there is clockwise [$\alpha \to \beta \to \beta'$], and again counter-clockwise [$\alpha \to \gamma \to \beta'$] between the Other as such, as locus of the treasure trove of metonymies, and the metonymic object itself, insofar as it is constituted in the system of metonymies.

What was it I explained to you last time concerning what I called the preparation for a joke? The best thing is sometimes not to prepare it – but it is clear that it is not a bad thing to do so. We only have to recall what happened when I didn't – you were left high and dry. Something as simple as the '-t' that I related to you one day seems to have left some of you stumped. If I had prepared you on the reciprocal attitudes of the little count and the well-bred young lady, perhaps you might have been sufficiently tantalized and the 'Ahhht' might have more easily overcome something. Because some of you were paying close attention, you took the time to understand. By contrast, last time you laughed much more easily at the joke about the horse because it included a lengthy preparation, and while you were having a good time with the candidate's remarks that struck you as marked by the powerful insolence that lingers at the bottom of ignorance, you were then quite well disposed to see this flying horse come in at the end of the joke and really give it its punchline.

What I produce with this preparation is the Other. This, of course, is what in Freud is called '*Hemmung*', inhibition. This is merely the opposition that is the fundamental basis of the dual relation, and which, here, is comprised of all the objections you could make against what I was presenting as the object. That is quite natural, you were preparing yourself to be shocked by it, its approach and its pressure. What is organized in this way is what we habitually refer to as 'defence', which is the most elementary of forces. It is very much what is involved in these preludes that can be performed in a thousand ways. Non-sense sometimes plays the role of a prelude in the form of an inducement that draws the mental gaze in a certain direction. It is a lure in this sort of bullfight. Sometimes it's comical, sometimes obscene.

In effect, this is all about focusing the Other on an object. Let's say that, in the opposite sense to the metonymy of my discourse, it's a matter of bringing about a kind of fixation of the Other as discoursing on a particular metonymic object. In a way, this could be any object. It is not at all necessary that it have the slightest connection with my own inhibitions. It makes no difference, it will work with anything provided that the Other is occupied with some object at that particular moment. That is what I was explaining to you last time when I spoke about the imaginary solidification of the Other, which is the first position in making a witticism possible.

We must, then, find a place in our schema for the homologue of the object relation at the level of the Other, whom we are taking here as a subject, and this is why I am giving you another system, which I have drawn [see dotted lines]. I am plotting the homologue of the line that I call β - β', which is the Γ's relationship with the metonymic object for the first subject. I am thereby indicating the superimposition of the system of the Other subject onto the system of the first.

123
124

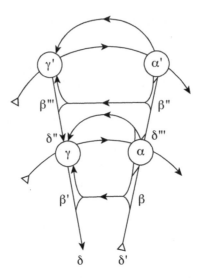

For the baton to be passed from the Other towards the message that authenticates a joke as a joke, it has to be bound up in its own system of signifiers, that is, as it were, the problem is referred back to him [the Other] in such a way that he himself, in his own system, authenticates the message as a joke.

In other words, my γ - α presupposes the inscription of a parallel γ' - α', which is just what is recorded on this schema. A requirement inherent in jokes gives them a theoretical perspective of reproduction ad infinitum, given that a good joke is made for being recounted and is not complete until it has been recounted and others have laughed at it. The very pleasure of recounting it includes the fact that others can, in turn, try it out on others.

While there is no necessary relationship between what metonymic captivation I must produce in the Other to leave the way open for the witty words, there is, on the other hand, necessarily a relationship between the systems of the two subjects. This is made sufficiently clear on the schema by the relationship between the signifying chain, as organized in the Other, which goes from δ''' to δ'' here, and the one that goes from δ' to δ. There has to be a relationship, and this is what I was expressing last time when I said that the Other has to be from the same church, of like mind. It is not enough that he more or less understands French, even though this is the first way to be of like mind. If I make a joke in French, for it to work and succeed there are many other things assumed known and that the Other must share.

Here, then, represented on the schema, are two conditions that we could write as follows. The β'' – β''' designates an inhibition

125

produced in the Other. Here I am using a sign with two small arrowheads going in opposite directions, and which is equal to, and goes in the opposite direction to, my metonymy, that is, opposite to $\gamma - \alpha$. By contrast, there is a sort of parallel between $\gamma - \alpha$ and $\gamma' - \alpha'$, which can be expressed by saying that $\gamma - \alpha$ can find its certification, which I have indicated by putting a rough breathing incidentally, on α' and γ'. The Other certifies it as a message and authenticates it as a witticism.

This has at least the advantage of clarifying these ideas by visualizing them, since that is one of the mental organs most familiar to the intellect. It visualizes for you what I meant when I was talking last time about the subjective conditions for the success of a witticism, namely, what is demanded of the imaginary other so that, within the goblet that this imaginary other proffers, the symbolic Other understands it.

I leave to ingenious minds the task of aligning this with what, curiously, I previously managed to say in a metaphor, when I was above all interested in imaginary images and in the conditions of the appearance of imaginary unity in a particular organic reflection. I must have had a reason to employ almost the same formal schema when I used the image of a concave mirror in relation to narcissism. But let's not engage in a parallel that would only be forced, as suggestive as it might be.

I am now going to put this schema to one little supplementary use, since, whatever interest there may be in thus reminding you of the meaning of what I said last time, it would be fairly limited if it did not take us any further.

The initial schema that we have been using since the start of the year has been transformed, then, by the modifications I have been making to the formula of the Other as a subject. We have $\gamma - \alpha$, here, for the subject, and $\beta - \beta'$ for the relation to the metonymic object. Beyond this, at the next level up, this same arrangement is reproduced and this means that the Other also has a relation to the metonymic object, $\beta'' - \beta'''$, whereas here the $\gamma - \alpha$ becomes $\gamma' - \alpha'$, and so on indefinitely. The final loop, the one through which need, on its return, passes on the way to indefinitely deferred satisfaction, has to run across the entire circuit of Others, before returning here to its endpoint in the subject.

126

2

We will use this schema again shortly. For the moment, let's pause at a special case that Freud considers immediately following his analysis of the mechanisms of jokes, on which this is nothing but a commentary. He speaks about what he calls the social motives of jokes, and from there he goes on to the problem of the comic.

That's what we're going to try to explore today, without exhausting it. Freud explicitly says that he is only exploring it from the perspective of jokes, for there is a field here that is much too vast for him even to think about taking it on, at least on the basis of his experience. To introduce his analysis of the comic, Freud foregrounds what, in the comic, is closest to jokes. It is striking that with the sureness of orientation and touch that is his, what he presents us as being the closest to jokes is very precisely what at first sight might seem to be the furthest from jokes, namely the naive [*SE* 8: 182].

Naivety, he says, is based on ignorance, and quite naturally he gives examples of it taken from children. I've already mentioned the scene where children enact an entire and very pretty little story for the benefit of the adults. A couple separate, the husband goes off to seek his fortune. He returns several years later, having become rich, and on his return the woman greets him with these words, 'You see, I have behaved wonderfully, I haven't wasted my time either while you were away.' And she draws the curtain on a line of ten dolls. It's like a little scene of marionettes. The children are astonished, perhaps simply surprised – they perhaps know more than one thinks – by the outburst of laughter from the adults in the audience.

This is the type of naive joke Freud presents. He also gives it to us in a form that is technically much closer to the processes of language in the story about the little girl who offers a '*Bubizin*' to her brother who has a bit of a tummy ache. Having heard mention of a '*Medizin*' for her, since '*Mädi*' designates little girls and '*Bubi*' little boys, she thinks that if there is a '*Medizin*' for little girls, there must 127   also be a '*Bubizin*' for little boys. It's still a story that, provided one has the key to it, which is that one understands German, can easily be presented as a joke.

Although the reference to children is not unfashionable, what is essential is not there but in a feature that we won't say is one of ignorance but which Freud defines very specifically and whose easily substitutive character in the mechanism of jokes he emphasizes. What pleases us in jokes, says Freud, and this plays precisely the same role as what earlier I called fascination or metonymic captivation, is that we sense a lack of inhibition in the speaker. It's the lack of inhibition that makes it possible for us to convey what is essential in a joke – namely, the beyond that it evokes – to the Other we are telling it to and who is himself already fascinated by this absence of inhibition. Here, in the case of the child, in the cases that I have just referred to, what is essential does not consist in the humour, but in evoking the time in childhood when there is such a close relationship to language that it thereby directly evokes for us the relationship of language to the desire that constitutes the specific satisfaction of a joke.

I will take another example, one from an adult, which I think I already quoted at one time. One of my patients, who was not normally known for making very elaborate circumlocutions, was telling me one of those stories that are just a little sad, as he would do fairly regularly. He had made a date with a young woman he had met on his peregrinations and, as would often happen to him, the aforementioned stood him up. He concluded his story, 'I understood, once again, that it was a case of a knockback [*femme de non-recevoir*].'

He wasn't being witty; he thought that the expression was in use and that he was saying something completely innocent, which, however, has a highly amusing quality and satisfies something in us that goes well beyond the comical perception of this character in his disappointment.

If this story evokes a feeling of superiority in us, which is entirely doubtful, it is surely much inferior in this respect. I am alluding here to one of the mechanisms that have often been unduly elevated to the origin of comical phenomena, namely, the feeling of superiority over others. This is entirely questionable. Although it was a very great mind who attempted to sketch out the mechanism of the comic in this sense, namely Lipps, it's entirely refutable that this is where the essential pleasure of the comic lies. If there is anyone who happens to retain his superiority intact, it is our character, who possibly finds on this occasion a reason for his disappointment that is far from wounding his unshakeable confidence in himself. If any feeling of superiority takes shape in relation to this story, it acts more like a lure. Everything momentarily engages you in the mirage created by the way you situate the person who is recounting the story, or situate yourself, but what is going on here goes well beyond this.

Effectively, what is looming behind the term '*femme de non-recevoir*' is the fundamental disappointment, in itself, whenever one approaches desire, well beyond the satisfaction of this or that specific approach. What amuses us here is the satisfaction that the subject who has let drop this innocent phrase derives from his very disappointment. He finds that his disappointment is sufficiently explained by a locution that he thinks is an accepted locution, a ready-made metonymy for such occasions. In other words, he rediscovers his disappointment in a top hat in the guise of a baby's stuffed bunny that he thinks is the living rabbit of the valid explanation, and which is actually imaginary. Always expecting the rabbit

128

that constitutes his very disappointment to turn up yet again, he will remain unshaken and constant, without otherwise being affected by it, when he nears the object of his illusion.

You see, therefore, that a joke by an ignorant or naive person, by the person from whom I've borrowed this phrase and made it into a joke, is complete on this occasion, as it were, at the level of the Other. No longer do I need to bring about anything in the Other that constitutes this solid cup. It has already been given to me in its entirety by the one from whom I gather the precious words which when communicated will form the basis of the joke, and which my story thus raises to the dignity of a master word. In short, the entire dialectic of a naive joke is located in the upper part of my schema. What has to be brought about in the Other in the imaginary order so that a joke in its standard form is admitted and received is formed here by its naivety, ignorance and self-satisfaction. And to elevate this blunder to the level of a joke, I simply have to present it and have it ratified by a third party, the big Other, to whom I communicate it.

Promoting the imaginary other in this analysis of metonymies and in the pure and simple satisfaction he finds in language – and uses to avoid appreciating the extent to which his desire is leading him on – introduces us, and this is why Freud places it at the intersection of witticisms and the comic, to the domain of the comic.

We haven't come to the end of our pains, for, in fact, on the subject of the comic there has been no shortage of more or less unsatisfactory theories advanced – and it's certainly not an idle question to ask why this is so and also why they have been propounded. They have been presented in all sorts of forms that we don't need to spell out here, but their summation, succession and past history, as we say, do not lead us to anything fundamental. Let's leave all that behind and say that, in any case, the question of the comic is evaded when one undertakes to examine it, and I'm not saying resolve it, solely at the psychological level.

At the psychological level, both wit and the comic can obviously be easily combined under the category of what provokes laughter. Now you cannot fail but be struck by the fact that even though I have stressed that a witticism has been more or less well received and registered by the fact that you sanction it with a discreet laugh, or at the very least with a smile, till now I have not examined the question of laughter.

The question of laughter is far from having been resolved. Everyone agrees on making laughter an essential characteristic of what occurs in the witty and the comic, but as to linking it to its expressive character or even simply describing which emotion this phenomenon might correspond to – where it is possible to say, although this is not absolutely certain, that it is unique to man – one generally enters into matters that are extremely difficult. From some, one gets the impression that in trying to examine the relationship between laughter and phenomena that are thought to correspond to it in an analogical way, they are skirting around the issue. But even those who have said the most defensible or prudent things about the phenomenon of laughter hardly do more than note that it can leave 'oscillatory traces'. For Kant, it is a spasmodic movement with a particular mental oscillation, which passes from tension that is being reduced to nothing, an oscillation between an active tension and its sudden collapse in the face of the absence of anything that, supposedly, might resist it once the tension is activated. Similarly, the sudden passage from a concept to its contradiction emerges with a psychologist from the last century, Léon Dumont, whom Dumas refers to in his article on the psychology of laughter – a very Dumasian article, very fine and subtle, which this fortunate man didn't go to much effort over, but which is well worth reading, for even without making an effort he contributes some very nice elements.

In short, the question of laughter goes a lot further than that of wit or the comic.

It is not rare to see the different varieties of the phenomenon discussed. There is the mere communication of laughter, the laughing at laughter, there is the laughter that is linked to the fact that one must not laugh. The mad laughter of children under certain conditions also deserves to attract our attention. There is also the laughter of anxiety, and even the laughter of an imminent threat, the nervous laughter of the victim who suddenly finds himself threatened by something that goes well beyond the limits of his expectation, the laughter of despair. There is even the laughter over a bereavement that one has just learned about. I leave it there, for I do not intend to treat all these forms of laughter, nor is it my aim to give you a theory of laughter.

I would simply stress, in passing, that nothing is further from what we should be satisfied with than Bergson's theory about the mechanical appearing in the midst of life. His work on laughter reapplies in a condensed and schematic way the myth of vital harmony, of *élan vital*, characterized by its supposedly endless novelty and permanent creation. You cannot fail to appreciate how outrageous this is when you read that one of the characteristics of the mechanical as opposed to the vital is said to be its repetitive character – as if we don't piss in the same way every day, or go to sleep in the same way every day, or as if one is reinventing love

130

whenever one has a fuck. There is something truly incredible there. This explanation by means of the mechanical appears throughout the book like a mechanical explanation. What I mean is that it lapses into a lamentable stereotype that entirely leaves out what is essential in the phenomenon.

If the mechanical really were at the origin of laughter, where would we go? What would we do with Kleist's subtle remarks about marionettes, which run completely contrary to the supposedly amusing and inferior character of the mechanical? Very subtly, he stresses the fact that a true ideal of grace is achieved by these little objects which, controlled by nothing more than pieces of string, create movements whose elegant paths are linked to the stability of the centre of gravity of their curves, provided they are properly made – that is, according to the precise features of articulations in humans. No dancer, he says, can rival the grace of a skilfully operated marionette.

Having simply remarked how much Bergson's theory neglects even the most elementary understanding of the mechanism of laughter, let's leave it aside even before we involve it in anything as elaborate as the witty or the comic. Laughter effectively touches everything that is an imitation, a doubling, a *Doppelgänger* or a mask, and if we look at it more closely it's not just a matter of masks, but of unmasking – and unmasking at moments that are worth thinking about. You go up to a child with your face covered by a mask, he laughs in a nervous or embarrassed way. You move a bit closer, a manifestation of anxiety starts to appear. You take off the mask, the child laughs. But if you are wearing another mask beneath this mask, he won't laugh one bit.

131

All I want to indicate here is that a study is called for, one that can only be experimental – but can only be experimental if we begin to have some idea of the direction in which it is pursued. In any case, this phenomenon, like others that I could bring in in support of my affirmation if I intended to highlight it, shows us that there is a very intense, very close relationship between the phenomena of laughter and the function of the imaginary in man.

Images as such have a captivating character beyond their corresponding instinctual mechanisms, as is shown in both sexual and combative animal display. There's an extra touch to it in man due to the fact that in him the other's image is very closely linked to the tension I mentioned earlier, which is always elicited by the object at which the tension is directed, leading it to be placed at a certain distance with a connotation of desire or hostility. I am referring to the ambiguity that is at the very foundation of the ego's formation and this means that for the ego its unity lies outside itself, that it is in relation to its semblable that it is established and that it finds this unity of defence which is the unity of its being as a narcissistic being.

The phenomenon of laughter is located in this field. And it is here that the collapse of tension, to which authors attribute the instantaneous triggering of laughter, is produced. If someone makes us laugh simply by falling over, it is as a result of his more or less pompous image that we hadn't paid all that much attention to before. The phenomena of stature and status are so rife in our lived experience that we do not even notice them. We burst out laughing when in our imagination the imaginary character goes on in his affected way, whereas what he is supported by in the real is lying spreadeagled on the ground. This is about the liberation of or from the image. Take this in the two senses [in French] of this ambiguous expression – on the one hand, something is freed from the constraints of the image while, on the other, the image is also free to wander off on its own. This is why there is always something comical about the duck with its head cut off taking a few more steps around the farmyard.

This is why, somewhere, the comic connects with what makes one laugh. I locate it at the level of the direction I $\rightarrow$ object, $\beta \rightarrow \beta'$ or $\beta'' \rightarrow \beta'''$. Certainly, inasmuch as the imaginary is somehow implicated in the relationship to the symbolic, laughter, insofar as it connotes and accompanies the comic, reappears at a higher level, which interests us infinitely more than the totality of the phenomena of pleasure.

Let's move on to the comic.

132

3

To introduce the notion of the comic today I'll go back to the joke about the Golden Calf.

Soulié's quip in talking about the Golden Calf in relation to the banker – it's almost a witticism already, it's at least a metaphor – meets with this response, then, from Heinrich Heine. 'For a calf, he seems a bit past it to me.' Observe that if Heinrich Heine had said that quite literally, it would be because he hadn't understood, and he would be like my ignoramus from before who said, '*la femme de non-recevoir*'. In this case, his retort would have been comical.

It's this that constitutes the underside of this witticism. Heine's retort is in effect something of a flat rejection [*fin de non-recevoir*], he puts Soulié in his place, makes him feel uncomfortable, as it were. After all, Soulié didn't say anything particularly funny, and Heine checkmates him by showing that it can be dealt with differently.

He erects a metonymic object different from the first calf. In this respect, he is playing at the level of comic opposition.

One cannot avoid noticing one essential difference at the outset. On the occasion of a *Witz*, the comic is grasped in a fleeting state, in a trait, a word, in the repartee – but, really, the comic goes much further. A witticism doesn't need to be massaged at length for it to work, whereas for the comic a simple, brief encounter is not enough. Here I am, then, addressing all of you, whatever your current position, without knowing where you're from, nor even who you are – well, in order for there to be comical relations between us, there has to be a relationship that involves us with one another much more personally. That's what you can already see taking shape in the relationship between Soulié and Heine, and it concerns a mechanism of seduction, because, all the same, Heinrich Heine's response does rebut something on Soulié's side just a little.

To put it briefly, for the comic to be possible it is necessary that the relationship between demand and satisfaction be inscribed, not in an instantaneous moment, but in a dimension that gives it stability and constancy and its own pathway in relation to a determinate other. Now, if, in what underpins witticisms, we have located one of the essential structures of demand according to which, insofar as it is taken up by the Other, it has to be essentially unsatisfied, there is nevertheless a solution, the fundamental solution, the one that all human beings seek from the start of their lives to the end of their existence. Since everything depends on the Other, the solution is to have an Other of one's own. This is what we call love. In the dialectic of desire it's about having an Other of one's own.

The field of full speech, as I've said to you in the past, is defined in this schema by the very conditions under which, as we have just seen, something equivalent to the satisfaction of desire can and must be realized. We have an indication that it can only be satisfied in something beyond speech. The link uniting the Other, the *I*, the metonymic object and the message defines the zone in which full speech has to reside [see graphs pp. 85 and 112]. As an image of the message it is typically constituted by, I have given you 'You are my master' and 'You are my woman'. 'You, the other, are my woman.' I would therefore say to you that this is the form in which a man gives an example of the full speech in which he commits himself as subject, founds himself as the man of the woman to whom he is speaking and declares it to her in an inverted form. I also showed you its strangely paradoxical character, which is that everything rests on what must close the circuit. The metonymy that it contains, the passage from the Other to this unique object that is constituted by the statement, nevertheless requires that the metonymy be received, that something subsequently pass from γ to α, namely that the 'you' in question does not simply reply, 'Ah, no! No way!'

Even if he does not answer like that, something else happens much more often. It's that, by virtue of the very fact that no preparation as clever as a witticism comes along so that the line β″ - β‴ merges with the line parallel to it at the lower level, the two lines remain completely independent of one another – so much so that the subject in question well and truly retains his own system of metonymic objects. We will thus see produced the contradiction that is established in the circle of the four βs – namely, that since everyone has, as they say, his own little idea, this foundational speech comes up against what I will call, since we are in the presence of a square, the problem not of squaring the circle, but of 'circling' the metonymies, which remain quite distinct, even with the most ideal partner. 'There are good marriages, but no delightful ones,' said La Rochefoucauld.

Now, the problem of love and the Other is at the centre of the comic. To see this, it is a good idea first to remember that, if one wants to inform oneself about the comic, it would not perhaps be such a bad thing to read comedies.

Comedy has a history, comedy even has an origin – something that many people have studied. The origin of comedy is narrowly bound up with the id's relationship to language.

What is this id that we occasionally talk about? It is not purely and simply some original radical need, one that is at the root of the individualization of an organism. The id can only be grasped beyond the elaboration of desire in the network of language, only actualized at its limit. Here, human desire is not initially caught in the system of language that defers it indefinitely and leaves no place for the id to be constituted and named. However, beyond all of this elaboration of language, it is what represents the realization of the first need which, at least in man, has no chance of ever being known. We don't know what the id of an animal is, and there is very little chance that we ever will, but what we do know is that the id of man is entirely caught up in the dialectic of language and that it conveys and preserves the first existence of tendencies.

Where does comedy originate? We're told that it comes from the banquet at which, in a word, men say 'Yes' in a kind of orgy – leave this word in all its vagueness. The meal is constituted by offerings to the gods, that is, to the Immortals of language. Ultimately, the entire process of the elaboration of desire in language comes back to and comes together in consumption at a banquet. The whole detour is only taken so as to come back to jouissance, and the most elementary at that. That is how comedy makes its entrance into what, with Hegel, we can regard as the aesthetic face of religion.

134

What does Classical comedy show us? It would be a good thing for you to poke your nose into Aristophanes from time to time. This is always where the id gets the upper hand, pulls on the boots of language for its own use of the most elementary kind. It is well known that in *The Clouds* Aristophanes makes fun of Euripides and Socrates, particularly Socrates, but how does he portray this to us? He shows us an old man making use of all his beautiful dialectics to satisfy his cravings by all sorts of tricks – escaping his creditors, getting money from people – or a young man using them to escape his commitments, fail in all his duties, rail against his ancestors and so on. This is the return of need in its most elementary form. What enters at the start in the dialectic of language – namely, sexual needs most especially, all hidden needs in general – is what you see produced right before your eyes on Aristophanes' stage. It's powerful stuff.

I particularly commend to your attention the plays involving women. In the return to the elementary needs that underlie the entire process, a special role devolves upon women, insofar as it's by their intermediary that Aristophanes invites us, at the moment of imaginary communion that comedy represents, to appreciate what can only be appreciated retroactively, which is that if the State – and the City – exist, it's for one's benefit, so that the table of plenty, which, moreover, nobody believes in, is established on the Agora. After good sense has been thwarted by the perverse evolution of a city subject to all the indecision of a dialectical process, one emerges from it through the intermediary of women, who are the only ones who really know what men need, and one returns to this good sense, which naturally assumes the most excessive forms.

This is of interest to us only because of what it shows us about the violence of certain images. It also makes us imagine a world in which women were not quite what we are made to imagine they were by authors who depict a civilized Antiquity to us. In Antiquity, or so it seems to me, the women – I'm talking about real women, not the Venus de Milo – would have had lots of hair and not smelt good, if we are to believe the insistence that is placed on the role of the razor and on certain perfumes.

Be that as it may, in this Aristophanesque twilight, especially the one that concerns the vast insurrection of women, there are some quite beautiful images that one cannot but be struck by. There's one image that is suddenly expressed in the words of one of a group of women who are in the process of not just dressing up as men but also sporting beards to suggest omnipotence – it is simply a matter of knowing which beard it is. She starts laughing and says to them, 'How funny! We look like a school of grilled cuttlefish with beards!'

This vision from the shadows seems like it could suggest an entire foundation of relations in Classical society.

What did this comedy evolve into? Into the New Comedy which began with Menander and has continued right up to our day. What is the New Comedy? It shows us people engaged in the most fascinated and obstinate of manners, in general, with some metonymic object. We encounter every human type there. They are the same characters as the ones you find in Italian comedy. They are defined by having a certain relationship to an object. Something has taken the place of the irruption of sex, and it's love – love that is named as such, the love that we would call naive love, ingenuous love, the love that unites two young and, in general, fairly bland people. This is what forms the pivot of the intrigue. Love plays the role of being the axis around which the entire comedy of the situation revolves, and it will remain so until the appearance of Romanticism, which we will leave to one side for today.

Love is a comedic sentiment. The high point of comedy is readily locatable. The highpoint of comedy in the strict sense, in the sense in which I am presenting it to you here, is found in a unique masterpiece.

The latter is situated in history at the pivotal moment at which the presentation of relations between the id and language, in the form of a taking possession of language by the id, is about to give way to the introduction of the dialectic of man's relations with language in a blind, closed form, which is achieved in Romanticism. It is very important in the sense that without knowing it Romanticism turns out to be a confused introduction to the dialectic of signifiers as such, of which psychoanalysis is, in short, the articulated form. But in the, let's say, Classical line of comedy, the high point is reached when the comedy of which I'm speaking, which is by Molière and is called *The School for Wives*, raises the problem in an absolutely schematic way because it is indeed a question of love, but love as a tool of satisfaction.

Molière presents the problem to us in a manner that gives it a matrix. It possesses a clarity that is absolutely comparable to one of Euclid's theorems.

The play is about a person named Arnolphe. As a matter of fact, the rigour of the thing would not even have required that he be a person with just one idea. It just so happens that it works better that way, but in the same way in which a witticism uses metonymy to fascinate us. We see him enter right at the start with an obsession about not being cuckolded. That is his principal passion. It's a passion just like any other. All passions are equivalent, all are equally metonymic. It's the principle of comedy to present them as such, that

136

is, to focus the attention on an id that believes entirely in its metonymic object. It believes in it, which doesn't mean that it is tied to it, for it is also one of the characteristics of comedy that the id of the comedic subject, whatever it may be, always remains intact at the end. Whatever happens during the comedy is like water off a duck's back. *The School for Wives* ends with a 'Phew!' from Arnolphe, and yet God only knows what extremes he has been through.

I will try briefly to recount what it's about. Arnolphe is, then, taken with a young girl who, with her 'sweet and poised appearance', 'inspired me with love for her at the age of four'. He has, then, chosen his little woman, he has already instituted the 'You are my woman'. It's even for this reason that he gets so upset when he sees that this dear angel is about to be taken from him. The fact is that, at the point he has come to, he says, she is already his wife, he has already established her socially as such, and he has found an elegant solution to the matter.

'He is an enlightened man,' says his friend, who is called Chrysalde, and enlightened he is indeed. He has no need to be the monogamous person that we were talking about at the start – behind this monogamy he is an educator. Old men have always been preoccupied with the education of girls and have even proposed principles for it. Here, he's found a very happy principle, one that consists in keeping her in a state of being a complete idiot. He himself sets the programme of care supposedly contributing to this end. 'And you won't believe', he says to his friend, 'how far this can go. Just the other day didn't she ask me if children were made through the ears?' This was something that really should have made him prick up these very same ears, for if the girl had had a healthier physiological understanding of things, she might have been less dangerous.

'You are my woman' is full speech whose metonymy is the duly explained duties of marriage that have to be read out to little Agnès. 'She is a complete idiot,' he says, and he thinks, like all educators, that his scheme is thereby guaranteed.

What do the story's developments tell us? It could be called 'How girls grow wise'. The originality of the character of Agnès seems to have created a real enigma for psychologists and critics – is she a woman, a nymphomaniac, a flirt, is she this or is she that? Absolutely not. She's a being who has been taught to speak, and she does so.

She is captivated by the words of a character, a complete dimwit of a young man, moreover. This Horace comes into the picture on this question, when, in the important scene in which Arnolphe tells her he would tear half his hair out, she calmly replies, 'Horace could do more than you with two words.' She thus perfectly punctuates what is present throughout the play, namely that what has come to her in her encounter with the character in question is precisely that he says things that are amusing and sweet to the ear, that delight her. She is quite incapable of telling us, and of telling herself, what he says, but it comes through speech – that is, through what ruptures the system of learned and educational speech. This is how she gets captivated.

138

The sort of ignorance that is one of the dimensions of her being is simply connected with the fact that for her there is nothing but speech. When Arnolphe explains to her that the other held her hands, her arms, she asks, 'What else is there?' She is very interested. She is a goddess of reason, this Agnès. Moreover, the word 'reasoner' comes back to choke Arnolphe when he reproaches her for her ingratitude, her lack of sense of duty, her betrayal, and she answers him with admirable pertinence, 'But what do I owe you? If it is only for having made me stupid, your expenses will be reimbursed.'

At the beginning we thus find ourselves with the reasoner alongside the ingenuous, and what constitutes the comical mainspring is that as soon as the girl starts becoming clever we see the emergence of a reasoner alongside a character who, for his part, becomes the ingenuous one – for in words that leave no ambiguity he then tells her that he loves her, and he tells her in every possible way, telling her to the point where his declaration culminates in telling her more or less the following, 'You will do exactly everything you want to, you can also have Horace if it so happens that you want him.' Ultimately, the character overturns even the very principle of his system. He even prefers to be cuckolded, which was his principal starting point in the matter, rather than lose the object of his love.

Love – I am saying that this is the point at which the highpoint of Classical comedy is located. Love is here. It is curious to see to what extent we no longer perceive love except through all kinds of partitions, romantic partitions, that stifle it, whereas the mainspring of love is essentially comical. It is precisely in this respect that Arnolphe is truly in love, much more authentically in love than the said Horace, who is always vacillating. The romantic change in perspective that took place around the term of love means that we can no longer grasp it so easily. It's a fact – the more the play is performed, the more Arnolphe is played as Arnolphe, the more people lean over and say to one another, 'This Molière is so noble and profound, you laugh when you should be crying.' People almost never find the comic compatible with the authentic and overwhelming expression of love as such. However, love is comical when the love that declares itself and shows itself is love that is love at its most authentic.

That, then, is the outline of the story. Still, I must also tell you how it ends.

139   The story is brought to an end by the stupidity of the third person, namely Horace, who happens to conduct himself like a little baby, going so far as to hand back the very person he has just taken out of the hands of her legitimate possessor, without even having been able to identify him as the jealous party whose tyranny Agnès was suffering from, and who, moreover, is her chosen confidant. This doesn't matter. He is a secondary character. Why is he there? So that the problem is posed in these terms – namely, that Arnolphe is kept informed at every instant, hour by hour, minute by minute, about what is happening in reality, by the very person who is his rival and, also, in a manner that is just as entirely authentic, by his pupil herself, the said Agnès who hides nothing from him.

Indeed, she is a complete idiot, as was his wish, uniquely in the sense that she has absolutely nothing to hide, says everything and says it simply, in the most pertinent manner. But from the moment she is in the world of speech, whatever the power of her educational formation, her desire lies beyond. Her desire is not simply on the side of Horace whom – here we are in no doubt – she will in the future subject to the very same fate so feared by Arnolphe. It's just that, by virtue of the fact that she is in the domain of speech, her desire lies beyond, she is charmed by words, she is charmed by wit and – insofar as something lies beyond this metonymic actuality that Arnolphe is attempting to impose on her – she slips away. Even as she always says the truth to Arnolphe, she is still deceiving him, because everything that she does is tantamount to deceiving him.

Horace is aware of this himself when he recounts how she threw his little stone out of the window, telling him, 'Off you go, I do not want to hear any more of your words, and that is my response', which sounded like it meant, 'Here is the stone that I am throwing to you', but the stone was also the vehicle for a little letter. Horace emphasizes it very well – for a girl that Arnolphe wanted to keep in extreme ignorance, there is an ambiguity here that is not at all badly done, and that is the start of these double meanings and an entire game that augurs well for the future.

That is the point at which I wanted to leave you today. By its very nature, the id lies beyond desire's capture in language. The relationship to the Other is essential inasmuch as the path of desire necessarily passes through it, but not insofar as the Other is the unique object, but rather insofar as the Other is the correspondent of language and subjects it to its entire dialectic.

18 December 1957

THE LOGIC OF
CASTRATION

VIII

FORECLOSURE OF THE NAME-OF-THE-FATHER

Mrs Pankow expounds the double bind*
Typography of the unconscious
The Other in the Other
Psychosis between code and message
Symbolic triangle and imaginary triangle

I get the impression that I pushed you a bit too hard last trimester – I got some feedback about it. I hadn't noticed, otherwise I wouldn't have done it. I was under the impression that I was repeating myself and getting nowhere. This still didn't prevent me from perhaps leaving behind some of the things I wanted to get you to understand, and it's worth retracing our steps a little and, let's say, looking back over how I have been approaching things this year.

1

What I am trying to show you concerning jokes, for which I have extracted a schema whose usefulness may not be immediately clear to you, is how things fit together and how they mesh with the earlier schema. Ultimately, you have to be aware of something constant in what I teach you – although, certainly, you shouldn't just view this constant as a little flag on the horizon by which you can get your bearings, but you should understand where it is taking you and where the detours are. What is constant is my belief that fundamental to understanding what is in Freud is that one recognize the importance of language and speech. I was the first to say this, but the closer we get to our object, the more aware we become of the importance of signifiers in the economy of desire – let's say, in the formation and information of signifieds.

You could appreciate this when listening to the interesting things Mrs Pankow was saying at our scientific meeting last night. It so happens that in America people are concerned with the same thing as I am explaining to you here. They are trying to introduce the fact of communication and what they call the message into the economic determination of psychical disturbances. You were able to hear Mrs Pankow talking about someone who certainly wasn't born yesterday, namely Mr Bateson, anthropologist and ethnographer, who has contributed something that makes us think a little bit beyond the end of our noses concerning therapeutic action.

Bateson tries to locate and formulate the basis of the genesis of psychotic disturbances in something that is established at the level of the mother–child relationship and is not simply an elementary effect of frustration, tension, retention, relaxation and satisfaction, as if interhuman relationships take place at the ends of a piece of elastic. He introduces the notion of communication from the outset, insofar as it is not merely centred on contact, a relationship or an entourage, but on a meaning. He places it at the beginning of what was originally conflicting and harmful in the child's relationship to its mother. What he designates as being the essentially conflicting element in this relationship is the fact that communication is presented in the form of a double bind.

As Mrs Pankow put it so well last night, in the message in which the child has deciphered the behaviour of its mother there are two elements. They are not defined in relation to one another, in the sense in which one would be presented as the subject's defence in relation to what the other means, which is the common notion that you have of a defence mechanism when you analyse. You consider that the intention behind what the subject says is to misrecognize some signification somewhere there inside him, and that what he says to himself – and says to you – is something else [*la couleur à côté*]. That is not what it is about. It's about something that concerns the Other, which the subject receives in such a way that, if he answers one way, he knows, by virtue of this alone, that he's going to find himself cornered with respect to the other. The example that Mrs Pankow gives is this – if I respond to my mother's declaration of love, I provoke her withdrawal, and if I don't listen, that is to say, if I don't respond to her, I lose her.

We are thereby introduced to a true dialectic of double meaning, where the latter already involves a third party. There are not two meanings one behind the other, with a second meaning, located beyond the first and the more authentic of the two. There are two simultaneous messages in the one single meaningful utterance, as it were, which creates a position in the subject whereby he finds

himself at an impasse. This proves that even in America they are   145
making huge progress.

Am I saying this is adequate? Mrs Pankow nicely highlighted
what is there at the ground level or, one might say, at the empirical
level, in this attempt – though it's not a matter of empiricism, of
course. If there were not very important work on game theory in
America alongside this, Mr Bateson would not have dreamed of
introducing into the analysis what is, after all, a reconstruction
of what is thought to have occurred early on, or of determining a
subject position that is deeply rent or falsified with respect to what
in the message is constitutive for him. I say 'constitutive for him'
because if his conception did not imply that the message is constitutive for the subject, it is difficult to see how one could attribute such
major effects to the original double bind.*

The question that arises concerning the psychoses is what the
nature of this process of communication is, precisely, when it fails
to be constitutive for the subject. We have to look for another point
of reference. Up to this point, when you read Mr Bateson, you see
that while everything is, to put it simply, centred on the double
message, it is centred on the double message as double meaning.
This is precisely where the system fails, and it fails precisely because
this conception neglects the signifier's constitutive role in meaning.

Last night I jotted something down in passing – it has now gone
missing – where I recorded a remark by Mrs Pankow about psychosis, which amounted more or less to this. There is no speech, she
said, that grounds the act of speech. In speech itself, there has to be
speech that grounds speech as an act in the subject. This is in line
with what I am coming to now.

By stressing the fact that somewhere in speech there has to be
something that grounds speech as true, Mrs Pankow was exhibiting
a demand for the stabilization of the entire system. To this end, she
had recourse to the perspective of 'personality', which at the very
least has the merit of demonstrating her sense of the inadequacy of a
system that leaves us in a state of uncertainty and fails to deliver an
adequate deduction or construction.

I absolutely do not think that it can be formulated this way.
I believe that this personalist reference is only psychologically
grounded in the sense that we cannot fail to feel and sense that
meanings create the impasse that supposedly triggers this profound
disturbance in the schizophrenic subject. But, also, we cannot fail to
feel and sense that something must be the cause of this deficit, and
that this something is not simply the registration of the experience of   146
impasses in meaning, but rather the lack of something that founds
meaning itself, and that what is lacking is a signifier – and something

more, which is precisely what I am going to explore today. It is not something that presents itself simply as the personality, as what grounds speech as an act, as Mrs Pankow was saying last night, but something that presents itself as giving the law its authority.

By 'law', here, I mean that which is properly articulated at the level of the signifier, namely the text of the law.

Saying that there has to be a person there in order to sustain the authenticity of speech is not the same as saying that there is something that authorizes the text of the law. Effectively, it is sufficient that what authorizes the text of the law is at the level of signifiers. This is what I call the Name-of-the-Father, namely the symbolic father. It's a term that subsists at the level of signifiers and that, in the Other as the seat of the law, represents the Other. This is the signifier that gives the law its support, that promulgates the law. It is the Other in the Other.

This is just what the myth of the Oedipus complex, necessary for Freud's thought, expresses. Look at it closely. If he is obliged to procure the origin of the law in this mythical form, if there is anything that makes it the case that the law is founded on the father, it is necessary for the father to be murdered. The two things are closely linked – the father, insofar as he promulgates the law, is the dead father, which is to say the symbol of the father. The dead father is the Name-of-the-Father, who is there, constructed over the content.

This is quite essential. I will remind you why.

What has been the nub of everything that I have taught you about psychosis these last two years? It's what I have called *Verwerfung*. I have tried to make you sense that it is different from *Verdrängung*, that is, different from the fact that the signifying chain continues to unfold and continues to be organized in the Other, whether you know it or not. This is essentially Freud's discovery.

Verwerfung, as I have said, is not simply what is inaccessible to you, that is, what exists in the Other as repressed and as signifiers. That is *Verdrängung*, and it is the signifying chain. The proof of this is that it continues to act, even though you do not attach even the slightest signification to it yourself, and determines even the slightest signification without your knowing it to be the signifying chain.

I have also told you that there are other things which, on occasion, are *verworfen*. There may be a missing signifier or a missing letter in the chain of signifiers, one that is always missing in the typography. The space of the signifier, the space of the unconscious, is effectively a typographical space, which we must try to define as being constituted along lines and little squares, and as corresponding to topological laws. There may be something lacking in a chain of signifiers. You have to understand the importance of the lack

147

of the particular signifier I have just mentioned, the Name-of-the-Father, that grounds, as such, the fact that the law exists, that is, its articulation in a certain order of signifiers – the Oedipus complex, the Oedipal law or the law of prohibition of the mother. It is the signifier that signifies that, within these signifiers, the signifier exists.

That is the Name-of-the-Father and, as you see, it is an essential signifier in the Other, and on which I have tried to centre what takes place in psychosis – namely, that the subject must compensate for the lack of the signifier, the Name-of-the-Father. Everything that I have called the chain reaction or disarray produced in psychosis is organized around that point.

2

What should I do now? Should I immediately go back over what I have said concerning President Schreber? Or should I first show you, more precisely, in detail, how to formulate what I have just been showing you at the level of this year's schema?

To my great surprise, not everybody finds this schema interesting – though some do. It has been constructed, don't forget, so as to represent what occurs at a level that deserves to be called a technique, which is the technique of witticisms. This is something quite unusual, since a *Witz* can obviously be constructed by a subject in the most unintentional way in the world. As I have shown you, a witticism is sometimes only the converse of a slip, and experience shows that many witticisms are born in this way – one realizes after the fact that one has been witty, but it happened all by itself. In some cases, this could be taken for exactly the contrary, a sign of naivety, and last time I alluded to naive witticisms.

It was around witticisms, with the satisfaction that results from them and is particular to them, that I tried to organize this schema for you last trimester. I was trying to work out how to think about the source of the special satisfaction they give. This brings us back to nothing less than the dialectic of demand on the basis of the ego.*

148

Recall the schema for what I managed to refer to as the primordial ideal symbolic moment, one that is completely non-existent.

The moment at which a demand is satisfied is represented by the simultaneous arrival at the Other of the intention, as it appears in the message, and the message as such. The signifiers – this is what is at stake, since this chain is a chain of signifiers – arrive at the Other. The perfect identity, simultaneity, or exact superimposition between the manifestation of the intention, insofar as it is the ego's* intention, and the fact that the signifiers are ratified, as such, in the Other is at the heart of the very possibility of the satisfaction of speech. If this moment, which I am calling the ideal primordial moment, exists, it must be constituted by the simultaneity, the precise coextensivity, of desire, insofar as it manifests itself, and the signifiers, insofar as they carry and convey it. If this moment exists, then, what follows, that is, what succeeds the message in its passage into the Other, is thus realized both in the Other and in the subject and corresponds to what is necessary for there to be satisfaction. This is, very precisely, the required starting point for understanding that this never happens.

That is, the nature and the effect of signifiers are such that what happens here at M [see graph, p. 85] appears as the signified, that is, as something that is the result of the transformation or refraction of desire when it passes through signifiers. This is why these two lines cross over one another – so as to get you to sense the fact that desire is expressed through, and passes through, signifiers.

Desire crosses the signifying line, and what does it encounter at the level at which it crosses the signifier line? It encounters the Other. We shall see shortly, since we will have to come back to it, what the Other is on the schema. I am not saying it encounters the Other as a person. It encounters it as the treasure trove of signifiers, as the locus of the code. This is where the refraction of desire by the signifier occurs. Desire, then, as the signified, is different when it arrives from what it was at the start, and there you have – I won't say why the moon is not made of blue cheese – but why your desire is always cuckolded. Or, rather, it's you who are cuckolded. You yourself are betrayed in that your desire has slept with signifiers. I do not know how I could articulate these things better to get you to understand them. The entire meaning of the schema is to get you to visualize the idea that the mere passage of desire – as the expression, the high point of the radical ego* – through the chain of signifiers introduces an essential change in the dialectic of desire.

149　　It is quite clear that, concerning the satisfaction of desire, everything depends on what passes through point A, originally defined as the locus of the code, which, in itself, *ab origine*, merely by virtue of its signifier structure, introduces an essential modification to a desire at the level at which it passes through signifiers. Here, everything else is implied, since not only is the code here, there is more besides. I locate myself here at the most radical level – but, of course, there is the law, there are prohibitions, there is the superego and so on. But in order to understand how these various levels are constructed, we have to understand that, even at the most radical level, as soon as you speak to someone, there is an Other, another Other in him, as subject of the code, and that we already find ourselves subject to the dialectic of the cuckoldification of desire. Therefore, everything depends, as it turns out, on what happens at this point of crossover, A, at this level of crossing.

The possibility of satisfying any human desire happens to depend on how it fits into the signifying system, insofar as it is formulated in the subject's speech, and, as M. de la Palice would have said, on the system of signifiers insofar as it resides in the code – that is, at the level of the Other as locus and seat of the code. A child would be convinced on hearing this, and I am not claiming that what I have just explained to you moves us forward one little bit. But it still needs to be spelt out.

This is where we are going to explore the connection I want to make between this schema and what I was telling you before about the essentials of the question of the Name-of-the-Father. You'll see it being prepared and sketched out, not being engendered, and above all not engendering itself, for it involves making a leap to get there. Not everything happens in continuity, it being a characteristic of signifiers to be discontinuous.

What does the technique of jokes bring to our experience? This is what I have been trying to get you to appreciate. While a joke gives no particular immediate satisfaction, it consists in the fact that something happens in the Other that symbolizes what could be called the necessary condition of all satisfaction – namely, that you are understood beyond what you say. In no case, effectively, can what you say really make you understood.

Witticisms unfold in the dimension of metaphor, that is, beyond signifiers, insofar as when you try to signify something with a signifier, you will always signify something else, whatever you do. It is a signifier that gives the appearance of stumbling that satisfies you, simply by virtue of the fact that, by this sign, the Other is acknowledging this dimension of the beyond where what is at issue has to be signified and which you cannot signify as such. This is the dimension   150
that witticisms reveal to us.

This schema is thus grounded in our experience. I realized I had to construct it to explain what goes on in witticisms. What, in witticisms, replaces the failure of desire to be communicated via signifiers, to the point of giving us a kind of happiness, comes about in this way – the Other confirms that a message has stumbled or failed and, in this very stumbling, recognizes the dimension that lies beyond and where true desire is located, that is, what, because of signifiers, never gets to be signified.

You see that the dimension of the Other is a little bit more extensive here. Effectively, here it is not just the seat of the code any more. It intervenes as a subject, ratifies a message in the code and renders it more complicated. That is, it is already at the level of who it is that constitutes the law as such, since he is capable of adding this trait or message to it as supplementary – that is, as itself designating something beyond the message.

This is why, when the theme came to be formations of the unconscious, I began the year by speaking about witticisms. Let's now try to look at this Other a little more closely – and in a less unusual situation than that of witticisms – insofar as in this dimension we are seeking to discover the necessity for the signifier that founds signifiers, the signifier that institutes the legitimacy of the code or the law. Let's return, then, to our dialectic of desire.

When we address the other, we don't always express ourselves by means of witticisms. We'd be all the happier if we could in a way. This is what I try to do in the brief time I have for the discourse I address to you. I'm not always successful. Whether it is your fault or mine is completely indiscernible from this point of view. But, in the end, at the banal level of what happens when I address the other, there is a word that makes it possible for us to found him in the most elementary way, and which is absolutely marvellous in French if one thinks about all the ambiguities and puns it lends itself to – which I would be embarrassed to make use of here except in the most discreet way possible. As soon as I say this word, what I am evoking will immediately come back to you. It is the word 'you' ['*tu*'].

This 'you' is quite essential to what on several occasions I have called full speech, speech as foundational in the subject's history, the 'you' of 'you are my master' or 'you are my woman'. This 'you' is the signifier of the appeal to the Other, and I remind those of you who were so kind as to follow my entire chain of Seminars on psychosis about the use I put it to, the demonstration that I tried to bring alive for you around the distance between '*Tu es celui qui me suivras*', 'You are the one who shall follow me' and '*Tu est celui qui me suivra*', 'You are the one who will follow me'. What I was already exploring for you at that time and was trying to engage you in is precisely what I am going to allude to now, which I have already given a name to.

In these two sentences, with their differences, there is an appeal. It is more present in one than in the other, and even completely present in one and not at all in the other. In the 'You are the one who shall follow me', there is something that is not in the 'You are the one who will follow me', and it is what is called invocation. If I say, 'You are the one who shall follow me', I invoke you, I pick you out as being the one who will follow me, I solicit in you the 'Yes' that says, 'I am yours, I devote myself to you, I am the one who will follow you.' But if I say, 'You are the one who will follow me', I do nothing

151

of the kind, I announce, I state, I objectify, and even, on occasion, I reject. It can mean, 'You are the one who will always follow me, and I'm sick of it.' In the most ordinary and most consequential way that this sentence is pronounced, it is a refusal. Of course, the invocation requires quite another dimension, namely that I make my desire depend upon your being, in the sense that I call upon you to follow the pathway of this desire, whatever it happens to be, unconditionally.

This is the process of invocation. The word means I make an appeal to the voice – that is, to what supports speech. Not to speech, but to the subject insofar as he carries it, and that is why I am there at the level that earlier I called the personalist level. Indeed, this is why the personalists pile it on with their 'thou', 'thou, 'thou', 'thou', all day long, with their 'thou' and their 'thine'. Mr Martin Buber, for example, whose name Mrs Pankow mentioned in passing, is an eminent name in this register.

There is, of course, an essential phenomenological level there, and we cannot do without it. Nor must we give in to its mirage and prostrate ourselves. The personalist attitude – this is the danger that we encounter at this level – lends itself fairly freely to mystical prostration. And why not? We don't refuse any attitude to anyone, we simply request the right to understand these attitudes, and this moreover is not forbidden from the personalist side, though it is forbidden from the scientistic side – if you begin to attach authenticity to the mystical position, you yourself are thought to be succumbing to some ridiculous indulgence.

Every subjective structure, of whatever kind, to the extent that we can follow what it articulates, is strictly speaking equivalent to every other from the point of view of subjective analysis. Only stupid idiots like Mr Blondel, the psychiatrist, can object, in the name of some supposedly ineffable morbid consciousness of the lived experience of another, to what seems ineffable but is articulated. This should be rejected out of hand, because there is a confusion here arising from the fact that one thinks that what is not articulated lies in the beyond, whereas it is nothing of the sort – that which lies beyond can be articulated. In other words, we don't need to speak of the ineffable concerning the subject, whether delusional or mystical. At the level of subjective structure, we are in the presence of something that cannot be presented in any other way than the way it is presented, and which, as such, as a consequence, is presented with full value at its own level of credibility.

If there is something ineffable, whether in the delusional or mystical order, by definition he doesn't say it, because it's ineffable. So we are not to judge what he articulates, namely his speech, on the basis of what he cannot say. If it can be supposed that the ineffable exists, and we are very happy to suppose that it does, we never turn away from grasping whatever is demonstrated as structure in speech, of whatever kind, under the pretext that the ineffable exists. It is possible we will get lost in it, and then we abandon it. But if we don't get lost in it, the order that this speech demonstrates and unveils is to be taken for what it is. In general, we notice that it is infinitely richer to take it as it is and try to articulate the order that it establishes, provided we have the right reference points – and that is what we are trying to do here. If we were to set out with the idea that speech was essentially made for representing the signified, we would go under immediately, because this would be to fall back upon previous oppositions, namely that we have no knowledge of the signified.

The 'you' in question is the 'you' we invoke. For sure, when we invoke it, this subjective personal impenetrability is involved, but this is not the level at which we are trying to reach it. What is involved in an invocation? The word 'invocation' has a historical usage. It's what was performed in a particular ceremony that the ancients, who had more wisdom than us on certain points, carried out before combat. This ceremony consisted of doing what was necessary – they probably knew what this was – to get the gods of the others on their side. This is exactly what the word 'invocation' means, and it's where the essential relationship that I am now leading you to resides – at this second stage, that of the appeal, the necessary appeal for desire and demand to be satisfied.

153 It is not enough just to say to the Other, 'you', 'you', 'you', and obtain his assistance in a heartbeat. One needs to give him the very voice we want him to have and evoke this voice, which is present in witticisms as their true dimension. A witticism is a provocation, one that does not achieve any great feat, one that does not achieve any great miracle of invocation. An invocation is located at the level of speech insofar as it is articulated vocally in conformity with one's desire.

At this level we find the fact that all satisfaction of demand, to the extent that it depends on the Other, will hinge on what happens here, in this to-and-fro between message and code, code and message, which enables the Other to authenticate my message in the code. We come back to the earlier point – that is, to what constitutes the essence of our interest that together we are bringing to witticisms this year.

I would simply have you remark, in passing, that if you had had this schema, that is to say, that if I had been able, not to give it to you, but to forge it for you at the time of my Seminar on the psychoses, if together we had come to the same witticisms at the same time,

I would have been able to use this to picture what is essentially happening in President Schreber, insofar as he fell prey to, and became
a subject absolutely dependent upon, his voices.

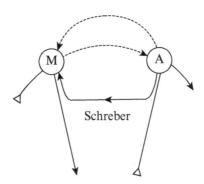

Schreber

Pay close attention to this schema behind me and simply suppose
that everything in the Other that might correspond, in whatever
way possible, to the level that I am calling the Name-of-the-Father,
which incarnates, specifies and particularizes what I have just been
explaining to you – that is to say, which represents the Other as what
gives the law in the Other its significance – were *verworfen*. Well
then, if you imagine the *Verwerfung* of the Name-of-the-Father, that
is, that the signifier is absent, you will see that the two links in dotted
lines here – namely the to-and-fro between message and code and
code and message – are thereby destroyed and rendered impossible.
This makes it possible to enter on this schema the two fundamental
types of voice phenomena experienced by President Schreber as a
substitute for this defect or lack. Let me add that when this hollow
or void appears, it's because the Name-of-the-Father has been
evoked at least once – because what has been appealed to at the level
of the 'you' at a given moment is precisely the Name-of-the-Father,
insofar as it is capable of endorsing the message and insofar as, by
virtue of this fact, it is the guarantor of the fact that the law as such
presents itself as autonomous. That's where the tipping point is, the
turning point that tips the subject into psychosis – and I am leaving
to one side for the moment in what way, at what moment, and why.

That year I began my discussion of psychosis with a sentence I
had extracted from one of my patient interviews. People grasped
very well the moment at which the sentence muttered by the patient,
'I have just come from the butcher's', tipped over onto the other
side. It was when the word 'sow' appeared in apposition. No longer
able to be assumed or integrated by the subject, it tipped over,
through its own movement, through its own inertia as a signifier,

154

from being one of her lines in her own script, into the Other. This was elementary phenomenology, pure and simple. In Schreber what was the result of the exclusion of the links between the message and the Other? The result presented itself in the form of the two broad categories of the voice and hallucinations.

First, there are the utterances at the level of the Other, involving the signifiers of what is presented as the *Grundsprache*, the fundamental language. They are the original elements of the code articulable in relation to one another, for this fundamental language is so well organized that it literally covers the world with its network of signifiers. Nothing else in it is sure or certain, except that total, essential signification is involved. Each of these words has its own weight, emphasis and mass as a signifier. The subject articulates them to one another. Whenever they are isolated, the properly enigmatic dimension of signification, insofar as the latter is infinitely less apparent than the certitude it conveys, is altogether striking. In other words, here the Other only transmits beyond the code, as it were, without there being any possibility of integrating into it what might come from the place in which the subject articulates his message.

From another perspective, if you put the little arrows back in here, messages come. They are not in any way authenticated by the Other's return, as the support of the code, back to the message, nor are they integrated into the code with any intention of any kind. They come from the Other, as does every message, since there is nowhere for a message to come from except from the Other, given that it is made from a language that is the language of the Other – even when it comes from one of us as a reflection of the other. These messages, then, issue from the Other, they leave this reference point behind and become articulated in this sort of proposal, 'And now I want to give you . . .', 'Specifically I want this for myself . . .', 'And now, that must however . . .'.

155

What's missing? The principal thought, the one expressed at the level of the fundamental language. The voices themselves, which know the entire theory, also say, 'Reflection is missing'. This means, in effect, that messages of the other category of messages come from the Other. They are a type of message that cannot be ratified as such. The message appears here, in that pure and broken dimension of signifiers, as something whose signification is only contained beyond oneself, as something that, by virtue of not being able to contribute to authentification by the 'you', appears as having no other aim than to present as lacking the position of the 'you', where signification is authenticated. Of course, the subject is driven to complete the signification himself, and therefore gives the sentence its complements. 'I do not now wish', say the voices, but elsewhere he says to himself that he, Schreber, 'cannot acknowledge that he is a . . .'. The message remains broken in that it is unable to go via the path of the 'you' and can only arrive at point gamma as an interrupted message.

I think I have indicated well enough that in order for the dimension of the Other to be fully able to exercise its function as Other, as the locus of the depot or treasure trove of signifiers, it must include the following, which is that it also contain the signifier of the Other as Other. The Other also has, beyond itself, this Other capable of giving the law its foundation. This is a dimension which, of course, is also of the order of signifiers, and is embodied in people who underpin this authority. The fact that on occasion these people are absent, that for example the father is deficient in the sense that he is too stupid, is not what's essential. What is essential is that, in one way or another, the subject has acquired the dimension of the Name-of-the-Father.

Of course what actually happens, and you can glean this from biographies, is that the father is often there in the kitchen doing the dishes and wearing his wife's apron. This is not at all sufficient to make a schizophrenic.

3

156

I am now going to write up on the blackboard the little schema with which I will introduce what I will talk about next time and which will make it possible for us to find a way to draw the distinction, which might seem a bit scholastic to you, between the Name-of-the-Father and the real father – the Name-of-the-Father insofar as it may possibly be missing and the father who doesn't seem to need to be there for him not to be lacking. I will therefore introduce what will be the theme of my Seminar next time, namely what, as of today, I will call the paternal metaphor.

A name is never a signifier just like any other. To be sure, it is important to have one, but that does not mean for all that that one has access to it, any more than one has access to the satisfaction I was talking to you about earlier – the satisfaction of desire, cuckolded in principle. This is why, in the famous speech act Mrs Pankow was talking about yesterday, the invocation I was talking about earlier is going to be actualized concretely, psychologically in a dimension that we call metaphorical.

In other words, you have to have the Name-of-the-Father – but you also have to know how to use it. It's on this that the destiny and outcome of the entire affair may largely depend.

There are the real words that flow around the subject, notably in his childhood, but the essence of the paternal metaphor, which I announce to you today and which we will talk about at greater length next time, consists of the following triangle:

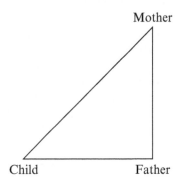

157   And we also have this schema:

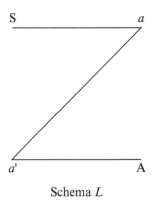

Schema *L*

Everything that happens at S, the subject, depends on what signifiers are placed at A. If A truly is the locus of signifiers, it must itself carry some reflection of the essential signifier that I represent here by this zigzag, and which elsewhere, in my article, 'The Purloined Letter', I called schema L.

Three of these four cardinal points are given by the three subject terms of the Oedipus complex as signifiers, which we encounter at each of the vertices of the triangle. I will return to this next time, but I ask you for the moment to grant me what I am telling you – a story to whet your appetite.

The fourth term is the S. He – not only do I grant you this but this is where one starts – is in effect ineffably stupid, for he does not have his own signifier. He lies outside the three vertices of the Oedipal triangle, and he is dependent on what takes place in this game. He is the dummy in the game. It's even because the game is structured in this way – I mean that it is conducted not only as a particular game, but as a game that is correctly instituted – that the subject will find himself dependent upon the three poles called ego-ideal, superego and reality.

But to understand the transformation of the first triad into the second, you have to see that, dummy that he is, the subject – and there is a subject – gets little reward for his efforts in this game. From the unconstituted point where he is, it will be necessary for him to contribute to it – if not with his dollars, which perhaps he doesn't have as yet, then at least with his hide, that is to say with his images, his imaginary structure and all that follows. This is how the fourth term, the S, is going to be represented in something imaginary that is opposed to the signifier of the Oedipus complex and which, if it is to work, has to be ternary.

Of course, there is an entire stock, the entire baggage of images.   158
To see this, open the books by Mr Jung and his school, and you'll see that there is no end to such images – they sprout and they vegetate everywhere. There is the serpent, the dragon, tongues, the flaming eye, the green plant, the pot of flowers, the concierge. They are all fundamental images, incontestably stuffed with signification. It is just that we can do strictly nothing with them, and if you move about at this level, you will only succeed in losing yourself, along with your little lamp, in the vegetating forest of primitive archetypes.

As to what interests us, namely the intersubjective dialectic, there are three images selected – I am articulating my thought a little too strongly here – to take on the role of guides. This is not difficult to understand, since something is in some way already ready, not only for being the homologue of the base of the triangle mother–father–child, but for merging with it – it is the relationship between

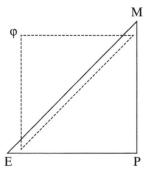

the body, fragmented and by the same token enveloped by a good number of these images we have been talking about, and the unifying function of the total image of the body. In other words, the ego's relationship with the specular image already gives us the base of the imaginary triangle, here indicated by the dotted line.

The other point [φ] is where we will see the effect of the paternal metaphor.

I gave you this other point in my Seminar last year on the object relation, but now you will see what place it has in formations of the unconscious. I think that you will have recognized this point just in the fact of seeing it here in the third position with the mother and the child. We see it here in another relation, which I did not at all hide from you last year, since we ended on the relation between the Name-of-the-Father and what caused the fantasy of the little horse to emerge in our little Hans. This third point – I will name it, finally, I think you already have it on the tip of your tongue – is nothing other than the phallus. And this is why the phallus occupies such a central place as an object in the Freudian economy.

This alone is enough to show us where *La psychanalyse d'aujourd'hui* is in error, which is moving further and further away from it. It eludes the fundamental function of the phallus, with which the subject imaginarily identifies himself, reducing it to the notion of part object. This brings us back to comedy.

I will leave you there for today, having shown you the ways in which the complex discourse, in which I am trying to bring together everything I have been presenting to you, comes together and holds together.

8 January 1958

IX

THE PATERNAL METAPHOR

Superego, reality, ego-ideal
Ways the father can fail
The delicate question of the inverted Oedipus complex
The phallus as a signified
The dimensions of something Other

I made an exception and announced the title of what I am going to talk about today, namely the paternal metaphor.

Not long ago, someone, slightly worried, I imagine, about the direction in which I was taking things, asked me, 'What do you intend to speak about for the rest of the year?' And I replied, 'I intend to address questions of structure.' That way, I didn't compromise myself. Nevertheless, I actually do intend to talk to you about questions of structure this year concerning formations of the unconscious. To put it simply, it's a matter of putting in place things that you talk about every day and by which you get confused every day in a way that in the end you don't even worry about any more.

The paternal metaphor, then, is about the father's function, as one might say in terms of interhuman relations. You encounter complications every day in the way in which you might have to make use of it as a concept that has taken on a certain familiar appearance since you started talking about it. What you need to know is precisely whether you are talking about it in the form of a coherent discourse.

The father's function has a place, a fairly large place, in the history of analysis. It lies at the heart of the question of the Oedipus complex. And that's where you see it presented. Freud introduced it right at the start, as the Oedipus complex appears as early as *The Interpretation of Dreams*. What the unconscious reveals in the beginning is first and foremost the Oedipus complex. The importance of the revelation of the unconscious is what infantile amnesia relates to. What it relates to is the existence of the child's desires for the mother and the fact that these desires are repressed. And not only are they suppressed, but it has been forgotten that these desires are primordial. And not only are they primordial, but they are always there. That is where analysis started, and that is the basis on which a number of clinical questions arise.

I have tried to organize the questions that have been raised in the history of analysis in relation to the Oedipus complex in a number of directions.

1

I distinguish three historical poles, which I will briefly situate for you.

In the first, I will inscribe a question of historical importance. It's the question whether the Oedipus complex, initially promoted as fundamental in neurosis but which Freud's work turns into something universal, was to be encountered not only in neurotics but also in the normal person. And the question arose for a good reason, since the Oedipus complex has an essentially normalizing function. On the one hand, then, one could consider that it's an accident of the Oedipus complex that produces neurosis, but also raise the question whether there exist neuroses without an Oedipus complex.

A number of observations seem to indicate, effectively, that the Oedipal drama doesn't always play the essential role but, for instance, that the child's exclusive relationship to its mother does. Experience thus obliged us to admit that there could be subjects presenting with a neurosis in which one did not at all find an Oedipus complex. I remind you that 'Névrose sans complexe d'Oedipe?' ['Neurosis without Oedipus Complex?'] is precisely the title of an article by Charles Odier.

The notion of a neurosis without an Oedipus complex correlates with the totality of questions raised about what has been called the maternal superego. At the time at which the question of neurosis without an Oedipus complex was raised, Freud had already formulated that the superego was of paternal origin. And so the question arose – is the superego really uniquely of paternal origin? Is there not, in neurosis, behind the paternal superego, a much more demanding, more oppressive, more devastating and more insistent maternal superego?

I do not want to go on at length, for we have a long road to travel. That, then, is the first reference point, where the exceptional cases and the relationship between the paternal superego and the maternal superego are grouped together.

Now for the second pole.

Independently of whether the Oedipus complex is present or lacking for a subject, the question has been raised whether an entire field of pathology that falls under our jurisdiction and presents itself to our jurisdiction should not be referred to what we can call the pre-Oedipal field.

There is the Oedipus complex. This Oedipus complex is thought   163
of as representing a phase, and while maturity is present at a certain moment in the subject's evolution, the Oedipus complex is always there. But what Freud had himself put forward in the early stages of his work, five years after *The Interpretation of Dreams*, in *Three Essays on the Theory of Sexuality*, was likely to make it understood that what happens prior to the Oedipus complex also has its importance.

This assumes importance in Freud, to be sure, but via the Oedipus complex. It's just that at no point at that time was the notion of retroaction highlighted, the *Nachträglichkeit* of the Oedipus complex, to which as you know I am always insistently drawing your attention. This notion seemed to have escaped thought. People have only thought about the demands of the temporal past.

Certain parts of our field of experience refer especially to this field of pre-Oedipal stages in the subject's development – namely, perversion on the one hand, and psychosis on the other.

For some people, perversion was the primary, untouched state. We are no longer at that point, thank goodness. While in the early days this was a legitimate conception, at least in the name of an approximation to the question, it's certainly less so in our day. Perversion was essentially thought to be a pathology whose aetiology supposedly referred specifically to the pre-Oedipal field, a pathology conditioned by an abnormal fixation. It is, moreover, for this reason that perversion was only ever thought to be an inverted neurosis or, more precisely, a neurosis that hadn't been inverted, with the neurosis remaining patent. What in neurosis had been inverted was openly apparent in perversion. Because perversion had not been repressed, since it had not passed through the Oedipus complex, the unconscious was there, out in the open. It's a conception that nobody entertains any longer, which, however, doesn't mean that we have advanced any further.

I make the point, then, that questions of perversion and psychosis are grouped around the question of the pre-Oedipal field.

Everything that is involved here can now be clarified for us in a number of ways. Whether we are dealing with perversion or psychosis, it's always a matter of the imaginary function. Even without being particularly familiar with the use we make of the image here,

each and every one of you is able to appreciate the special importance it has in these two registers – from quite different angles, of
course. An endophasic invasion comprised of words heard doesn't
have the troublesome, parasitic character of an image in a perversion, but, in both cases, it's a matter of pathological manifestations
in which the field of reality is profoundly disturbed by images.

164

The history of psychoanalysis shows us that our experience,
the concern for coherence and the manner in which theory is constructed and makes sense have led to some occasionally profound
disturbances to the field of reality by the invasion of the imaginary being attributed to the pre-Oedipal field. Moreover, the term
'imaginary' seems to render better service than the term 'fantasy',
which would be unsuitable for talking about the psychoses and the
perversions. An entire direction in analysis committed itself to the
exploration of the pre-Oedipal field, even to the point that one could
say that this is the direction in which all essential progress since
Freud has been made.

In this respect I emphasize the paradox, essential to today's
theme, of the testimony that Mrs Melanie Klein's work constitutes.

In any work, as with anything that is put into words, there are two
levels. On the one hand, there is what she says, what she formulates
in a discourse and what she wants to say, insofar as, if we separate
the wanting and the saying, her intention is there in the meaning.
And then, we would not be analysts in the sense in which I am trying
to get you to hear things here, if we did not know that she sometimes says a little bit more beyond that. This is even habitually what
our approach consists in – grasp what one is saying beyond what
one means to say. Mrs Melanie Klein's work says things that are
full of importance, but sometimes through nothing other than the
internal contradictions of her texts, which may be subject to certain
criticisms – which have been made. Then, there is also what she says
without meaning to say it, and one of the most striking things in this
respect is the following.

This woman has contributed views that are so profound and
enlightening, not only about pre-Oedipal times, but about the
children that she examines and analyses at a stage that, in a first
approximation of the theory, is presumed to be pre-Oedipal. This
analyst, who forcibly explores, in children, in terms it seems that are
sometimes preverbal, almost at the emergence of speech – well then,
the further back she goes into the supposedly pre-Oedipal time of
history, the more she sees there, the more she always, all the time,
permanently, sees the Oedipal question there.

Read her article on the Oedipus complex, specifically. She
describes an extremely precocious stage of development, the

so-called stage of the formation of bad objects, which is prior to the so-called paranoid-depressive phase and is bound up with the appearance of the mother's body in its totality. Listening to her, the predominant role in the evolution of the child's initial object relations is played by the insides of the mother's body as the centre of the child's entire attention. Now, you will be surprised to observe that, basing herself on drawings, words and an entire reconstruction of the psychology of children at this stage, Mrs Melanie Klein testifies to us that amongst the bad objects present in the mother's body – including all the rivals, the bodies of brothers and sisters, past, present and future – there is, quite precisely, the father represented in the form of his penis.

165

This is indeed a discovery that merits our attention, since it's situated at the initial stages of imaginary relationships, to which the properly schizophrenic functions, and psychotic functions in general, can be attached. This contradiction is a highly valuable one, when Mrs Melanie Klein's intention was to go off and explore pre-Oedipal states. The further back she goes on the imaginary plane, the further back she discovers – very difficult to explain if we cling to a purely historical notion of the Oedipus complex – the appearance of the paternal third term, and this is so from the child's earliest imaginary phases. This is why I say that her work says more than she means to say.

Here, then, we have already defined two poles in the evolution of interest around the Oedipus complex – first, questions of the superego and neuroses without the Oedipus complex and, second, questions concerning disturbances that are produced in the field of reality.

The third pole, equally deserving of comment – the Oedipus complex's relationship with genitalization, as one says. This is not the same thing.

On the one hand – a point that so many explorations and discussions in history have moved into the background, but which always remains implicit in everything clinical – the Oedipus complex has a normative function, not simply in the subject's moral structure, nor in his relations with reality, but concerning the assumption of his sex, which, as you know, still retains a certain ambiguity in analysis. Moreover, the properly genital function is the object of a maturation that follows an initial sexual spurt in the order of the organic, for which an anatomical support has been sought in the double growth of the testicles and the creation of spermatozoa. The relationship between this organic growth and the existence of the Oedipus complex in the human species has remained a phylogenetic question over which a lot of obscurity hovers, to the point where nobody takes the risk of writing articles on the subject any more. But, actually, this question has been no less present in the history of analysis.

The question of genitalization is therefore twofold. There is, on the one hand, growth which carries an evolution or a maturation. There is, on the other hand, in the Oedipus complex, the subject's assumption of his own sex – that is, to call things by their name, what makes it the case that a man assumes the virile type and that a woman assumes a certain feminine type, recognizes herself as a woman and identifies with her functions as a woman. Virility and feminization are the two terms that translate what is essentially the function of the Oedipus complex. Here we find ourselves at the level at which the Oedipus complex is directly tied to the function of the ego-ideal – it has no other meaning.

Here, then, are the three chapters into which you can classify every discussion that has been produced around the Oedipus complex and, consequently, around the function of the father – for they are one and the same thing. There is no question of the Oedipus complex if there is no father, and, inversely, to speak about the Oedipus complex is to introduce the function of the father as essential.

I will repeat for those who take notes. On the historical subject of the Oedipus complex, everything revolves around three poles – the Oedipus complex in relation to the superego, in relation to reality and in relation to the ego-ideal. The ego-ideal, to the extent that genitalization – insofar as it has been assumed – becomes an element in the ego-ideal. Reality, insofar as it concerns relations between the Oedipus complex and the afflictions that involve a disruption of the relationship to reality – perversion and psychosis.

I will summarize this on the blackboard, with an addition whose signification you will see later.

Superego	R.i
Reality	$S \leftarrow S'.r$
Ego-ideal	I.s

Now let's try and go a bit further.

2

Now that you have these broad, global groupings, underlined by history, amply present to assist you, we are going to move forward into the third chapter – the function of the Oedipus complex insofar as it directly affects the assumption of one's sex – and what has been so little clarified with respect to the castration complex.

We are happy enough to take things from the clinical angle and naively ask, concerning cases, 'And what about the father? What was he doing during that time? What was his involvement in the situation?'

167

The question of the father's absence or presence, of his beneficial or harmful nature is clearly not hidden. We have even seen the term 'paternal deficiency' appear recently, which was not a minor topic to take on – knowing what people have said on the matter, and whether it holds up, is another question. But in the end, this paternal deficiency, whether known by this name or not, is a topic on today's agenda in the evolution of analysis that is becoming increasingly environmentalist, as it's elegantly expressed.

Not every analyst falls into this trap, thank goodness. A lot of analysts, if you bring them biographical information as interesting as, 'But the parents didn't get on, there was marital conflict and that explains everything', will answer, even those with whom we are not in agreement, 'So what? This proves absolutely nothing. We would expect no particular kind of effect', and they would be right.

That said, when one is seeking this paternal deficiency, what is one interested in concerning the father? Questions in the biographical register come flooding in. Was the father there or not? Did he travel? Was he away? Did he return often? And also – can an Oedipus complex be constituted in a normal manner when there is no father? These are questions that are very interesting in themselves, and I would say even more. It was from this angle that the first paradoxes were introduced, those that led to raising the questions that followed. It was then noticed that an Oedipus complex could be very well formed even when the father was not there.

At the very beginning, it was always thought that it was some excess in the father's presence, or excess in the father, that created all the dramas. This was the time when the image of the terrifying father was considered a damaging element. In neurosis, it was very soon observed that it was even more serious when he was too nice. We were slow to learn these lessons, and now we are at the other extreme, wondering about paternal deficiencies. There are weak fathers, submissive fathers, subjugated fathers, fathers castrated by their wife, and, finally, ill fathers, blind fathers, bankrupt fathers and whatever you want. We should nevertheless try to detect what can be extracted from such a situation and find the minimum of formulas that will enable us to move forward.

First of all, the question of his concrete presence or concrete absence, as someone in the surroundings. If we place ourselves at

168   the level at which these researches take place, that is to say at the
level of reality, one can say that it's completely possible, conceivable, actualized and palpable in our experience that the father is
there even when he isn't there, which should already encourage us
to adopt a certain level of prudence in the use of the environmentalist point of view concerning the father's function. Even in cases in
which the father isn't there, or the child has been left alone with its
mother, completely normal Oedipus complexes – normal in both
senses, normal as normalizing on the one hand, and also normal
insofar as they denormalize, I mean by their neuroticizing effect, for
example – are established in a manner that is exactly homogeneous
with other cases. First point that should grab our attention.

Concerning the deficiency of the father, I would simply point out
to you that one never knows in what respect the father is deficient.
In certain cases, we're told he's too nice, which would seem to mean
that he should be nasty. On the other hand, the fact that, manifestly,
he can be too nasty, implies that it would perhaps be better if from
time to time he were nice. In the end, we went around this little
merry-go-round a long time ago. We discerned that the problem of
the father's deficiency did not directly concern the child in question,
but, as was obvious from the outset, that one could begin to say
things that were a little more effective concerning this deficiency by
taking it in the context of the place he has to occupy as a member
of the fundamental trio of the family. But one did not, for all that,
manage to formulate what was at stake any better.

I do not want to dwell on this at length, but last year we spoke
about it with respect to little Hans. We saw the difficulties that we
had in pinpointing where the deficiency of the paternal character
lay, taken solely from the environmentalist point of view, whereas
he was far from being deficient in his family – he was there, close to
his wife, he fulfilled his role, he talked about things and she would
tell him where to shove it a bit too often, but in the end he was very
involved with his child, he was not absent, and so little absent that
he even had his child analysed, which is the best outlook that one
could expect from a father, at least in this sense.

It's worth coming back to the question of the father's deficiency,
but one enters here into a world that is so much in movement that
we should try to draw a distinction that makes it possible to see in
what way the research falls down. It falls down, not because of what
it finds, but because of what it seeks. I believe that the fault in the
orientation is that one is confusing two things that have a relation-
169   ship but are not to be confused – the father as normative and the
father as normal. Of course, the father can be very denormativizing
insofar as he himself isn't normal, but that is to reject the question at

the level of structure – neurotic, psychotic – of the father. Therefore, the father's normality is one question, that of his normal position in the family is another.

The third point I put forward – his position in the family isn't to be confused with an exact definition of his normativizing role. Speaking of his deficiency in the family isn't the same as speaking of his deficiency in the complex. Effectively, to speak about his deficiency in the complex, we have to introduce another dimension than the realist dimension defined by his characterological, biographical or other mode of presence in the family.

It's in that direction that I am going to take my next step.

3

Now that you can see the current state of the question, more or less, I am going to attempt to introduce a little bit of order and get a broader view of these paradoxes. Let's now introduce the father's role more accurately. Since it's his place in the complex that can give an indication of the direction in which to move forward and establish a correct formulation, let's now investigate the complex and go back to the ABC of it.

At the outset, the terrifying father. Still, this image summarizes something much more complex, as the name indicates. The father intervenes at several levels. First, he prohibits the mother. That is the function and origin of the Oedipus complex. It's where the father connects to the primordial law of the prohibition of incest. It's this father, we are told, who is charged with representing this prohibition. Sometimes he has to directly, as when the child is too effusive, demonstrative or indulges in its inclinations, but he plays his role well beyond this. It's through his entire presence, through his effects in the unconscious, that he succeeds in prohibiting the mother. You are waiting for me to say, 'under the threat of castration'. It's true, it has to be said, but it's not so simple. It's understood that castration has a manifest role here, one that is increasingly confirmed. The link between castration and the law is essential, but let's see how this presents itself to us clinically. I feel obliged to remind you of this because my remarks produce all sorts of textual echoes in you.

Let's start with the boy. The relationship between the boy and his father is regulated – this is taken for granted – by the fear of castration. What is this fear of castration? How are we to take it? We encounter it in the initial experience of the Oedipus complex, but in what form? We encounter it as a form of retaliation within

170

an aggressive relationship. The aggression arises in the boy insofar as his privileged object, the mother, has been prohibited him and is directed towards the father. It returns to him as a function of the dual relationship, insofar as he imaginarily projects intentions onto the father that are equivalent to or reinforced in relation to his own but which find their point of departure in his own aggressive tendencies. In short, the fear experienced towards the father is clearly centrifugal – I mean it has its centre in the subject. This presentation agrees both with experience and with the history of analysis. It's from this angle that, as experience very quickly taught us, the effect of the fear experienced in the Oedipus complex with respect to the father has to be assessed.

Although castration is profoundly bound up with the symbolic articulation of the prohibition of incest, it appears, then, in our entire experience, and particularly with respect to those who are its privileged objects, namely neurotics, on the imaginary level. That is where it starts. It doesn't start with a commandment of the type that the law of Manu formulates – 'Whosoever should sleep with his mother shall cut off his genitals, and holding them in his right hand' – or left, I don't remember which very well – 'will go towards the west until he dies.' That's the law, but this law has not particularly, as such, reached the ears of our neurotics. In general, it's even somewhat left in the shadows. There are, moreover, other ways of dealing with it, but I do not have the time to spend on it today.

And so, the manner in which a neurotic embodies the castrating threat is bound up with imaginary aggression. It's retaliation. Just as Jupiter is quite capable of castrating Chronos, our little Jupiters fear that Chronos will do the job himself first.

Our examination of the Oedipus complex, the way it presents itself in experience, was introduced by Freud and has been articulated in theory, gives us something different again, which is the delicate question of the inverted Oedipus complex. I do not know if it seems self-evident to you, but in reading Freud's article, or any other article by any other author on the subject, whenever the question of the Oedipus complex arises, one is always struck by the extremely shifting, nuanced and disconcerting role that the function of the inverted Oedipus complex plays.

171   The inverted Oedipus complex is never absent from the function of the Oedipus complex – I mean, the element of love for the father cannot be avoided. It's what brings the Oedipus complex to an end, its dissolution, in a dialectic that remains very ambiguous between love and identification, identification as rooted in love. Identification and love, these are not the same thing – one can identify with someone without loving them, and vice versa – but the two

terms are nevertheless closely tied to and absolutely indissociable from one another.

In Freud's article about the dissolution of the complex, '*Die Untergang des Ödipuskomplexes*' ['The Dissolution of the Oedipus Complex'], from 1924, read the explanation he gives of the final identification which is its outcome. It's insofar as the father is loved that the subject identifies with him and discovers the final solution to the Oedipus complex in a composite of amnesic repression and the acquisition within himself of this ideal term, owing to which he becomes the father. I am not saying that he is henceforth and immediately a little male, but he too can become someone, he already has the titles in his pocket, the matter in reserve, and when the time comes, providing things go well and the little piglets don't eat it, at the time of puberty he will have his penis all ready with its certificate – 'Daddy was there to confer it on me at the right moment'.

That's not how it happens if a neurosis declares itself, precisely because something's not in order in the title in question. However, the inverted Oedipus complex isn't so simple either. It's via the same pathway, that of love, that the position of inversion can be produced – namely, in lieu of a beneficial identification, the subject finds himself affected by a nice little passive position at the unconscious level which will reappear in due course, placing him in a kind of angle bisector – *squeeze-panic*. It's a position the subject is caught in, which he has discovered all alone, and it is quite advantageous. It consists in placing oneself in the right place to gain the favours of this redoubtable father who has forbidden so many things but who is otherwise quite nice – that is to say, getting him to love one. But since getting him to love one consists first of all in joining the ranks of women, and since one still retains one's little virile self-love, this position, as Freud explains, carries the danger of castration – hence this form of unconscious homosexuality that places the subject in a conflictual situation with multiple consequences. On the one hand, the constant return of the homosexual position with respect to the father and, on the other, its suspension, that is, its repression, by virtue of the threat of castration that this position entails.

None of this is simple. Well, we are trying to develop something that allows us to conceptualize it in a more rigorous manner and ask better questions in any given case.

So let's summarize. As before, the summary will consist of introducing a number of distinctions that serve as a prelude to realigning the point that isn't working. Already, earlier, we were getting to this – that the question has not been raised with respect to the ego-ideal. Let us also try here to carry out the reduction that we have

172

just started to undertake. I put the following to you – it's not too great a claim to say here and now that, here, the father comes to the position of intruder. And not simply because his sheer volume makes him an encumbrance, but because he prohibits. What does he prohibit, exactly?

Let's press on and draw some distinctions. Do we have to bring the emergence of the genital drive in and say that, in the first instance, he prohibits its real satisfaction? On the one hand, the latter seems to take place earlier. But it's also clear that something revolves around the fact that he prohibits the small child from making use of his penis at the time at which the tendencies of the said penis start to manifest themselves. We will say, therefore, that it's a question of prohibition by the father with respect to the real drive.

But why the father? Experience shows that the mother does too. Recall the observation of little Hans, where it's the mother who says, 'Put it away, you don't do that.' In general, it's most often the mother who says, 'If you keep on doing that, we will call the doctor who will cut it off.' It's therefore correct to point out that the father, as he who prohibits at the level of the real drive, isn't so essential. Let's return, in this connection, to what I contributed last year – as you see, these things always end up being useful – my table with three levels.

real father	castration	imaginary
symbolic mother	frustration	real
imaginary father	privation	symbolic

What is the issue at the level of the threat of castration? The issue is the real intervention of the father concerning an imaginary threat, R.i, since it's a fairly rare occurrence that he gets it cut off in reality. I point out to you that on this table castration is a symbolic act, the agent of which is someone real, the father or the mother who tells him, 'You will have it cut off', and whose object is an imaginary object – if the child feels it has been cut off, it's because he imagines it. I point out to you that this is paradoxical. You could make the following objection – 'This is the actual level of castration, and you are telling me that the father isn't all that useful!' That is indeed what I am saying. Yes, it is.

Also, what does the father prohibit? This is the point we started with – he prohibits the mother. As object, she is his, she isn't the child's. This is the level at which this rivalry with the father, which engenders aggression quite by itself, is established. The father does indeed frustrate the child of its mother.

Here you have another level, that of frustration. Here, the father intervenes as having rights and not as a real person. Even if he isn't there, even if he calls the mother on the telephone, for example, the result is the same. Here it's the father as symbolic who intervenes and frustrates – an imaginary act concerning an object that is quite real, which is the mother insofar as the child needs her, S'.r.

Then we have the third level, that of privation, which intervenes in the articulation of the Oedipus complex. This level involves the father insofar as he is preferred by the mother, which is a dimension that you are absolutely obliged to bring into the final function, the one that results in the formation of the ego-ideal, $S \leftarrow S'$.r. It's inasmuch as the father becomes, in whatever way, through strength or weakness, an object that the mother prefers that the final identification can be established. The question of the inverted Oedipus complex and its function is established at this level. I would go even further – this is where the question of the difference of the effect of the complex upon the boy and the girl is centred.

Everything proceeds smoothly as far as the girl is concerned, and it's for this reason that the function of the castration complex is said to be asymmetrical for the boy and the girl. It's the entry that she finds difficult, whereas at the end the solution is made easier, since the father, as bearer of the phallus, has no difficulty in getting himself preferred over the mother. For the boy, on the other hand, it's a different matter, and this is where there remains a gap. How does the father get himself preferred over the mother insofar as this is how the exit from the Oedipus complex occurs? We find ourselves faced with the same difficulty we encountered with respect to the establishment of the inverted Oedipus complex. It seems to me as a consequence that, for the boy, the Oedipus complex is always the least normativizing, whereas, really, the implication of what we are told is that it's the most, because virility is assumed via identification with the father.

In the end, the problem is how, in the case of the boy, it comes about that the father's essential function of prohibition doesn't result in what is the very clear conclusion on the third level – namely, the privation that is correlated with identification with the ideal, which tends to be produced for both boy and girl. It's to the extent that the father becomes her ego-ideal that the girl's recognition that she doesn't have the phallus occurs. But this is good for her – whereas for the boy it would be an absolutely disastrous outcome, as it sometimes is. Here, the agent is I, whereas the object is s – I.s.

174

In other words, at the time of the normativizing outcome of the Oedipus complex, the child recognizes not having – not truly having what he has, in the case of the boy, and what she doesn't have, in the case of the girl.

What happens at the level of identification with the ideal, a level at which the father gets the mother to prefer him, and not at all at the exit from the Oedipus complex, must literally result in privation. For the girl, this result is entirely admissible, and entirely conformizing, even though it's never completely achieved, for there always remains a little aftertaste, which is called *Penisneid*, proof that it doesn't really work rigorously. But in the case where it must work, if we stick to the schema, the boy should always be castrated. There is, therefore, something that doesn't work, that is missing in our explanation.

Let me now attempt to introduce the solution.

What is a father? I am not saying 'in the family', for in the family he is whatever he wants to be – he is a shadow, he is a banker, he is whatever he has to be, he is or he isn't it. This is of overriding importance sometimes, but it may also be of none at all. The question is entirely about what he is in the Oedipus complex.

Well then, there, the father isn't a real object, even if he has to intervene as a real object to embody castration. If he isn't a real object, what is he?

He isn't solely an ideal object either because, on that side of things, it's only accidents that can happen. Well, the Oedipus complex is, nevertheless, not solely a catastrophe since it's the foundation of our relationship to culture, as one says.

And so, naturally, you are going to tell me, 'The father is the symbolic father, you have already said as much.' In effect, I have already said it to you often enough for me not to repeat it to you today. What I am bringing you today is giving precisely a bit more precision to the notion of the symbolic father. It's this – the father is a metaphor.

What is a metaphor? Let's state it straight out and put it up on our table, which will enable us to rectify the difficult consequences of the table. A metaphor, as I have already explained to you, is a signifier that comes to take the place of another signifier. I am saying that this is the father in the Oedipus complex, even if that must be astonishing to the ears of some people.

I am saying exactly this – the father is a signifier substituted for another signifier. That is the mainspring, the essential and unique mainspring, of the father's intervention in the Oedipus complex. And if you don't look for the paternal deficiencies at this level, you won't find them anywhere else.

175

The father's function in the Oedipus complex is to be a signifier substituted for the first signifier introduced into symbolization, the maternal signifier. According to the formula that, as I once explained to you, was the formula for metaphor, the father comes to the place of the mother, S in the place of S', S' being the mother insofar as she is already linked to something that was x, which is the signified in relationship to the mother.

$$\frac{Father}{Mother} \cdot \frac{Mother}{x}$$

The mother comes and goes. It's because I am a small being who is already caught up in the symbolic, because I have learnt to symbolize, that it's possible to say that she comes and goes. In other words, I perceive her or I do not perceive her, the world changes with her arrival, and it may disappear.

The question is – what is the signified? What does she want? I would really like it to be me that she wants, but it's very clear that it's not just me that she wants. There are other things at work in her. What is at work in her is the x, the signified. And the signified of the mother's comings and goings is the phallus.

The child, more or less shrewdly, or with more or less luck, may come to discern very early on what the imaginary x is and, once he has understood this, may make himself the phallus. But the imaginary way isn't the normal way. Moreover, it's for this reason that it leads to what one calls fixations. And also, this way isn't normal because in the end it's never pure, it's not completely accessible, it always leaves something that is approximate and unfathomable, even something dual, which makes for all the polymorphism of perversion.

What is the symbolic way? It's the metaphorical way. I will give you the schema that will serve as our guide first and explain it to you later, since we have come more or less to the end of today's discussion – it's insofar as the father is substituted for the mother as signifier that the usual outcome of metaphor will be produced, the one that is expressed in the formula on the blackboard.

176

$$\frac{S}{S'} \cdot \frac{S'}{x} \rightarrow S\left(\frac{1}{s'}\right)$$

The intermediary signifying element falls, and the S enters into possession of the object of the mother's desire by way of the metaphor, which henceforth presents itself in the form of the phallus.

I am not saying that I am giving you the solution in an already transparent form. I am giving it to you in the form of its end result to show you where this is going. We shall see how one gets there and what the point of going there is – that is, everything that this solution resolves.

I leave you with this rough affirmation in your hands – my claim is that the entire question of the impasses of the Oedipus complex can be resolved if we regard the father's intervention as the substitution of one signifier for another signifier.

4

So as to begin to explain the thing to you a little bit, I will introduce a remark which, I hope, will nourish your dreams for the week.

A metaphor is located in the unconscious. Now, if there is one thing that is truly surprising, it's that no one discovered the unconscious earlier, since it has always been there and, moreover, it's still there. The fact of the matter is, no doubt, that one needed to know it on the inside in order to perceive that this place existed.

I would simply like to give you something with which you, who wander about the world as, I hope, so many apostles of my word, could introduce the question of the unconscious to people who have never heard it mentioned. You would say to them, 'How astonishing it is that ever since the world has been the world none of these people who call themselves philosophers has ever dreamt of producing' – at least not in the classical period, these days we have lightened up a bit, but there is still some way to go – 'this essential dimension that I have spoken to you about under the name of "something Other".'

I have already spoken to you about the desire for something Other – not as you feel it at the moment, perhaps, the desire to go out and eat a sausage rather than listen to me, but at any rate, and whatever it's about, the desire for something Other as such.

This dimension isn't present solely in desire. It's present in many other states that are permanent. Wakefulness, for example, what do we call wakefulness? It's not something we think about enough. 'To be awake, so what?' you will tell me. Being awake is what Freud evokes in his study of President Schreber when he speaks to us about 'Before Dawn', a chapter of Nietzsche's *Zarathustra*. This is indeed the type of reference that reveals to us the extent to which Freud lived in this something Other. When I spoke to you formerly about the day, the peace of the evening and some other little things like that which more or less reached you, it was centred entirely on

177

this suggestion. Before sunrise, is it really the sun that is going to appear? It's something Other that is latent, expected at the moment of waking.

And then, claustration. Isn't this an essential dimension? As soon as a man arrives somewhere, in the virgin forest or in the desert, he commences by closing himself in. If needs be, he'll put up two doors, like Cami, to get the air circulating between them. It's a matter of setting oneself up inside, but it's not simply a notion of interior and exterior; it's the notion of the Other, of what the Other is as such, of what is not the place in which one is shut off.

I would go even further – if you were to explore the phenomenology, as some might say, of claustration, you would realize to what extent it's absurd to limit the function of fear to a relationship with a real danger. The close relationship fear has with security should be obvious to you via the phenomenology of phobia. You would know that, for the phobic, his moments of anxiety occur when he observes that he has lost his fear, when you start to alleviate his phobia for him a little bit. It's at that moment that he will tell himself, 'This is not good. I no longer know at what places I have to stop. In losing my fear, I have lost my security.' In short, everything I said to you last year about little Hans.

There is also a dimension that you do not think about enough, I'm convinced of it, because you live in it as if it were the air you breathe – it's called boredom. You have perhaps never thought enough about the extent to which boredom is typically a dimension of this something Other that even manages to be formulated as such in the clearest of manners – you would like something Other. We are happy to eat shit, but not always the same shit. These are types of diversion, formulated diversions, already symbolized, away from the essential relationship with something Other. 178

You are going to think that, all of a sudden, I am falling into romanticism and melancholy. You can see it – desire, claustration, wakefulness – I was on the point of offering a prayer while I was at it, why not? 'Where is he headed? Where's he going?' No, no.

I would like to end by drawing your attention to the various manifestations of the presence of something Other insofar as they are institutionalized. You can classify the human formations that men institute wherever they go, and everywhere they go, what we call collective institutions, according to the satisfaction they give to the different ways of relating to something Other.

As soon as man arrives somewhere, he builds a prison and a brothel – that is, the places where desire truly is – and he waits for something, a better world, a future world. He is there, he conducts a vigil, he waits for the revolution. But above all, above all, as soon as he arrives somewhere, it's excessively important that all his occupations ooze boredom. An occupation only begins to become serious when what constitutes it – that is to say, in general, regularity – has become perfectly boring.

Think in particular of everything in your analytic practice that has been very precisely set up to make you bored. Being bored, that's the key. A large part, at least, of what are called the technical rules to be observed by analysts are nothing other than the means for giving this occupation a guarantee of professional standards – but if you look very closely at things, you will see that it's insofar as they approve, sustain and maintain the function of boredom at the heart of practice.

That is a little introduction that doesn't yet introduce you to what I will be talking about next time when I will show you that it's at the level of this Other, as such, that the dialectic of the signifier is located and that it's from there that it's best to explore the function, the impact, the precise pressure and the inductor effect of the Name-of-the-Father, also as such.

15 January 1958

X

THE THREE MOMENTS OF THE OEDIPUS COMPLEX (I)

From the Name-of-the-Father to the phallus
The key to the decline of the Oedipus complex
Being and having
Caprice and the law
The a-subject child

We will continue our examination of what I have been calling the paternal metaphor.

We got to the point where I was claiming that all possibilities of clearly articulating the Oedipus complex and its mainspring – namely, the castration complex – resided in the structure that I have been advocating as that of metaphor.

To those of you who might be astonished that I have come so late to formulating the question that has been so central in the theory and practice of analysis, I would reply that it was impossible to do so without having demonstrated to you, in various theoretical and practical areas, the deficiencies in the formulas that are commonly used in analysis and, above all, without having shown how it's possible to give more adequate formulas, as it were. To begin to formulate the problems, I first need to accustom you, for example, to think in terms of the subject.

What is a subject? Is it something that is purely and simply confused with the individual reality opposite you when you say 'the subject'? Or is it rather that, from the moment you get him to speak, something else is necessarily implied? What I mean is this. Is speech like an emanation floating above him, or does it develop? Does it, yes or no, by itself, impose a structure like the one I have been commenting on at length and familiarizing you with? A structure that says that once there is a speaking subject there is no longer any question of simply reducing the question of the subject's relations, insofar as he speaks, to an other, but that there is always a third party, the big Other, who is constitutive of the subject's position, insofar as he speaks, which is also to say, insofar as you analyse him.

180   This is not simply a supplementary theoretical requirement. It actually makes things easier when it comes to understanding where the effects you are dealing with are located, namely what happens when you encounter in a subject demands, desires, a fantasy – which is not the same thing – and, also, what, in short, seems to be the most uncertain and difficult to grasp and define of all, a reality.

We will get the chance to see this at the point we have now arrived at in explaining the term 'paternal metaphor'.

1

What is the paternal metaphor? Strictly speaking, in what has been constituted out of a primordial symbolization between child and mother, it's the substitution of the father as a symbol or signifier in the place of the mother. We shall see what the meaning of this 'in the place of the mother' is, which constitutes the turning point or the motor nerve essential to the Oedipus complex's forward movement.

The terms I set out for you last year concerning the child's relations with its mother are summarized in the imaginary triangle that I taught you how to use. Now, introducing the child–father–mother triangle as fundamental is bringing in something that is undoubtedly real, but that already places a symbolic relationship, I mean an established one, in the real. It places it objectively, as it were, insofar as we ourselves are able to make an object of it, are able to look at it.

The initial reality relationship takes shape between the mother and the child, and it's here that the child experiences the first realities of its contact with the living world. In order to describe the situation objectively, we will bring the father into the triangle, whereas for the child he has not yet made his entry.

The father, for us, *is*, he is real. But let's not forget that he is only real for us insofar as the institutions confer upon him, I am not even going to say his role and function as father – it's not a sociological question – but his name as father. That the father is, for example, the real agent of procreation is in no case a truth of experience. It so happens that at a time when analysts still discussed serious matters it was observed that, in some primitive tribe, procreation was attributed to, I don't know, a fountain, a stone or an encounter with a spirit in some far-off place. On this point Mr Jones

181   had made the remark, very relevant moreover, that it was entirely unthinkable that this truth of experience would elude intelligent

beings – and we attribute a minimum of this intelligence to all human beings. It's quite clear that, barring exceptions – but exceptional exceptions – a woman does not give birth unless she has had coitus and, moreover, within a very precise timespan. But in making this particularly pertinent remark, Mr Ernest Jones was quite simply leaving out everything important in the matter.

What is important, in effect, is not that people know perfectly well that a woman can only bear a child if she has had coitus. It's that they acknowledge with a signifier that the one with whom she has had coitus is the father. For otherwise, in the way that the order of symbols is intrinsically constituted, absolutely nothing precludes the 'something' responsible for procreation from continuing to be maintained, in the symbolic system, as identical to whatever you like – that is, a rock, a fountain or an encounter with a spirit in some far-off place.

The father's position as symbolic doesn't depend on people's having more or less recognized the need for a certain sequence of events as different as coitus and giving birth. The Name-of-the-Father's position as such, the attribution of father as procreator, is something that is located at the symbolic level. It can be brought about in various cultural forms, but as such it does not depend on its cultural form. It's a requirement of the signifying chain. Merely by virtue of the fact that you institute a symbolic order, something corresponds to, or does not correspond to, the function defined as the Name-of-the-Father. And within this function you place significations that may be different according to the case, but which in no case depend on any other necessity than the necessity of the father's function, to which the Name-of-the-Father corresponds in the signifying chain.

I believe I have stressed this sufficiently already. Here, then, is what we can call the symbolic triangle, as it is instituted in the real when there is a signifying chain or the articulation of speech.

I'm saying that there is a relationship between this symbolic ternary and what I brought here last year in the form of the imaginary ternary to represent the child's relationship to the mother, insofar as the child finds itself dependent on the mother's desire, on the first symbolization of the mother as such, and nothing else. Through this symbolization, the child detaches its effective dependence on the mother's desire from the pure and simple lived experience of this dependence, and something that is subjectivized at an initial or primitive level is instituted. This subjectification consists simply in posing the mother as this primordial being who may be there or not. In the child's own desire this being is essential. What does the subject desire? It's not simply a matter of appetition for the

182

mother's care, contact or even her presence, but of appetition for her desire.

Immediately following this first symbolization in which the child's desire takes shape, all the subsequent complications of symbolization begin. As a result, a dimension opens up by which what the mother – as a being who lives in the world of symbols, a world in which symbols are present, a speaking world – objectively desires is inscribed virtually. Even if she only lives in it partially, or even if she is, as sometimes happens, a being ill-adapted to this world of symbols or who has refused certain elements within it, this primordial symbolization nevertheless opens up, for the child, the dimension of whatever else it is that the mother may desire on the imaginary plane.

This is how the desire for something Other that I spoke about last week makes its entry, in a manner that is still confused and completely virtual – not in the substantial manner that would enable it to be recognized in all its generality, as I did in the last seminar, but in a concrete manner. There is in her the desire for something Other than to satisfy my own desire, which is starting to pulse with life.

Down that path, there is both access and there is no access. In this relationship of illusion by which the first being reads or anticipates the satisfaction of his desires in the hint of a movement in the other, in this dual adaptation of image to image which occurs in all inter-animal relations, how are we to conceptualize that what is Other in what the subject desires is able to be read therein as in a mirror, as it's expressed in Scripture?

Surely, it's both difficult to think about and too difficult to bring about, since this is the whole issue around what happens at this primitive level of a switch point for perversions. It's difficult to bring about, in the sense that it's brought about in a faulty way, though it's brought about nevertheless. It's certainly not brought about without the intervention of a little more than the primordial symbolization of this mother who comes and goes, whom one calls when she is not there and whom, when she is there, one pushes away so that one can call her back again. This something extra, which must be there, is precisely the existence behind her of this entire symbolic order on which she depends, and which, since it's always there more or less, permits a degree of access to the object of her desire, which is already such a specialized object and so marked with the necessity the symbolic system institutes that in its prevalence it's absolutely unthinkable in any other way.

183   This object is called the phallus, and it's what I made our entire dialectic of the object relation revolve around last year.

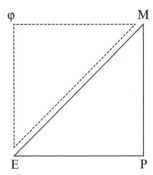

Why? Why would this object be necessary in this place unless it was privileged in the symbolic order? This is the question I want to enter into now in greater detail.

In this drawing there is a relationship of symmetry between 'phallus', which is here, at the vertex of the imaginary ternary, and 'father', at the vertex of the symbolic ternary. As we will see, there is not simply a symmetry here, but rather a connection. How is it that I can already claim that this connection is metaphorical in kind?

Well, this is precisely what takes us to the dialectic of the Oedipus complex. Let's try to articulate what is at issue step by step, as Freud did and as others have done after him.

Not everything is always completely clear therein, nor clearly symbolized. We shall try to go further, and not just for the satisfaction of our intellect. If we articulate step by step the genesis, if I can use this term, that makes the position of the signifier of the father in the symbolic foundational for the position of the phallus on the imaginary plane, if we can manage to clearly distinguish the logical moments, as it were, of the constitution of the phallus on the imaginary plane as a privileged and predominant object, and if, as a result of these distinctions, we are better able to orient ourselves and better able to question the patients we interview, the meaning of our clinical work and the management of the treatment, then we shall regard our efforts as justified. Given the difficulties we encounter in our clinical work, interviews and examinations and in the management of the therapy, these efforts are justified in advance.

Take this desire of the Other, which is the mother's desire, and which contains something beyond. Just reaching this beyond alone requires mediation, and this mediation is given precisely by the father's position in the symbolic order. 184

Rather than proceeding dogmatically, let's think about the way in which the question arises in concrete terms. We shall see that there are very different states, cases and also stages where the child identifies with the phallus. That was the point of the course we adopted last year. We showed an exemplary perversion in fetishism, in the sense that the child there has a particular relationship with the object of what lies beyond in the mother's desire, whose predominance and value of excellence, as it were, he has observed and to which he attaches himself to by way of an imaginary identification with the mother. I also pointed out that in other forms of perversion, and notably in transvestism, it's in the contrary position that the child assumes the difficulty of the imaginary relation with the mother. It has been said that he identifies himself with the phallic mother. I think it's more correct to say that he identifies with the phallus as hidden under the mother's clothing.

I am giving you this reminder to show you that the child establishes a relationship to the phallus insofar as it is the object of the mother's desire. Moreover, experience proves to us that this element plays an active and essential role in the child's relations with the parental couple. I recalled this last time at the theoretical level in the commentary on the decline of the Oedipus complex in relation to the so-called inverted Oedipus complex. Freud emphasizes cases where the child identifies with the mother and, having adopted this position that is both significant and promising, fears the consequences – namely, the privation of his virile organ that will result from it for him, if he's a boy.

This is indicative, but it goes much further. Analytic experience proves that the father, as the one who deprives the mother of the object of her desire, namely the phallic object, plays an absolutely essential role in, I won't say the perversions, but in every neurosis and in the entire course, even the easiest and most normal, of the Oedipus complex. In experience, you will always find that the subject has adopted a position of a particular kind, at a moment of his childhood, towards the role the father plays in the fact that the mother does not have a phallus. This moment is never left out.

The reminder I gave last time left the question of the favourable or unfavourable outcome of the Oedipus complex suspended around the three planes of castration, frustration and privation exercised by the father. It's the level of privation that we are concerned with here. At this level, the father deprives someone of what, in the final analysis, he does not have, namely something that only exists insofar as you bring it into existence as a symbol.

185

It's quite clear that the father does not castrate the mother of something that she does not have. For it to be posited that she does not have it, it has to have already been projected onto the symbolic plane as a symbol. But it's well and truly privation, given that every real privation requires symbolization. It's therefore at the level of privation of the mother that at a given moment of the evolution of the Oedipus complex the question arises for the subject whether to accept, register, symbolize for himself and render meaningful this privation of which the mother proves to be the object. The child subject either assumes or does not assume this privation, accepts or refuses it. This point is an essential one. You will rediscover it at every crossroads, whenever your experience takes you to a certain point that I am now trying to define as nodal in the Oedipus complex.

Let's call it a nodal point, since this has just occurred to me. I am not essentially committed to it. What I mean by it is that it does not coincide, far from it, with this moment to which we are seeking the key, which is the dissolution of the Oedipus complex, its result and the fruit it bears in the subject – namely, the child's identification with the father. But there is the earlier moment at which the father enters into his function as depriver of the mother – that is, he is profiled behind the mother's relationship to the object of her desire as 'that which castrates', but I am only putting it there in quotes because what is castrated, in the event, is not the subject. It's the mother.

This point is not very new. What is new is to focus on it and for you to turn your gaze towards this point insofar as it makes it possible for us to understand what comes before, about which we already have some enlightenment, and what follows.

Don't be in any doubt about it, and you will be able to verify it and confirm it whenever you have occasion to see it. Experience proves that, insofar as the child does not cross this nodal point, that is to say, does not accept the privation of the phallus carried out on the mother by the father, he maintains, as a rule – it's a correlation grounded in the structure – a certain kind of identification with the mother's object, this object that I present to you from the outset as a rival object, to use the term that comes up here, and this is so whether it's a question of phobia, neurosis or perversion. This is a point of reference – there is perhaps no better word – around which you are able to regroup the elements of the observations by asking yourself this question in each particular case – what is the special configuration of the relationship to the mother, the father and the phallus that makes it the case that the child does not accept that the mother is deprived of the object of her desire by the father? To what extent is it necessary in any given case to emphasize the fact that, in correlation with this relationship, the child maintains its identification with the phallus?

186

There are degrees, of course, and this relationship is not the same in neurosis, psychosis and perversion. But the configuration is nodal in every case. At this level, the question that arises is, 'To be or not to be*' the phallus? On the imaginary plane, the question for the subject is one of being or not being the phallus. The phase that is to be passed through places the subject in the position of choosing.

Put this 'choosing' in quotes, moreover, since the subject is as much passive as active there, for the good reason that he is not the one pulling the strings of the symbolic. The sentence started before him, it was started by his parents, and what I am leading you towards is, precisely, the relationship each of these parents has with this sentence that has been started and with the way it's agreed that this sentence is supported by a certain reciprocal position of the parents in relation to this sentence. But let's say, because it's necessary to express oneself, that, in the neuter, there is an alternative between being and not being the phallus.

You get the sense that there is a huge step required to understand the difference between this alternative and the one in question at another moment, and which, all the same, we do have to expect to find, which is that of 'to have or have not' – to draw on another literary reference. In other words, having or not having the penis is not the same thing. Between the two, there is the castration complex, let's not forget. What is at issue in the castration complex is never articulated and is made almost completely mysterious. We know, however, that the following two facts depend on it – that on one side the boy becomes a man, that on the other side the girl becomes a woman. In both cases, the question of having or not having is settled by the intermediary of the castration complex – even for him who in the end has the penis by right, that is, the male. This presupposes that, in order to have it, there must have been a time at which he didn't have it. What is involved would not be called the castration complex if, in some way, it didn't put in the foreground the fact that in order to have it, it first of all has to be the case that one might not have it – so much so that the possibility of being castrated is essential to assuming the fact of having the phallus.

This is a step that has to be taken, and it's one where at some moment the father has to intervene effectively, really and efficaciously.

2

Till now, as the direction of what I have been saying suggests, I have only been able to speak to you from the point of view of the subject, saying to you, 'He accepts or does not accept, and if he does not accept, that leads him, man or woman, to being the phallus.' But now, for the following step, it's essential to have the father intervene effectively. I'm not saying that he wasn't already intervening effectively before, but till now I've been able to leave him in the background of what I've been saying and I could even have left him out altogether. And now that it's a question of having it or not having it, we are obliged to bring him into consideration. First of all, I would emphasize that, along with the subject, he needs to be constituted as a symbol. For if he isn't, no one will be able to actually intervene under the sign of this symbol. It's as a real person under the sign of this symbol that he will now effectively intervene at the next stage.

What can we say about this real father as the conveyor of a pro-hibition? I have already pointed out that, regarding the prohibition of the first appearance of the sexual instinct as it comes to its initial maturity in the subject, when the latter starts to draw attention to his tool, even displays it and offers its good offices to the mother, the father is not necessary. I would go even further – when the subject exhibits himself to his mother and propositions her, which is a moment still very close to that of imaginary identification with the phallus, what occurs unfolds most of the time – as we saw last year with respect to little Hans – on the plane of imaginary deprecation. The mother is quite capable of showing the child to what extent what he offers her is insufficient, and she is also capable of placing a prohibition on the use of his new tool.

However, the father enters into play – this is not in doubt – as the vehicle of the law and prohibitor of the mother as object. This is fundamental, as we know, but it's completely separate from the question that is actually brought into play for the child. We know that the father's function, the Name-of-the-Father, is bound up with the prohibition of incest, but nobody has ever dreamt of placing the fact that the father actually promulgates the law of pro-hibition of incest in the foreground of the castration complex. It's said sometimes, but it's never articulated by the father qua legislator *ex cathedra*, as it were. He is an obstacle between the child and its mother. He is the vehicle of the law, but *de jure*, whereas *de facto* he intervenes in a different way, and it's also in a different way that his failures to intervene manifest themselves. This is what we are exam-ining close up. In other words, insofar as culturally he is the vehicle of the law, insofar as he is invested with the signifier of the father, the father intervenes in the Oedipus complex in a more concrete, more graduated manner, as it were, and this is what I want to spell out today. This is the most difficult level at which to understand anything, whereas it is, however, the level where, we are told, the key to the Oedipus complex, namely its outcome, is found.

188

This is where the little schema I was commenting on for you in the first trimester – so massively boring for some of you, it seems – turns out, however, not to have been completely useless.

I remind you what one must always come back to – it's only after having traversed the already constituted order of the symbolic that the subject's intention – by which I mean his desire once it has passed over to the state of a demand – encounters what he addresses himself to, which is his object, his primordial object, namely his mother. Desire is something articulated. The world it enters into and progresses through, this world, this world here below, is not simply an *Umwelt* in the sense that one can find a way to satiate one's needs in it, but a world in which speech reigns, and this submits the desire of each of us to the law of the desire of the Other. The young subject's demand more or less satisfactorily crosses the line of the signifying chain, which is here, latent and already structuring. By this fact alone, the first test that he undergoes in his relationship with the Other, he undergoes with this first Other that is his mother, insofar as he has already symbolized her. It's insofar as he has already symbolized her that he addresses her in a manner that is articulated regardless of how much of a squawk it is, for this first symbolization is linked to the first articulations we have located in the *Fort-Da*. It's therefore insofar as this intention, or this demand, has traversed the signifying chain that it can come to the attention of the maternal object.

Therefore, the child who has made its own mother a subject on the basis of the first symbolization finds itself entirely subject to what we can call, but purely in advance, the law. This is only a metaphor. We have to unpack the metaphor contained in the term, 'the law', if we are to give it its proper place when I use it.

The mother's law is, of course, the fact that the mother is a speaking being, and this suffices to justify saying 'the mother's law'. Nevertheless, this law is, if I may say so, an uncontrolled law. It consists simply in the fact, at least for the subject, that something in his desire is completely dependent upon something else that is doubtless already articulated as such and is of the order of the law, but it is a law that lies entirely within the subject that supports it, namely within the good or bad will of the mother, the good or bad mother.

189   This is why I am about to propose a new term to you which, as you will see, is not as new as all that, since you only need to force it a little and it will join up with something that language has discovered, and not by chance.

Let's begin with the principle I am proposing here, which is that there is no subject unless there are signifiers that found it. It's insofar as primary symbolizations have been formed by the signifying couple *Fort-Da* that the mother is the first subject. In the light of this principle, what can we say about the child at the start of its life? One wonders whether for the child there is a reality or not, autoerotism or not. You will see things become especially clear as soon as you centre your questions on the child as a subject from whom demand emanates and in whom desire forms – and all analysis is a dialectic of desire.

Well then, I say that the child takes shape as a 'subject-to'. He is a subject-to because he experiences himself and feels himself initially as profoundly subject-to the capriciousness of what he is dependent on, even if this capriciousness is articulated capriciousness.

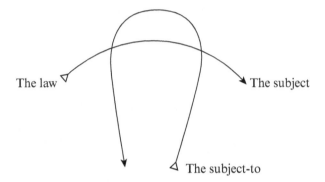

The law

The subject

The subject-to

What I am proposing is a necessity in all our experience, and I will illustrate it by taking the first example that comes to mind. Last year you could see how little Hans found an atypical solution to his Oedipus complex, which is not the outcome that I am about to try to describe, but a suppletion. Effectively, he needs his all-purpose horse as a suppletion for everything that he lacks during this time of transition, which is nothing other than the stage of assuming the symbolic in the form of the Oedipus complex, which is where I am taking you today. His suppletion is, then, this horse which is at one and the same time the father, the phallus, the little sister and what-ever else you want, but which essentially corresponds to what I am about to show you now.

Remember how it ends for him, and how this ending is symbol-ized in the final dream. What he summons to the father's place is this imaginary and all-powerful being called a plumber. The plumber is precisely there to desubjectify something, for little Hans's anxiety is essentially, as I told you, the anxiety of subjectification. Literally, at a certain moment, he realizes that in being subjected in this way, there's no knowing where it might lead. You remember the schema of the carts that come and go, and which embody the core of his fear.

190

It's precisely from this moment on that little Hans establishes in his life a number of centres of fear around which the re-establishment of his sense of security will revolve. Fear, which is something that has its source in the real, is a component of a child's security. He uses his fears to provide a beyond to this anxiety-provoking subjectification that he produces when the lack of this external domain, this other plane, appears. Something to make him afraid has to emerge if he is not to be purely and simply a subject-to.

Here it's appropriate to observe that this Other to whom he addresses himself – specifically, the mother – has a relationship with the father. Everyone realizes that many things depend on her relations with the father, especially when – experience has shown this to be the case – the father fails to play his role, as they say. I don't need to remind you that last week I spoke about all the types of paternal deficit concretely designated in terms of interhuman relations. Our experience effectively requires that this is how it is, but no one fully formulates what is involved. It's not so much a question of the mother's relations with the father, in the vague sense in which there would be a kind of rivalry of prestige between them, one that is supposed to converge upon the subject of the child. Undoubtedly, this schema of a convergence is not false, and that there be two is more than a requirement – without them there could not be this ternary. But this is not sufficient, even if what happens between the two, as everybody admits, is essential.

We come, then, to these bonds of love and respect around which some people make the entire analysis of the case of little Hans revolve, namely – was the mother nice, affectionate enough towards the father, and so on? And we fall back into the rut of environmental sociological analysis. Now, it's not so much a question of the personal relations between the father and the mother, nor whether they are each up to the task or not, as it is of a moment that has to be lived through as such, concerning the relations, not simply of the person of the mother to the person of the father, but of the mother with the father's speech – with the father insofar as what he says is not completely equivalent to nothing.

191

What matters is the function in which three things intervene – first, the Name-of-the-Father, second, the father's spoken words, third, the law insofar as the father has a more or less intimate relationship to it. What is essential is that the mother establish the father as the mediator of what lies beyond her law and her capriciousness – namely, the law as such, purely and simply. It is, therefore, a question of the father qua Name-of-the-Father, closely tied to the declaration of the law, as the entire development of the Freudian doctrine declares and promises. This is the respect in which he is accepted or not accepted by the child as the one who deprives or does not deprive the mother of the object of her desire.

In other words, in order to understand the Oedipus complex, we must consider three moments that I am going to try to schematize for you with the help of our little diagram from the first trimester.

3

First moment. What the child is seeking, qua desire for desire, is to be able to satisfy the mother's desire, that is to say, 'to be or not to be' the object of the mother's desire. He therefore introduces his demand, here, in Δ.

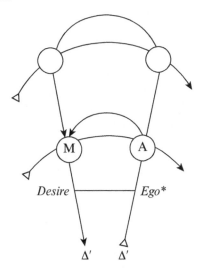

The fruit or result of this will appear here, in Δ'. Two points are plotted on this path – one that corresponds to the ego* and, opposite, one that here is his other, with which he identifies, this something other that he is going to seek to become, namely the object that satisfies the mother. As soon as something begins to stir at the base of his stomach, he will start to show it to his mother, a matter of finding out 'what I am capable of', with the disappointments that ensue. He will seek it and he will find it, insofar as the mother is questioned by the child's demand. She herself is also pursuing her own desire, and its components are located somewhere thereabouts.

At the first moment and first stage, it is, then, a matter of the following – the child identifies in the mirror with the object of the mother's desire. This is the primitive phallic stage, the one in which

192

the paternal metaphor per se acts inasmuch as the primacy of the phallus is already instituted in the world by the existence of symbols, discourse and the law. But the child himself is only ever aware of its outcome. In order to please the mother, if you will allow me to go quickly and employ words of imagery, it's necessary and sufficient to be the phallus. At this stage, many things come to a halt and in a certain sense become fixed. Depending on the more or less satisfactory way the message at M is realized, a number of disturbances and perturbations can be established, including the identifications I have been calling perverse.

Second moment. I told you that on the imaginary plane the father definitely intervenes as the depriver of the mother, which means that the demand addressed to the Other, provided it's relayed as it should be, is referred to a higher court, if I may express myself in these terms.

What the subject effectively questions the Other about, provided he traverses it completely, will always encounter in the Other, in some ways, the Other of the Other, that is, its own law. At this level, what occurs is what brings it about that what comes back to the child is purely and simply the law of the father, insofar as the subject imaginarily construes it as depriving the mother. This is the nodal and negative face, as it were, by which what detaches the subject from his identification at the same time reattaches him to the initial appearance of the law in the form of the fact that the mother is dependent upon an object that is no longer simply the object of her desire, but an object that the Other either has or does not have.

The close connection between the mother's deferral to a law that is not hers but an Other's and the fact that the object of her desire is in reality sovereignly possessed by this same Other to whose law she defers provides the key to the Oedipal relation. What gives it its decisive character is to be identified as a relation, not to the father, but to the father's speech.

Recall little Hans from last year. The father is as nice as can be, he is as present as can be, he is as intelligent and as friendly towards little Hans as can be. He does not seem to have been an idiot at all. He took little Hans to Freud, which at the time really was proof of an enlightened mind, and yet he is nevertheless totally inoperative, insofar as what he says is exactly as if he were whistling in the dark – I mean as far as the mother is concerned. This is perfectly clear, whatever the relations were between the two parental characters.

Observe that the mother is in an equivocal position in relation to little Hans. She prohibits, she plays the castrating role that one might see attributed to the father on the real plane and says to him, 'Don't touch it, it's disgusting' – which does not prevent her, on the

193

practical level, from admitting him into her intimacy, and not only allowing him to retain the function of her imaginary object, but encouraging him to do it. He effectively renders her the greatest of services, he well and truly incarnates her phallus for her, and thus finds himself maintained in the position of 'subject-to'. He is 'subjected to', and that's the whole source of his anxiety and his phobia.

This is a problem to the extent that the father's position is called into question by the fact that his speech does not lay down the law to the mother. But that's not all – it seems that in the case of little Hans what should occur at the third moment fails to. That's why I emphasized last year that the outcome of the Oedipus complex in the case of little Hans was skewed. Although, thanks to his phobia, he came through it, his love life will remain completely marked by this imaginary style the repercussions of which I showed you in the case of Leonardo de Vinci.

The third stage is as important as the second, for the outcome of the Oedipus complex depends on it. The father testified that he was giving the phallus insofar as, and only insofar as, he is the bearer, or the *supporter*, if I may put it like that, of the law. Whether the maternal subject possesses this phallus or not depends on him. Now that the stage of the second moment has been traversed, it's necessary, at the third moment, that the father deliver what he has promised. He can give or he can refuse to give, insofar as he has the phallus, but he must give proof that he has it. It's insofar as he intervenes at the third moment as the one who has, and not who is, the phallus that the shift can occur that restores the instance of the phallus as the mother's desired object and no longer only as an object of which the father can deprive one.

It's the all-powerful father who is the depriver. That's the second moment. It's at this phase that the analyses of the Oedipus complex ceased at the time it was thought that all the ravages of the complex depended upon the father's omnipotence. One was only thinking of this second moment, except that no one emphasized that the castration that is in operation here is the privation of the mother and not the child.

The third moment is this – the father is able to give the mother what she desires and can give it to her because he has it. Here, then, the fact of potency in the genital sense of the word intervenes – let's say that the father is a potent father. By dint of this fact, the mother's relationship to the father moves back onto the real plane.

The identification with the paternal instance that may occur has, therefore, been achieved here in these three moments.

First, the paternal instance is introduced in a veiled, or not yet apparent, form. This does not prevent the father from existing in mundane reality, I mean in the world, by virtue of the fact that the law of the symbol reigns therein. By virtue of this fact, the question of the phallus is already posed somewhere in the mother, which is where the child has to locate it.

Second, the father affirms himself in his privative presence, insofar as he is the one who supports the law, and this no longer happens in a veiled manner but in a manner mediated by the mother, who accords him the place of the one who lays down the law to her.

Third, the father is revealed as having it. This is the exit from the Oedipus complex. The exit is favourable insofar as the identification with the father occurs at this third moment, where he intervenes as the one who has it. This identification is called 'the ego-ideal'. It's inscribed on the symbolic triangle at the pole where the child is located, insofar as it's at the maternal pole that everything that will subsequently become reality starts to form, whereas it's at the level of the father that everything that will subsequently become the superego starts to form.

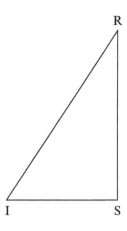

At the third moment, then, the father intervenes as real and potent. This moment succeeds the privation, or castration, that bears upon the mother, the imagined mother, in her own imaginary position of dependency at the level of the subject. It's insofar as the father intervenes as the one who has it that he is internalized in the subject as ego-ideal, and that, henceforth, let's not forget, the Oedipus complex declines.

What does that mean? It doesn't mean that the child is going to enter into possession of all his sexual powers and deploy them, as you well know. On the contrary, he does not deploy them at all, and one could say that he is apparently disappointed by the deployment of the functions that had begun to awaken. Nevertheless, if what Freud formulated makes any sense, the child has all the titles in his pocket for later use. The paternal metaphor plays a role here, which is precisely the role we would expect from a metaphor – it results in the institution of something which is of the order of signifiers, which is there in reserve and whose signification will develop later. The child has all the entitlements for being a man, and what may be challenged in him later, at the time of puberty, is to be referred to something that has not entirely fulfilled the metaphorical identification with the image of the father, insofar as it has formed across these three moments.

I point out to you that this means that, insofar as he is virile, a man is always more or less his own metaphor. This is even what places this touch of ridicule, which should be mentioned all the same, upon the term 'virility'.

I should also point out that the outcome of the Oedipus complex is, as everyone knows, different for the woman. For her, in effect, this third stage, as Freud emphasizes – read his article on the decline of the Oedipus complex – is much simpler. She does not have to carry out this identification nor retain this title to virility. She knows where it is, and she knows where she has to go to get it. It's on the side of the father and she goes to him as having it.

This is also indicative of the respect in which femininity, true femininity, always has a bit of a dimension of escape. True women always have something a little lost about them.

I only make this suggestion so as to stress the concrete dimension of this development.

Today, this is still only a diagram, as you will be well aware. We will return to each of these three stages, and we will see what we can add to them. I will conclude by justifying my term 'metaphor'.

Note that what is at stake here is, at the most fundamental level, exactly the same thing as the long metaphor common in the field of mania. Effectively, the formula that I have given you of metaphor means nothing but this – that there are two chains, the Ss of the upper level, which are signifiers, while underneath one finds all the wandering signifieds that are circulating because they are always sliding around. The pinning down I have spoken about, the quilting point, is only a mythical affair, for nobody has ever managed to pin a signification to a signifier. On the other hand, what one can do, is pin one signifier to another signifier and see what happens. In this case, something new is always produced, which is sometimes as unexpected as a chemical reaction – namely, a new signification emerges.

196

The father is the signifier in the Other that represents the existence of the locus of the signifying chain as law. He places himself, if I may say so, above the signifying chain.

$$\frac{\mathrm{S}}{\mathrm{S\ S\ S\ S\ S}}$$
$$\overline{}$$
$$\textit{S\ \ S\ \ S\ \ S\ \ S}$$

The father is in a metaphorical position inasmuch as, and solely to the extent that, the mother makes him the one who, by his presence, sanctions the existence as such of the locus of the law. Immense latitude is therefore left to the modes and means by which this can be realized, and this is why it is compatible with diverse concrete configurations.

On account of this, the third moment of the Oedipus complex can be gone through, which is the stage of identification at which, for the boy, it's a question of identifying with the father as possessor of the penis and, for the girl, of recognizing the man as the one who possesses it.

We will continue this next time.

22 January 1958

THE THREE MOMENTS OF THE OEDIPUS COMPLEX (II)

Desire for desire
The metonymic phallus
La Châtre's beautiful letter
'Inject' and 'adject'
Male homosexuality in the clinical field

I've been talking about the paternal metaphor. I hope you have noticed that I am talking about the castration complex. It's not because I am talking about the paternal metaphor that I am talking about the Oedipus complex. If my remarks were centred on the Oedipus complex, that would introduce an enormous number of questions, and I can't say everything at once.

The schema I brought you last time brings together what I have tried to get you to understand under the heading of the three moments of the Oedipus complex. What is at stake, I stress this for you at every moment, is a structure that is formed somewhere else than in the subject's own experiences and into which he has to insert himself. Other people may take an interest in this on a number of counts. Let the psychologists who project individual relations in the interhuman, interpsychological or social field into the tensions within groups attempt to inscribe that on this schema, if they can. Likewise, sociologists will have to take into account the structural relations that make up our common measure, for the simple reason that it is the ultimate basis and that the very existence of the Oedipus complex cannot be justified socially – I mean, cannot be founded on any social teleology. As for us, we find ourselves in the position of having to see how a subject is introduced into the relation that is the Oedipus complex.

It wasn't I who discovered that he is not introduced into it without a leading role being played by the male sexual organ. The latter is the centre, the pivot and the object of everything that refers to this order of events – quite confused and very poorly discerned events, it has to be said – that one calls the castration complex. Everyone continues to refer to it just as much, in terms that, surprisingly, don't produce greater dissatisfaction amongst the public.

As for me, in this sort of psychoanalytic diatribe that I am engaged in here, I am trying to give you a letter that will not cloud over. I mean that I am trying to use concepts to differentiate the various levels that are involved in the castration complex.

It has come into play both at the level of a perversion that I would describe as primary, on the imaginary plane, and at that of a perversion that we will perhaps talk a bit more about today, and which is intimately bound up with the end of the Oedipus complex, namely, homosexuality.

To try to show this clearly, I will return, since it's fairly new, to the way I formulated the Oedipus complex for you last time, focusing on the phenomenon linked to the particular function as object that the male sexual organ plays therein. Once I have gone back over this ground and clarified it, I will show you, as I told you, that this throws light on the familiar but poorly situated phenomena of homosexuality.

1

On the schemas I've been giving you, which are extracted from the heart of our experience, I am trying to create a number of moments. They are not necessarily chronological moments, but that doesn't matter, since logical moments also can only unfold in a particular sequence.

You have therefore, in a first moment, as I have told you, the child's relation, not, as people say, with the mother, but with the mother's desire. It's a desire for a desire. I have become aware that this is not such a common formulation, and that some of you have been having a bit of trouble getting used to the notion that desiring something is different from desiring a subject's desire. What needs to be understood is that this desiring a desire implies that one is dealing with the primordial object, which is the mother, and that she has been constituted in such a way that her desire can be desired by another desire, namely, the child's.

Where do we put the dialectic of this first stage? The child is particularly isolated and bereft of everything but the desire for this Other whom he has already constituted as the Other capable of being present or absent. Let's try to get a good grip on what the child's relation is with what is at issue, namely the object of the mother's desire. What has to be traversed is this D, namely the mother's desire, the desire that is desired by the child, D (D). The question is knowing how he is going to be able to reach this object when the latter is constituted in an infinitely more elaborate way at the level of the mother who is a bit more advanced in existence than the child.

199

I have suggested that this object is the phallus as the pivot of the entire subjective dialectic. It is the phallus insofar as it is desired by the mother. From the point of view of structure, there are several different states in the mother's relationship to the phallus. It plays a primordial role in the subjective structuring of the mother and it can be in different states as an object – it is even what makes what comes next so complicated. But for the moment, we will limit ourselves to taking it as it is, because we think we are only able to introduce order and a correct perspective on everything that is an analytic phenomenon by starting out from the structure and circulation of signifiers. If our reference points are always stable and certain, it's because they are structural and because they are linked to the pathways of signifying constructions. This is what we use to guide ourselves, and it's why we don't otherwise have to be particularly worried here about what the phallus is for an actual mother in a specific case. No doubt there are distinctions to be made here. We'll come back to this.

If we simply place our trust in our customary little schema, the phallus is located here, and it is a metonymic object.

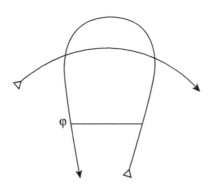

We can settle for situating it amongst signifiers here – it is a metonymic object. Because of the existence of the signifying chain, it will in any case circulate, like the ferret, everywhere amongst the signifieds – being, amongst the signifieds, what results from the existence of signifiers. Our experience shows us that this signified plays a major role for the subject – that of universal object.

That's the surprising thing. It's what creates a scandal for those who would like the situation concerning the sexual object to be symmetrical for both sexes. Just as the man has to discover the use of his implement and then adapt to a series of experiences, it should be the same for the woman, namely that the *cunnus* be at the centre of her entire dialectic. This is not at all the case, and it's precisely what analysis has discovered. This is the best ratification of the fact that there is a field that is the field of analysis, which isn't that of a more or less vigorous instinctual development that on the whole is superimposed on anatomy, that is, on the real existence of individuals.

How are we to understand the fact that the child who has the desire to be the object of the mother's desire arrives at satisfaction? He has no other means, of course, than to come to the place of the object of her desire.

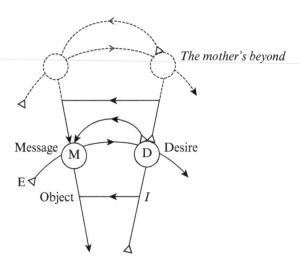

The mother's beyond

Message — M   D — Desire

E

Object — I

What does this mean? Here, the child is at E. We have already had to represent him many times through the relationship between his demand and the existence of articulation of signifiers as such, which is not only in him but also encountered by him.

At the place marked *I*, there is not yet anything, at least not in principle. The subject's constitution as the *I* of discourse is not at all necessarily differentiated yet, even though it is already implied from the first modulation of signifiers. The *I* doesn't need to be designated as such in discourse for it to be its support. In an interjection, in a command, 'Come here!', or in an appeal, 'You!', there is an *I*, but it is latent. We could express this by putting a dotted line between D and *I*. Similarly, the metonymic object, opposite, hasn't yet been constituted for the child.

The expected desire of the mother comes here at D. What results when the child's appeal encounters the mother's existence as Other, namely, a message, is placed opposite. What does it take for the child to successfully become the object of the mother's desire, which we can characterize, already at this level, as what is immediately within its grasp?

Let me begin by drawing what lies beyond the mother as a dotted line – but for a different reason, because this one is completely inaccessible to him.

It is necessary and sufficient that the *I* that is latent in the child's discourse comes to be constituted here, at D, at the level of this Other that is the mother, that the *I* of the mother becomes the child's Other, and that what circulates at the level of the mother at D, insofar as she herself expresses the object of her desire, arrives at M where it fulfils its function as a message for the child – which ultimately implies that the latter momentarily renounces absolutely everything that is his in his own speech. But this isn't difficult for him to do, because at that time his own speech is still being formed. The child therefore receives, at M, the completely raw message about the mother's desire, whereas underneath, at the metonymic level in relation to what the mother says, his identification with her object occurs.

This is highly theoretical, but if you don't grasp it at the outset, it's impossible to conceptualize what has to happen next, which is the entry of the mother's beyond constituted by its relationship to another discourse, that of the father.

Therefore, it is insofar as the child first adopts the mother's desire – and he only adopts it in such a way that the reality of this discourse has something raw about it – that he is open to being in the place of the metonymy of the mother, that is, to becoming what the other day I called her 'subject-to'.

You have seen on what displacement primitive identification, as we will call it in this case, is founded. It consists in an exchange that brings the *I* of the subject to the place of the mother qua Other, except that the *I* of the mother becomes his own Other. That's what is expressed by this new rung on the little ladder of our schema, which has just been introduced at this second moment.

This second moment revolves around the moment when the father makes his presence felt as the prohibitor. He appears as mediated in the mother's discourse. Earlier, at the first stage of the Oedipus complex, the mother's discourse was grasped in its raw state. Saying now that the father's discourse is mediated doesn't mean we are bringing what the mother makes of the father's words back into play, but that the father's words effectively intervene in the mother's discourse. It therefore now appears less veiled than it did at the first stage, but it isn't completely revealed. That is what this use of the term 'mediated' corresponds to on this occasion.

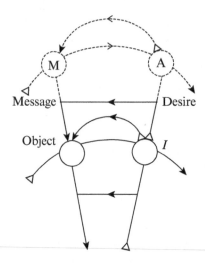

At this stage, the father intervenes by way of a message for the mother. He speaks at **M**, and what he declares is a prohibition, a 'not', transmitted at the level at which the child receives the expected message from the mother. This 'not' is a message about a message. It's a particular form of a message about a message – which, to my great surprise, linguists do not differentiate as such, and one thereby sees the importance of working with them – namely, the message of prohibition.

This message isn't simply the 'You will not sleep with your mother' already addressed to the child at this period. It is a 'You will not reintegrate your own product' addressed to the mother. Thus, all well-known forms of what is called the maternal instinct encounter an obstacle here. In fact, the primitive form of the mater-nal instinct, as everyone knows, manifests itself – in certain animals perhaps even more than in humans – by the oral reintegration, as we elegantly say, of what has come out the other end.

This prohibition arrives as such at **A**, where the father appears as the Other. As a result, the child is profoundly called into ques-tion and disturbed in his position as the subject-to – a potentiality or virtuality that is ultimately salutary. In other words, it is insofar as the object of the mother's desire is affected by the paternal pro-hibition that the circle doesn't completely close up on the child and that he doesn't purely and simply become the object of the mother's desire. The process could have stopped at the first stage, given that the child's relationship to the mother implicitly comprises three

203

elements, since it isn't her that he desires, but her desire. This is already a symbolic relationship, one that, for the subject, facilitates an initial closure of the desire for a desire and an initial success – the discovery of the object of the mother's desire. Nevertheless, everything is called back into question by the paternal prohibition, which leaves the child at a loss as to locating the desire for the mother's desire.

This second stage is a little less loaded with potentialities than the first. It is palpable or perceptible, but essentially instantaneous, as it were, or at least transitory. It is no less crucial, for it is ultimately this one that is the kernel of what can be called the privative moment of the Oedipus complex. It is insofar as the child is driven out, and for his greatest good, of this ideal position that he and the mother could be happy with, and in which he fulfils the function of being her metonymic object, that the third relation is able to be established, the following stage, which is a fruitful one. Indeed, he becomes something else there, for it includes this identification with the father that I was telling you about last time as well as the virtual title to having what the father has.

If last time I gave a quick outline of the three moments of the Oedipus complex, it was so I wouldn't have to go through it all again today, or, more exactly, it was so as to have time today to go back over it point by point.

2

Let's pause here for a moment to make place for what is almost a parenthesis, important nevertheless, concerning psychosis.

It is extremely important to consider the manner in which the father intervenes at this moment in the dialectic of the Oedipus complex. You will see this more clearly in the article that I have given for the next issue of the review *La Psychanalyse*, which presents an overview of what I said the year in which we spoke about the Freudian structures of psychosis. The level of publication that this represents did not allow me to give the foregoing schema, which would have required far too much explication, but when you've read this article, before too long I hope, you will be able to return in your notes to what I am now going to tell you.

In psychosis, the Name-of-the-Father, the father as symbolic function, the father at the level of what happens here between message and code, and code and message, is *verworfen*. As a result, what I have represented by the dotted lines, namely, that by means of which the father intervenes as law, is not there. There is the raw intervention of the message 'not' upon the mother's message to the child. This message, insofar as it is completely raw, is also the source of the code that lies beyond the mother. This is perfectly clear on this schema of the conduction of signifiers.

Referring to the case of President Schreber, because he has been called upon, at an essential vital detour, to bring the Name-of-the-Father to respond from its place, which is where it is incapable of responding from because it has never come to that place, he sees this structure appear in its place. This structure is brought about by the massive, real intervention of the father beyond the mother, insofar as she is absolutely not backed up by him as protector of the law. As a result, at the major, fertile point of his psychosis, what does President Schreber hear? Very precisely, two fundamental types of hallucination that are never identified as such in the classic manuals.

To understand something about hallucinations, it is better to read the exceptional work of a psychotic like President Schreber than to read the best psychiatric authors who have explored the problem of hallucination with the famous 'scholar's ladder' they learnt in their philosophy classes at school all ready in their pocket – sensation, perception, perception without an object and other rubbish.

President Schreber himself differentiates two orders of things very well.

First, there are the voices that speak in the fundamental language, a characteristic of which is to teach its code to the subject via this very speech. The messages that he receives in the fundamental language, which are composed of words which, whether neologisms or not, are always neologisms in their own way, consist in teaching the subject what they are in a new code, one that literally repeats a new world to him, a signifying universe. In other words, the first series of hallucinations consists of messages on a neo-code which presents itself as coming from the Other. It is what is the most terrifyingly hallucinatory.

On the other hand, there is another form of message, the interrupted message. You remember these little bits of sentences – 'He must namely . . .', 'Now I want . . .' and so on. They are the beginnings of orders and, in certain cases, even of veritable principles – 'Finish what you have started', and so on. In short, these messages present themselves as pure messages, as orders, or as interrupted orders, as pure forces of induction in the subject, and they are perfectly localizable on the two sides, message and code, insofar as they are dissociated.

205   That's what the intervention of the father's discourse resolves into, when what makes discourse coherent – namely, the self-ratification by which the father, at the completion of his discourse,

goes back over it and ratifies it as law – is abolished from the start and has never been integrated into the life of the subject.

Let's now move on to the following stage of the Oedipus complex, which, under normal conditions, assumes that the father enters into play, as we said last time, insofar as he has it. He intervenes at this level to give what is involved in phallic privation – a central term in the evolution of the Oedipus complex and its three moments. He effectively appears in the act of giving. It is no longer in the comings and goings of the mother that he is present and therefore still half-veiled, but he appears in his own discourse. In some ways, the father's message becomes the mother's message insofar as he now permits and authorizes. My schema from last time means nothing other than this, that the father's message, insofar as it is incarnated as such, is capable of producing this new rung on the schema – so much so that the subject is able to receive from the father's message what he had attempted to receive from the mother's message. Through the intervention of the gift or the permission accorded to the mother, he is finally given permission to have a penis for later. There you have what is effectively brought about by the phase of the decline of the Oedipus complex – he really does have, as I was saying last time, the title in his pocket.

To evoke a historical and amusing citation – a woman whose husband wanted to be sure that she was faithful to him had certified to him in writing that she was faithful to him, following which she went about the world declaring, 'Ah! What a beautiful letter La Châtre has!' Well then, this La Châtre and our little castrated one are of the same order. They both have, at the end of the Oedipus complex, this beautiful letter that is not nothing, since they can rely upon the fact that in the best of cases they can calmly assume that they will have a penis – in other words, that he is someone identical to his father.

But this is a stage in which you can clearly see that the two sides are always liable to switch. There is something abstract and yet dialectical in the relationship between the two moments I have just been speaking about, the one where the father intervenes as prohibiting and depriving, and the one where he intervenes as permissive and gift-giving – gift-giving at the level of the mother. Other things may happen, and to see this, we must now place ourselves at the level of the mother and once again pose the question of the paradox represented by the central character of the phallic object as imaginary.

The mother is a woman who, we suppose, has arrived at the fullness of her capacities of feminine voracity, and the objection that is made to the imaginary function of the phallus is completely valid. If this is what the mother is, then the phallus isn't purely and simply

206

that, this beautiful imaginary object, for she gobbled that up some time ago. In other words, the phallus at the level of the mother isn't uniquely an imaginary object. It is also perfectly well something that fulfils its function at the instinctual level, as a normal implement of the instinct. It is the 'inject', if I can put it like that – a word which doesn't simply mean that she introduces it into herself, but that one introduces it into her. This 'in' equally signals its instinctual function.

It is because man has to traverse an entire forest of signifiers if he is to reunite with his instinctively valuable and primitive objects that we are dealing with the entire dialectic of the Oedipus complex. This doesn't prevent him from succeeding at it from time to time, nevertheless, thank goodness, otherwise things would have become extinct a long time ago through lack of combatants, given the excessive difficulty of attaining the real object.

That is one of the possibilities on the mother's side. There are others, and we would need to try to find out what her relationship to the phallus means for her, insofar as it is dear to her heart, as it is for every human subject. We can for example differentiate, along with the function of the inject, that of the 'adject'. This term designates the imaginary appurtenance of something which, at the imaginary level, is either given to her or not given to her, which she has permission to desire as such, and which she lacks. The phallus intervenes, then, as lack, as the object of which she has been deprived, like the object of this *Penisneid*, this privation that is always felt and whose incidence we are familiar with in female psychology. But it can also intervene as an object which has been given to her nevertheless, but from where it is it enters into consideration in a very symbolic manner. This is a different function, that of the adject, even though it can be confused with that of the primitive inject.

In short, while she has all the difficulties entailed by the fact of having to introduce herself into the dialectic of symbols if she is to succeed in integrating herself into the human family, a woman also has every kind of access to something primitive and instinctual that puts her in a direct relationship with the object, no longer of her desire, but of her need.

Having clarified this, let's now talk about homosexuals.

3

People talk about homosexuals. We treat homosexuals. We don't cure homosexuals. And what is most incredible is that we do not cure them despite the fact that they are absolutely curable.

If there is anything that emerges in the clearest of fashions from observations, it's that masculine homosexuality – the other one is too, but we are going to limit ourselves today to the male for reasons of clarity – is an inversion concerning the object, which is structured at the level of a full and completed Oedipus complex. More exactly, even as a homosexual realizes this third stage that we have just been talking about, he modifies it appreciably. You will say to me, 'We know this already, they realize the Oedipus complex in an inverted form.' If that is sufficient for you, you can stay with that, I am not forcing you to follow me. But I consider that we have the right to be more demanding than to say, 'Why is the moon made of blue cheese? Well, it's because of an inverted Oedipus complex.'

What we have to seek in the very structure of what is shown by clinical experience regarding homosexuals is whether we are able to understand any better at what precise point the completion of the Oedipus complex is located. One has to consider, in the first instance, his position with all its characteristics and, second, his extreme adherence to the said position. The homosexual, effectively, should you so much as offer him the ways and means, adheres to his homosexual position strongly, and his relationships with feminine objects, far from being abolished, are on the contrary profoundly structured.

I think that only this way of schematizing the problem enables us to point out where the difficulty of shaking his position stems from, and, much more, why once this position has been flushed out, analysis generally fails. This isn't because of any impossibility internal to this position, but is due to the fact that all sorts of conditions are required, and that it is necessary to wend our way through the detours by which his position has become precious and primordial to him.

There are a number of traits that we can note in the homosexual – and, first, a profound and perpetual relationship to the mother. The mother is presented to us, according to the average case, as having a directive and eminent function in the parental couple, and as being more occupied with the child than with the father. It is also said, and this is already another matter, that she has been occupied with the child in a very castrating manner, and that in raising him she has taken great care, been very meticulous and lingered to excess. No one seems to doubt whether all this leads us in the same direction. We have to add some little supplementary links to get to the point of thinking that the effect of such a castrating intervention would have an effect of overvaluation of the object for the child, in the general form in which it presents itself in homosexuals, such that no partner capable of interesting him can be deprived of it.

I don't want to keep you waiting, nor do I want to give the impression of creating new riddles. I believe that the key to the

208

problem concerning homosexuals is this – if homosexuals, in all their nuances, grant a prevailing value to the blessed object to the point of making it an absolute requirement of the sexual partner, it's insofar as, in one form or another, the mother lays down the law to the father, in the sense in which I have taught you to describe him.

I told you that the father intervenes in the Oedipal dialectic of desire insofar as he lays down the law to the mother. Here, what is at stake, and which can don diverse forms, always comes down to this – it's the mother who turns out to have laid down the law to the father at a decisive moment. This means very precisely that, at the time at which the prohibiting intervention of the father should have introduced the subject to the phase of the dissolution of his relationship to the object of the mother's desire, and cut off at the root all possibility for him to identify himself with the phallus, the subject discovers, on the contrary, in the structure of the mother, the support and the reinforcement which prevents this crisis from taking place. At the ideal moment, at the dialectical time at which the mother should be grasped as deprived of the adject in such a way that the subject is literally at his wit's end over her, he finds therein, on the contrary, his security. That holds up perfectly well by virtue of the fact that he feels it is the mother who holds the key to the situation and that she won't let herself be either deprived or dispossessed of it. In other words, the father can say whatever he wants, they are completely indifferent to it.

This doesn't mean, then, that the father has not come into play. Freud said a long time ago – I ask you to refer to the *Three Essays on Sexuality* – that it isn't rare – and he isn't expressing himself idly, he isn't saying 'it isn't rare' out of vagueness, it's because he has seen it frequently – for an inversion to be determined by the *Wegfall*, the failure, of an excessively prohibitive father. There are two moments in this – namely, prohibition, but also that this prohibition has failed. In other words, in the end it is the mother who lays down the law.

This also explains to you why, in quite different cases, if the mark of the prohibitive father is broken, the result is exactly the same. In particular, in cases in which the father loves the mother too much, where, through his love, he appears too dependent on the mother, the result is exactly the same.

I am not in the process of telling you that the result is always the same, but that it is the same in certain cases. The fact that the father loves the mother too much may have another outcome than homosexuality. I am not at all taking refuge in constitution, I am only pointing out in passing that there are differences to be acknowledged and that it is possible to observe for example an obsessional neurosis type of effect, as we will see on another occasion. For the moment, I am simply emphasizing that different causes can have a common effect, namely that in cases in which the father is too much in love with the mother, he finds himself in fact in the same position as one to whom the mother lays down the law.

There are still other cases – the interest of this perspective is that it brings together different cases – in which the father, as the subject will testify to you, has always remained a person very much at a distance, his messages only arriving via the intermediary of the mother. But analysis shows that in reality he is far from being absent. In particular, behind the tense relationship with the mother – very often marked by all sorts of accusations, complaints and manifestations of aggressiveness, as they say – which constitutes the text of the analysis of a homosexual, the presence is revealed of the father as a rival, not at all in the sense of the inverted Oedipus complex, but in the sense of the normal Oedipus complex, and revealed in the clearest of fashions. In this case, one makes do with the remark that the aggressiveness against the father has been transferred onto the mother, which isn't very clear but at least it has the advantage of sticking to the facts. What one needs to know is why this is how it is.

This is how it is because the child has found his solution in the critical position in which the father was effectively a threat to him – a solution that consists in the identification represented by the homology of these two triangles.

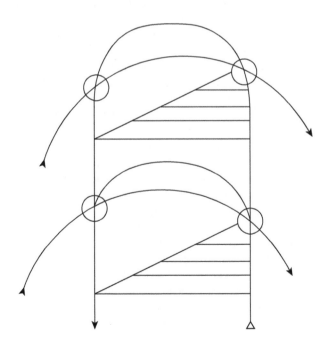

The child has considered that the best way to cope is to identify with the mother, because the mother has not let herself be shaken. It is therefore in the position of the mother, thus defined, that he finds himself.

On the one hand, when he gets involved with a partner who is a substitute for the paternal figure, it is a matter for him, as it frequently appears in the fantasies and dreams of homosexuals, of disarming him, even checkmating him, in a manner that is completely clear in certain cases, and rendering the person who is the substitute for the father incapable of being valued by a woman or women.

On the other hand, the homosexual's requirement of encountering the penile organ in his partner corresponds precisely to this, which is that in the primitive position, the one that the mother who lays down the law to the father occupies, what is called into question – not resolved but called into question – is whether, truly, the father has one or doesn't have one. And this is very exactly what is demanded by the homosexual well before anything else, and in a way that prevails over everything else. Afterwards, we will see what one does with it, but it is a question above all of showing that he has one.

I would go even further, to the point of indicating to you here what the value of the dependence that is represented by the father's excessive love for the mother consists in. You remember, I hope, the formula that I chose for you, namely, that to love is always to give what one doesn't have, and not to give what one has. I shall not come back to the reasons why I gave it to you, but be convinced by it and take it like a key formula, like a little ramp which, with the touch of a hand, will take you to the right floor even if you don't understand anything about it, and it's much better if you don't understand anything about it. To love is to give to someone who has or doesn't have what is in question, but it is certainly to give what one doesn't have. To give, on the other hand, is also to give, but it is to give what one has. There's a world of difference.

In any case, insofar as the father truly shows himself to be in love where the mother is concerned, he is suspected of not having it, and this is the angle from which the mechanism comes into play. I point out to you in this respect that these truths are never completely obscure, nor are they unknown – when they are not articulated, one has an intuition about them at the very least. I don't know if you have observed that this burning issue is never explored by analysts, even though it is at least as interesting to know whether the father loves the mother as it is to know whether the mother loves the father. One always raises the question in that direction – the child had a castrating phallic mother and whatever else you can think of, she had an authoritarian attitude towards the father, a lack of love, of respect for him, and so on – but it is very curious to see that we never emphasize the father's relationship to the mother. We don't very well know how to think about it, and it doesn't seem to us possible, all things considered, to say anything very normative about it. Thus, we carefully leave this aspect of the problem to one side, at least till today, and I will very probably have to return to this.

Another consequence. There is also something that comes up very frequently, and it is not the least of the paradoxes of the analysis of homosexuals. At first sight, it seems very paradoxical in relation to the demand for a penis in the partner that they are terrified of seeing the organ of a woman, because, or so we are told, that suggests the idea of castration to them. It's perhaps true, but not in the way you think, because what it is about the organ of a woman that stops them is precisely that, in many cases, it is presumed to have ingested the phallus of the father, and that what is dreaded in penetration is precisely an encounter with this phallus.

Dreams – I will quote some for you – well recorded in the literature, and which also occur in my practice, make it apparent in the clearest of manners that what sometimes emerges in a possible encounter with a woman's vagina is a phallus that develops as such and represents something insurmountable, before which not only is the subject brought to a stop but he is invaded by all sorts of fears. This gives a completely different meaning to the danger of the vagina from the one that one thought necessary to put under the heading of *vagina dentata*, which also exists. It is the feared vagina insofar as it contains the hostile phallus, the paternal phallus, the phallus that is both fantasmatic and absorbed by the mother, and whose real power she holds in the feminine organ.

This is an adequate formulation of all the complexity of the homosexual's relationships. It's a stable situation, and not at all a dual one, a fully secure situation, a situation with three legs. It's precisely because it is only ever envisaged from the aspect of a dual relation, and because one never enters into the labyrinth of the homosexual's positions, that, through the fault of the analyst, the situation never comes to be completely clarified.

Even though the situation has the closest of relations with the mother, it only has its importance in relation to the father. What ought to be the message of the law is quite the contrary, and, whether ingested or not, it ends up in the mother's hands. The mother holds the key, but in a manner that is much more complex than the one implied by the global and massive notion that she is the mother equipped with a phallus. If a homosexual turns out to have identified with her, it isn't at all insofar as she has or doesn't have the adject, purely and simply, but insofar as she holds the key to the particular situation that prevails at the exit of the Oedipus complex, where judgement is passed as to which of the two ultimately holds the power. Not just any power, but very precisely the power of love, and insofar as the complex bonds of the construction of the Oedipus complex, as they have been presented to you here, allow you to understand how the relationship to the power of the law metaphorically reverberates through the relationship to the phallus as fantasmatic object, insofar as it is the object with which the subject must identify at a particular moment.

I will continue next time with a little side commentary on what have been called states of phallic passivity – the term is Löwenstein's – to account for certain disturbances to sexual potency. It fits in here too naturally for me not to do it. Then I will show you how, across the different avatars of this same object, from its origins – namely its function as the mother's imaginary object – through to the moment where it is taken on by the subject, we can outline the general and definitive classification of the different forms in which it intervenes. That's what we will do next week.

The time after that, after which I will leave you for three weeks, we will conclude on the subject's relationship to the phallus in a way that may perhaps interest you less directly, but which I hold to dearly.

Effectively, last trimester I concluded with what I brought for you concerning comedy. When I said that the essence of comedy was when the subject takes the whole dialectical matter in hand and says, 'After all, this entire dramatic affair, tragedy, the conflicts between father and mother – none of that has the same value as love, and now let's amuse ourselves, let's begin the orgy, let's bring all these conflicts to a close, all of that is made for man', it wasn't very well taken. I was quite astonished to have surprised, even scandalized, some people. I am going to let you in on a secret – it's in Hegel.

By contrast, I will bring something new to this topic, something that seems much more demonstrative to me than anything it has ever been possible to formulate on the various phenomena of the mind. The fact is that by taking this path one rediscovers a surprising confirmation of what I am claiming, namely, the crucial character for the subject, and for his development, of imaginary identification with the phallus.

I therefore invite you to come back for the last day of this period so that I can show you the extent to which this applies, the extent to which it is demonstrable and how sensational it is – so as to give a key to, a unique term for, and a univocal explanation of, the function of comedy.

20 January 1958

XII

FROM IMAGE TO
SIGNIFIER – IN PLEASURE
AND IN REALITY

The connection between the two principles
Winnicott's paradox
Kleinism's dead-ends
From the *Urbild* to the Ideal
The girl who wants to be whipped

The world is preoccupied with symbolization. An article appeared in the *International Journal* in May–June 1956 under the title 'Symbolism and Its Relationship to the Primary and Secondary Processes', in which Mr Charles Rycroft tries to give symbolism a meaning in the current state of analysis. Those of you who read English would do well to familiarize yourselves with this article, where you will see the difficulties that have always been present concerning the meaning to give in analysis, not only to the word 'symbolism', but to the idea one has of the process of symbolization.

Since 1911 when Mr Jones carried out the first important comprehensive study, the question has gone through various phases, and it has encountered, and still encounters, huge difficulties in what currently constitutes the most developed position on this subject, that is, the one arising from the considerations by Mrs Melanie Klein on the role of symbols in the ego's formation.

The matter at hand has the closest of relationships with what I am currently explaining to you, and I would like you to sense how useful the point of view I am trying to communicate to you is for introducing a little bit of clarity into some obscure directions.

I don't know from what angle I am going to approach it today, for I don't have a plan for how I am going to present things to you. Since this is our third-last session, and since I told you that next time the Seminar would be centred on the phallus and comedy, today I would like simply to pause here and show you several directions

214 in which what I have expounded for you regarding the castration complex makes it possible to raise a number of questions.

I will start by taking theses as they come. It's not always possible to impose a strict order on this subject, above all when, as is the case today, we're at a crossroads.

1

You have just seen the terms 'primary' and 'secondary' process in the title of Rycroft's article, which I have never spoken to you about, to the point where some of you were astonished to come across them some time ago in the context of a vocabulary definition.

The opposition between primary process and secondary process dates from the time of the *Traumdeutung*, and, without being completely identical with this, it covers the contrasting notions of pleasure principle and reality principle. I have alluded to these two terms more than once here, and always in order to get you to observe that the use made of them is incomplete unless one considers them in relation to one another and senses their link and their opposition as being constitutive of the position of each.

I will come straight to the heart of the matter.

When one isolates the notion of pleasure principle as the primary process principle, one ends up where Rycroft does – he thinks that he has to define the primary process, set aside all its structural characteristics and place in the background condensation, displacement and so on, everything that Freud began to enquire into when defining the unconscious so that he can characterize it in terms of what the final formulation of Freudian theory in the *Traumdeutung* contributes. Specifically, he turns it into an originary, original mechanism – whether you understand this as a historical stage or as the underlying ground – on the basis of which something else would develop. It would be a kind of base or psychical depth, or, taking it in the logical sense, an obligatory point of departure for reflection. In response to impulses from the drives, there is, supposedly, always a tendency in the human subject – it obviously cannot be anything else, but the point isn't very clearly defined – towards the hallucinatory satisfaction of desire. This would be a virtual possibility – constitutive, as it were – of the subject's position with respect to the world.

I doubt this will come as a surprise to you, for you find that this reference to a primitive experience on the model of the reflex arc is

215 abundantly expressed by all authors. Even before need corresponds to an impulse internal to the subject, triggering the instinctual cycle, the movement, however uncoordinated, of appetite, then the

searching and the locating in reality, it is satisfied via the pathway of the memory traces of what previously satisfied the desire. This, quite simply, is how satisfaction tends to be reproduced on the hallucinatory plane.

Doesn't this notion which has become almost consubstantial with our analytic conceptions, and which we make use of in an almost implicit manner when we speak about the pleasure principle, seem so excessive as to warrant clarification? Because, in the end, if it's in the nature of the cycle of psychical processes to create their own satisfaction, why don't people satisfy themselves?

Of course, it's because a need continues to insist. Fantasmatic satisfaction is unable to fulfil every need – though we are only too well aware that in the sexual order, in every case without any doubt, it's highly likely to confront a need when it's the need of a drive that is at stake. For hunger, it's a different matter. What is appearing on the horizon is that it's ultimately a question of the quite possibly illusory nature of the sexual object.

This conception of the relationship between a need and its satisfaction does exist and it may effectively be sustainable, at least at one level – that of sexual satisfaction. It has so profoundly impregnated the whole of analytic thought that what has come to the foreground are the primitive or primordial gratifications or satisfactions, and frustrations as well, that are produced at the beginning of the subject's life – that is, in the subject's relations with its mother. Psychoanalysis has thus, on the whole, entered more deeply into a dialectic of need and its satisfaction the more it has become interested in the early phases of the subject's development. Down this path, one has come to formulations whose character – no less necessary than significant – I would like to point out to you.

From the Kleinian perspective, which is the one I am referring to at the moment, the subject's entire learning, as it were, about reality is primordially prepared and underpinned by the essentially hallucinatory and fantasmatic constitution of its first objects, which are classified into good and bad objects, insofar as they establish an initial primordial relation which, in the subsequent life of the subject, will give the subject the principal types of the relations he will have with reality. We thus arrive at the notion that the subject's world is made up of a fundamentally unreal relationship that the subject has with objects that are merely the reflection of his fundamental drives.

For example, this world of 'phantasy'*, in the way this concept is used in the Kleinian school, is organized, in a series of projections of the subject's needs, around the subject's fundamental aggressiveness. A series of more or less favourable experiences, and it's desirable that they be favourable, intervenes on the surface of this world. In this way, little by little, the world of experience makes possible a certain rational locating of what in these objects is, as one says, objectively definable as corresponding to a certain reality, where the background of unreality remains absolutely fundamental.

Here, we have what one can truly call a psychotic construction of the subject. From this perspective, a normal subject is, in short, a psychosis that has turned out well, a psychosis in harmony with experience. What I am saying to you isn't a reconstruction. The author I am going to speak about now, Mr Winnicott, expresses it exactly so in a text he wrote on the use of regression in analytic therapy. It absolutely affirms, as such, the fundamental homogeneity of psychosis with a normal relationship to the world.

There are huge problems with this approach, even just in managing to formulate it. As phantasy [*fantaisie*] is only the fabric underlying the world of reality, what can the function of phantasy, when it is recognized as such, be in a subject at an adult and completed state and who has successfully constituted his world? This is also the problem that presents itself to any self-respecting Kleinian – that is, to any self-declared Kleinian – and also, one can currently say, to virtually every analyst, insofar as the register in which he inscribes the subject's relationship to the world becomes more and more exclusively one of a process of learning about the world carried out on the basis of a series of more or less successful experiences of frustration.

I invite you to refer to Mr Winnicott's text, which can be found in volume 26 of the *International Journal of Psychoanalysis* under the title 'Primitive Emotional Development'. The author makes an effort to explain the emergence of this world of phantasy insofar as it's consciously lived by the subject and stabilizes his reality, as we necessarily observe in the very text of experience. For those interested, I refer them to a remark by the author the need for which one clearly senses, given how it leads to a very curious paradox.

The emergence of the principle of reality – in other words, the recognition of reality – on the basis of the child's primordial relations with the maternal object, the object of its satisfaction and also of its dissatisfaction, doesn't at all show how the world of phantasy in its adult form can emerge from there – unless it's by way of an artifice that Mr Winnicott becomes aware of, and which no doubt makes possible a coherent enough development in the theory, but at the price of a paradox that I want to get you to see.

217

There is a fundamental discordance between the hallucinatory satisfaction of need and what the mother gives the child. It's within this very discordance that a gap opens up to make it possible for the child to attain its first recognition of the object. This presupposes that, despite appearances, the object turns out to be disappointing. Now, in order to explain how the thing that sums up everything for modern psychoanalysis concerning the world of fantasy and imagination, namely what in English is called wishful thinking,* can arise, he makes the following observation.

Let's suppose that the maternal object turns up at the appointed hour to fulfil a need. As soon as the child begins to act so as to get the breast, the mother gives it to him. Winnicott quite rightly pauses here and raises the following problem – what enables the child, under these conditions, to distinguish between the hallucinatory satisfac tion of his desire and reality? In other words, with this point of departure we necessarily come to the following equation – in the beginning, it's absolutely impossible to distinguish a hallucination from a fulfilled desire. The paradox of this confusion is unavoidably striking.

From the perspective that rigorously characterizes primary process as naturally having to be satisfied in a hallucinatory manner, we arrive at this, which is that the more satisfying reality is, the less it constitutes a test of reality – omnipotent thought in the child is henceforth originally founded on everything that has succeeded in reality.

This conception may be coherent in some way, but do recognize that in itself it presents a paradoxical aspect. The very need to have to resort to such a paradox to explain a pivotal point in the subject's development gives one pause for thought and even makes one question it.

As paradoxical, and blatantly paradoxical, as this conception already is, it inevitably has several consequences, which I already pointed out to you last year when I alluded to this same article by Mr Winnicott. That is, in the rest of his anthropology, it has no other effect than to lead him to classify almost everything that might be called free speculation as part of the same register as the fantasmatic aspects of thought. He completely assimilates everything of the order of speculation, however highly developed it is, namely everything that can be called a conviction – pretty much whatever it might be – whether political, religious or other, to fantasmatic life. That is a point of view that fits in well with British humour, and with a certain attitude of mutual respect, tolerance and also reserve. There is a series of things that one only ever speaks about in inverted commas, or that one doesn't speak about at all, amongst well-brought up people. They are, however, things that do count just a bit, since they form part of the internal discourse that one is far from being able to reduce to wishful thinking*.

But let's not go into the finer details of the matter. I simply want to show you what, in contrast, a different conception can suggest.

218

2

First, is it so clear that one can purely and simply call satisfaction what is produced at the hallucinatory level, and in the different registers in which we can embody the fundamental thesis of the hallucinatory satisfaction of primordial need at the level of the primary process?

I have already introduced the problem several times. We are told, 'Take a look at dreams,' and one always refers to children's dreams. Freud himself shows us the way on this. From the perspective that he was exploring, which was the fundamental nature of desire in dreams, he was effectively led to give us the example of the dream of a child as typical of hallucinatory satisfaction.

From that point on, the door was open. Psychiatrists rushed in – they had for a long time been looking for an idea about their subjects' disturbed relationship to reality in their delusions – by referring them, for example, to structures analogous to those of dreams. The approach I have presented you with here doesn't introduce any essential modifications on this point.

From where we are now, where we can see the difficulties and impasses of a conception in which a purely imaginary relation of the subject to the world is at the origin of the development of his relationship to so-called external reality, it's important to return to the little schema that I never tire of using.

I will return to its simplest form and remind you, even if I should seem to be drumming it in a little, what it's about.

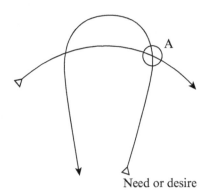

Need or desire

Here one finds something that could be called need, but which I am already calling desire because there is no original or pure state of need. From the outset, need is motivated at the level of desire, that is, at the level of something that is destined in man to have a particular relationship to signifiers. Here, we have this desiring intention crossing what is laid down for the subject as the signifying chain – either the requirements of the signifying chain have already been imposed on his subjectivity, or, from the start, he only ever encounters it in the following form, which is that it's always and already constituted in the mother and that it imposes its requirements and its barrier on him, in the mother. The subject, as you know, initially encounters the signifying chain in the form of the Other, and it arrives at this barrier in the form of a message – whose projection you can see on this schema.

Where is the pleasure principle located on this schema? One may consider it possible, from some angles, to find a primitive manifestation of it in the form of dreams. Take the most primitive of dreams, the most confused, a dog's dream. You can occasionally see a dog's legs moving when he is asleep. He must be dreaming, therefore, and perhaps his desire, too, has a hallucinatory form of satisfaction. Can we conceptualize this? How do we situate it in humans? Here's what I suggest to you so that it exists at least in terms of a possibility in your minds and so that you are aware that in this case it applies in a more satisfying way.

A hallucinatory response to need isn't the emergence of a fantasmatic reality at the conclusion of a circuit initiated by the insistence of a need. At the conclusion of this insistence that started to awaken in the subject, this movement towards something that, effectively, must begin to take shape for him, what appears does not, of course, bear no relationship to the subject's need, does not bear no relationship to an object, but bears a relationship to the object of such a kind that it deserves to be called a signifier. It's effectively something that has a fundamental relationship to the object's absence and already possesses the characteristics of a discrete element, a sign.

If you consult Letter 52 to Fliess, which I have already cited, you will see that when he sets about articulating the birth of unconscious structures, when he begins to formulate a model of the psychical apparatus that makes it possible to explain the primary process, all Freud can do is grant from the outset that the mnesic inscription that hallucinatorily corresponds to the manifestation of need is nothing but a sign, *Zeichen*.

A sign isn't characterized merely by its relationship to an image in the theory of instincts. It's not the sort of lure that is sufficient to awaken need but not fulfil it. It's located in a particular relationship with other signifiers, with for example the signifier that is its direct opposite and signifies its absence. It has a place in a set of already organized signifiers, already structured in a symbolic relationship, insofar as it appears at the intersection of a play of presence and absence, of absence and presence – a game that is itself ordinarily linked to a spoken articulation in which discrete elements that are signifiers are already present.

In fact, the experience we have of the simplest of children's dreams isn't one of simple satisfaction, as when it's a matter of the need of hunger. It's already something that presents itself with the character of excess, as exorbitant. What the little Anna Freud dreams of is precisely what the child has been forbidden, 'cherries, strawberries, raspberries, pudding', everything that has already adopted a properly signifying character through being prohibited. She doesn't dream simply of what corresponds to a need, but of what is present in the mode of a feast, going beyond the limits of the natural object that satisfies a need.

This feature is crucial. You will find it at absolutely every level. It's there, at whatever level you consider what appears to be hallucinatory satisfaction.

Conversely, approaching things from the other end, from the angle of delusions, for a while, before Freud, you might be tempted, for want of anything better, to endeavour to make it too correspond to a kind of desire on the part of the subject. You get there via a number of insights, some oblique flashes like this one, where something may effectively seem to represent the satisfaction of desire. But isn't it obvious that the major phenomenon, the most striking, the most massive and the most invasive of all the phenomena of delusions isn't at all the phenomenon that refers to a reverie of satisfaction of desire, but something as frozen as verbal hallucinations?

People have wondered about the level at which this verbal hallucination is produced, whether there is in the subject something like an internal reflection in the form of a psychomotor hallucination which it's extremely important to observe, or whether there is projection, or something else, and so on. But doesn't it seem from the outset that what dominates in the structuration of this hallucination, and which should serve as the first element of classification, is that it has the structure of signifiers? Hallucinations are phenomena structured at the level of signifiers. One cannot, not even for an instant, think about the organization of these hallucinations without seeing that the first thing to be emphasized in the phenomenon is that it's a phenomenon of signifiers.

Here, then, is something that must always remind us that, while it's true that one can explore the pleasure principle from the angle of the fundamentally unreal satisfaction of desire, what characterizes the hallucinatory satisfaction of desire is that it's formed in the domain of signifiers and that, as such, it implies a locus of the

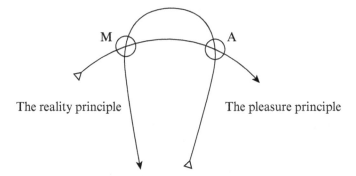

The reality principle   The pleasure principle

Other. This is, moreover, not necessarily an Other. It's a locus of the Other, insofar as it's necessary for the position of the instance of signifiers.

You will notice that on this little schema we see need come into play in that part of the circuit that is external in some way, formed by the part on the [lower] right. Need manifests itself in the form of a sort of tail of the signifying chain, as something that only exists at the limit, and where, however, you will always recognize the feature of pleasure as being attached to it. This is the case every time something reaches this level of the schema.

For a witticism to result in pleasure, it's necessary that what takes place at the level of the Other only comes to an end virtually by tending towards what lies beyond sense, which in itself carries a kind of satisfaction.

If the pleasure principle gets schematized in the external part of the circuit, the reality principle is, likewise, situated in the opposite part. As for the human subject insofar as we have dealings with him in our experience, there is no other possible apprehension or definition of the reality principle, inasmuch as he enters it at the level of the secondary process. How can we neglect, concerning reality, that signifiers effectively enter into play in the human real as an original reality? There is language, it speaks in the world, and by virtue of this fact there is an entire series of things, objects that are signified and that would absolutely not be objects if there were no signifiers in the world.

Introducing the subject into any kind of reality is absolutely unthinkable on the basis of any kind of pure and simple experience, frustration, discordance, shock, burn or whatever else you might think of. There is no bit-by-bit spelling out of an *Umwelt*, explored in an immediate and tentative manner. For animals, instinct comes to the rescue, thank goodness for that. If animals needed to reconstruct the world, life would not be long enough. And so, why wish

222

that man, who has very poorly adapted instincts, somehow fashion an experience of the world with his own hands? The fact that there are signifiers is absolutely essential to it, and the principal means of expression of his experience of reality – it's almost banal, foolish to say this – is surely the voice. The teaching he receives comes to him essentially from the speech of adults.

But the significant margin that Freud achieves over this element of experience is the following – even before language acquisition is elaborated at the motor level, at the auditory level and at the level at which he understands what one tells him, there is already symbolization – from the outset, from the first relations with the object, from the child's first relationship to the maternal object as the primordial, primitive object on whom its subsistence in the world depends. This object has effectively already been introduced as such into the process of symbolization and it plays the role of introducing the signifier's existence into the world – and at a very early stage.

Take note of this – as soon as the child merely starts to be capable of opposing two phonemes to one another, there are already two vocables. And with two, the one who pronounces them and the one to whom they are addressed, that is the object, his mother, you already have four elements, which is enough to contain potentially, within itself, the entire combinatory from which the organization of signifiers will emerge.

3

I am now going to move to a new and different little schema – one that, moreover, I have already started here, and which will show you what the consequences are of what I have been telling you as well as recalling for you what I was trying to get you to see at our last session.

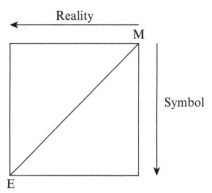

I said that, primordially, we have the child's relationship with the mother. If it's along the E–M axis that one wants the initial relationship with reality to be established, and if one makes the constitution of reality depend uniquely on the relationship of the child's desire with the object insofar as it satisfies him or doesn't satisfy him, then this reality cannot be deduced and can only be reconstructed in experience with the aid of continual sleights of hand.

If it's possible, in very extreme cases, to find something that corresponds to this in a number of cases of childhood psychosis, it's always, ultimately, the so-called depressive phase of the child's development that one is referring to whenever one brings this dialectic into play. But insofar as this dialectic comprises an infinitely more complex development, it's in fact a question of something quite different – the child doesn't simply have a relationship with an object that satisfies him or that doesn't satisfy him, but, owing to this minimum thickness of unreality that the initial symbolization gives, there is already a triangular mapping of the child, namely, a relationship, not with what brings satisfaction to his need, but a relationship with the desire of the maternal subject there with him.

If the child does manage to locate his position, it's solely insofar as the dimension of symbols has already been inaugurated. This dimension is represented here as the axis called the axis of ordinates in mathematical analysis. It's what enables us to conceptualize how the child is to locate himself with reference to two poles. It is, moreover, what Mrs Melanie Klein is searching around for without being able to find the formula for it. It's effectively around a double pole of the mother – which she calls the good mother and the bad mother – that the child begins to take up its position. It's not the object that he situates, it's initially himself that he situates. He is then going to situate himself at all sorts of points along this axis, trying to reach the object of the mother's desire, trying to respond to her desire. That is the essential element, and it might take quite some time.

In truth, no species of dialectic is possible if we only consider the child's relationship with the mother – first because it's impossible to deduce anything from this, but also because it's equally impossible, on the basis of experience, to conceive how the child is in this ambiguous world that Kleinian analysts present us with, in which the only reality is that of the mother. According to them, the child's primitive world is both suspended from this object and entirely autoerotic, in that the child is so closely tied to the maternal object that he literally forms a closed circle with her.

In fact, we all know this, and you only have to see a small, living child – he isn't at all autoerotic. He is interested normally, just like

224

any young animal, and, as he is, when all is said and done, a young animal who is more particularly intelligent than the others, he takes an interest in all sorts of other things there in reality. Obviously, they are not random things. There is one to which we attach a certain importance and which appears at the limit of this reality, on the axis of the abscissa, which here is the axis of reality. This isn't a fantasy, it's a perception.

For Mrs Melanie Klein all is forgiven, for she is a woman of genius, but for her followers, and in particular those trained in matters of psychology, like Susan Isaacs who was a psychologist, it is unforgivable – in the wake of Mrs Melanie Klein, she manages to articulate a theory of perception on which there is no way of distinguishing a perception from an introjection in the analytic sense of the term.

I cannot, in passing, go through all the impasses of the Kleinian system. I am only trying to give you a model that will enable you to articulate what happens more clearly.

What happens at the level of the mirror phase? The mirror phase is a subject's encounter with what is and isn't a reality, strictly speaking, namely a virtual image, which plays a decisive role in a particular crystallization of the subject which I call his *Urbild*. I put it in parallel with the relationship that arises between the child and the mother. This is basically what it's about. The child acquires this point of support for the thing at the limit of reality that appears for him in a perceptual form, but which one can also call an image, in the sense in which an image has the property of being a captivating signal that is singled out in reality and attracts and captures some of the subject's libido, some of its instinct, owing to which a number of reference points, of psychoanalytic points in the world, make it possible for the living being more or less to organize his behaviour.

For the human being, it ultimately seems that this is the sole point that subsists. It plays a role there, as deceptive and illusory. This is where it comes to the aid of an activity which the subject already only engages in insofar as he has to satisfy the Other's desire and, therefore, with the aim of creating an illusion for this desire. That's the whole point of the child's jubilatory activity in front of the mirror. His image of the body is acquired as something that both exists and doesn't exist at the same time, and he positions his own movements as well as the image of those who are there with him in front of the mirror in relation to it. What's special about this experience is that it presents the subject with a reality that is virtual, unrealized, grasped as such, and is to be acquired. Every possible construction of human reality literally passes through here.

225

For sure, the phallus, as this imaginary object that the child has to identify with in order to satisfy the mother's desire, cannot yet be put in place. But the possibility for this is greatly enriched by the ego's crystallization in this positioning, which opens up all sorts of possibilities for the imaginary.

What are we observing? A double movement. On the one hand, the experience of reality introduces, in the form of the image of the body, an illusory and deceptive element as the essential foundation for mapping the subject in relation to reality. On the other hand, the margin that this experience opens up for the child gives him the possibility of entering into another field and acquiring, in the opposite direction, his first ego identifications.

The field of experience of reality is represented here by the triangle, M-*i*-*m*, which sits on the axis of the previously defined abscissa, whereas the more enigmatic, homologous and inverse triangle, M-*m*-E, creates the subject's field for him, insofar as he has to identify himself, define himself, learn about himself and subjectify himself.

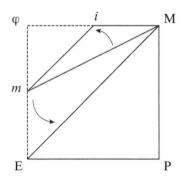

226

What is this triangle, M-*m*-E? What is this field? And how is this trajectory which starts with the specular *Urbild* of the ego, in *m*, going to enable the child to master himself, to identify himself, to progress? How can we define it? How is it constituted?

Answer. The ego's *Urbild* is this initial self-conquest or self-mastery that the child acquires in his experience once he has split the real pole in relation to which he has to situate himself. This brings him into the trapezium *m*-*i*-M-E, insofar as he identifies multiple elements of signifiers in reality. Through his successive identifications along the segment *m*-E, he himself takes on the role of a series of signifiers, understand by that a series of hieroglyphs, types, forms and presentations that punctuate his reality with a number of reference points, thus making it a reality riddled with signifiers.

What constitutes the limit of the series is this formation in E that we call the ego-ideal. This is what the subject identifies with when he goes in the direction of the symbolic. He sets out from imaginary reference points – which are, in some ways, instinctually preformed in his relationship with his own body – and engages in a series of signifying identifications whose direction is defined as the opposite of the imaginary and which use it as a signifier. The reason the ego-ideal identification occurs at the paternal level is that at this level there is greater detachment in relation to the imaginary relationship than at the level of the relation with the mother.

This little construction of schemas one on top of the other, these little dancers standing on one another, the legs of one on the shoulders of the other – that's what this is about.

The third of these little constructions is the father insofar as he intervenes to prohibit. As a result, he brings the object of the mother's desire to the properly symbolic rank, in such a way that it's no longer a purely imaginary object – it's also destroyed, prohibited. It's insofar as the father intervenes as a real person, as *I*, in order to fulfil this function that the *I* will become an eminently signifying element and constitute the nucleus of the final identification, the ultimate outcome of the Oedipus complex. This is why the formation called the ego-ideal relates to the father.

The ego-ideal's oppositions to the object of the mother's desire are expressed on this schema. The subject's virtual and ideal identification with the phallus, insofar as it's the object of the mother's desire, is located at the vertex of the first triangle of the relationship with the mother [φ-M-E]. It's situated there virtually, at one and the same time always possible and always under threat – so much under threat that it will effectively be destroyed by the intervention of the purely symbolic principle represented by the Name-of-the-Father.

The latter is there in the form of a veiled presence. His presence isn't unveiled progressively but by an initially decisive intervention, insofar as he is the prohibiting element.

What does he intervene in? In this kind of groping about on the part of the subject who, without this intervention, would end up in, and in certain cases does end up in, an exclusive relationship with the mother. This exclusive relationship isn't one of pure and simple dependence but manifests itself in all sorts of perversions through a particular essential relationship with the phallus because either the subject assumes it in a number of forms, or turns it into a fetish, or because we are at the level of what can be called the original root of the perverse relationship with the mother.

In general terms, the subject may, at a particular phase, effectively attempt to identify his ego with the phallus. It's inasmuch as he is

227

transported in the other direction that he constitutes and structures a certain relationship, marked by the endpoints i-M which lie along the axis of reality, with the image of his own body, that is, the imaginary pure and simple, namely the mother.

Also, his ego, as a real term, is apt not merely to recognize itself, but, having recognized itself, to become a signifying element and no longer simply an imaginary element in its relationship with the mother. This is how these successive identifications that Freud spells out for us in the strongest of terms, and which form the theme of his theory of the ego, can occur along m-E. This theory effectively shows us that the ego is made of a series of identifications with an object that lies beyond the immediate object, the father beyond the mother.

It's essential to retain this schema. It shows you that, in order for it to turn out correctly, completely and in the right direction, there has to be a particular relationship between the subject's direction, his rectitude and his accidents, and the always growing development of the father's presence in the dialectic of the child's relationship with the mother.

This schema comprises a double seesawing movement. On the one hand, reality is mastered by human subjects inasmuch as it reaches one of its limits in the virtual form of the image of the body. Correspondingly, it's insofar as the subject introduces the unreal elements of signifiers into his field of experience that he manages to enlarge the field of this experience to the scale it has for a human subject.

This schema is made for constant use. If you don't refer to it, you will find that you are forever sliding into a series of confusions and literally taking the smoke for the fire – an idealization for an identification, an illusion for an image, all sorts of things that are far from being equivalent and that we shall have to come back to later with reference to this schema.

It's quite clear, for example, that it is easy to show our conception of the phenomenon of delusion through the structure set out on this schema. Delusion is a phenomenon that, surely, deserves to be called regressive, but not because it reproduces an earlier state, which would be completely incorrect. The idea that the child lives in a world of delusion, which seems to be implied by the Kleinian conception, is one of the most difficult things to agree to, for the good reason that while this psychotic phase is required by the premises of the Kleinian articulation, we have no kind of experience of anything at all in the child that represents a transitory psychotic state.

On the other hand, we can very well conceptualize it at the level of a structural, and not a genetic, regression, which the schema makes

228

possible to illustrate by means of a movement in the direction opposite the one indicated here by the two arrows. The invasion of the world of objects by the image of the body is manifest in delusions of a Schreberian type, whereas, inversely, signifier phenomena are gathered around the ego to the point where the only thing supporting the subject is a continuous thread of verbal hallucinations which constitutes a withdrawal to an initial position of the genesis of his world or of reality.

229

4

Let's see what our aim has been today. Our aim is to definitively locate the meaning of the question we raise concerning the object.

The question of the object is fundamental for us analysts. We experience it constantly, all we ever do is concern ourselves with it. The question is essentially this – what is the source and the genesis of the illusory object? The question is whether we can form an adequate conception of this object as illusory by referring simply to the categories of the imaginary.

My reply to you is, 'No, that's impossible.' The illusory object has been known about for such a long time, for as long as there have been people who think, philosophers who attempt to express what forms part of everyone's experience. The illusory object has been spoken about for ages. It's the veil of Maya. It's well known that sexual need manifestly produces aims that go beyond the subject. We did not have to wait for Freud for that. Mr Schopenhauer, and many others before him, had already seen a ruse of nature in the fact that a subject thinks about kissing such and such a woman, and that he is purely and simply subject to the requirements of the species.

The fundamentally imaginary character of the object, most especially the object of sexual need, was recognized long ago. The fact that the subject is only sensitive to the image of the female of his species, very roughly speaking, has the character of a lure that, supposedly, seems to be realized in nature – but that doesn't help us one little bit in understanding what is nevertheless essential, which is that one small woman's shoe may very precisely be what provokes in a man the emergence of this energy that is said to be intended for the reproduction of the species. The whole problem is there.

It can only be solved on condition that one realizes that the illusory object doesn't fulfil its function in the human subject as an image – however deceptive, however naturally well organized as a lure you suppose it to be. It fulfils it as a signifying element, taken up into a signifying chain.

We have come to the end of a session today that is perhaps particularly abstract. I apologize, but if we don't set these terms down we will never get to understand what's here and what's there, what I'm saying and what I'm not saying, what I am saying so as to contradict others, and what others say in all innocence, without being aware of their contradictions. We really do have to take this route via the function played by this or that object, fetish or not, and even simply via all the instruments of a perversion.

I really have no idea what one would have had to be thinking about to be satisfied with, for example, terms like 'masochism' or 'sadism', which provide all sorts of admirable considerations on stages and instincts and on the fact that there is some sort of aggressive motor need in order to be able just to accomplish the aim of genital coupling. But, then, why does the fact of being beaten – there are other ways of practising sadism and masochism – very specifically with a switch, or anything else analogous, play an essential role in sadism and masochism? Why does one minimize the importance to human sexuality of this implement commonly known as the whip, in a more or less elided, symbolic or generalized manner? There really is something here that deserves to be taken into consideration.

Mr Aldous Huxley depicts a future world in which everything will be so well organized concerning the reproductive instinct that little foetuses will simply be placed in bottles when those chosen for providing the best embryos have been selected. It all goes very well, and the world becomes particularly satisfactory. Because of his personal preferences, Mr Huxley declares it boring. I'm not taking sides, but what is interesting is that by engaging in these sorts of predictions, to which I personally attach no kind of importance, he remakes the world that he is familiar with, just as we are, through the intermediary of a person who isn't just anybody – a girl who expresses her need to be whipped. There seems to him to be no doubt that there is something here that is closely bound up with the character of humanity in the world.

I am simply pointing this out to you. What is accessible to a novelist, who no doubt has some experience concerning sexual life, should give us analysts pause for thought, all the same.

See the turning point in the history of perversion in analysis. To get away from the idea that perversion was purely and simply the drive coming to the surface – that is to say, the contrary of neurosis – we waited for a sign from the conductor, which came when Freud wrote '*Ein Kind wird geschlagen*' ['A Child is Being Beaten'], a text that is totally sublime, where everything that has been said about it since is merely small beer. It's through the analysis of this whipping fantasy that Freud really brought perversion into his real analytic dialectic. It doesn't appear as the pure and simple manifestation of a drive, but proves to be attached to a dialectical context that is as subtle, composite, rich in compromise and ambiguous as a neurosis.

Perversion is therefore not to be classified as a category of the instinct or of our tendencies, but is to be articulated precisely in all its detail, in its instruments and, let's say the word, in its signifiers. Whenever you deal with a perversion, moreover, it's a misrecognition not to see to what extent it is fundamentally attached to a scenario that is always liable to be transformed, modified, elaborated and enriched. In certain cases, experience makes it clear that perversion is chemically linked in the closest of ways to the appearance, disappearance and entire compensatory movement of a phobia, which obviously exhibits both a front and a back, but in quite a different sense, in the sense in which two articulated systems are mutually composed, offset one another and alternate with one another. This encourages us to talk about the drive in quite another domain than that of tendencies pure and simple.

I am particularly drawing your attention to the traces of a signifier that the components and the instruments of perversion itself correspond to, since we are interested in the object for the moment.

What does all this mean? We have an object, a primordial object, one that, without any doubt, remains dominant for the rest of the subject's life. We have certain imaginary elements that play a crystallizing role, in particular all the material of the body's parts, its members, the subject's reference to their domination, the image of a whole. But the fact of the matter is that the object is caught in the function of signifiers.

A relationship is formed here between two series – a series of S, S′, S″, which symbolizes the existence of a signifying chain, and a series of significations underneath. While the upper chain moves in one direction, this something that is in the significations moves in the opposite direction. This is a signification that is always sliding, flying and fleeing, which means that ultimately, by virtue of the existence of signifiers, man's basic relationship with all signification is a special type of object. I call this object a metonymic object.

What is the nature of this object insofar as the subject has a relationship with it? The subject imaginarily identifies with it in a totally radical manner, not with this or that of its object functions that supposedly correspond to this or that partial tendency, as they say. Something requires that somewhere at this level there be a pole that represents in the imaginary what is always evasive, what is induced by a certain tendency of the object to take flight into the imaginary, because of the existence of signifiers. This pole is an object. It's pivotal, central in the entire dialectic of perversions, neuroses and even, purely and simply, in subjective development. It has a name. It's called the phallus.

This is what I will be illustrating for you next time.

5 February 1958

XIII

FANTASY, BEYOND THE PLEASURE PRINCIPLE

Reading 'A Child is Being Beaten'
The hieroglyphics of the whip, the law of the rod
The negative therapeutic reaction
The pain of being
So-called feminine masochism

By way of bibliographical information, I draw your attention to the following three articles that I will have occasion to refer to. The first is by Ernest Jones, 'The Phallic Phase', published in the *International Journal*, volume 14, 1933, and reprinted in his collection, *Papers on Psychoanalysis*, where it's the last one. The second is in German. It's by Hanns Sachs, '*Genese der Perversion*' ['The Genesis of Perversion'], and you will find it in the ninth volume of the *Zeitschrift für Psychoanalyse*, 1923. Finally, I give you the English reference for the third, 'Perversion and Neurosis', by Otto Rank, in the *International Journal of Psychoanalysis* of the same year.

I will add to these Freud's initial article from 1919, '*Ein Kind wird geschlagen*' ['A Child is Being Beaten'], which was the signal he gave of a turnaround or a step forward in his own thought and, thereby, for the entire theoretical development of subsequent analytic thought concerning the neuroses and the perversions.

On close examination, the best formula one can give of what occurred at that moment is a formula that the register I am trying to elaborate here by showing you the essential role of signifiers in the formation of symptoms enables me to give – it's effectively a question, in Freud, of the intervention of the notion of a signifier.

Once Freud had shown this, it became clear that the instinct, the drive, has no right to be promoted as any more naked, as it were, in perversion than in neurosis. Hanns Sachs's entire article on the genesis of perversions is there to demonstrate that there is exactly the same structure of compromise, evasion, and dialectic of the repressed and return of the repressed as in neurosis. That is the essence of this article that is so remarkable, and he gives absolutely convincing examples for it. There is always something in perversion that the subject does not wish to recognize, with what this '*veut*', 'wish', conveys in our language – what the subject does not wish to recognize can only be conceived as being articulated therein and, nevertheless, not only misrecognized by him, but also repressed for essential reasons of articulation.

This is the mainspring of the analytic mechanism of repression. If the subject were to recognize the repressed, he would be forced to recognize a series of other things, which are strictly intolerable to him, and this is the source of the repressed. Repression can be conceptualized only insofar as it's linked to an articulated signifying chain. Whenever you have repression in neurosis, it's insofar as the subject does not wish to recognize something that it would be necessary to recognize – and this term 'necessary' always carries an element of signifying articulation that cannot be otherwise conceived than as internal to the coherence of a discourse. Well then, for perversion, it's exactly the same thing. There you have it. In 1923, following Freud's article, Sachs and all psychoanalysts recognized that if you look closely, perversion carries exactly the same mechanisms of elision of the fundamental – that is, Oedipal – terms as we find in the analysis of neuroses.

If there is, all the same, a difference, it deserves to be studied very closely. In no case can one rest content with an opposition as summary as that which consists in saying that in neurosis the drive is avoided, whereas in perversion it declares itself nakedly. The drive does appear here, but it only ever appears here partially. It appears in something which, in comparison with the instinct, is a detached element, strictly speaking a sign and, one can even say, a signifier of the instinct. This is why last time, as I was finishing up, I emphasized the role of instruments that is present in an entire series of so-called perverse fantasies – limiting ourselves to just these for the moment.

Effectively, it's preferable to begin from the concrete and not from some general idea that we might have of what is called the instinctual economy of a tension, aggressive or not, and its reflections, turnings around and refractions. At least, isn't this what will explain the prevalence, insistence and predominance of these elements the nature of which is not only emergent but also isolated in the form that perversions take as a species of fantasy, that is, as that by which they provide imaginary satisfaction?

Why do these elements occupy this special place? The other day I spoke about the shoe and also the whip – we can't link them to a

234

235

pure and simple biological economy of the instinct. They are instru-
mental elements isolated in a form that is too obviously symbolic
for it to be possible to misunderstand this for a moment, once one
has explored the lived reality of perversion. The constancy of such
elements across the transformations that the evolution of a subject's
perversion is capable of showing over the course of his life – a point
on which Sachs also insists – is very likely to emphasize the need to
view it, not just as a primordial, ultimate and irreducible element
whose place we have to see in a subject's economy, but also as a
signifying element of perversion.

Let's turn to Freud's article.

1

Freud starts with a fantasy that he has detected in a group of eight
patients, six girls and two boys, presenting fairly nuanced pathological forms, of which quite a large portion are neurotic, but not
all are.

This is a systematic and very careful study pursued, step by step,
with a scrupulousness that distinguishes the investigations carried
out by Freud himself from all others. Beginning with these subjects,
as diverse as they are, he sets out to follow the transformations in
the economy of the fantasy, 'a child is being beaten', through the
stages of the Oedipus complex. He begins to articulate what will
subsequently develop in his thought into the period where he investigates perversions, and which will, I insist on this point, show us
the importance of the play of signifiers in this economy even more.

I can only point out in passing that one of Freud's last articles,
'Constructions in Analysis' – I don't know if you have noticed
this – shows the central importance of the notion of the subject's
relationship to signifiers for thinking about the mechanism of
remembering in analysis. It's clearly shown in this article that this
mechanism, as such, is linked to the signifying chain. Similarly, the
last work that Freud wrote for us, the last article by him that we
have, from 1938, the one that in the *Collected Papers* was translated
with the title 'Splitting of the Ego in the Process of Defence', which
I translate as 'The Division or Splitting of the Ego in the Mechanism
of Analytic Symptoms', and whose German title is '*Die Ichspaltung
im Abwehrvorgang*', the one that Freud stopped writing – the article
is unfinished – closely links the economy of the ego with the dialectics of perverse recognition, as it were, of a particular theme that
confronts the subject. An unbreakable knot ties the ego's* function
to the imaginary relationship in the subject's relations with reality,

and it does so insofar as this imaginary relationship is utilized as integrated into the mechanism of signifiers.

Let's now turn to the fantasy, 'a child is being beaten'.

Freud pauses at what is signified by this fantasy, into which at least a significant part, if not all, of the libidinal satisfactions of the subject seem to be absorbed. He insists on the fact that the great majority of cases he has encountered it in are female subjects, less often male subjects. We're not dealing with just any sadistic or perverse fantasy, we're dealing with a fantasy that culminates in and stabilizes into a form the theme of which the subject discloses with great reticence. It seems that a great deal of guilt is bound up with even communicating this theme which, once revealed, cannot be put into any other words than 'a child is being beaten'.

Being beaten. *Ein Kind wird geschlagen.* This means that it isn't the subject who beats, he is there as a spectator. Freud begins by analysing the thing as it occurs in the imagination of female subjects who were the ones who revealed it to him. Taken in its totality, the person who is speaking comes from the line of those who are in authority. It isn't the father, it's on occasion a schoolteacher, an all-powerful man, the King or a tyrant – it's occasionally a very romanticized figure. One recognizes, not the father, but someone who, for us, is equivalent to him. We will have to situate him in the full form of the fantasy, and we shall very clearly see that there is no reason for us to be content with a homology with the father. Far from being assimilated to the father, he should be placed beyond the father, in that category of the Name-of-the-Father that we carefully distinguish from the effects of the real father.

There are several children involved in these fantasies, a kind of group or crowd, and they are always boys. This raises problems, and enough of them for it not to be possible for me to think of covering them all today – I ask you simply to refer to Freud's article. The fact that it's always boys that are beaten, that is, subjects of the opposite sex to that of the subject of the fantasy, is something on which one can speculate indefinitely – try for example relating it initially to themes such as that of the rivalry between the sexes. This is where Freud ends his article, showing the profound incompatibility with the clinical facts of theories such as Adler's and their inability to explain a finding like this one. Freud's argumentation is largely sufficient, and this isn't what creates our essential interest.

What creates our interest is the way Freud goes about examining the problem. He gives us the findings of his analyses. He begins by speaking about what happens in the girl's case, which he does for the requirements of his exposition, so as not to have to be constantly beginning again twice over – this for the girl, that for the boy. Then

237

he takes what happens in the boy's case, where, moreover, he has less material. In short, what does he tell us? He observes some constants, and he tells us about them. What seems essential to him are the avatars of this fantasy – its transformations, its antecedents, its history and what underlies it – which analytic investigation has given him access to. The fantasy effectively undergoes a number of successive states over the course of which it's possible to observe that something changes and something remains constant. For us it's a matter of learning from the result of this painstaking investigation, which carries the mark that gives almost everything that Freud wrote its originality – precision, insistence, working on the material to the point where the articulations that seem irreducible to him have been properly detached. This is how, in the five major psychoanalyses, and in particular in the admirable 'Wolf Man', we see him constantly returning to rigorously examine the part that we can call the symbolic origin and the part that is the real origin, in the primitive chain of the subject's history. Here, similarly, he discerns three moments.

The first stage, he tells us, that in this instance one always finds in the case of girls is the following. At a certain moment of the analysis, the child who is being beaten, and who discloses his real face, is a sibling, a little brother or a little sister, whom the father is beating. What does this fantasy signify?

We are unable to say whether it's sexual or sadistic, is the surprising affirmation that comes from Freud's pen, supported by a literary reference to the witch's response to Banquo in *Macbeth* – it's made from the stuff from which the two, the sexual and the sadistic, will come. Here we find what Freud will emphasize in an article in 1924, 'The Economic Problem of Masochism', and which is necessitated by *Beyond the Pleasure Principle*, namely this first stage at which, we have to think, there is originally, at least in considerable part, *Bindung*, binding or fusion of the libidinal instincts, or life instincts, with the death instincts, whereas the evolution of the instincts comprises a more or less premature defusion, *Entbildung*, of these instincts. Certain types of prevalence or certain arrests in a subject's evolution can be attributed to the premature isolation of the death instinct.

Although this fantasy is primitive, in that one doesn't find any more archaic stage, Freud also emphasizes that its signification is located at the level of the father. The father refuses his love to or withholds his love from the beaten child, the little brother or the little sister. Inasmuch as there is the denunciation of any relationship of love and humiliation, this subject is targeted in his existence as a subject. He is the object of abuse, and this abuse consists in denying him as subject, reducing his existence as desiring to nothing and reducing him to a state that aims to abolish him as a subject. 'My father does not love him' is the meaning of the primitive fantasy and it's what gives the subject pleasure – the other isn't loved, that is, isn't established in a properly symbolic relationship. This is the perspective from which the father's intervention acquires its primary value for the subject, on which everything that follows depends.

This archaic fantasy is thus initially born into a triangular relationship, one that isn't established between the subject, the mother and the child, but between the subject, the little brother or little sister and the father. We are prior to the Oedipus complex, and yet the father is there.

Whereas this first moment of the fantasy, the most archaic, is recovered by the subject in analysis, the second, on the other hand, never is and has to be reconstructed. This is unbelievable. If I stress the daring of Freud's deduction, it isn't so that we can pause for a moment and ask whether it's legitimate or not. It's so that we do not allow ourselves to be led along blindfolded, it's so that we are aware of what Freud is doing, owing to which his construction can be continued. The analytic material therefore converges on this state of the fantasy which has to be reconstructed since it never appears, according to Freud, in memory.

This second moment is tied to the Oedipus complex as such. It has the meaning of a privileged relationship between the little girl and her father – it's she who is being beaten. Freud thus acknowledges that this reconstructed fantasy may testify to the return of Oedipal desire in the little girl, the desire to be the object of the father's desire, with the guilt that that comprises, requiring that she have herself beaten. Freud speaks in this respect of regression. What should we understand by that? Given that the message in question is repressed and can't be recovered in the subject's memory, a correlated mechanism, which Freud here calls regression, causes the subject to have recourse to the figuration of the previous stage in order to express, in a fantasy that is never brought to light, the frankly libidinal relationship, already structured in the Oedipal mode, that the subject then has with the father.

At a third moment, after emerging from the Oedipus complex, there remains nothing more of the fantasy than a general schema. A new transformation has been introduced, and it's a double one. The figure of the father, now outmoded, is transposed and referred to the general form of an omnipotent and despotic person in a position to beat, whereas the subject himself is presented in the form of these multiple children, not all of whom are even of a determinate sex, but form a kind of neutral series. This final form of the fantasy, in which

239

something is thus maintained and fixed, one might say memorized, remains invested for the subject with the property of forming the privileged image in which whatever genital satisfaction he will be able to experience will find its support.

This deserves our attention, and it deserves to arouse a reflection using the terms whose primary use I am trying to teach you here.

What might they represent here?

2

I return to my imaginary triangle and my symbolic triangle. The first dialectic of the symbolization of the child's relationship with the mother is essentially made for what is signifiable, which is what is of interest to us. There are no doubt other things beyond. There is the object that the mother as bearer of the breast can present, and there are the immediate satisfactions that she can bring to the child, but if that were all there is, there wouldn't be any kind of dialectic, no opening in the edifice. Later, the relationship with the mother does not consist merely of satisfactions and frustrations, it consists in the discovery of what the object of her desire is. The subject, this little child who has to constitute himself in his human adventure and enter the world of the signified, effectively has to make the discovery of what signifies her desire for her. Now, what has always posed a problem in analytic history, for theory as for practice, has been to know why the privileged function of the phallus appears at this point.

When you read Jones's article, 'The Phallic Phase', you will see the unfathomable difficulties that he has with Freud's remark that for the two sexes there is an original stage in their sexual development where the theme of the other as desiring other is linked to the possession of the phallus. This is literally incomprehensible by nearly everybody around Freud, even though they contort themselves in order to get it to fit into their own elaborations, notwithstanding, because the facts impose it on them. What they do not understand is that Freud is positing there a pivot-signifier around which the entire dialectic of what the subject must conquer in himself, in his own being, revolves.

240   For want of understanding that this is a signifier and nothing else, commentators have worn themselves out looking for its equivalent in talking about a defence of the subject in the form of a belief in the phallus. Of course, they gather numerous extremely valuable facts about this, and they discover a thousand traces of it in their various experiences, but these are only ever particular cases or pathways

that still don't explain why it's this privileged element that is taken up as the central, pivotal point of the defence. Jones, in particular, gives belief in the phallus a function in the boy's development which, if you read him, you will notice is taken from the case of a homosexual, which is far from being the general case. Whereas, with the phallus, it's a question of the most general of functions.

Allow me a dense formulation that will strike you as quite bold, but we won't have to come back to it if you will be kind enough to agree to accept it momentarily for its operational use. Just as I have told you that within the signifying system the Name-of-the-Father has the function of signifying the entire system of signifiers, authorizing its existence, making it law, I will tell you that we frequently have to consider that the phallus enters into play in the signifying system when the subject has to symbolize, in contrast with the signifier, the signified as such – I mean signification.

What matters to the subject – what he desires, desire as desired – the subject's desired, when it comes to the neurotic or pervert symbolizing it, is literally carried out, ultimately, with the help of the phallus. The phallus is the signifier of the signified in general.

This is essential. If you start there, you will understand many things. If you do not start there, you will understand far fewer and you will be obliged to take some sizeable detours in order to understand some exceedingly simple things.

The phallus enters into play immediately the subject addresses the mother's desire. This phallus is veiled and will remain veiled to the end of time for one simple reason, which is that it's an ultimate signifier in the signifier's relationship with the signified. There is, effectively, little chance that it ever unveils itself in any other way than in its nature as a signifier, little chance, that is, that it truly reveals what it signifies as a signifier.

Nevertheless, consider what happens – a case that we have not envisaged till now – if in this place something intervenes that is much less easy to articulate or symbolize than anything that is imaginary, namely a real subject. This is just what is in question at this first phase that Freud designates.

The mother's desire here isn't simply the object of an enigmatic search that has to lead the subject, over the course of his development, to trace out this sign, the phallus, therein so that the latter will subsequently enter into the dance of the symbolic, become the exact object of castration and be finally rendered to him in a different form, so that it does and is what it's meant to do and be. It is that and it does do that, but here we are right at the origin, where the subject comes face-to-face with the imaginary place in which the mother's desire is located. And this place is occupied.

241

We can't speak about everything at once, and anyway it was quite fortunate that we didn't immediately think of the role of younger siblings even when we all know that this is of decisive importance in the triggering of neuroses. A minimum of analytic experience is sufficient for one to know how much the appearance of a little brother or little sister acts as a crossroads in the evolution of every neurosis. It's just that if we had thought about this immediately, it would have had exactly the same effect on our thought as we observe it having on the neurotic subject – dwelling on the reality of this relationship makes one miss its function completely. The relation to the little brother or little sister, to any rival, does not acquire its decisive value at the level of reality, but insofar as it's inscribed in a completely different development, the development of symbolization. This complicates it and requires a completely different solution, a fantasmatic solution. What is that? Freud spelt out the nature of this for us – the subject is abolished on the symbolic plane insofar as he is a nonentity who is denied any consideration as a subject. In this particular case, the child discovers the so-called masochistic fantasy of beating that constitutes a successful solution to the problem at this level.

We don't have to limit ourselves to this case, but initially we need to understand what is happening. And what's happening is a symbolic act. Freud stresses it strongly – this child who thinks he is someone in the family, well, a single slap is often enough for him to plummet from the pinnacle of his omnipotence. Well then, we're dealing with a symbolic act, and the very form that comes into play in fantasy – a whip or a switch – carries within itself the character of, has the nature of, some sort of thing which expresses itself on the symbolic plane as an erasure. Before it becomes something else, *Einfühlung*, empathy of some kind, that can be attributed to a physical relationship between the subject and the one who is suffering, what intervenes before anything else is something that strikes out the subject, crosses him out, or abolishes him – this something is the signifier.

This is so true that when later – all of this is in Freud's article, I'm following him line by line – the child effectively encounters the act of beating, namely, when at school he sees a child being beaten before his eyes, he doesn't find it at all amusing, says Freud, trusting to the text of the experience of subjects from whom he has obtained the history of this fantasy. The scene inspires something in the order of an *Ablehnung* – I am correcting the translation – an aversion, a turning away of the head. The subject is obliged to endure it, but he has no involvement and keeps himself at a distance. The subject is by no means taking part in what really takes place when he is confronted by an actual scene of a thrashing. And also, as Freud precisely indicates, the very pleasure of this fantasy is manifestly tied to its non-serious, inoperative character. The thrashing has no other effect upon the subject's real and physical integrity. It really is its symbolic character that is eroticized as such, and eroticized from the outset.

At the second moment – and this is important for the validation of the schema I introduced you to last time – the fantasy is going to acquire a completely different value and change its meaning. It's here that the whole enigma of the essence of masochism resides.

Where the subject is concerned, there is no way of getting out of this impasse. I am not telling you that this is easy to grasp, explain or unpack. We must first of all hold on to the fact, which is that that is how it is, and, afterwards, we will try to understand how it can be like that.

The radical introduction of signifiers comprises two distinct elements. There is the message and its signification – the subject receives the news that the little rival is a child who is beaten, that is, a nonentity, someone one can sit on. There is also a signifier that has to be picked out as such, namely, what one wields, the instrument.

The fundamental character of the masochistic fantasy as it actually exists in a subject – and not in some kind of model or ideal reconstruction of the evolution of the instincts – is the existence of the whip. It's what, in itself, merits being emphasized by us. We are dealing with a signifier that merits having a special place in the series of our hieroglyphs, and initially for a simple reason, which is that the hieroglyph of the one holding the whip has always designated the director, the governor and the master. We mustn't lose sight of the fact that that exists and that it's what we are dealing with.

The same duality occurs again at the second moment. However, the message in question, 'My father is beating me', doesn't reach the subject – this is how what Freud says is to be understood. The message which had first meant, 'The rival does not exist, he's a nonentity', now means, 'You exist, and you are loved, even.' That is what serves as a message at the second moment, whether it's in a regressive or repressed form doesn't matter. And it's a message that does not arrive.

When Freud addresses the problem of masochism as such, one year later, in *Beyond the Pleasure Principle*, and looks for the radical value of this masochism that he encounters in analysis in the form of an opposition or radical enemy, he will be obliged to present it in various terms. Hence the interest we have in thinking about this enigmatic moment of the fantasy, which, he says, is the entire essence of masochism.

243

3

Let's take it step by step. We have to start off by seeing the paradox, and seeing where it lies.

There is, then, the message, the one that does not arrive at the place of the subject. On the other hand, the one thing that remains is the material of the signifier, this object, the whip, which remains as a sign right to the end, to the point of becoming the pivot and, I would almost say, the model of the relationship to the other's desire.

Effectively, the final fantasy's character of generality, the one that remains, is reasonably well indicated by the indefinite reduction in the number of subjects. This highlights the relationship with the other, the others, the little others, the little *a* as libidinal, and it means that human beings, as such, are all under the stick. To enter into the world of desire is for the human being to undergo, right at the outset, the law imposed by this something that exists beyond – that we were calling it the father is no longer of any importance, it doesn't matter – the law of the rod. This is how, for a determinate subject entering the matter by particular pathways, a certain line of evolution is defined. The function of the final fantasy is to reveal an essential relationship between the subject and the signifier.

Now let's move on a little bit, and remind ourselves what Freud introduces that is new regarding masochism in *Beyond the Pleasure Principle*. It's essentially this – if we consider a subject's mode of resistance or inertia to a certain normative or normalizing form of treatment intervention, we are led to articulate the pleasure principle as the tendency of life to return to the inanimate. The last resort of libidinal evolution is to return to the stillness of a stone. This is the great scandal that Freud contributes for everyone who till then had made the notion of libido the law of their thought.

If this contribution is paradoxically new, even scandalous when expressed as I just have, it's in other respects merely an extension of the pleasure principle, which Freud characterized as a return to zero tension. There is, in effect, no more radical a return to zero than death. However, at the same time, you can see that we're still obliged, in order to distinguish them, to locate this formulation of the pleasure principle beyond the pleasure principle.

I should say some words here about one of the most unusual problems in the life and person of Freud – his relationship to his wife, to which we will perhaps have occasion to return one day. His existence was very deprived of, or denied itself, women. He is scarcely known to have had any more than two women, his own and this sister-in-law who lived in the couple's shadow. We really have no

244

trace of anything else that was a properly romantic relationship. On the other hand, he had a fairly deplorable tendency to take suggestions readily from the constellation of women that formed around him, and whose members wished to be the upholders or assistants of his thought. It was thus sufficient for him that a person like Barbara Low should suggest a term to him that was so mediocrely suited, if I may say so, as 'the Nirvana principle' for him to endorse it. The relationship that perhaps exists between Nirvana and the notion of the return of nature to the inanimate is just a little bit approximate – but since Freud was happy with it, let's be happy with it too.

If the Nirvana principle is the rule and the law of the evolution of living things, there must be a trick somewhere so that, at least occasionally, it isn't the decrease in pleasure that gives pleasure but, on the contrary, its increase – except that, as Freud is aware, we are completely incapable of saying why. There must be something in the genre of a temporal rhythm, a concordance of terms, pulsations. He allows that on the horizon there may possibly be recourse to explanations which, were they able to be given, aren't vague, but they remain very much out of reach – they go in the direction of music, of harmony of the spheres.

In any case, as soon as one allows that the principle of pleasure is a return to death, actual pleasure, the pleasure we concretely deal with, requires a different order of explication. We really need some trick of life that makes subjects believe, as it were, that it actually is for their pleasure that they are here. One thus returns to the greatest philosophical banalities, namely that it's the veil of Maya that sustains us in life by deceiving us. Beyond, the possibility of obtaining either pleasure or pleasures by taking all sorts of detours, would [then] be based on the reality principle. This is what would be beyond the pleasure principle.

It takes nothing less than a Freud to justify the existence of what he calls the negative therapeutic reaction. We must pause here for a moment, nevertheless, because, well, this negative therapeutic reaction isn't some kind of stoic reaction by the subject. It manifests itself in all sorts of extraordinarily annoying things as much for him as for us and for his entourage. They are even so troublesome that, all things considered, 'not having been born' can seem like a better fate for everything that has come into being. This remark that Oedipus ends up making, his μή φύναι (*me phunai*), as the final word that gives the meaning in which the adventure of tragedy culminates, does not abolish the latter, far from it. On the contrary, it eternalizes it, for the simple reason that, if Oedipus was unable to succeed in stating it, he would not be the supreme hero that he is. It's precisely insofar as he does say it – that is, makes himself eternal – that he is this hero.

245

What Freud discovers for us as beyond the pleasure principle is that there is perhaps, effectively, an ultimate aspiration for rest and eternal death, but, in our experience, and this was the entire meaning of the second year of my Seminar, we encounter the specific character of the negative therapeutic reaction in the form of this irresistible inclination towards suicide that becomes recognizable in the last resistances we encounter in these subjects who are more or less characterized by the fact of having been unwanted children. As what must bring them closer to their history as a subject becomes better articulated, they increasingly refuse to play the game. They literally wish to quit it. They do not accept being what they are. They want nothing of this signifying chain into which their mother has only regretfully admitted them.

What appears to us analysts in these cases is exactly what can be found in others, namely the presence of a desire that is articulated, and articulated not only as a desire for recognition, but as the recognition of a desire. The signifier is the essential dimension here. The more the subject, with the aid of signifiers, asserts himself as wishing to exit the signifying chain, and the more he enters it and integrates himself into it, the more he himself becomes a sign in this chain. Should he do away with himself, he is a sign more than ever. The reason for this is simple – it's precisely when the subject is dead that he becomes an eternal sign for others, and those who have committed suicide even more than others. This is indeed why suicide has a horrific beauty which makes it so terribly condemned by people, and also a contagious beauty which gives rise to these suicide epidemics that are as real as it gets in experience.

246   Once again, in *Beyond the Pleasure Principle*, Freud stresses the desire for recognition as such, as forming the basis of what constitutes our relation to the subject. And, after all, in what Freud calls beyond the pleasure principle, is there anything else besides the subject's fundamental relation to the signifying chain?

If you think about it, resorting to some supposed inertia in human nature for the model of what life aspires to is an idea that must make us smile slightly, given where we have come to. In fact nothing is less assured than a return to nothing. Moreover, Freud himself – in a tiny parenthesis that I would ask you to go back to in the article 'The Economic Problem of Masochism', where he mentions his *Beyond the Pleasure Principle* – points out to us that if the return to inanimate nature is actually conceivable as the return to the lowest level of tension, to the state of rest, nothing assures us that, in reducing to nothing everything that has risen and is life, nothing stirs therein either, as it were, and that, at bottom, there is no pain of being. I am not springing this pain on you, I'm not extrapolating it. As pointed out by Freud, it's what we have to regard as the final residue of the bond between Thanatos and Eros. No doubt Thanatos comes to be released through the subject's motor aggressiveness in relation to what is in his surroundings, but some part of it remains internal to the subject in the form of this pain of being that, for Freud, seems to be linked to the very existence of living beings. Now, there's no reason to think that this pain stops at living beings – according to everything we now know about a nature that is much more animated, rotting, fermenting, bubbling and even explosive, than we have been able to imagine up till now.

On the other hand, what we do not have to imagine, what is there at the tip of our fingers, is that in his relationship to signifiers a subject may occasionally, insofar as he is asked to constitute himself in signifiers, choose not to do so. He can say, 'No, I will not be an element in the chain.' That really is what lies at the bottom of the matter. But the bottom, the back, is exactly the same thing as the front. What does the subject do, in effect, when he chooses, in some way, not to pay a debt that he has not contracted? He does nothing but perpetuate it. His successive refusals have the effect of making the chain rebound, and he always finds himself tied to this same chain even more. The *Absagüngzwang*, this eternal necessity to repeat the same refusal, is, as Freud shows us, the ultimate mainspring of everything that in the unconscious appears in the form of symptomatic reproduction.

Nothing less than this is necessary in order to understand in what respect signifiers, once they have been introduced, have a fundamentally double value. How does the subject feel affected, as desire, by signifiers, inasmuch as it's he who is abolished, not the other with the imaginary and, of course, signifying whip. As desire, he feels he is running up against what, as such, sanctions and valorizes him even as it profanes him. In masochistic fantasies, there is always a degrading and profanatory aspect, one that indicates both the dimension of recognition and the subject's prohibited mode of relation with the paternal subject. This is what constitutes the depths of the misrecognized part of the fantasy.

The subject's access to the radically double-meaning nature of a signifier is facilitated by something I have not yet brought into play on the schema, so as to spare your tiny minds, because last time there were frightful complications as soon as I introduced the parallel line *i-m* – namely, the relationship between the image of the body and the ego of the subject.

We cannot misrecognize the fact that the rival does not purely and simply intervene in the triangular relation, but that he is already present at the imaginary level as a radical obstacle. This is what

247

provokes what Saint Augustine describes for us in his *Confessions* –
the deathly pallor of the suckling watching its brother at the
mother's breast. There is, in effect, something radical there, truly
deadly for the subject, which is well expressed in this passage. But
the rivalry with the other isn't all, since there is also an identification with the other. In other words, the relationship that binds the
subject to every image of the other has a fundamentally ambiguous
character, and it gives the subject a completely natural introduction to the back-and-forth which, in fantasy, takes him to his rival's
place, where the same message will henceforth reach him with a
completely opposite meaning.

We can, then, see this, which makes us better understand what the
issue is – it's inasmuch as part of the relation develops a connection
with the subject's ego that successive fantasies are organized and
structured. It's not for nothing that it's in this dimension between
the primitive maternal object and the subject's image – a dimension
in which the entire range of the intermediaries where reality is constituted is laid out – that all these others who are the support of the
significant object, namely the whip, come to be located. From this
moment on, in its signification the fantasy – I mean the fantasy in
which the subject appears as the child who is being beaten – becomes
the relation with the Other by whom it's a question of being loved,
insofar as he himself is not recognized as such. This fantasy is, then,
situated somewhere in the symbolic dimension between the father
and the mother, between whom, moreover, he effectively oscillates.

248   Today I have taken you down a path that was no less difficult
than the one I took you down last time. Let's wait and test its value
and its validity, which I will be able to tell you about at a later stage.
To terminate on a brief suggestive note, I will make the following
remark, which will show you how our terms are applied.

It's commonly said in analysis that a woman's relation to the
man comprises a certain masochism on her part. It's one of these
errors of perspective to which some kind of sliding of our experience
into confusion and into a rut leads us all the time. It's not because
masochists display certain signs or fantasies of a typically feminine position in their relations with their partner that, inversely, a
woman's relation to the man is a masochistic relation. The idea that,
in the relations between a man and a woman, the woman is someone
who receives the blows may well be a masculine subject's perspective as someone who is interested in the feminine position. But, in
order for a constitutively feminine position to effectively be there,
it isn't enough that the masculine subject perceive, from certain
perspectives – whether his own or those of his clinical experience –
a certain connection between adopting a feminine position and

such-and-such a signifier of the subject's position that is supposed to have more or less of a relationship with masochism.

It's extremely important to make this correction, which I am doing for you in passing, to the term 'feminine masochism' introduced by Freud in his article on the economic problem.

I have had no time at all to start what I was going to tell you about the relations between the phallus and comedy. I regret it, and I'll defer it till next time.

12 February 1958

THE SIGNIFICANCE
OF THE PHALLUS

XIV

DESIRE AND JOUISSANCE

The masks of a woman
André Gide's perversion
The Balcony by Jean Genet
Comedy and the phallus

Dear friends, to pick up the thread after a three-week break, I will begin with what we were rightly recalling last night, which was that our discourse has to be a scientific discourse. That said, it seems that the paths to achieving this aim are not so easy as far as our object is concerned.

Last night I simply pointed out the originality of this moment in the examination of the phenomena of man that bringing this privileged element called desire to the foreground, by way of the entire Freudian discipline, constitutes.

I pointed out to you that prior to Freud this element had, in itself, always been reduced and in some respects prematurely elided. It's this that makes it possible to say that until Freud every study of human economy more or less started from a concern with morals, with ethics in the sense in which it's less about studying desire than already reducing it and training it. Now, it's the effects of desire in a very large sense – desire is no side-effect – that we have to deal with in psychoanalysis.

What manifests itself in the phenomenon of human desire is its fundamental subduction, not to say subversion, by signifiers. That is the meaning of everything I am striving here to make you aware of – desire's relationship to signifiers.

I am not going to develop this for you again today, even though we should go back and recommence from there, but I am going to show you what, from the rigorous perspective that maintains the originality of the conditions of man's desire, is signified by a notion that is always more or less implicated in your handling of the notion of desire, and which deserves to be distinguished from it – I would go further – which can only begin to be articulated once we are sufficiently inculcated with the complex conditions under which this desire is formed. This notion I am speaking about will be the other pole of my discourse today. It's called jouissance.

We will briefly return to what forms, as such, desire's deviation or alienation in signifiers, and we will ask what it means, from this perspective, that the human subject is able to take possession of what in his world are the very conditions imposed upon him as if these conditions were made for him and succeed in satisfying him.

I point out to you that this brings us to a theme – and I hope to get there today – that I announced to you at the start of the year when we were approaching things from the perspective of witticisms, namely the nature of comedy.

1

Remember for a start that desire is established in relation to the signifying chain, that it first poses and proposes itself as a demand in the evolution of the human subject, and that frustration in Freud is *Versagung*, which is refusal or, even more precisely, retraction.

If, along with the Kleinians, we go further back into the origins, which is an exploration that surely constitutes progress for analysis, in the majority of problems in the evolution of the neurotic subject we are led back to so-called oral-sadistic satisfaction. Simply observe that this satisfaction takes place in fantasy, and does so immediately, as retaliation for fantasized satisfaction.

We are told that everything starts with the sometimes aggressive need to bite in the small child, in relation to the mother's body. Don't forget, though, that none of this ever consists of actual biting, that they are fantasies and that this reasoning can only move forward by showing that the fear of being bitten in return is the essential thread in what is being demonstrated.

Moreover, one of you with whom I was chatting last night, and who, after Susan Isaacs, is trying to retrieve some valid definitions of fantasy, was quite correctly telling me about his total confusion as to pursuing any reasoning whatsoever that was founded purely and simply on the imaginary relation between subjects. It's absolutely impossible to distinguish, in any valid way, unconscious fantasies from this formal creation that is the play of imagination, if we do not see that unconscious fantasy is already dominated and structured by the state of the signifiers.

Good and bad primordial objects, and primitive objects on the basis of which all analytic reasoning is carried out, constitute a range of objects in which several series of substitutive terms destined to be equivalent appear. Milk, the breast, subsequently become – what? – sperm – what? – the penis. These objects are already, as it were, 'signifierized'.

What the relation with the most primordial object, the maternal object, initially produces operates on signs, on what we might call, to give an image of what I mean, the currency of the Other's desire. Still, the close study – close so as to see it clearly – we undertook last time of this work that Freud considers decisive –and I stressed to you that it was effectively groundbreaking in the real analytic understanding of the problem of perversion – was intended to get you to see that these signs can be divided in two. Effectively, they are not all reducible to what, as I have already pointed out to you, are property titles, fiduciary values, representative values or money for exchange, as I just said – signs constituted as such. Some of these signs are constitutive – I mean whereby the creation of value is assured, whereby this something real, which is locked into this economy at every moment, is struck by the bullet that turns it into a sign.

We saw one such bullet last time, formed by the sign of the stick, the switch or whatever else is used for hitting. This is an element whereby even a disagreeable effect can create a subjective distinction and can establish the very relation in which demand can be recognized as such. What was initially a means to annul all rivalrous reality with the brother secondarily becomes that by which the subject finds himself differentiated, recognized or picked out as something that can be either recognized or rejected into nothingness. Henceforth, the subject presents himself as a surface on which everything that can be given subsequently can be recorded, or even, as it were, as a blank cheque where all gifts are possible. And since all gifts are possible, the fact is that what can be given or not given is not what's at issue, because what's at issue is a relation of love, which, as I have said, consists in the fact that the subject essentially gives what he doesn't have. Everything possible about the introduction to the order of love presupposes this fundamental sign for the subject, who may be either annulled or recognized as such by it.

I asked you to read a number of things over the break. I hope you have done so and that you occupied yourselves at least a little bit with Mister Jones's phallic phase and the early development of feminine sexuality.

Since I have to move on today, I will punctuate with a completely

254

local example that I rediscovered when rereading the issue of the *International Journal of Psychoanalysis* commemorating Jones's fiftieth anniversary, at the time when this phallic phase was in the foreground of the interest of English psychoanalysts. In this issue, volume 10, I reread once again, with great interest, Joan Riviere's article, 'Womanliness as a Masquerade'.

The article is about the analysis of a specific case, and not about the function of femininity in general, which Joan Riviere situates in relation to various branches that offer a number of possible pathways to femininity.

The subject in question presented as endowed with a femininity that was all the more remarkable for apparently being completely embraced, and for the fact that her entire life appeared – in her day much more than in ours – to indicate that she assumed all the masculine functions. In other words, she was someone who had a perfectly independent, developed and free professional life, which, I repeat, stood out much more in those days than in our own, and which nevertheless manifested itself in her correlative assumption to the maximum, to the highest degree, of her role as a woman – both in the public form of her functions as housewife and in her relations with her spouse, everywhere displaying the superiority of qualities which, in our social state just as in all social states, come under what is necessarily the woman's responsibility, and, in another register, quite specially at the sexual level, her relations with her man proved to be entirely satisfying with respect to her jouissance.

Now, beneath the apparently total satisfaction of her feminine position, this analysis highlighted something very hidden and which nonetheless formed its basis. This is without any doubt something that one doesn't find without the instigation of some tiny, infinitely tiny discord appearing on the surface of a state that was in principle completely satisfying.

You are aware of the emphasis our experience can place on *Penisneid*, the claim for a penis, in many developmental disorders of female sexuality. Here, what is hidden is quite the contrary. I cannot repeat the history of this woman, this is not my aim today, but the source of the satisfaction that supports what apparently flourishes in this favourable libido is the hidden satisfaction of superiority over the parental characters. This is the term that Mrs Joan Riviere uses, and which she considers to be the very source of the problems in this case – which, as I have said, has a character of freedom and fullness that is not so secure in the evolution of female sexuality for it not to be remarked upon. Detecting this hidden mainspring of her personality produced the effect, if only a transitory one, of profoundly disturbing what had been presented as a complete, mature and happy relationship to the point of producing for a time the disappearance of a satisfying outcome to the sexual act – which, according to the author, proves her case.

With this woman, we therefore find ourselves in the presence, as Mrs Joan Riviere emphasizes, of the need to avoid reprisals from men motivated by the surreptitious theft that she carries out on the source and very symbol of their power. As the analysis progresses, the meaning of her relations with persons of one or the other sex appears more and more obviously to be given, guided and dominated by her concern to avoid punishment and reprisals from the men whom she has in her sights here.

This very fine scansion, which appears as the analysis progresses, as I say, was, however, already discernible in small, anomalous traits. Whenever she had displayed her phallic power, she would rush into a sequence of steps that were either a seduction or even a sacrificial procedure – 'Do everything for others', thereby in appearance adopting the highest form of feminine devotion, as if she was saying, 'But look, I do not have this phallus, I am a woman and purely a woman.' She would adopt a mask, particularly in her professional activities in relation to men – although she was highly qualified, she would suddenly adopt, with a kind of self-effacement, an excessively modest even anxious attitude to the quality of what she had done, thus in reality playing a game of coquettishness, as Mrs Joan Riviere puts it, which would function not so much to reassure as to deceive those who might take offence at what, in her, was presenting fundamentally as aggression and the need for, and jouissance of, supremacy as such, and which was structured on a history of rivalry, first with the mother and then with the father.

In short, with respect to an example like this, as paradoxical as it may seem, we can clearly see that what is at stake in an analysis and in the understanding of a subjective structure is always something that shows us the subject engaged in the process of recognition as such – but recognition of what? Let's clarify this.

The subject is unconscious of the need for recognition, and indeed this is why it's necessary, completely necessary, for us to locate it in an alterity with qualities that were unknown before Freud. This alterity stems purely and simply from the place of signifiers, whereby being is separated off from its own existence.

The fate of a human subject is essentially tied to his relationship with his sign of being, which is the object of all kinds of passions and presentifies death in the process. In his link to this sign, the subject

256

is in effect sufficiently detached from himself to be able to have this apparently unique relationship to his own existence in creation – and this constitutes the ultimate form of what, in analysis, we call masochism, namely that by which the subject apprehends the pain of existing.

The subject, qua existence, finds himself constituted as divided from the outset. Why? Because his being has to become represented elsewhere, in signs, and signs themselves are in a third location. This is what structures the subject in this splitting of himself, and without it it's impossible for us, in any valid way, to found what we call the unconscious.

Take the slightest dream and you will see, provided you analyse it correctly and refer to the *Traumdeutung,* that it isn't in the articulated signifiers, even after you have carried out the initial decoding, that the unconscious is embodied. Freud is constantly stressing and returning to this – there are, he says, hypocritical dreams, and they are nonetheless the representation of a desire, even if only the desire to deceive the analyst. Recall what I emphasized in a fully explicit passage from the analysis of the young homosexual woman. The unconscious discourse is not the last word of the unconscious, it's supported by what truly is the ultimate mainspring of the unconscious and which cannot be expressed in any other way than as the subject's desire to be recognized. And this is so, even where it's through a lie already articulated at the level of mechanisms that escape consciousness – a desire for recognition that is here underlying the lie itself, and which from a false perspective may seem like a lie by the unconscious.

This gives you the meaning of and the key to the necessity we find ourselves under to place this schema, around which I am trying to advance the authentic course of the experience of formations of the unconscious, at the foundation of any analysis of the full subjective phenomenon as it's given in analytic experience. This is the one I recommended to you recently in a form that today I can present more simply. Of course, it's always the simplest forms that have to be introduced last.

257

2

What do we have in this triangle with the three poles, E, P and M, which forms the position of the subject?

We see the subject in a relation to a triad of terms that form the signifying foundations of his entire progress. Namely, M, the mother, insofar as she is the first symbolized object and insofar as

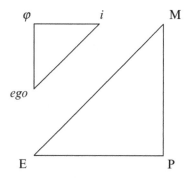

Desired child = ego-ideal

her absence or presence will become, for the subject, the sign of the desire onto which his own desire will hook, and which will make him or not make him, not simply a satisfied child or not, but a desired or undesired child.

This is not an arbitrary construction. Be aware that our experience has taught us to discover, step by step, what I am putting in place here. Experience has taught us what the flow-on consequences are, what almost infinite structuration for a subject, before his birth, flows from the fact of having been a child that is not desired. This term is essential. It's more essential than having been, at this or that moment, a more or less satisfied child. The term 'desired child' corresponds to the establishing of the mother as the seat of desire and to the dialectic of the child's relationship with the mother's desire that I have been attempting to demonstrate to you, which is concentrated in the primordial fact of the symbol of the desired child.

Here, P, the term for the father insofar as he is, as a signifier, the signifier through which signifiers are founded as such. It's for this reason that the father is essentially a creator, I would even say an absolute creator, who creates out of nothing. Signifiers effectively have, within themselves, this original dimension of being able to contain the signifier that defines itself as the emergence of signifiers.

In relation to this, something essentially confused, indeterminate, undetached from its existence and yet made for being detached from it – namely, the subject insofar as he must be signified – has to get its bearings.

If identifications are possible, if the subject in his lived experience succeeds in giving this meaning or that meaning to what has been given to him by his particular human physiology, it's always structured in this triadic relationship formed at the level of signifiers.

258

I don't need to go back over the homology of terms at the level of signifieds, the side where the subject is, in relation to these three symbolic terms. I have partly demonstrated it, and in the end that's all I'm doing here. I ask you to take my word on this, at least till you are better informed, till we get a fuller demonstration.

In the subject's relationship to his own image, he rediscovers the duality of maternal desire in relationship to himself as a desired child, which is only symbolic. He feels it, experiences it in this relationship with this image of himself on which many things can end up being superimposed.

I'm immediately going to give you an example that illustrates this, since I made an allusion last night to the fact that I had been looking quite closely at the history of Gide's childhood, as Jean Delay sets it out for us in a truly exhaustive manner in the pathography that he has given us of this case, under the title *La Jeunesse d'André Gide*.

We know that Gide, this graceless child – as the author says somewhere on seeing a photograph the sight of which made the person tremble – would indulge in the most deformed images in his erotics, his primitive autoerotism, since, as he says, he could achieve an orgasm by identifying with situations of catastrophes. For example, he was able to achieve an orgasm very early on by reading Madame de Ségur, whose books are fundamental with all the ambiguity of primordial sadism, but where this sadism is perhaps not fully developed. Equally, one finds other examples – a child who has been beaten, a servant who drops something with a great 'Crash!', destroying what she was holding in her hands, or again identification with this character of Gribouille in a tale by Hans Christian Anderson, who is carried off by the current and ends up on a far-off bank, transformed into a branch. These are amongst the least humanly constituted forms of the pain of existence.

We can't do anything but grasp something abyssal here that was formed in the subject's first relationship with his mother who, as we know, had both very high and remarkable qualities and something completely elided in her sexuality, in her life as a woman, which, in her presence, clearly left the child in his early years in a completely unsituated position.

259

The turning point at which the life of the young Gide regains, as it were, meaning and human constitution is to be located in a crucial moment of entification that we are given, as clearly as is possible, in his memory, and which without the slightest doubt marks his entire existence. This is his identification with his young female cousin.

Identification, for sure, but it's not enough to use the term in this vague form. He recounts the precise moment, and nobody pays enough attention to its unusual nature. It's the moment when he discovers his cousin in tears on the second floor of this house he has rushed to, attracted not so much by her as by her taste for, her love of, the clandestine that festers in that household. It's after he passes the first floor, where his cousin's mother is – his aunt, whom he sees more or less in the arms of a lover – that he encounters his cousin in tears – and then, the height of euphoria, exaltation, love, distress and devotion. From that point on, he dedicates himself to the protection of this child, as he will later tell us. Let's not forget that she was older than he – at the time, Gide was thirteen years old and Madeleine fifteen.

We can absolutely not understand the meaning of what happened at this moment unless we place it in a threefold relation. The young André doesn't find himself only in the presence of his cousin, but also with a woman who is at the height of her passion on the floor below, namely, the said cousin's mother, who, as he presents it to us in *La Porte Étroite*, had previously made an attempt at seducing him.

What happened at that moment? At the time of the seduction, he became the desired child, and, moreover, he fled in horror effectively because nothing had ever contributed the elements of an approach and a mediation that would have made this anything other than a trauma. Still, he had found himself in the position of a desired child for the first time. This new situation, which in some respects was to be his salvation, would nevertheless fixate him on a profoundly divided position, by reason of the atypical, late and – I repeat this – unmediated way this encounter took place.

What did he acquire from this for the constitution of the symbolic term that had been missing till then? He acquired nothing less than the place of the desired child, which he would eventually be able to occupy by the intermediary of his cousin. In that place where there had been a hole, there is now a place, but nothing more, for in that place he denies himself at the same time, insofar as he is unable to occupy it because he is unable to accept the desire of which he is the object. On the other hand, his ego, undeniably, doesn't stop identifying – and forever, and without knowing it – with the subject of the desire upon which he is now dependent. He falls in love forever, for the rest of his existence – this little boy that for an instant had been in the arms of his aunt, this aunt who stroked his neck, his shoulders and his chest. His entire life is there.

260

We can report the fact, since he admitted as much, that during his honeymoon – everyone is astounded and scandalized by this – and virtually in front of his wife, he would think about the 'excruciating delights', as he expresses it, of being stroked on the arm and shoulder by young boys he had met in the train. This page has become famous, it's part of literature, one in which Gide displays what, for him, will remain the privileged point of the entire fixation of his desire.

In other words, what has been subtracted at the level of what becomes his ego-ideal, namely the desire of which he is the object and which he is unable to bear, he adopts for himself, he falls in love forever and for all eternity with this same caressed little boy he had no wish to be.

The term 'desired child', this signifier which primordially constitutes the subject in his being, is pivotal here. Something must be created here, and the ego must combine with it in one way or another at this point x where he is, which is designated by E. This is where the ego-ideal, which marks the entire psychological development of a subject, is formed.

First, the ego-ideal is marked with the sign of the signifier. Second, the question is – where does it start? It can be formed gradually with the ego as its point of departure, or, alternatively, without the ego being able to do anything but undergo what is produced, unbeknownst to the subject, solely by a succession of accidents subject to the fortunes of the signifier, and which allow him to subsist in the signifying position of a child who is desired to a greater or lesser extent.

The schema thus shows us that it's in the same place – depending on whether it is produced via the conscious pathway or via the unconscious pathway – that what, in one case, we call the ego-ideal and, in the other, perversion is produced.

Andre Gide's perversion doesn't consist so much in the fact that he can only desire little boys, only the [image of] the little boy that he had been, *i*. Andre Gide's perversion consists in the fact that, there, at E, he is able to constitute himself only by perpetually relating himself, only by submitting himself to this correspondence that for him is the heart of his work, only by being the one who makes himself valued in the place occupied by his cousin, the one whose thoughts are all turned towards her, the one who literally gives her, at every moment, everything that he doesn't have, but nothing but that, and who constitutes himself as a personality in her, through her, and in relation to her.

This is what places him, in relation to her, in a deadly dependency, which makes him exclaim somewhere, 'You cannot know what the love of a Uranist is. It's something like an embalmed love.'

This entire projection of his own essence into this relationship is the basis of his existence, the heart and root of his existence as a man of letters, as a man totally in signifiers, and totally in what he communicates to this woman. This is how he exists objectively in his interhuman relations. This woman that he does not desire can effectively be the object of a supreme love for him, and when this object with which he has filled the hole of love without desire disappears, he utters this miserable cry whose similarity to the comical cry par excellence, that of the miser, 'My money box! My precious money box!' I pointed out to you last night.

All passions, insofar as they are the alienation of desire in an object, are on the same footing. Of course the miser's money box makes us laugh more easily – at least, if we have in us a touch of humanity, which is not universally the case – than the disappearance of Gide's correspondence with his wife. Obviously, that was of value to all of us. It doesn't make it any less true that, fundamentally, it's the same thing, and that Gide's cry at the moment his correspondence disappeared is the same cry as that of Harpagon.

What is this comedy I'm referring to?

3

Comedy comes to us in a thousand varied remarks. Comedy is not the comical.

If we want to give a correct theory of comedy, we have to begin with the fact that, at least for a time, comedy was produced for the community, insofar as the latter represents a group of men, that is, insofar as, above itself, it constitutes the existence of a Man as such. Comedy was what it seems to have been at a time when the representation of the relationship between man and woman was the object of a spectacle with a ceremonial value. I am not the first to compare the theatre and Mass, since everybody who has examined the question of theatre has noted that, surely, our day is the only one in which the drama of the Mass represents what the full development of the functions of theatre could represent at a certain moment in history.

At the time of the great period of Greek theatre, tragedy represented man's relationship to speech, insofar as this relationship seizes him in his fatality – a fatality in conflict, insofar as the chain that binds man to the law of signifiers is not the same at the level of the family as at the level of the community. That is the essence of tragedy.

Comedy represents something else, which is not without a link to tragedy, since, as you know, a comedy always completes the tragic trilogy, and we cannot consider it independently. I will show you that we even find both the trace and the shadow of this comedy in the marginal commentary on the Christian drama itself. Of course, this is not to be found in our epoch of constipated

262

Christianity, where, certainly, no one would dare accompany the ceremonies with these robust farces formed by what used to be called the *risus paschalis*. But let's leave that to one side.

Comedy arises at the point at which the subject and man attempt to adopt a different relationship to speech from that in tragedy. It's no longer a matter of committing to or adopting contrary necessities, nor is it a question of it being only one's own affair. It's a matter of that in which he has to express himself as a person whose destiny it is to absorb the substance and matter of this communion, profit from it, enjoy it and consume it. Comedy, one might say, is something like the representation of the end of the communion meal on the basis of which tragedy has been evoked. It's ultimately man who consumes all his substance and common flesh that has been presented there, and it's a matter of finding out what the outcome is.

To see this, I believe there is no other way than to refer to classical comedy, of which all subsequent comedies are merely a degradation in which the traits of their origin are, however, still recognizable. I refer you to the comedies of Aristophanes, *The Assembly of Women*, *Lysistrata*, *Women at the Thesmophoria*, to see where it leads. I started showing this to you – comedy manifests, by a kind of internal necessity, the subject's relationship to his own signifieds, as the result or fruit of the relationship between signifiers. The signifieds must arrive fully developed on the scene of comedy. Comedy embraces, gathers and takes enjoyment from the relationship with an effect that has a fundamental relation to the signifying order, namely the appearance of this signified called the phallus.

It just so happens that, having given you this term, in the days following the brief sketch I gave of Molière's *The School for Wives* as representing the essential comical relationship, I only had to open this text, which I think I can regard as a very unusual and extraordinary resurgence of the master works of comedy, if what I think I read in Aristophanes is right. It's nothing other than Jean Genet's *The Balcony*.

What is *The Balcony*?

You know that there was some fairly lively opposition to its being performed. We shouldn't be astonished by this, in a state of the theatre whose substance and interest can be said to consist primarily in the actors' self-promotion on the stage in various capacities, which delights and titillates those who are there to identify with what we can call by its name – a display. If the theatre is anything else, I certainly believe that this play is well made to get us to appreciate it. It's uncertain whether the public is in a state to view it. It seems to me difficult, though, not to find it dramatically interesting.

Genet speaks of something that means more or less what I am going to try to expound for you. I am not saying that he knows what he is doing. Whether he knows or not is of no kind of importance. Corneille probably didn't know what he was writing as Corneille either, but this didn't prevent him from doing it with great rigour.

Human professions enter the stage of *The Balcony* insofar as they refer to the symbolic: the power that Christ confers on the posterity of Saint Peter and all episcopacies to bind and unbind the order of sin and transgression; the power of the person who condemns and punishes, namely the judge; the power of the person who assumes command in this great phenomenon, war, the power of the warlord, more typically the general. Each of these characters represents functions from which the subject finds himself alienated – they are functions of speech of which he finds himself the support but which go well beyond his singularity.

Now, as it happens these characters are all of a sudden going to be subject to the laws of comedy. That is, we begin to imagine what it is like to enjoy these functions. Disrespectful, no doubt, to pose the question in this way, but the disrespect of comedy is not something one should stop at without trying to discover what it leads to later.

That always starts to emerge in a period of crisis. It's at the highest point in the crisis of Athens – resulting from precisely the aberration of a series of bad choices and a submission to the law of the city that literally seem to lead to its downfall – that Aristophanes attempts this wake-up, which consists in saying that we are ruining ourselves in this war without end and that there is nothing to do but stay at home, keep warm and rediscover one's wife. This is not something that is put forward as a moral, exactly. What is being suggested is that man resume his essential relationship with his state – moreover, without our knowing whether its consequences are all that salubrious.

Thus, we see the bishop, the judge and the general posited there before us on the basis of the question – what is it really like to enjoy the status of a bishop, a judge or a general? This explains the device by which this balcony is nothing other than what is known as a 'house of illusions', a brothel. What happens at the level of different forms of the ego-ideal is not, as is thought, the result of sublimation, in the sense in which this means the progressive neutralization of deeply rooted internal functions. On the contrary, it's a formation that is always more or less accompanied by an eroticization of the symbolic relationship. The person who, in his position and function as bishop, judge or general, enjoys his station can thus be assimilated to this person well known to the keeper of the brothel, such as the little old man who comes for his satisfaction in a strictly

264

calculated fashion, which momentarily places him in a role – the strangest diversity is encountered at this level – adopted in relation to a partner-accomplice who is always willing to play the role of respondent.

Thus, we see a bank employee come and dress up in the garments of a priest and take confession from a prostitute. The confession is of course nothing but a sham, though it must approximate the truth to some extent. In other words, something in the intention of his accomplice needs to make it possible for him at least to believe that she is taking part in some guilty jouissance. Mounting the grotesque on an even grander scale by having the character in question wear buskins to heighten his caricatured position is not the least original aspect of the art and lyricism with which the poet Jean Genet is well able to mount the dialogue of this grotesque character for us. We thus see this clearly perverse subject basking in the pleasure of seeking his satisfaction in this image, insofar as it's the reflection of a function essentially of signifiers.

In other words, in three long scenes Genet presents us with what, at the level of perversion, gets its name from there, namely what, in explicit language, we can at times of great disorder refer to as the brothel in which we live. Effectively, society cannot be defined in any other way than as a more or less advanced state of degradation of culture. All the confusion that builds up in the relations, however fundamental, of man to speech is there represented in its place. We know what he is getting at.

What is this about? It's about something that for us embodies the subject's relationship to the functions of faith in their diverse and most sacred forms, and presents them to us through a series of degradations. This leap made momentarily – namely that we see the bishop himself, the judge and the general here in the place of 'specialists', as they say in the language of perversion – challenges the subject's relationship to the function of speech.

And so, what happens? This is what happens. This relationship, however degraded, however adulterated it is – and it's a relationship where everyone has failed, in which nobody finds himself – continues nonetheless to be staged there before our eyes, sustains itself and subsists, purely and simply. Despite not being recognized as legitimate, it subsists, at the very least, as something linked to the existence of what one calls order.

Now, what does this order come down to when a society has ended up in the most extreme disorder? It comes down to what we call the police. This last resort, this final right, this final argument of order which is called maintaining order, symbolized by the establishment at the centre of the community of a house of ill repute, of what was presented originally as the three crossed pikes – this reduction of everything that is of the nature of order to the maintenance of order is embodied by the pivotal character in the drama, namely the Chief of Police.

Genet's hypothesis, and it's truly a very nice one, is that the image of the Chief of Police, the one who essentially knows that maintaining order depends on him and that he is the ultimate foundation and residue of all power, is not elevated to sufficient nobility for any of the little old men who come to the brothel to ask for his ornaments, attributes, role and function. Some know how to play at being a judge and in the presence of some little prostitute who confesses to being a thief, adopt the role themselves to obtain this confession, for 'How could I be a judge if you weren't a thief?' says the judge. I'll pass over what the general says to his mare. On the other hand, nobody asks to be the Chief of Police.

This is pure hypothesis. I do not have enough experience of brothels to know whether the Chief of Police was not elevated long ago to the dignity of characters whose role one might enjoy. But in the play, the Chief of Police, who is the good friend of the manageress of the whole brothel – I am not at all seeking here to do theory, any more than I am saying that it's about concrete things – comes and anxiously asks, 'Has anyone asked to be the Chief of Police?' And it never happens.

Similarly, there is no Chief of Police's uniform. We see a habit displayed, a judge's wig, a general's hat, though without the latter's pants, but no one has ever assumed the role of a Chief of Police in order to make love. That is the nub of the drama.

266

Now, note that everything that takes place inside the brothel takes place while, outside, there is a revolution raging. Everything that unfolds – and I will pass over the detail, you will gain a lot of pleasure from studying this comedy – everything that unfolds inside – and it's far from being as schematic as I am telling you, there are cries, there are blows, in short they're having a good time – is accompanied, outside, by the rattle of machine guns. The city is in revolt, and all these women are expecting to perish in their beauty, massacred by the dark and virtuous workers who here are supposed to represent the whole man, the real man, the man who is in no doubt that his desire will ultimately prevail and triumph as such in a harmonious manner. Proletarian conscience has always believed that morality will prevail – whether it's right or wrong is irrelevant.

I need to speed up a bit. What is relevant is that Jean Genet takes us to the heart of the adventure in the fact that the Chief of Police is in no doubt, because this is his function, and it's for this reason that the play unfolds as it does, that after the revolution, just as before, it will still be a brothel. He knows that, in this sense, the revolution is a game.

There is one more very beautiful scene in which the blue-blood diplomat comes and enlightens this amiable group who find themselves in the heart of the brothel about what's happening in the Royal Palace. There, in her state of the most complete legitimacy, the Queen is embroidering and is not embroidering. The Queen is snoring and is not snoring. The Queen is embroidering a little handkerchief. There is a swan in the middle, and one doesn't know yet whether it will be on a sea, on a pond or on a cup of tea. I'll pass over what relates to the ultimate disappearance of this symbol.

The one who makes herself the voice and words of the revolution is one of the prostitutes. She has been abducted by a virtuous plumber, and consequently finds herself fulfilling the role of the woman in the Phrygian bonnet on the barricades, with this extra thing that she is a sort of Joan of Arc. Knowledgeable about the ins and outs of masculine dialectics, because she has been in places where one hears it being developed in all its phases, she knows how to speak to them and how to respond to them. The said Chantal disappears in the blink of an eye – she gets shot – and the power appears immediately incarnated in Irma, the manageress of the brothel. The latter adopts, and with such superiority, the functions of the Queen. Has she not also passed over to the pure state of a symbol, since, as the author expresses it somewhere, with her nothing is real apart from her jewels?

267

We then come to the regimentation of the perverts we saw displaying themselves during the entire first act, and to their authentic and integral assumption of the reciprocal functions they embodied in their little, diversely amorous frolics.

A fairly forthright political dialogue takes place between them and the character of the Chief of Police, who needs them to represent the powers that will have to take the place of the previously overturned order. They don't do it without reluctance, understanding very well that it's one thing to enjoy where it's warm, in the shelter inside the walls of one of these houses about which one doesn't sufficiently reflect that it's the very place in which order is the most carefully preserved, but another thing to place oneself at the mercy of the elements, even quite simply of responsibilities that these really absurd functions include. Obviously, here, we are openly at the level of farce.

It's the conclusion of this farce in high taste that, in the end, I would like to emphasize.

In the middle of all this dialogue, the Chief of Police is still concerned. 'Has anyone come and asked to be the Chief of Police? Has

there been anyone who has fully recognized his greatness?' Aware
that he is looking for satisfaction difficult to obtain, discouraged by
having to wait indefinitely for the event that for him would be the
endorsement of his accession to the order of respected – because
profane – functions, the Chief of Police maintains that he has
succeeded in demonstrating that he alone is the order and hub of
everything. This means that there is nothing other, in the end, than
a firm hand, which doesn't lack meaning, insofar as Freud's discovery of the ego-ideal coincided more or less with the inauguration in
Europe of this type of character who offers the political community
a unique and easy identification, namely the dictator. The Chief of
Police, then, consults the people around him on the subject of the
appropriateness of a kind of uniform as well as a symbol that would
be the symbol of his function, and does so not without timidity, just
in case. In fact, he shocks the ears of his listeners just a little – he
suggests a phallus.

Wouldn't the Church take objection? And he leans over to the
bishop who, in effect, shakes his mitre for a moment, hesitates, but
suggests that in the end, if one were to make it like the dove of the
Holy Spirit, it would be more acceptable. Similarly, the general suggests that the said monogram be painted in the national colours.
Some other suggestions of this kind tend to indicate that they
will arrive fairly quickly at what in such circumstances is called a
concordat.

It's at this moment that events take a dramatic turn. One of the
girls, whose role in this play truly swarming with significations
I have passed over, enters the scene, speechless because of the
emotion of what she has just experienced. This is nothing less than
the following. The friend, the saviour of the prostitute, who has
risen to the state of revolutionary symbol – the character of the
plumber, then – who is known in the house, came to see her and
asked her for everything he needed in order to look like the person
of the Chief of Police.

Total uproar. Tightening of the throat. Our worries are over.
Everything was there, including the Chief of Police's toupee. The
latter, startled, asks, 'How did you know?' Someone answers him,
'You are the only person who thinks that nobody knows you wear a
toupee.' Once the character – who is actually the heroic figure in the
drama – has been clothed in all the trappings of the Chief of Police,
the prostitute makes the gesture of throwing in his face, after he has
cut it off himself, that with which, as she coyly puts it, he will never
deflower anybody again. With this, the Chief of Police, who was
very close to arriving at the zenith of his satisfaction, nevertheless
makes the gesture of checking that he still has his. He still does have

268

his, effectively, and his passage to the state of being a symbol in the form of the proposed phallic uniform is henceforth useless.

The conclusion is completely clear. This subject, the one who represents the simple desire of man to encounter and embrace his own existence and thought authentically, a value that is not separate from his flesh – this subject who is there, representing man, the one who has fought so that something that until now we have been calling the brothel can rediscover a basis, a norm, a state that can be accepted as fully human – this subject reintegrates himself into it, once he has passed the test, only on condition of being castrated. That is to say, only on condition of bringing it about that the phallus is again promoted to the status of signifier, as this something that can be given or withheld, conferred or not conferred by the one who at this time is confused, in the most explicit manner, with the image of the creator of the signifier, the 'Our Father', the 'Our Father who art in heaven'.

The comedy ends there. Is it blasphemous? Is it comical? We can place the accent wherever we like.

These terms, which I will come back to, will serve as reference points for the essential question of desire and jouissance, a taste of which I wanted to give you today.

5 March 1958

XV

THE GIRL AND THE PHALLUS

The aporias of the Kleinian approach
The phallus, signifier of desire
The theory of the phallic phase
Critique of Ernest Jones
A step forward

The first presupposition of our task is that you appreciate what we are trying to do here. It is, namely, always to bring you to the point where the difficulties, contradictions and impasses that form the fabric of your practice appear to you in their true significance, whereas you avoid them by referring to partial theories and even by dodging the issue and fudging the meaning by the very terms you use, which are also the locus of all one's excuses.

Last time, I spoke about desire and jouissance. I would like to move ahead today by showing you, in the text itself, Freud's contribution to a precise theoretical point by observing the difficulties that he provokes amongst his followers. In his attempt to be more precise about things, starting from certain preconceived requirements, moreover, something emerges that makes the difficulty even greater. As for us, perhaps we can take a third step.

This has to do with the phallic position in women, or, more precisely, with what Freud calls the phallic phase.

1

I remind you what it is that we have been emphasizing and where it is that we have come to. Over the last three or four sessions, I have begun to articulate this desire that, as such, is placed at the heart of analytic mediation. By condensing what I have said, I have formulated it here in a concentrated form as a 'signified demand'.

You have two terms here that work as one. 'I demand, I notify you of my demand', as we say, 'I notify you of an order, I notify you of a judgement.' The demand therefore implies the other, the one of whom the demand is made, but also the one to whom this demand makes sense, an Other who has, amongst other dimensions, the dimension of being the locus in which this signifier acquires its significance. The second term, the term 'signified', in the sense in which 'I signify something to you, I signify my wish to you', is the important point that I particularly had in mind. The term implies the structuring action in the subject of signifiers that have been constituted, in relation to need, in an essential modification due to the entry of desire into demand.

Let me pause for a moment to make a parenthetical remark.

Up till now, for reasons of time and economy, I have left dreams to one side this year even though I have been discussing formations of the unconscious. You know Freud's statement concerning dreams – that a dream expresses a desire. But, in the end, we have not even started to wonder about what this desire in dreams we talk about actually is. There is more than one in a dream. There are the desires of the day which provide it with its occasion and its material, whereas, as everyone knows, what matters is the unconscious desire.

Why, in short, did Freud recognize this unconscious desire in dreams? In the name of what? How is it recognized? Apparently, there is nothing in a dream that corresponds to the way in which a desire is expressed grammatically. There is no text of a dream except for what has to be translated into an underlying articulation, but at the level of this articulation, which is masked and latent, what differentiates, what identifies what dreams articulate? Nothing, apparently.

Notice that ultimately what Freud recognizes as desire in dreams is clearly indicated by what I am telling you, namely, by the modification of need – which is fundamentally masked because it is articulated in a medium that transforms it. That goes through a number of modes and images which are there as signifiers, and this presupposes that an entire structure has come into play.

This structure is undoubtedly the structure of the subject inasmuch as a number of instances have to be brought into operation, but we only recognize it through the fact that whatever enters into a dream is subject to the modes and transformations of signifiers, to the structures of metaphor and metonymy, condensation and displacement. What gives the law for the expression of desire in dreams is, effectively, the law of signifiers. It is through an exegesis of what is articulated in a particular dream that we can discern something, which is what, ultimately? Something that we assume

wants to be recognized, which partakes of a primordial experience,
which is inscribed therein, is articulated, and which we always relate
to something that originally took place in childhood and has been
repressed. This is ultimately what we give primacy of meaning to in
what is articulated in dreams.

Something quite crucial with respect to structuring the subject's
desire occurs there. Now we can say what it is – it is the primordial
experiences that occurred during the desires of childhood, the essential desires, that is the desire for the Other's desire, or the desire to
be desired. What has been inscribed in the subject over the course
of these events remains there, permanently subjacent. It's what gives
the final word on what interests us in a dream. An unconscious
desire finds expression through the mask of what fortuitously provides a dream with its material. It is signified through the always
specific conditions that the law of the signifier imposes upon desire.

I am trying to teach you to substitute the fundamental notion
of the subject's primordial dependence upon the Other's desire for
the mechanics or economy of gratifications, needs, fixations and
aggressions – which remains more or less confused in the theory
because it is always partial. What is structured in the subject always
passes through the intermediary of this mechanism, which means
that his desire is already shaped by the conditions of demand. That
is what is inscribed in his structure, over the subject's history – these
are the twists and turns, the avatars, of the constitution of desire,
insofar as it is subject to the law of the Other's desire. This is what
makes the most profound of the subject's desires the desire that
remains suspended in the unconscious, the sum, the entirety I would
say, of this capital D, the Other's desire.

Only this can make sense of the developments in analysis that you
are familiar with, which have placed so much emphasis on the primordial relationship with the mother that all of the later dialectic,
even the Oedipal dialectic, has ultimately eluded it, or seems to have.

This movement both heads in the right direction and formulates it
in a way that misses the point. What is important, effectively, is not
merely frustration as such, namely, more or less what in the real has
been given or not given to the subject. It's in what way the subject
has looked for and located this desire of the Other that is the mother's desire. And what matters is to get him to recognize, in relation
to this x of desire in the mother, in what way he has been brought to
become, or not brought to become, the one who corresponds to it,
to become, or not, the desired being.

This is essential. In neglecting it even as she approaches it, in
penetrating as deeply as possible into what happens in the child,
Melanie Klein discovered many things. But by formulating it simply

as the child's encounter with the maternal person, she ends up with a specular, mirroring relation. Consequently, the body – and it is already very striking that the body is in the foreground – the maternal body, becomes the enclosure and habitat for everything in the child's drives that can be located in it through projection, and which themselves are motivated by aggression due to fundamental disappointment. Ultimately, nothing in this dialectic is able to get us out of a mechanism of illusory projection, a construction of the world based on a sort of autogenesis of primordial fantasies. The genesis of the outside as the locus of the bad remains purely artificial and subjects all subsequent access to reality to a pure dialectic of phantasy.

To complement the Kleinian dialectic, it is necessary to introduce this notion that for the subject the outside is already given, not as something that is projected out from the subject's inside, out of his drives, but as the place or the locus in which the Other's desire is located, and where the subject has to go to encounter it.

That is the only way in which we can discover the solution to the aporias engendered by the Kleinian approach, which has shown itself to be so fertile at many points, but ultimately causes the primordial dialectic of desire, as Freud discovered it, to disappear, misses it completely, or reconstructs it in some implicit manner, which she herself does not notice, but in a manner that is illicit because without grounds. This primordial dialectic includes a third relationship, which, beyond the mother, or even through her, brings into play the presence of the character, whether desired or a rival, but invariably a third party, of the father.

This is what justifies the schema I gave you when I told you it is necessary to initially put into place the fundamental symbolic triad, namely the mother, the child and the father.

The mother's absence or presence offers the child – placed here as a symbolic term, this is not the subject – the possibility of being or not being a wanted child and does so merely by virtue of the introduction of the symbolic dimension.

The third term is essential in that he is what permits or prohibits all that. He is placed beyond the mother's absence or presence, as a meaning or signifying presence, which does or doesn't enable him to appear. The subject has to situate himself in relation to this, once the signifying order has come into play.

The subject extends his concrete and real life to him, a life which already consists of desires in the imaginary sense, in the sense of capture, in the sense in which images fascinate him and in the sense in which, in relation to these images, he feels like an ego, a centre, or like a master, or as if dominated.

As you know, the image of oneself, of the body, plays a pri- mordial role in the imaginary relationship in man and comes to dominate everything. The fascination of this image in man is closely bound up with the fact that he is open to this dialectic of signifiers we are talking about. Reducing captivating images to the central image of the image of the body is not unconnected to the fundamental relationship that the subject has with this signifying triad. This relationship to the signifying triad introduces the third term by which the subject, beyond his dual relationship, beyond his relationship of captivation with images, demands, as it were, to be signified. And it is for this reason that there are three poles on the imaginary plane.

In the minimal constitution of the symbolic field beyond the ego and its image, by virtue of the fact that I have to enter under the conditions of the signifier, something must mark the fact that my desire has to be signified, insofar as it necessarily passes through a demand that I must signify on the symbolic plane. In other words, a general symbol of this margin that always separates me off from my desire is required, a margin by virtue of which my desire is always marked by the alteration it undergoes through entering into the signifier. There is a general symbol of this margin, this fundamental lack necessary for my desire's admission into the signifier and for making it the desire that I have to deal with in the analytic dialectic. This symbol is what designates the signified insofar as it is always signified, distorted or even signified to the side.

We can observe this in the schema I gave you [see p. 241]. This triangle is in the subject at the level of the imaginary. Here, his image, *i*. Here, the point at which the ego, *m*, is constituted. Here, what I designate for you with the letter φ, namely the phallus.

The constitutive function of the phallus in the dialectic of the subject's introduction to his pure and simple existence and to his sexual position is impossible to deduce if we don't make it the fundamental signifier by which the subject's desire has to be recognized as such, whether in the case of a man or a woman.

The fact is that desire, whatever it may be, has this phallic reference in the subject. It's the subject's desire, of course, but, insofar as the subject himself has received its signification, he must draw his power as a subject from a sign, and he only obtains this sign through mutilating himself and losing something, by which everything comes to have value.

This is not a deduction. It is given in analytic experience. It's the essence of Freud's discovery.

It's what makes it the case that Freud, writing '*Über die weibliche Sexualität*' ['Female Sexuality'] in 1931, lays down an affirmation

274   that, at first sight, is no doubt problematic, insufficient and in need
of elaboration, and which provokes responses first from all the
women analysts – Helene Deutsch, Karen Horney, Melanie Klein,
Josine Müller along with many others – and then, summarizing all
of that and expressing it in a manner that is more or less compatible
with how Freud puts it, is Ernest Jones's intervention.

This is what we are going to examine today.

2

Let's take up the question at its most paradoxical point.

Initially, the paradox presents itself at the level of a sort of scientific observation. It's as a natural scientist that Freud says to us,
'What my experience shows me is that the phallus is also central for
a woman, and not only for a man.'

Consistent with the general formula that I was trying to give
you just now, he showed us that the subject cannot be introduced
into the dialectic that enables him to take up place and rank in the
transmission of human types and enables him to become a father
in his turn, without what a moment ago I called this fundamental
mutilation owing to which the phallus will become the signifier of
power, the sceptre, and also owing to which virility can be assumed.
Up to that point, we have understood Freud. But he goes further
and shows us how this same phallus appears at the centre of the
feminine dialectic. Here, something gaping seems to open up.

Until now, it was in terms of struggle or biological rivalry that,
at a pinch, we were able to understand man's accession to the qualities of man via the castration complex. But in the woman's case this
affirmation surely presents a paradox, and Freud introduces it initially as a pure and simple fact of observation, one that therefore
presents itself – like everything observed – as a part of nature, as
natural.

This does indeed seem to be how he effectively introduces things
when he tells us – I'll say this as it's written – that the girl, like the
boy, initially desires the mother. There is only one way to desire.
The girl initially thinks she is equipped with a phallus, just as she
also thinks that her mother is equipped with a phallus.

What that means is that the natural evolution of drives brings
it about that, from one transfer to another across the instinctual
phases, from the form of the breast and on through a number
275   of other forms, one arrives at this phallic fantasy by which it is
ultimately in a masculine position that the girl presents herself in
relation to the mother. It's consequently necessary that something

more complex for her than for the boy intervenes for her to recognize her feminine position. In Freud's description, not only is there nothing to support recognition of the feminine position, but it is assumed to be lacking from the outset.

It is no minor paradox to make an affirmation that runs so counter to nature, which, on the contrary, might suggest a symmetry in relation to the position of the boy, by distinguishing the vagina, or even, as someone has said, the vaginal mouth, for the girl. We have observations which go, I would say, contrary to the Freudian data. There are primitive lived experiences the primordial trace of which we can find in young subjects, and which show that, contrary to the claims about a primitive misrecognition, something can stir within the subject, at least as a reaction it seems, at the time of the procedure of breastfeeding. The baby girl still at the breast shows some no doubt vague emotion, but it isn't completely unjustified to refer it to a profound bodily emotion, no doubt difficult to localize behind the memories, but which would, in short, make it possible to equate, through a series of transmissions, the mouth during feeding with the vaginal mouth, and moreover, in the developed state of femininity, with the function of an absorbing or even sucking organ.

There is something here that is locatable in experience, and it provides the continuity by which, if it were merely a question of the migration of the erogenous drive, we could see the royal road to the evolution of femininity traced out at the biological level. It's of this that Jones is effectively making himself the advocate and theoretician when he thinks it is impossible, for all sorts of in-principle reasons, to admit that the evolution of sexuality for a woman is destined for this detour and this artificialism.

Jones proffers, then, a theory that, point by point, opposes what Freud describes as a given of observation – the phallic phase of the little girl rests, according to him, on a drive whose natural supports he demonstrates in two elements. The first, accepted, is primordial biological bisexuality. But this is a point, as we must recognize, that is purely theoretical and a long way from what we can access, so we can be very much in agreement with him when he says it. But there is something else – the presence of the beginnings of a phallic organ. Effectively, the clitoral orgasm of her first pleasures linked to masturbation can give rise to the beginnings of the phallic fantasy that plays the decisive role Freud describes. And this is what he emphasizes – the phallic phase is a clitoral phallic phase, the fantasmatic penis is an exaggeration of the small penis effectively present in female anatomy.

Freud sees the source of the little girl's entry into her feminine position in disappointment. The exit from her phallic phase is

276

engendered by this disappointment, a detour that in his view is, however, founded on a natural mechanism. And it's at this moment, he tells us, that the Oedipus complex plays the normative role it has to play, but in the little girl it plays it inversely to the little boy. The Oedipus complex gives her access to this penis she lacks through perceiving the male's penis, whether she discovers it in a playmate, or places it or, equally, discovers it in the father.

It is through disappointment or disillusionment in relation to this fantasmatic phase of the phallic phase that the little girl is introduced to the Oedipus complex, as was theorized by one of the first analysts to follow Freud in this field, Mrs Lampl-de-Groot. As she quite correctly observed, the little girl enters the Oedipus complex through the inverted phase of the complex. The girl is initially present in the Oedipus complex via her relationship with the mother, and it is the failure of this relationship with the mother which opens up the relationship with the father for her, with what, subsequently, will be found to be normativized by an equivalence between this penis, which she will never possess, and the child that she will effectively be able to have and give in its place.

Note that a number of the reference points I have been teaching you can be found here. *Penisneid* here finds itself to be the essential point of articulation for a woman's entry into the Oedipal dialectic, just as castration finds itself at the heart of the dialectic in a man. No doubt the criticisms I am going to formulate for you, like those that Jones has contributed, will call into question this conception, which, of course, from the outside, when one begins to study analytic theory, looks like an artificial construction.

First, let's pause here for a moment to emphasize the ambiguity with which the term '*Penisneid*' is used at different moments in the girl's Oedipal evolution – as Jones's discussion points out, moreover. *Penisneid* effectively presents itself in three distinct modes, from the entry into to the exit from the Oedipus complex, as Freud describes them concerning the phallic phase.

There is *Penisneid* in the sense of fantasy. It's this wish, this long-maintained wish, sometimes maintained one's whole life – that the clitoris be a penis. Freud insists upon the irreducible character of this fantasy whenever it is kept in the foreground.

There is another meaning, when *Penisneid* intervenes at the moment at which what is desired is the father's penis. This is when the subject attaches herself to the reality of the penis, there where it is, and can see where to go to get it. She is as much deprived of it by Oedipal prohibition as by reason of physiological impossibility.

Finally, in the evolving series, the fantasy of having a child by the father emerges – that is, of having the penis in symbolic form.

277

Remember what I have taught you to distinguish with respect to the castration complex – castration, frustration and privation – and ask yourselves which of these three forms corresponds to each of these three terms.

Frustration is imaginary, but it bears upon an object that is very real. It's in this respect that the fact that the little girl does not receive the penis from the father is frustration.

Privation is completely real, even though it only bears upon a symbolic object. Effectively, when the little girl doesn't have a child by the father, it has ultimately never been any question of ever having one by him. She is incapable of having his child. The child, moreover, is there only as a symbol, and a symbol precisely of that of which she is really deprived. It is, therefore, in the name of privation that the child's desire for the father intervenes at a certain moment in the evolution.

There remains, then, what corresponds to castration, which symbolically amputates the subject of something imaginary. The fact that in this case this is a fantasy corresponds to it quite closely.

Whatever we make of Freud's conception, he's heading in the right direction when he details the little girl's position in relation to her clitoris – at some time she would have to renounce what she was keeping in store, at least as a hope, namely, that sooner or later it would become something as important as a penis. This is the level at which what corresponds structurally to castration is located, if you remember what I thought necessary to spell out when talking to you about castration at the elective point at which it manifests itself – that is, in the boy.

One can dispute whether everything in the girl effectively revolves around the clitoral drive. One can probe the detours of the Oedipal drama, as happens to have been done. You are now going to see this through Jones's critique. But first we cannot fail to notice the rigour, from the structural perspective, of the point that Freud designates as corresponding to castration. It is at the level of a fantasmatic relation – insofar, of course, as it takes on a signifying value – that the symmetrical point was found.

278

It is now a matter of understanding how this comes about. It isn't because that point is used that it gives us the key to the matter. It apparently gives it to us in Freud insofar as he gives the impression of showing us here a story about an anomaly of the drive, and it is this that is going to make a number of subjects revolt and rebel, and do so precisely in the name of biological preconceptions. But you will see, in the very formulation of their objections, what they end up saying. They are, by the nature of things, forced to articulate a number of characteristics that will make taking the next step possible.

It is, effectively, a matter of going beyond the theory of natural drives and seeing that the phallus really does intervene in the way that I have been expounding to you in the premises of today's class. This is nothing other than what I have just been outlining in other ways, namely that the phallus intervenes here as a signifier.

But let's now turn to Jones's exposition, which comes in reply.

3

There are three important articles by Jones on the topic. One, written in 1935, is called 'Early Female Sexuality', and it is this one that we shall be talking about today. It was preceded by the article on 'The Phallic Phase', presented at the Congress of Wiesbaden three years earlier in September 1932, and, finally, by 'Early Development of Female Sexuality', communicated to the Innsbruck Congress in September 1927, which Freud alludes to in his 1931 article when, very contemptuously I must say, he refutes the positions taken by Jones in several lines, who replies in 'The Phallic Phase' by spelling out his position against Freud, in sum, even as he attempts to remain as close as possible to the letter of Freud.

The third article, which I will draw on today, is extremely significant for what we want to demonstrate. It is also the most developed point in Jones's position. It is located four years after Freud's article on female sexuality. It was presented at the request of Federn, who at the time was vice president of the Viennese Society. Jones was brought to Vienna in order to put before the Viennese circle what he straightforwardly formulated as being the London point of view, which was, as it turns out, already centred on the Kleinian experience.

279   In true London fashion, Jones draws some sharp distinctions, his intervention thereby gaining greater purity and clarity, and it's a good basis for discussion. It's very interesting to pause over a number of his remarks, referring as much as possible to the text.

Jones first observes that experience shows us how difficult it is, when one studies a child, to grasp the supposedly masculine position of the little girl in relation to her mother at the time of the phallic phase. The further one goes back towards the origin, the more we find ourselves confronted there with something that is critical. I apologize if by following this text we find ourselves looking at positions that are sometimes a little tangential in relation to the line that I am tracing out for you here, but they deserve our attention for what they reveal.

Jones's suppositions – I am going to tell you this straight off – are essentially directed at what he openly states at the end of the article. Is a woman a being who is born a woman, as such? Or is she a being who is made a woman? That is where he locates his question, and it's what makes him rebel against Freud's position. These are the alternatives towards which his thinking is heading. No doubt his work results from a sort of summary of facts arising from concrete experience with children and which enable one either to object or sometimes to confirm, but, in any case, to rectify Freud's conception – but what informs his entire demonstration is the fact that at the end he raises it as a question, 'Yes or no?' In fact, there is no possibility of a choice in his eyes, one of the two responses being absolutely unacceptable – from his perspective, it would not be possible to maintain a position which implies that half of humanity consists of beings that are made* in the defiles of the Oedipus complex.

He doesn't seem to observe in this respect that the Oedipal defile no less makes men, if this is what it's about. Nevertheless, the fact that women enter with luggage that is not their own seems to him to be sufficiently different from the boy for him to object.

In substance, this claim consists in saying this – it's true that in the little girl we observe, at a particular moment in her evolution, the foregrounding of the phallus and a demand, a desire, which manifests itself in the ambiguous form, so problematic for us, of *Penisneid*. But what is this? Everything that he explains to us consists in this – it's a defensive formation, a detour comparable to a phobia, and the exit from the phallic phase has to be thought of as the recovery from a phobia that is, in short, a very widespread phobia, a normal phobia, but of the same order and with the same mechanism as a phobia.

Since, in short, as you can see, I am choosing to jump right into   280
the heart of his demonstration, it does have to be said that there is something there that is, all the same, extraordinarily opportune for our own reflections, inasmuch as you may still remember the way I attempted to spell out the function of phobia for you. If it is indeed the case that the little girl's relation to the phallus has to be conceived as Jones says, then we are undoubtedly getting closer to the conception I am giving you when I say to you that the phallus intervenes in the little girl's Oedipal relations as a privileged signifying element.

Am I saying that we are about to rally to Jones's position here? Certainly not. If you recall the difference I have drawn between a phobia and a fetish, we can say that here the phallus is playing the role of a fetish rather than of a phobic object. We will come back to this later.

Coming back to the beginning of Jones's critical exposition, let's discuss how this phobia is formed. For him, this phobia is a defensive construction against the danger engendered by the child's primitive drives, both the little girl's and the little boy's. But here it is a question of the little girl, and he observes that her original relationship to the mother – this is where I paused just before when I told you that we were going to encounter some highly unusual things – is proof of a primitive feminine position. He says that she is a long way from behaving towards her mother like a man towards a woman. 'Her mother she regards not as a man regards a woman, as a creature whose wishes to receive something it is a pleasure to fulfil' [p. 265]. He would have us believe that a man considers a woman as a creature whose desires to receive something it is a pleasure to accede to, to fulfil.

We have to acknowledge that it is paradoxical at the very least to introduce a position that is as developed as the relationship between a man and a woman into the level we are at. It is quite certain that when Freud speaks of the masculine position of the little girl, in no way does he make mention of this most complete effect of civilization, if indeed it is ever truly attained, where man is there to fulfil all the desires of a woman. But coming from the pen of someone who enters into this domain with such naturalistic ambitions at the outset, we cannot fail to single out this characteristic as evidence, I would say, of one of the difficulties in this field, and which cannot be such a minor one for him to run up against at this point in his demonstration and, moreover, right at the start. At least he does not confuse, but instead contrasts, man's position with respect to the woman and that of the child with respect to the mother.

281 He then brings in, in the wake of Melanie Klein, the mother as milk jug, whom the child considers – I am translating Jones – as 'a person who had been successful in filling herself with just the things the child wants so badly' [p. 265]. This 'successful' carries a lot of weight because it implies, although Jones is not aware of this, that by basing things on the text of what one finds in the child, the maternal subject is indeed a desiring being. The person who has been successful is the mother, since she has been fortunate enough to succeed in filling herself with the things that the child desires so badly, namely with this pleasant material of both a solid and liquid kind.

One only has access to the child's original experience from a distance, but Melanie Klein has come as close to it as one possibly can by analysing three- to four-year-old children, and has given us the discovery of a relationship to the object that is structured in a form I have characterized as the empire of the maternal body. It's not possible to misrecognize that merely representing that to us is a distinguished contribution.

You will find this in her contributions concerning what she calls the very early Oedipus complex in the child. The latter's drawings show us that the maternal empire carries within it what I have called, with reference to Chinese history, the Warring States. The child is able to draw what she locates as signifiers – brothers, sisters, excrement – inside this field. All of that cohabits in the maternal body, everything is already inside her, since she also identifies what the dialectic of the treatment enables one to describe as the paternal phallus. The latter is supposedly already present as a particularly harmful and rivalrous element in relation to the child's demands concerning possession of the contents of the maternal body.

It is very difficult for us to fail to see that these data call into question and deepen the problematic character of relations that are presented to us as so-called natural, whereas we already see them as structured by what last time I called an entire battery of signifiers articulated in such a way that no natural biological relation could ever account for them.

It is, therefore, already at the level of this primitive experience that the phallus makes its entry onto the stage in the child's dialectic. Although this reference is presented to us by Melanie Klein as deduced from what the child offers, the fact remains no less stupefying. The introduction of the penis as a breast that is more accessible, more convenient and, in some way, more perfect is supposed to be accepted as a fact of experience.

Of course, if this is a given, then it's valid. Nevertheless, it remains the case that it's not self-evident. What can possibly make the penis something more accessible, more convenient and more enjoyable than the primordial breast? It is a question of what this penis signifies and, therefore, of the child's early introduction into a signifying dialectic. Moreover, everything in Jones's demonstration subsequently does nothing but raise this question in an increasingly pressing manner.

As required by his premises, Jones is led to tell us that the phallus can only intervene as the means of and the pretext for a kind of defence. He therefore supposes that at the outset the little girl finds herself interested libidinally in a certain primitive apprehension of her own female organ, and from there he goes on to explain to us why it is necessary that she repress this apprehension of her vagina. The female child's relationship with her own genitals evokes greater anxiety than does the little boy's relationship with his genitals because, as he says, the organ is more internal, more diffuse, more

282

profoundly specific to her first motions. Hence the role that the clitoris will therefore play.

If Jones does not resile here from relatively naive observations, it is, I am convinced, so as to highlight the necessities that they imply. The subject will use the clitoris, he says, insofar as it is external, to project her anxieties onto it, and it will more easily be a reassuring object on her part, because she will be capable of experiencing, through her own experimentations, even visually at a pinch, the fact that the organ is still there. Later in her evolution it will always be external objects, namely her appearance and her clothing, that a woman will make the focus of what he calls the need for reassurance, which thus enables her to temper anxiety by displacing it onto an object that is not its point of origin. The result of this is that precisely this origin turns out to be particularly misrecognized.

As you can see, here we find once again the implied requirement that the phallus come to the foreground as externalizable and representable, as the limiting term at which anxiety stops. That is Jones's dialectic. Let's see whether it is adequate.

This dialectic leads him to present the phallic phase as a phallic position which enables the child to keep anxiety at a distance by centring it on something accessible, whereas her own oral or sadistic desires directed at the interior of the maternal body immediately evoke the fear of reprisals and appear to her as a danger capable of threatening her inside her own body. That is the genesis that Jones gives to the phallic position as a phobia.

283

It is certainly as a fantasized, but accessible, exteriorized organ that the phallus comes into play and will subsequently be capable of disappearing from the scene again. The fears linked to hostility will be capable of being dampened by being referred to other objects than the mother. The erogeneity and anxiety linked to the internal organs will be capable of being displaced through the process of a number of masturbatory practices. Ultimately, he says, the relation to the feminine object will become less partial and will be able to be displaced onto other objects, and the original unnameable anxiety, linked to the female organ, which corresponds in the girl-child to the castration anxieties in the boy, can subsequently vary and transform itself into this fear of being abandoned which, in the words of Jones, is characteristic of female psychology.

That, then, is the problem we find ourselves faced with, and you see how Freud intends to resolve it. His position is that of an observer, and therefore his elaboration presents itself as an empirical observation.

The link with the phallic phase is in the nature of a drive. The entry into femininity occurs on the basis of a libido which, by its nature, is, let's say, active – in order to put things exactly in their place, without following Jones in his critique, which is a bit of a caricature. One arrives at the feminine position to the extent that, through a series of transformations and equivalences, disappointment manages to give birth in the subject to a demand with respect to the paternal figure, that something that will fulfil her desire come to her.

Ultimately, Freud's presupposition, fully spelt out moreover, is that the primordial infantile demand is, as he says, *ziellos*, aimless. What she demands is everything, and it's by virtue of the disappointment of this demand, moreover impossible to satisfy, that little by little the child enters into a more normative position. That is, surely, a formulation which, as problematic as it may be, comprises an opening that will enable us to elaborate the problem with the terms 'desire' and 'demand', which are the ones I have been trying to emphasize.

Jones's response to this is that this is a natural history, a naturalist's observation – which is not as natural as all that – 'and I will make it more natural for you'. He says as much. The history of phallic phobia is only a detour along the path to a primordially determined position. A woman is born, born a woman, in a position that is already that of a mouth, of an absorbent mouth, a sucking mouth. Following the decline of her phobia, which is nothing but a simple detour, she will rediscover her primitive position. What you call phallic drive is only the artificialism of a counter-described phobia provoked in the child by its hostility and aggression towards the mother. It is nothing but a pure detour in an essentially instinctual cycle, and the woman subsequently and rightfully enters her place, which is vaginal.

That, in summary, is Ernest Jones's conception.

4

In reply, what I will try to spell out for you is this.

The phallus is absolutely inconceivable in Kleinian dynamics or mechanics. It is only conceivable if it is already implied that it is the signifier of lack, the signifier of the distance between the subject's demand and his desire. To accede to this desire, something must always be deducted at the necessary entrance into the cycle of signifiers. If the woman has to go via this signifier, however paradoxical that is, it's insofar as it's not a question for her of fulfilling a primitively given female position, but of entering into a defined dialectic of exchange. Whereas the man, the male, is isolated by virtue of the signifying existence of all the prohibitions that constitute the Oedipal relation, she has to inscribe herself in the cycle of exchanges of alliance and kinship in the name of herself becoming an object of exchange.

What structures the Oedipal relation to begin with is, as every analysis effectively shows us, that the woman must propose or, more exactly, accept being an element in the cycle of exchanges. This fact is huge in itself, and infinitely more important from the natural point of view than all the anomalies in her instinctive evolution that up till now we have been able to observe. We must expect, effectively, that we will find a kind of representative of this at the imaginary level, at the level of desire, in the convoluted ways she has to take to enter it.

The fact that she must – like the man, moreover – inscribe herself in the world of signifiers, is for her punctuated by this desire which, qua signified, will always have to remain at a certain distance from, in the margin of, whatever can be put down to a natural need. Effectively, introduction into this dialectic requires that something in the natural relation has to be amputated, sacrificed – and to what end? Precisely so that it can become the very element that signifies the entry into demand.

285   You will observe a return, which I will not say is surprising, of the necessity – which I have just announced with all the brutality carried by this sociological remark founded on everything we know, most recently articulated by Lévi-Strauss in his *Elementary Structures of Kinship* – the necessity for one half of humanity to become a signifier of exchange, according to various laws, more simply structured in elementary structures, bearing much more sophisticated effects in the complex structures of kinship. What we observe, effectively, in the dialectic of the child's entry into the system of signifiers is in some ways the other side of the woman's passage as signifying object into what we can call the 'social dialectic', in quotation marks, for the entire accent has to be placed here on the dependence of the social with respect to the signifying and combinatory structure. Now, in order for the child to enter into this signifying social dialectic, what do we observe? Very precisely this, that there is no other desire on which it depends more closely and more directly than the woman's desire, and insofar as it is signified precisely by what she lacks, the phallus.

What I have shown you is that everything that we encounter as obstacle or accident in the child's evolution, and this includes the most radical of these obstacles and accidents, is linked to this, that the child doesn't find itself alone with the mother, but that along with the mother there is the signifier of her desire, namely the phallus. We find ourselves here faced with what will be the theme of my next class.

One of two things is true. Either the child enters into the dialectic, makes itself the object in the current of exchanges and, at a given moment, renounces his father and his mother – that is, the primitive objects of his desire. Or he keeps these objects. That is, he retains something in them that is much more than their value, for their value is precisely what can be exchanged. From the moment he reduces these objects to pure signifiers even as he clings to them as objects of his desire, the Oedipal attachment is invariably preserved – that is to say, the infantile relation with parental objects does not pass. And to the extent that it does not pass, and strictly to that extent, we see appear – let's say, in a very general form – these inversions or perversions of desire which show that within the imaginary relation with Oedipal objects, no normativization is possible.

Why not? Very precisely for this reason, which is that, even in the most primitive relation, that of the child to the mother, the phallus as object of the mother's desire is always there in a third place, and this raises an insurmountable obstacle to the satisfaction of the child's desire, which is to be the exclusive object of the mother's desire. And this is what pushes him to a series of solutions, which will always be to reduce or to identify with this triad. If it is necessary for the mother to be phallic, or for the phallus to be put in the mother's place, then we have fetishism. If it is necessary that he bring about within himself, intimately, the conjunction of the phallus and the mother without which nothing in him can be satisfied, then we have transvestism. In short, it's inasmuch as the child – that is, that being who enters with natural needs into this dialectic – does not renounce his object that his desire does not succeed in being satisfied.

286

Desire only succeeds in being satisfied on the condition of a partial renunciation – which is essentially what I initially elaborated by saying that it has to become a demand, that is, a desire qua signified, signified through the existence and intervention of signifiers, that is, in part, alienated desire.

12 March 1958

XVI

INSIGNIAS OF THE IDEAL

Karen Horney and Helene Deutsch
Masculinity complex and
homosexuality
The process of secondary identification
Mother and woman
The metaphor of the ego-ideal

I would like to start today by introducing the question of identifications. For those who were not here last time, as well as for those who were, I will recall the gist of what was said.

I attempted to draw attention to the difficulties that the notion of the phallic phase raises. One finds it quite difficult, in effect, to fit what Freud extracted from experience into any biological rationality, whereas things become clear immediately if we assume that the phallus is taken into a certain subjective function where it has to play the role of a signifier.

This phallus-signifier didn't just come out of the blue. At its origin, which is an imaginary origin, it must have had some property for it to fulfil its signifying function. This isn't just any function – it's one more especially adapted than others to hook the human subject into the entire mechanism of signifiers.

In some ways it's a crossroads-signifier. More or less whatever takes place over the course of the human subject's capture in the signifying system converges upon it inasmuch as one's desire has to pass through this system if it's to gain recognition and inasmuch as it's profoundly modified as a consequence. This is a fact of experience – we encounter the phallus at every turn in our experience of the Oedipal drama, at its entry and at its exits.

One may even say, in a certain problematic way, that it extends beyond this Oedipal drama, since, also, one cannot but be struck by the presence of the phallus, and specifically the paternal phallus, in the primitive Kleinian fantasies. It's precisely this presence that raises for us the question of the register into which these Kleinian fantasies are to be inserted. Should it be the register that Melanie Klein herself proposed in accepting a very early Oedipus complex? Or, on the contrary, should we accept a primitive imaginary functioning classified as pre-Oedipal? The question can be left open for the moment.

To clarify the function of the phallus that is present here in a completely general manner, precisely because it presents itself as a signifier function, we have to see, before we push our formulas to the limit, in what signifying economy the phallus is involved. This means investigating the moment that Freud explored and formulated as the exit from the Oedipus complex, where, following the repression of Oedipal desire, the subject emerges new – and equipped with what? The answer is – with an ego-ideal.

1

In the normal Oedipus complex, the effect of the repression that results from the exit from the Oedipus complex is to constitute an identification in the subject that has an ambivalent relationship with the latter. It's best if we proceed step by step on this. One thing at least emerges unequivocally, I mean in just one way, from what Freud was the first to raise, and no author has neglected to raise it as a minimal formulation – this is an identification distinct from the ego's identification.

Whereas the ego's structure rests on the subject's relationship to the image of the semblable, the ego-ideal's structure raises a problem specific to it. Effectively, the ego-ideal is not put forward – it's almost stating the obvious to say this – as an ideal ego. I have often stressed that the two terms are distinct in Freud, and this is so in the very article, '*Zur Einführung des Narzissmus*' ['On Narcissism'], but you need to look at it with a magnifying glass, for the difference is very difficult to detect in the text, to the point where some people confuse the two. First, this is not accurate, but if it were, by convention we should note that there is no synonymy between what is attributed to the ego-ideal's function in Freud's texts, inspired by clinical experience, and the meaning we may attribute to the ego's image – however much we glorify it by making it an ideal image with which the subject identifies, or a successful model, as it were, of himself, which he confuses himself with and thereby reassures himself of his wholeness.

For example, what is under threat when we make an allusion

to fears of narcissistic attacks on the body, what we are referring to when we speak of the necessity for narcissistic reassurance, can be placed in the register of the ideal ego. As for the ego-ideal, it intervenes in functions that are often depressive, even aggressive, with respect to the subject. Freud brings this into play in diverse forms of depression. At the end of Chapter 7 of *Massenpsychologie* [*Group Psychology and the Analysis of the Ego*], which is called '*Die Identifizierung*' ['Identification'], where for the first time he introduces the notion of the ego-ideal decisively and in an articulated manner, he is inclined to place all forms of depression in the register, not of the ego-ideal, but of some vacillating relationship of conflict between the ego and the ego-ideal.

Let's grant that everything that takes place in the depressive register or, conversely, in that of elation, is to be considered from the angle of open hostility between the two instances, whichever of the instances the declaration of hostilities starts in, whether it be the ego that rebels, or the ego-ideal that becomes too severe, with the consequences and repercussions of the imbalance of this excessive relationship. The fact remains that the ego-ideal presents us with a problem.

We're told that the ego-ideal results from a late identification, that the latter is linked to the three-party relationship in the Oedipus complex, and that desire and rivalry, aggression and hostility mix with one another in a complex manner. Something is being worked out, a conflict, the outcome of which is in the balance. Even if the outcome of the conflict is uncertain, it's nevertheless suggested that it introduces a subjective transformation by virtue of the introduction – introjection, as they say – into a certain structure, which is called the ego-ideal, and which henceforth turns out to be a part of the subject himself – even as it retains, however, a relation to an external object. Both things are there, and we are here touching on the fact that, as analysis teaches us, intrasubjectivity and intersubjectivity cannot be separated. Whatever the modifications that intervene to affect the subject's entourage and milieu, what he acquires as ego-ideal is like the country of an exile which he carries stuck to the soles of his shoes – his ego-ideal does indeed belong to him, it's something acquired. It's not an object, it's something extra in the subject.

We are reminded, with a great deal of insistence, that intrasubjectivity and intersubjectivity must remain connected in the analytic process. In the current use of analysis, people speak of the relations between the ego and the ego-ideal as relations that can be either good or bad, in conflict or harmonious. One brackets, or doesn't succeed in formulating, what has to be formulated and which is imposed by the minimal requirements of our language, namely, that these relationships are always structured as intersubjective relationships.

The same mode of relations that exist between subjects is repro-   290
duced internally to the subject – and, as you well know, it can only be reproduced on the basis of a signifying organization. We are unable to think – even though we say it, and even though it may work when we do say it – that the superego is effectively something severe that spies on the ego and inflicts dreadful misery on it. It is not a person. It functions inside a subject in the way one subject acts towards another subject, and precisely in the sense that a relation-ship between subjects doesn't necessarily imply the existence of a person – conditions introduced by the existence and functioning of signifiers as such are sufficient for the establishment of intersubjec-tive relationships.

It's this intersubjectivity inside the living person that we are dealing with in analysis. It's at the heart of this intersubjectivity that we have to form an idea of what the ego-ideal's function is. You will not find this function in a dictionary, you will not get an unequivo-cal response, you will only find the greatest confusion. This function is, for sure, not to be confused with that of the superego. They came along together almost, but, for this very reason, they were distin-guished from one another. Let's say that they are conflated in part, but that the ego-ideal plays more of a classificatory function in the subject's desire. It does seem to be linked to the adoption of one's sexual type, insofar as the latter is implicated in an entire economy that is at times a social one. It's a matter of masculine and feminine functions, not simply insofar as they result in the act necessary for reproduction, but insofar as they comprise an entire world of rela-tions between men and women.

Of what interest are the findings of analysis on this point? Analysis has made it possible for us to get inside a function that only shows itself at the surface and through its results. It has done this by taking cases where the outcome has been a failure, here fol-lowing the well-known method, called psychopathological, which consists in breaking a function down and dismantling it by grasp-ing it at the point where it turns out to be imperceptibly displaced or deviant, and where, as a result, what is usually inserted more or less normally into all its surroundings appears with its roots and branches laid bare.

I would like to refer here to our experience of the impact on a certain type of subject of the failure of identification, or that we assume to be partial or provisional failure, with what can be called their regular, satisfying type. We will need to choose a particular

291   case. Let's therefore take that of those women where we can discern what has been called the 'masculinity complex' that has been linked to the existence of the phallic phase. We can do this because I have already emphasized the problematic aspect of the existence of this phallic phase.

Is there something of the instinctual here? Could a sort of flaw in instinctual development for which the existence of the clitoris would be solely responsible be the cause of what translates at the other extreme into the masculinity complex? We are already ready to recognize that it can't be that simple. When you look at it closely in Freud, it's not that simple – he saw clearly that it isn't purely and simply a matter of a detour in feminine development required by a natural anomaly or the famous bisexuality. Anyway, the debate that followed shows us that it's not so simple, even if the debate itself was poorly conceived, beginning as it did with the question-begging assumption that it couldn't be so.

The issue is definitely more complex. However, we are not immediately able to formulate what this is, but we clearly see that the vicissitudes of what presents itself as the masculinity complex in women already indicate a connection with the phallic element, a game with or a use of this element – and this is worth hanging onto, since, also, the use to which an element can be put is, still, of a kind to clarify for us what this element is, fundamentally.

What are analysts telling us, then, especially women analysts, who have explored this topic?

2

I won't mention everything they tell us today. I will quite especially refer to two of these analysts that are in the background of Jones's discussion of the problem, Helene Deutsch and Karen Horney. Those of you who read English will be able to go to the article by Helene Deutsch that is called 'The Significance of Masochism in the Mental Life of Women', January 1930, *International Journal of Psychoanalysis*, volume 11, on the one hand, and, on the other, to an article by Karen Horney, January 1924, volume 5, 'On the Genesis of the Castration Complex in Women'.

Whatever one might think of the positions Karen Horney comes to in both theory and technique, she has undeniably been an innovator on the clinical plane from the outset and through to the middle
292   of her career. Her discoveries are still completely valid, however strong or weak are the deductions she might have made from them concerning the anthropological situation of psychoanalysis. What

she emphasizes in her article on the castration complex can be sum-marized as follows. She observes in women an analogy between everything that, clinically, is organized around the idea of castra-tion, and the claims [*revendications*] subjects make concerning the organ as something they lack. In these claims we find the resonances and clinical traces of castration. Using a series of examples, she shows – you should consult this text – that there is no difference in kind' between these cases of phallic demand and certain cases of homosexuality in women, namely those in which the subject, in a certain position with respect to her partner, identifies with the paternal image. There is a seamless continuity between the two. The moments are composed in the same manner. The fantasies, dreams, inhibitions and symptoms are the same. It isn't even possible to say, it seems, that the former constitute an attenuated form of the others, but simply that one has or has not gone beyond a particular thresh-old, which in itself remains vague.

The point that Karen Horney stresses in this respect is the fol-lowing. What happens in these cases encourages us to focus our attention on a particular moment in the Oedipus complex that is placed very close to the end of the period, since it presumes that one has arrived at the moment at which not only is the relationship with the father formed, but it's so well formed that it manifests itself in the little girl subject in the form of an explicit desire for the father's penis, which – and for me this is quite correctly emphasized – therefore implies a recognition of the penis, not as fantasmatic, not in general, not in this ambiguous half-light that constantly makes us wonder what the phallus is, but well and truly a recognition of the reality of the penis. We are not at the level of the question, is it or is it not imaginary?

Of course, in its central function, the phallus implies this imaginary existence. At various phases in the development of this relation, the female subject may, in the face of all opposition, main-tain that she has it, even as she knows full well that she doesn't have it. She has it simply as an image – she has either had it or has to have it, as is frequently the case. But here, we are told, something else is at stake. It's a question of a penis actualized as real and longed-for as such.

I could not put this forward if I had not already modulated the Oedipus complex in its three moments by pointing out to you that it turns up at each of these three moments in different ways. The father as possessing the real penis intervenes at the third moment. I described it especially for the boy, and here things are perfectly situ-ated for the little girl.

What happens, according to what we are told? We are told that, in the cases in question, what results from the privation of what is longed-for is a phenomenon that was not invented by Karen Horney, and is constantly being implemented in Freud's own text – the shift, the mutation that transforms what had been love into identification.

Effectively, it is insofar as the father disappoints an expectation or a demand, with a particular orientation, by the subject that an identification forms. This assumes that the situation is already at an advanced stage. One could say that the subject has reached the peak of the Oedipal situation, were it not that its function consists in the fact that it has to be gone beyond, since it's by going beyond it that the subject will have to find a satisfactory identification with her own sex.

The identification with the father that occurs here is described as a problem, even a mystery. Freud himself stresses that the transformation of love into identification, the possibility of which is manifest here par excellence, is not self-evident. We accept it at this moment, however, and in the first place because we observe it. The thing is to describe how it works, that is, to give a formula that enables us to conceptualize this identification insofar as it is linked to a moment of privation.

I would like to try to give you several formulas for this, because I consider that they are useful for distinguishing what it is from what it is not. If I am introducing this essential element of an articulation in signifiers, it's not for the pleasure, as it were, or simply out of a taste for finding ourselves back amongst words. It's so that we don't use words and signifiers to commit errors of numbing grossness. Let's not take things that are inadequately articulated for things that are sufficiently enlightening. It's by formulating them properly that we will be able effectively to weigh up what's occurring and distinguish what occurs in one case from what occurs in another.

What happens when a female subject takes up a particular position of identifying with the father?

The situation, if you will, is as follows. There is the father, something has been expected at the level of the child, and the singular, paradoxical result is that, from a certain angle and in a certain way, the child becomes this father. She doesn't really become the father, of course, she becomes the father as ego-ideal. A woman in this case can actually say in the most explicit manner, you just have to listen, 'I cough like my father.' This is indeed an identification. Let's try and follow the economy of the transformation step by step.

Still, this little girl is not transformed into a man. We find signs or stigmata of this identification, they are partly expressed and the subject can be aware of them and she may pride herself on them up to a point. What are they? There is no doubt that they are signifying elements.

If a woman says, 'I cough like my father,' or 'I stick my stomach, or my body, out like him,' they are signifying elements. More precisely, in order to get at what is in question, I will use a special term for them, because they are not signifiers brought into play in a signifying chain. I'll call them insignias of the father.

The psychological attitude shows this on the surface – to call things by their name, the subject appears behind the mask of the insignias of masculinity and she places them over what, in every subject as such, is partly undifferentiated.

It's perhaps appropriate here, with the slowness that must always keep us from error, to ask ourselves what becomes of desire in this approach. Where does it all begin? The desire, after all, was not a masculine desire. What becomes of it when the subject adopts the insignias of the father? In relation to whom will these insignias be put to use? In relation, experience shows us, to what takes the place that the mother had occupied in the primitive evolution of the Oedipus complex. From the moment the subject adorns herself with the insignias of that with which she has identified, and the desire that comes into play is transformed in the direction of a passage to the state of a signifier, to the state of an insignia, it is then no longer the same.

What desire are we talking about? At the point in the Oedipus complex we have arrived at and seen what was expected from the relationship with the father, we can suppose that it had been a passionate desire, a properly female appeal and extremely close to a passive genital position. It's quite clear that it's no longer the same desire that is there after the transformation.

Let's leave the question of knowing what has happened to this desire for the moment, and let's return to the term 'privation' that I mentioned earlier. One could also talk about frustration. Why privation rather than frustration? I will point out here that this was left up in the air.

Whatever the case may be, the subject who is here [Child] has also been there [Father] insofar as she has an ego-ideal. Something has thus occurred within her, which is structured as in intersubjectivity. This subject will now deploy a particular desire – what is it?

295

The father's relations with the mother appear on this schema. Now, it's clear that when we analyse a subject like this what we find in her analysis is not the duplication or the reproduction of what takes place between the father and the mother, for all sorts of reasons – if only because the subject has only attained this point

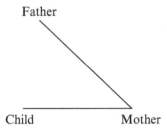

Father

Child   Mother

imperfectly. Experience shows, on the contrary, that what comes up is the entire past, the vicissitudes of the extremely complex relations that to this point have modulated the child's relations with its mother from the outset. That is to say the frustrations, the disappointments linked to the mishaps and fits and starts that necessarily exist, with the entire, extraordinarily complicated relationship that the latter entail, and that bring into play, with a very special emphasis, aggressive relations in their most original form, along with relations of rivalry, marked by the impact, for example, of the arrival of elements external to the trio, namely the brothers or sisters who might have come along more or less inconveniently in the subject's evolution and relations with her mother. That all has an impact, and one rediscovers its trace and its reflection tempering or reinforcing what will then appear as a claim upon the insignias of masculinity. That will all be projected into the young subject's relations with her object. These relations will henceforth be determined on the basis of this point of identification in which the subject adopts the insignias of what she has identified with and which, for her, play the role and function of ego-ideal.

Of course, what I am describing for you is a way of imagining the places in question, but this obviously presupposes, if you want to understand it, that one adds to it some sort of coming and going. The subject carries these insignias with her after this to-and-fro movement and finds herself formed in a new way and with a new desire.

296   What does the mechanism of this transformation entail? Three moments are to be distinguished.

First, there is the subject and one other term, one that has a libidinal value for her.

Next, there is a third term with which the subject has a distinct relationship, and this requires that the radically differentiating element – competition – has intervened in past relations with this term.

Finally, an exchange occurs – what was the object of the libidinal relation becomes something else and is transformed into a signifying function for the subject, and the latter's desire passes over onto another plane, the plane of desire established with the third term. In the process, this other desire comes to be substituted for the initial desire, which is repressed and re-emerges fundamentally transformed.

That is what constitutes the process of identification.

There first has to be a libidinal element that picks out a particular object qua object. This object becomes a signifier in the subject, occupying the place that will henceforth be called the ego-ideal. Desire, on the other hand, undergoes a substitution – another desire takes its place. This other desire doesn't come from nothing, it's not nothing. It existed before – it related to the third term – and it emerges transformed.

That's the schema I ask you to keep in mind, because it's the minimal schema for every process of identification in the true sense of the word, identification at the secondary level, insofar as it grounds the ego-ideal. It never lacks any of these three terms. This to-and-fro is the result of the transformation of an object into a signifier that takes place in the subject and forms the identification that we find at the base of what forms an ego-ideal. This is always accompanied, moreover, by what we can call a transference of desire – another desire comes from somewhere else, from the relationship with a third term that had nothing to do with the first libidinal relation, and this desire is substituted for the first one, but, in and through this substitution, it itself turns out to be transformed. This is absolutely essential. Again, we can explain it differently if we return to our schema in the form in which I am currently presenting it.

In her initial relationship with the primordial object – that's the general formula – the child finds herself adopting a position symmetrical to the father's. She becomes his rival and places herself in opposition to him in relation to the primitive relationship with the object, at a point x, marked with the sign φ. There, she becomes something capable of assuming the insignias of the one whose rival she has become, and it's for this reason that she will subsequently rediscover a place, there where she necessarily is, that is to say at 'Child' – opposite this point x where the events occurred – and where she comes to constitute herself in this new form that is called I, the ego-ideal, thus retaining something from this passage in the most general form.

No longer is it a matter, here, as you can clearly see, of the father or the mother, it's a matter of relations with the object. The mother is the primitive object, the object par excellence. What the subject retains from the comings-and-goings, which have made her the

297

rival of a third term in relation to the object, is characterized by what can be called the common factor resulting from the existence of signifiers in the human psyche. Inasmuch as men have dealings with the world of signifiers, it's the signifiers that constitute the defile by which desire has to pass. Consequently, this toing-and-froing always implies the factor common to the impact of signifiers upon desire, common to what signifies it and to what necessarily makes it a signified desire – this common factor is precisely the phallus.

The phallus is always there. It's the lowest common denominator of this common factor. And this is why we always find it there in every case, whether it's a man or a woman. This is why we place the phallus, the small φ, here, at this point x.

The phallus is the third party in what is the subject's imaginary relationship with himself, $m - i$, always formed in a more-or-less fragile manner. This is the ego's primitive identification, which is always more-or-less ideal, with an always more-or-less disputed image. It has nothing to do with the fundamental relationship the subject maintains with that to which he has addressed his demands, that is, his object.

In these comings-and-goings, the ego-ideal, I, is always formed in opposition to the virtual point at which the rivalry, the competition, the contest* with the third term, this 'P' here, occurs and is in opposition to the common metonymic factor, the phallus, which is found everywhere. Of course, what happens at the level of the ego-ideal consists in having this common factor as a minimum. The ideal is composed in a way that prevents it from being seen, or that only lets it be seen as something that is always slipping between your fingers. It still remains there, circulating at the bottom of every kind of acquisition of signifiers.

Note the following – signifiers always eat into the signified. The ego-ideal is formed in the relationship with this third term, which is here, the father, and it always implies the phallus, and does so solely insofar as this phallus is the common, pivotal factor in the instance of the signifier.

3

Karen Horney has shown us the castration complex's continuity with female homosexuality. What does Helene Deutsch tell us?

She speaks of something else. She, too, tells us that the phallic phase does indeed play the role Freud says it does, except that what matters to her is to follow its subsequent vicissitude, where the girl adopts the masochistic position that is constitutive, she says, of the female position. Inasmuch as clitoral jouissance happens to be forbidden for the little girl, she will find her satisfaction in a position that will, then, no longer be purely passive, but in a position of jouissance that is assured in this very privation of clitoral jouissance that has been imposed on her.

There's a paradox here. But it's a paradox that Helene Deutsch underpins with observations from experience that go so far as to be guidelines for technique. I am reporting the experiential data of a woman analyst, which, without any doubt, are subject to the choice of material that she makes but are nevertheless worth making the effort to consider.

For Helene Deutsch, the question of feminine satisfaction presents itself in a way that is sufficiently complex for her to consider that a woman, in her nature as a woman, is able to find complete satisfaction – complete enough for nothing to appear that presents itself as neurotic or atypical in her behaviour, in her adaptation to her female functions – without, in any clearly marked way, genital satisfaction fully taking place for her.

I repeat, this is Mrs Deutsch's position. For her, satisfaction in the female position can be totally achieved in the maternal relation, in all the stages of the function of reproduction – namely, in the satisfactions specific to the state of pregnancy, breastfeeding and maintaining the maternal position. The maturation of the satisfaction attached to the genital act, orgasm itself, to call it by its name, is something else – it's linked to the dialectic of phallic privation.

In subjects more or less implicated in the phallic dialectic and presenting a certain degree of masculine identification, Helene Deutsch has thus encountered a personality necessarily in conflict, whose equilibrium is therefore precarious and which has been formed on this basis. Reducing this complex relationship too far, pursuing the analysis too far, would be liable to frustrate such a subject of what jouissance she has more or less managed to achieve on the genital plane up to this point. This type of case goes so far as to comprise, according to her, an indication to leave the subject her penis-identifications, which have been more or less successful but are at least established. To decompose, analyse and reduce these identifications would risk placing the subject in a position of loss in comparison with what the treatment reveals to have been the basis of the jouissance she had established before her analysis. What she would acquire on the plane of genital jouissance would be linked to the subject's past as it relates to her identifications. If, effectively, her jouissance consists in the masochistic frustration that the acquired

299

position comprises, by the same token it requires that the position from which this frustration is capable of being exercised be maintained. In other words, under certain conditions, reducing the properly masculine identifications has the capacity to threaten what the subject has achieved at the level of jouissance in the very dialectic of these identifications.

That's worth what it's worth. The issue for us here is simply that that has actually been asserted, and by a female analyst who is not at all lacking in experience and reveals herself to be, surely, if only through her reflections, someone who thinks about her trade and the consequences of what she is doing. It's on this basis – and this basis alone – that that deserves to be kept in consideration.

To summarize Mrs Deutsch's position on interhuman relations – I'm not saying that the genital act presents itself in the same way in robin redbreasts or in praying mantises – in the human species, the centre of gravity of the female's position and its element of major satisfaction is said to be located in what lies outside genital relations as such.

Everything that a woman can find in genital relations is said to be linked to a dialectic whose intervention here should be no surprise to us. What does that mean? It means, first, the extreme importance of what is called preliminary pleasure – which is also quite apparent in the man's position regarding the genital act, although it's perhaps simply more accentuated in the woman. These are the libidinal matters that are to be brought into question. But they are effectively only brought into play when they are captured in the subject's history, in a signifying dialectic that implies the intrusion of possible identification with a third object – the father, in the event. Phallic demands, as an identification with the father complicated by the woman's relationship with her object, are thus said to be only the signifying elaboration of this earlier pleasure from which, it turns out, the satisfactions produced in the genital act have been borrowed. As for the orgasm itself insofar as it's to be identified in the moment of the act, it effectively raises a problem in the woman that deserves to be raised, given what we know physiologically about the absence of an organization of nerves directly designed to produce pleasure in the vagina.

300   This leads us to attempt to formulate the relationship between the ego-ideal and a particular vicissitude of desire in the following manner. As much in the case of the boy as in the case of the girl, at a certain moment there is a relationship with a certain object already formed in its reality as an object, and this object becomes the ego-ideal through its insignias. Why has the desire in question in this relationship with the object been called privation in this

case? Because, we are told, it's not typical for it to relate to a real object.

Of course, when the father intervenes in the girl's evolution – this is the first example I gave – it's necessary, effectively, that he be a being real enough in his physiological constitution for the phallus to pass to a stage of evolution that goes beyond the purely imaginary function, which it is capable of retaining for a long time, in *Penisneid*. This is certain, but what constitutes the privation of desire is not that it's directed at something real, but that it's directed at something that can be demanded. A dialectic of privation can only be instituted, properly speaking, with respect to something that the subject is able to symbolize. It's insofar as the father's penis can be symbolized and demanded that what happens at the level of the identification in question today can occur.

This is completely distinct from what intervenes at the level of the prohibition of phallic jouissance. Clitoral jouissance, to call it by its name, can be prohibited at a given moment in its evolution. What is prohibited rejects the subject, throwing her into a situation in which she can no longer find anything suited to signify herself. This is what gives it its painful character, and inasmuch as the ego finds itself in this position of reject on the part of the ego-ideal, for example, a melancholic state sets in. We shall come back to the nature of this rejection, but you can understand already that what I am alluding to here can be brought into relation with this German term that in our vocabulary I have linked to rejection, namely *Verwerfung*. It's inasmuch as, on behalf of the ego-ideal, the subject in her living reality can find herself in a position from which every possible signification is excluded that the depressive state as such sets in.

The process in question in the formation of the ego-ideal is completely the opposite. The object finds itself faced with what I called privation, inasmuch as it's a question of a negative desire, of an object that can be demanded, and insofar as it's on the level of demand that the subject sees his desire refused. The link between desire that is refused and the object is there at the start of the constitution of this object as a particular signifier that occupies a particular place, is substituted for the subject and becomes a metaphor of the subject.

This occurs in the identification with the object of desire in the case where the girl identifies with her father. This father whom she has desired and who has refused the desire of her demand takes its place. The formation of the ego-ideal thus has a metaphorical character and, just as with a metaphor, what results is the modification of a desire that has nothing to do with the desire involved in

301

constituting the object, a desire that is elsewhere, the one that had bound the little girl to her mother.

Let's call it small *d* in contrast to big D. All the little girl's prior experience with her mother occupies a place here in the question and undergoes the consequences of this metaphor to which desire comes to be bound. Here we rediscover the formula for metaphor that I gave you previously. The result is a change of signification in the relations that have been established to that point in the subject's history.

Since we are still at the first example of the little girl with her father, let's say that it's establishing this new function called the ego-ideal within her that modifies her history and will henceforth mould the subject's relations with her object.

19 March 1958

THE FORMULAS OF DESIRE

Critique of the early Oedipus complex
Desire and mark
On *Totem and Taboo*
The sign of language
The signifier of the barred Other

$$d \longrightarrow \mathcal{S} \lozenge a \rightleftarrows i\,(a) \longleftarrow m$$

$$D \longrightarrow A \lozenge d \rightleftarrows s\,(A) \longleftarrow I$$

$$\Delta \longrightarrow \mathcal{S} \lozenge D \rightleftarrows S\,(A) \longleftarrow \Phi$$

I have started by writing these three formulas on the blackboard so as to avoid writing them incorrectly or incompletely when I come to refer to them. I hope to be able to clarify them all before the end of today's discussion.

Picking things up from where I left off last time, I have learned, not without some satisfaction, that some of my propositions managed to provoke some emotion, namely because I seemed to be endorsing the opinions of a certain female psychoanalyst who felt obliged to put forward the view that some analyses of women did not necessarily benefit from being taken right to the end, for the reason that the very progress of the treatment might deprive the said subjects of the point that they had come to in their sexual relations and threaten the level of jouissance they had acquired and achieved. I was subsequently asked whether I endorsed this position and whether analysis should effectively stop at a certain point for reasons external to the laws of its very progress.

My answer to this would be that everything depends on what one considers the aim of analysis to be – not its external aim, but what it's regulated by, as it were, theoretically. There is, effectively, a perspective according to which the very notion of the development of analysis implies the idea of an adjustment to reality. It takes it as a given that in the condition of man and in the condition of woman, a full explication of this condition must necessarily lead the subject to an adaptation that is in some way preformed and harmonious. It's a hypothesis. In actual fact, there's nothing in experience that would warrant it.

The question of a woman's development and her adaptation to a certain polyvalent register in the human order is clearly a sensitive point in analytic theory. To give you some signposts and to use terms that are the very ones that will return today, in a completely concrete sense this time, doesn't it immediately seem quite certain that it's right, concerning a woman, not to confuse what she desires – I give this term its full meaning – with what she demands? Not to confuse what she demands with what she wants either, in the sense in which one says, 'A woman always gets what she wants'?

These simple reminders, which, if not self-evident, then at least arise from our experience, are intended to show that the question one raises concerning what is to be achieved in analysis is no simple one.

1

What I spoke to you about last week came into the discussion at a tangent. What I wanted to lead you to, and will bring you back to today to create a general formula for it, will function in what follows as a reference point precisely for the critique of normative identifications for men and women.

Last time I gave you an initial glimpse into the identification that produces the ego-ideal, insofar as the latter is the exit point, pivotal point and endpoint of the crisis of the Oedipus complex which analytic experience began with and has not stopped revolving around since, even though it's adopting increasingly centrifugal positions. I insisted on the fact that every identification of the ego-ideal type stemmed from the fact that the subject is placed in a relationship with signifiers in the Other that I called insignias, and on the fact that this relationship grafts itself onto another desire than the desire that had brought the two terms together, the subject and the Other as bearer of these insignias.

That about summarizes it. Of course, it didn't satisfy everybody, even though, speaking to this or that person, that was the only reference I gave. For example, can't you see that it's insofar as a woman identifies with her father that she makes all the accusations against her husband that she had made against her mother? This is pointed out as a prominent feature by Freud, as it is by every author.

There's no question of being fascinated by this example, for we can find the same formula in different forms, but it is a good illustration of what I have just been telling you – the fact that identification occurs when a subject assumes signifiers characteristic of his relations with another includes and implies that the relations of desire between this subject and a third party will rise to the fore. You will discover the subject S, the big A and the little *a*. Where is the big A, where is the little *a*? It doesn't matter – what's important is that there be the two of them.

Let's go back to a remark that pertains to the maxim of La Rochefoucauld's concerning the things that cannot be gazed at steadily, the sun and death. There are things in analysis like that. It's quite curious that it's precisely the central point in analysis that one looks at obliquely and, increasingly, from a distance. The castration complex is one of those things.

Notice what's happening and has been happening ever since Freud's initial understanding of it. There was an essential, pivotal point there in the subject's formation – a strange thing, it has to be said, one that had never been advanced or articulated till then. The step Freud takes is to make the subject's formation revolve around a threat that is precise, particularized, paradoxical, archaic and even horror-provoking in the strict sense of the term, and which arises at a decisive moment that is no doubt pathogenic, but also normative. This threat is not there alone and in isolation, but is coherent with the said Oedipal relationship between the subject, the father and the mother – the father here in the role of vehicle of the threat, and the mother being the intended object of a desire that is profoundly hidden.

You rediscover there, at the origin, precisely what needs to be elucidated – this third relationship in which the relationship to certain insignias will be entered into – insignias that are indicated in the castration complex, but in an enigmatic manner, since these insignias themselves have a singular relationship to the subject. They are under threat, we are told, and, by the same token, it's they that need to be gathered and received, and this in a relationship of desire with respect to a third term, which is the mother.

That's what we find at the start, and, having said that, we are faced with an enigma. We, those of us who are practitioners, have to grasp, coordinate and articulate this relationship, complex by definition and in its essence, which we encounter in the life of our subject. We find a thousand forms, a thousand reflections, a dispersion of images and fundamental relationships, all of whose repercussions, effects and multiple psychological facets we have to grasp in the experience of the neurotic subject. And then what happens?

What happens is this phenomenon that I will call the phenomenon of psychologizing motivation. We start by looking for the origin and meaning of the fear of castration in the individual, and this leads us to a series of displacements and transpositions. I will summarize them for you.

First, the fear of castration is related to the father as object, to fear of the father.

Considering the impact of this fear leads us to appreciate its relationship to a tendency or a desire in the subject, that of his bodily integrity. Consequently, we find the notion of narcissistic fear promoted.

Then, still pursuing a line that is necessarily genetic – that is, one that goes back to origins – as soon as we look for the genesis of what subsequently takes place in the individual, we discover the fear of the female organ, there in the foreground and supported by clinical material, which is always there for us to grasp the ways in which a particular effect is embodied. And in an ambiguous manner – either this organ becomes the locus of the threat against the incriminated organ, or on the contrary it's the model for this organ's disappearance.

Finally, even further back, going back even further still, to the first moment – a striking and singular endpoint at which we have gradually arrived, and I won't go through the list of authors again today, but for this first moment, you know that it's Melanie Klein – what is there at the origins of the fear of castration is the phallus itself, hidden in the depths of the maternal organ. Right at the origins, the paternal phallus is perceived by the child as having its seat inside the maternal body, and this is what the subject dreads.

Is it not already quite striking to see the threatening organ appear as a mirror image before the threatened organ, and in a way that I would describe as more and more mythical the more distant its origins? For the final step to be taken, the father's organ inside the mother's vagina must be regarded as threatening, by virtue of the fact that the subject himself, at the roots of what is called his aggressive, sadistic and primordial tendencies, makes it his ideal weapon. At the first moment, everything thus comes down to a sort of pure reflection of the phallic organ considered as the support of a primitive tendency that is one of pure and simple aggression.

The castration complex is here reduced to the isolation of a partial, primordial, aggressive, and henceforth disconnected, drive.

As a result, all the efforts of authors then tend to reintegrate the castration complex into its context as a complex, which is where it began, and where it was the profound motivation for being the central feature of subjective economy in the original exploration of the neuroses. Authors thus go to the greatest lengths to restore it, all the same, to this place, so much so that when we consider these things, what we see emerging is a set of concepts vainly circling one another. This is how it looks if we closely examine the economy of what Melanie Klein describes as taking place at the level of the early Oedipus complex. This expression is nothing but a contradiction in terms – it's like saying 'pre-Oedipal Oedipus complex'. It's the Oedipus complex before any of the characters in the Oedipus complex have emerged. The interpretative signifiers that she uses to name the drives she encounters, or thinks she encounters, in the child, her very own signifiers, imply the entire dialectic that was at issue in the first place.

And so, we have to go back over this dialectic, in its essence, from the start.

307

2

Castration is an essential feature, if we consider it in the way it has been promoted by analytic experience and analytic theory, and by Freud, and from the start. Let's now work out if we can see what it means. Prior to being fear, prior to being lived, prior to being psychologizable, what does castration mean?

Castration is not actual castration. It's linked to a desire, as I have said. It's even linked to the evolution, progress and maturation of desire in the human subject.

While it's castration, it's quite clear, furthermore, that it is difficult to centre the link with this organ on the notion of the castration complex. It has often been observed that castration is not directed at the genital organs in their totality, and indeed it's for that reason that in the woman it does not take on the aspect of a threat against the female genital organs as such, but the female genital organs insofar as they are something else – specifically, the phallus. Similarly, it has been possible to legitimately pose the question whether in the man it was necessary to single out the penis as such in the notion of the castration complex, or include in it the penis and the testicles. In truth, these discussions are a good indication that what is at stake is something other than this or that. It's something

308   that has a particular relationship with the organs, but a relationship whose signifying character is not in doubt from the outset. It is
its signifying character that is predominant.

Let's just say that, at the very least, a minimum has to be retained
to define what the castration complex is in its essence – it's the relationship of a desire to what for the moment I will call a mark.

In order for desire to successfully traverse phases and come
to maturity, both Freudian experience and analytic theory teach
us that something as problematic to situate as the phallus has
to be marked by the fact that it's retained only insofar as it has
experienced the threat of castration.

This must be maintained as the essential minimum beyond which
we go off into synonyms, shifts in meaning, equivalences and, as a
consequence, obscurity. We literally no longer know what we are
saying if we do not retain these characteristics as essential. Isn't
it better to look, first, in the direction of the relationship as such
between these two poles, between desire and the mark, before
heading off to look for it in the various ways in which it's embodied
for a subject? As soon as we deviate from this starting point, the
reason for this link can only become increasingly enigmatic, problematic and, before long, avoided.

I insist upon this feature of the mark. Moreover, outside analysis, in all its other interpretative or meaningful manifestations, and
certainly in everything that embodies it ceremoniously, ritually or
sociologically, the mark is the sign of what supports this castrating
relation whose emergence in anthropology analysis has made it possible for us to appreciate. Let's not forget the religious incarnations
in which we recognize the castration complex – circumcision, for
example, to call it by its name, or again, in the rites of puberty, this
or that form of inscription, marking or tattooing, linked to a particular phase which unambiguously presents itself as the accession
to a certain stage of desire. All of that always present itself in the
form of a mark and an impression.

You are going to tell me, 'Here we are, then, the mark – not
something difficult to come across. Even where there are flocks,
each shepherd has his little mark in order to distinguish his ewes
from everybody else's.' This is not such a stupid remark, for indeed
there is a relationship, even if it's only that the mark presents itself
as a kind of transcendence in relation to the formation of a flock.
Should that be sufficient for us? It's indeed true that, in a certain
way, circumcision presents itself as constituting a particular flock,
the flock of God's chosen ones. Are we not merely rediscovering
309   that? Certainly not. What analytic experience, and Freud, brought
us at the beginning is that there is a close, even intimate relationship

between desire and the mark. The mark is not simply there as a sign of recognition for the shepherd, whom we would have difficulty locating if required. Where man is concerned, the marked living being has a desire which does not fail to have a certain intimate relationship with the mark.

We mustn't go too quickly and say that this mark modifies desire. In this desire, there is perhaps, from the outset, a gap that makes it possible for this mark to have its special effect. What is certain is that there is a close relationship between what is characteristic of desire in man and the effect, role and function of the mark. Once again, we see here signifier and desire together, which is what the entire investigation we are developing here is about.

I would not like to stray too far, but here is one small parenthesis, all the same. Let's not forget that the question quite obviously leads to the function of signifiers in man, and you are not hearing it said here for the first time. If Freud wrote *Totem and Taboo*, if he had an essential need to do so and derived an essential satisfaction from it – read Jones's text and you will see the importance it had for him – it was not just under the heading of applied psychoanalysis. His satisfaction wasn't in rediscovering the little human animal that he found himself occupied with in his consulting rooms, magnified to the dimensions of the heavens. It was not the celestial dog in relation to the terrestrial dog, as in Spinoza. For him, it was an absolutely essential myth – so essential that, for him, it was not a myth. What is the meaning of *Totem and Taboo*?

The meaning of it is that, if we want to understand anything about Freud's specific enquiry concerning the experience of the Oedipus complex in his patients, we are necessarily led to the theme of the murder of the father.

This is not something that Freud wonders about. But, I ask you, what can it mean that in order to conceptualize the passage from nature to humanity one has to pass via the murder of the father?

According to his method, which is the method of an observer and a natural scientist, he groups facts together and amasses all the documents that his researches bring him concerning this crossroads. There's no doubt we see, occupying the foreground, the point at which his own experience and the ethnological material meet. It doesn't matter that the latter is more or less outdated. It's not important any more. What counts is the fact that the point at which he ends up, which he was happy with, and where he saw that the signs whose tracks he was following were converging, was the point at which the function of a phobia meets the theme of the totem. And this is indistinguishable from a development that places the function of signifiers in the foreground.

310

A phobia is a symptom in which the signifier is isolated, and promoted as isolated, in the foreground. I spent last year explaining this to you by showing you how the signifier of a phobia can have thirty-six thousand significations for the subject. The key point is the missing signifier that would make it possible for the significations, at least for a time, to settle down a little. Without it, the subject is literally overwhelmed by them. A totem is the same thing – a signifier of all trades, a key signifier, the one owing to which everything falls into place, and first and foremost the subject, for the subject discovers what he is in this signifier, just as it's in the name of this totem that what is prohibited comes to be organized for him.

But what is this still veiling or hiding from us, in the end? What is being hidden by the father's murder, inasmuch as taking place around him is the revolution whereby the young males of the horde are seeing that what will become the primitive law – that is, the prohibition of incest – is emerging? To put it simply, it hides the close link that exists between death and the emergence of signifiers.

We all know that in the ordinary course of events life scarcely pauses over the corpses it creates. Big fish eat little fish – or even, once they have killed them, don't eat them. The movement of life reduces down to the same level whatever is there for life to abolish, and it's already a problem to know in what way a death is memorized, even if that memorization remains implicit in some ways, that is, even if, as seems to be the case, it's in the nature of this memorization for the fact to be forgotten by the individual, whether it concerns the murder of the father or the murder of Moses. It's in the nature of a mind to forget what remains absolutely necessary as the key or pivotal point around which it revolves. For a death to be memorized, a link needs to have been turned into a signifier in such a way that this death exists in the real in some other way, in life's abundance. There is no existence of death. There are the dead, and that's it. And when they're dead, nobody in life pays attention to them any longer.

In other words, what is it that accounts both for Freud's passion when he writes *Totem and Taboo* and for the dazzling impact of a book that is very generally rejected and reviled on its publication? And everyone says, 'What's this guy telling us? Where has this come from? What right does he have to be telling us this? We ethnographers have never seen anything like it before.' This doesn't prevent this book from being one of the major events of our century, one that has profoundly transformed the entire inspiration for critical, ethnological, literary and anthropological work.

What does this mean, if not that Freud conjugates two things – desire and the signifier. He conjugates them in the sense in which

311

one says one conjugates a verb. He brings the category of this conjugation into the heart of thinking about man that before him had remained, I should say, academicizing – designating thereby an ancient philosophical affiliation which, from Platonism up to the Stoic and Epicureans sects, and passing via Christianity, has had the profound tendency to forget the organic relationship between desire and signifiers, to exclude desire from signifiers, to reduce it, to account for it in a particular economy of pleasure, to include what is absolutely problematic, irreducible and, strictly speaking, perverse within it, and to avoid what is the essential, living characteristic of the manifestations of human desire, at the forefront of which we must place not only its unadapted and unadaptable, but its fundamentally marked and perverted, character.

It's the state of this link between desire and mark, desire and insignia, and desire and signifier that we are trying to work out here.

3

Let's now turn to the three little formulas I have written out for you.

Today, I merely want to introduce them and tell you what they mean, because we will not be able to progress any further than that. To my mind, these formulas are the ones that make it possible for us to articulate not only something of the problem that I have just put to you, but even all the meanderings, or even wanderings, of analytic thought concerning what still remains our fundamental problem, which is, let's not forget, the problem of desire.

Let's start by clarifying what is meant by the letters that are up there. The little d is desire. The $\math$ is the subject. The little a is the little other, the other insofar as he is our semblable, insofar as his image grabs, captivates and supports us, and insofar as we constitute around him this first order of identifications which I have defined for you as narcissistic identification, which is the small e, the ego.

The first line places these letters in a certain relationship to one another where the arrows indicate that it cannot go from one side to the other, no matter which side it starts from, but that it stops at the point where one directional arrow meets another with the opposite sign. The egoic or narcissistic identification finds itself here in a particular relation with the function of desire. I will come back to this commentary.

The second line is about what I constructed my entire discourse around at the start of the year when I was trying to get you to see in jokes a certain fundamental relationship that desire has, not with signifiers as such, but with speech – namely, with demand. The D

312

written here stands for demand. The big A that comes next is the big Other, the locus, seat or witness that the subject makes reference to as the locus of speech, in his relationship with any kind of little *a*. There is no need here to remind you how much, over a long period of time, and by coming back to it incessantly, I have declared that the big Other as the locus of speech, articulated as such, is necessary. The little *d* is found here, and also, for the first time, the little *s*, with the same signification that it normally has in our formulas, namely that of the signified. The little *s* of big A designates what in the Other is signified, and signified with the help of signifiers – that is, what in the Other, for me as a subject, takes on the value of a signified – that is, what earlier I was calling insignias. It's in relation to these insignias of the Other that the identification occurs whose product and outcome is the constitution of the big I, which is the ego-ideal, in the subject. The mere constitution of these formulas presents you with the fact that access to the identification of the ego-ideal is only possible once the term 'the big Other' is taken into account.

As with the previous lines, the third is trying to articulate a problem in a reference chain [*chaîne-repère*]. This is the problem that I am formulating here with you today.

The delta is precisely what we are enquiring about, namely the very mainspring by which the human subject is placed in a certain relationship with the signifier, the human subject in his essence as a subject, as total subject, as subject in his completely open, problematic and enigmatic character – and which this symbol expresses.

Here we see the subject returning again, this time in relation to the fact that his desire goes through a demand, that he speaks it and that this has a number of effects. Next, you have the big S which is, as usual, the letter I use to designate the signifier. The formula explains that the big S of barred A is precisely what Φ, the phallus, produces. In other words, the phallus is the signifier that introduces something new into A, introduces it only into A, and at the level of A – owing to which this formula will be illuminated by the effects of signifiers. This precise point of impact on the Other is what this formula will enable us to clarify.

313

Let's now return to the matter at hand.

Man's relationship to desire is not a pure and simple relationship of desire. In itself, it isn't a relationship with an object. If the relationship with an object were already established, there would be no problem for analysis. Men would, as we can assume for the majority of animals, go to their object. Man would not have this second relationship, as it were, to the fact that he is a desiring animal, which conditions everything that happens at the level we call perverse – namely, that he enjoys his desire. The entire evolution of desire has

its origins in these lived facts that are classed in, let's say, the masochistic relation, because this is the one we are told to consider first in
the genetic order, although one comes to it by a kind of regression.
The one that suggests itself as the most exemplary and the most
pivotal is either the so-called sadistic relationship or the scopophilic
relationship.

It's quite clear that it's through a reduction, the manipulation or
second-order artificial decomposition of what is given in experience
that we isolate them in the form of drives that are interchangeable
and equivalent to one another. The scopophilic relationship, insofar
as it conjugates exhibition and voyeurism, is always ambiguous –
the subject sees himself being seen, one sees the subject as seen, but,
of course, one does not just see him, but sees him in his jouissance,
in that species of irradiation or phosphorescence that emerges by
virtue of the fact that the subject finds himself in a position that
comes from some sort of primitive gap, in some way extracted from
his relationship of involvement with an object, and from there he
fundamentally grasps himself as the patient in that relation. The fact
that what we find at the core of the analytic exploration of desire is
masochism stems from there – the subject grasps himself as suffering, and he grasps his existence as a living being as one of suffering,
that is, as being a subject of desire.

Where is the problem now? Human desire will always remain
irreducible to any form of reduction and adaptation. No analytic
experience goes against this. The subject does not simply satisfy a
desire, he derives enjoyment from desiring, and this is an essential
dimension of his enjoyment. It's completely erroneous to omit this
primitive datum which, I have to say, the so-called existentialist
investigation has illuminated and cast in a certain light. If what I am
saying here for you, as best I can, is to mean anything, it requires
you to refer to our daily experience, but that is elaborated over the
course of pages that are masterful in a variety of ways by Mister
Sartre in *Being and Nothingness*. It isn't always absolutely rigorous   314
philosophically, but it's certainly the work of an undisputed literary
talent. What is striking is that it has only been possible for things
of this order to be articulated so brilliantly since analysis gave the
dimension of desire freedom of the city.

Mister Jones, whose usefulness to and function in analysis are in
direct proportion to what he didn't understand, very quickly tried
to expound the castration complex by finding an equivalent for it.
To be frank, the phallic signifier was the object of what one could
perhaps call a veritable phobia throughout his entire existence as a
writer and analyst. The best of his writing, which culminates in his
article on the phallic phase, consists precisely in saying this – why

privilege this damned phallus that we find here under our feet at every moment, this inconsistent object, moreover, whereas other things are just as interesting? The vagina, for example. And, effectively, the man is right. It's quite clear that this object is no less interesting than the phallus. We know this. It's just that what astonishes him is that they don't have the same function. He was, strictly speaking, condemned to understand nothing, insofar as, from the outset, from his first sentence, as soon as he tried to spell out what the castration complex is in Freud, he felt the need to produce an equivalent for it, instead of clinging to what there is in the Oedipus complex that might be tough, even irreducible, namely the phallus signifier.

Jones didn't lack an orientation. Perhaps he had only one failing, which was to think that God created them man and woman. This is the sentence with which he ends his article, 'The Phallic Phase', thereby clearly showing the biblical origins of his conviction. Since God created them man and woman, they are therefore well made to go together, and that is where it has to culminate, and if not, we need to say why.

Now, precisely, in analysis we appreciate that when one is asked to say why, one gets into all sorts of complications. This is why, from the start, he substituted the term '*aphanisis*' for the castration complex, which is a word he went looking for in a Greek dictionary, and which, it has to be said, is not one of the words most commonly used by authors. It means disappearance. Disappearance of what? Disappearance of desire. It's what the subject is afraid of in the castration complex, according to Mister Jones. With his jaunty little step of a Shakespearean character, he seems to be unaware that it was already an enormous problem that a living being might feel threatened, as if by some danger, by the disappearance, lack or withdrawal, not of his object, but of his desire. There is no other way of making *aphanisis* equivalent to the castration complex than by defining it as he does, namely as the disappearance of desire. Isn't there something there that completely lacks foundation? That there is already something there that stands at a second or third degree in relation to a relation described in terms of need is not in doubt. However, he does not give the slightest impression of being aware of this.

That said, even if we allow that all the complications suggested by merely posing the problem in these terms have already been resolved, the subject's relationship to the Other remains to be structured, insofar as it's in the Other, in the gaze of the Other, that he apprehends his own position. It's not for nothing that I am singling out the scopophilic position – it's because it's effectively at the core, not only of this position, but also of the Other's attitude, insofar as, although the sadistic position can be described as sadistic in the strict sense, there is no sadistic position that is not accompanied by a degree of masochistic identification. The human subject is, thus, in a detached relationship to his own being, which places him in a position with respect to the Other such that, in both what he grasps and what he enjoys, we are dealing with something other than a relation to the object, we are dealing with a relation to his desire. What we now need to know is this – what does the phallus as such do there? That's where the problem is.

To solve it, let's refrain from trying to engender or imagine the term in question through a genetic reconstitution founded on what I would call the fundamental references of modern obscurantism. I am thinking of formulas that, in my opinion, are so much more stupid than what you find in the little books of catechism, of which an example is: ontogenesis recapitulates phylogenesis. When our great-grandchildren come to know that in our day this was sufficient to explain a heap of things, they will say to themselves that man really is a weird thing – moreover, without realizing what they will have in its place in their time.

It is, then, a question of knowing what the phallus is doing there. For today, let's set out what the existence of the third line comprises, namely that the phallus plays the role of a signifier. What does that mean?

To clarify, let's start with the second line, which means that man has a certain relationship with the little other which is structured like what I have just called human desire, in the sense in which this desire is already fundamentally perverse, and that as a consequence all his demands are marked by a particular relationship, represented by this new little lozenge symbol that we keep coming across in these formulas. It simply implies – this is its entire meaning – that everything here is controlled by this quadratic relationship that from the outset we have always placed at the foundation of our way of articulating the problem, and which says that there is no conceivable – nor articulable, nor possible – $ that is not sustained by the ternary relationship A-a'-a. That's all the lozenge means. In order for demand to exist, to have a chance, or to be something, there needs to be a certain relationship between $s(A)$ and desire as it's structured, A $\lozenge$ d. This refers us back to the first line.

There is, effectively, an organization to these lines. The first indicates that narcissistic identification, namely what constitutes the subject's ego, takes place in a certain relationship all of whose variations, differences and nuances we have seen over the course of time – prestige, presence, domination – in a certain relationship with

316

the image of the other. You find what corresponds to the ego, its correlate, in what lies on the other side of the point of revolution of this table, namely the double line of equivalence there in the middle. The very possibility of the existence of an ego is thus brought into relationship with the subject's fundamentally desiring nature, tied to the avatars of desire, which is expressed here in the first part of the first line.

Similarly, what does all identification with the insignias of the Other, that is, of the third party as such, depend on? On demand. On demand and on the Other's relations with desire.

This is quite clear and quite apparent, and it enables the term by which Freud designates what we quite incorrectly call – I will say why – frustration to be given its full value. Freud says *Versagung*. We know from experience that it's insofar as something is *versagen* that the phenomenon of secondary identification, or identification with the insignias of the Other, is produced in the subject.

What does that imply? That in order for anything to be able to be established for the subject between the big Other as the locus of speech and the phenomenon of his desire – which is located on a completely heterogeneous plane, since it has a relation to the little other as his image – in order to explain human desire as perverse desire, it's necessary that something introduce, into the Other, this same relationship with the little other that is required, necessary and phenomenologically tangible. It's the need for this problem to be spelled out that I am proposing today.

This may seem obscure to you. I will only tell you one thing – it's this. To say that not only does this become increasingly obscure, but that it's also all a muddle, is to say nothing at all. It's possible, on the other hand, that in saying this we will manage to contribute a little bit of order.

317   I propose that Φ, the phallus, is this signifier by which the relationship to *a*, the little other, is introduced into A as the locus of speech, and insofar as the signifier plays a part.

There you are. This looks like it's biting its own tail – but it has to bite its own tail. It's clear that the signifier plays a part, since we encounter this signifier every step of the way. We have encountered it from the outset, since man would not enter into culture – or rather into society if we distinguish between culture and society, but it's the same thing – if the relationship to the signifier were not there at the origin.

Just as we have defined the paternal signifier as the signifier which establishes and authorizes the play of signifiers in the locus of the Other, there is another privileged signifier which has the effect of instituting in the Other the following, thereby changing its nature – and this is why on the third line the symbol for the Other is barred – namely, that it isn't purely and simply the locus of speech, but that it is, like the subject, implicated in the dialectic located on the phenomenal plane of reflection with respect to the little other. What this adds is that this relationship exists inasmuch as the signifier inscribes it.

I ask you to keep this in mind, no matter how difficult it might be for you. You will stop there for today. I will show you what this makes possible to illustrate and formulate another time.

26 March 1958

XVIII

SYMPTOMS AND THEIR MASKS

My interpretations and his
The case of Elisabeth von R.
Dissociating love and desire
Articulated desire is not articulable
Laughter and identification

Today I would like to bring you back to one primitive understanding of the object of our experience, that is, the unconscious.

My aim, in short, is to show you the pathways and possibilities that the discovery of the unconscious opens up for us, without having you forget the limits it places on our powers. It is, in other words, about my showing you from what perspective, from what approach we get an insight into the possibility of normativization – therapeutic normativization – when the entire analytic experience is there to remind you that it nevertheless runs up against the antinomies internal to all normativization in the human condition.

Analysis even makes it possible for us to go into the nature of these limits in depth.

1

One cannot but be struck by the fact that, in one of his last articles – the one whose title has been incorrectly translated as 'Analysis Terminable and Interminable', whereas in fact it's about the finite or the infinite, and where the question is whether an analysis comes to an end or must be situated in a kind of infinite range – Freud points out the projection to infinity of the aim of analysis in the clearest way possible, at the level of concrete experience, as he says, emphasizing what for man is irreducible in the castration complex, for woman in *Penisneid*, that is, in a particular fundamental relationship to the phallus.

What was it that the Freudian discovery emphasized at the outset? It emphasized desire. What Freud essentially discovers, what he apprehends in every kind of symptom, whether they are pathological symptoms or whether they are what he interprets in what till then had presented itself as more or less reducible to normal life – namely, dreams for example – is always a desire.

Moreover, in dreams, he doesn't just talk about desire but about the fulfilment of desire, *Wunscherfüllung*. We should not fail to be struck by this fact – namely, that he speaks about the satisfaction of desire, precisely, in dreams. He also indicates that, in symptoms themselves, there is something that resembles this satisfaction, but it's satisfaction whose problematic character is quite marked, since it's also satisfaction turned upside down.

It already seems, then, that desire is linked to something that is its appearance and, to use this word, its mask. In the way desire presents itself to us in analytic experience, the close link that it maintains with what cloaks it, problematically, invites us to reflect upon this as an essential problem.

Several times recently, I have emphasized the way desire, insofar as it appears in consciousness, manifests itself in a paradoxical form in analytic experience – or, more precisely, how much the latter has promoted this characteristic inherent in desire qua perverse desire, which is a second-order desire, an enjoyment of desire qua desire.

Speaking generally, it's not analysis that discovered the function of desire, but it has made it possible for us to see just how far down goes the fact that human desire is not directly implicated in a pure and simple relationship with the object that satisfies it, but that it's just as much linked to the position that the subject adopts in the presence of this object as it is to the position he adopts outside his relations with the object, in such a way that nothing in his relations with an object is ever completely exhausted.

Moreover, analysis is well placed to remind us of the fact, which has always been known, that desire is restless, fleeting and elusive in nature. It evades synthesis by the ego and leaves it no other way out than that of being nothing but an illusory affirmation of synthesis. While it's always me who desires, this can only be grasped in me in the diversity of these desires.

Behind this phenomenological diversity, behind the contradiction, the anomaly and the aporia of desire, it's certain, moreover, that there exists a deeper relationship, which is the subject's relationship to life and, as one says, to the instincts. By taking this approach, analysis helps us make progress on the subject's situation in relation to his position as a living being. But analysis makes us experience the intermediaries through which the aims or ends, not only of life, but perhaps also of what lies beyond life, are realized. What Freud envisaged, effectively, was some sort of teleology of first vital ends, of ultimate ends that life supposedly aims at lying beyond the pleasure principle – and this is a return to the equilibrium of death. Analysis enabled us, I won't say to define all that, but to catch a glimpse of it, insofar as it has also made it possible for us to follow the course of the fulfilment of desires.

There have always been glimpses of human desire in its internal relations with the Other's desire. One doesn't need to refer to the first chapter of Hegel's *Phenomenology of Mind* to encounter the paths that a reasonably in-depth reflection would enable this research to take. This is in no way to detract from the originality of the new phenomenon that Freud contributes, and which makes it possible for us to throw such essential light on the nature of desire.

The approach that Hegel takes in his first study of desire is far from being, as one thinks from the outside, a uniquely deductive approach. It's a matter of capturing desire through the intermediary of the relations of self-consciousness with the constitution of self-consciousness in the other. The question that this raises, then, is how the dialectic of life itself can be introduced via this intermediary. This can only be translated in Hegel through what, when the occasion arises, he calls a synthesis. Freudian experience shows us quite a different pathway, even though, very curiously and also very remarkably, desire appears there just as profoundly tied to the relationship with the other as such, even though it appears as unconscious desire.

Now let's go back and place ourselves at the level of what this approach to unconscious desire was in the experience of Freud himself, in his experience as a human being. We have to imagine the first moments at which Freud encountered this experience with its quality of surprising novelty, appealing, I won't say to intuition, but rather to divination, since it was about comprehending something beyond a mask.

Now that psychoanalysis is established and has developed into a discourse that is so broad and shifting, we can imagine – but we imagine this fairly poorly – what the significance was of what Freud introduced when he started reading his patients' symptoms and his own dreams and started bringing us the notion of unconscious desire. Indeed, that is what is missing for us to evaluate the true value of his interpretations. We are always quite astonished by what very often appears as their extraordinarily interventionist

322

nature compared to what we allow ourselves to do, and, I would say, compared to what we may and may no longer allow ourselves to do.

One may even add that to some extent his interpretations strike us as wide of the mark. Have I not pointed out to you a thousand times, concerning the case of Dora for example, or his interventions in the analysis of the young homosexual woman whom we have discussed at length here, to what extent Freud's interpretations – and he recognizes this himself – were connected with his incomplete knowledge of psychology, in particular that of homosexuals in general, but also of hysterics? The inadequate knowledge that Freud possessed at that time means that, in more than one case, his interpretations look too directive in nature, almost forced and pre-cipitate all at once, which effectively gives full value to the term 'an interpretation wide of the mark'.

Still, it's certainly true that these interpretations, at that moment, and up to a point, looked like they had to be made and looked like efficacious interpretations for resolving a symptom. What does that mean?

Obviously, this raises a problem. To begin to solve it, we have to mention that when Freud gave interpretations of this nature, he found himself faced with quite a different situation from the present one. Effectively, everything that in a verdict-interpretation emerges from the mouth of an analyst, insofar as there is interpretation in the strict sense – this verdict, what is stated, proposed and given as true literally gets its value from what is left unsaid. The question, therefore, is what is the background of the unsaid against which an interpretation is being given.

At the time when Freud was giving Dora his interpretations, he was telling her, for example, that she was in love with Herr K. and he would indicate to her, in no uncertain terms, that normally she should be redoing her life with him. This comes as a surprise for us, and all the more so because we know that this was out of the question for the best of reasons, and ultimately Dora wants to have nothing to do with it. Nevertheless, an interpretation of this order, when Freud made it, appeared against a background that carried no presumption for the patient that her interlocutor was there to rectify her understanding of the world or bring her object relation to maturity. For a subject to expect such things from the mouth 323 of an analyst, there has to be an entire cultural atmosphere and none of this had been formed as yet. In actual fact, Dora does not know what to expect, she is taken by the hand, and Freud tells her, 'Speak', and there is nothing else on the horizon of an experience conducted in this way – unless implicitly, for, merely by virtue of the fact that she is told to speak, something of the order of truth has to come into play.

This situation is far from being like ours. Today, the subject comes to analysis already with the idea that the maturation of the personality, the instincts and the object relation is a reality that is already organized and normativized, and the analyst stands as the measure of this. The analyst seems to be like the possessor of the pathways into and the secrets about what initially presents itself as a network of relations, and, while not all are known to the subject, at least their general outline is available to him – at least in the notion that there are these grand lines. He has the idea that pauses in his development are conceivable, that progress is an achievement. In short, there is an entire background concerning the normativization of his person, his instincts and so on – add whatever you like to the list. This all implies that when an analyst intervenes he intervenes from a position, it's said, of judgement, of ratification – there is an even more precise word that I will point you to later – which gives his interpretation a completely different weight.

To get a good grasp of what is in question when I speak to you of unconscious desire in the Freudian discovery, one has to return to these times of freshness in which nothing was implied in the analyst's interpretation, except for immediately detecting, behind something that paradoxically presented itself as completely closed, an x that lies beyond.

Each and every one of you here goes crazy over the term 'meaning'. I don't think that this term is anything but a weakening of what was originally involved, whereas the term 'desire', in what it binds and gathers together as identical with the subject, gives what was encountered in the initial understanding of the analytic experience its impact. That's what we should return to if we wish to bring together both where we are now and what is essentially signified not only by our experience but by its possibilities – I mean, by what makes it possible.

This is also what has to keep us from sliding down the slope and giving into the tendency, I would almost say the trap, in which we are ourselves implicated along with the patient that we introduce into the experience – this would be to lead him down a path that would rest upon a number of circular arguments, I mean upon the idea that an ultimate solution can be given to his condition that would in the end allow him to become, let's use the word, identical to some object or other.

324

Let's return, then, to the problematic character of desire such as it presents itself in analytic experience, that is, in every type of symptom.

2

Here, what I am calling a symptom in the most general sense is a morbid symptom as well as a dream and anything that's analysable. What I am calling a symptom is anything that is analysable.

A symptom appears behind a mask, appears in a paradoxical form.

The pain of one of the first hysterics that Freud analyses, Elisabeth von R., initially appears to present itself in a way that is completely closed off. Freud, little by little, with patience that can truly be said here to be inspired by some kind of instinct of a sleuth, relates it to the patient's lengthy presence at the side of her ill father and to the impact, while she was caring for him, of something else that at first he glimpses as if through a fog – namely, the desire that bound her at that time to one of her childhood friends whom she had hoped to make her spouse. Something else presents itself subsequently, also in an incompletely unveiled form, namely her relations with the spouses of her two sisters. The analysis makes us dimly aware that, in various forms, they represented something of importance for her – she detested one of them for some kind of indignity, vulgarity or masculine loutishness, the other on the other hand she seems to have found infinitely seductive. It effectively seems that her symptom precipitated around a number of encounters, and around a sort of oblique meditation concerning the otherwise very good relations between this brother-in-law and one of her sisters. I am going back over these details so as to focus the mind by way of examples.

It's clear that there we are at a primitive period of analytic experience. That Freud should purely and simply say to the patient, as he did not fail to do, that she was in love with her brother-in-law and that her symptoms, namely the pain in her leg, crystallized around this suppressed desire. We now feel and we know, after all the experiences we have had since, that, for a hysteric, this is forcing things – like telling Dora that she was in love with Herr K.

When we come across an observation like this, we experience first hand the above view that I am putting to you. You don't need to turn the observation upside down to do it, for – while Freud doesn't formulate it like this, diagnose it or discern it – he provides all its elements in the clearest of manners. Up to a point, beyond the words that he puts into his paragraphs, the very composition of his observation allows it to appear in a way that is infinitely more convincing than anything he says.

What does he highlight concerning Elisabeth von R.'s experience? Precisely the fact that, in his words and in his experience, in

325

many cases the appearance of hysterical symptoms is bound up with the experience, in itself so difficult, of being entirely devoted to the care of a sick person and playing the role of nurse – and even more so, when one considers the impact that this function has when it's taken on by the subject with respect to someone close. Then, all the ties of affection, even passion, attach the carer to the cared for. The subject thus finds herself in the position of having to satisfy, more so than on any other occasion, what can be emphatically described as a demand. The subject's entire submission, indeed abnegation, in relation to demand is really given by Freud as one of the essential conditions of the situation, insofar as it turns out to be hysterogenic here in this case.

This is made all the more important by the fact that for this hysteric, in contrast with others that he also gives as examples, both the personal and family history is extraordinarily vague and underemphasized, and that, as a consequence, the term 'hysterogenic situation' here becomes highly significant. Freud, moreover, indicates as much.

In the middle formula of my three formulas, I thus isolate, here, the function of demand. Correlatively, as a function of this background position, I would say that essentially the question is about the interest that the subject takes in a situation of desire.

Freud makes only one mistake here, if I may say so, and it's that he is somewhat led along by the requirements of language, orientates the subject prematurely and implicates her in this situation of desire in an overly defined way.

There is a situation of desire and the subject takes an interest in it. But now that we know what an hysteric is, we cannot even add 'whatever side she takes'. This would effectively already imply that she takes one side or another – that she is interested in her brother-in-law from the perspective of her sister or in her sister from the perspective of her brother-in-law. An hysteric's identification is perfectly capable of subsisting, in a correlative manner, in several directions. Here it's twofold. Let's say that the subject is interested, that she is implicated, in the situation of desire and that that's essentially what is represented by a symptom – and this reintroduces the notion of a mask.

The notion of a mask means that desire presents itself in an ambiguous form that does not make it possible for us to orientate the subject in relation to this or that object in the situation. The subject is interested in the situation as such, that is to say, in the relations of desire. This is exactly what is expressed by the symptom that appears, and it's what I call the element of a mask in a symptom.

This is the respect in which Freud can say to us that symptoms speak in the session. The 'it speaks' that I am always talking to you about is there from the first of Freud's formulations, expressed in the text. He will later say that the stomach noises of his patients, when they come to be audible in a session, have the signification of words. But here, what he is telling us is that the pains that reappear, worsen and become more or less intolerable during the session itself are part of the subject's discourse, and that he measures the extent of the heartburn, the impact and the revelatory value of what the subject is avowing and releasing into the session by the tone and modulation of his speech. The trace, the centripetal direction of this trace, the progress of the analysis, is measured by Freud by the very intensity of the modulation by which the subject registers a greater or lesser intensification of his symptom during the session.

I took this example – I could just as well take others, I could just as well take the example of a dream – in order to centre on the problem of symptoms and unconscious desire. The question is that of the link with desire, which remains a question mark, an x, an enigma, which the symptom cloaks itself in – the link, that is, with the mask.

We are told that, insofar as a symptom is unconscious, it is, in short, and to a certain extent, something that speaks and of which one can say with Freud – with Freud from the outset – that it's articulated. A symptom, therefore, goes in the direction of the recognition of desire. But what was the nature of this symptom that is the desire to be recognized, before Freud turned up and, following him, his whole crowd of disciples, the analysts? This recognition has a tendency to surface, to find its own way, but it only manifests itself through the creation of what I have been calling a mask, which is something closed. This recognition of desire is recognition by nobody, it doesn't target anybody, since nobody was able to read it till someone began to discover the key.

This recognition is presented in a form that is closed off to the other. Recognition of desire, then, but recognition by nobody. 327

On the other hand, insofar as desire is a desire for recognition, this is something other than a desire. Moreover, we are told as much – this desire is a repressed desire. It's for this reason that our intervention adds something more to a simple reading. It's a desire that the subject excludes insofar as he wants it to be recognized. As a desire for recognition, it's perhaps a desire, but, at the end of the day, it's a desire for nothing. It's a desire that is not there, a rejected, excluded desire.

This twofold characteristic of unconscious desire, which, by identifying it with its mask, turns it into something different from anything that can be directed towards an object – we must never forget this.

3

That's what enables us literally to read the analytic meaning of what is presented as one of the most essential of Freud's discoveries, namely, the debasement, the *Erniedrigung*, of love life, which stems from the depths of the Oedipus complex.

Freud presents the mother's desire as being at the bottom of this debasement for certain subjects, who, we are specifically told, have not abandoned their incestuous object – well, they have not abandoned it sufficiently, for, ultimately, we learn that no subject ever abandons it completely. There must, of course, be something that corresponds to this greater or lesser abandonment, and we diagnose – fixation on the mother.

These are cases in which Freud presents to us the dissociation of love and desire.

These subjects are incapable of contemplating being with a woman who for them has the full status of being lovable and human, of being in the sense of complete, of a being who, as the saying goes, is able to give and give herself. There is an object there, we are told, which of course means that it's there under a mask, for it isn't the mother that the subject addresses, but the woman who succeeds her and takes her place. Here, then, there is no desire. On the other hand, Freud tells us, these subjects get their pleasure from prostitutes.

What is the meaning of this? As we are at the moment of an initial exploration of the obscurity surrounding the mysteries of desire, I will say – it's inasmuch as the prostitute is the complete opposite of the mother.

Is this entirely sufficient? Is she the complete opposite of the mother? We have made enough progress since then in learning about images and fantasies of the unconscious to know that what the subject seeks in prostitutes is, as it happens, nothing other than what ancient Rome openly displayed, sculptured and represented at the entrance to brothels – namely, the phallus – the phallus insofar as it's what inhabits the prostitute.

What the subject seeks in a prostitute is the phallus of all the other men; it's the phallus as such, the anonymous phallus. There is something problematic here, in an enigmatic form behind the mask, which binds desire to a privileged object whose importance we have only too well come to appreciate by following the phallic phase and the defiles through which subjective experience has to pass in order for the subject to be able to reconnect with his natural desire.

What we are here calling the mother's desire is a symbolic label or designation of what we observe in the facts, namely, the correlative and fractured promotion of the object of desire into two irreconcilable halves. On the one hand, what on our own interpretation can be put forward as being the substitute object, the woman insofar as she is the heir to the mother's function, and insofar as she is dispossessed and deprived of the element of desire. On the other hand, this element of desire itself, which is tied to something extraordinarily problematic and, also, presents itself with the characteristic of a mask and a mark – with the characteristic, let's use the word, of a signifier. Everything happens as if, as soon as it's a question of an unconscious desire, we find ourselves in the presence of a mechanism, a necessary *Spaltung* which makes desire – which for a long time we have presumed alienated in a quite special relationship with the other – appear here as marked, not only by the need for an intermediary in the other as such, but also by the mark of a special signifier, a chosen signifier, which here happens to be the obligatory path which, as it were, the course of the vital force, desire in this case, must follow.

The problematic feature of this particular signifier, the phallus, is the question. That's where what we are considering is located. What raises all the difficulties for us is there. How are we to think about the fact that we have encountered this obstacle along the path to so-called genital maturation? Besides, it's not simply an obstacle, it's an essential defile which makes it the case that it's only through the intermediary of a certain position adopted in relation to the phallus – for the woman, as lack, for the man, as threatened – that what presents itself as what will be, let's say, the best outcome necessarily comes about.

We see here that by intervening, interpreting and naming something, we are always doing more, whatever we do, than we think. The precise word that I wanted to give you on this point earlier is the verb 'to ratify'. We identify the same with the same, and we say, 'That's it.' We substitute someone for this 'nobody' to whom the symptom is addressed inasmuch as it is there on the path to the recognition of desire. We thus always misrecognize, to some extent, the desire that wants to be recognized, inasmuch as we assign an object to it, whereas it's not about an object – desire is desire for this lack which, in the Other, designates another desire.

That will now introduce us to the second of these three formulas that I am proposing to you here, namely the chapter of demand.

329

4

In the way I am tackling things and returning to them, I am trying to spell out for you the originality of this desire which is in question at every moment of an analysis by leaving aside the monitoring we can bring to it in the name of a more or less theoretical idea about an individual's maturation.

I think you must be starting to understand that when I speak of the function of speech, or the instance of the letter in the unconscious, it's clearly not in order to eliminate what is irreducible and unformulatable in desire – not the preverbal, but what lies beyond words.

I say this with respect to a comment that, in the event, was recently made by some very ill-advised person about the fact that certain psychoanalysts – as if there are all that many – gave too much importance to language with respect to this famous 'unformulated' that some philosophers, I do not know why, have made their personal property. This person whom I describe as ill-advised, as it happens, which is the least of what I think, declared that the unformulated is not unformulatable. I would answer them in the following way, which one would do better to pay attention to rather than strive to implicate each and every one in his personal squabbles, for it's a remark that philosophers don't yet seem to be aware of. The perspective is the opposite – the fact that desire is not articulable is no reason for its not being articulated.

What I mean is that in itself desire is articulated, insofar as it's tied to the presence of signifiers in man. Still, this does not mean that it's articulable. Precisely because it essentially involves a link with signifiers, it's never fully articulable in any given case.

Let's now return to this second chapter, which is that of demand, where we are in the articulated articulable, in the actually articulated.

For the moment we are concerned with the link between desire and demand. We won't get to the end of this discussion today, but I will devote the next time to these two terms, desire and demand, and to the paradoxes in desire as masked desire that I designated just before.

Desire is articulated in demand necessarily, because we are only able to approach it through some demand or other. As soon as the patient contacts us and comes to see us, it's to demand something, and we are already getting very involved and being very specific about the situation simply by saying to him, 'I'm listening'. It's appropriate, therefore, to start again on what one might call the premises of demand, on what produces a demand about demand, on what constitutes the situation for a demand and on the way in which demand takes effect inside an individual's life.

330

What institutes a demand? I am not going to redo the 'Fort-Da' dialectic for you. Demand is linked above all to something that is there in the very premises of language, namely the existence of an appeal, which is both the basis of presence and the term that makes it possible to reject it, a game of presence and absence. The object called for by the first words is already no longer an object pure and simple, but a symbol-object – it becomes what the desire for presence makes of it. The initial dialectic is not that of the part object, breast-mother, nourishment-mother or total mother-object as in some kind of Gestaltist approach, as if it were a question of an ever-expanding acquisition. The baby at the breast is well aware that the breast extends to the armpit, neck and hair. The object in question is the symbolic parenthesis of presence, inside of which is the sum of all the objects it can bring. This symbolic parenthesis is already more precious than any good. None of the goods it contains are capable by themselves of satisfying the appeal for presence. As I have already observed several times, none of these goods in particular can be used for anything other than crushing this appeal at its source. The child feeds, perhaps begins to sleep, and at this moment, obviously, there is no longer any question of an appeal. Any relationship with any part-object, as we say, within the maternal presence, is not satisfaction as such, but a substitute, the crushing of desire.

The causal role of the object's symbolization, this object appealed to as object, as the object in its presence, is already marked by the fact – we, too, have read this, but, as always, we don't know how to extract all the consequences from what we read – that an aspect of the mask appears in the object.

What does our good friend, Mister Spitz, contribute, if not that? What is initially recognized by the baby at the breast is the headpiece [*frontal grec*], framework or mask, with a characteristic of the beyond that characterizes this presence as symbolized. His researches effectively go beyond this presence insofar as it's masked, symptomatized and symbolized. With no ambiguity in his behaviour, the child shows us that he possesses the general outline of this beyond.

In another connection, I have already spoken of the very unusual character of the child's reaction to the mask. You put on a mask, you take it off and the child beams – but if, from under this mask, another mask appears, then he no longer laughs and even becomes quite anxious.

There is not even any need to undertake these tiny little exercises. One has to have never observed a child over the course of his development in his first months to be unaware that even before speech, the first true communication – that is, communication with what is beyond what you are for him as a symbolized presence – is laughter. Before talking, the child laughs. The physiological mechanism of laughter is always linked to smiling, relaxation and a level of satisfaction. People have spoken about the outline of a smile on a sated child, but the child laughing at you laughs at you present and awake and in relation not only to the satisfaction of desire but, after and beyond, to what lies beyond presence insofar as it is able to satisfy him and possibly match his desire. The familiar presence, the presence he is accustomed to, which he knows is capable of satisfying his desires in their diversity, is appealed to, apprehended and recognized in this so special code that in the preverbal child is his first laughter in the presences that care for him, feed him and respond to him.

Laughter is also a response to all the maternal games that are the first activities in which modulation and articulation, as such, are brought to him. Laughter is rightly linked to the beyond, as I called it in all the early remarks in my lectures this year on witticisms – beyond the immediate, beyond all demand. Whereas desire is linked to a signifier which happens to be the signifier of presence, the first laughter is addressed beyond this presence, to the subject behind it.

From that moment, from the beginning, as it were, we find the root of the identification that will take place successively, over the course of the child's development, with the mother first and then with the father. I am not saying that this step exhausts the question, but identification is precisely the correlate of this laughter.

The opposite of laughter is, of course, not tears. Tears express colic, they express need. Tears are not a communication, tears are an expression, whereas laughter, inasmuch as I am obliged to articulate it, is a form of communication.

What is the opposite of laughter? Laughter communicates, it's an address to the one who, beyond the signified presence, is the mainspring, the resource of pleasure. Identification? That is the contrary. You are no longer laughing. You are as serious as a Pope, or as a Papa. You act nonchalantly because the person who is there is scowling, because it's no doubt not the moment to laugh. It's not the moment to laugh because this is not the point at which needs are to be satisfied. Desire models itself, as they say, on the person who holds the power to satisfy it and brings the resistance of reality up against it – where reality is perhaps not entirely what one says it is, but it is surely present here in some form and, frankly, already in the dialectic of demand.

According to my old schema, we can see what is at issue in laughter appear when demand reaches its destination, which is beyond the mask, and there it encounters not satisfaction, but a message of presence. When the subject acknowledges the fact that he does indeed have before him the source of all his goods, that is surely when laughter breaks out and the process does not need to be taken any further.

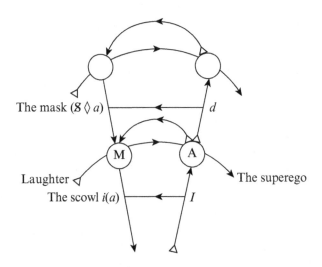

The process may also have to be taken further, however, if he gets scowled at and the demand is rejected. Then, as I've told you, what is at the origin of this need and desire appears in a transformed form. The scowl gets transferred into the circuit and ends up here [$i(a)$], the place where it's not for nothing that we encounter the other's image. What is known as the ego-ideal is produced at the conclusion of this transformation of demand. However, on the signifying line, the principle of what is called prohibition and superego, articulated as coming from the Other, emerges.

Analytic theory has always had great difficulty in reconciling the existence, the coexistence, the co-dimensionality of the ego-ideal and the superego, whereas they correspond to different formations and productions. However, it's sufficient to draw this essential distinction between need and the words in which need is expressed to understand how these two products can be both co-dimensional and different. Even in its most primitive forms, the superego is formulated along the [lower] line of the articulation of signifiers, the line of prohibition, whereas the ego-ideal is produced along the [upper] line of the transformation of desire, insofar as it's always linked to some kind of mask.

In other words, the mask is constructed in dissatisfaction, via the intermediary of rejected demand. This is the point I wanted to bring you to today.

333

But, then, what is the outcome of this? There should be, in sum, as many masks as forms of dissatisfaction.

Yes, that is actually how things seem, and you can take that as your guide with certainty. In the psychological dimension that unfolds following frustration, so alive for some subjects, you can pick out this relationship between dissatisfaction and the mask in their very declarations, and this would mean that, up to a point, there would be as many masks as there are forms of dissatisfaction. The plurality of a subject's relationships with others, according to the diversity of his dissatisfaction, poses a problem here. It's possible to say that, up to a point, it would make every personality a moving mosaic of identifications. What enables a subject to see himself as a subject requires the intervention of a third dimension, which I will leave aside for today and keep in reserve for next time.

334   This dimension is not introduced by genital maturation, as is said, nor by the gift of oblativity, nor by any of the other moralizing blatherings that are the completely secondary features of the question. It's no doubt necessary that a desire intervene therein – a desire that is not a need, but *eros*, a desire that is not autoerotic, but, as they say, alloerotic, which is another way of saying the same thing. It's just that saying that is not enough, since genital maturation is not sufficient to bring about the decisive subjective reworking that will enable us to grasp the link between desire and the mask.

Next time we will see the essential condition that binds the subject to a prevailing, privileged signifier that we call – not by chance, but because concretely it is this signifier – the phallus. We shall see that this is the stage at which, paradoxically, what enables a subject to see himself as one across the diversity of masks is realized, but also, moreover, to see what makes him fundamentally divided, marked by an essential *Spaltung* between what is desire and what is mask.

16 April 1958

XIX

SIGNIFIER, BAR AND PHALLUS

Desire is eccentric to satisfaction
Outline of the graph of desire
Friday's footprint
Aufhebung of the phallus
The Other's castration

Today, we are going to keep exploring the distinction between desire and demand, which we think of as so essential to a well-conducted analysis that we believe that, without it, it will irresistibly slide into a practice of speculation founded on the terms 'frustration' on the one hand and 'gratification' on the other, which, to my mind, constitutes a real deviation in its approach.

What we will do, then, is continue along the direction that we have already given a name to – the distance between desire and demand, their *Spaltung*.

'*Spaltung*' is not a term I choose at random. It was, if not introduced, at least strongly emphasized in Freud's last work, the one he was in the middle of writing when he died. This '*Ichspaltung*' is truly a point of convergence in Freud's final meditation. We cannot say that it brought him back to it again and again because we only have a fragment of several pages which is in volume 17 of the *Gesammelte Werke* and which I advise you to read if you wish to get a sense of the question that this *Spaltung* raises in Freud's mind. You will see, however, the force with which he emphasizes that the ego's synthetic function is far from being everything as far as the psychoanalytic *Ich* is concerned.

I am, therefore, going to pick up from what I was saying last time, for I believe that one can only make progress here by taking three steps forward and two steps back, by starting again and advancing one small step at a time. I will move fairly quickly, all the same, and remind you of what I insisted on when I spoke about desire, on the one hand, and demand, on the other.

336   **1**

As far as desire is concerned, I emphasized that it's inseparable from the mask, and I quite especially illustrated this for you by recalling that it's too swift a move to make a symptom the simple underside in relation to an outside.

I spoke to you about Elisabeth von R., about whom, as I was telling you, by simply reading Freud's text, one is able to formulate, since he himself articulates it, that her pain in the upper-right thigh *is* her father's desire and her childhood friend's desire. In effect, this pain comes up when the patient evokes the time she was entirely enslaved to her sick father's desire and demands, and when her attraction to her childhood friend's desire, which she reproached herself for having taken into consideration, was at work in the margins. The pain in her left thigh *is* the desire of her two brothers-in-law, one of whom, the spouse of her younger sister, represents the good masculine desire, and the other, the bad – the latter was considered, moreover, by all these women as quite a nasty man.

Beyond this remark, what we have to consider before we can understand what our interpretation of desire means is that in a symptom – and this is what 'conversion' means – desire is identical to somatic manifestation. The latter is the front, as the former is the back.

Moreover, since, if we have made any progress, it's only because things have been introduced in problematic form, I introduced the problematic of desire insofar as analysis reveals it to us as determined by an act of signification. But the fact that desire is determined by an act of signification does not at all yield its meaning in any final form. It's possible that desire is a by-product, as it were, of the act of signification.

I cited a number of articles that formed a true introduction to the question of perversion, insofar as it presents itself as a symptom and not as the pure and simple manifestation of an unconscious desire. For me, these articles re-establish the moment at which the authors realize that there is just as much *Verdrängung* [repression] in a perversion as in a symptom. In one of these articles, published in the *International Journal*, fourth year, with the title 'Neurosis and Perversion', the author, Otto Rank, considers the fact that a subject, a neurotic, immediately after having successfully performed his first coitus with satisfaction – this is not to say that others won't also be subsequently – commits a mysterious act, unique in his existence. Returning home from the place of the woman who had granted him her favours, he performs a particularly successful exhibition – I think I already alluded to this in a seminar last year – in the sense that it's performed with the greatest abundance and security at one and the same time. He drops his pants, effectively, and displays himself on the embankment of the railway line, lit up by a train as it goes past. He thus happens to display himself to a whole crowd of people without running the slightest risk. The author interprets this act within the general economy of the subject's neurosis in a way that is more or less successful.

I am not going to elaborate on this aspect, but I will pause at the following – to be sure, for an analyst, it's certain that this is a significant act, as one says, but what does it mean?

I repeat, he has just engaged in his first act of copulation. Does his act mean that he still has it? That it's at everyone's disposal? That it has become, as it were, his personal property? What does he want, then, by displaying it? Does he want to efface himself behind what he is displaying, to be no longer anything but the phallus? All of this is equally plausible about this one same act, and within the one same subjective context.

What, however, seems worth emphasizing more than anything – and this is underlined and confirmed by the patient's words, the context of the observation and the very sequence of things – is that this first coitus was fully satisfying. His satisfaction is captured and realized. But what the act in question shows especially, prior to any other interpretation, is what is left to be desired beyond satisfaction.

I'm only recalling this little example so as to focus your minds on what I mean when I speak about the problematic of desire as being determined by an act of signification – this is distinct from any graspable meaning. Considerations of this kind, which display desire's profound coherence and coalescence with a symptom, or a mask's with what appears in a desire's manifestation, put many futile questions back in their place, questions that one always asks oneself about hysteria, but even more so about all kinds of sociological, ethnographical and other facts, where one always sees people tying themselves up in knots over the question.

Let's take an example. An excellent small book by Michel Leiris has just appeared in a tiny collection by *L'Homme*, published by Plon, about the facts of possession and the theatrical aspects of possession, which he discusses on the basis of his experience amongst the Ethiopians of Gondar. Reading this book, you can clearly see how perfectly the incontestably consistent facts about trances line up or match up with the externally typified, determined, expected, known and mapped-out-in-advance features of the said spirits. The latter supposedly take possession of the people who are the site of all these singular manifestations. This can be observed in the ceremonies known as ceremonies of *wadāgā*, for what's involved can be found there, in the region indicated. There is more. One is struck not only by the conventional part played in the manifestations that are reproduced with the incarnation of this or that spirit, but also by their disciplinable character – to the point where subjects perceive it as a veritable training of these spirits who are, however, supposed to be taking possession of them. The order is reversed – the spirits have to behave themselves, they have an apprenticeship to undertake.

Possession, and everything it implies concerning phenomena powerfully inscribed in the emotions, in a 'pathetics' by which the subject is totally possessed for the duration of its manifestation, is perfectly compatible with the entire signifying richness linked to the domination that the insignias of the god or genie exercise. Attempting to inscribe the thing in the category of simulation, imitation and other terms of this nature would create an artificial problem in order to satisfy the demands of our own mentality. The very identity between the manifestation of desire and its forms is quite apparent here.

The other term to inscribe in this problematic of desire, and on which, in contrast, I insisted last time, is desire's eccentricity in relation to all forms of satisfaction. This term makes it possible for us to understand what, in general, desire's deep affinity with pain is. Ultimately, what desire borders on – not in its developed, masked forms, but in its pure and simple form – is the pain of existence. The latter represents the other pole, the area within which its manifestation presents itself to us.

By describing thus, at the other pole of the problematic, what I call the wandering movement of desire, its being off-centre in relation to satisfaction, I am not claiming to solve the question. This is not an explanation I am giving here, it's a view of the problem. This is what we have to go into more deeply today.

I return to the other element of the diptych I proposed last time, that is, the identificatory and idealizing function, insofar as it comes to depend on the dialectic of demand. Effectively, everything that takes place in the register of identification is founded on a relationship to signifiers in the Other – signifiers which, in the register of demand, are characterized on the whole as a sign of the Other's presence. Something is also instituted there that must bear a relationship to the problem of desire, which is that the sign of presence comes to dominate the satisfactions that this presence brings. This is what makes it the case that, so fundamentally, in such an extended and constant manner, the human being engages as much in empty speech as in more substantial satisfactions – or at least in an appreciable and quite measurable proportion in comparison with the latter. The fundamental characteristic of what I have just been discussing is about this.

Here, again, a complementary parenthesis to what I said last time. Does this mean that the human being is the only being who engages in empty speech? Up to a point, it isn't out of the question that some domestic animals have certain satisfactions linked to human speech. I have no need to evoke these things, but we do learn quite strange things if we can trust the words of those who are called, more or less appropriately, specialists, and who seem to have a degree of credibility. I thus allow myself to say that minks that have been kept in captivity for money, namely, to derive profit from their pelts, waste away and will yield the furriers only fairly mediocre products unless one converses with them. This makes rearing minks very onerous, apparently, and adds to the overall cost. What's apparent here, and we lack the means to pursue this any further, has to be linked to the very fact of being enclosed, that minks in their natural state, to all appearances and till further notice, do not have the possibility of having this satisfaction.

I would simply like to go from there to giving you an indication of the direction from which, in connection with our problem, we can refer to Pavlovian studies on conditioned reflexes. At the end of the day, what are conditioned reflexes?

In their most widespread form, which occupies the greater part of experience, the existence of conditioned reflexes rests on the intervention of signifiers in a more or less predetermined, innate cycle of instinctive behaviours. All the little electrical signals, the little buzzers and little bells which are drummed into the poor animals so as to make them secrete, on command, their various physiological productions, their gastric juices – they are all actually signifiers, really, and nothing but. They are the fabrication of experimenters for whom the world is very clearly constituted by a number of objective relations – a world an important part of which is formed by what one can rightly single out as properly signifying. In any case, the purpose of dreaming up and constructing all these things is to show the path of progressive substitution by which psychical progress can be conceived.

One might wonder why, at the end of the day, when these animals are so well trained, they don't end up having acquired

339

340

some kind of language. Now, precisely, this leap isn't made. When the Pavlovian theory became interested in what happens in man with respect to language, Pavlov took the very correct position, where language is concerned, of speaking, not of a prolongation of significations as it's brought into play in conditioned reflexes, but of a second system of significations. This is to recognize – implicitly, for this is perhaps not fully articulated in the theory – that there is some difference between them. To try to define this difference, I would say that it's due to what I call the relationship to the big Other, insofar as it is the locus of a unitary system of signifiers. I would also say that what the discourse of animals lacks is concatenation.

Ultimately, I would state the simplest formula in this way – no matter how elaborate these experiments, what is not found, and what there is perhaps no question of finding, is the law by which the signifiers involved are organized. This comes down to saying that this is the law by which the animals would be organized. It's completely clear that there is no trace of reference to any such law, that is, to anything that goes beyond a signal or a short chain of signals, once they've been introduced. No kind of law-like extrapolation is visible there, and that's why one can say that no one has ever managed to establish a law. I repeat, this is still not to say that there is no dimension of the Other with a big 'O' for animals, but only that, effectively, nothing like a discourse ever comes of it for them.

Where are we now? If we summarize what is involved in a subject's relationship to signifiers in the Other, namely what is happening in the dialectic of demand, it's essentially this. What characterizes a signifier is not that it's substituted for the subject's needs – which is the case in conditioned reflexes – but that it's capable of being substituted for itself. A signifier is essentially substitutive in nature in relation to itself.

In this direction, we can see that what is dominant, what matters, is the place it occupies in the Other. What points in that direction, and this is what I am trying to formulate here in various ways as essential to the signifying structure, is this topological, not to say typographical, space whose law is the law of substitution. The numbering of places provides the fundamental structure of a signifying system as such.

What one calls identification emerges – this is a fact highlighted by experience – inasmuch as the subject presents himself within a world that is structured in this way in the position of Other. In the absence of satisfaction, a subject will identify with the subject who is able to accede to his demand.

341

2

I left you last time with this question – so, why not the greatest plurality of identifications? As many identifications as there are unsatisfied demands? As many identifications as there are Others that place themselves in the subject's presence as responding, or not responding, to his demand?

This distance, this *Spaltung*, is reflected here in the construction of this little schema that I am putting on the blackboard for you for the first time today.

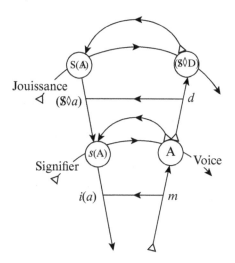

Here, we again find the three lines I have already repeated twice for you [see the formulas at the start of Chapter XVII, p. 285]. I think that you have them in your notes, but I can go over them for you.

The first line links the small *d* of desire to the image of *a* [*i(a)*], on the one hand, and, on the other, to *m*, which is the ego – by the intermediary of the subject's relation to small *a* [$ \, \lozenge \, a$].

The second line represents demand, inasmuch as it goes from demand to identification, passing through the position of the Other in relation to desire. Thus, you see the Other split in two. Desire is there beyond it. This line passes through the signified of A [*s(A)*], which is placed here, on the schema at this first stage that I detailed for you last time when I told you that the Other only corresponds to demand. Because of the something that is what we are looking for, at a second moment it will divide in two and establish itself in a relationship that is not single but double – and which I have already started through other avenues – with two signifying chains.

342

The first chain, which is here when it's single and the only one, is situated at the level of demand – this is a signifying chain which demand has to pass through to emerge. Then, something intervenes to double the signifying relation.

What does this doubling of the signifying relation correspond to? The bottom line can, for example, amongst other things – not in a univocal way, naturally – be identified, as has been done till now, with the mother's response. This is what happens at the level of demand where the mother's response lays down the law all by itself – that is, subjects the subject to its arbitrariness. The other line represents the intervention of another instance, corresponding to the paternal presence, and to the modes under which this instance is felt beyond the mother.

Of course, it's not so simple. If it were all only a question of Mummy and Daddy, I would find it difficult to see how we could explain the facts we are dealing with.

We shall now go into the question of the *Spaltung* – the gap between desire and demand responsible for this discordance or divergence that establishes itself between these two terms. This is why we still need to go back over what a signifier is.

I know, you ask yourselves this every time we part – 'So, what on earth does he mean?' You are right to ask because, to be sure, things are not said this way, it's not so common.

Let's return to the question of what a signifier is at the elementary level. I propose that you stop and think about a number of remarks. For example, do you not think that with signifiers we are touching on something with respect to which one could speak of 'emergence'?

Let's begin with what a trace is. A trace is an imprint, not a signifier. One does, however, get the sense that there may be a relationship between the two, and in actual fact what is called the material of signifiers always partakes in something of the evanescent character of a trace. That even seems to be one of the conditions for the existence of signifying material. It is not a signifier, however. Friday's footprint that Robinson Crusoe discovers during his walk on the island is not a signifier. On the other hand, if we suppose that for one reason or another he, Robinson Crusoe, effaces this trace, then the dimension of signifiers is clearly introduced. As soon as it's removed, where removing it has a meaning, that of which there is a trace is manifestly constituted as signified.

If the signifier is thus a hollow, it's insofar as it bears witness to a past presence. Conversely, in what is a signifier, in fully developed signifiers in speech, there is always a passage, that is, something following each of the elements that are articulated together and that are, by nature, fleeting and evanescent. It's this passage from one

343

to the next that constitutes the essential feature of what I call the signifying chain.

This passage, insofar as it's evanescent, is the very thing that becomes voice – I won't even say 'signifying articulation', for it's possible that the articulation remains enigmatic, but it's the voice that sustains this passage. It's also at this level that what corresponds to what we initially designated as the signifier as bearing witness to a past presence emerges. Conversely, when the passage is present, something emerges that deepens it, that is beyond it and that makes it a voice.

What we still find there is that if there is a text, if the signifier is inscribed among other signifiers, what remains after the effacement is the place where one has done the effacing, and this place also sustains transmission. Transmission is something essential there, since it's due to it that what is linked together in the passage adopts the consistency of voice.

As to the question of emergence, this is one essential point to grasp, which is that a signifier as such is something that can be effaced, leaving nothing but its place – that is, it can no longer be found. This is an essential property, and it means that, while one can speak of emergence, one cannot speak of development. In reality a signifier contains this property within itself. I mean that one of the fundamental dimensions of a signifier is to be able to cancel itself out. It is a possibility that in this context we can describe it as a mode of the signifier itself. It's materialized by something very simple which we are all familiar with, and we cannot allow the trivial nature of its use to hide its originality – it's the bar. Every kind of signifier is by nature something that can be barred.

Ever since there have been philosophers who think, a great deal has been said about *Aufhebung*, and they have learnt to make a more or less cunning use of it. The word essentially means cancellation – for example, I cancel my subscription to a newspaper, or my reservation somewhere. It also means, owing to an ambiguity of meaning that renders it valuable in the German language, raise to a power, to a higher situation. It doesn't seem that one dwells enough on the fact that properly speaking there is only one kind of thing that, in general terms, can be annulled, and that is a signifier. In truth, when we cancel anything else, whether it's imaginary or real, we thereby elevate it to the grade, to the title of a signifier.

There is, therefore, in signifiers, in a chain of signifiers, in operating with or using them, something that is always apt to demote them from their function in a line or in a lineage – the bar is a sign of bastardry – to demote them as such by virtue of the properly signifying function of what I will call 'high regard'. I mean that a signifier can

344

have a place in what is pre-given in a battery of signifiers, insofar as this battery forms a particular system of signs that are available in an actual, concrete discourse, and also that it can always lose the function its place creates for it and be torn from this place in the constellation that the signifying system introduces when it applies itself to the world and punctuates it. From there, it falls from dis-credit [*déconsidération*] into desideration [*désideration*], where it's marked by the fact that it leaves something to be desired.

I am not just amusing myself by playing on words. I merely wish, through the use of words, to show you which direction brings us closer to our object, which is desire, by exploring its links with the play of signifiers. Contrasting 'consideration' with 'desideration' marked by the bar of the signifier is, of course, only a beginning and doesn't solve the question of desire, whatever homonymy the conjunction of these two terms which meet in the Latin etymology of the French word '*désir*' lends itself to.

The fact remains that it's when a signifier is present as struck out, marked by the bar, that we have what one can call a product of the symbolic function. It's a product insofar as it's isolated and distinct from the general chain of signifiers and the law it establishes. It's only when it can be barred that a signifier acquires its proper status, that is, enters into this dimension which makes every signifier, in principle – to specify what I mean here – revocable.

The term '*Aufhebung*' is used by Freud, and in some quite amusing places where no one seems to have thought of looking for it. Ah! All of a sudden, when Freud uses it, we wake up. It's not that the word has the same resonance for him as it does for Hegel.

Every signifier is revocable in principle. As a result, for anything that is not a signifier – that is, for the real in particular – the bar is one of the surest and shortest ways to raise it to the dignity of a signifier.

I have already pointed this out to you in an extremely precise manner with respect to the fantasy of the child being beaten.

3

At the outset, this sign that the child is being beaten by the father is the sign of the hated brother's humiliation. I showed you that at the second stage of this fantasy's evolution, the one that Freud indi-cates as having to be reconstructed, as never having been perceived, except obliquely and in exceptional cases, when it's a question of the subject himself, this sign becomes on the contrary the sign of love. He, the subject, being beaten, is loved. The change in the meaning of this action in the interval does not fail to raise a problem, however. The same act which, when it applies to the other, is taken to be abusive and perceived by the subject as the sign that the other is not loved, assumes an essential value when it's the subject who becomes its support. This is only conceivable, properly speaking, via the function of signifiers.

It is inasmuch as this act raises the subject himself to the dignity of a signifier-subject that at this moment he is brought into its positive inaugural register. It institutes him as a subject with whom there can be a question of love.

This is what Freud – we must always come back to Freud's sentences, they are always lapidary – expresses in 'Some Psychical Consequences of the Anatomical Distinction between the Sexes' when he says that the child who is being beaten, then, becomes loved, valued on the plane of love. And then he introduces a remark that was merely implicit in '*Ein Kind wird geschlagen*' ['A Child is Being Beaten'], a text I started to analyse and comment on. Here, Freud formulates it explicitly, without absolutely explaining it, but orientating it with this prodigious flare of his. It's exactly what is in question in the dialectic of the recognition of the beyond of desire. I will summarize what he says: this very peculiar rigidity, *Starrheit*, that can be detected in the monotonous formula 'a child is being beaten' probably allows of only one meaning – the child who is being beaten, and thereby valued, *nichts anderes sein, als die Klitoris selbst*, is nothing other than the clitoris itself [see *SE* 19: 254]. In this study we are dealing with young girls.

'*Starrheit*' – the word is very difficult to translate into French because it has an ambiguous meaning in German. It means both a stare, in the sense of a fixed look, and rigid. They are not absolutely unrelated, although there is contamination of two meanings which have an analogy in history. That's actually what is at issue, namely that here we see something highlighted whose place as a knot to be untied I have already indicated, and this is the relationship that exists between the subject as such, the phallus as problematic object and the essentially signifying function of the bar insofar as it enters into play in the fantasy of the child that is being beaten.

For that, it isn't enough to be satisfied with this clitoris which leaves a lot to be desired in many respects. It's a matter of seeing why it's there in a particular position that is so ambiguous that, ultimately, although Freud recognizes it in the child being beaten, the subject on the other hand does not recognize it as such. It's in fact a question of the phallus inasmuch as it occupies a certain place in the economy of the subject's development and is the indispensable support of subjective construction as the pivot of the castration complex and *Penisneid*. It now remains to be seen how it enters into play in the subject's capture by the signifying structure, one of whose essential terms I have just recalled – or conversely.

For this we should pause for a moment at the mode in which the phallus can be considered. Why does one speak of the phallus, and not simply of the penis? Why do we effectively see that it's one thing to bring the phallus into play in the way we do, but that the way the penis comes in as a substitute for it in a more or less satisfactory manner is another thing, both for the masculine subject and the feminine subject? To what extent is the clitoris possibly involved in what we can call the economic functions of the phallus?

Observe what the phallus is originally. It's the phallos, φαλλός.

We find it attested for the first time in Greek Antiquity. If we go to the texts, to different places in Aristophanes, Herodotus, Lucian and so on, we see first of all that the phallus is not at all identical to the organ as an appendage of the body, a prolongation, a member or a functioning organ. The use of the word that dominates by far is its employment with respect to a simulacrum, an insignia, in whatever way it's presented – a raised staff with the male organ hanging from it, an imitation of the male organ, a piece of wood, a piece of leather and other varieties in which it's presented. It's a substitute object and, at the same time, this substitution has one property very different from substitution in the sense we have just been hearing about, sign-substitution. One could almost say that this object has all the features of a real substitute, of what in a good story we call, and with always more or less of a smile, a dildo, a *gode michet*, from *gaude mihi*, one of the most unusual of objects, by their rarity, that exist in human industry. All the same, it's something whose existence, and whose very possibility, one cannot fail to take into account.

I also note that the olisbos is often confused in Greek with the phallus.

There is no doubt that this object played a central role at the heart of the Mysteries, since the final veils that the initiation raised were placed around it. That is, at the level of the revelation of meaning, it was considered to have an ultimate meaningful character.

Doesn't that put what this is about – namely, the prevailing economic role of the phallus, insofar as it represents desire in its most manifest form – on the right path?

I would contrast it term for term with what I was saying about the signifier, which is essentially hollow and introduces itself as such into the fullness of the world. Conversely, what presents itself in the phallus is what in life manifests itself in the purest manner as turgescence and growth. We get the clear sense that the image of the phallus goes to the very heart of the term *'pulsion'* [drive],

347

which we use to translate the German term '*Trieb*' into French. This is the privileged object of the world of life, and its Greek appellation relates it to everything belonging to the order of flux and sap, and even the vein itself, for it seems that this is the same root as in '*phleps*', 'φλεψ' and '*phallos*'.

It seems, then, that things are such that this extreme point of the manifestation of desire in its vital appearances can only enter the field of signifiers by unleashing the bar. Everything in the order of the intrusion of vital growth as such is here highlighted or maximized in this form or image. And, as experience shows – all we are doing here is reading it off – this is precisely what introduces what appears in the human subject who does not possess the phallus with the connotation of absence there where it is not to be since it is not, which makes her regarded as castrated, whereas, conversely, the one who has something, and can claim to resemble it, is taken to be threatened with castration.

I alluded to the Mysteries of Antiquity. It's altogether striking to see that on the rare frescoes conserved remarkably intact, those of the Villa of the Mysteries in Pompeii, it's very precisely just along-side the place where the unveiling of the phallus is represented that different kinds of demons appear, represented on an impressive, life-size scale and able to be identified by a number of cross-references. There is one on a vase in the Louvre and others in other places. These demons – winged, booted, not helmeted, but almost, and in any case armed with a *flagellum* – are beginning to administer the ritual punishment to one of the applicants or initiates who are in the image. Thus, the fantasy of flagellation emerges in the most direct of forms and in the most immediate of connections with the unveiling of the phallus.

We don't need to undertake any kind of investigation into the depths of the Mysteries to know what texts of all sorts attest to – that, in every ancient cult, as one gets closer to the cult, that is to say, to the signifying manifestation of the fertile power of the Great Goddess, the Syrian goddess, everything that has a reference to the phallus is the object of amputations, marks of castration or prohibition that are increasingly accentuated. Specifically, the eunuch character of the priests of the Great Goddess is attested in texts of all kinds.

The phallus always finds itself covered by a bar placed over its accession to the domain of signifiers, that is, over its place in the Other. And this is how castration is introduced into development. It's never – you see this directly in observations – by means of a prohibition on masturbation, for example. If you read the observation on Little Hans, you will see that the first prohibitions have no effect

348

on him. If you read the history of André Gide, you will see that his parents fought during all his early years to stop him from it, and that Professor Brouhardel, showing him the huge pikes and the long knives that he had on his wall – because it was already the fashion amongst doctors to have a whole second-hand shop at one's place – promised him that if he did it again it would be sawn off. And the child Gide recounts very well that he did not believe in such a threat for one single moment, because he thought it was excessive – in other words, nothing more than the occasion for the emergence of Professor Brouhardel's own fantasies.

That's not at all what this is about. As the texts show us, and observations as well, this has to do with that being in a world who, in reality, would have the least cause to consider herself castrated, namely, the mother. It's in the place where castration in the Other manifests itself, where it's the Other's desire that is marked by the signifying bar – it's essentially here, in this way that, for a man as for a woman, this something specific that functions as the castration complex is introduced.

349

When we spoke about the Oedipus complex at the start of last trimester, I stressed the fact that the first person to be castrated in the intersubjective dialectic is the mother. This is where the position of castration is encountered in the first instance. If the destinies of the boy and the little girl are different, it's because castration is first of all encountered in the Other.

The little girl combines this perception with what it is that the mother has deprived her of. What is perceived in the mother as castration is, then, also perceived as castration for her and initially presents itself in the form of a reproach against the mother. This rancour then comes to be added to those that earlier frustrations have given rise to. It's in this mode that the castration complex first presents itself to the girl.

The father only enters here in the position of a replacement for what she initially finds herself deprived of, and this is why she moves onto the plane of the experience of privation. It's because the real penis of the father – which, we are told, she expects as a substitute for what she perceives to be what she has been deprived of – already appears at the symbolic level that we are able to speak of privation, with both the crisis that the latter engenders and the crossroads that presents itself to the subject of either renouncing her object, which is the father, or renouncing her instinct by identifying with the father.

This produces a curious consequence. Precisely as a result of having been introduced into the woman's castration complex in the form of a symbolic substitute, the penis is the source in the woman of all sorts of conflicts of the conflicts-of-jealousy type. The partner's infidelity is experienced in her as a real privation. The emphasis is quite different here from the same conflict seen from the side of the man.

I'm going through this quickly. I will come back to it, but there is one more thing that we really must see. If the phallus is encountered in the barred form where it has the place of indicating the Other's desire, what about the subject? In my remaining comments I will show that the subject also has to find his place as a desired object in relation to the Other's desire. Consequently, and as Freud indicates to us with such remarkable insight in 'A Child is Being Beaten', it's always insofar as the subject is and is not the phallus that he will ultimately have to be situated and find his identification as subject. In short, as we can see, the subject is, as such, himself a subject marked by the bar.

This is manifest in the woman. Today I have been exploring the effects of her development concerning the phallus in one simple indi- | 350 cation. The woman – the man also, moreover – finds herself caught in an insoluble dilemma, around which it's necessary to place all the typical manifestations of her femininity, whether neurotic or not. As to finding her satisfaction, there is first of all the man's penis, then, by substitution, the desire for a child. I'm doing no more here than indicating what is current and classical in analytic theory. But what does that mean? That, ultimately, she will only obtain satisfaction that is as deep, fundamental and instinctual as that of maternity, and as demanding moreover, via the pathways of lines of substitutions. It's inasmuch as the penis is initially a substitute – I would go so far as to say a fetish – that the child, he too, is, then, in a certain way, a fetish. There you have the pathways by which the woman finds what is, let's say, her instinct and her natural satisfaction.

Conversely, for everything that is aligned with her desire, she will find herself tied to the necessity that to a variable degree is implied by the function of the phallus, to be this phallus, insofar as it's the very sign of what is desired. However *verdrängt* the phallus's function may be, it's what the manifestations of what is thought of as femininity correspond to. The fact that she displays herself and offers herself as an object of desire identifies her in a latent and secret manner with the phallus and situates her being as subject as the desired phallus, the signifier of the Other's desire. This being locates her beyond what one may call feminine masquerade, since everything that she displays of her femininity is ultimately linked to this profound identification with the phallic signifier, which is the most linked with her femininity.

What we see appear here is the root of what, in the subject's completion on the path to the Other's desire, can be called her profound

Verwerfung, her profound rejection, qua being, of how she appears as a woman. Her satisfaction goes via a substitutive path, whereas her desire manifests itself on a plane where it can only end in a profound *Verwerfung*, a profound estrangement of her being in relation to how she feels she is obliged to appear.

Don't think that the situation is any better for the man. It's even more comical. The phallus, he has it, the poor bastard, and indeed it's the knowledge that his mother doesn't have it that traumatizes him – for then, since she is much stronger, where does that leave us? Karen Horney revealed one of the most essential sources of the disturbances of the castration complex in the primitive fear of women. Just as the woman is caught in one dilemma, so the man is caught in another. For him, masquerade is established along the lines of satisfaction, because he resolves the question of the danger that threatens what he effectively has, we well know how, namely by simply identifying with the one who possesses its insignias and gives every appearance of having escaped the danger – that is, with the father. Ultimately, man is only virile through an indefinite series of proxies that come to him from all his male ancestors, passing via his immediate ancestor.

But conversely, in line with desire, that is, inasmuch as he has to find his satisfaction with a woman, he also is going to seek the phallus. Now – we all have testimony of this, clinical and other, I will come back to it – it's because he does not find this phallus there where he is looking for it, that he looks for it everywhere else.

In other words, for the woman, the symbolic penis is inside, as it were, the field of her desire, whereas for the man it's outside. This explains why men always have centrifugal tendencies in monogamous relationships.

Inasmuch as she is not herself, that is, inasmuch as in the field of her desire she has to be the phallus, the woman experiences the *Verwerfung* of subjective identification, the one that arises where the second line, the one starting with the capital D, ends. [See the formulas on p. 285.] And it's inasmuch as he is not himself either, insofar as he satisfies, that is, insofar as he obtains the Other's satisfaction, but only perceives himself as the instrument of that satisfaction, that the man finds himself in love outside his Other.

The problem of love is the problem of the profound division it introduces into the subject's activities. What is at issue for a man, following the very definition of love, 'to give what one does not have', is to give what he does not have, the phallus, to a being who is not it.

23 April 1958

THE DIALECTIC
OF DESIRE
AND DEMAND IN THE
CLINICAL STUDY
AND TREATMENT
OF THE NEUROSES

XX

THE DREAM BY THE BUTCHER'S BEAUTIFUL WIFE

The Other's desire
Unsatisfied desire
The desire for something other
Barred desire
Dora's identification

If the things of man, which we are concerned with in principle, are marked by his relationship to signifiers, one cannot use signifiers to speak about these things in the way one does when speaking about things that signifiers help him pose. In other words, there has to be a difference between the way we speak about the things of man and the way we speak about other things.

We know very well today that things are not indifferent to being explored by signifiers, that they bear a relationship to the order of the logos and that this relationship has to be studied. We are well placed, more so than our predecessors were, to appreciate that language penetrates things, makes furrows in them, raises them up and disrupts them even if only modestly. But in the end, at the point where we are now, we know, at least we suppose, that unless we're wrong things did not develop in language. That, at least, was where one started for the work of science as it's currently constituted, the work of the science of *phusis*.

Think, first, of purifying language – that is, of reducing it to the necessary minimum for it to be able to grasp onto things, which is the principle of what is called the transcendental analytic. In short, people have contrived to disconnect language as much as possible – not totally, of course – from the things with which it was deeply connected up until a certain period that corresponds more or less to the beginning of modern science, in order to reduce it to its interrogative function.

Now, everything has become complicated. Do we not observe

strange upheavals in things, which are certainly not unconnected to the way in which we question them? And, moreover, curious impasses in language, which, as soon as we start speaking about things, becomes strictly incomprehensible to us? But that is not our concern. We are dealing with man. And, here, I want you to observe that the language in which to question him has not yet been discovered.

We think we have discovered it when we employ the discourse of the Academy or of psychiatric psychology – until otherwise informed, they are the same thing – for the things of man. We ourselves can very adequately perceive the poverty, and moreover the immutability, of the constructions that we engage in, for, if the truth be known, over the century since in psychiatry one has been speaking about hallucinations, almost no progress has been made and they can still not be defined in any other than a ridiculous manner.

The entire language of psychiatric psychology presents the same handicap, moreover, and makes us aware of its profound stagnation. We say that such-and-such a function is being reified, and we feel the arbitrariness of these reifications, when for example we speak in a Bleulerian language about dissociation in schizophrenia. And when we say 'reify' we get the impression that we are formulating a valid critique. What does that mean? It's not at all that we are reproaching this psychology with having turned man into a thing. If only it did make a thing of him, for that is indeed the aim of a science of man. But, precisely, it makes of him a thing that is nothing other than prematurely frozen language, which hastily substitutes its own form of language for something that is already woven into language.

What we call 'formations of the unconscious', what Freud presented us with under this heading, are nothing other than the grip of a certain primary in language. This is why he called it 'primary process'. Language marks this 'primary', and this is why the ground for Freud's discovery, that of the unconscious, can be said to have been prepared by the enquiry into this primary, inasmuch as its structure as language was detected first.

I said 'prepared'. Freud's discovery effectively made it possible for the enquiry into this 'primary' to be prepared for and for an accurate enquiry into primary tendencies to be commenced. But we will not be at that point as long as we haven't first focused on what has to be recognized, namely that this primary is first and foremost woven from language. This is why I am returning you to it. Those who dazzle you with the synthesis of psychoanalysis and biology are showing you that it's obviously a lure, not only by virtue of the fact that till now there have been absolutely no developments in this direction, but because until further notice it's a swindle even to promise them.

I am, then, now at the point of trying to show, project and situate here, with you, what I am calling the texture of language. That does not mean that we exclude the primary inasmuch as it's something other than language. It's what we are looking for as we move forward.

357

1

In previous classes, we got to a point where we were touching on what I called the dialectic of desire and demand.

I was saying to you that, in demand, identification is with the object of a sentiment. Why, in the end, is that so? Precisely because nothing intersubjective can be established unless the Other with a big 'O' speaks. Or, again, because the nature of speech is to be the speech of the Other. Or, again, because everything that is a manifestation of primary desire is necessarily established on what Freud, following Fechner, calls the other scene, because that is necessary for man's satisfaction inasmuch as, being a speaking being, his satisfactions have to pass through the intermediary of speech.

This one fact introduces an initial ambiguity. Desire is obliged to be mediated by speech, and it's apparent that it is only in the Other as the locus of speech that this speech gains its status, becomes established and develops in its nature. Now, it's clear there is no reason why the subject should be aware of this. I mean that the distinction between the Other and him himself is the most difficult of distinctions to make at the outset. Freud thus emphasizes the symptomatic value of this moment of childhood in which the child thinks his parents know all his thoughts, but he explains the link between this phenomenon and speech very well. Since the subject's thoughts have been formed in the Other's speech, it's quite natural that in the beginning his thoughts should belong to this speech.

On the imaginary plane, on the other hand, at the start there is only a weak border between the subject and the other, an ambiguous border in the sense that it can be crossed. The narcissistic relation is open, effectively, to permanent transitivism, as the child's experience shows here also.

These two forms of ambiguity, these two limits – one located on the imaginary plane, the other belonging to the symbolic order whereby desire is grounded in the Other's speech – these two forms of crossing-over which mean that the subject is alienated are not to be confused with one another. As experience shows, it is, on the contrary, their discordance that opens up an initial possibility for the subject to differentiate himself as such. Of course, he differentiates himself most particularly on the imaginary plane, establishing himself in a position of rivalry with his semblable in relation to a third object. But there always remains the question of what happens when there are two of these subjects, namely, when it's a question of the subject sustaining himself in the presence of the Other.

This dialectic is limited to the one called the dialectic of recognition, of which you have some idea, at least some of you do, due to what I have communicated about it here. You know that a certain Hegel sought the mainspring of this in the conflict of enjoyment and in the struggle called the struggle to death from which he extracted his entire master–slave dialectic. All this is very important to know, but of course this does not cover the entire field of our experience, and for the best of reasons. The fact is that there is something other than the dialectic of the master–slave struggle. There is the child's relationship to its parents, and there is, precisely, what occurs at the level of recognition when what is involved is not a struggle, not a conflict, but a demand.

It is, in short, a question of seeing when and how the subject's desire, alienated in demand, profoundly transformed by the fact of having to pass through demand, can and must be reintroduced. These are simple things I am telling you today.

Primitively, the child, in its impotence, finds itself entirely dependent on demand, that is, on the Other's speech, which modifies, restructures and profoundly alienates the nature of its desire. This dialectic of demand corresponds more or less to the period that is called, rightly or wrongly, pre-Oedipal and, surely rightly, pre-genital. By virtue of the ambiguity of the limits between the subject and the Other, we see introduced into demand the oral object, an object which is incorporated inasmuch as it's demanded on the oral level, and the anal object, the support of the dialectic of the primitive gift, essentially tied in the subject to the fact of satisfying or not satisfying an educative demand, that is, the demand to accept or not to accept to let go of a certain symbolic object. In short, the profound reworking of initial desires by demand is permanently palpable for us in the dialectic of the oral object and particularly in that of the anal object – and the result of this is that the Other with whom the subject is involved in the relation of demand is itself subject to a dialectic of assimilation, incorporation or rejection.

Something different, then, has to be introduced – something by which the originality, irreducibility and authenticity of the subject's

desire is re-established. The progress that is made at the time of the
so-called genital stage means nothing else. It consists in the fact that
the subject, installed in the initial, pre-genital dialectic of demand,
encounters another desire at some point, a desire that has not yet
been integrated, and cannot be integrated without much greater
critical and even more profound reworkings than is the case for the
initial desires. The usual way in which this other desire is introduced
for the subject is as the Other's desire. The subject recognizes a
desire beyond demand and locates it beyond the first Other to whom
he addresses his demand – let's say, to focus our minds, the mother.

What I am saying here is just one way of expressing what people
have always taught, which is that it's via the Oedipus complex that
genital desire is assumed and takes its place in subjective economy.
But what I intend to draw your attention to is the way this desire
of the Other's functions, insofar as it makes it possible for the real
distinction between the subject and the Other to become established
once and for all.

At the level of demand, there is a situation of reciprocity between
the subject and the Other. If the subject's desire depends entirely
on his demand of the Other, what the Other demands also depends
on the subject. This is expressed in the relations between child and
mother by the fact that the child knows full well that he, too, holds
some part of the mother's demand that he can refuse – by refusing
for example to accede to the request for excremental regulation.
This relationship between the two subjects over demand demands
to be completed by the introduction of a new dimension which
makes the subject something other than a dependent subject, whose
relation of dependence makes this being essential. What must be
introduced, and which is there right from the start, latent from the
outset, is that beyond what the subject demands and beyond what
the Other demands of the subject, there has to be the presence and
the dimension of what the Other desires.

Initially, this is profoundly veiled for the subject but nevertheless
immanent to the situation, and it's what is going to unfold, little
by little, in the experience of the Oedipus complex. It is essential in
the structure, and it is more original and more fundamental than
the perception either of the relations between the father and the
mother, which I have expanded on in what I have called the paternal
metaphor, or of any point that results in the castration complex and
constitutes a development in what lies beyond demand.

The fact that the subject's desire is initially located and discovered
in the existence as such of the Other's desire – desire as distinct from
demand – is what I want to illustrate for you today with an example.
Which example? It is a requirement that it be the first one.

Effectively, if what I am suggesting really is an introduction to everything regarding the structuration of the unconscious in relation to signifiers, then we ought to find our example immediately.

2

I have already alluded here to what we can point to in the initial observations Freud makes on hysteria. Let's go, then, to the time when Freud spoke about desire for the first time.

He speaks about it in relation to dreams. I have previously commented on what Freud extracts from the inaugural dream of Irma, the dream of her injection, and I won't go back over it. The second dream is one of Freud's own dreams – since he also analyses some of his own dreams in the *Traumdeutung* – the dream of Uncle Joseph. I will analyse it some other time, because it's so entirely convincing, and it illustrates very well the schema of the two intertwined loops in particular – nothing shows better the two levels on which a dream unfolds, the properly signifying level which is the level of speech, and the imaginary level where in some way the metonymic object is embodied.

I will, then, take the third dream Freud analyses. It appears in the fourth chapter, '*Die Traumentstellung*', 'Distortion in Dreams'. It's the dream by the woman whom we shall call the butcher's beautiful wife. Here is the dream. Freud says:

> I wanted to give a supper-party, but I had nothing in the house but a little smoked salmon. I thought I would go out and buy something, but remembered then that it was Sunday afternoon and all the shops would be shut. Next I tried to ring up some caterers, but the telephone was out of order. So I had to abandon my wish to give a supper-party. [*SE* 4: 147]

That is the text of the dream. Freud scrupulously notes the manner in which the text of a dream is verbalized, and it's on the basis of this verbalization, a kind of written text of the dream, that the analysis of a dream always and only seems conceivable to him.

> I answered, of course, that analysis was the only way of deciding on the meaning of the dream. [*SE* 4: 147]

In fact, the patient had contradicted him with this dream, saying:

> You're always saying to me that a dream is a fulfilled desire. Here, I have the greatest difficulty fulfilling my desire. [*SE* 4: 146]

Freud continues:

> I admitted that at first sight it seemed sensible and coherent and
> looked like the reverse of a wish-fulfilment. 'But what material
> did the dream arise from? As you know, the instigation to a
> dream is always to be found in the events of the previous day.'
>
> ANALYSIS. – My patient's husband, an honest and capable
> wholesale butcher, had remarked to her the day before that
> he was getting too stout and therefore intended to start on
> a course of weight-reduction. He proposed to rise early, do
> physical exercises, keep to a strict diet, and above all accept
> no more invitations to supper. She laughingly added that her
> husband, at the place where he regularly lunched, had made the
> acquaintance of a painter, who had pressed him to be allowed
> to paint his portrait, as he had never seen such expressive fea-
> tures. Her husband however had replied in his blunt manner
> that he was much obliged, but he was sure the painter would
> prefer a piece of a pretty young girl's behind to the whole of
> his face. She was very much in love with her husband now and
> teased him a lot. She had begged him, too, not to give her any
> caviare. [*SE* 4: 147]

361

What did that mean?

> She had wished for a long time that she could have a
> caviare sandwich every morning but had grudged the expense.
> [*SE* 4: 147]

Or, rather, she didn't grant herself that licence.

> Of course her husband would have let her have it at once if she
> had asked him. But, on the contrary, she had asked him *not* to
> give her any caviare, so that she could go on teasing him about
> it. [*SE* 4: 147]

Then Freud makes this parenthesis:

> This explanation struck me as unconvincing. Inadequate
> reasons like this usually conceal unconfessed motives. They
> remind one of Bernheim's hypnotized patients. When one of
> these carries out a post-hypnotic suggestion and is asked why
> he is acting in this way, instead of saying that he has no idea, he
> feels compelled to invent some obviously unsatisfactory reason.

The same was no doubt true of my patient and the caviare. I saw that she was obliged to create an unfulfilled wish for herself in her actual life; and the dream represented this renunciation as having been put into effect. But why was it that she stood in need of an unfulfilled wish? [*SE* 4: 147–8]

A further parenthetical remark by Freud:

The associations which she had so far produced had not been sufficient to interpret the dream. I pressed her for some more. After a short pause, such as would correspond to the overcoming of a resistance, she went on to tell me that the day before she had visited a woman friend of whom she confessed she felt jealous because her [my patient's] husband was constantly singing her praises. Fortunately this friend of hers is very skinny and thin and her husband admires a plumper figure. I asked her what she had talked about to her thin friend. Naturally, she replied, of that lady's wish to grow a little stouter. Her friend had enquired, too: 'When are you going to ask us to another meal? You always feed one so well.'

The meaning of the dream was now clear, and I was able to say to my patient: 'It is just as though when she made this suggestion you said to yourself: "A likely thing! I'm to ask you to come and eat in my house so that you may get stout and attract my husband still more! I'd rather never give another supper-party." What the dream was saying to you was that you were unable to give any supper-parties, and it was thus fulfilling your wish not to help your friend to grow plumper. The fact that what people eat at parties makes them stout had been brought home to you by your husband's decision not to accept any more invitations to supper in the interests of his plan to reduce his weight.' All that was now lacking was some coincidence to confirm the solution. The smoked salmon in the dream had not yet been accounted for. 'How', I asked, 'did you arrive at the salmon that came into your dream?' 'Oh,' she replied, 'smoked salmon is my friend's favourite dish.' I happen to be acquainted with the lady in question myself, and I can confirm the fact that she grudges herself salmon no less than my patient grudges herself caviare. [*SE* 4: 148]

It's at this point that Freud introduces the text of the dream that bears another interpretation, one that enters into the dialectic of identification:

She had 'identified' herself with her friend. I believe she had in fact done this; and the circumstance of her having brought about a renounced wish in real life was evidence of this identification. [*SE* 4: 149]

I think you must already sense the outline that is being drawn in this simple text. I could have opened the *Traumdeutung* at any other page, we would have found the same dialectic. This dream, which was the first to fall into my hands, will show us the dialectic of desire and demand, which is particularly straightforward in the hysteric.

Let's keep on reading, so that we can pursue to the end what this very important text articulates for us. It is in short one of the first very clear articulations, by Freud, of what hysterical identification signifies. He spells out its meaning. I will leave out several lines so as not to go on too long. He discusses what is called hysterical imitation, the hysteric's sympathy for the other, and criticizes, with great energy, the simple reduction of hysterical contagion to pure and simple imitation.

The process of hysterical identification, he says,

363

is a little more complicated than the common picture of hysterical imitation; it consists in the unconscious drawing of an inference, as an example will make clear. Supposing a physician is treating a woman patient, who is subject to a particular kind of spasm, in a hospital ward among a number of other patients. He will show no surprise if he finds one morning that this particular kind of hysterical attack has found imitators . . . but the psychical infection has occurred along some such lines as these. As a rule, patients know . . . [*SE* 14: 149]

You have to be aware of the importance that such a remark carries, I am not saying simply at the time at which it was made, but for us still.

. . . more about one another than the doctor does about any of them; and after the doctor's visit is over they turn their attention to one another. [*SE* 4: 149]

An essential comment. In other words, the human object continues to live out its little special relationship to signifiers, even after the observer, whether a behaviourist or not, has shown an interest in his photography.

Let us imagine that this patient had her attack on a particular day; then the others will quickly discover that it was caused by a letter from home, the revival of some unhappy love-affair, or some such thing. Their sympathy is aroused and they draw the following inference, though it fails to penetrate into conscious-ness: 'If a cause like this can produce an attack like this, I may have the same kind of attack . . .' [*SE* 4: 150]

Articulation of the elementary symptom with an identification in discourse, with a situation articulated in discourse

. . . since I have the same grounds for having it.' If this inference were capable of entering this consciousness, it might possibly give rise to a fear of having the same kind of attack. But in fact the inference is made in a different psychical region, and consequently results in the actual realization of the dreaded symptom. Thus identification is not simple imitation but assim-ilation on the basis of a similar aetiological pretension; it expresses a resemblance and is derived from a common element which remains in the unconscious. [*SE* 4: 150]

The term '*appropriation*' [in the French, the English gives 'assimi-lation'] is not a particularly good translation. It's rather, 'made one's own'. Freud says:

A hysterical woman identifies herself in her symptoms most readily – though not exclusively – with people with whom she has had sexual relations or with people who have had sexual relations with the same people as herself. Linguistic usage takes this into account, for two lovers are spoken of as being 'one'. [*SE* 4: 150]

The problem raised by Freud is the relation of identification with the jealous friend. In this respect I want to draw your atten-tion to the following – the desire we encounter from the very first steps of the analysis, and on the basis of which the solution to the puzzle will unfold, is desire as unsatisfied. At the time of this dream, the patient was preoccupied with creating an unsatisfied desire for herself. What is the function of this unsatisfied desire?

What we effectively read in the dream is the satisfaction of a wish, a wish to have an unsatisfied desire. And what we discover in this connection is the underlying situation, which is man's fundamental
364   situation, between demand and desire, to which I am trying to intro-duce you, and which effectively I am introducing you to via hysteria, because the hysteric is suspended between this necessary split, as I was showing you earlier, between demand and desire. Here, it could not be any clearer.

What was she asking for before the dream, in her life? What is this patient, very much in love with her husband, asking for? It's love, and hysterics, like everybody else, ask for love – except that, for them, it's more of an encumbrance. What does she desire? She desires caviar. You just have to read. And what does she want? She wants not to be given caviar.

The question is precisely knowing why, for a hysteric to enter into a commerce of love that she finds satisfying, it's necessary, first, that she desire *something else*, and the caviar has no other role than to be this something else, and, in the second place, that in order for this something else to fulfil the function that is its task to fulfil, precisely, one doesn't give it to her. Her husband would ask for nothing better than to give her caviar, but she imagines it would probably be so that he would be left alone. But what Freud tells us in so many words is that she wants her husband not to give her caviar so that they can continue to be madly in love, that is, tease one another and make each other's lives endlessly miserable.

These structural elements, apart from the fact that we have stopped to think about them, are not particularly original, but they are beginning to take on meaning here. What is expressed is a structure which, beyond its comical side, has to represent something necessary. The hysteric is precisely a subject who finds it difficult to establish a relation – one that enables her to retain her place as a subject – with the constitution of the Other as big Other and bearer of the spoken sign. This is the very definition that one can give of the hysteric. In a word, the hysteric, man or woman, is so open to suggestion through speech that there must be something in it.

In *Group Psychology and the Analysis of the Ego* Freud enquires into the way in which hypnosis arises, when its relation to sleep is far from being transparent, and when the tendency that suits it to certain people, whereas others refuse it and radically distance themselves from it, remains enigmatic. But everything seems to show, however, that what occurs in hypnosis is made possible in a subject by the purity of certain circumstances – I would even say by libidinal attitudes. What is at issue, if not places or positions that we are in the process of throwing light on? The unknown element Freud speaks of revolves around the way demand and desire are articulated. That is what I will try to show later.

If a subject has to create an unsatisfied desire for himself, it's because this is the condition for a real Other to be constituted for him, that is, one that is not entirely imminent to the reciprocal satisfaction of demand or to the entire capture of the subject's desire by the Other's speech. That the desire in question is, by its nature, the Other's desire is very precisely what the dialectic of

365

dreams introduces us to, since the patient does not want this desire for caviar to be satisfied in reality. And this dream incontestably tends to satisfy her with respect to the solution to the problem she is pursuing.

What is the desire for caviar represented by in the dream? By the intermediary of the person in the dream, the friend with whom – Freud points out the signs – she identifies. Her friend is also an hysteric, or not, it doesn't matter, it's all pure hysterico-hysterical. The patient is hysterical, and the other is as well, to be sure, and all the more easily because the hysterical subject is almost entirely constituted on the basis of the Other's desire. The desire that the subject makes clear in the dream is the preferred desire of her friend, the desire for salmon, and even when she is unable to give a dinner party, this is all that she is left with, smoked salmon, which is an indication of the Other's desire as well as of the fact that it's capable of being satisfied, but only for the Other. 'Besides, there is nothing to worry about, we have some smoked salmon.' All the same, the dream does not say that things come to the point where she gives it to her friend, but the intention is there.

On the other hand, what gets stranded is her friend's request, the dream's genetic element. She asked her if she could come to dinner at her place where one eats so well, and where, moreover, one can meet the handsome butcher. This amiable husband who always speaks so well of her friend must also have his own little desire inside his head, and the backside of the young girl evoked so promptly in relation to the proposition by the amiable painter who would like to draw him and sketch such an interesting, expressive face is certainly there as proof. In a word, everyone has his little desire beyond, simply more or less intensified.

Except that, in the specific case of an hysteric, desire as lying beyond all demand, that is, as having to occupy its function in the name of a refused desire, plays a role very much in the foreground. You will never understand anything about hysterics, him or her, if you don't start with this primary, structural element. Moreover, in man's relationship to signifiers, the hysteric is a primordial structure. Should you push the dialectic of demand far enough with a subject, you will always encounter the *Spaltung* between demand and desire at some point in the structure, at the risk of committing major errors, that is, of rendering the patient hysterical, for everything that we analyse there is, of course, unconscious for the subject. In other words, an hysteric does not know that he cannot find satisfaction in the demand, but it's quite essential that you yourself know this.

These notations are now going to enable us to begin to point to what the little diagram that I drew for you last time means, the interpretation of which it was a little premature to give you then. [See the diagram on p. 321.]

As I have told you, what manifests itself as a need must be expressed in demand, that is, must be addressed to the Other [A]. An encounter takes place opposite, or does not take place, and it occupies the place of the message [s(A)] – that is, what in the Other is signified. Then, a relic of demand is produced, which consists in the alteration of what manifests itself in the still unformed state of the subject's desire, which manifests itself in principle in the form of the subject's identification. I will come back to this next time, with Freud's text in hand, and you will see that the first time he speaks in a fully articulated manner about identification – you can already look it up if your heart is in it – primitive identification is not articulated in any other way than I have noted for you here.

You are aware, moreover, that down the path along which the narcissistic short-circuit is introduced, there already exists a possibility, an opening, an outline.

What's essential in what I gave you when describing the function of the phallus is that it's the signifier that is the mark of what the Other desires insofar as it itself, as a real, human Other, is, in its economy of being, marked by the signifier. It's this formula that we are precisely in the process of studying. It's precisely insofar as the Other is marked by the signifier that a subject can through there, and only through there – through the intermediary of the Other – recognize that he, too, is marked by the signifier, that is, that there is always something that remains beyond what can be satisfied through the intermediary of the signifier, that is, through demand. This split created around the action of signifiers, this irreducible residue linked to signifiers, also has its own sign, but this sign is going to be identified with this mark in the signified. This is where a subject must encounter his desire.

In other words, it's insofar as the Other's desire is barred that the subject will recognize his own barred desire, his own unsatisfied desire. It's at the level of this desire, barred through the intermediary of the Other, that the subject's encounter with his most authentic desire, namely genital desire, occurs. It's for this reason that genital desire is marked by castration, in other words by a particular relationship to the signifier phallus. The two things are equivalent.

What we find first off corresponds to demand, that is, at an initial stage, the mother's speech. This speech itself has a relation to a law that lies beyond, and which, as I have shown, is incarnated by the father. This is what constitutes the paternal metaphor. But you have the perfect right to think that not everything is reducible to this

367

layering of speech, and I think that this sort of lack must have left you – you too – with something to be desired when I explained it to you.

Effectively, beyond speech and beyond over-speech, beyond the law of the father, whatever one calls it, something else is required. This is the capacity in which this chosen signifier, the phallus, is introduced and, naturally, it's situated at the same level as the law. Under normal conditions, it's located at a second order of the encounter with the Other. This is what, in my little formulas, I have called S(Ⱥ), the signifier of barred A. It's precisely the question of what I have just now defined as being the function of the signifier phallus – namely, the function of marking what the Other, as marked by the signifier, that is, as barred, desires.

Where is the subject? When we are no longer dealing with the ambiguous subject, at one and the same time perpetually dipping into the speech of the Other and getting caught up in the specular, dual relationship with the little other, but rather with the constituted and completed subject of the Z-shaped formula – this is the subject insofar as the bar has been introduced, namely, insofar as he himself is also marked somewhere by the relationship to signifiers. This is why we find it here, in [$ ◊ D], where the subject's relation to demand as such happens.

How are we to explain the necessary stage by which the Oedipus complex is integrated with the castration complex, namely, the structuration of the subject's desire through them? How does that happen? You can see it set out on this diagram. This beyond-the-relationship-to-the-Other's-speech is introduced through the signifier phallus. But, of course, once it is constituted and the signifier phallus is there in this place as the Other's desire, it doesn't remain there, but becomes integrated into the Other's speech and, with all the consequences that follow, occupies its place this-side-of, in the primitive place of the speech relationship with the mother. It's here that it plays its role and takes on its function.

In other words, this beyond I have posited, inasmuch as I am attempting to determine the requisite stages for the integration of speech to enable desire to take its place for the subject, remains unconscious for the subject. Henceforth, this is where the dialectic unfolds for him, without him knowing that this dialectic is only possible insofar as his desire, his true desire, finds its place in a relationship, which therefore remains unconscious for him, with the Other's desire. In short, these two lines are normally interchangeable [see lines 2 and 3 on p. 285].

Solely because they have to be interchangeable, all sorts of accidents can happen in the interval. We will encounter these accidents

368

in various forms. I simply wish to point out to you today the elements of the deficiency that is always to be found in hysterics.

3

Take the Dora case.

In her we see this beyond-the-Other's-desire produced in its pure state, and we can point out why a portion of the set of elements is missing. There is absolutely no mention of the mother. You have perhaps observed that she is completely absent from the case. Dora is exposed to her father. It's from her father that she wants love.

It has to be said that before the analysis Dora's life is neatly balanced. Before the drama explodes, she had come up with a very good solution to her problems. Her demand is addressed to her father, and things go very well because her father has a desire, and things go even better because this desire is an unsatisfied desire. Dora, as Freud does not hide from us, knows full well that her father is impotent and that his desire for Frau K. is a barred desire.

But what we also know – Freud only found this out a little too late – is that Frau K. is the object of Dora's desire, because she is the father's desire, the father's barred desire.

Just one thing is necessary to maintain this equilibrium. It's that Dora succeed in achieving somewhere self-identification that stabilizes her and enables her to know where she is, and to do so as a function of her demand which is not satisfied, a demand for love from her father. This works so long as there is a desire, a desire that cannot be satisfied, neither for Dora, nor for her father.

That all depends on the place in which the identification called the ego-ideal takes place. You can see it on the schema [p. 321], normally it's always produced after the line of the Other is crossed twice, at $I(A)$. It's the same in the Dora case, except for the fact that the father's desire is represented by the second line. It's after the two lines cross that the hysteric's identification becomes actual, here, in $[\mathcal{S} \lozenge a]$. It's no longer a question of an identification with the father, as is the case when the father is purely and simply the one to whom demand is addressed. Don't forget, there is now a beyond, and this suits the hysteric very well for her satisfaction and equilibrium. The identification is with a little other who is in a position to satisfy her desire. This is Herr K., the husband of Frau K., this Frau K. who is so seductive, charming and radiant, the real object of Dora's desire. Identification occurs here because Dora is an hysteric and because in the case of an hysteric, the process cannot go any further.

369

Why? Because desire is the sole element to have charge of taking the place of the beyond located by the subject's own position with respect to demand. Because she is an hysteric, she does not know what she is demanding. She simply has the need for this desire to be there beyond, somewhere. But for her to be able to draw upon this desire, complete herself with it and discover her identification, her ideal in it, there needs to be, at least at the level of this beyond-demand, an encounter that enables her to rely upon and locate herself on this line, and this is where Herr K. comes in, where, as is obvious to all observation, she finds her other, in the sense of little *a*, the other in whom she recognizes herself.

This is the reason that she is extremely interested in him, to the point of initially deceiving her world, that is, to the point where Freud believes that she loves this Herr K. She doesn't love him, but he is indispensable to her, and even much more indispensable to her for desiring Frau K. As I have already pointed out to you a hundred times, that is super-demonstrated by the fact that the circulation completely short-circuits, and that vis-à-vis the little *a* Dora falls back into a situation of aggressive fury that manifests itself with one huge slap. This is fury towards the other insofar as he is your semblable, and that, being your semblable, he quite simply steals your existence from you. The fatal words that Herr K. says to her – he knows nothing of what he is saying, the poor unfortunate man, and does not know that he is the support of Dora's identification – namely, that his wife means nothing to him, are precisely what Dora cannot tolerate. She cannot tolerate it. Why?

One says, and with very good reason, except that it's incomplete, that Dora is manifestly structured in a homosexual way, inasmuch as any hysteric can be. After what Herr K. says to her, normally she should be very pleased. Not at all. This is precisely what triggers her fury, because at that moment her beautiful hysterical construction of identification with the mask, with the insignias of the Other – namely with the abundant masculine insignias that Herr K., and not her father, presents her with – collapses. She then simply falls back onto the demand, onto the claim for love from her father, and she enters into a quasi-paranoid state when she much more objectively thinks of herself as what she effectively is for her father, namely an object of exchange, someone to amuse Herr K., while he, her father, can take care of Frau K. As vain as this is, that's all it takes, and you get a good sense, in this case, of the very function of desire.

Following Herr K.'s words, our hysteric falls from on high and returns to the entirely primitive level of demand. She simply demands that her father take care of her, that he give her his

370

love – in other words, according to our definition, everything that he does not have.

Today, I've performed the first little exercise at the barre for you in an attempt to show you what the meaning of the relationship between desire and demand is. As you become more and more accustomed to it, you will be able to go much further and with much greater confidence.

30 April 1958

XXI

THE 'STILL WATERS RUN DEEP' DREAMS

Madame Dolto and the phallus
An hysteric's jacket
The unconditional in the demand for love
The absolute condition of desire
The Other become object of desire

We'll start with recent events which those of you who attended the society's scientific presentation last night will be able to appreciate. Someone spoke about heterosexual relationships. This is exactly what I, too, am trying to talk about.

1

From the point of view that was presented to us, a heterosexual relationship proves to be essentially formative. It was, in short, a primary given in the evolving tension between parents and child. From another perspective, which is our point of departure, this is precisely what is in question – is the heterosexual relationship between human beings something simple?

The truth of the matter is that if we hold fast to primary experience, it seems that it is not. If it were simple, it should constitute a series of harmonious islands within the human world, at least for those who had managed to clear away the worst of the undergrowth. It doesn't seem that up till now we can consider that analysts – but, after all, do we need to invoke analysts on the matter? – speak with a single voice and say that, even when it has come to completion, the heterosexual relationship presents itself to man as anything other than unstable, since the least one can say is precisely that the entire problem with it revolves around this. Take for example Balint's writings, which are quite focused on this, since even the title of his collection is *Genital Love* – which attests to the existence of a completely ultimate *Spaltung* and the juxtaposition of the current of desire and the current of tenderness. The entire problem of the heterosexual relationship is constructed around this juxtaposition.

The remarks I have just been making detract none of the interest from what was said last night, far from it – even if only for the terms of reference that were used and, for example, the conscious and aesthetic valorization of the sexual organ, to use the speaker's own terms, which from her perspective constitute the fundamental stage of the Oedipus complex. As Madame Dolto was saying, the sexual organ, its symbol, presents itself as a beautiful and good form. The sexual organ is beautiful, she added. It's a question, obviously, of a remark coming from the speaker's perspective, and it is clearly flattering for those who possess this male organ.

Nevertheless, this doesn't seem to be a given that we can embrace in any univocal manner, even if merely by reference to the reservations of one of the people who intervened, authoritatively, on the subject, giving us what one can call ethnological observations. Primitive peoples, good old primitive peoples, have always been a reference point for anthropologists, but it doesn't seem, if the truth be known, that any of the earliest data – if primitive people were in fact the earliest – about the beautiful and good form of the phallus is to be found there either.

If you refer to these documents as a whole – I'm not talking about learned documents, those things that are devised in the ethnographer's study, but about testimonials of the experience of those ethnographers who have been in the field, amongst the said primitives, good or bad – it seems that it is truly a basis and a principle of the relations between the sexes, even in the most backward tribes, that the phallus's erection at least be hidden. It's striking to note that even in tribes that possess only the most primitive forms of clothing, the existence of something that is used precisely to hide the phallus, a penis sheath for example, is the one remaining remnant of clothing.

Also, quite a large number of ethnographers have recorded the sort of irritation, as if with a truly primary response, that the persons of female sex experience in the presence of manifestations of an erection of the phallus. There are the very rare cases where there is no clothing at all, amongst the Nambikwara for example, whom as you know our friend Lévi-Strauss visited on several occasions and has spoken about at length. On the question that I put to him in this connection, Lévi-Strauss told me, repeating what he says in his book, *Tristes Tropiques*, that he never observed an erection in the presence of the group. Sexual relations occur without any special

372

373

concealment, a few feet away from the group, during the evening round the campfire, but an erection, either during the day or at that time, doesn't occur in public. This isn't entirely irrelevant to our subject.

There is the notion of the beautiful-and-good form. Situating the meaning of the phallus in such terms seems to arise from a fairly unique natural perspective. On the other hand, I am well aware that there is the beautiful and good form of a woman. It's certainly valued by every element of civilization, but, well, even if only because of the individual variety, it can't be said that we can, in this respect, speak univocally of a beautiful and good form. Let's say, in any case, that this beautiful and good form leaves more room for variation than the other. Undoubtedly, behind every woman there is the silhouetted form of the Venus de Milo or Aphrodite of Cnidus, but ultimately it's not always with unambiguously favourable results. Daumier has been much criticized for having given the Greek gods the rather crumpled forms of the bourgeois men and women of his time. He was criticized for it as if it were a sacrilege. This is precisely the point at which the problem I am indicating is situated – if it is obviously so deplorable to humanize gods, it is undoubtedly because humans are not always so easily deified.

In short, if what's necessary for the perpetuation of the human race lies in the hands of this beautiful and good form, the overall indication is that we make do with middling requirements, which the term 'beautiful and good form' perhaps doesn't tend to evoke. It at least remains fairly puzzling.

In fact, everything remarkable and appropriate that has been said to emphasize this beautiful and good form of the phallus is precisely what is being called into question here. This doesn't of course eliminate its typical prevalence as a form. The discourse that I am maintaining here, inasmuch as it is founded on and directly continues both Freud's own discourse and his experience, is intended to give a different idea of the meaning of the phallus.

The phallus is not a form. It doesn't have the form of an object, insofar as a form remains a captivating and fascinating form – at least not in one sense, for the problem remains intact in the other. The attraction between the sexes is something infinitely more complex than an imaginary attraction, as the entire economy of analytic doctrine shows us. As for us, we are committed to following the path that gives the solution to the problem in accordance with this formula, which itself is none other than a statement that needs to be developed if it is to be understood – the phallus is neither a fantasy, nor an image, nor an object, not even a part object, not even an internal one. It's a signifier. It's solely the fact

that it is a signifier that makes it possible to conceptualize and
articulate the diverse functions it assumes at different levels of the
intersexual encounter.

374

A signifier. It's not enough to say it's a signifier. Which signifier?
It's the signifier of desire. That of course throws up the further question – what does 'signifier of desire' mean? It's certain that the scope
of this affirmation implies that first we say what desire is.

Desire isn't something self-evident in the function it fulfils in our
experience. It's not simply intersexual appetite, intersexual attraction or the sexual instinct. It's also well understood that this notion
doesn't eliminate the existence of tendencies that are more or less
accentuated, that vary from one individual to the next, and have the
primary characteristic of expressing – in general let's say – greater or
less power in each individual with respect to sexual union. This in no
way resolves the question of the constitution of desire as we locate it
in this or that individual, whether neurotic or not. The constitution
of his desire is something other than whatever sexual potency he
carries around with him.

They are some remarks to put us back on track after the sense of
disorientation that the point of view perhaps gave us last night – we
will now quietly return to Freud's text.

2

Today isn't the first time I have made this remark, but I will convey
it to you today – one is filled with awe at the existence of this text,
Die Traumdeutung. One is filled with awe at it as if it were a kind of
miracle, because it is actually not too much to say that it can be read
as thought in motion. But it's a lot more than this.

At times things are brought in that correspond to a composition
that is overdetermined – here the word would apply well – on several
levels. Merely by taking this text in the way I said I would last time,
that is, by selecting the first dreams, one can see that the significance
of what comes first goes well beyond the reasons put forward for
placing them first in the chapters. For example, it's regarding the
day's residues, insofar as they enter into account in the determinism
of dreams, that a number of the initial dreams are presented there,
like the one I commented on last time, the dream by the butcher's
beautiful wife, as I call it.

As you saw, I chose it in order to examine the question of demand
and desire. It wasn't I who put demand and desire in the dream,
they're there. And Freud didn't put them there, he read them in it.
He saw that the patient has a need to create an unsatisfied desire

375

for herself, it's he who tells us. Of course, when Freud wrote *Die Traumdeutung*, he wasn't there to give this name along with a little lamp. But if he approached and composed things in this order, it's because he was urged on by a concern that may well go beyond the divisions of the chapters. Effectively, this dream presents a characteristic that especially offers an introduction to the problem that is fundamental to the perspective that I am trying to promote here, that of desire.

As to demand, it is hardly necessary to say that it, too, is everywhere. The reason the dream occurred is that a friend asked the patient if she could come to dinner at her place. In the dream itself, the request is there in the clearest of forms. The patient knows that everything was closed that day and that she was unable to make up for her inadequate provisions and offer the dinner as she should, and then she requests, in the clearest and most isolated manner in which one could present a request, since she makes it over the telephone, which at the time – this text is in the first edition – was not in widespread use. The telephone is actually there with its full symbolic power.

Let's go on a bit further. What are the first dreams that we encounter in the chapter on the 'Material and Sources of Dreams'?

The first dream we encounter is the dream of the botanical monograph, which is one of Freud's own. I am going to leave that one – not that it doesn't contribute exactly what we can expect today as I try to show you how the phallic signifier's relations with desire function, but simply because it's one of Freud's dreams, and so it would take a little bit longer and it would be a little bit more complicated to show you this. I will do it later if I have the time, for it is absolutely clear and structured exactly along the lines of the little schema I started drawing for you in relation to the hysteric's desire. But Freud is not purely and simply an hysteric. If he has the relation to hysteria that every relationship with desire comprises, it's in a slightly more elaborate manner.

We will therefore skip the dream of the botanical monograph and come to the patient who, as Freud tells us, is an hysteric. We are therefore returning to the hysteric's desire.

An intelligent and cultivated young woman, reserved and undemonstrative in her behaviour, reported as follows: *I dreamt that I arrived too late at the market and could get nothing either from the butcher or from the woman who sells vegetables.* An innocent dream, no doubt; but dreams are not as simple as that, so I asked to be told it in greater detail. She thereupon gave me the following account. *She dreamt she was going to the market with*

her cook, who was carrying the basket. After she had asked for
something, the butcher said to her: 'That's not obtainable any
longer', and offered her something else, adding 'This is good too.'
She rejected it and went on to the woman who sells vegetables,
who tried to get her to buy a peculiar vegetable that was tied up
in bundles but was of a black colour. She said: 'I don't recognize
that; I won't take it.' [*SE* 4: 183]

Freud's commentary is essential here, since we weren't the ones who analysed this patient. At the time *Die Traumdeutung* appeared, it was more or less as if the first work on atomic theory had appeared without any kind of link with the physics that preceded it. Besides, the book was greeted with almost total silence.

It is, then, on the first pages of this book that, when speaking of the presence of recent and indifferent material in dreams, Freud calmly laid out for his readers the following comments. 'She had actually gone to the market too late and had got nothing.' An attempt to attach this dream to the events of the day. 'One is tempted to say: the butcher's shop was already closed.' Here he isn't saying that he is reporting the words of the patient, he is putting himself forward by saying that that is what the utterance obviously is. 'But, stop – *Doch halt.* Was not that, or rather its opposite, a vulgar description of a certain sort of slovenliness in a man's dress?' It seems in effect that in the language of the Viennese, at least in familiar terms, it's customary to say to someone who has forgotten to button up his pants, 'Your butcher's shop, the door of your butcher's shop, is open – *Du hast deine Fleischbank offen.'* As Freud recognizes. 'However, the dreamer herself did not use the phrase.' And he adds, 'She may have perhaps avoided using it' [*SE* 4: 183].

That said, let's go on a little further. 'When anything in a dream has the character of direct speech, that is, when it is said or heard and not merely thought (and it is easy as a rule to make the distinction with certainty).' It's therefore a question of words inscribed in a dream as if written on a banner. One doesn't escape the implications of the situation. It's something that can be easily distinguished, Freud tells us – namely, the factor of language, which he invites us always to take as a factor that has its own value. 'It is derived from something actually spoken in waking life – though, to be sure, this something is merely treated as raw material and may be cut up and slightly altered and, more especially, divorced from its content. In carrying out an interpretation, one method is to start from spoken phrases of this kind. What, then, was the origin of the butcher's remark, *'That's not obtainable any longer'*?'

This sentence, '*Das is nicht mehr zu haben*', is recalled by Freud at the time he is writing the case of the Wolf Man, as an indication of the fact that for a long time he has been interested in the difficulty involved in reconstructing what is pre-amnesic in the subject's life prior to infantile amnesia. Indeed, it is in relation to this that he said that to the patient.

377

> A few days earlier I had explained to the patient that the earli-est experiences of childhood were '*not obtainable any longer as such*', but were replaced in analysis by 'transferences' and dreams. So *I* was the butcher and she was rejecting these trans-ferences into the present of old habits of thinking and feeling. What, again, was the origin of her own remark in the dream, '*I don't recognize that; I won't take it*'? '*Das kenne ich nicht, das nehme ich nicht.*' For the purposes of the analysis this had to be divided up. '*I don't recognize that*' was something she had said the day before to her cook, with whom she had had a dispute; but at the time she had gone on: '*Benehmen Sie sich anständig*', '*Behave yourself properly!*' [*SE* 4: 184]

As Freud says, what has been retained in the dream is precisely the element of language, the part that has no signification, '*Das kenne ich nicht*', whereas the censor has moved the second sentence over onto the servant. What therefore appears in the dream, '*Das kenne ich nicht, das nehme ich nicht*', gives meaning to what has been retained from '*Das kenne ich nicht, Benehmen Sie sich anständig.*'
Freud continues:

> At this point there had clearly been a displacement. Of the two phrases that she had used in the dispute with her cook, she had chosen the insignificant one for inclusion in the dream. But it was only the repressed one, '*Behave yourself properly!*' that fitted in with the rest of the content of the dream: those would have been the appropriate words to use if someone had ventured to make improper suggestions and had forgotten 'to close his meat-shop'.
>
> The allusions underlying the incident with the vegetable-seller were a further confirmation that our interpretation was on the right track. A vegetable that is sold tied up in bundles (lengthways, as the patient added afterwards) and is also black, could only be a dream-combination of asparagus and black (Spanish) radishes. No knowledgeable person of either sex will ask for an interpretation of asparagus. But the other vegetable – *Schwarzer Rettig* ['black radish'] – can be

taken as an exclamation – '*Schwarzer, rett' dich!*' ['Blacky! Be off!'] –; and accordingly it too seems to hint at the same sexual topic which we suspected at the very beginning, when we felt inclined to introduce the phrase about the meat-shop being closed into the original account of the dream. We need not enquire now into the full meaning of the dream. So much is quite clear: it *had* a meaning and that meaning was far from innocent. [*SE* 4: 184–5]

I apologize if this might have seemed a bit long. I would simply like to refocus things on this little dream, now that we know so much and have a tendency to read a little too quickly.

Here, we find represented in the clearest of manners another   378
example of the hysteric's relationship to desire as such, the place of which, as I indicated last time, the hysteric has a need for in her dreams and symptoms – a need for its place to be marked some-where. But here something else is in question, namely, the place of the phallus signifier.

Let's mix our theoretical discourse in with references to dreams so as to vary things a bit and not to lose our attention. Three other dreams by the same patient are subsequently mentioned, and we will make use of them at the appropriate moment. Let us pause for a second over what needs to be stressed.

Like the other day, the question is what place to give desire. But this time, this place isn't marked in the field external to the subject. It's not about desire, insofar as the subject rejects it for herself beyond demand and only accepts it in the dream as the Other's desire, who, here, is her friend. It's about desire insofar as it is supported, by hypothesis, by the phallus signifier. Let's see what function the signifier plays in this case.

As you can see, Freud introduces the phallus signifier here without hesitation or ambiguity. The only element that he has not stressed as such in his analysis, since he has to leave something for us to do, is the following, and it is altogether striking. The entire ambi-guity of the subject's behaviour in relation to the phallus resides in this dilemma, which is that the subject may either have or be this signifier.

The reason that this dilemma arises is that the phallus isn't the object, but the signifier, of desire. The dilemma is absolutely essen-tial. It lies at the heart of all the shifts, transmutations and sleights of hand, I would say, of the castration complex.

Why does the phallus come into this dream? From this perspec-tive, I think that it's not at all overstepping the mark to say that the phallus is, as such, actualized in this hysteric's dream around

Freud's sentence, '*Das ist nicht mehr zu haben*', that is, 'That's not obtainable any longer.'

I obtained confirmation about the absolute use of the verb '*avoir*', to have, as in the linguistic usage that has us say, '*l'avoir*', to have it, or, even better, '*en avoir ou pas*', to have some or not, which also has significance in German. It's a question here in this sentence of the phallus insofar as it emerges as the object that is lacking.

Who is it that lacks the object? This is, of course, what it would be good to know, but nothing is more uncertain than that it is purely and simply the object that the biological subject lacks. Let's say, first, that it presents itself in signifying terms as linked to the sentence that expresses the fact that it is what is no longer obtainable – *Das ist nicht mehr zu haben*. This isn't an experience of frustration. It's a signification, a signifying articulation of the object lack, as such.

This of course tallies with the notion that I am placing in the foreground, that here the phallus is the signifier insofar as – who doesn't have it? – insofar as the Other doesn't have it. With the phallus it is effectively a matter of something that is articulated on the plane of language, and which therefore is located as such on the plane of the Other. It's the signifier of desire insofar as desire is articulated as the Other's desire. I will return to this presently.

We'll now take the second dream by the same patient. It's a dream that is purportedly innocent.

> Her husband asked her: 'Don't you think we ought to have the piano tuned?' And she replied: 'It's not worth while ['*Es lohnt nicht*' – which means something like, 'it's not worth it']; the hammers need reconditioning in any case.'

Freud comments in these terms:

> This was the repetition of a real event of the previous day . . .. But what was the explanation of her dreaming it? But why does she dream about it? She told me that the piano was a *disgusting* old *box*, that it made an *ugly noise*, that it had been in her husband's possession before their marriage, and so on.

In a footnote, he says, 'This last was a substitute for the opposite idea [that is that her husband did not have it before their marriage], as the course of the analysis will make clear.'

> '*It's not worth while.*' These were derived from a visit she had paid the day before to a woman friend. She had been invited to take off her jacket, but had refused with the words: 'Thank

you, but *it's not worth while*; I can only stop a minute. As she was telling me this, I recollected that during the previous day's analysis she had suddenly caught hold of her jacket, one of her buttons having come undone. Thus it was as though she were saying: 'Please don't look; *it's not worth while.*' In the same way the 'box' ['*Kasten*'] was a substitute for a chest ['*Brustkasten*']; and the interpretation of the dream led us back at once to the time of her physical development at puberty, when she had begun to be dissatisfied by her figure. We can hardly doubt that it led back to still earlier times, if we take the word '*disgusting*' into account and the '*ugly noise*', and if we remember how often – both in *doubles entendres* and in dreams – the lesser hemispheres of a woman's body are used, whether as contrasts or as substitutes, for the larger ones. [*SE* 4: 185–6]

We find ourselves here on the other side of the question. If the phallus is the signifier of desire, the Other's desire, and the problem that presents itself to the subject from the very first step of the dialectic of desire, then the other side is this – a question of being or not being the phallus.

Let's put all our faith in this function as a signifier that we are granting the phallus, and let's say the following – just as 'one cannot be and have been', so too 'one cannot be and not be'. If it is necessary that what one is not is what one is, what remains is not to be what one is, that is, what remains is to reject what one is in appearance, which is very precisely the woman's position in hysteria. As a woman, she makes a mask of herself. She makes a mask of herself precisely so that, behind this mask, she can be the phallus. The entire behaviour of hysterics manifests itself in the gesture of this hand placed on her button – the meaning of which Freud's eye accustomed us to see a long, long time ago – accompanied by this sentence, 'It's not worthwhile.' Why isn't it worthwhile? Because there is, of course, no question of looking further, because further on is where the phallus should be. But it's truly not worthwhile looking, '*Es lohnt nicht*', because you won't find it there.

For the hysteric, it is a matter of seeing and knowing, as Freud immediately gives us in a note addressed, '*Für Wissbegierige*' ['For anyone curious to know'], which is translated into French as, '*A ceux qui voudraient l'approfondir*', 'For anyone who would like to go into it in depth'. More rigorously, 'To lovers of knowledge'.

This brings us to the heart of what I have perhaps already referred to with this term – borrowed from a morality that despite everything bears the imprint of a human experience that is perhaps richer than a lot of others, moral theology – the *Cupido sciendi* [the curiosity or desire to know]. We can choose this term for translating '*le désir*', although the equivalences between languages always raise delicate questions. With respect to desire, I have already obtained '*Begierde*' ['desire'] from my German-speaking friends, which one finds in Hegel, but which some find too animal. It's funny that Hegel has employed it for the master–slave, a theme which isn't overly imbued with animality.

'If anyone is curious to know,' Freud says in this footnote, 'I may add that the dream concealed a phantasy of my behaving in an improper and sexually provocative manner, and of the patient putting up a defence against my conduct' [*SE* 4: 185fn]. Being provocative towards an hysteric is liable to produce the desire, but beyond what is known as a defence. That is, it indicates the place – beyond appearance, beyond the mask – of something that is presented to desire, something which, of course, it can't be offered access to, since it is something that is presented behind the veil but which can't be found there either. It's not worthwhile unbuttoning my jacket, because you will not find the phallus there, but if I place my hand on my jacket, it is so that you desire, inside my blouse, the phallus, which is the signifier of desire.

These remarks lead me to think about how to define this desire in a fully rigorous way, in such a way as to give you a good sense of what we are talking about.

3

Someone I was in conversation with called my little interwoven lines, the ones I have been refining for you over time, a little Calder mobile. It's quite a well-chosen expression, to my mind. The issue is not to stop there but to try to spell out what we mean by desire as such.

In this dialectic, we locate desire as what on this little mobile is located beyond demand. Why does there need to be anything beyond demand? There needs to be something beyond demand, inasmuch as, for the requirements of articulation, demand diverts, changes and transposes need. Therefore, there is the possibility of a residue.

Insofar as man is caught in the signifying dialectic, there is something that doesn't work – whatever optimistic people think when they point to all the positive things that take place between children and their parents, in terms of locating the other sex. Now this is precisely the level at which we come in.

There is, then, a residue. What form does it take? What form does it take, necessarily? It's now no longer a question of sexual desire, and we shall see why later, why it must come to this place. But we are considering the general relationship between a man's needs and signifiers, and we find ourselves faced with the following question. Is there anything that restores this margin of deviation marked by the impact of signifiers on needs? And in what form does that beyond appear, if indeed it appears at all? Experience proves that it does appear. And it's what we call desire. This is how we can formulate one possible form of its appearance.

The manner in which desire in the human subject must manifest itself depends on what is determined by the dialectic of demand. If demand has a particular effect on needs, it also has its own characteristics. I have already formulated the characteristics belonging to it. Demand, merely by virtue of being articulated as a demand, even when it isn't a demand for the Other, explicitly establishes the Other as absent or present, and as giving or not giving this presence. That is, demand is fundamentally a demand for love – a demand for what is nothing, no particular satisfaction, a demand for what the subject brings purely and simply by responding to the demand.

This is where the originality of introducing the symbolic in the form of demand shows its originality. The originality of the introduction of demand in comparison with need is located in what is unconditioned in demand, namely, that demands are made against a background of the demand for love.

382

If the introduction of demand carries some loss with it, in whatever form, in relation to need, does what is thereby lost have to end up beyond demand? It's clear that if it has to end up beyond demand, that is, beyond the distortion introduced by the dimension of demand, it's inasmuch as we must rediscover in this beyond something where the Other loses its predominance, and where need, insofar as it stems from the subject, occupies the primary place.

However, since need has already passed through the filter of demand onto the plane of the unconditioned, it is only in the name of a second negation, as it were, that we encounter there, beyond, the margin that was lost in demand. What we find in this beyond is precisely the feature of absolute condition that is present in desire as such.

This feature is, of course, borrowed from need. How could we form desires, if it were not by borrowing the raw materials from our needs? But that passes to a state that isn't one of unconditionality, since it involves something borrowed from a particular need, but one of absolute condition, one that is without measure and incommensurate with the need for an object of any kind. This condition can be deemed absolute for the precise reason that it abolishes the dimension of the Other, that it's a requirement where the Other doesn't have to respond yes or no. This is the fundamental characteristic of human desire as such.

Every desire in its pure state is something that, uprooted from the soil of needs, assumes the form of an absolute condition in relation to the Other. It's the margin or result of the subtraction, as it were, of the requirements of need from the demand for love. Conversely, desire presents itself as what, in the demand for love, rebels against being reduced to a need, because in reality it satisfies nothing other than itself, that is, desire as an absolute condition.

This is the reason that sexual desire will come to that place, insofar as it presents itself, in relation to the subject or the individual, as essentially problematic and on the two planes of need and the demand for love.

On the plane of need, Freud wasn't the first to emphasize this – ever since the world has been the world, people have wondered how the human being, who has the property of recognizing what is to his advantage, can bear and accept this sexual need which undeniably pushes him to aberrant extremes that correspond to no immediately rationalizable need, and which introduces, let's say, what is called the dialectic of the species into the individual. Thus, by its very nature, sexual need already presents itself as problematic in the subject, as we define him – even if philosophers have articulated this differently – that is, as someone who is able to rationalize his needs and articulate them in terms of equivalences, that is, in terms of signifiers.

Moreover, with respect to the demand for love, this sexual need will become desire, specifically, since it can only place itself at the level of desire as we have just defined it. Sexual desire presents itself in a problematic manner from the perspective of the demand for love, whatever one says, whatever holy water one tries to cover it with in the name of 'oblation'. With respect to what in all languages is called 'stating one's demands', the question of desire is problematic, inasmuch as – in order to express things in the most common form of language, which here is revealing – in whatever manner demand is formulated, what takes shape is that the Other comes into play in the form of the instrument of desire as soon as sexual desire is in question.

It's for this reason that sexual desire, insofar as it is a question, is placed at the level of desire. Insofar as it is a question, it can't really be articulated. There are really no words for it – hear it from the horse's mouth, since it perhaps won't do any harm for me to say that not everything is reducible to language. I have always said so, of course, but I haven't been heard. I repeat it – there are no words to express something, something that has a name, which is desire.

383

For expressing desire, as popular wisdom knows very well, there are only sweet nothings.

The question of the signifier of desire, then, arises as such. What it is expressed by isn't just any ordinary signifier. It's effectively something that borrows from prevailing forms of thrust or vital flux, but it is still as a signifier that it is less caught up in the dialectic, along with what the mortification that passing into the register of signifiers always comprises for anything that attains the dimension of signifiers.

Here, the ambiguous mortification presents itself in the form of a veil, one that we see reproduced every day in the form of the hysteric's jacket. This is the fundamental position of woman in relation to man where desire is concerned, namely that above all don't take a look there, inside her jacket, because of course there is nothing there, there is nothing but the signifier. But it is nothing other than the signifier of desire.

384

Behind this veil, there is, or there is not, something that must not be shown, and this is why the demon I was talking about concerning the unveiling of the phallus in the sacred Mysteries is called the demon of shame. 'Shame' has a different meaning and significance in man and woman, whatever its origin, whether it is the horror of it that a woman has, or something that quite naturally arises from the oh-so delicate souls of men.

I alluded to the veil that quite often covers the phallus in man. It's exactly the same thing that normally covers a woman's being almost entirely, inasmuch as what is precisely there lying behind, and which is veiled, is the signifier phallus. What Freud called, concerning the female sex, *Abscheu*, the horror that corresponds to absence as such, the Medusa, is connected with the unveiling that would only show nothing, that is, the absence of what is unveiled.

We are told that sexual progress or maturation would entail passing from a partial object to a total object. What I have managed to introduce on the perspective that I am giving you on the play between the subject of desire and the signifier of desire, and which is far from having been exhausted, already suffices to completely reverse notions like this that obscure the whole dialectic about approaching the other in the sexual relation. There is, here, a real camouflage or evasion. In coming to the place of desire, the other does not in any way become the total object, but on the contrary the problem is that the other totally becomes an object as instrument of desire. The problem is maintaining the two positions compatible with one another.

There is, on the one hand, the position of the Other as Other, as the locus of speech, to whom demand is addressed and whose radical irreducibility manifests itself in the fact that it can give love, that is, something that is all the more totally gratuitous because there is no support for love, since, as I have been telling you, to give one's love is to give nothing of what one has, for it's precisely insofar as one doesn't have it that love is at issue. But there is discordance between what there is that is absolute in the subjectivity of the Other who gives or doesn't give love and the fact that, to gain access to the Other as object of desire, it is necessary for it totally to become an object. It's in this vertiginous or nauseous, to call it by its name, gap that the difficulty of accessing sexual desire is located.

385   In the *Studies on Hysteria*, Breuer connects the manifestation of hysterical symptoms in the form of nausea and disgust to the phenomena of dizziness. He refers to the work of Mach on motor sensations, showing, with an extraordinary intuition, that the essential source of this labyrinthine phenomenon, in which we see this series, dizziness, nausea, disgust, appear, lies in the discordance between optical sensations and motor sensations [*SE* 2: 210–11].

I have in fact already observed in more than one person, to the point where the analysis of such a thing is possible, the sort of short-circuit that is established between the phallus signifier, in the form of which the perception of the Other in desire is actualized, and what, at that moment, can only appear empty to the subject, namely, the place that the organ would normally occupy, I mean between the legs, and which is at that moment evoked only as a place. I have ten observations I could give you on this point, in all sorts of forms, whether totally clear and raw or variously symbolic, with the subject stating it clearly, nevertheless – it's insofar as the Other as object of desire is perceived as the phallus and insofar as, as such, he is perceived as a lack at the place of his own phallus, that the subject experiences something that resembles a very curious form of dizziness. Someone has even gone so far as to compare it to a kind of metaphysical dizziness experienced in other circumstances, the rarest of circumstances, with respect to the notion of being itself, insofar as it lies subjacent to everything that is.

I will end there today. We will come back to the dialectic of being and having in the hysteric, and we will progress further when we see what point this takes us to in the obsessional.

I will tell you this straightaway, and you must feel it anyway – this isn't unconnected to an entire dialectic, a different one, an imaginary one, for which a theory has not only been proposed to you, but patients have been more or less forced to swallow it with a particular technique concerning obsessional neurosis, and where the phallus as imaginary element plays the dominant role therein.

We shall see what theoretical and technical rectifications we can contribute by no longer regarding the phallus as an image or a fantasy, but as a signifier.

7 May 1958

XXII

THE OTHER'S DESIRE

Three articles by Maurice Bouvet
The graph of desire
The third 'still waters run deep' dream
The future of the obsessional's fixed ideas
The supports of desire

Fonderung : Demand	*Wunsch* :
Begehren : Desire	The dream's desire
Bedürfnis : Need	

Our trajectory, in which the theme of the phallus plays an essential role, has brought us to the point of grasping more fully what in analysis is advanced concerning the notion of object.

We must both centre our attention on the effective function that the object relation plays in contemporary analytic practice, the way it's used and the services that that renders, and at the same time attempt to spell out more fully what we have specified in speaking about the phallus.

1

As to the first part of this programme, we can refer to an article that with time has come to assume historical value, published in 1953 in the *Revue Française de Psychanalyse,* authored by Maurice Bouvet and on '*Le moi dans la névrose obsessionelle*' ['The Ego in Obsessional Neurosis']. In reality, it's solely about object relations in the obsessional, and something to explore would be why the author gave it this unsuitable title, when he actually says nothing about the ego in obsessional neurosis, except – it's weak, it's strong.

The author has, at the end of the day, adopted an attitude of prudence on this matter that one can only praise.

I will mention two earlier articles by the same author. One, dated 388 December 1948, appeared in 1950 in the same journal under the title '*Incidehces thérapeutiques de la prise de conscience de l'envie du pénis dans la névrose obsessionnelle féminine*' ['Therapeutic Effects of Becoming Aware of Penis Envy in Obsessional Neurosis in Women']. The freshness of this first approach to the function of the penis in obsessional neurosis gives this article its value. It enables one to gauge how much things have gone rather downhill since, for this still new experience provides an interesting reflection on the question. The other was published in the July–September 1948 issue, '*Importance de l'aspect homosexuel du transfert dans quatre cas de névrose obsessionnelle masculine*' ['Importance of the Homosexual Aspect of the Transference in Four Cases of Obsessional Neurosis in Men'].

These are the three things to read, since there are not all that many articles written in French on the topic. They show reasonably well the level that things are now at on these problems. Moreover, rereading them can't fail to create an overall impression that will provide a basis for what we can manage to explore, or so it seems to me, concerning the exact articulation of the issue, and will enable us to situate the value and significance of a therapeutic approach centred thereon. When one sees object relations being articulated in synoptic tables enabling one to follow the object's progressive constitution, one realizes that these are, at least in part, false windows. I do not believe that either the genital object or the pre-genital object has any other significance here than to embellish the beauty of the said synoptic tables.

What gives the object relation its value and is its pivot, what introduced the notion of object into the analytic dialectic, is above all what is known as the part object. The term is taken from Abraham's vocabulary, in a manner that isn't quite exact, since what the latter spoke of was the partial love for the object, and this shift in meaning is itself already significant. It requires no great effort to identify the part object purely and simply with this phallus we are talking about – and must all the more readily talk about given that we have endowed it with such significance, which removes any discomfort we might have over treating it as a privileged object. We know that it deserves this privilege as a signifier. It's because of their extraordinary discomfort at giving such privilege to a particular organ that authors have ended up not mentioning it at all, whereas it's in virtually every analysis.

If you reread these articles, you will see that there is one enormous fact, centre stage, across every page, which is that the phallus is taken – not only by the psychoanalyst in question, but by all those who listened to him – at the level of fantasy. From the author's perspective, the treatment for obsessional neurosis entirely revolves around the incorporation or imaginary introjection of this phallus that appears in the analytic dialogue in the form of a phallus attributed to the analyst and to which all fantasies refer.

389

There are, supposedly, two phases. In the first, fantasies of incorporation and devoration of this fantasmatic phallus have a clearly aggressive and sadistic character at the same time as it's experienced as horrible and dangerous. These fantasies have the value of being capable of revealing the subject's position in relation to the object constitutive of its stage, which, in this instance, is that of the second phase of the anal-sadistic stage, marked by fundamental tendencies to destroy the object. From there, one moves to a second phase in which one begins to respect the object's autonomy in an at least partial form.

The entire dialectic of the moment – the subjective moment, I would say here – at which obsessional neurosis is situated is, it's claimed, suspended at the point of maintaining a certain form of the part object. A world can be established around this object – a world that isn't completely destined to be fundamentally destroyed by the stage immediately subjacent to the precarious equilibrium which the subject has achieved. The obsessional is effectively presented as always ready to lapse into destruction of the world, since, from the perspective from which the author expresses himself, one also thinks in terms of the subject's relationship to his environment. It is through maintaining the part object – maintenance that requires an entire scaffolding, which is precisely what constitutes obsessional neurosis – that the subject is said to avoid lapsing into a permanently threatening psychosis. This is quite clearly what the author considers to be the very basis of the problem.

Still, one can't fail to object that whatever the obsessional's parapsychotic symptoms – depersonalization, for example, disturbances of the ego and feelings of estrangement and the darkening of the world, all feelings obviously touching on mood [*couleur*], even perhaps on the structure of the ego – the cases of transition from obsession to psychosis, while they have always existed, have always been extremely rare. Authors observed long ago that, on the contrary, there was a sort of incompatibility between the two afflictions. When a real obsessional neurosis is involved, the idea that one runs the risk in analysis of not curing the subject but of seeing him lapse into psychosis is a risk that seems extraordinarily fantasmatic, for it's really the thing that one runs the least risk of. That an obsessional, in the course of an analysis, even subsequent to an unfortunate or even wild therapeutic intervention, lapses into psychosis is very, very, very rare. Personally I've never seen it in my practice, thank God. Nor have I ever had the impression that this was a risk I was running with these patients.

An appraisal like that must betray a little more than a simple lack of discernment in clinical experience. One can assume that the author's concern to assure the coherence of his theory leads him further than he wants. Very probably there is, no doubt, also something that goes even further, and which derives from the author's own particular position when faced with the obsessional. It's not a question of speaking about the countertransference of a particular person, but of the countertransference in a more general sense, where one may consider it as formed by what I often call the analyst's prejudices, in other words, the background of things said or not said against which his discourse is articulated.

This practice is led, then, in the specific therapeutics with obsessional neurosis, to take as its pivot the fantasy of the imaginary incorporation of the phallus, the analyst's phallus. It's a bit difficult to see at what moment, or why, the about-turn occurs, unless it's through what one may suppose is a kind of effect by attrition. It's actually a bit mysterious. We are told there is a moment where, by virtue of the 'working through' or of insistence in the treatment, the incorporation of phallic fantasies seems to have a completely different value to the subject. What appears to have been the incorporation of a dangerous and in some way repudiated object in these fantasies suddenly changes in nature, provoking acceptance and becoming a welcome object, an object that is a source of power – 'source', the word is there, I am not the one creating this metaphor.

Doesn't this introjection, which has become, we are told, conservative, 'have traits in common with religious communion in which one swallows without chewing?' [p. 172] One adds by way of commentary that the 'feelings of happiness' that this fantasy supposedly brings 'comprises no destruction, similar in that respect to the sucking fantasies of Abraham's melancholics' [p. 172].

These traits are not chosen in any tendentious way. We do get the sense that in an analysis conducted in this way something effectively occurs like a kind of ascesis that plays principally on fantasies, no doubt in doses, with barriers, with the brakes on and in stages, with all the precautions that the technique carries, and that it enables the subject of an obsessional neurosis to enter into new relationships with the object. It is more difficult to see what one wants out of it, which the author calls the distance from the object. If I understand well, it's a matter of enabling the subject to get closer to the object and pass through a phase in which this distance is nullified and, no doubt, then recovered – at least, we have to hope so. An object which has all the powers of fear and danger successively concentrated upon itself subsequently becomes the symbol by which a libidinal relation that is considered more normal and described as genital is established.

From our perspective, we remain perhaps a little more strict than the author who congratulates himself on having achieved the aim of having garnered from a patient, after a number of months of treatment, the following declaration – 'I had an extraordinary experience, that of being able to enjoy my husband's happiness, I was extremely moved to observe his joy, and his pleasure was my pleasure' [p. 164].

I ask you to weigh these terms. They are certainly not without value. They describe very well an experience that implies no lifting of the said patient's prior frigidity. The extraordinary experience of being able to enjoy her husband's happiness is something frequently observed, but it still doesn't signify that the patient has in any way attained orgasm. The patient remains, we are told, semi-frigid. This is why one remains a little surprised when the author immediately adds: 'Is this not the best way to characterize adult genital relations?' [p. 164].

The notion of adult genital relations is obviously what gives this entire perspective the character of being a construction of false windows. It's not very clear what 'adult genital relation' means when you examine it closely.

As soon as the author tries to explain himself, he doesn't seem to find either the simplicity or the unity that that seems to imply. 'As to affirming the ego's coherence, not only does it emerge from the disappearance of an obsessional symptomatology and phenomena of depersonalization, but also it translates into the achieving of a sense of freedom of unity which is a new experience for these subjects' [p. 164]. Nor do these optimistic approximations exactly correspond to our experience of what progress and cure really represent in obsessional neurosis.

We clearly see here what kind of mountain, wall or ready-made conception we are dealing with when it's a question of appraising what an obsessional structure is, the manner in which it's lived and the manner in which it evolves. Here we are trying to articulate things in a completely different register. I don't think I am any more complicated than others, and if you can manage to familiarize yourselves with the measures I bring into play here, and count them, you will see that, in the end, there are not that many more things and that this is simply articulated in another less unilinear way.

I am well aware that the desire to have a synoptic table corresponding to or contradicting the one by Mrs Ruth Mack Brunswick lies deep in the heart of many in the audience. We will perhaps get there one day, but before we do it's perhaps best to proceed step by step and start by criticizing the notion of the phallus as a part object whose present use, which involves clear dangers, has to be put in its proper place.

We are trying to articulate this place with the use of this little schema.

392

2

It would be possible to cover the entire schema with signs and equations, but I do not want to give you the impression of something artificial, even though I have tried to reduce things to their essential necessity.

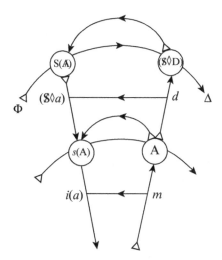

We've already placed here the big A, the big Other, which is where the code is located and receives demands. It's in the passage from A to the point where the message is that the signified of the Other [s(A)] is produced. And then, need, which begins here, finds itself transformed there [at A], and is characterized differently at the different levels. If we take this line [that starts bottom right and ends bottom left] as the line of the realization of the subject, at the end it translates into something that always emerges more or less as an identification, that is, as the remodelling, as the transformation also and ultimately the passage of the subject's need through the defiles of demand.

Now, we know that this isn't sufficient to constitute a satisfactory subject, a subject who holds together over the requisite number, let's say four, of points of support. This is why there is a field beyond demand.

What I have already tried to define by characterizing it as the signifier of desire is initially articulated there, in its topological place, and I have explicitly presented it to you as this Φ. There is, effectively, a necessity linked to this topology, which is that it's in the field lying beyond demand that sexual desire comes to be situated and, at the same time, undergoes the articulation particular to this beyond.

The line on which the drive, the tendency as such, is inscribed and the place assigned to the capital Phi in the beyond-demand coincide here by virtue of the structural necessity that something come and superimpose itself on the set of signifiers to make a signified of it, which is what we usually place below the bar of our formulation, big S over small s. Here the signified is initially a 'to be signified'.

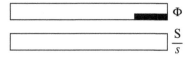

The phallus is this particular signifier which, in the body of signifiers, is specialized for designating the overall effects of the signifier, as such, on the signified. That goes a long way, but there is no way of not going this far to give the phallus its signification. It occupies a privileged place here in what of the signifier will be produced in the beyond of desire – that is, the entire field located beyond the field of demand.

To the extent that this beyond of desire is symbolized, there is the possibility – this is simply articulating the sense of what I am saying – that there is a relationship between the subject and demand as such: [$ ◊ D]. It is quite clear that such a relationship assumes that the subject isn't completely included therein prior to the moment at which this beyond is constituted, even if, by hypothesis, the subject is constituted through being articulated, thanks to the phallus signifier.

On the near side, which is the field of demand, the pure and simple Other creates all the law of the subject's constitution – even if only taken simply at the level of the existence of his body – by virtue of the fact that the mother is a speaking being. The fact that she is a speaking being is absolutely essential, whatever Spitz might think. It's not only the little kisses and cuddles and dabs of eau de cologne that constitute a relationship to the mother. The mother has to speak to him or her, everyone knows that. Not only does she speak to him, undoubtedly, but a mute nurse would not fail to produce certain fairly visible consequences on the infant's development.

Beyond this Other, if something called the beyond of desire is constituted by signifiers, we then have the possibility of the relationship [$S \lozenge D$]. S is the subject as such, a less complete, barred subject. That means that a complete human subject is never a pure and simple subject of knowledge, as all of philosophy constructs it, well and truly corresponding to the *percipiens* of this *perceptum* that is the world. We know that there is no human subject who is a pure subject of knowledge, save reducing him to a photoelectric cell or an eye or, again, to what in philosophy is called a consciousness. But as we are analysts, we know that there is always a *Spaltung*, that is, there are always two lines along which he is constituted. This, moreover, is where all our problems of structure originate.

Here on the upper left, what has to be formed? It's precisely what I no longer call the signified of A, $s(A)$, but the signifier of A, $S(\text{Å})$, insofar as the subject knows this *Spaltung*, is structured by it and has already undergone its effects. That means that he is already marked by this signifier-effect that is signified by the phallus signifier. This is, therefore, the A insofar as the phallus is barred within it and brought to the state of a signifier. This Other as castrated is represented here in the place of the message. The terms are inverted in relation to the message at the lower level. Desire's message is that.

Nevertheless, this isn't to say that this message is easy to receive, precisely because of this difficulty of articulating desire, which brings it about that there is an unconscious. In other words, we must imagine, in fact, that what is presented here as on the upper level of the schema is ordinarily on the lower level and not articulated in the subject's consciousness, although well and truly articulated in his unconscious. It's even because it's articulated in his unconscious that it exists. This is the question we are asking here – it's articulable in the subject's consciousness, but up to a point, and the question is knowing precisely what point.

What does the hysteric who we spoke about last time show us? The hysteric, of course, isn't psychoanalysed, otherwise, by hypothesis, she would no longer be an hysteric. The hysteric, as I have said, situates this beyond in the form of a desire that is the Other's desire. I will justify that to you a little bit more later, but for now – because, if one is trying to articulate something, it's quite necessary to start by commenting on it – I will tell you that things happen as follows.

In the first loop, the subject, via the manifestation of need, its tension, crosses the first signifying line of demand, and we can place here, so as to topologize things, the ego's [m] relation to the image of the other, the imaginary little a [i(a)]. Similarly, in the second loop the little d of desire – which in the Other as big Other enables the subject to access this beyond that is to be signified and which is the field we are in the process of exploring, that of his desire – occupies the corresponding place to that of the little m. This simply expresses the fact that the subject will encounter the desire of the Other as such, in the place at which the subject has sought to articulate his desire.

I have been developing this using other terms over a long period of time, but also using the formula that the desire in question, namely desire in its unconscious function, is the Other's desire. This is a formula founded on [analytic] experience and which was verified last time when I spoke about the hysteric with reference to dreams.

Let's pick up this thread.

3

These are not selected dreams, any more than I give you selected texts of Freud.

If you apply yourselves to reading Freud, as it seems is starting to happen, I can't advise you too much to read him entirely, failing which you run the risk of coming across passages that will perhaps not have been selected, but which will be no less a source of all sorts of errors, even of *fausses reconnaissances*. You have to see what place such-and-such a text fits into in – I won't say the development of a thought, even though it would be right to say so, but ever since we started talking about thought, the term has become so hackneyed that we never quite know what we are talking about – the development of the research, the efforts of someone who has a certain idea about his magnetic field, as it were, and can only achieve it through a particular detour. Each of these detours has to be judged by the road taken overall.

Thus, I didn't choose the two dreams from last time, the hysteric's dreams, at random. I explained to you how I chose them. I chose the first dream because I came across it after other dreams, and I explained the reasons why I didn't choose them first. I will come back to this. The dream of the botanical monograph can help us understand what there is to demonstrate, but since it's one of Freud's dreams, it's best to explain it later.

First, I will continue the discussion of the hysteric's dream.

The hysteric showed us that what she discovers in the Other's 396
desire is what can be called her point of support – this isn't a term
whose use I reserve for myself, and if you read Mr Glover on obsessional neurosis, you will see that he uses exactly the same term to
say that when one has withdrawn obsessional neurotics' obsessions
from them, they lack their point of support. You'll see that the
terms I make use of I have in common with other authors – we are
all trying to metaphorize our experience, our little impressions. The
hysteric, then, takes her point of support, as I was saying, from a
desire that is the Other's desire. It's this creation of a desire beyond
demand that is essential, and I think I have articulated it adequately.

One might mention here the third dream that I did not have time
to explore last time, but I can easily read it out to you now.

> She was putting a candle in a candlestick; but the candle broke
> so that it wouldn't stand up properly. The girls at her school
> said she was clumsy; but the mistress said it was not her fault.
> [*SE* 4: 186]

This is Freud's comment on the dream: 'The occasion for the dream
was a real event. The day before she had actually put a candle into
a candlestick, though it did not break.' That is symbolic, and, to be
frank, we know what a candle signifies. 'If it won't stand up properly, it means that the man is impotent.' And Freud emphasizes the
'It was not her fault, *Es sie nicht ihre Schuld*' [*SE* 4: 186].

'But could a carefully brought-up young woman, who had been
screened from the impact of anything ugly, have known that a
candle might be put to such use?' [*SE* 4: 187]. On this point we
learn that during a boating trip, she had heard a rather unseemly
students' song about the use that the Queen of Sweden made of
Apollo's candles, behind closed shutters. She did not understand.
Her husband explained the Apollo to her, behind closed shutters of
course, and it all re-emerges and suitably frolics around when the
occasion arises.

Here we see the phallus appear in a raw state, one might say,
and appear isolated, with the status of a part, if not a flying, object.
Although we don't know from what moment of this patient's
analysis – for she is clearly in analysis – this dream was extracted,
the important point is obviously in the 'It was not her fault'. The fact
is that it's at the level of the others. It takes place in the presence of
all the others, and it's because of the teacher that all the little class-
mates stop their mocking. The symbol of the Other is evoked, and
it corroborates and confirms – this is what I want to get to – what
was already present in the dream called the dream by the butcher's

397

beautiful wife, that is, that in hysteria, which is in short a mode of constitution of the subject precisely concerning her sexual desire, the stress is to be placed not only on the dimension of desire insofar as it's opposed to that of demand, but above all on the Other's desire, the position or the place of desire in the Other.

I reminded you how Dora lives up till her hysterical position collapses. She is very much at ease, apart from some minor symptoms, but they are precisely those that constitute her as an hysteric and can be read in the *Spaltung* of these two lines. We shall return to the overdetermination of symptoms, which is tied to the existence of these two signifying lines. What we saw the other day is that Dora subsists as a subject insofar as she demands love, like every good hysteric, but also insofar as she supports the Other's desire as such – it's she who supports it, it's she who is its support. Everything is going along very well, rolling along as happily as can be, and without anyone having anything to be worried about. Saying that she supports the Other's desire is the most suitable expression for the style of her position and action in relation to her father and to Frau K. As I have been indicating, it's inasmuch as she comes to identify with Herr K. that the whole little construction is possible. In the face of desire, she is the support, in that place, of a certain relationship with the other, the imaginary other, indicated by [$ ◊ a$].

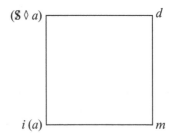

Here I've drawn a little square whose four corners are represented by the ego, the image of the other, the now constituted subject's relationship to the imaginary other, and desire. These are the four feet on which a human subject can normally stand, a human subject constituted as human – that is, who is neither more nor less aware of the functioning and strings of the mechanism controlling the marionette of the other in which he sees himself, that is, in which he is capable, or more or less capable, of orientating himself.

The hysterical subject is here, opposite the Other's desire, and, as I showed last time, without things actually going beyond, because, ultimately, one can say that, in the hysteric, the line of return from

398

[$ ◊ a] back to i(a) is weaker. This, moreover, is the reason that the hysteric has all kinds of difficulties with her imaginary, here represented by the other's image, and that she is susceptible to seeing effects of fragmentation and various forms of disintegration appear in it, which are what she makes use of in her symptoms.

So much for the hysteric. How do we now formulate what occurs in an obsessional structure?

Obsessional neurosis is much more complicated than hysterical neurosis, but not so much more. If one succeeds in pointing out the essential things, one can formulate it, but if one doesn't, which is certainly the case with the author that I was speaking about before, Bouvet, one literally ends up lost in it, one floats around between the sadistic, the anal, the part object, incorporation and distance from the object. One literally doesn't know where to turn. It's exceedingly diverse clinically, as the author shows in his cases – which it seems scarcely possible to bring under one single clinical rubric – that go by the names of Pierre and Paul, without mentioning the Moniques and the Jeannes. In the clinical material in the article, '*Le moi*', there are only Pierre and Paul. Now, obviously, Pierre and Paul are completely different subjects from the point of view of the object's features. One can hardly place them under the same heading – which isn't an objection in itself, since for the moment we are not in a position to articulate any other nosological categories ourselves.

It is very striking to see that, ever since we have been treating obsessional neurosis, we are incapable of dismembering it, as would obviously be required of us clinically given the diversity of aspects it presents us with. One recalls the fine words of Plato about the knife of the good cook, the one who knows how to cut at the joints. In the current state of things, no one, and particularly no one who has ever worked with obsessional neurosis, is capable of formulating it correctly. This is quite an indication of some theoretical deficiency.

Let's go back to where we were.

What does the obsessional do in order to consist as a subject? He is like the hysteric, rest assured. Immediately before any serious elaboration – namely, before Freud – a Mr Janet managed to carry out a very curious exercise of geometrical superimposition, a point-by-point correspondence of images, as they say in geometry, of transformation of figures, where the obsessional is thought of, as it were, as a transformed hysteric. The obsessional, too, is orientated towards desire. If it were not a question of desire above all else, there would be no homogeneity in the neuroses.

399

Except, there you have it. What, in his final formulation, does Freud tell us? What is his final word on obsessional neurosis, which classical theory echoes?

Freud said many things over the course of his career. He initially observed that what one may call the obsessional's primitive traumatism contrasts with the hysteric's primitive traumatism. In the hysteric, there is a sudden seduction, an intrusion or an irruption of the sexual into the subject's life. In the obsessional, inasmuch as the psychic traumatism supports the critique of reconstruction, the subject has, on the contrary, played an active role from which he has derived pleasure.

That was the first approximation. This was followed by all the developments in the *Rat Man*, namely the appearance of the extreme complexity of his affective relations, and notably the emphasis placed on affective ambivalence, the active–passive, masculine–feminine opposition and, most important thing of all, the love–hate antagonism. You must reread the *Rat Man* like the Bible, moreover. The case is rich with everything that still remains to be said on obsessional neurosis. It's a topic for study.

Where did Freud ultimately end up, in his final metapsychological formulation? Clinical experiences and metapsychological developments brought aggressive tendencies to light, which brought him to draw the distinction between life instincts and death instincts that has not stopped tormenting analysts since. According to Freud, in the obsessional there is a defusion of the early intrications of life instincts and death instincts. The detachment as such of destructive tendencies took place at too early a stage in him for it not to have marked all his subsequent development and installation in his particular subjectivity.

How is this to be inserted into the dialectic that I am presenting to you? Much more immediately, concretely and perceptibly. If these terms 'demand' and 'desire' begin to find their logic in your head, you will find a daily use for them, at least in your analytic practice. On a daily basis you will be able to use them before they wear out, but you will always come back to asking yourselves whether it's a question of desire and demand or desire or demand.

What does what I have just gone over for you concerning the instincts of destruction mean? The latter manifest themselves in clinical experience, which at first we have to take at the common and ordinary level of what we know about obsessionals – not even those that we analyse, but those whom, simply as informed psychologists, we see living and breathing and on whose behaviour we are capable of assessing the effect of neurosis. It is quite clear that the obsessional has a tendency to destroy his object. It's merely a matter of not being satisfied with what is almost a self-evident truth of experience and seeing what the obsessional's destructive activity is close up.

That is what I propose to do.

As clinical experience clearly demonstrates, the hysteric lives entirely at the level of the Other. She emphasizes being at the level of the Other, and that is the reason that the Other's desire must exist, for without it, what would the Other be, apart from the law? The centre of gravity of the hysteric's constitutive movement is initially located at the level of the Other. Likewise, for reasons that are not impossible to spell out, and which are, in sum, identical with what Freud says when speaking of the early defusion of instincts, it's the aim of desire as such, of this beyond-demand, that is constitutive of the obsessional. But with one obvious difference from the hysteric.

I would like you to have some experience with a child who is going to become an obsessional. I believe that there are no young subjects where it's more tangible that what I called desire is located in the margin of need. As I tried to spell out for you last time when I presented to you that the margin of need, whose range is necessarily a limited range – as when one speaks of a company of limited liability, for need is always something whose range is limited – the margin, then, exists between need and the unconditional character of the demand for love. How did I define this desire as such? As something that, precisely because it has to be situated beyond, negates the element of otherness that is included in the demand for love.

But, so as to preserve the unconditional character of this demand by transforming it into an absolute condition of desire, into desire in a pure state, the Other is negated. By virtue of the fact that the subject has had to know, and break through, the unconditioned in the demand for love, which has a limit-character, this character remains and finds itself transferred onto need.

The young child who becomes an obsessional is this young child of whom the parents say – everyday language and the language of psychologists converge – 'He does have his fixed ideas [idées fixes]'. The ideas he has are no more extraordinary than those of any other child, if we think about the things he demands. He will demand a little box. It's not such a big deal, a little box, and there are lots of children where one won't pause for a moment over this demand for a little box – except psychoanalysts, of course, who will find all sorts of fine allusions here. In fact, they wouldn't be wrong, but I find it more important to see that there are some children, amongst all children, who demand little boxes, and their parents find that this demand for a little box is strictly speaking intolerable – and it is intolerable.

One would be wrong to think that it would be enough to send the said parents to parenting school for remediation, because, contrary to what people say, the parents are implicated. It's not for nothing

401

that one is obsessional. One has to have a model for that some-where. So much is granted, but in the reception itself, the fixed-idea aspect that the parents point to is completely discernible, and is always immediately discerned, even by people who are not part of the parental couple.

In this very particular requirement that manifests itself in the way the child demands a little box, what is intolerable for the Other and which people loosely call a fixed idea, is that it isn't a demand just like any other, but that it presents with the characteristic of being an absolute condition, which is the very characteristic that I have been referring to as specific to desire. For reasons whose correspondence you can see with what might in this case be called strong drives, the emphasis for the subject is placed on what will be the element of the initial foundation of this tripod – which must subsequently have four legs if it's to stand up – namely, on desire. And not merely on desire, but on desire as such, that is, insofar as, in its constitution, it entails the Other's destruction. Desire is the absolute form of need, need that has passed to the state of an absolute condition, insofar as it lies beyond the unconditional demand for love, of which it can sometimes become the proof.

As such, desire negates the Other as such, and this is what renders it, like the desire for the little box in the young child, so intolerable.

Pay close attention here, because when I say that desire is the destruction of the Other I am not saying the same thing as when I say that the hysteric seeks her desire in the Other's desire. When I say that the hysteric seeks her desire in the Other's desire, it's the desire that she attributes to the Other as such. When I say that the obsessional puts his own desire before everything else, that means that he seeks it in a beyond by aiming for it as such in its constitution as desire, that is, insofar as it destroys the Other. That is the secret of the profound contradiction between the obsessional and his desire. Thus aimed for, desire carries within itself this internal contradiction, which constitutes the impasse of the obsessional's desire and which authors try to translate by speaking about this perpetual and instantaneous toing-and-froing between introjection and projection.

I must say that this is something extremely difficult to represent to oneself, above all when one has adequately indicated, as the quoted author does in certain places, the extent to which the mechanisms of introjection and projection bear no relationship to one another. I have spelt it out for you more powerfully than this author has, but it's where one has to start from, all the same – namely, that the mechanism of projection is imaginary, and that the mechanism of introjection is symbolic. They bear absolutely no relationship to one another.

402

On the other hand, you can see, and you will find this in your experience on condition that you are alert to it, how the obsessional is inhabited by desires which, provided you tackle them a little bit, you will see swarming with an extraordinary species of vermin. If you steer the culture of obsessional neurosis in the direction of fantasy – it doesn't take much, it's enough to have the elements of your transference that I was talking about before – you will see a proliferation of said vermin in just about anything you like. That's why the culture of obsessional neurosis doesn't last long.

But, in the end, to see what's essential, what happens when, from time to time, the obsessional, taking his courage in his two hands, endeavours to cross the barrier of demand, that is, sets out in search of the object of his desire? For a start, he doesn't find it easily, even though there are many things that he is already accustomed to and can use as a support, even if it's only a little box. It is clear that down this path the most extraordinary accidents will befall him – accidents that one will try to account for at different levels by bringing in the superego, and a thousand other functions which, of course, do exist. But, much more radically than all that, the obsessional, insofar as his fundamental movement is directed at desire as such, above all in its constitution as desire, is moved to aim for what I am calling the Other's destruction.

Now it's in the nature of desire as such to require the Other's support. The Other's desire isn't a means of access to the subject's desire, it's quite simply the place of desire, and all movement by the obsessional towards his desire runs into a barrier which is absolutely tangible in the movement of his libido, as it were. In an obsessional's psychology, the more something plays the role of the object, even momentarily, of desire, the more the subject's law of approach in relation to this object will literally manifest itself in a lowering of libidinal tension. And this, to the point where, when he possesses the object of his desire, nothing exists for him any longer. This is absolutely observable, and I will try to show it to you with some examples.

403

The problem for the obsessional is therefore entirely one of providing support for this desire – a desire which, for him, conditions the Other's destruction, where desire itself comes to disappear. There is no big Other here. I am not saying that the big Other doesn't exist for the obsessional, I am saying that there isn't one, where his desire is involved, and this is for the reason that he is seeking the only thing that, outside this point of reference, can maintain this desire as such in its place. The entire problem of the obsessional is to find the only thing that can give his desire a semblance of support, corresponding to this point that the hysteric, owing to her identifications, occupies so easily, namely what is opposite *d*, the formula $\mathbb{S}$ in relation to little *a*.

The hysteric finds support for her desire in her identification with the imaginary other. What takes its place and function in the obsessional is an object, one that is always – in a veiled form, no doubt, but recognizable – reducible to the phallus signifier.

I will end there today. In what follows, you will see the consequences for the behaviour of the obsessional vis-à-vis this object, and also vis-à-vis the little other. I will show you next time how a number of far more common truths can be deduced – for example, that the subject can only truly focus his desire by contrasting it with what I will call absolute virility, and also that insofar as he has to show his desire, since for him this is the essential requirement, he can only show it elsewhere, some place where he is required to surmount some exploit.

The performance aspect of all the obsessional's activity finds its reasons and motives here.

14 May 1958

THE OBSESSIONAL
AND HIS DESIRE

The duality of desire
The significance of fantasy
Sadistic scenarios
Permission, prohibition, exploit
The significance of acting out

Our exploration of neurotic structures as conditioned by what I call formations of the unconscious led us last time to the point of talking about the obsessional, and I ended by saying that he has to constitute himself in the face of his evanescent desire.

I started to show why his desire is evanescent on the basis of the formula 'Desire is the Other's desire'. The reason for that is to be found in a fundamental difficulty in his relationship with the Other, insofar as it's the locus where the signifier organizes desire.

It's this dimension that I am trying to articulate here, because I think that both the difficulties in theory and the deviations in practice were introduced by the failure to have identified it.

In passing, I want you to appreciate what Freud's discovery consists in and what the meaning of his work is, when it is considered once one has gone through it sufficiently and as a whole. The fact is that desire is organized by signifiers – but, of course, inside this phenomenon the subject tries to express, to manifest in an effect of signifiers as such, what is happening in his own approach to the signified.

Freud's work itself is inserted into this effort, up to a point. Many have spoken of naturalism with respect to him, of an effort to reduce human reality to nature. There is nothing of the sort. Freud's work is an attempt at a pact between the being of man and nature. This pact is without doubt sought elsewhere than in any innate relationship, since man is always experienced in Freud's work on the basis of the fact that he is constituted as a subject of speech, as the *I* of the speech act. How can one deny it, since in analysis he is experienced in no other way? He finds himself, then, opposite nature, in a position that is different from that of being an immanent vehicle of life. The subject's relationship to nature comes to be formulated internally to the experience he has of speech.

His relationship to life comes to be symbolized by the phallus signifier, this lure he extracts from forms of life, and it's here that the central point is located, the most tangible and most significant of all the signifier crossroads that we explore over the course of a subject's analysis. The phallus is its pinnacle, its point of equilibrium. It's the signifier par excellence of man's relationship to the signified and is in a privileged position as a consequence.

Man's insertion into sexual desire is destined to a special problematic, the primary feature of which is that it has to find a place in something that preceded it, which is the dialectic of demand, insofar as demand always demands something that is more than the satisfaction which it's appealing to, something that goes beyond. Hence the problematic and ambiguous character of the place in which desire is located. This place is always beyond demand inasmuch as demand aims for the satisfaction of need, and it lies on this side of demand inasmuch as the latter, by virtue of being articulated in symbolic terms, goes beyond all the satisfactions to which it appeals, inasmuch as it's a demand for love, which targets the being of the Other and aims to obtain from the Other this essential presentification, inasmuch as the Other gives his very being, which lies beyond all possible satisfaction and is precisely what is aimed at in love.

It's in the virtual space between the appeal for satisfaction and the demand for love that desire has to assume its place and be organized. This is why we can only locate it in a place that is always double with respect to demand, both beyond and short of, according to the aspect under which we are considering demand – demand in relation to a need, or demand structured in terms of signifiers.

As such, desire always goes beyond every possible kind of response at the level of satisfaction, in itself calls for an absolute response and henceforth projects its essential characteristic of being an absolute condition onto everything that is organized in the interval internal to the two planes of demand – the signified plane and the signifier plane. It's in this interval that desire has to find its place and be articulated.

For precisely this reason, the Other becomes the relay for the subject's access to his desire. The Other as locus of speech, insofar as demand is addressed to it, will also be the locus in which desire, or the possible formulation of desire, has to be discovered. This is where a contradiction is constantly operating, for this Other is possessed by a desire – a desire which, inaugurally and fundamentally, is alien to the subject. Hence, the difficulties in formulating desire, difficulties at which the subject will stumble, made all the more significant by the fact that we see him developing the neurotic structures that the analytic discovery has made it possible to describe.

These structures differ according as the emphasis is placed on the unsatisfaction of desire – and this is the mode in which the hysteric accesses its field and its necessity – or on the dependence on the Other for access to this desire, which is the mode in which this access is made available to the obsessional. By virtue of this fact, as I said at the end of the last session, something happens for the obsessional here in [$ \lozenge $ a], which is different from hysterical identification.

1

For the hysteric, desire is a point of enigma, and we always bring to it, as it were, this sort of forced interpretation that characterizes all Freud's early explorations of hysteria.

Effectively, Freud didn't see that for the hysteric desire is located in a position such that telling her 'This or that person is whom you desire' is always a forced, inexact interpretation, wide of the mark. Either in Freud's initial observations, or later in the case of Dora, or even, if we extend the meaning of the word 'hysteria' to the case of the young homosexual woman that I discussed at length here last year, there is no example where Freud didn't make this mistake, and which didn't, at least, result, with no exception, in the patient's refusal to agree to the meaning of the desire of her symptoms and acts, whenever he went about it this way. Effectively, an hysteric's desire is not a desire for an object, but a desire for a desire, an effort to maintain herself opposite this point at which she calls for her desire, this point where the Other's desire is situated.

She identifies with an object, on the contrary. Dora identifies with Herr K., Elizabeth von R. identifies with different characters in her family or in her entourage. To describe the point where she identifies with someone, the terms 'ego' and 'ego-ideal' are equally inappropriate – in fact, for her, this someone becomes her other ego. It's a matter of an object the choice of which was always explicitly articulated by Freud in a manner consistent with what I am now telling you, namely that it's insofar as she or he recognizes in another man or in another woman the signs of her or his desire, namely, that she or he is faced with the same problem of desire as the other is, that identification arises – with all the forms of contagion, crisis, epidemic and symptomatic manifestations that are so typical of hysteria.

The obsessional has different relations, for the reason that the problem of the Other's desire presents itself to him in a completely different way. To spell this out, I am going to try to get to it through the stages that our experience offers us.

In a certain manner, it doesn't much matter from what direction we approach the obsessional's lived experience. We mustn't lose sight of its diversity. The paths traced out by analysis, those by which our experience – where, it has to be said, we're groping around – have encouraged us to find the solution to the problem of the obsessional, are incomplete or biased. Of course, they give us material. We can explain this material and the manner in which it's used in different ways in relation to the results obtained.

First, we can criticize the approaches themselves. The critiques have to converge. In spelling this experience out in the way in which it has been effectively oriented, it incontestably emerges that both theory and practice have tended to be centred on the subject's use of his fantasies. Now, the role of fantasies in the case of obsessional neurosis has something puzzling about it inasmuch as the term 'fantasy' is never defined. We have spoken at length here about imaginary relationships, about the image's function as a guide for the instinct, so to speak, as channelling or indicating the path to the instinct's realizations. We also know to what extent the use – insofar as one can discern it with certainty – of the image's function is diminished in man, since it seems to be reduced to the specular, narcissistic image. It is, however, an extremely polyvalent and not neutralized function, since it functions on the level of relations that are both aggressive and erotic.

How can we articulate the essential, prevailing imaginary functions, the ones everybody speaks of, that are at the heart of analytic experience, those of fantasy, at the point we have come to?

I believe that at this place [$ \lozenge a$], the schema presented to us here opens up the possibility of locating and articulating the function of fantasies. I ask you to represent it to yourselves first of all through an intuitive aspect, taking into account the fact that this isn't a real space, of course, but a topology in which homologies can be sketched out.

The relationship to the image of the other, $i(a)$, is located at 409 the level of an experience integrated into the original circuit of demand where the subject initially addresses himself to the Other for the satisfaction of his needs. It's therefore somewhere along this circuit that transitivism and the effect of one's 'presence' are accommodated, placing the subject in a certain relationship to his semblable as such. The relationship to the image is thus found at the level of experiences from the time at which the child enters into the game of speech, at the limit of the passage from the infant state to the speaking state. Having said this, I would say that, in the other field, the one in which we look for the pathways to the realization of the subject's desire through access to the Other's desire, the function of fantasy is located at a homologous point – that is, at [$ ◊ a].

I will define fantasy, if you are happy with this, as the imaginary captured in a particular use of signifiers. Moreover, it manifests itself and is observable in characteristic ways, even if it's only when we speak of sadistic fantasies, for example, which play such an important role in the economy of an obsessional.

Do take good note that if I am describing it in these terms, if I qualify as sadistic the tendency that these manifestations represent for us, it's in connection with a particular work. This work itself is not presented as an investigation into instincts, but as a game which the term 'imaginary' would be very far from being adequate to characterize, since it's a literary work. I am referring to scenes, or to scenarios in fact – which are, therefore, profoundly expressed in signifiers. Well then, whenever we speak of fantasies, we must not misrecognize the scenario or story aspect, which constitutes one of their essential dimensions. They are not blind images of the instinct of destruction, they are not something in which the subject – I myself struggle to create an image of this that will explain to you what I mean – sees red all of a sudden when confronted with his prey, but a fantasy is not only something that the subject articulates into a scenario, but also something which the subject puts himself into. The formula, S with the little bar – that is, the subject at the most articulated point of his presentification in relation to the little *a* – is quite valid there for every kind of properly fantasmatic elaboration of what I call the sadistic tendency, inasmuch as it can be implicated in the economy of an obsessional.

You will notice that there is always a scene in which the subject is present in the scenario in different masked forms, in which he is implicated in a variety of images, in which another as semblable and also as the subject's reflection is presented. I would go even further – no one places sufficient emphasis on the presence of a certain type of instrument.

I have already alluded to the importance of whipping fantasies. Freud singled them out as seeming to play a very special role in the female psyche. This is one aspect of the precise contribution he made on this topic. He came at it from an angle that came out of his experience, but this fantasy is far from being limited to the field

410

and cases that Freud spoke of on that occasion. If you look closely, it was quite legitimate to limit it in that way, inasmuch as this fantasy plays a particular role at a turning point in the development of female sexuality and at one particular place – quite precisely, insofar as the function of the phallus signifier comes into play. But this function plays no lesser role in obsessional neurosis and in every other case where we see so-called sadistic fantasies appear.

What is the element that gives this instrument its enigmatic prevalence? No one can say that its biological function would be explained in any way. You might imagine it could by looking for it along the lines of some sort of relationship with superficial excitations, stimulations of the skin, but you sense to what extent these explanations would have an incomplete and almost artificial character. What becomes attached to the function of this element, which appears so often in fantasies, is a signifying multivalence that does rather tilt the balance towards the signified than towards anything of any kind that could be deduced from the order of biological needs, or from anything else.

This notion of fantasy as something that undoubtedly partakes of the imaginary order, but which, at whatever point of its articulation, only ever functions in the economy through its signifying function, seems essential to me, and it has not been formulated as such till now. I would go further – I do not believe that there is any other way of conceptualizing what are called unconscious fantasies.

What is an unconscious fantasy, if not the latency of something which, as we know through everything that we have learnt about the organization of the structure of the unconscious, is completely thinkable in terms of a signifying chain? The fact that in the unconscious there are signifying chains, subsisting as such, which, from there, structure and act on the organism and influence what appears externally as a symptom, is the heart of the analytic experience. It's much more difficult to conceptualize the unconscious impact of whatever is imaginary than it is to put fantasies themselves at the level of a common measure that presents itself to us at the level of the unconscious – that is, signifiers. Fantasy is essentially an imaginary embedded in a particular signifying function.

I am not able to develop this approach any further for the moment, and I intend simply to situate the fantasmatic effect at this point – barred S in relation to small *a*. It's characterized by being an articulated and always complex relation, a scenario, one able to remain latent for a long time at a certain point in the unconscious, even as it is organized nevertheless – just as a dream, for example, can only be conceptualized if the signifier function gives it its structure, consistency and, thereby, its insistence.

411

A common fact of experience, and one of the very first facts, concerning the analytic investigation of obsessionals is to observe the place that sadistic fantasies occupy for the obsessional. They occupy this place but do not necessarily occupy it in an overt and declared manner. On the other hand, in the obsessional metabolism, the various efforts the subject makes towards a re-equilibration make evident what the object of his equilibrating search is, namely, to successfully recognize himself in relation to his desire.

When we see a pure obsessional, in a state of nature, as happens to us or is said to happen to us in our published observations, we find someone who speaks to us above all about all sorts of impediments, inhibitions, barriers, fears, doubts and prohibitions. We also already know that at that point he won't speak to us about his fantasmatic life, but will take advantage of our therapeutic interventions or of his own autonomous attempts at a solution, at finding an outcome or elaborating his properly obsessional difficulty. He will reveal to us the more or less predominant invasiveness of his psychic life by fantasies. You know how much these fantasies are capable of assuming a truly invasive, absorbing and captivating form in certain subjects, capable of swallowing up whole areas of their psychic life, lived experience and mental occupations.

We describe these fantasies as sadistic – this is, as it happens, merely a label. In fact, they confront us with an enigma, insofar as we are unable to be satisfied with describing them as the manifestations of a tendency but must see in them an organization that itself signifies the subject's relations with the Other as such. Indeed, the question is about finding a formula for the economic role of these fantasies insofar as they are articulated.

It's characteristic of these fantasies in the obsessional subject to remain in the state of fantasies. They are only actualized in quite exceptional circumstances, and these actualizations are, moreover, always disappointing for the subject. In effect, we observe here the mechanics of the obsessional's relationship to desire – the more he strives to approach the object, by the means that have been proposed to him, the more his desire dies away to the point of extinction or disappearance. I would say the obsessional is a Tantalus, had Tantalus not been presented to us through what is quite a rich iconography as an image that is above all oral. But it is, however, not for nothing that I present it thus, because we shall see the oral underpinning of what constitutes the point of equilibrium of obsessional fantasies as such.

Still, this oral dimension must exist, since, in the end, this is the plane of fantasy attained by the analyst I alluded to in connection with the therapeutic line traced out in the series of three articles I have been referring to. Many analysts engaged in a practice of fantasmatic absorption in order to find a way for the obsessional to be given a new mode of equilibration, a certain temperament for him to realize his desire.

Some of the results there are undeniable, even if they remain subject to criticism.

2

You can already see that by approaching things from this angle we are only seeing one side of the problem. From the other side, one has to gradually deploy the whole range without misrecognizing what is present in the most apparent manner in the obsessional's symptoms, which are normally called the demands of the superego.

How should we think about these demands? What are their roots in the obsessional? That's what we will look at now.

We can identify, and we can read, what is going on in the obsessional at the level of this schema in a way that will subsequently prove to be no less fertile than what we have demonstrated so far.

One could say that the obsessional is always in the process of asking permission. You can see this concretely in what the obsessional tells you in his symptoms, where this is inscribed and frequently articulated. If we have confidence in the schema, this occurs at the level of [$ ◊ D]. To ask permission is, as a subject, to have a certain relationship to one's own demand. To ask permission, to the very extent that the dialectic with the Other – the Other as one who speaks – is called into question, challenged and even put in danger, is ultimately to apply oneself to restoring this Other and to place oneself in the most extreme dependence on him. This already shows us the extent to which it's essential for the obsessional to maintain this place. It's where we see the relevance of what Freud always calls '*Versagung*', refusal. Refusal and permission mutually imply one another. A pact is refused against the background of a promise. This is more valuable than talking about frustration.

It's not at the level of demand pure and simple that the problem of relations with the Other arises, at least not when it involves a complete subject. The problem only arises in these terms when we try to take recourse in development and imagine a small child, powerless with its mother, like an object at the mercy of someone. But as soon as the subject is in a relationship with the Other whom we have defined in terms of speech, there is a virtual point somewhere beyond any response from the Other, and very precisely insofar as

413

speech creates this point beyond his response. Not only is it virtual, but, in truth, if there were no analysis, we would not be sure that anyone attains this point – save through this spontaneous master analysis that we always assume is possible in someone who perfectly fulfils this 'know thyself'. But we have all kinds of reasons for thinking that till now this point has never been designated in any strict manner except in analysis.

What the notion of *Versagung* designates, properly speaking, is a situation in which the subject has a relation to demand. I ask you to take the same little step forward as the one I asked you to take concerning fantasy. When we talk about stages or fundamental relations with the object, and we describe them as oral, anal or even genital, what are we talking about? About a certain kind of relation that structures the subject's *Umwelt* around a central function and defines his relationship with the world over the course of his development. Everything that comes from his environment would thus have a special signification due to the refraction that is undergone through the typical oral, anal or genital object. There is a mirage here – the notion of it is only ever reconstructed after the fact and projected back into development.

The conception I am criticizing is not even usually articulated in such an elaborate manner and it very frequently turns out to be avoided. One speaks of the object, then, as a side issue. One speaks of the environment, without thinking for a single instant about what the difference is between the typical object of a relation that is defined by a stage – as a reject, for instance – and the actual environment with multiple instances of a plurality of objects to which the subject, whatever he is, is subjected, whatever one says, from earliest infancy.

Until further notice, we must similarly have the greatest doubts about the supposed absence of objects for the child at the breast, his supposed autism. If you want to take my word for it, you will consider this notion to be purely illusory. It's enough to resort to the direct observation of very young children to learn that this isn't so, that for them the objects of the world are as multiple as they are interesting and stimulating.

414

So, what's this about? What have we discovered? We can define it and articulate it as being effectively a certain style of demand in the subject. Where did we discover these manifestations that have us talking about successively oral, anal and indeed genital relationships with the world? We discovered them in the analyses of people who left the stages in question behind ages ago, the stages concerning the child's development. We say that the subject regresses to these stages – what do we mean by that?

Responding by saying that there is a return to one of the imaginary stages of infancy – if these are at all conceivable, but let's allow that they are – is a lure which doesn't yield the true nature of the phenomenon. Is there anything that looks like such a return? When we speak of fixation at a certain stage in the neurotic subject, what could we try to formulate that would be more satisfactory than what we are usually given?

What we effectively see in analysis is that over the course of regression – we shall see more clearly what this term means in what follows – the subject articulates his current demand in analysis in terms that enable us to recognize a particular relationship, respectively oral, anal or genital, with a particular object. This means that if these relationships of the subject have been able to exercise a decisive influence over the entire length of his development, it's insofar as, at a certain stage, they have shifted to the function of signifiers.

While, at the level of the unconscious, the subject articulates his demand in oral terms and articulates his desire in terms of absorption, he finds himself in a particular relationship [$ \lozenge $ D], that is, at the level of a virtual signifying articulation which is that of the unconscious. This is what makes it possible for us to describe as a fixation at a certain stage something that will present with a particular value at some moment in the analytic exploration, and we might think there is some interest in having the subject regress to this stage so that something essential about the mode in which his subjective organization presents itself can be clarified.

But what interests us is to give neither gravitation nor compensation nor even symbolic return to what at a given moment of development has been, more or less with reason, the subject's unsatisfaction on the plane of an oral, anal or other demand – unsatisfaction at which, supposedly, he is arrested. If we are interested in this, it's solely because this is the moment of his demand where the problems in his relationships with the Other arise, insofar as they have been determinant for setting his desire in place.

415

In other words, everything that comes under demand in the subject's experience is over, once and for all. The satisfactions and compensations we might give him will never be anything but symbolic, and giving them to him can even be considered a mistake, even if it were possible to do so.

It's not completely impossible, precisely, owing to the intervention of fantasies, of this more or less substantial something supported by fantasy. But I believe that this is a mistake in the orientation of analysis, for at the end of an analysis it leaves the question of relations with the Other not settled.

3

I would say that the obsessional, like the hysteric, needs an unsatisfied desire, that is, a desire beyond demand. The obsessional resolves the question of the evanescence of his desire by turning it into a forbidden desire. He has it supported by the Other through the Other's prohibition.

Nevertheless, this manner of getting the Other to support his desire is ambiguous, because a forbidden desire does not, however, mean a strangulated desire. Prohibition is there to sustain desire, but it has to be present for it to be sustained. This, then, is what the obsessional does, and the question is how.

The way in which he does this is, as you know, very complex. He displays it and doesn't display it at one and the same time. In short, he disguises it, and it's easy to understand why. His intentions are, as it were, not pure.

As has already been noted, this is what has been referred to as the aggressiveness of the obsessional. Every time his desire emerges is said to be, for him, an occasion where this projection, this fear of reprisal, will inhibit all of its manifestations. I think this is a first approach to the question, but I don't think it's everything. It is to misrecognize quite fundamentally what is at issue simply to say that the obsessional is switching back and forth and that when his desire appears it becomes aggressive by going too far, redescends or swings back into the disappearance of this aggressiveness, linked to the fear of effective retaliation on the part of the other, namely, the fear of himself undergoing destruction equivalent to that of the desire he displays.

I think there is room to take a global apprehension of what's at stake in the case at hand, and there is perhaps no better way of doing this than to pass through the illusions that the relationship with the other gives rise to in us, we other analysts, and inside analytic theory.

The notion of the relationship with the other is invariably influenced by a slippage that tends to reduce desire to demand. If desire is effectively what I have said it is here, that is, what is produced in the gap that speech opens up in demand, and if it's therefore, as such, beyond all concrete demand, it's clear that every attempt to reduce desire to something from which one demands satisfaction encounters an internal contradiction. Almost all analysts in their community presently take the summit and acme of the subject's happy attainment of what they call genital maturity to be access to 'oblativity' – namely, access to recognition of the other's desire as such. I gave an example of this, in a passage by the author I have

416

been examining, with the profound satisfaction brought by the satisfaction given to the other's demand, which is commonly known as altruism. It's precisely missing what is effectively to be resolved in the problem of desire.

When all is said and done, I think the term 'oblativity', as it's presented to us from this moralizing perspective, is, and one can say this without any distortion of terms, an obsessional fantasy. It's quite certain that in analysis, as things present themselves – for reasons that are very easy to understand, I am talking of temperaments that our practice theorizes – hysterical temperaments are much rarer than obsessional natures. One part of the indoctrination of analysis is constructed along the lines and according to the pathways of obsessional wishes. Now, the illusion, the very fantasy that is within reach of the obsessional is ultimately that the Other as such gives his consent to his desire.

In itself this carries extreme difficulties, since if it's necessary that he give his consent, it's necessary that it be given in a way that is completely different from a response to just any satisfaction, different from a response to a demand. But, all things considered, that is preferable to eluding the problem and giving him a short-circuited solution by thinking that ultimately it's sufficient to come to an agreement – that to find happiness in life it's enough not to inflict on others the frustrations that one has been the object of oneself.

417   Some of the unfortunate and utterly confusing outcomes of analysis find their origins in a number of presuppositions concerning what constitutes a good termination of analytic treatment, presuppositions whose effect is to exalt the obsessional subject via the perspective of his good intentions, which then become rapidly established and incite him to give himself over to one of the most common of these tendencies, which is expressed more or less as follows – 'Do not do to others what you would not like to be done to yourself.' This categorical imperative, structuring in morals, does not always lend itself to practical employment in existence, and it's completely beside the mark when it's a question of performing something like sexual intercourse.

The order of the relationship with the Other that consists in putting oneself in his place is a tempting slippage, and all the more so if the analyst, being precisely in an aggressive relationship vis-à-vis the little other, his semblable, is quite naturally tempted to occupy the position of sparing him, as it were. Sparing the other is what lies at the heart of an entire series of ceremonials, precautions and detours – in short, all the tricks of the obsessional. If the aim is to generalize what was manifesting itself in his symptoms – not without reason no doubt, and in a much more complicated manner – if the aim is to turn it into a moralizing extrapolation and propose to him what one calls the oblative outcome, that is, submission to the Other's demands, as the aim and outcome of his problems: well then, this detour is really not worth the effort. As experience shows, this is only substituting one symptom for another, and a very serious symptom, because it doesn't fail to engender the re-emergence – in other more or less problematic forms – of the question of desire, which has never been and can in no way be resolved by going down this path.

From this perspective, it can be said that the paths the obsessional finds for himself, and down which he seeks the solution to the problem of his desire, are otherwise adequate – even if they are not adapted – because at least the problem can be clearly read in them. Amongst the modes of solution, there are some for example that are located at the level of an effective relationship with the other. The manner in which the obsessional conducts himself with his semblable when he is still capable of doing so and not submerged by his symptoms – and it's rare that he is entirely – is in itself sufficiently indicative. This no doubt leads down a dead-end path but still gives what is not such a bad indication for the direction.

For example, I have spoken to you about the exploits of obsessionals. What are these exploits? For there to be an exploit, there have to be at least three people, because one does not carry out one's exploits all alone. There have to be at least two of you, there must be something like that for there to be a winning performance, a sprint. Then, there also has to be someone who records and is the witness. What the obsessional is striving to obtain in an exploit is very precisely what earlier I called the Other's permission, in the name of something that is very polyvalent. One can say – he earned what he strived to achieve. But the satisfaction he strives to obtain is not at all to be classified on the terrain on which he earned it.

Observe the structure of our obsessionals. What does what one calls 'an effect of the superego' mean? It means that they inflict upon themselves all kinds of particularly hard, punishing tasks, that they succeed at them, moreover, and that they succeed at them all the more easily because it's what they want to do – but there, they succeed very, very brilliantly, in the name of which they would have the right to a little holiday where you could do whatever you wanted, hence the well-known dialectic of work and holidays. For the obsessional, work is powerful, being done so as to free up the time for sailing, which will be holiday time – and the holidays habitually turn out to be more or less wasted. Why? Because what it was about was obtaining the Other's permission. Now, the other – I'm speaking now of the actual other, the other that exists – has

418

absolutely nothing to do with all this dialectic, for the simple reason that the real other is far too preoccupied with his own Other and has no reason to fulfil this mission of giving the obsessional's exploit its little crown – namely, what would be precisely the realization of his desire, insofar as this desire has nothing to do with the terrain on which the subject has demonstrated all his abilities.

This is all a very tangible phase, one whose humorous aspect is well worth making the effort to display. But it's not limited to that. The interest of concepts such as the big Other and the little other is to structure the lived relationships in many more than one direction. One may also say, from a certain angle, that in his exploit the subject dominates, tames and even domesticates a fundamental anxiety – this has been said by other people than me. But there again, one misrecognizes a dimension of the phenomenon, namely, that what's essential is not in the skill or in the risk taken, which for the obsessional is always a risk taken within very strict limits – a skilful economy strictly differentiates everything that the obsessional risks in his exploit from anything that resembles the risk of death in the Hegelian dialectic.

419   In the obsessional's exploit there is something that always remains irremediably fictitious, for the reason that death, I mean there where the real danger is, does not reside in the adversary he appears to be defying, but completely elsewhere. It's precisely on the side of this invisible witness, this Other who is there as the spectator, the onlooker, and who is going to say about the subject, 'Decidedly,' as it's expressed somewhere in Schreber's delusion, 'he's a horny bastard!' We re-encounter this exclamation, this way of feeling the effects, as implicit, latent and wished for throughout the dialectic of exploits. Here the obsessional is in a particular relationship to the other's existence as his semblable, as the one in whose place he can put himself, but it's precisely because he can put himself in his place that in reality there is no kind of essential risk in what he demonstrates in his effects of presence, sports and the risks more or less taken. Ultimately, this other with whom he is playing is only ever an other who is he himself and who, already, will in any case leave him with the laurels, from whichever side he approaches things.

But the important one is the Other before whom all of this takes place. He's the one that has to be preserved at any cost, the locus in which the exploits are registered and his history inscribed. This place has to be maintained at any cost. This is what makes the obsessional cling to everything that belongs to the verbal order, the order of the computus, recapitulation, inscription and falsification, too. What the obsessional wants to maintain above all without giving the appearance of doing so, giving the appearance of aiming at something else, is this Other where things are articulated in terms of signifiers.

That, then, is an initial approach to the question. Beyond all demands, beyond everything that this subject desires, there is the question of seeing what on the whole the obsessional's conduct aims at. It's quite certain that the essential aim is to maintain the Other. This is the primary, preliminary aim, solely inside of which the so difficult validation of his desire can be accomplished. What can, what will this validation be? This is what we will have to spell out subsequently. But first we needed to fix the four points of his conduct so that the trees didn't hide the forest from us.

The satisfaction of surprising one or other of the little mechanisms of his conduct, with its own style, must not fascinate and stop us. Obviously, stopping at any particular detail of an organism always produces satisfaction that is not entirely illegitimate, since, at least in the domain of natural phenomena, the detail always effectively reflects something of the totality. But in a matter which is about an organization that is as little natural as that of a subject's relations to signifiers, we can't totally trust the reconstruction of the entire obsessional organization on the basis of one mechanism of defence or another – if it's at all possible to enter all of that in the catalogue of mechanisms of defence.

420

I'm trying to do something different. I'm trying to get you to find the four cardinal points around which each of the subject's defences is orientated and polarized. Here we already have two today. We first addressed the role of fantasy. We can now see, with respect to the exploit, that the Other's presence as such is fundamental. There is a further point, which I would at least like to introduce you to.

Hearing me speak about exploits, you have no doubt been thinking about all sorts of behaviour by your obsessionals. There is one exploit that perhaps does not completely deserve to be pinned down by this same name. It's what in analysis is called 'acting out'.

On this, I undertook – I hope you will undertake it too, at my example, even if it would only be to confirm what I am advancing – some investigations in the literature. It's surprising to see how difficult it is to extract oneself from it. The best article on the subject is the one by Phyllis Greenacre, called 'General Problems of Acting Out', published in the *Psychoanalytic Quarterly* in 1950 – a completely remarkable article in that it shows that till now nothing valuable has been formulated on this.

I believe that we have to limit the problem of acting out, and that it's impossible to do this if one holds on to the general notion that it's a symptom, a compromise, that it has a double meaning or that it's an active repetition, for this is to drown it in compulsions to repeat in their most general forms. If the term has any meaning, it's insofar as it designates a kind of act that arises out of an attempt at a solution to the problem of demand and desire. That's why it's produced in a specific manner in the course of an analysis, because, whatever one effectively does with it outside analysis, it's an attempt to solve the problem of the relationship between desire and demand.

Acting out is certainly produced on the way to the analytic realization of unconscious desire. It's extremely instructive, because if we look carefully for what characterizes the effect of acting out, we will find there are all kinds of absolutely necessary components, and for example what absolutely distinguishes them from what is called a bungled action, or what I more correctly call a successful action – I mean a symptom, inasmuch as it clearly reveals a tendency. Acting out always comprises an element that is highly significant, and precisely because it's enigmatic. We will only ever call acting out an act that presents with a particularly unmotivated character. That doesn't mean that it doesn't have a cause, but that psychologically it lacks motivation, for it's an act that is always signified.

Moreover, an object always plays a role in acting out – an object in the material sense of the word, which I will be led to come back to next time to show you, actually, the limited function that the role of the object should be granted in this entire dialectic. There is almost an equivalence between fantasy and acting out. Acting out is in general structured in a way that comes very close to that of a scenario. In its own way, it's at the same level as fantasy.

One thing distinguishes it from fantasy and also from an exploit. Whereas an exploit is an exercise, a tour de force or a sleight of hand designed to give pleasure to the Other, who, as I've said, couldn't give a damn about it, acting out is different. It's always a message, and it's for that reason that we are interested in it when it occurs in an analysis. It's always addressed to the analyst in that the latter is not, in brief, all that badly placed, but not completely in his place either. It's in general a hint that the subject is giving us and this can sometimes go a long way and sometimes be very serious. If the acting out occurs outside the confines of the treatment, I mean afterwards, it's obvious that the analyst can hardly benefit from it.

Whenever we are led to designate, in a precise way, this paradoxical act that we try to circumscribe under the name 'acting out', we see that it's a question of bringing out into the open, along this line, the subject's relations with demand, which reveals that every relationship to this demand is fundamentally incapable of making it possible for the subject to gain access to the effective reality of the effect signifiers have upon him, that is, for him to place himself at the level of the castration complex.

421

It's possible to miss this – I will try to show it to you next time – inasmuch as, in this interval, this intermediary space in which one sees all these opaque acts that go from exploit to fantasy, and from fantasy to a passionate and indeed partial love – Abraham never spoke of part object, he spoke of partial love of the object – the subject has obtained illusory solutions concerning the object and, in particular, this solution that appears in the form of what one calls the homosexual transference in obsessional neurosis.

That's what I call the illusory solution. I hope next time to show you in detail why it's an illusory solution.

21 May 1958

XXIV

TRANSFERENCE AND SUGGESTION

Three forms of identifications
On two lines
Regression and resistance
Significance of an action
Technique – theirs and ours

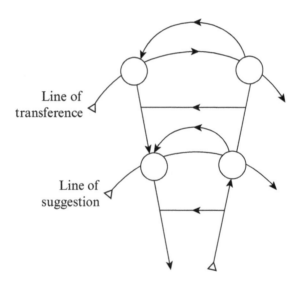

Line of
transference

Line of
suggestion

In the few remaining seminars we have left this year, we are going to move into the field that Freud opened up after the Second World War, during the 1920s – the field described as the second topography. Effectively, only the path we have taken this year, giving formations of the unconscious their full scope, makes it possible for us not to lose our way concerning the meaning of this topography.

We will, then, be led to indicate what this model means and, in particular, why the function of the ego in it has moved into the foreground. It has quite another meaning, so much more complex, than the one that it's customary to give it and which inspires the use that has been made of it since. That's the direction.

I will start by pointing out that Freud devotes a chapter to identification in *Group Psychology and the Analysis of the Ego*. You have to read this chapter to see the relevance of transferring the three types of identification distinguished by Freud onto this schema here. For us, at the point at which we find ourselves, this schema has to have the value of a mediation – it gives you a formulation or even an interpretation of what, on the one hand, the structure of the unconscious is insofar as it's fundamentally structured as speech and, on the other, the structure of the topography that emerges from it.

The various organs, as it were, of the Freudian model originate in a schema also – this famous schema in the shape of an egg, where you imagine you can intuit the relations between the id, the ego and the superego. In it you see an eye and a sort of pipette entering into the substance that is supposed to represent the superego. It's a very useful schema, and has precisely the inconvenience of representing topological things through spatial schemes. There is, however, a necessity here that I myself do not escape, since I too represent the schema by a spatial schema, but I have tried to do it with the least inconvenience possible. Thus, imagine that you take my little network, crumple it up, make it into a little ball and put it in your pocket. Well then, in principle, the relations still remain the same, inasmuch as they are relations of order.

It's obviously more difficult to do this with the schema of the egg, since it's entirely oriented towards spatial projection. Consequently, you imagine that Freud wants the id to designate an organ that exists somewhere and on which there is a protuberance representing the ego, which appears here like an eye. But read the text – no allusion is made to anything that might have this substantial character or that might authorize representing these instances as differentiated organs. The Freudian differentiations are of a different kind and are placed in a completely different order from the development of bodily organs precisely in that they are supported by identifications.

It's important to bear this in mind, even if only because it can be far-reaching. There are people who imagine that when they carry out a lobotomy they are taking out a slice of the superego. Not only do they believe it, but they write as much and they do it with this in mind.

1

Freud distinguishes three types of identification. This tripartition is spelt out clearly, and one finds it summarized in a single paragraph in the text.

The first type of identification is '*die ursprünglichste Form der Gefühlsbindung an ein Objekt*', 'the original form of emotional tie with an object' [*SE* 18: 107–8].

The second form is one that Freud particularly dwelt on at length in this chapter, which is the concrete basis of all his reflection on identification and is fundamentally linked to everything on the topic – '*sie auf regressivem Wege zum Ersatz für eine libidinöse Objektbindung wird, gleichsam durch Introjektion des Objekts ins Ich.*' The second form of identification occurs 'in a regressive way [and] it becomes a substitute for a libidinal object-tie, as it were by means of introjection of the object into the ego' [*SE* 18: 107–8]. This second form of identification is the one that throughout Freud's discourse in *Group Psychology*, but also in *The Ego and the Id*, presents him with the most problems, by virtue of its ambiguous relation to the object. It's here also that all the problems of analysis gather, in particular that of the inverted Oedipus complex. Why, at a particular moment, in certain cases, and in the form of the inverted Oedipus complex, does the object, which is an object of libidinal attachment, become an object of identification?

Sometimes it's more important to keep open the problem raised than to solve it. There is absolutely no obligation for us to represent to ourselves a possible solution to the question raised. This question is perhaps the central question, the question that we will always be condemned to fall short of, the one that forms the pivotal point. There must be such a point somewhere, because, wherever we place ourselves and consider every question solved, there will always remain the question why we are there – how did we get to the point where everything is clear?

Still, in the present case, it's clear that there must be a point that keeps us, precisely, immersed in the question. I'm not saying that this is the point in question, but Freud, in any case, circles around it and in no way claims to have solved it. What is important, on the other hand, is to see how the coordinates of this zero point vary.

I repeat, the essential question is that of the passage, attested in experience, of the love for an object to the ensuing identification.

The distinction Freud introduces here between libidinal erotic attachment to the loved object and the identification with the same is no different from the one I alluded to at the end of one of our recent seminars concerning the relation to the phallus, namely, the opposition between being and having. But added to this is what Freud says his experience gives him – this identification is always regressive in nature. The coordinates of the transformation of a libidinal attachment into an identification indicate that there is regression.

I think you know enough about this for there to be no need for me to dot the i's. At least I've already spelt out in previous sessions what regression confirms. There is still the question of how to articulate it. I articulate it by suggesting that it's the choice of signifiers that gives an indication of regression. Regression to the anal stage, with all its nuances and varieties, even to the oral stage, is always the presence of regressive signifiers in the subject's discourse.

There is no other regression in analysis. That the subject starts to whimper like a baby on your couch or even act like one – it sometimes happens, but in this sort of play-acting we are not accustomed to seeing the true regression that is observed in analysis. When that does happen, it generally doesn't augur very well.

From where we are now, we are going to try to see what these two forms of identification mean on our schema. Let's place ourselves here, at the level of the subject's need – the term is used in Freud.

I would point out to you in passing that Freud, and precisely in connection with the advent of identification in relation to investment in the object, tells us that it has to be admitted that investment in the object stems from the id which perceives the promptings, pressures and erotic tensions as needs, which clearly shows that the id puts itself forward as being quite ambiguous.

I also point out to you in passing that the French translation of these chapters renders them unintelligible and sometimes makes them say exactly the opposite of Freud's text. The term '*Objektbindung*', 'object-tie', investment in the object, is translated as concentration on the object, which is incredibly obscure.

However that may be from the perspective of need, these lines give us the two horizons of demand. Here we find demand as articulated demand, insofar as the demand for the satisfaction of a need must pass via the defiles of the articulation that language renders obligatory. Moreover, by virtue of the sole fact that it passes over to the level of the signifier, as it were, in its existence and no longer in its articulation, there is an unconditional demand for love, and, as a result, at the level of the one to whom demand is addressed, that is, the Other, it is itself symbolized – which means that it appears present against the background of absence and can be made present as absence. Note that even before an object is loved in the erotic sense of the term – in the sense in which the eros of the loved object can be perceived as a need – the position of demand, as such, creates the horizon of the demand for love.

On this schema, the two lines on which the subject's need is articulated as signifiers – that of demand as demand for the satisfaction of a need and that of the demand for love – are separated by reason of topological necessity, but the earlier comments apply. The separation does not mean that they are not one single, unique line on which what the child articulates for the mother is inscribed. There is an ongoing superimposition of the unfolding of what takes place on each of these lines.

You can see an immediate application of this. This ambiguity is very precisely that which, over the length of Freud's work, is maintained in a constant manner between the notion of transference – I mean, the action of transference in analysis – and the notion of suggestion.

Freud is always telling us that, after all, transference is suggestion and that we make use of it under that name – except, he adds, we do something completely different with it, since we interpret this suggestion. Now, if we are able to interpret suggestion, it's clearly because it has a background. The transference exists there potentially. We know very well that it exists, and I will immediately give you an example of it.

Transference is already potentially the analysis of suggestion, it's itself the possibility of the analysis of suggestion, a second articulation of what in suggestion simply imposes itself upon the subject. In other words, the horizon on which suggestion is based is there at the level of demand, the demand that the subject makes of the analyst simply by virtue of the fact that he is there.

This demand does not lack variety. What are these demands? How are we to situate them? It's interesting to take stock of them at the start, for there is enormous variation. There really are people for whom the demand to be cured is there, insistent at every moment. Others, more informed, know that it's to be deferred till tomorrow. There are others who are there for something other than for the demand to be cured, they are there to find out. There are those who are there to become analysts. But what is the importance of knowing the place of demand, given that the analyst, even if he does not respond to demand, responds to it simply by virtue of the fact that he is instituted, which is constitutive of all the effects of suggestion?

The idea one normally has is that the transference is that thanks to which suggestion works. Freud himself writes that if it's appropriate to allow the transference to establish itself, it's because it's legitimate to use the power of – what? Of the suggestion that the transference gives rise to. Transference is here thought of as the analyst's seizing power over the subject, as the affective tie that makes the subject dependent on him, and which it's legitimate for us to make use of for an interpretation to work. What does that mean, if not to declare in the clearest of manners that we use suggestion? To call things by their name, it's because the patient has come to love us that our interpretations are ingested. We're on the plane of suggestion. Now, of course, Freud does not intend to limit himself to that.

We are told, 'Yes, it's simple, we are going to analyse the transference. As you will see, this makes the transference completely disappear.' I stress these terms because they are not mine but those that are implicit in all discussions about the transference as an affective capture of the subject. To think that what differentiates one from someone who uses his power as the support for getting the patient to accept an interpretation, and who is therefore suggesting, is the fact that one is going to analyse this effect of power, is nothing other than an infinite deferral of the question – since it's still on the basis of the transference that one is going to analyse the fact that the subject has accepted the interpretation. There is no possibility of exiting the infernal circle of suggestion by that route. Now, we suppose, precisely, that something else is possible, which is, then, that the transference is something different from the use of power.

The transference is already in itself an open field, the possibility of a signifying articulation other than and different from the one that imprisons the subject in demand. This is why it's legitimate, whatever its contents might be, to place this line on the horizon. I will call it the line of transference. It's something articulated which exists potentially, beyond what is articulated on the plane of demand where you find the line of suggestion.

Now, there on the horizon is what demand as such produces, namely, the symbolization of the Other and the unconditional demand for love. This is where the object will subsequently come to be lodged, but as an erotic object that becomes the subject's aim. When Freud tells us that the identification that succeeds and replaces this aimed-at love object is regression, what that is about is the ambiguity between the line of transference and the line of suggestion.

I formulated this a long time ago, right at the outset – it's along   429
the line of suggestion that identification in its primary form occurs, the one we are so familiar with, which is identification with the insignia of the Other as the subject of demand, he who has the power to satisfy it or not satisfy it and marks this satisfaction at every moment with something that is in the foreground – his language, his speech.

I have stressed the essential importance of spoken relations with the child. All other signs, the mother's entire miming, as they were saying last night, are articulated in signifying terms that crystallize themselves into the conventional character of this so-called emotional mimicry by which the mother communicates with the child. Every type of expression of the emotions in man has a conventional character. You don't need to be Freudian to know that the supposedly spontaneous expression of the emotions turns out on examination to be not only problematic but massively variable. What in one particular area of signifying articulation signifies a given emotion may have a completely different expressive value in another.

Therefore, if identification is regressive, it's precisely insofar as the ambiguity between the line of transference and the line of suggestion remains permanent. In other words, in the developments and detours of analysis, we shouldn't be astonished to see regressions punctuated by a series of correlated identifications which mark their rhythm and tempo. They are different, moreover – there can't be both regression and identification at the same time. One is the halts and stops of the other. But it remains the case that if there is transference, it's precisely so that the upper line can be maintained on another plane than the plane of suggestion – that is, it is held in view, not as something to which no satisfaction of demand corresponds, but as a signifying articulation as such. That's what distinguishes one from the other.

You will say to me, 'What is the operation by which we keep them distinct?' Our operation is precisely abstinent or abstentionist. It consists in never ratifying demand as such. We know that, but although this abstention is essential, it isn't sufficient on its own.

But this is stating the obvious – these two lines can remain distinct because it's in the nature of things for them to remain distinct. In other words, they can remain distinct because for the subject they are distinct and because between the two there is this entire field which, thank goodness, is not slim, and which is never abolished. It's called the field of desire.

430   Henceforth, all that is asked of us is not to encourage this confusion by our presence there as Other. Now, by virtue of the simple fact that we are there to listen as Other, that is difficult – and all the more so if, in the way we enter into it, we accentuate the feature of analysis described as permissive. It's permissive purely on the level of verbal play, but that is sufficient. It's sufficient that things are permissive on the verbal plane for the patient to be satisfied, not, of course, on the real plane, but on the verbal plane. And it's enough that he be satisfied on the plane of demand for the confusion

between the line of transference and the line of suggestion to be irremediably established. This means that, by virtue of our presence, and insofar as we listen to the patient, we have a tendency to confuse the line of transference with the line of demand. We are therefore, in principle, harmful.

If regression is our path, it's a receding path. It doesn't designate the aim of our action, but its detour. We must keep this constantly in mind. There is an entire technique of analysis which has no other aim than to establish this confusion, and this is why it results in a transference neurosis. You will then see it in writing in a journal called *La revue française de psychanalyse* that, as to resolving the question of the transference, there is only one thing to do – sit the patient down, say nice things to him, show him how nice things are outside, tell him to go on his way and leave quietly so as not to disturb the flies. And that's from a great practitioner.

Thank goodness that there is something between the two lines that stops this irremediable confusion from becoming established. And it's obvious that the hypnotists, or simply those who have become interested in hypnosis, know full well that no suggestion, however successful it may be, will take hold of the subject completely.

Let's ask this question here – what resists?

2

It's desire that resists.

I won't even say this or that of the subject's desires, since this is obvious – but essentially the desire to have one's desire. This is even more obvious, but that is no reason not to say it.

What the schema enumerates and organizes are the forms necessary for maintaining desire, owing to which the subject remains a divided subject, which is in the very nature of the human subject. If he is no longer a divided subject, he is mad. He remains a divided subject because there is a desire, the field of which can't be so easy to maintain either, since I am explaining to you that a neurosis is constructed in the way it's constructed so as to maintain something articulated called desire.

431

That's the right definition. Effectively, neurosis is not a greater or lesser force or weakness of desire, nor is fixation to be imagined as the fact that at some point the subject has put his foot in a pot of glue. If fixation resembles anything, it's more like pickets that are designed to keep something in that would otherwise escape.

The force of desire in neurotics, what is called the quantitative element, is very variable. This variation constitutes one of the most convincing arguments for establishing the autonomy of what one calls the structural modification in neurosis. It's blatantly obvious in experience that neurotics who have the same form of neurosis are diversely gifted people with respect to what one of the authors in question calls somewhere, concerning an obsessional neurosis, 'the exuberant and precocious sexuality' of one of his patients.

In the event, this involves a subject of whom it's said that when he masturbated he would lightly pinch the outside part of his foreskin. Convinced that he would cause irreparable lesions, he didn't dare wash his penis, and he had to consult a doctor given the repeated failure of his attempts at coitus. We know very well that these are only symptoms and that the subject will show himself to be, in the midst of his analysis, very capable of fulfilling his duties as a husband and satisfying his wife. But in the end, whatever force we suppose his symptoms to be supported by, we are nevertheless not going to describe as 'exuberant' a sexuality that lets itself languish and be deceived to the point where one can give a similar description of a subject who is already at an advanced age. This does not mean that another obsessional neurotic will not show you a different picture, justifying one in describing his sexuality as exuberant, even as precocious.

This altogether tangible difference between clinical cases doesn't prevent us from recognizing that it's one and the same obsessional neurosis in every case. This is why an obsessional neurosis is situated somewhere else entirely than in the quantitative element of desire. If this does enter into play, it's solely insofar as it will have to pass through the defiles of structure, for what characterizes neurosis is structure.

In the case of the obsessional, whether his desire is strong or weak, whether the subject is in the midst of puberty or comes to us when he is forty or fifty years old – that is, at a time at which his desire is nevertheless in decline and he desires to get some idea about what's happened, that is, something he has never understood anything about in his existence till then – in every case it will emerge that he has been preoccupied during the whole of his existence with placing his desire in a strong position and constituting a stronghold for his desire, doing it on the plane of essentially signifying relations. In this stronghold there dwells either a weak or a strong desire, that's not the question. One thing is certain, it's that strongholds are always double-edged. Those that are built to protect one from the outside are even more annoying for those that are inside, and that's the problem.

The first form of identification is, then, defined for us as the original tie with an object. It is, to schematize things, the identification

432

with the mother. The other form of identification is the regressive identification with the love object, that is, identification insofar as it should occur somewhere else, at a point on the horizon that is not easy to reach because the demand is precisely unconditional or, more exactly, submitted to the one condition of the existence of signifiers inasmuch as, without the existence of signifiers, there is no possible opening for the dimension of love as such. The latter is therefore entirely dependent upon the existence of signifiers, but, within this existence, it isn't dependent on any particular articulation. It's for this reason that it isn't easy to formulate since nothing can complete it or fulfil it, not even the totality of my discourse throughout my entire existence, since it is, in addition, the horizon of my discourses.

This raises precisely the question of what the barred S means at this level. In other words, what subject is in question?

There is no reason to be astonished that this only ever forms a horizon. The entire problem is that of knowing what will be constructed in this interval. The neurotic lives the paradox of desire exactly like everybody else, for no human inserted into the human condition ever escapes it. The only difference that characterizes the neurotic with respect to desire is that he is open to the existence of this paradox as such, which of course doesn't simplify existence for him, but doesn't place him in such a bad position either from a certain point of view.

We might directly formulate the philosopher's point of view some time and call him into question in the same way. The neurotic is effectively on a path that has some kinship with what the philosopher formulates, or at the very least with what he should formulate, since, to be honest, have you ever seen this problem of desire well and truly carefully, correctly and powerfully articulated in the philosopher's approach? Until now, what appears to me to be one of the most characteristic things about philosophy is that this is one of the most carefully avoided things in its field.

That would encourage me to make another aside about the philosophy of action, which would end with the same conclusions, namely that what's said about it is nonsense. One sees in it some kind of intrusion of spontaneity or originality by man, insofar as he transforms the givens of the problem or the world, as we say. It's odd that no one ever highlights what, for me, is a truth of experience, namely the profoundly paradoxical character of action completely akin to the paradox of desire. I was beginning to introduce its traits and contours to you last time when alluding to the character of exploit, performance, demonstration and indeed even desperate outcome in an action.

433

The terms I am using are not my own, because Freud uses the term '*vergreifen*' ['to make a mistake'] to designate paradoxical, generalized action, human action. Human action is particularly present when one claims to designate it as concordant with history. My friend Kojève speaks of crossing the Rubicon as a point of concordance, a harmonious solution between Caesar's present, past and future, although the last time I crossed the Rubicon, I only saw it dry. It was immense when Caesar crossed it, but it wasn't the same season. Even if Caesar crossed the Rubicon with the genius of Caesar, there is always in the fact of crossing the Rubicon something that involves jumping into the water, since it's a river.

In other words, human action is not as harmonious as all that. For us other analysts, it's the most astonishing thing in the world that no one in psychoanalysis has proposed to formulate what pertains to action from this paradoxical perspective from which we constantly view it. Moreover, we never see anything but this, which makes it quite difficult to define acting out clearly. In a certain sense, it's an action just like any other, but one that stands out because it's brought about by our use of the transference – that is, we are doing something extremely dangerous, and all the more so since, as you can see from what I am suggesting to you, we do not have a very precise idea of what this is.

Perhaps a word, in passing, on resistance will clarify what I mean. In some cases, the subject does not accept the interpretations that we present to him on the plane of regression. It seems to us that it fits, and to him it doesn't seem to fit at all. So one says to oneself that the subject is resisting and that in the end he will give way if we insist, seeing that we are always ready to play the card of suggestion. Now, this resistance may not be without its value. What value does it have? Inasmuch as it expresses the necessity to articulate desire in some other way, namely on the plane of desire, it has the very precise value that Freud gives it in some of his texts. He calls it *Übertragungswiderstand*, transference-resistance, because it's the same thing as transference. It involves transference in the sense I am talking to you about at the moment. Resistance aims to maintain the other line, that of transference, where the articulation has another requirement than the one we give it when we respond to demand immediately. This reminder only corresponds to things that are self-evident, but self-evident things that needed to be articulated, nevertheless.

To conclude on the second identification, at what point do we judge that what happens is regressive? It's the fact that the transference is an appeal that makes possible this disruption by signifiers that we call regression, but it mustn't stop there. On the contrary, it must take us further. That's what we are trying to set our sights on for the moment, namely, how are we to operate with the transference? The transference quite naturally tends to deteriorate into something we can always satisfy in some way at its regressive level, hence the fascination with the notion of frustration, hence the various formulations that are expressed in a thousand ways in object relations and the conception of analysis that follows.

Every way of articulating analysis always tends to deteriorate, which does not prevent analysis from being something else, nevertheless.

3

Freud formulates the third form of identification for us as one that may arise with any new perception of a common quality shared with a person who is not at all an object of the sexual drive, '*sie drittens bei jeder neu wahrgenommenen Gemeinsamkeit mit einer Person, die nicht Objekt der Sexualtriebe ist*' [*SE* 18: 108]. Where is this third identification located?

Freud illustrates this for us in a manner that leaves no ambiguity over how it is to be recorded on the schema. As I have been telling you lately, in Freud it's always said in the clearest of fashions. He takes hysterical identification as an example. For the hysteric, her problem is focusing her desire somewhere, in the sense in which an optical instrument makes it possible to focus on a point. This desire comes to present special difficulties for her. Let's attempt to spell them out more precisely.

For her, her desire is destined to some sort of impasse since she can only actually focus it on the condition that she identify with something, a small trait, it doesn't matter what. Where I say 'an insignia', Freud speaks of a trait, a single trait, *einziger Zug*, it doesn't matter what, of someone else, someone with whom she can sense that there is the same problem of desire. This means that for the hysteric her impasse opens wide the doors to the other – at least, the doors to all the others, that is, to all possible hysterics, even to all hysterical moments of all others, insofar as for an instant she can sense in them the same problem, which is that of the question about desire.

For the obsessional, although the question is articulated a little differently, it's exactly the same from the point of view of the relation, the topology – and with reason. The identification in question is placed here, at [$ \cancel{S} \lozenge a$], which, as I pointed out to you last time, is where fantasy is. There is a point at which the subject has to establish

435

a certain imaginary relationship with the other, not in itself, as it were, but insofar as this relationship brings him satisfaction. Freud makes quite clear that it's a question here of a person who has no relationship with any sort of *Sexualtrieb*. This is something else – he is a support for, a puppet of fantasy.

Here, give the word 'fantasy' as large an extension as you like. This is fantasy such as I formulated it last time, insofar as it can be an unconscious fantasy. The only use for the other, which is not insignificant, is this – to enable the subject to maintain a particular position that avoids the collapse of desire, that is, that avoids the problem of the neurotic.

That's the third form of identification, which is essential.

It would take too long now to start reading Bouvet's article published in *La revue française de psychanalyse*, in which my paper '*L'agressivité en psychanalyse*', 'Aggressiveness in Psychoanalysis', also appears. This article is titled '*Importance de l'aspect homo-sexuel du transfert*', 'Importance of the Homosexual Aspect of the Transference', and I ask you to read it, as I will be returning to it. Today I would just like to spell out the precise point at which I indicate the error in the analytic technique in question.

What happens in analysis, insofar as the phallic object, and especially the analyst's phallus, appears in fantasies happens at a point of proliferation that has already been instituted, but which can always be stimulated. This is the point at which, through his fantasy, the subject as obsessional maintains the possibility of sustaining himself in the face of his desire – a possibility that is much more difficult and dangerous than for the hysteric. It's here, therefore, that ø, the fantasmatic phallus, appears. It's in this technique that I am referring to that the analyst becomes pressing and insistent through his interpretations, so that the subject agrees to enter into communion with, swallow and fantasmatically incorporate this part object into himself.

I am saying this is mistaking levels. It's moving the plane of demand, which is called into question here, onto the plane of suggestive identification. It's favouring a certain imaginary identification by the subject through benefiting, as it were, from the hold that the openly suggestive position gives the analyst on the basis of the transference. It's giving a false, diverted solution to what is being questioned – I am not saying in his fantasies, but in the material that he effectively brings to the analyst. This is visible in the observations themselves, upon which one intends to construct an entire theory about the part object, the distance from the object, the introjection of the object and all that follows. I will give you an example.

It's palpable at every moment in this observation that the solution to the analysis of the obsessional is that he come to discover castration for what it is, that is, as the law of the Other. This Other that is castrated. For reasons that have to do with his mistaken implication in this problem, the subject feels that he himself is threatened by this castration at a level that is so acute that he can't come near his own desire without feeling its effects. What I am saying is that the horizon of the Other, the big Other as such, distinct from the little other, is tangible in this observation at every turn.

The following memories come back to him – the first time he approaches a young girl, he flees in anxiety, goes and confides in his mother and feels completely reassured as soon as he says to her, 'I will tell you everything' [p. 432]. One can only take this material literally. His virtual subjective support immediately passes via a distraught reference to the Other as the locus of verbalization. This is where, henceforth, the subject will be entirely invested. It is his one possible refuge when confronted with the panic he experiences on approaching his desire. It's already inscribed and it's a matter of finding out what is going on underneath.

Once certain fantasies have come to light after all sorts of solicitations from the analyst, we come to a dream that the analyst interprets as the fact that the subject's passive homosexual tendency is becoming apparent. Here is the dream. 'I accompany you home. In your bedroom there is a big bed. I lie down on it. I feel extremely awkward. There is a bidet in the corner of the bedroom. I am happy, although I feel uneasy' [435]. We are told that following the subject's preparation over the earlier period of his analysis, he does not experience much difficulty in admitting the passive homosexual meaning of the dream.

Is this sufficient for this formulation, in your opinion? Without   437
even returning to the observation – where all the indications are there to demonstrate that this is not sufficient – if we limit ourselves to the text of the dream, one thing is certain, which is that the subject comes and puts himself, so to speak, in the Other's place: 'I am in your home. I am lying on your bed.'

Passive homosexual? Why? Until evidence arises to the contrary, nothing appears there that in this particular case makes the Other an object of desire. On the contrary, what I clearly see designated here, in a third position, and in the corner, is something that is fully articulated and that nobody seems to have paid attention to, whereas it is, however, not there for no reason. It's the bidet.

One can say about this object both that it presentifies the phallus and does not show it, since I do not see any indication in the dream that anybody is engaged in using it. The bidet is there, indicating what is problematic. It's not for nothing that this famous part object enters. It's the phallus, but, as it were, as a question – does the Other have it or does he not? This is the moment to show it. Is the Other it or is he not it? That's what's in the background. In short, it's a question of castration.

This obsessional is, moreover, prey to all sorts of obsessions of cleanliness, which clearly show that this instrument is a possible source of danger. The bidet has presentified the phallus for him, at least his own, for a long time. What is problematic for this subject is the question concerning the phallus.

[It is the question concerning the phallus] insofar as the latter enters into play as the object of this symbolic operation which, in the Other, at the level of signifiers, makes it the signifier of what has been struck by the action of signifiers, of what is subject to castration. The aim is not to know whether in the end the subject feels comforted by taking a higher power inside himself, by assimilating himself to one who is stronger than he, but to know how he will have effectively resolved the question implicit on the horizon, in line with what the structure of neurosis indicates, namely, the acceptance or not of the castration complex, insofar as castration can only be realized as a function of signifiers.

This is where the two techniques differ, independently of the legitimacy linked to the structure and very meaning of obsessional desire.

Merely on the plane of the therapeutic solution obtained, by simply considering the resulting knot, closure or, let's say, scar, there is no doubt that a certain technique is unfavourable to a correct outcome and doesn't correspond to what one may call a cure, nor even to any form of orthopaedics, not even one that limps.

Only the other one is capable of giving, not just the correct, but the effective solution.

438

4 June 1958

XXV

THE SIGNIFICATION
OF THE PHALLUS IN
THE TREATMENT

Reading the schema
The reduction to demand
From fantasy to message
The treatment of a female obsessional neurosis
Beyond the castration complex

I am going to return to my comments, still with the help of our little schema.

Some of you are wondering about the little lozenge sign that is being used when, for example, I write $ opposite little *a*. This doesn't seem extremely complicated to me, but well, since some of you are wondering about it, I will give a response.

1

I remind you that the lozenge in question is the same thing as the square in a much older fundamental schema that I reproduced in a simplified form for you here in January [see p. 142], and on which I inscribed the subject's relationship to the Other as the locus of speech and message. I gave this as a first approximation of what comes from the Other and encounters the barrier of the *a–a'* relationship, which is the imaginary relation.

The lozenge expresses the subject's relationship – whether barred or not barred, according to the case, that is, according to whether it's marked by the effect of signifiers or whether we are simply considering it as a still indeterminate subject, not split by the *Spaltung* that results from the action of signifiers – this subject's relationship, then, with what is determined by this quadratic relationship. When I write it like that [$ ◊ *a*], the subject's relationship to the little other – that is, to the semblable or the imaginary other – the other vertices

of this framework are not otherwise determined. If I write $ in rela-
tion to demand, namely [$ ◊ D], it's the same, this doesn't prejudge
the corner of this little square where demand intervenes as such, that
is, the articulation of a need in the form of signifiers.

On this year's schema [see Appendix A] we have a line at the
upper level, which is a signifying and articulated line. Since it's
produced on the horizon of every signifying articulation, it's the
fundamental background to every formulation of a demand. At the
lower level, this is articulated in general, however poorly. We have a
precise articulation, a succession of signifiers, of phonemes.

Let's comment on the upper line, which lies beyond all signifying
articulation.

This line corresponds to the effect of the signifying articulation
taken as a whole, insofar as, through its mere presence it makes
the symbolic appear in the real. It makes this horizon or possibility of demand, this power of demand which is essentially and by
nature – place as much ambiguity on that as you like – a demand
for love, a demand for presence, appear in its totality and insofar as
it's articulated.

The reason I'm talking about love here is to pin something down.
Hatred happens to have the same place. The ambivalence of love
and hate can only be conceptualized within this horizon. It's also
within this horizon that we are able to see this third term, ignorance,
a homologue of love and hate in relation to the subject, come to the
same spot.

On the upper line on the left, we have the signifier of the Other as
marked by the action of the signifier, that is, the barred A – S(Å).
This precise point is the homologue of the point at which, on the
line of demand, the return from demand's passage through the
Other, which is called the message, s(A), appears in the fundamental
schema of every demand. If you like, what has to be produced at
the point of the message on the second line is precisely the message
of a signifier that signifies that the Other is marked by this signifier.
That doesn't mean that this message is produced. It's there as the
possibility of being produced.

This is, moreover, also the homologue of this point at which
the demand arrives at the Other, that is, where it's subjected to
the code's existence in the Other, the locus of speech. Also, on
this horizon you have what can arise in the form of what is called
conscious awareness. But it's not simply conscious awareness, it's
the formulation by the subject as speaking subject of his demand
as such, in relation to which he situates himself – [$ ◊ D]. That
this has to be able to occur is the fundamental presupposition of
analysis itself. It's what occurs in the first steps in an analysis. In

the foreground, but not essentially, is the subject's renewal of his demands. Of course, in a certain way it is a renewal, but it's an articulated renewal. It's in his discourse that, through the form and nature of his demand, the subject reveals the signifiers in which his demand is formulated, either directly or implicitly in his discourse – and it's surely always much more important for us when it's implicit. It's insofar as this demand is formulated in archaic signifiers that we speak, for example, of anal or oral regression.

Last time I wanted to introduce the fact that everything that arises in the nature of transference is suspended from the existence of the upper line. We can mark its beginning with a Φ and its end with a Δ, the meaning of which I will speak about later. This line is the foundation of the effect of signifiers in subjective economy.

Transference, strictly speaking, is situated relative to this line. Everything that is of the order of transference, in accordance with the analyst's action or his non-action, in accordance with his abstention or his non-abstention, always tends to get played out in this intermediary zone, but, equally, can always be brought back to the articulation of demand. Even more, it's in the nature of verbal formulation in analysis that something is being articulated on the plane of demand at every moment. But if the analytic law is that none of the subject's demands are to be satisfied, it's for no other reason than that we speculate on the fact that demand will always tend to be played out elsewhere than on the plane of precise, formulated demands, ones that are susceptible to being satisfied or not satisfied. Everybody is in agreement – what is being played out isn't that we frustrate the subject of what he can ask us on a particular occasion, whether it be simply to answer him or, in the extreme case, to hold his hand. What is being played out is a more profound frustration, one that stems from the very essence of speech insofar as it makes the horizon of demand appear, which I have quite simply called, to focus the mind, the demand for love, and which can also be the demand for something else. For example, a particular demand concerning the recognition of his being, with all the conflicts that that brings out if the analyst, through his presence, and as a semblable, denies it – the Hegelian negation in the relationship between consciousnesses looms here, if needs be. Or again, a demand to know, which, naturally, is also on the horizon of the analytic relation.

What does that have to do with symptoms? In what way can it be used for the resolution of neuroses? This is where we have to introduce the intermediary zone.

The four vertices of that other locus of the subject's reference to the Other, which is the imaginary locus of reference inasmuch as here it's only a false vertex, are situated in a topological relationship

442

with these two lines insofar as they are formed by speech whenever it is articulated in speech in analysis.

The ego's narcissistic or specular relationship to the other's image is prior, lies on this, the near side and is entirely implicated in the first relation to demand. This relationship lies along the line m–a.

Beyond, the intermediary zone, the zone of all articulations, extends from the [lower] line of articulated demand to the [upper] line of its essential horizon. The upper line is also articulated, of course, since what supports it is articulated, but this doesn't mean that it's articulable, since nothing suffices to formulate what is here on the horizon – the final term, properly speaking – in any completely satisfactory manner, except by the indefinite continuation of the development of speech.

What is called desire, indicated by the small d, is located in this intermediary zone. It's desire that is properly called into question in the subject's entire economy and that is involved in what is revealed in analysis, that is, in what starts to budge in speech in a game of oscillation between the signifiers at the level of need, as it were, and what results, beyond the articulation of signifiers, from the constant presence of signifiers in the unconscious, insofar as signifiers have already moulded, formed and structured the subject. Desire, man's desire insofar as it's the Other's desire, is located in this intermediary zone. It lies beyond need, beyond the articulation of need that the subject is led to by the necessity to declare it for the Other, beyond all satisfaction of a need. It's present in the form of an absolute condition and is produced in the margin between the demand for the satisfaction of needs and the demand for love. Man's desire is always, for him, to be sought in the locus of the Other as the locus of speech, which means that desire is a desire structured in this locus of the Other.

That is the entire problematic of desire. It's what makes it subject to the dialectic and the formations of the unconscious. That is why we are involved with it and are able to have an influence on it, according to whether it is or is not articulated in speech in analysis. There would be no analysis if it weren't for this fundamental situation.

We have here, in [$ \mathcal{S} \lozenge a $], the guarantor and support of desire, the point at which it attaches itself to its object, which, far from being natural, is always formed by a particular position the subject takes in relation to the Other. Helped by this fantasmatic relation, man finds his bearings and situates his desire. Hence the importance of fantasies. Hence the rarity of the term 'instinct' in Freud – it's always a question of the drive, *Trieb*, the technical term we give to this desire insofar as speech isolates it, fragments it and places it in

443

this problematic and disjointed relationship to its aim that one calls the direction of the tendency, and whose object is, moreover, subject to substitution and displacement or, indeed, to all forms of transformation and equivalents, but is also offered to love, which makes it a subject of speech.

2

Last time we got to the point of focusing on some studies of an obsessional neurosis which I have several times invited you to read carefully, and which have to be relevant to what is being said here, even if only because some of the terms involved – 'distance from the object', 'phallic object', 'object relation' – can't fail to invite retrospective evaluation in the light of what I am bringing you here.

I took, then, the account of the treatment of two cases of obsessional neurosis drawn from the article '*Importance de l'aspect homosexuel du transfert*', ['Importance of the Homosexual Aspect of the Transference'] and I pointed out to you the problematic character of the result of this or that suggestion, let's say direction, or even interpretation. In reference to one dream in particular, I stressed how much certain presuppositions and certain simplifications of the system led to missing certain prominent elements and therefore the dream itself.

He speaks of a homosexual transference dream, as if that could have a meaning where the dream itself gives the image of what it is about, that is, a relation that is far from being dyadic. The subject, then, was transported into the analyst's bed, both at ease and in an attitude that one could describe as one of expectation, according to the manifest content, on the condition that one not neglect the explicit and essential presence of this bed. I showed you the presence of an object in the striking form of the famous bidet. One is even more astonished that the analyst doesn't dwell on this, since another text by the same author shows that he is far from ignoring the properly phallic signification of what some analysts have called the hollowed out or cuplike penis, inasmuch as it's one of the forms in which the phallus signifier can be presented at the level of the adoption of the phallic image by the female subject. This kind of Grail 444 was at least likely to capture the attention and even give rise to some caution in one who interprets in terms of a two-person relationship.

I have read this second article again. I have also read the earlier one, which isn't the most interesting to critique, since matters there are brought to the level of the self-evident. Let's randomly choose this intervention. One similar in nature had already been given previously, but he returns to it because the subject had been pulled so far in the direction of deepening the homosexual transference that the transference situation was becoming clearer and clearer, frankly homosexual, and so he had to insist to overcome a number of silences.

> I therefore alluded to the fact that if between men there exist affective relations that are referred to by the name 'friendship' and by which nobody feels humiliated, these relations always take on a certain character of passivity for one of the partners when he finds it necessary to receive teaching, directives or some encouragement from the other. At this difficult moment the idea came to me of using an analogy that would be able to be felt *de plano* by this former officer. Why do men get themselves killed in combat for a leader that they love, unless it's precisely because they accept his instructions and his orders with a total absence of resistance, that is, with total passivity? They thus embrace the sentiments and thoughts of the leader to the point of identifying with him, and they sacrifice their lives as he himself would if he were to find himself in their place. [p. 425]

You can see that an intervention of this kind has to require a fairly large chunk of silence, above all when one is aware that the analyst chooses this example because his patient is an officer.

> They can only act in this way because they passively love their leader. This remark did not make all the subject's reservations disappear immediately, but it enabled him to continue to be objective when he was going to revive other homosexual situations with me, ones that were more specific. [p. 426].

And this is effectively what happens.

It's perfectly clear that the orientation of the treatment opens the door to an entire imaginary collaboration in the two-person relation between the analysand and the analyst and proceeds in a way that, as the observation itself bears out, isn't only systematic, but truly insistent. On the two planes of remembering and the analytic situation, it chooses everything in the material that goes in the simplifying direction of elaborating the two-person relation insofar as it has a homosexual signification.

Whereas the interpretation must essentially bear upon the handling of signifiers, whereas this requires that it be brief, and whereas later I will insist upon the mark that the introduction of a signifier

445

must give it, we have here an intervention whose significant, under-standable and persuasive character is manifest and which consists in inducing the subject precisely to live the analytic situation as a simple two-person relation. One does not need to be an analyst to point out that such an intervention is akin to suggestion, if only by virtue of the sole fact that it chooses one signification that it returns to three times.

This study of approximately six pages shows us the stages of the analysand's relationship to the analyst in the form of facilitating an understanding of the two-person situation in terms of homosexual relations. To be sure, homosexuality is classically presented to us in Freudian doctrine as a libidinal relationship underlying all relations considered from the social angle, but this is announced in a highly ambiguous form that doesn't enable it to be distinguished from what is strictly speaking the homosexual drive, insofar as the latter is characterized by this choice of erotic object of the sex opposite the one that the norm may wish for – which is different in nature from the libidinal underpinnings of social relations.

Whatever the theoretical difficulties thus raised, the use of this reference in this observation, and I am not saying that it's illegitimate in itself, appears in a systematic form within the therapeutics as a veritable indoctrination, and this raises the problem of the direction of the treatment overall. We can clearly see to what extent this indoctrination can have certain effects, but do you not also see, by the same token, that there is a choice here over the type of intervention with respect to obsessional neurosis? All that you know, moreover, about this subject's relationship to himself, his existence and the world, which is called an obsessional neurosis, is infinitely more complex than a relationship of libidinal attachment to the subject of his own sex, at whatever level it happens to be articulated.

From Freud's first observations, we all know the role played by the destructive drive directed at one's semblable and consequently turned back upon the subject, and we all know that many other elements are involved – elements of regression and fixation in the libidinal evolution, which are far from being as simple as one makes the famous link between the sadistic and the anal, a link that can in no way be taken as simple, or even as having been elucidated.

In short, the fact that such a direction of the treatment is full of effects turns out to be articulated into a much fuller perspective on what is going on. I am not saying that what I am contributing is completely sufficient, but it already makes it possible to arrange better the different registers into which things can be put. We can situate here, in [$ ◊ a], what, in short, is a detail in the economy of the obsessional, namely the role that is played in it at one point by

446

identification with another who is a little *a*, an imaginary other. This is one of the modes thanks to which the subject somehow more or less balances his obsessional economy.

It may have some therapeutic effect to go along with this, to give the subject the satisfaction of validating his relationship – which appears with regularity in the history of obsessionals – with another who is his point of reference, whose approval and criticisms he demands, and with whom he identifies as someone who is stronger than he, as the author in question says, and on whom, one can truly say, he relies as in a dream, to endorse this mechanism, which is surely a defence mechanism by which the subject balances the problematic of his relationship to the Other's desire. This may have some therapeutic effect, but it's far from having any just by itself.

Equally, the evolution of the author's work shows that things have been pushed by him in a direction that places more and more emphasis on what he calls distance from the object, which ends up being quite especially centred on the elaboration of a fantasy, the fantasy of fellatio, and not with just any phallus, but with the phallus that is a part of the imagined body of the analyst. The imaginary support derived from the semblable, the homosexual other, is embodied, materialized in this experience that is given to us as being comparable to Catholic Communion, to the ingestion of the host.

We can thus see here an elaboration of the fantasy being pursued along the same lines, this time taken further, and we can see what it produces. What it's about can be located on the schema. The relationship [$ ◊ a] at the level of fantasy, that is, the level of the original fantasmatic production that makes it possible for the subject to place himself and come to terms with his desire, moves onto the level of a response to a demand, which is the level of the message. It's not for nothing that in this observation you now see the image of the good mother appear, the benevolent mother, or that he speaks of the creation of the infantile female superego. Ratifying the subject's fantasmatic production at the level of the signified of the Other, $s(A)$, reduces the complex formations of desire in the subject to the demand articulated in the subject's immediate relationship to the analyst.

'But what if it works?' you will say to me. Effectively, why not? Isn't this an idea one can have of analysis? I reply that not only is it not sufficient, but that these observations themselves enable us to see that, while this orientation doesn't fail to have certain effects, what is produced is very far from the cure-effect that we might expect, like the supposed genital satisfaction that is said to be attained. How can one not see the paradox of representing it by the fact that the

447

subject lets himself be loved by his analyst? On the contrary, we very obviously see the opposite in it. The subjective reduction of symptoms is achieved via a regressive process, not in the purely temporal sense, but in the topical sense as well, insofar as there is a reduction of everything in the order of desire – its production, organization and maintenance – onto the plane of demand. The stages of the treatment, very far from being interpretable in the sense of an amelioration and normalization of relations with the other, are marked by sudden outbursts which take various forms, including acting out.

I showed you one last year in the case of a subject strongly marked by perverse tendencies. The outcome of things was a true acting out by the subject who went to look through the door of the lavatories on the Champs-Élysées at women urinating – that is, who went in search of the woman as phallus, literally. This was the abrupt outbreak of something which was excluded under the influence of demand and made its re-entry here in the form of an isolated act in the life of the subject which had the compulsive form of an acting out and assured the presentification of a signifier as such. Further testimonies show us still other forms – for example a problematic and paradoxical infatuation in subjects for whom there are no grounds for considering them in themselves to be so-called latent homosexuals ignorant of the fact. They have what they have that is homosexual, and they have precisely no more of it than what one can see in the abrupt infatuation for a semblable when it's merely the forced production of the relationship to a – induced by this way of directing the analysis. This truly is the artificial product of the analyst's interventions. At this level, the practice lacks all critique and finesse, to a degree that discourages commentary.

This is also why I would like to take another example that issues from the work of the same author, and which, it seems to me, would have been much more interesting, and suited to showing the development that his elaborations on these subjects might have taken, had they been given a different orientation.

3

I have in mind the 1950 article entitled *'Incidences thérapeutiques de la prise de conscience de l'envie du pénis dans la névrose obsessionnelle féminine'* ['Therapeutic Effects of Becoming Aware of Penis Envy in Obsessional Neurosis in Women'].

This observation is of great interest because we do not have all that many analyses of obsessional neurosis in women and also because it contributes to painting a picture of the problem of the sexual specificity of the neuroses. Those who might think that it's for reasons that have to do with their sex that subjects choose this or that inclination in neuroses will see on this occasion how much what is in the order of structure in neurosis leaves very little place to being determined by the position of sex, in the biological sense. Effectively, here one rediscovers, and in a very interesting manner, the famous prevalence of the phallic object that we see at play in masculine obsessional neuroses.

This is how the author conceives and articulates the progress of the analysis.

> Like the male obsessional, the woman has a need to identify with man in a regressive manner so as to be able to free herself of the anxieties of early childhood; but whereas the former will rely upon this identification to transform the infantile love object into an object of genital love . . .

This corresponds closely to what I pointed out to you earlier in the paradox of identification in the male subject – with the analyst as it happens – since she effects the passage from infantile love object to genital love object on her own, which at the very least poses a problem.

> . . . she, the woman, basing herself at first on this same identifi-cation, tends to abandon this initial object and orientate herself towards a heterosexual fixation, as if she were able to proceed to a new feminine identification, this time with the person of the analyst. [pp. 215–16]

It's said with a striking, but necessary, ambiguity that the iden-tification with the analyst, specified as such here, and which bears upon an analyst of the male sex, ensures by itself, quite simply, as if it were self-evident, access to genitality. It's an assumption. Not imprudently, there are no great claims of extraordinary improve-ment in this case.

Concerning the identification with the analyst, one observes, not without a certain embarrassment, or even a certain surprise, that it occurs in two successive modes. The first is initially conflictual, that is, one of revendication and hostility with respect to the man. Then, to the extent that this relationship, as we are told, 'becomes more relaxed', a very unusual problematic present itself. The need to think of the progress of the treatment on the basis of identification obliges one to accept that the female identification with the analyst is rendered possible, we are told, by a 'fundamental ambiguity of the

449

person of the analyst'. This is, surely, not an explanation we're likely to be satisfied with.

> It goes without saying that the interpretation of the transference phenomena is here particularly delicate. If the personality of the male analyst is initially apprehended as that of a man, with all the prohibitions, fears and aggressiveness that that comprises, shortly after the desire to possess the analyst's phallus . . .

This is something we will have to evaluate.

> . . . and the correlative desire to castrate him are brought to light, and if by virtue of this fact the effects of the pre-cited detente have been obtained, this personality of the male analyst is assimilated to that of a benevolent mother. Does not this assimilation demonstrate that the essential force of the anti-male aggressiveness is to be found in the initial destructive drive of which the mother was the object?

Here a Kleinian horizon will always provide some support.

> Becoming conscious of one brings with it the right to the free exercise of the other, and the liberating power of this becoming conscious of the desire to possess the phallus then becomes manifestly understandable, even as the passage from one identification to the other as a function of a fundamental ambiguity . . .

Here we reencounter the phrase mentioned earlier.

> . . . of the person of the analyst whose male aspect is initially only apparent to the patient. [p. 216]

That effectively says it all. The direction of the treatment rests upon the interpretation that it's about a desire for phallic possession and, correlatively, a desire for the castration of the analyst. On closer inspection, this is far from representing what is effectively present in the observation. I will take things in the order in which they are presented to us.

She is a woman, fifty years of age, in good health, mother of two children, practising in a paramedical profession. She comes for a series of obsessional phenomena that are of a common kind – an obsession with having contracted syphilis, and she sees in it some kind of prohibition bearing upon the marriage of her children, which moreover she was unable to prevent concerning her oldest, an obsession with infanticide, an obsession with poisoning – in short, a whole series of common obsessions in obsessional manifestations in a woman.

Even before he lists them, the author tells us about the prevailing manner of obsessions with a religious theme. As with all obsessions with a religious theme, there are all kinds of insulting, scatological phrases that impose themselves on the subject in strict contradiction with her own convictions. One of the elements that the author stresses in the subject's relationship – she is a Catholic – to religious reality is the presence of Christ's body in the host. In place of the host, she represents to herself in her imagination the masculine genital organs, without there being any question of hallucinatory phenomena, as is made clear to us. Several lines further on, an important detail is pointed out concerning the principal religious theme of this obsessional woman, which is that her mother alone was responsible for her Catholic education, which only ever had the character of obligation and constraint. Her conflict with her managed to be referred onto the spiritual plane, we are told. We won't dispute that. It's a fact that has its significance.

Before we come to the type of interpretation that will be given subsequently, I would like to stop you for a moment at this symptom, which is in itself very apt to persuade me to make several remarks. The genital organs, we are told, are present there in the place of the host, and out front. What can that mean for us? I mean, for us analysts. Here, indeed, is a case where we must give this superimposition its value, if we are analysts. What do we call repression, and above all the return of the repressed, if not something that seems to influence one from below and rises to the surface, as Scripture characterizes it, or like a stain that with time floats to the surface?

Here, then, is a case in which, if we want to grant things their textual importance, as it's our position as analysts to do, we can try to articulate what it is that it's returning from.

This woman who has received a religious education must at least have, like anyone in the Christian religion, a religious sense of what Christ is. Christ is the Word, the Logos – this has been drummed into us by our Catholic education. That he is the Word made flesh isn't in doubt in the slightest, it's the most abridged form of the *Credo*. He is the totality of the Word. Now, what we see appearing and substituting itself for him is, in a manner that converges with all our efforts to formulate the analytic experience, what we have been led to call the privileged, unique signifier, insofar as it designates the effect of the signifier, as such, upon the signified. What is produced, then, in this symptom is the substitution, for the subject's relationship to the Word made flesh or even for the totality of the Word, of a privileged signifier which serves to designate the effect, mark, imprint or wound of signifiers as a totality, insofar as they bear upon the human subject and insofar as, via the instance of the signifier, there are things in it that come to be signified.

Let's continue with the case. What do we find further on? The subject says that she has dreamed that she was stomping on the head of Christ and crushing it, and this head, she adds, 'looked like yours'. Her associations – 'Each morning on my way to work I go past a funeral parlour in which four Christs are on display. When I look at them, I have the sensation of stepping on their penises. I feel a kind of intense pleasure and anxiety' [p. 225]. We find here, once again, the identification of Christ with the Other as locus of speech. The subject crushes the figure of Christ with her heel – let's not forget that Christ is here materialized in an object, namely the crucifix, and that it's possible that in this case he is, in his totality, the phallus. We can't fail to be struck by this, above all if we continue to spell out the details that the observation provides us with.

The reproaches that she will make to her analyst about the inconvenience that through her treatment he brings into her existence are going to be materialized in the fact that she is unable to buy herself shoes. The analyst doesn't fail to recognize here the phallic value of the shoe and, in particular, of the heel that she made good use of for crushing the head of Christ. Notice in this respect that fetishism, especially shoe fetishism, is almost never observed in women. Hence, the significance of the appearance of the phallic signification of shoes at this point in the analysis. Let's try to understand it.

One doesn't have to go very far to understand it, while the analyst does everything at this moment to suggest to the subject that there is in her a desire to possess the phallus. In itself, this is perhaps not, my goodness, the worst thing he could say, if it were not for the fact that for him that means that the subject has the desire to be a man. Which she doesn't stop contradicting and protests with the greatest energy, right to the end, that she has never had the desire to be a man. Effectively, perhaps desiring to possess the phallus and desiring to be a man are not the same thing, since analytic theory itself supposes that things can resolve themselves in a very natural manner, and who wouldn't inform themselves about it?

But let's see how the analysand replies at this point. 'When I am well dressed' – that is, when I'm wearing pretty shoes – 'men desire me, and I tell myself, with very real joy, "And now they too will get their comeuppance. I am happy imagining that they will suffer as a result"' [p. 223]. In short, she brings the analyst back to solid,

451

economical ground, namely – if there is a relationship to the phallus
in her relations with man, what is it?

Let's try to spell this out ourselves.

There are several elements here, and first off the relationship with
the mother, which we are told is profound, essential and truly coherent with the real subject. We are told about the mother's relations
with the father, which have manifested themselves in several ways,
in particular that the father had not been able to overcome the wife's
attachment to a first, incidentally platonic, love. If such a thing is
indicated in the observation, it must have occupied a certain place.

452

The subject's relations with her mother are presented to us thus –
she judges her in the most favourable manner in every respect, more
intelligent than her father, she is fascinated by her energy and so on.

> The rare moments when her mother relaxed filled her with an
> unspeakable joy . . . .. She always considered that her younger
> sister was preferred over her . . . .. Also, moreover, anybody who
> interfered in this union with her mother became the object of
> death wishes, as is shown by important material, either oneiric
> or infantile, relative to the desire for the death of her sister.
> [p. 219]

Is this not sufficient to show that what is in question is, as I have
stressed to you, what the subject's relationship to her mother's desire
is? The problem of desire is introduced into the subject's life early, is
particularly manifest in the history of obsessionals and results in the
fact that the subject envisages her end for herself, not as having this
or that, but as first being the object of the mother's desire, with what
that entails – that is, deducing what is, but is unknown. Everything
that, for the subject, henceforth binds approaching her own desire
to an effect of destruction and, at the same time, defines this desire's
approach as such to the phallus, insofar as in itself it is the signifier
of the effect of desire in the subject's life, will depend on the object
of the mother's desire.

For the subject in question, the problem is not, as in the phobic,
for example, whether the mother has the phallus or not, it's what
the effect in the Other is of this x that is desire, in other words, what
he himself will be – whether he is or isn't what the Other's desire is.
This is what we see coming into the foreground here. It's quite nice
that it's with respect to the Logos made flesh, namely the Other as
marked by the word, that the substitution of the phallus signifier
occurs at this point and at this level.

I will formulate my thoughts further. Freud saw and designated
the frontier of analysis as stopping at a point that in certain cases, he

says, prove to be irreducible, leaving this sort of wound that for the subject is the castration complex. Its prevailing manifestation can be summarized, in short, as this – man, the male, can only have the phallus against the background of the fact that he doesn't have it, and that the same thing exactly is present in woman, namely that she doesn't have the phallus against the background of the fact that she has it, for otherwise how would it be possible for her to be enraged by this irreducible *Penisneid*? Don't forget that *Neid* doesn't simply mean a wish but means that that renders me literally enraged. All the underpinnings of aggressiveness and anger are indeed in this original *Neid*, both in modern German and, even more so, in old forms of German and even Anglo-Saxon.

453

If on one occasion Freud recorded there the *unendlich*, infinite, projected to infinity, which was poorly translated as 'interminable', character of what can happen in an analysis, it's undoubtedly, after all, because there were things that he did not see or that he had not had the opportunity to encounter or articulate, although many indications in his work go in this direction, and specially his final article on the *Spaltung* of the ego, which I shall come back to. He doesn't see that the solution to the problem of castration in both man and woman doesn't revolve around the dilemma of having or not having the phallus, for the solution is only found when the subject perceives that there is one thing that is in any case to be recognized, which is that he isn't the phallus. It's from the moment of realization in analysis that the subject isn't the phallus that he is capable of normalizing his natural position, and that he either has it or doesn't have it. That's the final term, the ultimate signifying relationship around which it's possible to resolve the imaginary dead-end created by the function that the image of the phallus comes to adopt at the level of the signifying plane.

This is exactly what happens in the case of our subject under the effect of the first manifestations of her being caught in the mechanism of the transference, which is a more elaborate articulation of symptomatic effects. In a way that is completely recognizable in what I have just quoted to you today, she presents the shoe fantasy to herself.

It's a question of the possession or non-possession of feminine or phallic shoes, the shoes that in this particular case we will call fetishistic. What function does the shoe adopt for a masculine subject, inasmuch as what he rejects in his perversion is that the woman is castrated? The fetishist's perversion in the masculine subject consists in affirming that the woman has it against the background of not having it. Without that, there would be no need of an object to represent it – an object which, on top of everything else, is manifestly independent of the woman's body. Well then, as the transference is developing, the subject goes about fomenting the following, which in appearance is the same thing, namely that she has it. She stresses that she wants to have it in the form of clothing, in the form of these clothes that will excite men's desire, and owing to which, as she expresses it, she will be able to disappoint them in their desire. In appearance it's the same thing, but it's completely different according to whether it's posed by the subject herself, that is, by the woman, or by the man opposite. Also, what she demonstrates when the occasion arises is that by wanting to present herself as having what she knows perfectly well she doesn't have, at issue is something that for her has a completely different value, which I have called the value of masquerade. She makes a mask of her femininity.

On the basis of the fact that the phallus is for her the signifier of desire, the issue is that she presents the appearance of it, appears to be it. The issue for her is being the object of a desire, and a desire that she herself knows full well she can only disappoint. She expresses it explicitly when the analyst interprets it for her as being about a desire to possess the phallus, which shows us once again the divergence that is established between being the object of the Other's desire and having or not having the organ that bears its mark.

We come, then, to a formula, which is the following – the original desire is, 'I want to be what she, the mother, desires.' In order to be it, I must destroy what at present is the object of her desire.

The subject wishes to be what the mother's desire is. What she needs to be brought to see in the treatment is that man isn't the object of this desire in himself, that man is no more the phallus than woman is, whereas what constitutes her aggressiveness with respect to her husband as a man – I will show this to you even more clearly next time – is that she considers that he is, I'm not saying that he has, that he is the phallus, and it's in the name of this that he is her rival and that her relations with him are marked by the sign of obsessional destruction.

According to the essential form of obsessional economy, this desire for destruction turns back against her. The aim of the treatment is to bring to her awareness that 'you are yourself that which you want to destroy, insofar as you, too, wish to be the phallus'. In a certain way of pursuing the treatment, the 'You are this that you wish to destroy' is replaced by a desire for the destruction of the analyst's phallus, captured in improbable and fleeting fantasies. 'You want to destroy my phallus, the phallus of your analyst,' the analyst says, 'and so, I give it to you.' In other words, the conception of the treatment is that the analyst fantasmatically gives the phallus and consents to a desire of phallic possession. Now, this isn't what is at

454

issue, and one of the proofs of this is that at the almost final point to which the analysis seems to have been pursued, we are told that the patient retains all her obsessions except that they no longer cause her anxiety. They have all been ratified by the analysis, and they jam up. The fact that they still exist is of some importance.

What does the patient do? The observation states this in total innocence – she intervenes with her oldest son with all her force, a son of whom she has always been scared stiff, because in fact he is the only one whose masculine reactions she has never been able to master very well, by telling him that he urgently needs to go and do an analysis himself. What does that mean, if not that she hands back this phallus that the analyst thinks is the solution to the situation, insofar as he himself, taking the position of the benevolent mother, gives it to the patient. At the one point at which she effectively has the phallus, she returns it to him. Give-and-take.

The analyst has oriented the entire analysis around this, which is that the patient wishes to be a man. Right to the end, she is not entirely convinced of this. However, it's true that possessing or not possessing this phallus brought her some appeasement. But the heart of the matter, the essential, isn't resolved – the signification of the phallus as the signifier of desire.

11 June 1958

XXVI

THE CIRCUITS OF DESIRE

The basis of interpretation
The Other of the Other
Symptom and castration
Obsessional distance
Little theory of blasphemy

Today is the 18th June. The part the signifier plays in politics – the signifier 'no' when everybody is sliding towards dreadful consent – hasn't ever been studied to date. The 18th June is also the anniversary of the foundation of the French Society of Psychoanalysis. We also said 'No' at one moment.

Last time I began commenting on the case of an obsessional woman treated by one of our colleagues, and I started to outline several of the principles that can be deduced from the way we formulate things and that make it possible to form an opinion as to the well or poorly directed way in which a treatment is conducted when centred on a phenomenon that obviously exists in the material brought by the analysis, namely, the coming to consciousness of penis envy.

Although overall I think you see the value of the use we make of our schema and categories, there are naturally always some who are a little behind. Certain schemas that you have pondered and conceptual oppositions that you found easy to retain find themselves a little shaken up and put back in question by developments as we progress – and this disconcerts you.

Someone was wondering, for example, whether one wasn't compelled to see a contradiction between what I contributed last time and a principle that it was thought we could settle on. In summary, I am supposed to have said – at least this is what was heard – that the sexual development of women was obliged to go via this, which was that she has to be the phallus against the background of not

being it, and that for the man, the castration complex can be formulated as this, that he has the phallus against the background of
not having it, or of being threatened with not having it. These are
obviously schemas to which, from a certain angle, one can oppose
this or that phase of sexual development. It's completely insufficient
to remain there, since the dialectic of being and having also applies
to them both.

The man must also realize that he isn't it. This is even the direction in which we can situate a portion of the problems implicated in
the solution to the castration complex and *Penisneid*. We shall see
this in more detail, which will enable you, I hope, to reposition state-
ments that are not false in themselves, but which constitute partial
views.

With this aim in mind, we will start again from our schema today.

458

1

It's exceedingly important to suitably articulate the different lines
along which psychoanalysis develops. An article that I advise you
to read on the matter is one by Glover called 'Therapeutic Effects
of Inexact Interpretation', which appeared in October 1931 in the
International Journal of Psychoanalysis.

This is one of the most remarkable and intelligent articles that
could be written on such a subject. It truly clarifies the starting point
from which to examine the question of interpretation.

At the time Glover is writing Freud is still alive, but he has
already produced the great turning point in analytic technique
around the analysis of resistances and aggressiveness. Glover claims
that this orientation in analysis implies the path or the covering, one
might say, in the sense in which one has to cover ground, of the sum
of phantasy systems,* that we have learnt to recognize in analysis
owing to the accumulation of experience and the development of
acquired notions.

It's clear that we know a lot more about it now than right at the
start of analysis, and the question arises regarding the worth of our
therapeutics at the time at which we didn't know the whole range
of these fantasy systems. Were incomplete therapeutic treatments
less valuable than those we undertake today? It's a very interesting
question, and it leads Glover to draw up a general situation about
all the positions taken by whoever finds himself in the position of
consultant in relation to every kind of disorder. Having done this,
he generalizes and extends the notion of interpretation to every
formulated position taken by whomever one consults and draws

459

up a scale of the different positions of the doctor in relation to the patient.

There is here an anticipation of the doctor–patient relation, as we say today, but articulated in a manner which has not been developed along these lines, and which I regret, because it poses a sort of general law, namely, that insofar as we misrecognize the truth included in a symptom, we find ourselves complicit in symptomatic formations.

This begins with the general practitioner who says to the patient, 'Get a grip on yourself, go to the country, get a new pastime.' He resolutely places himself in a position of misrecognition, and by virtue of this fact immediately occupies a certain place, that isn't ineffective, since it can be very well recognized as the very place in which certain symptoms are formed. His function in relation to the patient can be situated using the very terms of analytic topography. I'll say no more.

Glover observes at one point that the tendency of the modern therapeutic analysis* of his time is to bring all interpretation to bear on sadistic systems and guilt reactions, and that till recently none of that had been emphasized. There's no doubt that one alleviated the patient's anxiety, but one left this famous sadistic system unresolved, unsuppressed and consequently repressed.

That's an example of the direction in which he takes his remarks, and it's indeed something it would be interesting to return to today.

What does it mean, for example, when one speaks of the advent of the analysis of aggressiveness? For a time, analysts were so impressed by the discovery they had made that it had become a standing joke. Analysts in training would greet one another by saying, 'And so, have you analysed your aggressiveness?' We can locate what this discovery represented, effectively, on our fundamental schema. It's what I was trying to do earlier, for in the end we can also wonder about this. When I was teaching you that the narcissistic system was fundamental to the formation of aggressive reactions, I would often observe how much our use of the term 'aggressiveness' was marked by ambiguity. The aggressiveness provoked in the imaginary relationship with the little other can't be confused with the sum of aggressive power.

To recall things that are self-evident, violence is essential to aggression, at least on the human plane. It isn't speech, it's even the exact contrary. What can be produced in any relationship between humans is violence or speech. If violence, in its essence, is differentiated from speech, the question arises of the extent to which violence as such – to differentiate it from the use we make of the term 'aggressiveness' – can be repressed, since we have made it a principle

460

that, in principle, only what reveals itself to have attained the structure of speech, that is, a signifying articulation, can be repressed. If what belongs to the order of aggressiveness comes to be symbolized and captured in the mechanism of what is repression, unconsciousness, what is analysable, and even, let's say, as a general rule, what is interpretable, it's from the angle of the murder of the semblable, who is latent in the imaginary relationship.

Let's again spell out our little schema in its simplest form, which shows us the intersection of the tendency – the drive, if you wish, insofar as it represents an individualized need – with the signifying chain into which it has to be articulated. This already makes it possible for us to make several remarks.

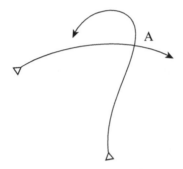

Let's make a supposition. Let's suppose that for the human being there is only reality, this famous reality that we make use of willy-nilly. Suppose that that's all there is. It isn't unthinkable that something signifying articulates this reality. To focus your mind, let's suppose that, as some schools say, a signifier is simply a kind of conditioning – I won't say of reflexes, but of something that is reducible to reflexes.

The fact that language belongs to another order than that which we artificially create in animals in the laboratory by teaching them to secrete gastric juices at the sound of a bell does not prevent the sound of the bell from being a signifier. One may therefore suppose a human world completely organized around a coalescence of each of the needs that are to be satisfied, with a number of predetermined signs. If these signs are valid for everyone, this must in principle make an ideally functioning society. Every expression of the drive commensurate with needs will be associated with a diverse and varied sound of the bell, which will function in such a way that he who hears it will immediately satisfy the said need.

This is how we arrive at the ideal society. What I am depicting is what has always been dreamt of by utopians, namely a perfectly

461

functioning society, and it culminates in the satisfaction of each according to his needs. One adds, to be honest, that everyone participates according to their merits, and that's where the problems start.

In short, if this schema remains at the level of the intersection of the signifiers and the thrust or tendency of need, where does it end? In the subject's identification with the Other, insofar as the latter articulates the distribution of the resources that are capable of responding to need. This isn't how it is, thanks to the sole fact that it is necessary to take the background of demand into account, even if it is only to explain the subject's articulation into an order that exists beyond the order of the real, which we call the symbolic order, and which complicates it, superimposes itself on it, but does not adhere to it.

However, already at this level, something of a natural, organic order intervenes, as soon as this simple state of the schema exists, and complicates it, at least in man.

The subject is here, the mythical child who acts as the background to our psychoanalytic speculations. He starts expressing his needs in the presence of his mother. It's here, in A, that he encounters the mother as a speaking subject, and it's here, in $s(A)$, that the message ends, at the point at which the mother satisfies him. As I have already pointed out, it's not at the point at which the mother does not satisfy him, frustrates him, that the problems begin. That would be too simple, although one always comes back to this, precisely because it is simple.

The interesting problem did not go undetected by a Winnicott, for example, whose mind and practice, as we know, cover the entire range of the current development and techniques of psychoanalysis up to and including an extremely precise consideration on the fantasmatic systems that are in the field bordering on psychosis. In his article on transitional objects, which I have mentioned to you, Winnicott shows with the greatest precision that the essential problem is to know how the child emerges from satisfaction, and not from frustration, to construct a world for himself.

462　　　Inasmuch as a world that comprises something beyond demand is articulated for a human subject, it's when demand is satisfied, and not when it's frustrated, that what Winnicott calls transitional objects appear, that is, these little objects that very early on we see assuming an extreme importance in the relationship with the mother – a piece of nappy that the child pulls at jealously, a scrap of anything, a rattle. It's essential to appreciate how early this transitional object is in the child's system of development.

That said, let's pause at frustration, that is, at what happens when the message does not arrive.

2

The relationship with the mother, where the mother imposes, more than her law, what I have called her omnipotence or capriciousness, is complicated by the fact that, as experience shows, the child – the human child and not just any young – is open to an imaginary-order relationship with the image of one's own body and the image of the other, and at a date we tried to determine three years ago when we were interested in the mirror stage.

The mirror stage hasn't just evaporated since. I am very fond of those of you who say that every year brings something different and that the system changes. It doesn't change, but I am simply trying to get you to cover the field. On our schema, we can see that the mirror stage is placed prior to what occurs on the line of the return from need, whether satisfied or not. The subject experiences, for example, reactions of disappointment, unease or dizziness in his own body in relation to the ideal image he has of it and which assumes a predominant value in him because of a feature of his organization that we have tied, with more or less justification, to the prematurity of his birth.

In short, from the outset we can see two circuits interfering with one another. The first is the symbolic circuit in which – let's say, so as to give you an idea, something familiar for you to hang your hat on – the subject's relationship with the infantile female superego is inscribed. There is, on the other hand, the imaginary relationship with the ideal self-image that finds itself more or less affected, even damaged, by frustrations or disappointments. Thus, it turns out that the circuit is being played out on two planes from the outset, a symbolic plane and an imaginary plane. On the one hand, the relationship to the primordial object – the mother or the Other as locus where the possibility of formulating need in signifiers is located. On the other, the image of the other, little *a*, where the subject has a kind of link to himself, to an image that represents the line of his own completion – imaginary completion, of course.

463

Everything that we have said since the beginning of the year, when we started to take things at the level of wit, has shown us the relevance of what this schema indicates, namely that nothing in mental life corresponding to what analytic experience gives us can be organized unless there exists, beyond the Other placed primordially in the position of omnipotence by its power – not of frustration, for that's insufficient, but of *Versagung*, with the ambiguity of promise and refusal that this word contains – the Other of this Other, as it were, that is, what makes it possible for the subject to become aware of this Other, the locus of speech, as itself symbolized.

You get the sense that the system of the familial Oedipal triangle comprises something more radical than anything that this social experiment of the family gives us, and indeed it is this that gives this Oedipal triangle and the Freudian discovery their permanence. This is why I told you that there the Father, with a capital F, is never just a father, but rather the dead father, the father as the vehicle of a signifier, a second-order signifier that authorizes and founds the entire system of signifiers and makes it possible for the first Other, that is, the first subject to whom the speaking subject addresses himself, itself to be symbolized.

The articulated, human world is able to assume its proper dimension solely at the level of this Other, the Other of the law properly so called, a law – I am going to insist on this – that is embodied. Experience shows us the extent to which an Other in the background in relation to the Other is indispensable and without which the universe of language cannot be articulated, this universe such as it shows itself to be effective in the structuration, not only of needs, but also of this thing called desire whose original dimensions I am trying to demonstrate to you this year.

If the Other qua locus of speech were able to be simply the locus of the sound of the bell I was talking about before, it would not be an Other strictly speaking, but only the organized locus of the system of signifiers that introduced order and regularity into the vital exchanges within a particular species.

It's difficult to see who could have organized this. It's possible to envisage that in a given society men full of benevolence spend their time planning it and getting it to work. It's even possible to say that this is one of the ideals of modern politics. It's just that that isn't what the Other is.

The Other isn't purely and simply the locus of this perfectly organized and fixed system. It is itself a symbolized Other, and this is what gives it its appearance of freedom. The Other, potentially the Father, the locus in which the law is articulated, is itself subject to the signifying articulation and, even more than subject to signifying articulation, it's marked by it, with the denaturing effect that the presence of signifiers entails.

What this is about is still far from having come to a state of perfect conceptualization, but, in the name of a working hypothesis to illustrate my thought, I would say that the effect of signifiers upon the Other, the mark that it suffers at this level, represents castration as such.

With respect to the triad of castration–frustration–privation, I have previously emphasized that in castration the agent is real, it's a real father that one needs, that the action is symbolic, and that

464

it bears upon an imaginary object. Here again we find that this is necessary. As soon as something real happens at the level of the law, and it matters not whether the father is more or less deficient here or whether something replaces him, takes his place, the following occurs – its background is reflected in the system of demand in which the subject is instated. Far from the system of demand being perfect, fully productive or in full use, it introduces into itself, in the background, the effect of signifiers on the subject, the mark of signifiers on the subject and the dimension of lack these signifiers introduce into the subject.

This introduced lack is symbolized as such in the system of signifiers as the effect of signifiers on the subject, that is, the signified. Strictly speaking, the signified does not arise so much from the depths, as if life lived on significations, but from language and signifiers, and this imprints this sort of effect that is called the signified upon life. This symbolization is primitive, as indicated by what I have contributed on castration.

What acts as a support for the symbolic action called castration is an image chosen from the imaginary system as its support. The symbolic action of castration chooses its sign, which is borrowed from the imaginary domain. Something in the image of the other is chosen to carry the mark of a lack, which is this very lack by which the living thing, because it's human – that is, has a relationship to language – sees itself as excluded from the omnitude of desires, as something limited, as local, as a creature, sometimes as a link in the lineage of life, one of those through whom life passes. Each animal is effectively only one of the individuals that realize the type, and in the name of this, in relation to the type, each individual may be considered already dead. We, too, we are already dead in relation to the movement of life. But through language, and by contrast with animals, we are capable of projecting this movement in its totality, and even more, in its totality as having arrived at its end.

This is exactly what Freud articulates in the notion of the death instinct. He means that for man life is already projected as having arrived at its conclusion, that is, at the point at which it returns to death. Man is this animal-being captured and articulated in a signifying system that makes it possible for him to dominate his immanence as a living thing and perceive himself as already dead. And he only does it in an imaginary, virtual or even speculative manner.

There is, of course, no corresponding experience of death, which is why it's symbolized in another way. It's symbolized by the specific organ where the thrust of life appears in its most tangible form. That

465

is why it's the phallus, insofar as it represents the rise of vital power, that takes its place in the order of signifiers and represents what is marked by signifiers – that which signifiers strike with the essential decline where this lack-in-being [*manque-à-être*], the scale of which signifiers introduce into the life of a subject, can be articulated.

This is what makes it possible for us to understand the order in which things presented themselves to us for analysis, once one has not simply gone from the School to the phenomenon, but starts with the phenomena as one sees them appear in the neuroses. They were the ground chosen to manifest that articulation in its essence, because it is here that it appears in its disorder. Our experience has proven to us that it has always been in disorder that we could more easily learn to uncover the inner workings and articulations of order.

What initially revealed itself, through Freud, to an experience that immediately made the underpinnings of the castration complex evident was the apprehension of subjects' symptoms.

3

What does 'symptom' mean? Where is it located on this schema?

It's located at the level of signification. This is what Freud contributed – a symptom is a signification, it's a signified. Far from involving solely the subject, his history and his entire anamnesis are implicated. That is why one can legitimately symbolize it in this place by a small $s(A)$, signified of the Other coming from the locus of speech.

466   But what Freud also taught us is that a symptom is never simple and that it's always overdetermined. There is no symptom whose signifier has not been provided by a prior experience. This experience is always located at the level involving what is suppressed. Now, the heart of everything that is suppressed in the subject is the castration complex. It's the signifier of barred A that is articulated in the castration complex but neither necessarily nor always totally articulated therein.

What is the famous traumatism we began with, the famous primal scene that enters into the subject's economy, which is in play at the heart and on the horizon of the discovery of the unconscious? What is it, if not a signifier whose impact on life I began describing to you earlier? The living being is grasped as living, as alive, but with this gap or distance that is precisely what constitutes both the signifying dimension's autonomy and the trauma or primitive scene. What is this, then, if it's not this life that grasps itself in a horrible apperception of itself, in its total foreignness and opaque brutality as the pure signifier of an intolerable existence for life itself as soon as it moves away from it to see the trauma and the primal scene? This is how life sees itself as a signifier in a pure state, which can in no way be articulated or resolved. When Freud begins to formulate what a symptom is, the signifiers in the background in relation to the signified are implicated by him in the formation of every symptom.

What we have been studying recently in the hysteric makes it possible for us to locate where the problem of neurosis is to be found. It stems from the relationship signifiers have with the position of the subject dependent on demand. This is why the hysteric has to articulate something that we will provisionally call her desire and this desire's object insofar as it isn't the object of need. This is what led me to insist somewhat on the so-called dream by the butcher's beautiful wife.

It appears there in a completely clear fashion, and Freud says it at the very dawn of psychoanalysis – that for the hysteric the question is one of making the object of desire subsist as distinct from and independent of the object of all need. The relationship to desire, to its constitution and to its being maintained in an enigmatic form in the background in relation to all demand is the hysteric's problem.

What is my hysteric's desire? It's what opens up for her, I won't say the universe, but an entire world that is already quite vast indeed, by virtue of what one can call the dimension of hysteria latent in every kind of human being in the world. The hysteric finds herself initially going straight to the point by means of anything that can pose as a question about her own desire, what I have called the x, the inexpressible desire, with whatever might happen in this order to all her hysterical brothers and sisters – and it's on that, as Freud formulates it, that hysterical identification is based. All hysterics respond to everything in the order of questions about desire as they currently arise for others, above all for hysterical others, but also for others who may be hysterical only occasionally, even in a latent manner, inasmuch as a hysterical way of posing the question is apparent in them.

For the hysteric, this question about her desire opens up the world to her, a world of identifications that place her in a special relationship with the mask, I mean with anything that in any way is able to fix and symbolize, according to a certain type, the question about desire. This question, which allies her to other hysterics and which is an appeal to hysterics as such, has essentially identified her with a sort of general mask under which every possible mode of lack is active.

467

We now come to the obsessional. The obsessional's structure, such as I am trying to make progress into it, is also indicated by a particular relationship to desire. This isn't the relationship d_x, but another, which today I will call d_o.

The obsessional's relationship to his desire is subject to the fact, which we are long familiar with thanks to Freud, that an early role is played therein by what is called the *Entbindung*, the unbinding of the drives, the isolation of destruction. The entire structure of the obsessional is, as such, determined by the fact that the initial access to his desire is through the Other's desire, as it is for every subject, and by the fact that the Other's desire is initially destroyed and annulled. In saying this, I am not saying anything terribly new, I am simply articulating it in a new way.

Those who already have an obsessional in hand may know that it's an essential trait of his condition that his own desire decreases, blinks, wavers and disappears the closer he gets to it. Desire shows itself here to bear the mark of the fact that desire has initially been encountered by the subject as something that destroys itself, inasmuch as it presented itself to him as that of his rival, and he responded to it in the style of this reaction of destruction that is subjacent to his relationship to the image of the other insofar as it dispossesses and ruins him. The obsessional's approach to his desire remains, therefore, struck by this mark such that every time he approaches it, it disappears.

468   This is what the author I am talking about and have been critiquing for several lessons perceives in the form of what he calls distance from the object, which he initially confuses with what he calls the object's destruction. He has the idea about the psychology of the obsessional that he is someone who has to perpetually defend himself from madness, defined as the object's destruction. That is only a projection which stems from the inadequacies of the said author's thought on the theoretical plan, but where personal factors also enter, for it's only a fantasy, a fantasy in some ways required by the imaginary perspective from which he engages with the solution to the problem of desire for the obsessional. Moreover, it's common experience that there isn't the slightest danger of psychosis for the typical obsessional, wherever you lead him – and I will tell you, when the moment comes, to what extent an obsessional differs in structure from a psychotic.

On the other hand, what has been perceived therein, although poorly translated, is that the obsessional only maintains a possible relationship with his desire from a distance. What has to be maintained for the obsessional is the distance from his desire and not the distance from the object. The object in this instance has quite

a different function. What experience shows us in the clearest of manners is that he has to maintain himself at a certain distance from his desire for this desire to subsist.

But there is another facet that can be observed in the clinical setting, concretely, when the obsessional establishes a relationship with the other that is fully formulated at the level of demand, whether it concerns his mother, initially, or his spouse. What can this term 'spouse' mean for us analysts? It becomes fully articulated at the level at which we are trying to situate things. He or she is the one with whom it's always necessary, one way or another, whether one likes it or not, to return to being in a relationship of demand. Even if one shuts up over a whole range of things, it's never painless. Demand demands to be pushed to the end.

What happens on the plane of the obsessional's relationships with his or her spouse? It's very exactly this, which is the most subtle thing to see, but you will observe it if you make the effort – the obsessional spends his time destroying the Other's desire. Entering into the obsessional's domain ends, in the normal case, if one gets taken in by it, with a muted attack or permanent erosion which tends to culminate in the abolition, devaluation and disparagement in the other of what is his own desire.

There are no doubt nuances. These are terms that require practice at handling, but in the absence of these terms, nothing would make it possible for us even to perceive the true nature of what is happening. I have already highlighted elsewhere, in the obsessional's infancy, the quite special, accentuated character that the articulation of demand assumes for him early on.

You are beginning to be able to situate him on this schema. This small child is always demanding something, and the surprising thing is that of all children who effectively spend their time demanding something, he is the one whose demand is always experienced, and by those who have the best intentions, as being properly speaking unbearable. He is a pest, as we say. It's not that he asks for things that are more extraordinary than others do. It's in the way he demands them. The specific character of the formulation of demand for one who is already obsessional when it manifests itself at the time of the decline of the Oedipus complex or in the so-called latency period lies in the subject's relationship to demand.

As for our hysteric, we have seen that in order to sustain her enigmatic desire, the little a for her is employed as an artifice. We can represent it with two parallel tensions – one at the level of the idealizing formation, $[\$ \lozenge a]$, the other at the level of the identification with a little other, $i(a)$. Think of Dora's feelings towards Herr

469

K. Incidentally, every hysteric has a comparable support in one or other phases of her history and comes to play the same role as *a*.

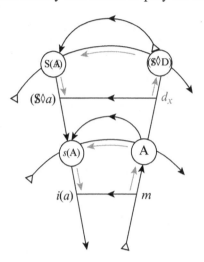

The hysteric's circuit

The obsessional does not take the same route. He is more centred on coming to terms with the problem of his desire. He starts from a different place and with other elements. It's in a certain early and essential relationship with his demand, [$ ◊ D], that he is able to maintain the necessary distance for this desire – annulled in its essence, this blind desire whose position must be assured – to be possible for him somewhere, but from a distance. We are going to circumscribe the obsessional's relationship with his desire. The subject's specific relationship to his demand is one of its first traits. There are more.

What is an obsession? You know the importance that the verbal form has therein, to the point where one can say that an obsession is always verbalized. Freud is in no doubt about this. Even when dealing with latent obsessional behaviour, he only considers that it has revealed its structure when it adopts the form of a verbal obsession. He even goes so far as to say that in the treatment of an obsessional neurosis the first steps have been taken only when one has obtained the full development of the subject's symptoms, which can present itself as a worsening, clinically.

What is at question in all obsessional forms is well and truly artic-ulated destruction. Is there a need to insist upon the verbal character of the formulas of undoing that are a part of the structure of the obsession itself? Everybody knows that what makes its essence and power phenomenologically anxiety-provoking for the subject is that

470

it's about destruction through words and signifiers. The subject finds himself prey to what one calls magical – I don't know why, why not quite simply say 'verbal'? – destruction of the Other, which is given in the very structure of symptoms.

You have seen the hysteric's circuit which terminates on the two planes – idealization or identification at the upper level is the symbolization paralleling what takes place on the imaginary plane. If I have allowed myself to use this schema to the end and inscribed the destructive schema of the relationship to the other on it, I would say that for the obsessional the circuit goes something like this.

471

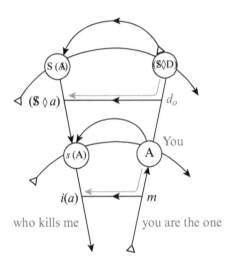

The obsessional's circuit

The fear of harming the Other with one's thoughts, tantamount to saying with one's words, brings us to an entire phenomenology which it would be worth dwelling on for a good bit of time. I don't know if you've ever been interested in the theme of blasphemy. It makes a very good introduction to verbal obsessions. What is blasphemy? I'd very much like some theologian to give me an answer. Let's say that blasphemy diminishes a pre-eminent signifier, where it's a question of ascertaining at what level of signifying authorization, as it were, it is located. This signifier is related to the supreme signifier called the Father, with which it should not be completely confused, even if it plays a homologous role. That God has a relationship to signifying creation as such isn't in doubt, nor is the fact that blasphemy is situated solely in this dimension. Blasphemy diminishes this signifier to the rank of object. In a way, it identifies the Logos with its metonymic effect and brings it down a notch. This remark undoubtedly does not constitute a full response to the question of blasphemy, but it's surely an approach to the phenomenon of the verbal sacrilege that can be observed in obsessionals.

As always, it's again in Freud that we find the most colossally exemplary things. Recall the episode in the case of the *Rat Man* of this furious anger that grips him towards his father at the age of four, if my memory is correct. He starts rolling around on the ground, calling him, 'You towel, you plate, and so on.' There is a veritable collision and collusion between the essential 'you' of the Other and this diminished effect of the introduction of signifiers into the human world, which is called an object and especially an inert object, an object of exchange, of equivalences. The multitude of substantives summoned up in the child's rage indicate this well enough. It's not a question of knowing whether the father is a lamp, a plate or a towel. It's about bringing the Other down to the level of an object and destroying it.

Since we're obliged to leave it there for today, I would say that what is happening here, the structure of which we shall see next time, shows us that it is only with a particular articulation of signifiers that the obsessional subject manages to preserve the Other, so much so that the effect of destruction is also the means by which he aspires to sustain it by virtue of the articulation of signifiers. You find here the very fabric of the world in which the obsessional lives. The obsessional is a man who lives amongst signifiers. He is very firmly installed amongst them. There is absolutely nothing to fear with respect to psychosis. This signifier suffices to preserve the dimension of the Other in him, but it is a dimension that in some way is idolized [*idôlatrée*]. French makes it possible to formulate this in a manner that I once introduced here – 'Thou art the one who will . . .'. That's what the subject formulates to the Other.

For the obsessional that is where it stops. Full speech in which the subject's engagement is articulated into a fundamental relationship with the Other can't be achieved, unless by this repetition that a comedian used to make use of. 'To be or not . . .', and the guy scratches his head before continuing, 'To be or not, to be or not', and so on. And it's in repeating it that he finds the end of the sentence, '*Tu es celui qui me, tu es celui qui me, tu es celui qui me tues*', 'You are the one who, you are the one who, you are the one who kills me.'

Here the French language gives us a fundamental schema of the obsessional relationship with the Other. The formulation that founds it ends on the Other's destruction, but because this is a signifying articulation, it makes the Other subsist as a result.

Within this formulation we see what the place of the phallus

472

signifier is with respect to being and having, which is where we stopped at the end of our last session. This will enable us to see the difference between a solution that enables the obsessional to show what really is his relationship to the phallus, as the signifier of the Other's desire, and one that consists in satisfying demand in a sort of imaginary mirage by granting him his object through the symbolization of an imaginary fantasy by the analyst. This is the dimension in which the entire observation that we have been critiquing unfolds. The illusory solution consists, in short, in saying to the woman, 'You envy the penis? Well then . . .'. This is what Casimir-Perier said to a guy who had him cornered up against a streetlamp: 'What do you want?' The guy replies, 'Freedom!' 'Well then, you have it,' Casimir says to him, slips through his legs and goes off, leaving him dumbstruck.

This may not be quite what we would expect from an analytic solution. The very termination of the case by a euphoric identification, intoxicating for the subject, the description of which completely matches a masculine ideal located in the analyst, perhaps brings a change in the subject's equilibrium, but this is surely not a genuine response to the obsessional's question.

18 June 1958

XXVII

EXITING VIA THE SYMPTOM

From the speech of the Other to the unconscious
The significance of regression
Why we are not monkeys
The psychotic and the Other's desire
The neurotic and the image of the other

We got to the point last time of starting to circle around the constellation of the obsessional's desire.

I spoke to you in this regard about the position of his demand, whose especially insistent character that renders it so difficult to tolerate is experienced very early by the Other, about his need to destroy the Other's desire, and about the function of some of his fantasies. My intention today is thus under way.

In the work I have chosen to make the object of a critique that stems less from a polemic than from a systematic analysis of all that emerges from what the author himself formulates, it isn't pointless that the phallic fantasy should present itself in the form of penis envy in the woman over the course of the analysis of an obsessional neurosis. This is not the work that will prove that I give an exaggerated importance to the phallus signifier. But the importance of the phallus signifier is not all I teach you. There's also the question of knowing how to make use of it – without, for all that, going in for a facile little game of criticizing and judging from the outside the outcome of a treatment that, in any case, is presented as unfinished and that we have not entered into. Let's simply say that none of what I give you as the significant elements in the direction of the treatment are not to be found. The general direction of the treatment is remarkable for its hesitations, even for a direction that is frankly opposed to the one that to us might seem logical.

My critique never starts just with the case considered as a factual report, but with the author's own questions, which you will always find expressed at the right moment, for it's one of the properties of the human mind that common sense in particular is, as has been said with reason and not without irony, the most fairly distributed thing in the world. There is no doubt that what is an obstacle here for us was already an obstacle in the mind of authors, and in this case these obstacles are clearly articulated. There are questions, there are even remarks concerning the paradoxical outcome, the non-outcome of what one was looking for, and there are, finally, contradictions which the author does not perhaps give as much importance to as he might have, but which may be described as contradictions since they appear in black and white in his text.

I will first go straight to the heart of the matter and raise the difference between, on the one hand, what is represented as articulated, and not as articulable, and, on the other hand, what the aim was and what was actually achieved in this treatment.

474

1

Let's take as our point of departure our schema on which a number of positions he completes appear, positions that enable us to orientate ourselves in what we are more familiar with. These positions are represented there in a particular order and topology.

Let's once more ask ourselves what the line at the top of our schema is. It's a signifying line, in that it's structured like a language. Also, while it's structured like a language, it's a sort of phrase that the subject is unable to articulate, which we have to help him articulate and which in sum structures the neuroses overall.

A neurosis is not identical to an object, it's not a kind of parasite, foreign to the personality of the subject. It's an analytic structure which is in his acts and his conduct. Progress in our conception of neurosis has shown that it's not only made up of symptoms that are decomposable into their signifying elements and the signified effects of these signifiers – since this is how I have retranslated what Freud articulates – but that the entire personality of the subject bears the mark of these structural relationships. In the way it's employed here, the word 'personality' goes well beyond its primary acceptation, with what that comprises that is static and confluent with what is called character. It's not that. It's the personality in the sense in which it designates, in behaviour, in relationships with the Other and with others, a certain movement that is always found to be the same, a scansion, a certain way of moving from the other to the Other and moreover to an Other that is always and endlessly being re-found and forming the very variations of obsessional action.

475

Obsessional or hysterical behaviour is overall structured like a language. What does that mean? It isn't enough to say that beyond articulated language, beyond discourse, all of a subject's acts would have this sort of equivalence to language that is there in what is called '*un geste*', gesture, inasmuch as a gesture is not simply a well-defined movement, but is also actually a signifier. The expression that fits perfectly is '*une geste*', a gest in the sense of a '*chanson de geste*', a gest such as *The Song of Roland* – that is, the sum of one's history.

It's ultimately speech, if you will. The sum of the neurotic's behaviour presents itself like speech, and even like full speech, in the sense in which we saw its original mode in the engagement in the form of a discourse. It's full, but entirely cryptographic speech, unknown to the subject as to its sense, even though he pronounces it with all his being, in everything he manifests, everything he evokes and has ineluctably realized down a certain path of completion and incompletion, if nothing in this order of oscillation called analysis intervenes. It's speech pronounced by the barred subject, barred to himself, which we call the unconscious. It's what we represent in the form of a sign, $.

We have now come to the point of introducing a distinction at the level of the Other. We have defined the Other as the locus of speech. This Other is instituted and takes shape through the sole fact that the subject speaks. By virtue of this sole fact, the big Other is born as the locus of speech. That does not mean, though, that it is realized as a subject in its alterity. The Other is invoked whenever there is speech. I think that there is no need to go back over this as I have insisted on it enough. But this beyond that is articulated in the upper line of our schema is the Other of the Other.

This is speech that is articulated on the horizon of the Other. The Other of the Other is the locus in which the Other's speech takes shape as such. There is no reason for it to be closed off from us. That the Other as locus of speech is immediately and effectively given to us as a subject, a subject who thinks of us as his Other, is even the root of the intersubjective relation. This is the principle of all strategy. When you play chess with someone, you attribute to him as many calculations as you make yourself. Well then, whereas we can say that this Other of the Other should be the most transparent to us and given along with the very dimension of the Other, why do we claim that this Other of the Other is the locus in which the discourse of the unconscious is articulated – articulated but not articulable by us? Why do we have to? By what right?

476   It's very simple. The conditions of human life mean that the latter is engaged in the conditions of speech, and we are subject to the Other by the conditions of demand, but without knowing what our

demand is for the Other. Why don't we know this? What gives it this opacity? These things are self-evident, but they're still self-evident things whose coordinates are not the least useful things to spell out, for we are always happy to obscure them in the form of premature objectifications.

We don't know how this Other, which becomes *unbewusst* and assumes a paradoxical position in discourse, receives our demand or intervenes in our strategy. That's what I mean when I say that the unconscious is the Other's discourse. This happens virtually on the horizon of the Other of the Other, inasmuch as it's here that the speech of the Other is produced insofar as it becomes our unconscious, that is, what necessarily presents itself in us solely by virtue of the fact that in this locus of speech we bring to life an Other capable of responding to us. This is why it's opaque for us, it's that there is something in it that we are not aware of and that separates us from its response to our demand. This is nothing other than what is called his desire.

This remark, self-evident in appearance only, derives its value as a function from the fact that this desire is located between the Other as pure and simple locus of speech and the Other insofar as it's a being of flesh whom we are at the mercy of for the satisfaction of our demand. That this desire is located there conditions its relationship to this symbolization of the signifier's action which forms what we call a subject, and which we symbolize with our $.

The subject is something other than a *soi-même*, for which in English one uses the elegant word 'self'. The fact of saying it in English isolates it and makes it possible to clearly distinguish what it signifies, namely what is irreducible in the individual's presence in the world. This self* becomes a subject, properly speaking, and a barred subject in the sense in which we symbolize it, inasmuch as it's marked by the condition that subordinates it not only to the Other as locus of speech, but also to the Other as itself. This is not the subject of the relationship to the world, of the eye's relationship to the world or of the subject–object relationship which is that of knowledge [*connaissance*]. This is the subject who is born at the moment of the human individual's emergence in the conditions of speech, and insofar, therefore, as it's marked by the Other, itself conditioned and marked by the conditions of speech.

What do we see, then, on this horizon that is rendered opaque by the obstacle of the Other's desire? Insofar as the Other no longer responds, the subject is referred back to his own demand, he is placed in a certain relationship to his own demand which is designated here by the symbol of the little lozenge that I explained to you last time. Here, 'big A is not answering' [*'grand A ne répond plus'*],

477

a very famous sentence with different initials. At the level of the subject, what tends to be produced on the horizon is that the subject is referred to a confrontation with his own demand, in the forms of signifiers that are, as it were, encompassing in relation to the subject and that the subject himself becomes the sign of. It's the horizon of this non-response from the Other that we see delineated in an analysis, inasmuch as at the start the analyst initially comes to be nothing other than the locus of speech, than an ear that listens and does not respond.

This is what is going to push the subject to detach himself from these forms of demand that appear to us implicitly in his discourse in the form of what we call anal phase, oral phase and whatever kind of phase you like. What do we mean when we speak of these phases? Don't forget that our subject does not progressively return to the state of an infant before our eyes. We do not go in for a fakir-like operation that would see the subject going back over the course of time and being reduced at the end to the seed that created him. It's all about signifiers. What we call oral phase or anal phase is the manner in which the subject articulates his demand via the appearance in his discourse, in the broadest sense of the term, in the manner in which his neurosis presents itself before us, of signifiers that were formed at such-and-such a stage of his development and that he uses to formulate his demand in recent or older phases.

What is called fixation is the prevalence retained by this or that form of oral, anal or other signifier, with all the nuances that you have learnt to formulate. It is the special importance that certain systems of signifiers have retained. Regression is what occurs when these signifiers are returned to in the subject's discourse by virtue of the fact that speech, simply through being speech, without having anything in particular to demand, appears in the dimension of demand. This is how the entire perspective is retroactively opened up to this condition of demand in which the subject has lived since his early and most tender childhood.

The whole question is what we do with regression. We are there to respond to it, or to say what happens when we don't respond to it, and whatever else we can do. This is the aim that is worth achieving.

478   Regression is the regression of discourse. The signifiers involved belong to the structure of discourse, and that's where we will always discover them. This is what is represented by these two lines.

$$\Sigma$$

$$\frac{S_1 \text{----} S_2 \text{----} S_3 \text{----} S_4}{S_2 \text{----} S_3 \text{----} S_4 \text{----} S_5}$$

The upper line is the line of signifiers. Underneath we find significations, always produced according to the law of the signifying chain. These two things are equivalent – the anticipation of the signifying sequence, where the signifying chain opens out before it the horizon of its own completion, and at the same time its retroaction once the signifying term has arrived that, as it were, completes the sentence and brings it about that what is produced at the level of the signified always has a retroactive function. Here, S_2 is already taking shape by anticipation when S_1 starts and is only completed when S_2 retroacts upon S_1. A certain lag always exists between signifier and signification, and it's what makes all signification – insofar as it's not natural signification linked to a completely momentary beginning of the instance of need in a subject – an essentially metonymic factor related to what binds the signifying chain together and constitutes it as such. These links and knots are indicated, for the moment and so as to differentiate them, by a sigma, if you will, thus designating this [plane] beyond the signifying chain.

Confronting the subject with demand brings about a reduction in the discourse in which we implicitly discern these elementary signifiers in what forms the crux of our experience. This is the way we re-encounter the same structural laws in all the subject's conduct, in the manner in which he sometimes expresses it to us, down to the scansion or the motor articulation of his discourse, inasmuch as a stammering, a mumbling or any other speech difficulty, as I have expressed myself elsewhere, may be significant for us and refer to a signifier of demand as oral or anal lack.

The small group of studies directed by the friendliest of my colleagues, namely Lagache, made the discovery, with an astonishment that must have arisen from a permanent misunderstanding, that everywhere we encounter the word '*instinct*' in the French translation of Freud, one never finds anything in the German text other than the term '*Trieb*'. I translate it as '*pulsion*', which, to be honest, rather obscures the thing. The English term is 'drive', whereas we have nothing in French able to translate it. The scientific word would be '*tropisme*', designating certain irresistible attractions considered as irreducible to physicochemical attraction, which supposedly operates in animal behaviour. This word is said to make it possible to exorcize the finalistic side that is always there in the term '*instinct*'. What we encounter here in the Freudian notion of *Trieb* is also of this order. One could translate it by '*attirance*', 'attraction', except that the human being is not this obscure subject that we encounter in gregarious forms of organic attraction towards an element of climate, for example, or of any other nature.

479

It's obvious that this is not where our interest develops, we in the field that we are called to explore in analysis, where we are led to speak of these various oral, anal, genital and other phases. In analytic theory, effectively, a certain necessity places the subject in a relationship of subordination, dependence, organization and attraction – in relation to what? To signifiers borrowed from the array of a certain number of his own organs.

This is to say nothing other than that an oral or anal fixation that survives in an adult subject depends on a certain imaginary relation. But what I am also articulating is that the latter is brought to the function of a signifier. If [this relation] were not isolated as such, mortified, it could not have the economic action that it has in the subject, and for a very simple reason, which is that the images are only ever tied to the arousal and satisfaction of need. Now, no one ever neglects to say that in analysis the subject remains attached to oral images there where there is no question of food, anal images there where there is no question of excrement. It's therefore the case that these images exist outside their text, that it's not purely and simply a question of need and that they have assumed another function. It's the signifying function that is involved. The drive, as such, is precisely the manipulable expression of concepts that are valid for us, and which express the subject's dependence in relation to a certain signifier.

What's important is that the subject's desire, encountered as beyond demand, renders it opaque to our demand and installs its own discourse as something that, even though necessary to our structure, is in certain respects impenetrable to us, which makes it an unconscious discourse. This desire, which is its condition, is therefore itself subject to the existence of a certain signifier effect, which I explained to you starting in January under the name of the paternal metaphor.

2

This metaphor is established on the mother's original, opaque and obscure desire, initially completely closed off to the subject, whereas, on the horizon, the Name-of-the-Father appears as the support of the order instituted by the signifying chain. I have already symbolized it for you in the relationship between two signifiers, one being in two different positions – the Name-of-the-Father over the Mother's Desire and the Mother's Desire over its symbolization.

What it determined as a signified is produced through a metaphoric effect.

$$\frac{S}{S'} \cdot \frac{S'}{x} \rightarrow S\left(\frac{S}{\text{phallus}}\right)$$

Where the Name-of-the-Father is lacking, the metaphorical effect is not produced and I cannot manage to bring to the light of day what makes the x designate the phallus signifier. This is what occurs in psychosis, insofar as the Name-of-the-Father is rejected, is the object of an original *Verwerfung* and does not enter into the cycle of signifiers, and this is also why the Other's desire, namely the mother's desire, is not symbolized there.

If we had to represent the place of psychosis on the schema, we would say that this desire as such – I don't mean as existing, for everyone knows that even the mothers of psychotics have a desire, though this is not always certain – is not symbolized in the system of the psychotic subject, and, as a consequence, the speech of the Other does not pass into his unconscious at all, but the Other as the locus of speech speaks to him incessantly. This does not necessarily mean you or me, but more or less the totality of what is offered to him as the field of perception.

This field speaks to him of us, naturally, and also, to take the first example that comes to mind, the well-known one that was recounted to us last night, a red car may mean for the delusional subject that he is immortal. Everything addresses him because nothing in the order of the symbolic organization intended to send the Other there where he should be, that is, into his unconscious, is achieved. The Other speaks to him in a manner homogeneous with the first and original speech, which is the speech of demand. This is why everything is in voices, and why the 'it speaks' that is in the unconscious for the neurotic subject is on the outside for the psychotic subject. There are no grounds for astonishment that it speaks and that it speaks out loud in the most natural manner. If the Other is the locus of speech, that's where it speaks, and that's where it resounds in all directions.

We find an extreme case of this at the height of the outbreak of psychosis, where, as I have always formulated it for you, what is *verworfen*, or rejected from the symbolic, reappears in the real. The real in question here consists of the hallucinations, that is, the Other insofar as it speaks. It's always in the Other that it speaks, but here it takes the form of the real. The psychotic subject is in no doubt that it's the Other who speaks to him, and who speaks to him with all the signifiers that one can collect by the bucketful in the human world, since everything we are surrounded by has the character of being marked by signifiers. Think of all the posters around our streets.

The qualities of desertion and dissolution will be more or less pronounced according to the state of the psychosis. As we see it, and as Freud articulates it for us, what psychosis articulates into is designed precisely to supplete this absence at its organized point, I mean dependent upon the signifying structure of the Other's desire. The forms of psychosis from the most benign to the extreme state of dissolution present us with a pure and simple discourse of the Other, scanded here, in $s(A)$, in the form of a signification.

Two years ago, I showed you some very curious cases of the decomposition of speech, which via the structure presented to us on this graph – I couldn't show you at the time – turn out to have arisen from a code of messages about the code. What is sent from A is everything that the subject possesses for bringing the Other's discourse to life. Schreber's 'fundamental language', each word of which itself comprises a kind of definition which comes with the issuing of the word itself, is a code of messages about the code. Conversely, these phrases, 'How is it . . .', 'You have only to . . . me', 'Perhaps he would like . . .' – and even the 'He would like' is too much – are a series of messages that only aim at what in the code refers to the message. The particles, personal pronouns and auxiliary verbs designate the place of the messenger. This can be precisely recorded on the graph, but as I do not want to linger too long, I refer you to my article on the psychoses that is going to be published, in which I synthesize my course from two years ago and what I am doing for you this year.

Take the delusion of jealousy. Freud formulates it as the subject's negation of a fundamental 'I love him' concerning less the homosexual subject than the semblable subject, which is, of course, thereby homosexual. Freud says, 'It is not me he loves, it's her.' What does that mean, if not that, in order to create an obstacle to the pure and simple outbreak of the speech of interpretation, the delusion of jealousy attempts to restore, to restitute the Other's desire. The structure of the delusion of jealousy consists precisely in attributing to the Other a desire – a kind of desire in outline, roughed out in the imaginary – that is the subject's desire. It's attributed to the Other – 'It is not me he loves, it's my spouse, he is my rival.' As a psychotic I try to establish in the Other this desire that is not given to me because I am psychotic, because this essential metaphor that gives the Other's desire its primordial signifier, the phallus signifier, has not been produced anywhere.

This phallus signifier nevertheless remains something fairly obscure to be acknowledged as essential, and in some way preferentially so in relation to all sorts of other objects that we occasionally see playing a homologous role. The phallus signifier is open to all sorts of equivalences, with the excremental signifier, for example, or the breast signifier, specifically the extremity of the breast, every

482

infant's object. It can be very difficult for you to perceive what gives
the phallus its privilege – it's obviously through being in a certain
place in what has the highest functions in the individual's relationship to the species, namely what one calls the genital phase.

It's for this reason that it's more especially dependent than any
other on a function of significance. Other objects – the maternal
breast or this part of the body which, in the form of excreta, present
themselves as able to be an occasion of loss for the subject – are, to
a certain degree, given to the outside as objects, whereas the phallus
is currency in the love transaction and needs to pass to the state of a
signifier in order to serve as a means in the way scoria or shells serve
as objects of exchange in certain remote tribes. That's already in the
natural order.

However, it's not quite the same for the phallus. In its real, organic
form, that of the penis or of what corresponds to it in the woman,
for it to become a detachable object, fantasmatically or otherwise,
there has to be a lot more than for the aforementioned objects
which are predetermined for this. One cannot insist too much on the
enigma contained in the castration complex or *Penisneid*, inasmuch
as what is involved here really is very much attached to the body,
and that, after all, is under no greater threat than any member, arm,
leg or even nose or ears.

This element is only a point of sensuality on the body, and this is
how the subject discovers it in the first place. Masturbatory autoerotism, which effectively plays such a big role in the subject's history,
is not at all in itself liable to trigger such catastrophes as those we
know about through experience, so long as the organ is not captured
in the play of signifiers, in the paternal metaphor, in the maternal or   483
paternal prohibition. This organ is for the subject originally nothing
but a point of sensuality on his own body, in his organic relationship to himself, and much less subject to obsolescence than any of
the other elements that have assumed the significance of a signifier
in earlier demands. It's precisely for this reason that the grasp of the
metaphorical chain must be playing its role, more for it than for any
other, in making it a signifier, which as a result becomes the privileged signifier of the relationship to the Other of the Other, and this
makes it a central signifier of the unconscious.

We can also grasp here how the dimension that analysis opened
up for us on this subject was completely unexpected in comparison
to everything that had been formulated previously, if one thinks
that it's only an organ with which a living being maintains innocent relations. Let's not forget how it is in our fraternal species,
the monkeys. It suffices to visit the Vincennes Zoo around the little
trenches circling a particular platform to appreciate with what

calmness this brave and brazen tribe of baboons and others, into which we would be wrong to project our own anxieties, pass their days engaged in florid sex, without the slightest concern in the world for what the neighbours think, except to help them from time to time with their collective festivities. There is a world between the relationship that this animal species, more or less erect in its posture, maintains with what hangs down below its belly and the relationship that man maintains with the same. Originally and signage-wise, this relationship makes the phallus the object of a cult. From the beginning of time, the erection as such has been a signifier, and it's not for nothing, we can sense it, that in our very ancient cultures the raised stone has such an impact as a signifier in the grouping of the human collectivity.

The emergence of the phallus in this essential role is certainly not primordial, but depends on something else, namely on its metaphorical passage to the rank of signifier, on which will depend, in turn, all possibility of situating the Other's desire, insofar as the subject has to find the place of his own desire therein and has to find out how to signify it. The encounter between the subject's desire and the Other's desire is subject to accidents, and this is where, quite naturally, we see the phallus signifier functioning for a subject who is placed in typical, abnormal, deficient or pathological conditions with respect to the four cardinal points of the definition of desire.

This constellation remains complete in the neurotic. It's incomplete for the psychotic.

484

3

As I've said, the obsessional is someone who, in this relationship to the Other's desire, finds himself primordially, originally marked by the defusion of instincts. Its first outcome, the result at the beginning, the one that is going to condition all later difficulties, will be to undo the Other's desire. What does that mean, if we give what I have just been formulating here its full meaning?

Undoing the Other's desire is not the same thing as having been unable to grasp the Other's desire owing to the inadequacies or deficiencies of the metaphorical act, of the Name-of-the-Father. Moreover, if in a real that is more or less delusional the Other's desire, instituted and symbolized by the phallus, is negated as such, the subject's original relationship to his own desire will be founded on the disavowal of the Other's desire. The term '*Verneinung*' applies here in the sense in which Freud shows us its two sides – that it's articulated, symbolized, but carries the sign 'No'. That's what the obsessional finds himself confronted with as the very basis of his position, and to which he responds with formulas of suppletion, of compensation.

I'm not saying anything new here, I am only rearticulating the triad emphasized by every author with respect to the obsessional – undoing, isolation, defence reaction. Observe simply that for us to be able to speak about undoing, it must involve signifiers, because one doesn't undo anything that is not a signifier. There is not the slightest conceivable undoing at the animal level, and if we did find something that resembles it, we would say that it's the beginnings of symbolic formation. Undoing is not simply the effacement of the trace, which I have spoken to you about, but on the contrary it's placing an elementary signifier in parentheses to say, 'That's not it' – but having said this, it's still posed as a signifier. It's still a matter of signifiers.

If the obsessional is led to undo so many things, it's because they are things that can be formulated. Namely, a demand, as we know. Except it's a demand for death. This demand for death, above all when it's premature, results in the Other's destruction, first and foremost the Other's desire and, along with the Other, equally, whatever the subject may have to articulate himself into. As a consequence, it's all the more necessary to isolate the parts of discourse to be retained in comparison with those that absolutely must be effaced and undone so that the subject himself is not thereby destroyed. It's a perpetual game of yes and no, of separating and sorting, of what in his speech and in his very demand destroys him, in contrast with what can preserve him and is also necessary for the preservation of the Other, for the Other only exists as such at the level of signifying articulation.

485

The obsessional subject is caught in this contradiction. He is constantly occupied in maintaining the Other and making him subsist through imaginary formulations which occupy him more than anyone. They are established to support the Other who is perpetually in danger of falling, of succumbing to the demand for death, for this Other is the essential condition for him to maintain himself as a subject. He could not subsist as a subject were this Other effectively undone.

What most particularly presents itself at the signifying level as having been undone is what marks the place of the Other's desire as such, namely the phallus. The d_0 I spoke about last time, which situates the obsessional's desire, is equivalent to the undoing of the phallus. Everything in analysis revolves around something that has the closest of relationships with the signifier. The resulting method is one that takes the function of the phallus as a signifier into account, while the other, for having failed to elucidate it, is thereby reduced to groping around in the dark.

What does this difference consist in? You will find the golden rule for it if you make the effort to read the article that I referred you to, at the risk of creating a gigantic demand of the publisher. But perhaps this risk is not so great. This rule of demarcation demands that one respond to the question of the basis on which, on what premises, the subject is liable to enter into a completed and complete relationship with his own desire. My response is that the subject, insofar as he must assume his genital desire as a human subject and not just as an animal, must make the phallus signifier function as an essential signifier of this desire. It's because the phallus signifier is there in the circuit of the subject's unconscious articulation that the human subject can be human, even when he fucks.

That doesn't mean that the human subject can't occasionally fuck like an animal. It's even an ideal fidgeting away in the very depths of the hopes of human subjects. I don't know whether the thing is often achieved, though some people have boasted that they have got to that point, and one does not see why one would not believe them, but what does it matter? For us, experience shows us that it's subject to much greater difficulties, which are signifier difficulties.

The endless ambiguities that surface with respect to the genital stage and the phallic stage – has either been attained? does the child attain the genital stage before the latency period? or is this simply a phallic stage? and so on – would perhaps be less obscure if one were to appreciate that 'phallic stage' simply means access to genital desire at the level of signification. The two things are different. On a first approach, it was possible to say that the child manages to accede to the phallic stage only, and this is very probably true, even though one can debate the point whether autoerotic activity is genital – which, ultimately, is also true. But that's not what is important for us. It's not a matter of genital desire that seems to appear, effectively, as representing the first spurt of physiological evolution, but of its structuration on the phallic plane, and this is what is subsequently decisive for neurosis.

It's a question of realizing something at the level of the unconscious, which is equivalent to what, at the lower level [of the graph], is full speech, there where the discourse articulated in the locus of the Other returns to the subject as a signified, involving the ego that the subject has concretely located in relation to the image of the other. At the upper level, attaining unconscious articulation assumes that the circuit, which starts from the subject's confrontation with his completed demand, is formulated in a desire that is articulated as such and satisfies the subject, to which the subject is

486

identical, and terminates in the place of the Other, who, here, is a human being marked by language and the drama of the castration complex, in other words, another me. What is formulated here is not 'I am the phallus', but, on the contrary, 'I am there in the very place that the phallus occupies in the articulation of signifiers.' This is the full meaning of '*Wo Es war, soll Ich werden.*'

The subject caught in the movement of signifiers must come to think, not that he is what he was confronted with as a child, the signifier of desire that took the total object, the mother, this phallus, away from him, but that he is merely subject to the requirement that this phallus occupy a certain place. It's only on the basis of the realization that he is not it that the subject is able to accept what over the entire process has been profoundly called into question, namely, to accept having it when he has it and not having it when he does not have it. This locates him in this place, S(A̶), in the articulation of the upper signifying chain. Only the elucidation of the subject's relationship to the phallus, insofar as he is not it but must come to its place, is properly suited to make it possible to conceptualize the ideal achievement that Freud formulates with his *Wo Es war soll Ich werden*.

That is the necessary condition for orientating our interventions and technique. How do we get to this point? This will be the aim of my Seminar next year, which I will call 'Desire and Its Interpretation'. What are the directions and directives that give us access to this final message designated by the Freudian formula with its pithy, pre-Socratic turn? We'll try to spell this out. In the absence of such access, what is produced is very precisely what neurosis, or any other anomalous form of evolution, spontaneously realizes.

For the hysteric, the place of desire is located in a deep incertitude which obliges him or her to take a detour and which she or he takes following the model of what makes it possible for him or her to situate his or her ego. Like all subjects, the hysteric fixes the place of his ego by detouring via the image of the other. It's characteristic of the hysteric to obtain the place for desire in exactly the same way at the upper level. The hysteric separates herself from and turns away from the Other and from the signified of the Other so as to come to locate herself in a certain ideal type by means of an image with which she identifies. It's by an analogous detour, as I have explained to you, that Dora identifies with Herr K. in order to locate the point on which the question of her desire bears, namely – how is it possible to desire a woman when one is impotent?

For the obsessional, the procedure is the same, with one small difference. Whereas the hysteric tries to locate the difficulties of her position at the level of the ideal, of the mask of identification, the obsessional, on the contrary, places himself at what can be called the

487

stronghold of his ego in an attempt to find the place of his desire. Hence these famous Vauban-like fortifications which I have spoken about elsewhere, these fortresses inside which a desire always under the threat of destruction barricades itself, and which are constructed on the model of his ego and in relation to the image of the other.

The obsessional's relationship to the image of the other consists very precisely in the signifier phallus insofar as it is always under the threat of destruction because it is caught in the negation of rediscovering it in the relationship with the Other. For every obsessional, man or woman, at some moment in their history you will always see appearing the essential role of identification with the other, a semblable, a friend, a brother scarcely older, a friend the same age, who, in every case, has for him the prestige of being more virile and of having the power. The phallus appears here in a form that is not symbolic but imaginary. We can say that the subject complements himself with an image stronger than himself, an image of power.

It's not I who formulate this, you will see it in its place in the article that I was quoting from, for functionally it is essential enough for it to be recognized by those who have been inspired by their own experience of these subjects. The emphasis is put on the image of the other as a phallic form, this time in the imaginary sense. That is what here takes on the value and function, no longer as the symbolization of the Other's desire, but as an imaginary formation of prestige, presence and precedence. I've already pointed out its function at the level of the narcissistic relation. This is what is produced as such in obsessional symptoms, in all the obsessional's history, and it's where the special function assumed by the subject's fantasmatic relationship to the imaginary other who is his semblable is marked.

488

The distinction between the presence of the Other with a big O and the presence of the other with a little o is tangible in the development of the case, if you read it carefully. You will note, for example, a very curious evolution between the beginning of the treatment when she *cannot* speak and later on when she does not *wish* to speak, because it's at the level of speech that the analysand's relationship with the analyst is instituted, and she denies herself at that level. Even if this is not how he expresses it, the analyst clearly perceives that she denies herself because her demand can only be a demand for death. Later, something else happens, and it's very amusing to see that the analyst clearly perceives that there is a difference, that relations have improved. Nevertheless, she is still not speaking, for now she does not want to speak. The difference between the two is that when one does not wish to speak it's because of the presence of the Other with a big O. However, what is disturbing is that, if she does not wish to speak, it's because what has come to the place of this Other is precisely the other with a little o that the analyst has done everything to present. Why? Because, following things closely as he does, he clearly sees that the content of what the subject brings indicates the place that the phallic fantasy plays in it. Of course, this is how the subject is defending herself, whereas her analyst spends his time drumming into her that she would like to be a man.

It depends on how one hears it. It's true that the subject, at the imaginary level, effectively makes this phallus a breast, and that the condition of man insofar as he is equipped with the phallus, and uniquely insofar as he is equipped with the phallus, represents an element of power for him. The question is why she has such a great need of the reference to this element of power that is the phallus.

From another angle, it's with complete authenticity that she absolutely denies having the slightest desire to be a man. However, on that, one does not let go of her, I mean that for example one interprets in summary terms of aggressiveness or, even, of a desire to castrate the man, things that are much more complex and that have to be articulated quite differently if we follow what I am outlining here. The entire evolution of the treatment, the manner in which it's directed – and this is the entire ambiguity that exists between interpretation and suggestion – tends, on the other hand, towards the fact that an Other (not to employ any other term, for it is indeed the Other, and nobody is in any doubt, if I may say so, the author himself emphasizes it sufficiently in the manner in which he formulates his own action and in other ways as well), that an Other, a benevolent mother, a much more gentle Other than the one whom the subject had to contend with, intervenes to tell her, according to the very formula that the author uses somewhere else in terms that are more or less the following – 'This is my body, this is my blood, this phallus, you can trust me, a man, absorb it, I authorize you to have it, this phallus, it's what must give you force and vigour, and it will resolve all your obsessional difficulties.'

In fact, the result is that not a single one of the obsessions has yielded, they are simply undergone and experienced without guilt. That is strictly modelled on what I have been telling you, and it's what would normally be the result of such a mode of intervention.

Conversely, as I have said to you, it's striking to see at the end of the treatment, at the point at which one has let her go, the patient send her own son to the analyst. This action is rather astonishing, because, we are told, the subject has experienced a holy terror of this son all her life, and one clearly feels, from the context and the images of it that the analyst creates for himself, that there has always been a problem with this son, which is the least one can say.

489

Wouldn't the fact that this son is offered to the analyst at the end be the acting out that marks precisely what has been missed? – at this point where the phallus is altogether something other than an accessory of power, where it's truly this signifying mediation by which what takes place between man and woman is symbolized. Didn't Freud show, in the woman's relations with the father, the equivalence between the desire for the symbolic gift of the phallus and the child that subsequently comes to be substituted for it? That is, the child occupies the very place that has not been worked through and elucidated in the treatment, that is, a symbolic place. The subject, despite herself, in a manner that is certainly unconscious and identical to an acting out when something has been missed in an analysis, shows that something else should have been realized.

The treatment effectively ends in a kind of intoxication of power and goodness, a quasi-manic intoxication, which is usual in and an indication of treatments that end with an imaginary identification. The fact is that the treatment has done nothing other than drive to its ultimate consequences and facilitate by way of suggestive approbation what was already to be found in the mechanisms of the obsession, namely, the absorption or incorporation of the phallus at the imaginary level, which is one of the mechanisms of obsession. It's down this same path, chosen from the mechanisms of defence, that the solution, as it were, is given. Added to this is the approval of what is now a good mother, the mother who allows the phallus to be absorbed.

490

Should we be satisfied with having, as the solution to a neurosis, what is only one of its components merely pushed to its final stage – a symptom that is more successful, in sum, and disengaged from the others?

I don't think that we can consider ourselves to be entirely satisfied. Nor do I think I have said everything that I could say with respect to this treatment, whereas time has caught up with us once again.

Between now and next time I will choose the three or four points in the observation that will highlight even more what I have just articulated for you today.

Then I will make some concluding remarks on our 'formations of the unconscious', to sum up the circuit that we have taken this year, following which all that will be left for us to do is wait for next year to undertake a new stage.

25 June 1958

XXVIII

YOU ARE THE ONE
YOU HATE

From the demand for death to the death of demand
Commandment, guilt without law, superego
Avatars of the phallus signifier
Misery of the gendarme
Not legitimating penis envy

We have come to the end of this year's Seminar, which I called 'Formations of the Unconscious'. Perhaps now you can at least appreciate the appropriateness of the title. Formations, forms, relations, topology perhaps – I had my reasons for avoiding scaring you off at the outset.

If something is to remain as a step on which we can place a foot to climb up onto the following rung next year, it's this – one can't articulate anything that arises from these mechanisms of the unconscious, which are at the foundation of Freud's experience and discovery, merely by referring to tensions, by considering them as inserted into a kind of maturational progress, fanning out from the pre-genital to the genital. Moreover, one cannot only stress relations of identification such as they are apparently – and I say 'apparently' – given over the course of Freud's oeuvre, as if one wanted to reduce the experience to a collection of characters in the style of an Italian comedy, where first would come the mother, then the father, capped off by several others. It's impossible to articulate anything concerning the progress and fixation of desire, or concerning this intersubjectivity that effectively occupies the foreground of our experience and preoccupations, unless we situate it in relation to the necessary relations that impose themselves not only on man's desire, but on the subject as such, and which are the relations between signifiers.

This is why over the course of this year I have tried to familiarize you with this little graph that for some while it has seemed to me, I'm speaking for myself, timely to make use of to support my experiences. It makes it possible to discern the places where this signifier manifests itself – this signifier encountered everywhere, and with reason, since it cannot fail to be involved directly or indirectly, whenever it's a question of not just any signification but signification insofar as explicitly engendered by the conditions imposed upon the living organism that has become the support, the prey or even the victim of speech, and which is called man. Today, I will place you at the edge of the pluripresence, I would say, of the phallus signifier, always the same, the one that we have been occupied with for several sessions. It's extremely important to clearly distinguish the places where this signifier makes its appearance in the subject in any given case.

That becoming conscious of penis envy is crucial in the analysis of a female obsessional neurosis goes without saying, for never to have encountered the phallus in the analysis of an obsessional neurosis, or any other kind of neurosis, female or not, would be really quite odd.

By dint of pushing the analysis in the sense indicated in the so-called *La psychanalyse d'aujourd'hui*, by dint of reducing fantasmatic products of the transference to what someone has called 'this so simple reality' of the analytic situation, namely that there are two people there who, of course, have nothing to do with these fantasies, it's perhaps possible that one can completely manage to do without the phallus in the interpretation of an analysis, but we're not there yet. In truth, no analysis ever takes place in the way outlined in this book.

We obviously have to do something with the phallus signifier. Saying that becoming conscious is the key to the solution of obsessional neurosis is not saying very much, for everything depends on the manner in which one interprets this signifier at the different points at which it appears and where the function it plays is not homologous. Not everything is reducible to penis envy in the sense in which it would concern rivalry with the male, as one ultimately ends up formulating it in this observation by lumping together the patient's relations with her husband, her analyst and others in general, which is falsified by the observation itself. That's obviously the angle from which the phallus appears. It appears at several points.

We are not going to claim to give an exhaustive analysis of an observation that is, moreover, given to us as an incomplete analysis and that we only have partial documentation for. But we have enough to get a good idea of it, nevertheless. I will start, then, by making some remarks about this observation which will introduce some other properties of the graph that we will make use of.

1

What is pointed out to us in this observation is the very lively sense   493
of guilt that accompanies the obsessions in the patient, for example,
her religious obsessions. The appearance of such a marked sense of
guilt in an obsessional neurosis presents a paradox, since surely the
subject considers correlatively that the parasitic thoughts that are
imposed on her are foreign to her, and that she is more the victim of
them than responsible for them. This will make it possible, perhaps,
to formulate something about the sense of guilt.

For some time now, hardly anyone ever speaks about anything
but the term 'superego', which seems to cover everything here. One
can't really say that it has thrown much light on things. The idea has
been put about that the superego is a much older formation, more
archaic, than what one had initially thought, namely that the superego could be considered as the creation corresponding to the decline
of the Oedipus complex and to the introjection of the Oedipal figure
considered to be eminently prohibitive, the paternal figure. You are
aware that experience has forced us to admit that there is an older
superego. What imposed this older origin upon us was not without
relationship to, on the one hand, the effects of introjection and, on
the other, the effects of prohibition. Still, let's try to get a closer look
at these things.

Here is an obsessional neurosis and, as in all neuroses, what we
have to make apparent initially, precisely insofar as we are not
hypnotists and do not work through suggestion, is a dimension
beyond, where, in some way, we offer to meet the subject at one
point. This is what is represented here by the upper line, the horizon
of signifying articulation. There, the subject, as I explained to you
at length last time, is confronted with his demand. This is what is
involved when we speak of an alternating process of successive
regressions and identifications. The two alternate to the extent
that when the subject encounters an identification when regressing
he stops along the path of this regression. Regression is entirely
inscribed, as I have shown you, in this retroactive opening that is
presented to the subject as soon as he speaks, inasmuch as speech
makes the whole history of this demand, in which his entire life as a
man who speaks has been inserted, emerge right down to its origins.

If we examine this closely, without doing anything but rediscover
what has always been formulated, there is a fundamental form that   494
we find on the horizon of every demand by an obsessional subject,
and it constitutes precisely the greatest obstacle to his formulating his demand. This is what experience teaches us to qualify as

aggressiveness and which has increasingly led us to take into consideration what can be called a death wish.

This is the major, inaugural difficulty, faced with which the obsessional's demand shatters, fragments and disarticulates, and it motivates the undoing, the isolation and all the defences – and, very primordially for the grand obsessionals, this silence that is often so prolonged that you have all the difficulty in the world overcoming it in the course of an analysis. I mention it here because it's precisely what is present in the case on which I am basing myself. It's very much the case that this demand is a demand for death. It's striking to see how it spreads throughout the text of the observation without ever being formulated, as if it were some kind of natural expression of a tension. In reality, it's a matter of the relationship between the demand for death and the difficulty of articulation itself, which is implied in the same pages, with the exception of several lines, and absolutely never brought into focus. Isn't that, however, the phenomenon that warrants being paid attention to?

If this demand is a demand for death, it's because the obsessional's first relations with the Other, as Freud and analytic theory teach us, essentially consist of the contradiction that the demand that is addressed to the Other, on which everything depends, has the demand for death as its horizon, and this is for a reason that is attached to the hook of our question mark. Let's not be precipitate, we shall see why and how this can be conceptualized. It's not so simple to speak with Mrs Melanie Klein of primordial aggressive drives if we start from there. Let's leave there this kind of primordial badness where, if he could, the infant's first movement, as the Marquis de Sade emphasizes, would be to bite and tear at the mother's breast.

It is, however, not fruitless that articulating the problem of desire in its fundamental perversity takes us back to the divine marquis, who was not alone in his day to have raised the question of the relations between desire and nature in a very intense and pressing manner. Is there harmony or fundamental disharmony between the two? This is the crux of the passionate questioning that is inseparable from the entire philosophy of the *Aufklärung* and which has contributed an entire literature. In my very first Seminars I drew on this to show a kinship or an analogy – I'll return to this next year with respect to desire – between Freud's initial inquiry and the philosophical inquiry of the *Aufklärung*, accompanied by all the literary eroticism that is its indispensable correlate.

495

We do not know, then, where this demand for death comes from. Before saying that it emerges from the most primordial instincts or from a nature turned against itself, let's start by situating it there where it is, that is, at the level – I won't say at which it's articulated – but at which it prevents any articulation of the subject's demand, where it creates an obstacle to the obsessional's discourse, both when he is alone with himself and when he begins his analysis, and finds himself in this disarray that our analyst occasionally describes from time to time. At the start of her analysis, the analysand effectively presents with an impossibility to speak that translates into reproaches, even insults, even listing everything that creates an obstacle to a patient speaking to a doctor – 'I know doctors well enough to know that they make fun of their patients amongst themselves. You are more knowledgeable than I am. It's impossible for a woman to speak to a man' [p. 221].

This is a deluge, which shows the emergence, in correlation with the activity of speech, of the difficulty of mere articulation. The crux of the demand that the simple fact of entering into the field of analytic therapeutics entails is immediately present. If the demand for death is located there where we placed it, that is, on the horizon of speech, implicated at the crux of all possible articulation of speech, and if it is what is creating an obstacle here, then this schema will perhaps show a little more clearly the logical articulation that supports it, not without some suspension of, or pauses in, thought.

For the obsessional subject, the demand for death represents a dead-end from which what one improperly calls ambivalence results, which is rather a seesaw or swinging movement where the subject is sent back and forth as if between the two buffers of a dead-end that she is unable to escape from. As the schema expresses, the demand for death necessarily has to be formulated in the locus of the Other, in the discourse of the Other, which means that the reason for it is not to be sought in any kind of history involving the mother, for example, as the object of this death wish over some particular frustration. The demand for death concerns the Other in an internal manner. The fact that this Other is the locus of demand effectively entails the death of demand.

The demand for death is unable to be sustained in the obsessional without itself bringing in this kind of destruction that here I am calling the death of demand. It's condemned to an endless to-and-fro, which means that as soon as it starts to be articulated, it dies out. This constitutes the crux of the difficulty of articulating the obsessional's position.

Between the obsessional subject's relationship to his demand [$ ◊ D], and the Other, A, which is so panic-inducingly necessary to him, sustains him and without which he would be something other than an obsessional, we find desire, d, annulled in him, but whose

496

place is maintained. We have described this desire as a *Verneinung*, for it is expressed but in a negative form. We see it appear, effectively, in this form when an analysand, after having said, 'It's not that I'm thinking about such a thing,' expresses to us an aggressive, disapproving or depreciative desire about us. He is effectively displaying his desire there, but he is only able to show it as disavowed. Now, how does it happen that this form of desire is still correlated with guilt feelings, when it has been disavowed?

This is where our schema makes it possible for us to move forward and make some distinctions that will be useful for us later.

2

The obscurities concerning the effects of the superego corresponding to the growth of our experience of this agency arise essentially from the absence of a fundamental distinction. We need to distinguish between guilt and the relationship to the law. There is a relationship between the subject and the law. As to guilt, it's born without any kind of reference to this law. This is the fact that analytic experience has contributed.

The naive move in the dialectic of the relationship between sin and the law was expressed in the words of St Paul, that is, that it's the law that makes the sin. From which it results, as in the sentence of old Karamazov on which I insisted at one time – 'If God does not exist, everything is permitted'.

One of the strangest things there is, and it required analysis to bring it to us, is that there is no need of any kind of reference, either to God or to his law, for man to be literally swimming in guilt. Experience shows us. It even seems that one is able to formulate the contrary expression, namely that 'if God is dead, nothing is permitted'. I have already spoken about this in its time.

How, then, do we formulate the appearance of guilt feelings in the life of the neurotic subject?

Let's go back to the first steps of analysis. In what respect did Freud initially show the sense of guilt to be fundamental, an essential subjective manifestation of the subject? It was with respect to the Oedipus complex. The contents of analysis revealed a desire that till then had been profoundly hidden, the desire for the mother, in her relationship with the intervention of a character who is the father as he emerged from the initial observation of the Oedipus complex, a terrifying and destructive father. This is effectively what becomes apparent in the form of castration fantasies, a discovery of analysis that one did not have the slightest suspicion of before – and whose

497

character, as I think I have spelt out for you this year, is necessarily unthinkable, unless we hold that the phallus is a privileged vital image raised to the signification of a signifier. It assumes here the function of castration as that which marks the impact of the prohibition that strikes desire. In fact, everything that refers to the superego in our experience has to be articulated in three stages which correspond strictly – one, two, three – to the three lines schematized here: the upper line, the line of desire and the line of demand.

For the neurotic, this line on the horizon is not formulated, and that's why he is neurotic. Here the command reigns supreme. Call it what you like, call it the Ten Commandments, why not? I have previously told you that the Ten Commandments were most likely the laws of speech, that is, that all disorders start to affect the way speech functions when they are not respected. Concerning the demand for death, it's obviously the '*Tu ne tueras point*', 'Thou shalt not kill', that is on the horizon and makes it so dramatic. But punishment doesn't derive its impact from the response that comes to that place. The fact is that, for reasons that have to do with the structure of the Other for man, the demand for death is equivalent to the death of demand.

This is the level of the commandment. It exists – so much so that, in truth, it emerges on its own. If you read the notes Freud made on his case of the Rat Man – this is the very nice supplement published in the *Standard Edition*, where one finds certain chronological elements that are valuable to know – you will see that the first obsessional content the subject speaks to him about is that of the commands he receives: You will sit your examination before such and such a date, or what would happen if I received the command, 'You will slit your throat'?, and you know in what a state of panic he enters when the command comes to mind – 'You will slit the old lady's throat', since she is keeping his girlfriend away from him.

We also see these commands appear in the clearest of manners in another context, in psychotics. They receive these commands, and one of the key points of classification is to know to what extent they obey them. In a word, psychosis places the autonomy of this function of command on the horizon of the subject's relationship to speech, an experience that we can only take as fundamental. The command may remain veiled. For the obsessional, it's veiled and fragmented and only appears in bits.

498

Where, and on what line, do we locate guilt?

Guilt, as M. de la Palice would say, is a demand experienced as prohibited. Everything is normally drowned in the term 'prohibition', the notion of demand remaining avoided, whereas it seems that the two go together – which is not certain either, as we shall see. Why is this demand experienced as prohibited? If it were simply experienced as prohibited because, as one says, it has been defended against, there would be no problem. At what level, at what point, do we see the phenomenon appear in clinical work that makes us say that guilt has emerged? What does neurotic guilt consist in? It's truly stupefying that no analyst, not even any phenomenologist, mentions this essential dimension, articulates it or makes a criterion of it – the sense of guilt appears in connection with approaching a demand experienced as forbidden because it kills desire, and this is precisely where it differs from diffuse anxiety, and you know to what extent that differs from the emergence of the sense of guilt.

Guilt is inscribed in the relationship between desire and demand. Everything that goes in the direction of a particular formulation of demand is accompanied by the disappearance of desire, and does so through a mechanism whose threads we can see on this little graph. Precisely because it is on this little graph, the subject can't perceive or determine it in its lived mainspring, inasmuch as the subject is always condemned to be in one of these places, but can't be in all of the places at the same time. That's what guilt is. That's where prohibition appears, but this time not insofar as it is formulated – insofar as the prohibited demand strikes desire down, makes it disappear, kills it.

That, then, is clear. It's insofar as the obsessional is condemned to carry out his battle to save his subjective autonomy, as they say, at the level of desire that everything that appears at this level, even in a disavowed form, is linked to this aura of guilt.

Underneath, in this instance, I will call the third level, unless someone disputes this way of situating it, that of the superego.

In the case we are following, I have no idea why but it's called the female superego, whereas it's ordinarily considered to be the maternal superego in all the other texts in the same register – an anomaly that is no doubt to be attributed to the theme of penis envy that concerns woman as such. The archaic, maternal superego, the one to which the effects of the primordial superego of which Melanie Klein speaks are attached, is linked to the first Other as the support of the subject's first demands of the emerging, I would almost say innocent, demands at the level of the first vague articulations of his need and his first frustrations on which there is so much insistence these days. We can now understand how, through confusing these lines, this superego could be placed on the same line of sight as what is produced at the upper level, that of the command and guilt, which is linked to the Other of the Other.

499

What do we have here at the level of the first Other and its first demands? We have the phenomenon that has been called dependence. Everything about the maternal superego is articulated around this. What makes it possible for us to place them in the same register? Placing them in the same register is not to confuse them, as if at the outset there were only the infant and the mother and the relation was dual. If this were the case, it would be quite different from what we have articulated in the relationship of demand as well as in that of guilt. In reality, initially there is the two-tiered structure that we see here, because it has to be admitted at the outset that, solely by virtue of the fact that signifiers are involved, there are two horizons of demand. I explained this to you by telling you that behind even the most primitive demand – for the breast and the object that represents the maternal breast – there is this doubling-up created in demand by the fact that demand is a demand for love, an absolute demand, a demand that symbolizes the Other as such, which therefore differentiates the Other as a real object, capable of giving satisfaction, from the Other as symbolic object which gives or refuses presence or absence – a matrix in which those fundamental relationships on the horizon of all demand – love, hatred and ignorance – will crystallize.

The first relationship of dependence is threatened by the loss of love and not simply by the privation of maternal care, and this is why it's already in itself homogeneous with what will subsequently become organized according to the perspective of the laws of speech. The latter are already instant, virtual and preformed from the very first demand. Doubtless, they are not complete and formulated, and this is why an infant doesn't begin to be an obsessional from its first feed. But from its first feed, it can very well already start to create this gap, which will mean that it will be in the refusal to feed that he will find the evidence he requires of his maternal partner's love. In other words, we can see signs of anorexia appearing very early.

What is specific to the case of the obsessional? The case of the obsessional is suspended from the early formation, along this horizon of demand, of what I have been calling the demand for death. The demand for death is no pure and simple drive to kill. It's an articulated demand, and solely by virtue of the fact that it's articulated, it's not produced at the level of the imaginary relationship with the other. This is not a dual relation. It looks beyond the imaginary other to the symbolized being of the other, and it's also for that reason that it's experienced and lived in the subject on its return. The fact is that the subject, because he is a speaking subject, and solely for this reason, is unable to harm the other without

500

harming himself, so much so that the demand for death is the death of demand.

It's internal to this that what I will call the avatars of the phallus signifier are located.

3

How can one not fall about in astonishment and stupor when one sees, effectively, if one knows how to read, the phallus signifier re-emerging at all points of the obsessional's phenomenology? Nothing makes it possible to conceptualize this polypresence of the phallus in various symptoms if not its function as a signifier. This confirms the signifier's impact on the living being, which is destined by speech to fragment into all sorts of signifier effects.

We are told in this observation that the woman is possessed by *Penisneid*. That's all very good, but then why is the first of her obsessions to be cited the obsessive fear of having contracted syphilis? This will lead her, as he writes, to oppose, in vain moreover, the marriage of her oldest son, the one I have placed so much emphasis on for the signification he has throughout the observation.

We would always do well to pay attention to the miracles and sleights of hand that are performed on us in both observations and theory. We would do well from time to time to polish up and shine our capacity for being surprised. What do we see in the male obsessional subject? The fear of being contaminated and of contaminating, the widespread experience of which shows us how important it is for him. The male obsessional has in general been initiated fairly early on to the dangers of so-called venereal diseases, and everyone knows the place that, in a large number of cases, this fact can have in his psychology. I am not saying that it is a constant, but we are accustomed to interpret it as going well beyond the rationality of things. As always, this is in Hegel. Even though for some time things have been going so well owing to the use of medication, it nevertheless remains the case that the obsessed remains very obsessed about anything that can create impulsive acts in the libidinal order. As for us, we remain accustomed to seeing an aggressive impulse showing through the libidinal drive, which means that in some way the phallus is something dangerous.

If we hold to the idea that the subject has a relation of narcissistic demand to the phallus, it seems very difficult to explain this first obsession. Why? Precisely because at this level, the use this woman makes of the phallus is strictly equivalent to that of a man, that is, by the intermediary of her son, she takes herself to be dangerous.

When the occasion arises she gives it as her prolongation, which is to say that as a consequence no *Penisneid* stops her. She has the phallus in the form of this son, she actually does have this phallus, since it's on it that she crystallizes the same obsession as male patients do.

I won't go on endlessly about the obsessions of infanticide that follow, the obsessions of poisoning and the rest. I will limit myself to saying very quickly that the case, with all its significance, confirms what I have been putting forward on this topic. I will read this because it's worth it. 'The violence of her complaints against her mother were testimony to the immense affection that she had for her' [p. 219]. After having several times circled around the possibility or not of a truly Oedipal relation by introducing arguments foreign to the question, he writes, 'She considered her to be from a higher milieu than her father, judged her to be more intelligent and was above all fascinated by her energy, character, decisiveness and authority' [p. 219].

That's the start of a paragraph about getting us to see the imbalance in the parental relation, which undeniably exists, and stressing the oppressed, I would say even depressed, aspect of the father in the presence of a mother who may have been virile, since this is how one interprets the fact that the subject requires that the phallic attribute be linked, in one way or another, to the mother.

'The rare moments when the mother relaxed filled her with unspeakable joy' [p. 219]. But up to this point there had never been any question of a frankly sexualized desire to possess the mother. Effectively, there is no trace of anything like it. See how he expresses himself – the patient 'was tied to her', the mother, 'on an exclusively sadomasochistic plane. And then there came to light the mother–daughter alliance that operated extremely rigorously here, and any transgression of the pact produced a movement of extreme violence, which, up till recently, was never objectified. Every person who meddled in this union was the object of death wishes' [p. 219].

This is a truly important point, and you will come across it again, and not only in obsessional neuroses. From whatever angle we look at the frequency of this in our analytic experience, these powerful daughter–mother links, this sort of knot, once again places us before a phenomenon that goes well beyond the bodily differences between beings. What is expressed there is exactly the ambiguity or ambivalence which makes the demand for death and the death of demand equivalent. This shows us moreover that the demand for death is really there. I'm not saying anything new here, for Freud sometimes very clearly saw this demand for death, which Mrs Melanie Klein tried to relate to the subject's primordial

502

aggressive drives, whereas it's there in the link that binds the subject to the mother.

This observation shows us, however, that that is not all. The demand for death is the mother's own demand. The mother carries this demand for death within herself, and she exercises it upon the unfortunate paternal character, a corporal in the Gendarmerie, who, despite his goodness and gentleness which the patient initially speaks of, shows himself to be unhappy, depressed and taciturn throughout his life, never manages to overcome the mother's rigidity, nor to prevail over his wife's attachment to a first, incidentally platonic, love, is jealous, and breaks his silence only to explode in emotional outbursts which always end in his defeat. No one doubts that the mother played a part in this.

One glosses this in terms of what is called the castrating mother. Perhaps that is the place to examine things more closely and to see that here, much more than a question of castration for this man, it's a question of the privation of the loved object that the mother seems to have been for him and of the onset of this depressive position in him that Freud teaches us to recognize as determined by a death wish against oneself – and which is directed at what? What else, if not at a loved and lost object. In short, the demand for death was already present in the subject's previous generation. Is it the mother who embodies it?

At the level of the subject, the demand for death is mediated by an Oedipal horizon that makes it possible for it to appear on the horizon of speech and not in its immediacy. If it were not thus mediated, we would not have an obsessional, but a psychotic. On the other hand, in the relations between the father and the mother, this demand for death is not mediated for the subject by anything that would indicate any respect for the father, to his being placed by the mother in a position of authority and support of the law. The demand for death in question at the level at which the subject sees it involved in the relationship between the parents is a demand for death directly directed at the father, who turns the aggression in against himself, hence the misery, the partial deafness and the depression. This is thus quite different from the demand for death always involved in all intersubjective dialectic, which finds expression in a court of law when the prosecutor says, 'I demand the death penalty.' He is not demanding it from the subject in question, he is demanding it from a third party who is the judge, which is the normal Oedipal position.

This, then, is the context in which the subject's *Penisneid,* or what one is calling such, is led to play its role. We see it here in the form of this dangerous weapon, which is there only as a signifier of the

503

danger manifested by the emergence of desire in the context of this demand. We shall also see this characteristic of signifiers manifest itself in the detail of a number of the subject's obsessions.

One of her first obsessions is a very nice one. It's the fear of putting pins in her parents' bed. And why? To prick her mother, not her father. This is the first level of the appearance of the phallic signifier. Here it's the signifier of desire as dangerous and guilty. It doesn't have the same function at another moment, when it appears altogether clearly, but in the form of an image. Wherever I have shown it to you here, it's been veiled, it's been in the symptom, it has come from elsewhere, it has been fantasmatic interference. For us, as analysts, it suggests the place where it exists as a fantasy, but it's something different when it gets projected out before the image of the host.

I have already alluded to these profane obsessions the subject is obsessed by. To be sure, the religious life is present in the obsessional in a profoundly reworked form, one infiltrated by symptoms, but, by a curious sort of conformity, his religious life, and especially his sacramental life, shows itself to be perfectly suited to giving the obsessional's symptoms the groove, the mould into which he so easily flows, especially in the Christian religion. I do not have much experience of obsessions in Muslims, for example, but it would be worth the effort to see how they manage it, I mean how the horizon of their belief, such as it's structured in Islam, gets implicated in an obsessional phenomenology. Whenever Freud had an obsessional with a Christian background, whether the Rat Man or the Wolf Man, he clearly showed the importance of Christianity in their evolution and economy. One cannot fail to see that with its articles of faith the Christian religion places us before this astonishing, bold – to say the least – and cheeky solution, which consists in having this function of the signifier whose action marks life as such borne by an incarnated person, a god-man. The Christian Logos as incarnated Logos gives a precise solution to the system of the relations between man and speech, and it's not for nothing that God incarnate was called the Word.

504

Also, we should not be astonished that in this observation it's at the level of the ever-renewed symbol of this incarnation that this subject conjures up the phallus signifier, which is substituted for her therein. Of course, this signifier doesn't form part of the religious context as such, but if what we say is true, it's no surprise to see it appear in this place.

In this place, it's clear that it plays quite a different role from where it was when we interpreted it at the beginning. When it appears again at a later point in the observation, it would be equally erroneous to interpret its function as homogeneous with the manner in which it intervenes here at the level of the symptom.

When, at a much later period of the observation, the subject communicates this fantasy to her analyst – 'I dreamt that I was crushing the head of Christ under my feet, and this head looked like yours' [p. 225], the function of the phallus is not, as one feels obliged to say, identified there with the analyst as the vehicle of the phallus. If the analyst is identified with the phallus, it's insofar as, at this moment in the history of the transference, he incarnates the effect of signifiers for the subject and the relationship to speech, whose horizon she then begins to project a little bit further owing to a number of the effects of the detente that has taken place in the treatment. To interpret this at the time in a homogeneous manner in terms of *Penisneid* was to miss the opportunity to relate the patient to what is more profound in her situation. Perhaps she would then have been able, effectively, to perceive the relationship that, in the distant past, she had formed between this x that fundamentally provoked the Other's demand as a demand for death and the very first perception that she would have had of the intolerable rivalry in the form of the mother's desire attached to this far-off love that distanced her from both her husband and her child. The phallus has to be situated here at the level of the signifier of the Other as barred, S(Ⱥ), as identical to the profoundest signification that the Other has attained for the subject.

The phallus appears again in the same place at a slightly later moment in the analysis, at a time when many dreams that have brought it to light from this angle have come under consideration. In one of these dreams that are the most commonly observed in the majority of neuroses, the patient sees herself as a phallic being, seeing one of her breasts replaced by a phallus, or a phallus located between her two breasts. That is one of the most frequent oneiric fantasies that one can encounter in any analysis.

505   Is this, as we are told, about a 'desire for a masculine identification with possession of the phallus'? [p. 224]. He has a go at speculating – 'If she sees her own breasts transformed into a penis, isn't she transferring the oral aggressiveness primitively directed against the maternal breast onto the man's penis?' [p. 224]. That is one kind of reasoning. But on the other hand he observes how extensive the phallus is in its given form. We well know that its presence can be polyphallic. As soon as there is more than one phallus, I would almost say that we find ourselves before the outline of this fundamental image that is quite well represented by Diana of the Ephesians, whose body consists of a cascade of breasts.

At a time when the analyst has already drawn an equivalence between shoes and the phallus, a dream immediately follows the two first attempts which, according to the analyst, confirms it. 'I get my shoe repaired at the shoemakers, then I climb onto a balcony decorated with blue, white and red paper lanterns, where there are only men – my mother is in the crowd, admiring me' [pp. 224–5]. Can we be satisfied here with speaking of *Penisneid*? Isn't it obvious that the relationship to the phallus is of a different order? The dream itself indicates that it's linked to a relationship of exhibition, and not in the presence of those who carry it, the other men there with her on the balcony – whose blue, white and red paper lanterns, this is almost too good to be true, evoke for us all sorts of variously obscene backgrounds – but in the presence of her mother.

We find here this compensatory fantasmatic relationship I was talking about last time, a relationship of power, no doubt, but in relation to a third party, who is her mother. The presence of the phallus in the subject's relationship to the image of her semblable, the little other, the image of the body, is precisely the image whose true function in the subject's equilibrium is to be studied, rather than interpreted and purely and simply assimilated to its function at the time of its other appearances. This is testimony here to a flagrant lack of criteria in the orientation of interpretation.

Finally, then, where are all the analyst's interventions in this observation going? Towards facilitating in the subject what he calls the becoming conscious of some sort of lack of or nostalgia for the penis, by facilitating her exit from her fantasies by centring her on a less powerful fantasy, whereas the majority of the facts go against this interpretation.

The analyst has changed the meaning of the phallus for the patient, he has rendered it legitimate for her. This comes down more or less to teaching her to love her obsessions. This is the evaluation of this therapeutics that we are given – the obsessions have not diminished, the patient simply no longer feels guilty about them. The result is brought about by an intervention essentially centred on the fabric of her fantasies and their value as fantasies of rivalry with man, rivalry supposed to transpose some kind of aggressiveness towards the mother, the roots of which are never touched.

506

We end up with this. The analyst's operation of authorization disconnects the fabric of her obsessions from a fundamental demand for death. In operating in this way, he authorizes and ultimately legitimates her fantasy and, as one can only legitimate in a block, her abandonment of the genital relationship is, as such, consummated. When the subject learns to love her obsessions, inasmuch as they are invested with the full signification of what happens to her, we see at the end of the case all kinds of extremely euphoric intuitions develop.

I invite you to refer to it, since it's getting too late for me to read it out to you today. You will certainly find this style of narcissistic effusion – a phenomenon at the end of analyses that some people have emphasized. The author doesn't have too many illusions on this count. 'The positive transference', he writes, 'became clearer with these very strongly pregenitalized Oedipal characteristics' [p. 233]. And he concludes on a note of profound incompleteness, with very few illusions over the possibility of a truly genital solution, as one says.

What, it seems to me, has not at all been seen is the close correlation between this result and the very mode of interpretation, namely, that it targets the reduction of demand rather than its elucidation. It's all the more paradoxical since these days one is accustomed to stressing the importance of the interpretation of aggressiveness. Perhaps this term is just too vague for practitioners to be always able to use it to find their way around. The term 'demand for death' could be profitably substituted for it, as it is in German, to indicate the level of subjective articulation of demand that one can be required to achieve.

4

Since I alluded to the commandments earlier and also spoke of Christianity, I would like to finish by drawing your attention to what is not one of the least mysterious of the commandments. It's not a moral commandment, since it's founded on identification. It's the one that, on the horizon of all the commandments, is promoted in its Christian wording in the formula 'You will love your neighbour as yourself.'

507   I do not know if you have ever paused over what that entails. It entails all sorts of objections. First, the beautiful souls cry, '"As yourself!" But more! Why "as yourself"? That's so little!' The more experienced people say to themselves, 'But seriously, is it so certain that one loves oneself?' Experience effectively proves that we have the strangest and most contradictory feelings about ourselves. And then, this 'yourself' may seem, if we take it from a certain perspective, to place egoism at the heart of love. How is one to make it the measure, the model and the paragon of love? This is what surprises one most.

These objections are completely valid, in fact, and one can make them apparent by the impossibility of responding to this sort of interpellation in the first person. No one has ever suggested that 'I love my neighbour as myself' could be a reply, because then the weakness of the formulation of the commandment would become apparent to the eyes of all. If, however, it is worth dwelling on, it's because it illustrates what earlier I called the horizon of the words of the commandment.

If we formulate it where it has to begin, that is, in the locus of the Other, it reveals itself to be something quite different, namely a circle, symmetrical and parallel to the one that, as I showed you, is subjacent to the position taken by the Other at the simple level of the first demand, and which says, 'You are the one who kills me.' The 'as yourself' at the level at which the commandment is formulated in being completed by it can't be the expression of any kind of egoism, inasmuch as the 'you' leads us to recognize in this 'yourself' nothing other than the '*tu*', thou. The Christian commandment henceforth reveals its value in being extended – '. . . as yourself you are, at the level of speech, the one you hate in the demand for death, because you are unaware of it'.

This is where it meets the point on the horizon at which Freud's counsel is formulated, his '*Wo Es war, soll Ich werden*'.

It's also what another wise saying expresses in its 'You are that.'

This is what must in the end come to mark the subject's authentic and full assumption in his own speech.

This means that the subject must recognize where he is on this horizon of speech without which nothing in analysis can be formulated except the tracing out of false pathways and the production of misrecognition.

                                                                2 July 1958

APPENDICES

A

THE GRAPH OF DESIRE

The definitive version of the major schema elaborated over the course of the Seminar, subsequently called 'The Graph of Desire', can be found on page 692 of *Écrits*. This 'complete graph' was preceded by several versions that represent the stages of its development (pp. 681, 684 and 690). The complete form is reproduced below.

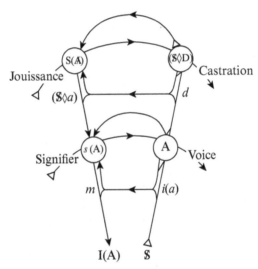

B

EXPLANATION OF
THE SCHEMAS

On 31 January 1958, between weeks eleven and twelve, Lacan met with a small group of participants who had asked him for further explanation of the schemas he had introduced at his Seminar. This discussion (perhaps in the form of a response to questions) was not taken down in full and the notes taken by Paul Lemoine, which consist of a summary plus some drawings, are the only record. These are reproduced below in expanded form, and should be read with the obvious caveat: this is not one of Lacan's written texts, nor is it a class from his Seminar.

1 The signifying chain

It is not possible to define the analytic field without establishing the structuring function of signifiers in relation to the subject and their constitutive value in the subject qua speaking subject. In a word, the human subject cannot be disconnected from discourse – more precisely, from the signifying chain.

Some authors have managed to avoid this fact in the name of mechanistic or biologistic prejudices, but the psychoanalytic experience is of the highest importance for showing that it is unavoidable. It shows, effectively, that at the level of the signifying chain as such, subjects are captured in the Other, that is, the unconscious, and no subject has access to the unconscious without the Other's intervention.

The theme of the father, which is one of the themes of social life, but which is also present in the unconscious closest to the primitive instincts, can only be identified on the condition that the Name-of-the-Father as a signifying knot be brought into play. A signification that stems from the signifying chain's relation to itself converges on this signifier. If this were not so, the Name-of-the-Father could not enter into any form of intersubjectivity whatsoever. It's effectively the signifying chain that differentiates the human subject from animal life. For the animal, there is, in a certain sense, a form of intersubjectivity, but it is completely different in kind. The same goes for identification: no system of identification is conceivable unless one brings into play something that is foreign to animal life, namely the signifying chain.

This has major consequences for [analytic] practice. For want of having understood this, a certain analyst (Bouvet) leaves himself open to deviations in technique by virtue of the prevailing impor- 514
tance he gives to the homosexual relationship between the analyst and the analysand, and to imaginary fellatio, a term that is ambiguous with 'imaginary filiation'. For him, everything takes place at the level of the imaginary relationship, the one that links the ego to the little other. On the contrary, Schema L [see *Écrits*, p. 53] is intended precisely to indicate that the question is whether, along the vector that goes from the Other to the subject, there is anything that traverses this imaginary relationship or not.

2 This year's schema

This year's schema is only a response to the quilting points that link the signifier to the signified.

The terms I have put there have a transformative role, in this respect. In themselves, their only originality is as signifiers. Our interest in them lies not so much in their meaning, which is necessarily ambiguous and even contradictory, but in their conjunction as signifiers.

This schema can be reduced to the following, which stands for the signifying chain.

I only have to bend the line you see there.

The retroactive effect of signifiers acts upon the signifieds. Whatever form we give this term 'signifying chain', as soon as there is a signifying chain, there is a sentence. And there is a sentence whenever something is complete at the level of signifiers, that is, all the signifiers that have been uttered, in their place, between the start and the punctuation. Meaning is formed when the final word of the sentence has been uttered. Consider my example of the line from Athaliah: 'Yes, I come into the temple to worship the Lord.' We can represent this retroaction of the signifier on the schema. When point p is attained, when it is produced, something is obtained at an earlier point, at p'.

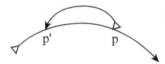

What comes next represents the discourse's intention for you, which also has to be indicated inasmuch as the discourse is not detached from the concrete individuality who is uttering it.

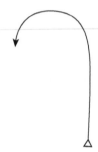

As analysts, we have at our disposal this middle term that enables discourse to be inserted into the human subject, namely, the term 'desire'. Desire's point of departure is at the same level as the point from which the signifying chain departs. Everything else is situated from there.

The duality of the subject operates in an 'intersubjective conjunction'. From its first cry, the newborn baby connects with the mother from whom it will acquire the use of the signifying chain. That's essentially the schema.

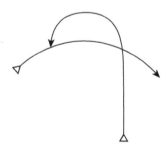

The encounter with the Other is projected onto that. The message is the result. For the message to be formed, it is sufficient that there be a receiver* and a sender*.

The support by desire is inscribed the length of the line of retroaction. The action of speaking has effects on the desire of the subject who articulated it, and these effects are produced retroactively. The result is inscribed at the end of the retrograde vector.

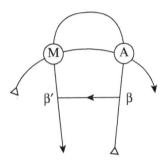

At the level of the short-circuit A, β, β', M, the subject is an animal. Everything that happens at the animal level happens at β, β'. The specular imaginary confrontation $a - a'$ is located at this level.

516

3 Concerning the Oedipus complex

This schema thus shows the place of the imaginary mother–phallus–child triad introduced last year with respect to the most primitive perversions like fetishism. I didn't feel comfortable about giving it to you without first being able to situate it like this today. There are other relations, also in the neuroses, that can be established prior to the Oedipus complex, but the subject has to be structured Oedipally for it to be possible to formulate anything about them.

The relationship to the mother in masculine homosexuality is structured in a current drama that is being played out between S, a, a', A. The notion of the phallic woman, which is usually brought into the account in such cases, is confused and doesn't fit what we learn from analysis. It's actually a question of the mother's relationship to the father's speech. The mother currently lays down the law.

Further verification of the significance of this schema reveals the meaning of the identification with the father that occurs at the end of the Oedipus complex. It makes it possible to situate the paradoxes of the subject's relations to the penis: the appendage required of the eroticized object, the threat of terror that is formed fantasmatically.

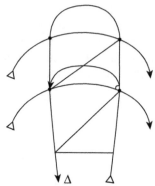

Inasmuch as I have been able to combine this schema and the schema where the code turns back upon the message – which introduces intersubjectivity and the relationship to the Other, not as present, but as produced by speech itself – we can start to give meaning to the term 'identification' by superimposing the two triangles.

Identification is Dante's condemned couple, who kiss on the mouth and each becomes the other.

EDITOR'S NOTE

The schema constructed over the course of this Seminar ('the graph of desire') acquired its definitive form in 'Subversion of the Subject and the Dialectic of Desire', written in 1962. See, in particular, *Écrits*, pp. 681–93.

For the first part of *Formations of the Unconscious*, Lacan refers to 'The instance of the Letter', a text from May 1957 (*Écrits*, pp. 412–41).

Following the first seven chapters of the Seminar, over December and January, Lacan wrote 'On a Question Prior to Any Possible Question of Psychosis' (*Écrits*, pp. 445–88).

Lacan wrote 'The Youth of Gide' (*Écrits*, pp. 623–44) over the February vacation and it was published in April. One finds an echo of it in Lesson XIV of the Seminar, the first lesson of the part, 'The Significance of the Phallus'.

The six lessons of this part, as well as the lesson of 7 May, are influenced by the prospect of the public lecture that Lacan was to give in Munich on 9 May called 'The Signification of the Phallus' (*Écrits*, pp. 575–84).

Finally, the last part coincides with 'The Direction of the Treatment and the Principles of its Power', a paper presented at Royaumont in July (*Écrits,* pp. 489–542).

*

I would like to express my gratitude to Judith Miller, the young girl of the 'Ahht!', who was the first reader of the manuscript and proofs, and made many useful suggestions.

I also express, once again, my gratitude to Gennie Lemoine, who placed at my disposal the totality of the notes taken at Lacan's Seminar by her husband, the late Paul Lemoine. I made use of his notes of this Seminar from January 1958 on. Paul does not seem to have attended the first trimester; he possessed a photocopy of the first seven lessons that had been typed up for Lacan.

Readers in a position to send me new information or offer corrections and improvements are kindly invited to write to me care of the publisher.

J.-A. M.

TRANSLATOR'S ENDNOTES

The following notes refer to page and paragraph of the present English edition.

Chapter I The Famillionaire

(3, 3) See 'The Instance of the Letter in the Unconscious, or Reason since Freud', *Écrits*, pp. 412–41.

(4, 4) See *The Seminar, Book I, Freud's Papers on Technique, 1953–1954*, ed. Jacques-Alain Miller, trans. John Forrester (Cambridge: Cambridge University Press, 1988).

(5, 1) See *The Seminar, Book II, The Ego in Freud's Theory and in the Technique of Psychoanalysis, 1954–1955*, ed. Jacques-Alain Miller, trans. Sylvana Tomaselli (Cambridge: Cambridge University Press, 1988).

(5, 2) See *Seminar II*, Chs 15 and 16; see also 'Seminar on "The Purloined Letter"', *Écrits*, pp. 6–48, esp. pp. 35–9 and the section titled 'Parenthesis of Parentheses', pp. 41–6, added in 1966.

(5, 2) See *Écrits*, pp. 35–8.

(6, 1) See *The Seminar, Book III, The Psychoses, 1955–1956*, ed. Jacques-Alain Miller, trans. Russell Grigg (New York: Norton, 1993).

(6, 1) The French term '*suppléance*' refers to the act of replacing someone unable to carry out their duties. It conveys the sense of making up for a lack. I have resurrected the old English term 'suppletion', which refers to remedying a deficiency or supplementing a lack. In *Écrits* the verb '*suppléer*' is translated as 'to make up for' or 'to supplement'.

(6, 3) See *Seminar III*, Ch. 21.

(7, 2) '*Point de capiton*' is translated here and in *Seminar III* as quilting point, and as button tie in *Écrits*.

(7, 4) See *Le séminaire, Livre IV, La relation d'objet (The Object Relation), 1956–1957*, ed. Jacques-Alain Miller (Paris: Seuil, 1998).

(7, 5)   See *Écrits*, pp. 428–9.

(8, 8)   Lacan is referring to Bertrand Russell's theory of 'logically
            proper names', set out in his 1918 paper, 'The Philosophy of
            Logical Atomism'. See Bertrand Russell, *The Philosophy of
            Logical Atomism* (London: Routledge, 2009), particularly the
            introduction by David Pears.

(16, 2)   Heinrich Heine, *Travel Pictures*, trans. Peter Wortsman
            (Brooklyn, NY: Archipelago Books, 2008); also available in
            his *Selected Prose*, trans. and ed. Ritchie Robertson (London:
            Penguin, 1993).

(16, 3)   See Heinrich Heine, *Travel Pictures*, trans. Peter Wortsman
            (New York: Archipelago Books, 2008), pp. 123 and 124.

(18, 6)   Freud compares witticisms and the comic in Chapter 7 of *Jokes
            and their Relation to the Unconscious*, *SE*, Vol. 8.

(18, 8)   The reference is to a remark found in the last paragraph on p. 430
            in *Écrits*, where '*alibi*' is translated as ruse.

Chapter II The *Fat-millionaire*

(20, *ch.title*)   Homophonic with '*famillionaire*', the '*fat-millionaire*' can
            mean the conceited, smug or fatuous millionaire.

(21, 3)   See Freud, *Jokes*, *SE* 8: 16ff and Heine, *Travel Pictures*, Bk. 3, Pt.
            2, Ch. 8.

(22, 2)   '*Tendance*' here renders Freud's '*Tendenz*', translated as purpose
            in *SE*. See, for example, 'The Purposes of Jokes', Ch. 3 in *Jokes*.

(22, 3)   See, for example, *SE* 8: 54, where Freud introduces the term
            'joke-work', along the lines of the 'dream-work'. The relation-
            ship between dreams and witticisms is discussed in Ch. 6 in *Jokes*.

(23, 1)   At this point the discussion constantly refers to Jacques Lacan
            'The Instance of the Letter in the Unconscious, or Reason Since
            Freud', in *Écrits*, pp. 412–41.

(23, 5)   See Roman Jakobson, 'Two Aspects of Language and Two
            Types of Aphasic Disturbances', in Roman Jakobson and Morris
            Halle, *Fundamentals of Language* (The Hague: Mouton, 1956),
            pp. 53–87.

(29, 3)   The speaker has unwittingly invented the expression, '*C'est signé
            que non*' ('It's signed with a "No"', we might say), through con-
            fusing it with the fixed expression, '*C'est signe que . . .*', which
            means 'It is a sign, or the proof, that . . . '.

(29, 4)   Sigmund Freud, *The Psychopathology of Everyday Life*, *SE*, Vol.
            6. See also Freud's 1898 paper, 'The Psychical Mechanism of
            Forgetfulness', *SE* 3: 289–97.

(30, 2)   The allusion is to the two-volume collection of articles, *La psy-
            chanalyse d'aujourd'hui* [*Psychoanalysis Today*], ed. Sacha Nacht
            (Paris: Presses Universitaires de France, 1956).

(30, 4)   See Freud, *Psychopathology*, *SE* 6: 9–11.

(36, 1)   *Le Prométhée mal enchaîné* was published in 1895. See *Marshlands
            and Prometheus Misbound,* trans. George Painter (New York:
            Mcgraw-Hill, 1965).

Chapter III The *Miglionaire*

(43, 3)   See above, p. 36.

(43, 4)   André Gide, *Paludes* (Paris: Gallimard, 1973) is a short novel originally published in 1895, translated as *Marshlands*. See Gide, *Marshlands and Prometheus Misbound*.

(43, 5)   That is, he plays no part in choosing who will receive the gift.

(45, 6)   See *Jokes*, *SE* 7: 140–2. Freud here speaks of the 'subjective determinants' of wit.

(47, 1)   The reference is to Émile Littré, *Dictionnaire de la langue française*, first published by Hachette 1863–1872, and now available online at <http://littre.reverso.net/dictionnaire-francais/>.

(47, 2)   See Charles Chassé, *Lueurs sur Mallarmé* (Paris: Editions de la Nouvelle revue critique, 1947) and Les *clés de Mallarmé* (Paris: Aubier, 1954).

(50, 3)   See the graph, Ch. 1, p. 10, where the metonymic object is located at β'.

(54, 5)   '. . . *le comte ne la contente pas, à ceci près que le comte, s'il est, comme je le dis, aussi peu contentant, peut ne s'apercevoir de rien.*'

(55, 1)   The response is a meaningless one that plays on the standard response to being asked how one is, which is to say '*Et toi?*' ('And you?') by instead giving a silly response, '*Et toile à matelas!*', 'And a mattress-cover!' To respond, '*Et toile à édredon!*', 'And an eiderdown-cover!', would ruin the effect.

Chapter IV The Golden Calf

(58, 1)   What is 'a bit too swift' is this one-line summary of the philosophical enterprise that goes from the formal logic of Aristotle to the transcendental logic of Kant.

(61, 4)   On metaphor, see *Seminar III*, Chs 17 and 18, esp. pp. 219ff, as well as 'The Instance of the Letter'.

(61, 5)   See *Jokes*, *SE* 8: 88.

(63, 3)   '*Le premier vol de l'Aigle*' plays on the two meanings of '*vol*', flight and theft. The expression 'the flight of the Eagle' refers to Napoleon I's successful return from exile on Elba in 1815 and reinstatement as Emperor.

(63, 4)   See *Jokes*, *SE* 8: 37.

(64, 6)   The reference is to Corneille, *Le Cid*, Act 4, Scene 3.

(65, 2)   See *Écrits*, p. 422.

(66, 5)   '*Un village de trente âmes*' (a village of thirty souls) means a small village with few inhabitants.

(67, 1)   '*Trente feux*' (thirty fires) refers to there being thirty houses in a settlement or village.

(67, 3)   'Without Poland there'd be no Poles' are the last words of Jarry's play *Ubu Roi*. See Alfred Jarry, *Ubu Roi*, trans. Beverly Keith and G. Legman (New York: Dover, 2003).

(70, 2)   See Félix Fénéon, *Novels in Three Lines*, trans. Luc Santé (New York: New York Review of Books Classics, 2007).

(71, 6)   For this and the following three paragraphs, see the diagram on page 10.

(72, 6)   In a footnote to *Capital*, Ch. 1, Sec. 3, Pt. A, 'Elementary or Accidental Form of Value', Marx writes: 'In a sort of way, it is with man as with commodities. Since he comes into the world neither with a looking glass in his hand, nor as a Fichtian philosopher, to whom "I am I" is sufficient, man first sees and recognizes himself in other men. Peter only establishes his own identity as a man by first comparing himself with Paul as being of like kind. And thereby Paul, just as he stands in his Pauline personality, becomes to Peter the type of the genus homo.' *Das Kapital: A Critique of Political Economy* (Washington, DC: Regnery, 2009), p. 18.

Chapter V A Bit-of-Sense and the Step-of-Sense

(76, 5)   See, in particular, *SE* 8: 131.

(77, 6)   Ernst Kris, 'Ego Psychology and Interpretation in Psychoanalytic Therapy', *Psychoanalytic Quarterly* 20/1 (1951): 15–29. Lacan mentions Kris's article in 'The Function and Field of Speech and Language in Psychoanalysis', *Écrits*, p. 244.

(78, 5)   Act 3, Scene 2. The scene was censored after the second performance.

(80, 4)   The delta is the small triangle at the lower right-hand side of the diagram.

(83, 1)   *The Interpretation of Dreams, SE,* Vols. 4 and 5; *The Psychopathology of Everyday Life, SE* Vol. 6; and *Jokes,* Vol. 8.

(84, 4)   See Octave Mannoni, *Prospero and Caliban: The Psychology of Colonization*, trans. Pamela Powesland, foreword by Maurice Bloch (Ann Arbor, MI: University of Michigan Press, 1990). Originally published as *Psychologie de la colonisation* (Paris: Seuil, 1950).

(85, 2)   The 'secondary circuit of need' refers to the level of pretext or invention mentioned in the preceding paragraph.

(85, 3)   These are the three moments numbered I, II and III on the diagram.

(87, 3)   '*Peu de sens*' means 'little sense' as in '*Cela a peu de sens*', 'That makes little sense', or even 'no sense', but Lacan is also drawing on the stand-alone meaning of the substantive as in '*un peu*', 'a bit', 'a little', to form '*le peu de sens*', 'the bit of sense'. '*Peu de sens*' is translated as 'scant meaning' in *Écrits*.

(87, 4)   An allusion to Albert Camus, who was awarded the Nobel Prize for literature in 1957, and his novel *The Outsider*.

(87, 4)   Lacan is playing on the homophony of '*veau*', veal, and '*vaut*', which is the third-person singular of '*valoir*', to be worth.

(88, 2)   See *Jokes, SE* 8: 143.

(89, 1)   '*Pas*' is an adverb of negation, as in the expression '*pas de sens*', which occurs in expressions such as '*Ça n'a pas de sens*', 'That makes no sense'. '*Pas*' is also a substantive. In Lacan's examples, a '*pas de vis*' is a screw thread, while a '*pas de quatre*' is a dance in ballet for four dancers; it appears as a geographical term in '*Pas de Suse*' which refers to Susa in Italy and in '*Pas de Calais*' which is the French term for the Straits of Dover.

(90, 3)   While '*motif*' and '*mobile*' mean roughly the same, namely motive, '*mobile*' is usually restricted to the legal context of motive for a crime. Lacan is referring to *Jokes*, *SE* 8, Ch. 5, 'The Motives of Jokes – Jokes as a Social Process'.

Chapter VI Whoah, Neddy!

(92, 6)   Lacan is referring to the 'subjective determinants' of the joke-work, *SE* 8: 142. Shortly after (144), Freud quotes Shakespeare's *Love's Labour's Lost*, V.ii:

> A jest's prosperity lies in the ear
>   Of him that hears it, never in the tongue
>   Of him who makes it . . .

(95, 1)   *SE* 8: 115. The example is discussed in 'The Instance of the Letter', *Écrits*, p. 436.

(96, 3)   Freud refers to the expression 'psychical scene of action', which is likely to be a reference to Fechner. See *Jokes*, *SE* 8: 176.

(99, 1)   Henri Bergson, *Laughter: An Essay on the Meaning of the Comic*, trans. Cloudesley Brereton and Fred Rothwell (London: Macmillan, 1935).

(107, 1)   *The Interpretation of Dreams*, *SE* 4: 283.

(107, 3)   Freud refers to the 'outer shell' of a joke in *Jokes*, *SE* 8: 55.

(107, 4)   'Être *de la même paroisse*' literally means coming from the same parish, but figuratively the expression indicates a shared perspective on things, having much in common, coming from the same background, thinking alike, and so forth.

Chapter VII *Une Femme de Non-Recevoir,* or: A Flat Refusal

(109, 1)   '*En esprit*'. '*Trait d'esprit*' and '*mot d'esprit*' are translated here as 'joke' or 'witticism'.

(113, 1)   'Rough breathing' refers to the diacritical mark in ancient Greek that is placed *inter alia* over the α to indicate that it is aspirate. It is represented here by an inverted comma.

(113, 3)   See the 'optical model' in 'Remarks on Daniel Lagache's Presentation: "Psychoanalysis and Personality Structure"', in *Écrits*, pp. 543–74 and the discussion in *Seminar I*, Chs 10 and 11.

(114, 2)   See Freud, *Jokes*, Ch. 7, 'Jokes and the Species of the Comic'.

(115, 2)   The French here is untranslatable. The expression '*une fin de non-recevoir*' is a legal expression meaning the rejection of a claim. In ordinary, somewhat elevated language it means a flat refusal, in the sense of dismissing out of hand. Lacan's patient unwittingly creates the new expression '*une femme* [a woman] *de non-recevoir*', which sounds very similar to the original expression, but doesn't exist in French.

(117, 1)   See Immanuel Kant, *Critique of Judgment*, trans. James Creed Meredith (Oxford: Clarendon Press, 1911), First Part, Sec. 54.

(117, 1)   Léon Dumont, *Des causes du rire* (Charleston, SC: Nabu Press, 2010); Georges Dumas, 'Les rires et les larmes', in *Traité de psychologie*, ed. Georges Dumas et al. (Paris: Alcan, 1923), Vol. 1, Bk. 3, Ch. 3.

(118, 2)   See Heinrich von Kleist, 'The Puppet Theatre', in *Selected Writings*, ed. and trans. David Constantine (Indianapolis, IN: Hackett, 2004).

(121, 6)   '*Die Kunst-Religion* [Religion in the Form of Art]' is Ch. 7, Pt. B, of Hegel's *Phenomenology of Mind*.

(122, 2)   Lacan has in mind Aristophanes' *Assemblywomen*. See Aristophanes, *The Assemblywomen* in *The Birds and Other Plays*, trans. David Barrett and Alan H. Sommerstein (Harmondsworth: Penguin, 1978).

(122, 4)   See *The Assemblywomen,* p. 127.

(124, 2)   Molière, *School for Wives*, trans. Ranjit Bolt (London: Oberon Books, 2012). Text references are to act, scene and line of this edition.

> Un air doux, et posé, parmi d'autres enfans,
> M'inspira de l'amour pour elle, dès quatre ans.
> (I. i. 28–9)

(124, 5)   A reference to Colette's 1919 novella, *Mitsou; or How Girls Grow Wise*, trans. Jane Terry (London: Victor Gollancz, 1930).

(124, 6)   'Horace avec deux mots en ferait plus que vous' (V. iv. 1605).

(125, 2)   The exchange takes place in Act 2, Scene 4.

Chapter VIII Foreclosure of the Name-of-the-Father

(129, 2)   The 'earlier schema' is schema L. See *Écrits*, p. 40.

(130, 1)   Gisela Pankow was at this time a colleague of Lacan's at the French Psychoanalytic Society. Her book, *L'Etre-là du schizophrène: Contribution à la méthode de structuration dynamique dans les psychoses* [*Being-There of the Schizophrenic: A Contribution to the Method of Dynamic Structuration in the Psychoses*] (Paris: Aubier, 1981), which presents her work on psychosis dating back to 1956. It was on a visit to the US in the 1950s that she met Gregory Bateson.

(130, 1)   See Gregory Bateson et al., 'Toward a Theory of Schizophrenia', *Behavioral Science* 1 (1956): 251–64; and Gregory Bateson, *Steps to an Ecology of Mind: Collected Essays in Anthropology, Psychiatry, Evolution, and Epistemology* (Chicago, IL: University of Chicago Press, 1972).

(135, 2)   *Une vérité de M. de la Palice* is a truism or tautology.

(136, 3)   '*Tu*' is the second-person singular personal pronoun. It is homophonic with '*tue*' and '*tues*', present-tense singular forms of the verb '*tuer*', to kill.

(136, 4)   See *Seminar III,* Chs 22–4, especially p. 272, fn. 3.

(137, 4)   Charles Blondel, *The Troubled Conscience and the Insane Mind*, trans. F. G. Crookshank (London: Kegan Paul & Co., 1928).

(139, 3)   See *Seminar III*, Ch. 4.

(140, 2)   The *Grundsprache* is briefly mentioned in *Seminar III*, p. 108, and at greater length in 'On a Question Prior to Any Possible Treatment of the Psychoses', *Écrits*, p. 450. See D. G. M. Schreber, *Memoirs of My Nervous Illness*, 2nd edn, trans. Ida MacAlpine and Richard A. Hunter (Cambridge, MA: Harvard University Press, 1988), pp. 12–13.

Chapter IX The Paternal Metaphor

(146, 5)   Charles Odier, 'Une névrose sans complexe d'Oedipe?', *Revue française de psychanalyse* 6 (1933): 298–343.

(151, 3)   See Henri Wallon, 'Les milieux, les groupes et la psychogenèse de l'enfant', *Enfance* 12/3–4 (1959): 287–96. Originally published in *Cahiers internationaux de sociologie* 16 (1954): 2–13.

(160, 7)   Friedrich Nietzsche, 'Before Sunrise', *Thus Spake Zarathustra*, trans. Thomas Common (New York: Start Publishing, 2012), pp. 244–8.

(161, 2)   Possibly a reference to French humourist, Pierre Henri Cami.

Chapter X The Three Moments of the Oedipus Complex (I)

(163, *line 2*)   Freud's 'Der Untergang des Ödipuskomplexes', translated as 'The Dissolution of the Oedipus Complex' in *SE* 19, is translated into French as 'Le déclin du complexe d'Oedipe'.

(166, 4)   The reference is to First Corinthians 3: 18, 'beholding as in a mirror the glory of the Lord'.

(170, 3)   Ernest Hemingway's *To Have and Have Not* was translated into French as *En avoir ou pas*. The French literally means to have some or not.

(171, 2)   See Sigmund Freud, *Analysis of a Phobia in a Five-Year-Old Boy*, *SE* 10: 5–149.

(177, 2)   See the final session of *Le séminaire IV*, Ch. 24.

Chapter XI The Three Moments of the Oedipus Complex (II)

(183, 4)   The 'ferret' is a reference to a children's song, '*Le jeu du furet*', the opening lines of which are:

> *Il court, il court, le furet*
> *Le furet du bois, mesdames,*
> *Il court, il court, le furet*
> *Le furet du bois joli.*

> He runs, he runs, the wood ferret does,
> The wood ferret, my Ladies,
> He runs, he runs, the ferret does
> The pretty wood ferret.

(187, 5)   This article is his 'On a Question Prior to Any Possible Treatment of Psychosis', *Écrits*, pp. 447–88. It was originally published in *La psychanalyse* 4 (1959): 1–50.

(192, 3)   This is most likely a reference to Freud's remark, added to the 1915 edition of *The Three Essays on Sexuality SE* 7: 146, n.1: 'The absence of a strong father in childhood not infrequently favours the occurrence of inversion.'

(196, 2)   See Rudolf Loewenstein, 'Phallic Passivity in Men', *International Journal of Psychoanalysis* 16 (1935): 334–40.

Chapter XII From Image to Signifier – in Pleasure and in Reality

(197, 1)   Charles Rycroft, 'Symbolism and Its Relationship to the Primary and Secondary Processes', *International Journal of Psychoanalysis* 37 (1956): 137–46.

(197, 2)   See Ernest Jones, 'Theory of Symbolism', *British Journal of Psychology* 9 (1918): 181–229.

(200, 2)   See D. W. Winnicott, 'Metapsychological and Clinical Aspects of Regression Within the Psycho-Analytical Set-Up', *International Journal of Psychoanalysis* 36 (1955): 16–26.

(200, 4)   D. W. Winnicott, 'Primitive Emotional Development', *International Journal of Psychoanalysis* 26 (1945): 137–43.

(203, 4)   The 'Letter 52' Lacan refers to is a letter from Freud to Wilhelm Fliess dated 6 December 1896. It was published in *The Origins of Psycho-Analysis: Letters to Wilhelm Fliess, Drafts and Notes, 1887–1902*, ed. Marie Bonaparte, Anna Freud and Ernst Kris, trans. Eric Mosbacher and James Strachey (London: Imago, 1954), 173–81. It appeared in a new translation as the letter of 6 December 1896 in *The Complete Letters of Sigmund Freud to Wilhelm Fliess, 1887–1904*, ed. and trans. Jeffrey Moussaieff Masson (Cambridge, MA: Harvard University Press, 1985), pp. 207–15.

(204, 2)   See *The Interpretation of Dreams, SE* 4: 130.

(208, 2) See Susan Isaacs, 'The Nature and Function of Phantasy', *International Journal of Psychoanalysis* 29 (1948): 73–97, esp. 94.

(209, 3) This diagram is a rudimentary version of the R Schema set out in Lacan, 'Question', *Écrits*, p. 462.

(212, 4) See Arthur Schopenhauer, *The World as Will and Representation*, trans. E. F. J. Payne (New York: Dover, 1958), Vol. 2, Ch. 42, 'Life of the Species', pp. 510–16.

(213, 4) Aldous Huxley, *Brave New World* (New York: HarperCollins, 2006).

(214, 6) '*Tendance*' here means drive.

(215, 1) Sigmund Freud, '"A Child is Being Beaten" A Contribution to the Study of the Origin of Sexual Perversions', *SE* 17: 179–204.

Chapter XIII Fantasy, Beyond the Pleasure Principle

(216, 1) Lacan will refer to three papers by Ernest Jones on female sexuality: 'The Early Development of Female Sexuality', *International Journal of Psychoanalysis* 8 (1927): 459–72; 'The Phallic Phase', *International Journal of Psychoanalysis*, 14 (1933): 1–13; and 'Early Female Sexuality', *International Journal of Psychoanalysis* 16 (1935): 263–73. All three are reprinted in his collection, *Papers on Psycho-Analysis*, 5th edn (1948; repr. London: Karnac, 1977), while the first and the third are also reprinted in Russell Grigg, Dominique Hecq and Craig Smith (eds), *Female Sexuality: The Early Psychoanalytic Controversies* (London: Rebus, 1999; repr. London: Karnac, 2015). Hanns Sachs's article was published in English as 'On the Genesis of Perversions', trans. Ruth B. Goldberg, *American Imago* 48 (1991): 283–93.

(216, 1) Otto Rank, 'Perversion and Neurosis', *International Journal of Psychoanalysis* 4 (1923): 270–92.

(218, 5) 'Constructions in Analysis', *SE* 23: 257–69.

(220, 3) 'Not clearly sexual, not in itself sadistic, but yet the stuff from which both will later come' ('A Child is Being Beaten', *SE* 17: 187). An allusion to the third witch's prophesy to Banquo, 'Thou shalt get kings, though you be none' (*Macbeth*, I. iii).

(220, 3) See Sigmund Freud, 'The Economic Problem of Masochism', *SE* 19: 159–70, esp. 164.

(227, 4) The line is spoken by the chorus in Sophocles' *Oedipus at Colonus*:

(228, 4) See Freud, 'Economic Problem of Masochism', *SE* 19: 159; see also a footnote by James Strachey in 'Instincts and Their Vicissitudes', *SE* 14: 121.

> Not to be born is best
> When all is reckoned in, but once a man has seen the light
> The next best thing, by far, is to go back
> Where he came from. (lines 1388–91)

(229, 1) See Freud, 'Economic Problem of Masochism', *SE* 19: 160.

Chapter XIV Desire and Jouissance

(236, 7)   The person in question would be either Jean Laplanche or Jean-Bertrand Pontalis whose joint publication, 'Fantasme originaire, fantasme des origines, origine du fantasme', appeared in *Les temps modernes* 215, in April 1964, and was published as a monograph by Hachette in 1985. It was published as 'Fantasy and the Origins of Sexuality' in *International Journal of Psychoanalysis* 49 (1968): 1–18, and reprinted in *Formations of Fantasy*, ed. Victor Burgin, James Donald and Cara Kaplan (London: Methuen, 1986).

(237, 4)   Lacan had neglected to mention 'The Early Development of Female Sexuality' the previous week.

(238, 1)   Joan Riviere, 'Womanliness as a Masquerade', *International Journal of Psychoanalysis* 10 (1929): 303–13; reprinted in Grigg et al. (eds), *Female Sexuality*, pp. 172–82.

(240, 3)   See *Le séminaire IV*, Ch. 8.

(242, 3)   Jean Delay, *La jeunesse d'André Gide* (Paris: Gallimard, 1956); *The Youth of André Gide*, abridged and trans. June Guicharnaud (Chicago: University of Chicago Press, 1963).

(242, 4)   The story Gide refers to is actually mentioned in Georges Sand, *Histoire du véritable Gribouille* (1850).

> Gribouille throws himself into the water one day that it is raining very hard, not to avoid the rain, as his wicked brothers say, but to avoid his brothers, who are laughing at him. For some time, he struggles in the water and tries to swim; then he lets himself go and as soon as he lets himself go, he floats; then he feels himself becoming tiny, light, odd, vegetal; leaves sprout out of him all over his body; and soon Gribouille turns into a slender, graceful sprig of oak, which the water gently deposits on the bank of the stream . . . no schoolboy was ever troubled by any page of Aphrodite so much as I – ignorant little boy that I was – by the metamorphosis of Gribouille. (André Gide, *If it Dies . . .*, trans. Dorothy Bussy (London: Penguin, 1977), pp. 60–1)

> Also see Lacan's detailed study of Gide in the article, published in 1958, 'The Youth of Gide, or the Letter and Desire', *Écrits*, pp. 623–44.

(243, 2)   André Gide, *Strait Is the Gate*, trans. Dorothy Bussy (Harmondsworth: Penguin, 1969).

(244, 7)   André Gide, *Madeleine*, trans. Justin O'Brien (Chicago, IL: Ivan R. Dee, 1989), pp. 30–1.

> *Personne ne peut soupçonner ce qu'est l'amour d'un uraniste, dégagé de toutes le contingences sexuelles: quelque chose de si fort, de si bien préservé, quelque chose d'embaumé contre quoi le temps n'a plus prise.* (No one has any idea what the love of a uranist is, devoid of all its sexual contingencies: something so strong, so well preserved, something embalmed against

which time is powerless.) (Jean Schlumberger, *Madeleine et André Gide* (Paris: Gallimard, 1956), p. 193)

(245, 2)   Harpagon is the protagonist of Molière's play, *The Miser*. When Madeleine Gide informed her husband that she had burnt all his letters, he wrote in his journal, 'I immediately felt ruined. I no longer have any heart for anything, and all the light in my heaven is extinguished' (*Madeleine*, p. 68).

(246, 5)   Jean Genet, *The Balcony*, trans. Bernard Frechtman (New York: Grove Press, 1966). The play premiered in Paris in 1957.

Chapter XV The Girl and the Phallus

(256, 1)   Melanie Klein introduced a distinction, not drawn by Freud, between largely unconscious 'phantasies' and 'fantasies' such as daydreams, reveries, imagined scenarios, and the like. Lacan is here using the term '*fantaisie*' for the former.

(268, 4)   Claude Lévi-Strauss (1949), *Elementary Structures of Kinship* revised edn (Boston, MA: Beacon Press, 1969).

Chapter XVI Insignias of the Ideal

(274, 1)   The term was introduced in 1917 by Johan H. W. van Ophuijsen. See his 'Contributions to the Masculinity Complex of Women', *International Journal of Psychoanalysis* 5 (1924): 39–49; repr. in Grigg et al. (eds), *Female Sexuality*.

(274, 5)   Helene Deutsch, 'The Significance of Masochism in the Mental Life of Women', *International Journal of Psychoanalysis* 11 (1930): 48–60, repr. in Grigg et al. (eds), *Female Sexuality*; Karen Horney, 'On the Genesis of the Castration Complex in Women', *International Journal of Psychoanalysis* 5 (1924): 50–65.

Chapter XVII The Formulas of Desire

(286, 2)   '*Ce que femme veut, Dieu veut*' is a French saying which literally means 'What a woman wants, God wants'.

(291, 3)   There is a passing simile in the *Ethics*, Pt. 1, Proposition 17, Corollary 2, where Spinoza contrasts the 'celestial' constellations *Canis Major* and *Canis Minor* with the 'terrestrial' barking animal.

Chapter XVIII Symptoms and Their Masks

(305, 3)   Elisabeth von R. was one of Freud's early patients. Her case is discussed in *Studies on Hysteria*, *SE* 2: 135–81.

(308, 2) See 'On the Universal Tendency to Debasement in the Sphere of Love', *SE* 11: 177–90.

(308, 5) *Donner et se donner. 'Aimer, c'est tout donner et se donner soi-même (to love is to give everything and to give oneself)'* is a line from a French hymn, popular at the wedding Mass.

(311, 3) See René Spitz, *The First Year of Life: A Psychoanalytic Study of Normal and Deviant Development of Object Relations*, in collaboration with W. Godfrey Cobliner (New York: International Universities Press, 1965). The book is based on the author's *'Genèse des premières relations objectales* (Genesis of the First Object Relations)', published in the *Revue française de psychanalyse* in 1954.

(314, 3) The French *'oblativité'*, here rendered as 'oblativity', means the propensity to give oneself to others or to God without an expectation of reciprocity, to dedicate oneself to a cause without expecting anything in return. In French psychoanalysis and psychology it has come to refer to something like authentic generosity and altruistic behaviour.

Chapter XIX Signifier, Bar and Phallus

(315, 3) See Sigmund Freud, 'Splitting of the Ego in the Process of Defence', *SE* 23: 275–8.

(316, 6) Otto Rank, 'Perversion and Neurosis', *International Journal of Psychoanalysis* 4 (1923): 270–92.

(317, 6) See Michel Leiris, *La possession et ses aspects théâtraux chez les Éthiopiens de Gondar* (Paris: Plon, 1958).

(330, 2) See Karen Horney, 'The Dread of Woman: Observations on a Specific Difference in the Dread Felt by Men and Women Respectively for the Opposite Sex', *International Journal of Psychoanalysis* 13 (1932): 348–60.

Chapter XX The Dream by the Butcher's Beautiful Wife

(334, 3) The reference is to Immanuel Kant. See his *Critique of Pure Reason*, trans. and ed. Paul Guyer and Allen W. Wood (Cambridge: Cambridge University Press, 1998).

(338, 4) Lacan is quoting from the French translation of *Die Traumdeutung*. This and following quotations are from *The Interpretation of Dreams, Standard Edition* 4: 147–50.

(347, 2) 'Fragment of an Analysis of a Case of Hysteria', *SE* 7: 7–122.

Chapter XXI The 'Still Waters Run Deep' Dreams

(351, 1) See Michael Balint, 'On Genital Love', *International Journal of Psychoanalysis* 29 (1948): 34–40. The article was subsequently included in his *Primary Love and Psychoanalytic Technique* (London: Hogarth Press, 1952), pp. 128–40.

(351, 2)   The phrase, '*la belle et bonne forme*', is something of a fixed expression in French. It reflects the ancient Greeks' usage of the term '*kalokagathia*' to indicate that which is beautiful-and-good, referring to Plato's identification of the two.

(351, 5)   Claude Lévi-Strauss, *Tristes Tropiques*, trans. John and Doreen Weightman (London: Jonathan Cape, 1973).

(358, 2)   '*En avoir ou pas*' is also the French title of Ernest Hemingway's 1937 novel, *To Have and Have Not*.

Chapter XXII The Other's Desire

(366, 3)   Maurice Bouvet, 'Le moi dans la névrose obsessionnelle', *Revue française de psychanalyse* 17 (1953): 111–96.

(367, 2)   Maurice Bouvet, 'Incidences thérapeutiques de la prise de conscience de l'envie du pénis dans la névrose obsessionnelle féminine', *Revue française de psychanalyse* 14/2 (1950): 215–43.

(367, 2)   Maurice Bouvet, 'Importance de l'aspect homosexuel du transfert dans quatre cas de névrose obsessionnelle masculine', *Revue française de psychanalyse* 13 (1948): 419–55.

(367, 4)   See Karl Abraham's table of the 'Stages of Libidinal Organization' in 'Origins and Growth of Object Love', Pt 2 of 'A Short Study of the Development of the Libido', *Selected Papers of Karl Abraham* (London: Hogarth Press, 1927), p. 497; reprinted in Grigg et al. (eds), *Female Sexuality*, p. 87.

(369, 4)   This is Karl Abraham's 'later anal-sadistic stage'. See 'Stages of Libidinal Organization', in Grigg et al. (eds) *Female Sexuality*, p. 87.

(371, 2)   I haven't been able to find the table Lacan is referring to.

(375, 1)   See Edward Glover, 'A Developmental Study of the Obsessional Neuroses', *International Journal of Psychoanalysis* 16 (1935): 131–44.

(378, 1)   See Freud's 1896 paper, 'Further Remarks on the Neuro-Psychoses of Defence', *SE* 3: 162–85.

(378, 2)   'Notes upon a Case of Obsessional Neurosis', *SE* 10: 155–318.

Chapter XXIII The Obsessional and his Desire

(390, 6)   '*Versagung*' is translated as 'frustration' in *SE*.

(397, 6)   Phyllis Greenacre, 'General Problems of Acting Out', *Psychoanalytic Quarterly* 19 (1950): 455–67.

Chapter XXIV Transference and Suggestion

(400, 1)   This is the id, ego, superego model, also referred to as the structural model.

(408, 2)   Bouvet, 'Importance de l'aspect homosexuel', p. 434.

Chapter XXVI The Circuits of Desire

(432, 1)   The date marks General de Gaulle's 'call to arms' of 18 June 1940 for the French to resist the German occupation of France.

(433, 4)   Edward Glover, 'The Therapeutic Effect of Inexact Interpretation: A Contribution to the Theory of Suggestion', *International Journal of Psychoanalysis* 12 (1931): 397–411.

(436, 5)   D. W. Winnicott, 'Transitional Objects and Transitional Phenomena – A Study of the First Not-Me Possession', *International Journal of Psychoanalysis* 34 (1953): 89–97. Lacan's article, 'Some Reflections on the Ego', was published in the same issue.

(446, 2)   See 'Notes upon a Case of Obsessional Neurosis', *SE* 10: 205.

(446, 4)   See *Seminar III*, Ch. 22.

Chapter XXVII Exiting via the Symptom

(449, 1)   'Common sense is the most fairly distributed thing in the world, for each one thinks he is so well-endowed with it that even those who are hardest to satisfy in all other matters are not in the habit of desiring more of it than they already have.' The opening words of René Descartes, *Discourse on the Method for Rightly Conducting One's Reason*.

(453, 3)   This study group included Jean Laplanche and Jean-Bertrand Pontalis, the authors of *The Language of Psycho-Analysis*, trans. Donald Nicholson-Smith (London: The Hogarth Press, 1973).

(455, 1)   Compare this diagram with the slightly different one in Lacan's 'Question', *Écrits*, p. 465.

(456, 2)   For further discussion, see Lacan, 'Question', *Écrits*, p. 452.

(456, 2)   See Sigmund Freud, 'Psycho-Analytic Notes on an Autobiographical Account of a Case of Paranoia (Dementia Paranoides)', *SE* 12: 59–65.

(456, 3)   See Sigmund Freud, *Introductory Lectures on Psychoanalysis*, *SE* 22: 80.

Chapter XXVIII You Are the One You Hate

(456, *ch. title*)   '*Tu es celui que tu hais*', 'You are the one you hate', and '*Tu es celui que tu es*', 'You are the one you are', are homophonic.

(466, 3)   Sacha Nacht (ed.), *La psychanalyse d'aujourd'hui* (Paris: Presses Universitaires de France, 1956).

(471, 3)   See Sigmund Freud, 'Notes Upon a Case of Obsessional Neurosis', *SE* 10: 187. '"If you received a command to take your examination this term at the first possible opportunity, you might manage to obey it. But if you were commanded to cut your throat with a razor, what then?" He had at once become aware that this command had already been given, and was hurrying to the cupboard to fetch his razor when he thought: "No, it's not so simple as that. You must go and kill the old woman.'"

Index